MANAGING AND LEASING COMMERCIAL PROPERTIES

SECOND EDITION

Alan A. Alexander
Richard F. Muhlebach, CPM®

IREM Institute of Real Estate Management

Printed in the United States of America
ISBN-13: 978-1-57203-242-2
SKU: 791-2

Publishing Department
Institute of Real Estate Management
430 North Michigan Avenue
Chicago, IL 60611–4090

Text and Cover Composition:
Nadia Geagea Pupa

Cover photos left to right: © Brus_Rus; © xijian; © zhudifeng; © imaginima;
© beijingstory; © lichaoshu; © ivo Gretener; © Maxiphoto / istock photos

IREM encourages diversity. We welcome individuals of all races, genders, creeds, ages, sexual orientations, gender identities, national origins, and individuals with disabilities. Our organization strives to provide an equal opportunity environment among its members, vendors, and staff.

IREM is dedicated to supporting real estate management strategies that advance an environmentally sustainable and economically prosperous future

Library of Congress Cataloging-in-Publication Data

Names: Muhlebach, Richard F., 1943- author. | Alexander, Alan A., author. | Alexander, Alan A. Managing and leasing commercial properties.
Title: Managing and leasing commercial properties / by Richard F. Muhlebach, CPM(r), Alan A. Alexander.
Description: Second Edition. | Chicago : Institute of Real Estate Management IREM, [2016] | Revised edition of the authors's Managing and leasing commercial properties, c2007. | Includes bibliographical references and index.
Identifiers: LCCN 2016023393 (print) | LCCN 2016033535 (ebook) | ISBN 9781572032422 (pbk. : alk. paper) | ISBN 1572032421 (pbk. : alk. paper) |
Subjects: LCSH: Real estate management. | Real estate management--United States. | Commercial buildings--United States--Management. | Commercial leases--United States. | Building leases--United States.
Classification: LCC HD1394 .M845 2016 (print) | DDC 333.33/87068--dc23
LC record available at https://lccn.loc.gov/2016023393

MANAGING AND LEASING COMMERCIAL PROPERTIES

SECOND EDITION

PROFESSIONAL REVIEW

Aaron M. Bosshardt, CPM®, CCIM

Sam Chanin, CPM®

David Domres, CPM®, CCIM

Carrie E. Woodring, CPM®

Kristine M. Moore, CPM®, CCIM, CPA

Mark Polatsek, CPM®

Jacqueline Harris, CPM®, CCIM

Richard H. Forsyth, CPM®, CCIM

IREM EDUCATION PUBLISHING

Nadia Geagea Pupa
Managing Editor, Publications

Ronald Gjerde
Vice President, Knowledge Center

To my loving wife of 37 years, Jeanne, thank you for your love, support, backing and encouragement in all that I do. You are always there for me in every way. The accomplishment of writing such books as this is made so much easier when one has someone to share the load and to provide loving guidance for the betterment of all that I attempt.

Thank you, Alan Alexander

In a few years from the date of this publication, Maria and I will celebrate 50 years in real estate management. Maria, for 50 years you supported me in my endeavor to change professions, start a career in a field I knew little about, and build a career and a company. While you served as the COO of our family, you encouraged and supported me through the excitement and challenges of venturing into the unknown while many nights you waited for me to come home from late meetings, teaching assignments, and business trips. Maria, thank you for being there for me over and over again!

I also want to thank IREM for serving as my mentor and jump starting my career by providing me with opportunities to network with real estate professionals, attend incredible courses and education forums, acquire publications that became invaluable desk references, and the opportunity to serve in leadership positions. Maria and I have made many lasting friendships with people we've met at local and national IREM meetings and conferences.

– Richard Muhlebach, CPM®

PREFACE

Managing and Leasing Commercial Properties, Second Edition provides practical and successful techniques for a proactive approach to operating, managing, marketing, and leasing commercial properties. This is not a book on the theory of real estate management; rather, it is a hands-on guide that provides problem-solving methods, procedures, tactics, and tips. The suggested approaches come from the combined experiences of the authors, who have more than 80 years' experience in the management, leasing, and marketing of all types of commercial properties, which include medical office buildings, high-rise office buildings, major industrial parks, regional enclosed malls, and large mixed-use developments.

In addition, Managing and Leasing Commercial Properties, Second Edition offers the philosophy that managing an income property is managing a business. Each real estate investment is the business of its investor—whether the property is a 10,000-square-foot strip shopping center, or one of the tallest office buildings in the world. Effective real estate managers do not manage brick and mortar, steel, and concrete—they manage people and relationships. These approaches ultimately lead to the long-term success of managing and leasing properties, and are the foundation which this publication has been written.

This book begins with a historical overview and evolution of commercial properties throughout the years, providing insight into how real estate management and leasing opportunities were created more than 100 years ago. The introductory chapter also identifies future opportunities in real estate management and leasing.

The second chapter provides information on managing income-producing real estate as a business, which contains the necessary information to develop a business plan for each property.

A study by the Institute of Real Estate Management (IREM) found that leasing and retaining tenants are the top concerns of real estate investors. There are greater opportunities to increase a property's cash flow and value through leasing compared to any other management activity. Therefore, a major portion of this book is devoted to the marketing and leasing of commercial properties. The daily responsibility of real estate managers has an impact on the marketing and leasing efforts and overall success of the properties they manage. Real estate managers must be proficient in developing an effective and efficient marketing and leasing program for every property they manage, along with being prepared to negotiate scores of lease provisions.

Effective management techniques for all types of commercial properties are discussed in the chapters on budgeting, maintenance management, and emergency procedures. Many commercial properties have common approaches to the management process, but where they differ, those differences are discussed as well. Specific approaches to management and leasing techniques are covered for shopping centers, office buildings, medical office buildings, and industrial properties.

The final section provides information on the development process and rehabbing commercial properties. The real estate manager has an important role in each of these development activities and should understand the responsibilities of each professional involved in developing and/or renovating all types of commercial properties.

The intention of this book is to provide a resource for real estate managers, property accountants, marketing personnel, leasing agents, and security and maintenance staffs to confront and exploit the opportunities and challenges in today's complex commercial property operations, management, marketing, and leasing. Without a doubt, this publication will be your handy reference guide for daily operations, management, marketing, and leasing of the properties in your portfolio.

– Alan Alexander and Richard Muhlebach

ACKNOWLEDGEMENT

Professionals in real estate management generously share their expertise and experiences with each other. This has enabled the real estate management profession to evolve and prosper and enables real estate managers to better serve their clients and the community. We have been beneficiaries of the generosity of our peers who have shared their knowledge and experiences with us. Without the guidance and mentoring from several real estate professionals, we would not have been able to write these and other real estate management and leasing books. We thank Eric Muhlebach of Bond Retail in San Francisco for his invaluable leasing and marketing advice.

This book would not have been possible without the experience, dedication, patience, and insight of Nadia Geagea Pupa, Managing Editor of IREM®.

We would also like to acknowledge the insights and experiences of the following Certified Property Managers® who served as reviewers of the book's manuscript:

Aaron M. Bosshardt, CPM®, CCIM

Sam Chanin, CPM®

David Domres, CPM®, CCIM

Carrie E. Woodring, CPM®

Kristine M. Moore, CPM®, CCIM, CPA

Mark Polatsek, CPM®

Jacqueline Harris, CPM®, CCIM

Richard H. Forsyth, CPM®, CCIM

We would like to acknowledge our long and valued association with the Institute of Real Estate Management® (IREM®). The opportunities for networking and training from the IREM® publications, courses, and conferences have been invaluable in the development of our careers.

– Alan Alexander

– Richard Muhlebach CPM, CSM, RPA, CRX, CRE

ABOUT THE AUTHORS

ALAN A. ALEXANDER, PRESIDENT OF ALEXANDER CONSULTANTS

Alan A. Alexander is the President of Alexander Consultants for more than 35 years, specializing in the management, leasing, and consulting for income-producing properties throughout the western United States and South America. He formed Alexander Consultants with a specialization in commercial real estate management and leasing, as well as involvement in large residential complexes. His company provided consulting services to the commercial real estate industry and managed and leased grocery-anchored shopping centers, specialty centers, and enclosed regional malls. He later sold that company to a large local developer.

Alan is the former Senior Vice President of Fox & Carskadon Management Corporation with a responsibility for a portfolio of commercial and residential properties worth in excess of $900 million dollars in four western states. As Director of Leasing for Fox & Carskadon Financial, Alan was responsible for the leasing of all shopping centers owned by the company throughout the United States with a total portfolio in excess of $2 billion dollars.

He was a member of the national faculty of IREM® as a senior instructor for both shopping centers and office buildings. In addition to classes taught in almost every major city in the United States, he has also instructed in Singapore, Canada, Mexico, Malaysia, Taiwan, Hong Kong, the Philippines, Poland, China, Thailand, Holland, India, Argentina, Turkey, and Jamaica. He was a frequent speaker for the International Council of Shopping Center (ICSC) programs including Idea Exchanges, the Annual Convention, Management Institutes, Maintenance Institutes, and the School for Professional Development. He represented the ICSC at their first three Asian Shopping Center Schools as an instructor.

Alan has been a moderator and speaker for more than 200 private seminars on developing and leasing of shopping centers, office buildings, and apartment properties for the Northwest Center for Professional Education. He has co-authored *Shopping Center Management* (1992, 2005), published by IREM®, and *Operating Small Shopping Centers* (1996), published by ICSC. He has also co-authored *Business Strategies for Real Estate Management Companies* (1997, 2003, and 2014), published by IREM.

He is a contributing author to the books *Managing Shopping Centers, Budgeting, CAM Operations and Leasing Shopping Centers,* all published by ICSC in 1998 and 2000. Alan was inducted into the Academy of Authors of the Institute of Real Estate Management in 1984. He is the past President of the San Francisco Bay Area Chapter of the Institute of Real Estate Management. He was awarded the "Distinguished Service Award" by the ICSC in 1992 for his contributions to education and publications.

ABOUT THE AUTHORS

RICHARD MUHLEBACH CPM, CRE, CSM, CRX, RPA

Richard Muhlebach is a commercial real estate professional with more than 40 years' experience as an executive with real estate firms that develop, lease, and manage commercial and residential properties. He served as the vice president of real estate management for two California developers and the vice president of leasing for a northwest developer. He founded, operated, and served for 19 years as the president of a real estate management and leasing company. He sold the firm to a national public real estate company, and served as its senior managing director for nine years.

Richard started a second real estate firm that provides brokerage and consulting services in the Northwest and California with offices in the Seattle and San Francisco areas. He also assisted his son in creating Bond Retail, a firm located in San Francisco, which acquires retail properties on great retail streets throughout the United States and provides retail brokerage services. He serves as the firm's vice president.

Richard has been responsible for the management and leasing of almost all commercial property types including regional open and enclosed malls, high-rise office buildings, medical office buildings, industrial parks, large multi-anchored strip shopping centers, street retail properties, and a two million square foot mixed-use development. He also managed, marketed, and leased large apartment developments.

Richard co-authored 23 books on commercial real estate including *Business Strategies for Real Estate Management Companies, Managing and Leasing Commercial Properties, Troubled Properties, Managing Your Maintenance Programs, Shopping Center Management and Leasing,* and *The Leasing Process: Landlord and Tenant Perspectives.* His books have been published by John Wiley and Sons, Aspen Publishing, International Council of Shopping Centers (ICSC), and the Institute of Real Estate Management® (IREM®). He has authored more than 130 articles including articles published in Asia and Europe. He is an instructor for the Commercial Brokers Association, IREM, Building Owners and Managers Association (BOMA), and the University of Washington. He served as an instructor for the ICSC, Northwest Center for Professional Education, and Orange Coast College. He's taught seminars and lectured throughout the United States and in Singapore, China, Taiwan, Spain, Hungary, Poland, Russia, Bulgaria, and Canada.

Richard served as the national president of IREM and the President of the Washington State Commercial Association of Realtors. He serves as a member of the Washington State Investment Board and he chaired the Real Estate Advisory Committee for the real estate program at North Seattle College. Richard is a Certified Property Manager® (CPM®), Counselor of Real Estate, Certified Shopping Center Manager, Certified Retail Property Executive, and Real Property Administrator (RPA).

For more information, visit *www.RichardMuhlebach.com.*

TABLE OF CONTENTS

SECTION II:

SECTION

I

The Profession of Commercial Real Estate Management

CHAPTER

1

Introduction to Commercial Real Estate Management

The development of every commercial property requires a team of real estate and other professionals to turn a vision into a structure that will serve the community—whether they are places for commerce, facilities for governmental activities, or venues for entertainment, dinning, and recreation.

Commercial properties of all types have an economic and physical life of several decades and even centuries, and it is the real estate manager who guides properties through the economic life and multiple real estate cycles. The real estate manager develops a business plan for the property consistent with the goals and objectives of the property ownership, and assembles a team of professionals to implement the business plan. The business plan is explained in more detail in Chapter 2.

This chapter provides an overview of the history of commercial real estate management in the U.S. The details of the last 40 years in the office building, industrial property, and shopping center industries serve as the backdrop for more in-depth consideration of the cyclical nature of the real estate industry. Opportunities in commercial real estate management in the U.S. and abroad are also explored in terms of the various commercial real estate professional associations. These organizations provide education, leadership growth, mentoring, and networking venues. This chapter also includes information about the various programs and professional designations that these associations offer.

THE HISTORY OF COMMERCIAL REAL ESTATE MANAGEMENT

The real estate management profession evolved during the 20th century, and continues to evolve into the 21st century. The real estate management profession changed from that of caretakers of properties in the early 1900s to a profession with the responsibility of managing properties as businesses to achieve or exceeding the goals and objectives of the property owners.

The history of commercial real estate management and the evolution of the roles and responsibilities of commercial real estate managers parallel the growth of the U.S. As the country evolved from an agricultural to an industrial society, populations shifted from farms and small communities to cities and urban areas. The concentration of people living and working in cities and metropolitan areas created development activities and these buildings needed to be managed. The real estate management industry was created out of necessity and evolved into a profession.

Early Years

Real estate management in the U.S. began as a service industry after the Revolutionary War when cities grew and new communities were established. Real estate was considered a good investment, but many property owners did not want the burden of managing their assets. A few entrepreneurs offered their services to manage those investments, thus, marking the beginning of the real estate management industry. A construction boom followed the Civil War. The population of the country grew rapidly and businesses prospered. With the development of office buildings and retail properties, downtown became the center of the community.

Development of Skyscrapers

Skyscrapers changed the field of real estate management; their history spans more than a century. The first skyscraper is reported to be the 180-foot Home Insurance Building developed in Chicago in 1885. Many major corporations built tall buildings that became symbols of their power, prestige, and status. The following lists in chronological order the tallest high-rise buildings in New York City as they were developed:

- 1908: The Singer Building; 612 feet
- 1909: The Metropolitan Life Building; 700 feet
- 1913: The Woolworth Building; 793 feet
- 1930: The Chrysler Building; 1,046 feet.
- 1931: The Empire State Building; 1,250 feet

In 1853, the invention of the elevator in by Elisha Graves Otis solved the problem of transporting people and materials up and down buildings. Prior to the use of steel beams, the foundation walls at the ground level of masonry buildings had to be very thick to support their load, thus, limiting the height of buildings. For example, the 16-story Monadnock Building in Chicago needed a six-foot-thick wall at its base to support it.

The Great Depression ended the era's competition to build the world's tallest building. The Empire State Building held the record for more than 40 years until the development of the World Trade Center in New York, followed by the 110-story Sears Tower in Chicago. Currently, the world's tallest building is the Burj Khalifa in Dubai, United Arab Emirates in 2010, following by the second tallest building, the Tokyo Skytree in Japan.

Throughout the 20th century, there were many more high-rise buildings created and developed for multiple uses, which also created new opportunities and challenges for real estate managers.

Beginning of the 20th Century to 1939

From 1900 until the 1920s, residential and commercial property occupancy and demand were high—except for a short period during World War I. In the 1920s, property owners found that modest real estate investments produced riches beyond their imaginations. The success of these investments allowed property owners the luxury of travel. Local real estate agents entered the real estate management business by offering to collect rents and pay the properties' operating expenses as a means to obtain the leasing and sales listings of the buildings. Even today, many brokerage firms provide real estate management services to obtain brokerage opportunities.

During the 1920s, private investors who financed their investments with mortgages owned most of the buildings. Unparalleled prosperity, growth, and a construction boom characterized that era. Financing was available for construction loans, which fueled the development of industrial properties and manufacturing plants, as well as retail chain store expansion. A strong economy and expanding commercial development created a need for multifamily housing for the new employees of the emerging industries and commercial growth. During this period, the real estate management industry experienced growth and recognition.

The age of the automobile and the availability of electricity brought about the development of the suburbs. In 1922, the J.C. Nicols Company developed the forerunner of the modern shopping center, Country Club Plaza in Kansas City. The nation's first planned, major suburban business and retail area, Country Club Plaza was developed with a coordinated architectural style and landscaping, and it was planned for shoppers to travel to it by driving. It was designed with the concepts of tenant synergism, easy access, convenient parking, and a pleasant environment that are the foundation of successful shopping centers. Designed to resemble a plaza in Seville, Spain, Country Club Plaza is still considered by many the most beautiful shopping area in the U.S. and continues to be very successful.

The Great Depression of 1929 brought about the foreclosure of thousands of real estate loans. The ownership of investment properties changed from investors to banks, insurance companies, saving societies, and trust companies that held the mortgages on the properties. Believing they could best manage the properties, many lenders created their own real estate management departments. Other real estate professionals, along with contractors, developers, and architects formed real estate management companies to take advantage of unprecedented opportunities. At first, the people responsible for the management of those properties believed building management was limited to rent collection and maintenance. Later, they realized that market research and property administration were required to effectively manage and lease these assets.

During the recovery years following the depression, the ownership of real estate transferred from the lender back to real estate investors. Real estate once again became a profitable investment for individuals and partnerships.

1940s and 1950s

In the 1940s, department stores such as Sears Roebuck and Co. and Montgomery Ward continued their expansion into the suburbs and built freestanding stores with self-contained parking. The expansion of department stores to the suburbs was significant because developers combined department stores and shop tenants with the concept of a planned retail and business district pioneered by J.C. Nicols at Country Club Plaza; that combination created the concept of shopping centers. This new type of property needed professional management, and that provided real estate management opportunities and expanded the real estate management industry.

The recovery period from the end of the depression to the beginning of World War II created a demand for residential and commercial buildings that caused rents to rise and property values to increase. The prosperity following the war, along with the demand for housing for the returning soldiers and their families, kept vacancies down and demand for space high. The real estate market remained strong through the mid-1950s.

Railroad companies were among the first developers of industrial areas. These areas were often developed along existing rail lines to attract business for the railroads. They were the predecessors of the industrial parks, which first appeared in the 1950s. The advent of industrial properties created another management opportunity.

The construction boom that followed World War II and continued through the mid-1950s eventually brought about an oversupply of space, and vacancies began to appear. The postwar period saw several societal changes, including a drop in the birth rate and increases in the divorce rate, the number of women in the workforce, and the lifespan of the American people. As automobiles became more common, the country became a mobile society. These changes created demands for new houses and multifamily buildings; high-rise residential buildings were developed in great numbers. As the economy improved, demand for office space increased.

1960s and 1970s

During the 1960s and 1970s, the growing popularity of two property types created new real estate management opportunities. Condominiums and cooperatives first appeared in the New York area several decades before they became popular throughout the U.S. Condominiums were first developed as primary residences and later as second homes in resort and recreation areas. Condominiums required professional management. Many of the apartment real estate management firms throughout the country added condominiums to their management portfolios.

The second property type to experience tremendous growth during this period was the shopping center. Developers of neighborhood shopping centers followed the growth patterns into the suburbs; they built shopping centers anchored by a grocery store and a small drugstore with several small local and chain fashion, gift, and jewelry stores. As the population in the suburbs continued to increase, shopping centers grew in size from neighborhood shopping centers to community shopping centers anchored by a supermarket or super drugstore. A combination of service and retail shops tenanted these shopping centers.

The size of shopping centers continued to increase. The first regional mall, Northgate Shopping Center, was developed in Seattle in the early 1950s. A few years later, the first enclosed mall, Southdale Mall, was developed in Edina, a suburb of Minneapolis. Specialty or theme shopping centers, such as Ghirardelli Square in San Francisco and Trolley Square in Salt Lake City were developed in the 1960s and 1970s. In the 1970s, large mixed-use developments (MXD) appeared. MXDs, such as Water Tower Place in Chicago and Newport Center in California, included three or more uses. Festive shopping centers, such as Faneuil Hall Marketplace in Boston first appeared in the 1970s.

1980s and 1990s

Power shopping centers came onto the scene in the 1980s. The first power center, 280 Metro Center, was developed near a regional mall just south of San Francisco in Colma. Entertainment was added to the retail experience with the development of the 5.2-million-square-foot West Edmonton Mall in Edmonton, Canada, in the mid-1980s, and the 4-million-square-foot Mall of America in the Minneapolis area.

In the early 1990s, one of the first lifestyle shopping centers was developed in Shrewsbury, New Jersey. These shopping centers are anchored by upscale specialty retailers with several fashion and gift stores and table-service restaurants. They have a main street design with parking in front of the stores. Lifestyle shopping centers are patterned after the first planned retail district, Country Club Plaza in Kansas City. Entertainment shopping centers first appeared in the 1990s.

Two or more new types of shopping centers were developed in great numbers in each decade from 1970 through 1990: enclosed malls, specialty centers, and MXDs in the 1970s, power shopping centers and outlet malls in the 1980s, lifestyle shopping centers, and entertainment shopping centers in the 1990s. By the end of the 20th century, downtown areas and urban neighborhood retailing once again became popular retail venues for merchants and shoppers. Each new type of shopping center created management opportunities for real estate management companies.

21st Century

During the early years of the 21st century, power shopping centers evolved into power towns with an expanded tenant mix and more amenities and landscaping. The lifestyle shopping center continued to evolve—first by adding two to four levels of residential units above the ground-floor retail and then by adding departments stores. Lifestyle shopping centers were added as a tail to some enclosed regional malls. Hybrid shopping centers were developed combining two or three types of shopping centers. For example, power centers and lifestyle centers were developed as one shopping center.

The oldest retail venue in America is making a comeback. Street retailing was the only form of shopping for most of our county's history. Today, many of the most dynamic retailing destinations are found on retail streets. These streets include 5th Avenue in New York, Michigan Avenue in Chicago, and Union Square in San Francisco. These and other retail streets survived the "malling" of America. Since the 1990s, many retail streets are reappearing stronger than ever. Retail streets that have been neglected for years are becoming the center of their neighborhoods. Many of these streets offer not only retailing but restaurants and a night life. These are 18-hour-per-day streets that cites love and communities cherish. As retail streets are reappearing across America, new management opportunities are created.

In the 21st century, the consumer has the choice of several retail venues. The shopping center industry consists of large strip shopping centers anchored by supermarkets; outlet, power, lifestyle, and entertainment shopping centers; ethnic malls, specialty, and festive shopping centers; and regional and super regional malls and hybrid shopping centers. Downtown and street retailing became the retail and entertainment choice for many urbanites.

Retailers must respond to the needs and wants of the consumers. Successful shopping centers must meet the ever-changing needs of retailers and be able to accommodate new retailing concepts. As new retailing concepts were created and new types of shopping centers developed, new real estate management opportunities emerged.

Office Building Industry

The office building industry entered the 1980s following a depressed market during the middle and late 1970s. Then, during the early 1980s, the office building market experienced a boom with low vacancies and unprecedented rent increases.

Effects of a Building Boom

Class A office building rental rates that nationally were in the $6- to $12-per-square-foot-per-year range in the mid-1970s doubled, tripled, and even quadrupled in many cities in the early 1980s. Vacancy rates that were high in most areas of the country in the second half of the 1970s dropped to well below five percent nationally in 1980. Cities as diverse as Anchorage, San Francisco, and Washington, D.C. experienced vacancy rates below two percent.

During the first two years of the 1980s, construction cranes became a common sight in every major city and throughout the suburbs. Real estate journals and other publications highly praised the wisdom of developing and investing in office buildings; every commercial developer wanted to build them—and many did. Office buildings became the preferred investment property type for many institutional investors.

Recovery from a Building Boom

The office building boom lasted only a few years, and by 1983, the country was glutted with vacant office space. Construction continued at a rapid pace due to the three- to seven-year lead time to develop and create mid- and high-rise office buildings.

A development takes on a life of its own, and the developer frequently cannot or will not stop its progress. Halting a project early in its development stage can have severe consequences to the developer. Land purchases, guaranteed land loans, pre-development costs, and architectural and other fees are commitments developers cannot avoid. In addition, development and other fees are often essential to the continued operation of the development firm. Many developers took a chance by continuing the development process when the market was already overbuilt, hoping that the market would turn by the time their office buildings were ready for occupancy; others believed their buildings were special and would outperform the other buildings. These buildings added to an already overbuilt market.

Vacancy rates in office buildings in the mid-1980s exceeded 10 percent in most areas. Many cities, especially those in oil-producing states, experienced vacancy rates ranging from 25 to 35 percent. When the price of oil plummeted from over $30.00 per barrel to less than $10 per barrel in the mid-1980s, vacancy rates skyrocketed in oil-dependent cities such as Houston, Dallas, Denver, Anchorage, and other cities in Texas, Oklahoma, and Louisiana.

By the early l990s, the supply of office space slowed because of limited new construction. In 1990, the national vacancy rate was just under 20 percent. By 1991, office building vacancy rates began to slowly diminish, rental rates gradually increased, and concessions were reduced. At the same time, the demand for office space continued to drop in many areas of the country. The imbalance in the supply and demand for space had three main effects: (1) rents dropped below most buildings' pro forma rents; (2) concessions increased to entice tenants to move to other buildings; and (3) vacancy rates continued to climb into the low double-digit range. There was also concern that in some areas of the country the office building market would not improve during the remainder of that decade.

Rental rates were still substantially below the rates necessary to support new development activities. Limited construction activities through the first half of the 1990s and a strong economy fueled in many areas by the new high-tech and dot-com industries caused the office building market to rebound by the end of the decade, just as limited construction of new buildings during the mid- and late-1970s was a major factor that created a strong office building market in the early 1980s.

A Long Recovery

At the end of the 1990s, the high-tech boom turned to a bust, and the economy suffered after the September 11, 2001 attack on the World Trade Center in New York and the Pentagon in Washington, D.C. Office building vacancy rate percentages climbed into the high teens in most major cities and even more than 20 percent in some. Rental rates dropped from the sudden jump they experienced during the last few years of the 1990s and started to stabilize by the second half of the first decade of the new century as vacancy rates started to decline.

The office building market experienced many more difficult years than good years during the 25-year period from 1980 though 2005. During those years, leasing and tenant retention were real estate managers' primary responsibilities. During the Great Recession from 2008 through 2014, rental rates plummet and vacancy rates soared. Real estate professionals who experienced three to five difficult markets during their careers stated that the worst market was during the Great Recession. Many believed this period was the most devastating real estate market since the depression. The recovery from the Great Recession was uneven geographically and by product type. The commercial property market in San Francisco and the Bay Area recovered two years before the market recovered in most of the rest of the country.

In less than 40 years, the office market experienced multiple booms and busts. Lessons learned and promises made during a bust were soon forgotten when the market started booming again. Office building managers approached each phase of the real estate cycle with a business plan designed to meet the goals and objectives of the building's investors.

Industrial Property Industry

In the 1980s, the industrial real estate market was overbuilt in most areas of the country. While the situation was serious, the problems were not as severe as those of the office building markets. The industrial real estate market entered the 1990s with a slow recovery.

A slowing of construction activity from the mid-1980s to the mid-1990s brought the industrial real estate market to equilibrium between supply and demand. During the last half of the 1980s, industrial properties outperformed office buildings. During the early l990s, industrial properties were among investors' preferred choices. By the late 1990s, many of the traditional areas to develop industrial properties had a shortage of buildable sites. Industrial areas were pushed further and further into the suburbs. The market in the beginning of the 21st century was between equilibrium and slightly overbuilt for many areas of the country. Rents were stabilized and often flat. Areas that had high concentrations of high-tech and dot-com companies had high vacancy rates and declining rental rates.

There are several different types of industrial properties to manage. The following industrial properties have evolved as the needs of industrial businesses evolve: manufacturing buildings, warehouse, distribution centers, truck terminal, flex space, call centers, and multi-tenant buildings.

The Green Building

The real estate management industry has a long history of developing energy conservation features and operations in building. Initially, the sole reason for these programs was to reduce utility expenses. During the beginning of the 21st century, sustainability became the focus of society. Real estate managers expanded their energy conservation practices to include building sustainability practices. These practices included using environmentally friendly cleaning products, recycling building material removed from buildings, developing recycling programs, and many more energy-efficient initiatives. Building owners began using a green lease, which includes sustainability practices added to existing provisions.

CONTEMPORARY COMMERCIAL REAL ESTATE MANAGEMENT

Armed with an understanding of the history of commercial real estate management and the cyclical nature of the real estate industry, commercial real estate managers have a context from which to contemplate current challenges and opportunities.

Restructuring of Real Estate Management

If the 1980s can be characterized as the decade of development, the first half of the 1990s can be characterized as the period of real estate management. The early 1990s were difficult years for most developers because they turned to real estate management as a source of income to offset some of the dramatic reductions in their primary sources of income. Regional and local brokerage firms that did not have a real estate management division created one and aggressively solicited third-party management business to generate additional income and to have the opportunity to acquire the leasing and sales listing of these properties. Many developers and property owners who hired third-party real estate management companies assumed the management of their properties to earn the management fees.

Creation of New Income Opportunities

Just as many real estate firms have entered the real estate management business to generate another source of income, real estate management firms began offering additional services, such as consulting, expert witness testimony, tax appeal, facility management, refinancing, leasing, lease administration, and brokerage to offset the reduction in their real estate management fees—their primary source of income. By the mid-1990s, the trend in the service sector of the real estate industry was merger and acquisition. National real estate companies acquired local firms to enter a new market or increased their existing market share. Even national firms were acquired by their competitors. During the late 1990s, major real estate firms were acquiring firms in other countries to create a platform to provide real estate services globally.

The Real Estate Manager's Evolving Role

Real estate managers of the 21st century learned from the experiences of real estate managers during the 1980s and 1990s that they must be able to manage through change. One cannot manage change that is occurring in the market and in society but one can develop strategies and tactics to manage through it. This requires a broad range of business and people skills. Real estate managers must be able to adapt to an industry that experiences cycles within cycles and they must be able to change their management focus to meet the needs of different property owners. The primary responsibility of the real estate manager is to achieve and hopefully exceed the property owner's goals and objectives.

Real estate managers must be proactive and anticipate problems and opportunities and respond in advance to manage and control events. A typical week's activities can bring the real estate manager in touch with legal issues, maintenance situations, marketing and leasing activities, HR issues, construction activities, customer service encounters, accounting issues, and a host of other diverse, but interrelated, activities.

Some of the personal traits necessary to be a successful real estate manager are having good judgment, people skills, self-motivation, and good work ethics. It's also important to be skilled at managing relationships. These relationships include those with residents and tenants, visitors and shoppers, contractors, government employees, neighborhoods, and professionals in varying fields. Those traits will always be requirements for success, but another trait must be added: the ability to adapt to change. The only constant in the real estate industry is change.

Real estate managers do not manage buildings they manage businesses. Each property is the owner's business. When managing a mega MXD or a successful super regional mall, the real estate manager is essentially managing a business worth in excess of one billion dollars. When a real estate manager is managing a small 10,000-square-foot office building, he or she is managing a small business for its owner. The small office building is just as important to its owner as the mega MXD is to its owner.

Opportunities in Commercial Real Estate Management

Commercial real estate management continues to more opportunities than ever before. Many of the changes in the real estate industry previously mentioned in this chapter—especially the changes during the weak markets of the late 1980s, early 1990s, and the Great Recession—created new opportunities for commercial real estate managers.

For years, real estate managers were employed primarily by third-party real estate management firms. Today, there are opportunities to work for several different types of real estate and other types of firms. Almost all of the *real estate investment trusts (REITs)* manage their own properties; they have hired real estate managers and promoted many of their staff to real estate management positions. Many private investors and developers have created in-house real estate management departments or subsidiary real estate management companies. National, regional, and local brokerage firms have added real estate management services to the portfolio of services they offer their clients. Major corporations and retailers have real estate departments to manage and lease their sites. Government agencies at all levels have real estate managers who are responsible for millions of square feet of commercial space ranging from small office buildings to airports. Opportunities will always be available with third-party management firms.

As discussed in the review of each property type, every decade developers are creating new property types and these properties create new management opportunities.

The responsibilities of commercial real estate managers are no longer limited to just managing properties; they are more involved than ever in transactions, consulting services, facility management, and expert witness testimony. Since commercial real estate management firms have increased their involvement in transactions, commercial real estate managers have more opportunities to lease, sell, and refinance properties. These activities give commercial real estate managers the opportunity to earn substantial commissions in addition to their salaries and other benefits.

Opportunities are plentiful in commercial real estate management in the U.S. The energetic and highly motivated person will seek out and capitalize on the increased opportunities to develop a fulfilling and rewarding career. Some career opportunities may lead commercial real estate managers beyond U.S. borders to the global community.

REAL ESTATE AS A GLOBAL COMMODITY

The real estate industry in the U.S. is the envy of real estate professionals throughout the world. They can practice their profession knowing that a standard of practice, laws, and regulations allow for the orderly conduct of real estate transactions. Investors have the assurance that business, real estate, and owner-tenant laws protect their property rights, while commercial tenants can rely on owner-tenant laws to protect their leasehold interests in spaces they occupy.

Real estate managers are able to manage and operate properties based on accepted industry standards. They also have the assurance that the owner-tenant laws provide a framework for dealing with commercial tenants. Real estate professionals in many underdeveloped and formerly communist countries operate in an environment that is clouded with uncertainty. Many of those countries have limited owner-tenant laws, no standards or limited standards of real estate practices, and archaic business practices.

U.S. Real Estate Industry Foundations

The real estate industry in the U.S. has six basic foundations that have enabled it to grow and prosper. These following six foundations bring discipline and order to every aspect of the real estate industry including land acquisition, financing, development, leasing, real estate management, ownership, and the sale of property:

1. Since the U.S. is a democratic country based on free enterprise, there are no barriers that keep individuals from entering the real estate profession—almost anyone can start a real estate management company.
2. Investing in income-producing real estate—whether purchasing commercial property or stock in a REIT—is available to most citizens.
3. Real estate regulations and laws in the U.S. protect consumers and communities while bringing order to developing, owning, and occupying commercial real estate. These regulations allow for the orderly flow of real estate transactions.
4. Several real estate professional and trade associations provide forums for networking and an exchange of ideas and experiences among real estate professionals. Such associations are advocates for the real estate industry, ensuring that property owners' rights and real estate practitioners' issues are represented.
5. Real estate education is readily available. Professional and trade associations, colleges and universities offer real estate seminars, designations, and degrees.
6. Many real estate associations and companies require their members and associates to abide by a code of ethics.

Real Estate Industry Country Classifications

The real estate industry in most countries can be classified into one of the following four categories.

1. Democratic countries with an advanced real estate industry such as the U.S., Canada, Australia, New Zealand, England, Singapore, Japan, and Western Europe encourage free enterprise and entrepreneurship.
2. Other industrialized countries with an advanced real estate industry offer limited real estate education and networking opportunities.
3. Formerly, communist countries that have become democracies and have a new generation of entrepreneurs have an emerging real estate industry. The best examples are the formerly communist Eastern European countries such as Poland, Hungary, and the Czech Republic. These countries are developing real estate laws and Western-style practices such as title to property and financing.
4. Under-developed countries have economies in which the government and a few wealthy individuals own almost all of the real estate. They have a small middle class, and the vast majority of the people are poor. Real estate education and networking opportunities do not exist. Ethics are unknown, while graft and kickbacks are common practices in many industries.

Though the challenges described in some of the countries seem overwhelming, the real estate professionals in many of the under-developed and formerly communist countries are working diligently to raise the standards of their industry to those of the democratic countries.

Real estate professional and trade associations have increased their international activities. The *Institute of Real Estate Management (IREM®)* offers courses in Asia, South America, Western Europe, Central and Eastern Europe, and it has developed partnerships with real estate associations in countries around the world. Some of its publications have been translated into other languages. IREM has awarded the Certified Real Estate Manager (CPM®) designation to real estate managers throughout the world.

Real Estate Management Opportunities Abroad

International real estate management opportunities are increasingly available for experienced U.S. real estate managers. International real estate management assignments are typically for 18 to 24 months. U.S. real estate managers who work abroad are paid well. American-style, high-rise apartment building usually occupied by other expatriates is typically part of the compensation. If the assignment is for a longer period, a housing allowance may be provided. Most U.S. real estate managers take an assignment abroad to experience another culture and to help develop the country's real estate management industry.

As U.S. real estate companies develop international operations, more opportunities will be created for experienced real estate managers to practice their profession in another country. Many of the large U.S. brokerage firms have purchased real estate firms headquartered in Europe with operations in Europe and Asia. These acquisitions give the U.S. firms a global network. Foreign real estate firms have acquired U.S. real estate companies for the same strategic purpose. Shopping center REITs, as well as major U.S. real estate investment firms are acquiring and developing properties in countries outside of North America.

PROFESSIONAL ASSOCIATIONS

When property owners hire real estate managers, they are hiring someone to essentially run their business. They are entrusting the real estate manager with an asset worth several to hundreds of million dollars; some developments exceed a billion dollars in value. They expect the manager of their business—the real estate manager—to increase the cash flow and value of their business.

Managing a property entails accounting, financial analysis, financing, reporting, marketing, sales (leasing), public relations, people skills, administration, maintenance, real estate and business law, and handling the unexpected; however, no one can be an expert in all these areas. Fortunately, the commercial real estate management industry is served by four professional or trade associations. They provide their members many benefits, including the following:

- Research
- Educational programs
- Periodicals, textbooks, and other publications
- Local, regional, and national meetings
- Professional designations

Each of these organizations is involved in promoting the real estate management profession internationally and has members around the world who have attended their seminars and courses and have earned their designations.

Institute of Real Estate Management (IREM)

IREM, founded in 1933, awards the Certified Property Manager (CPM®) designation to real estate managers who have distinguished themselves in experience, education, and ethical conduct. All CPM® Members must abide by a code of ethics established by IREM. Those violating the code are subject to revocation of their designation. To qualify for the CPM designation, a candidate must successfully complete an intensive series of IREM courses.

Commercial Real Estate Education

IREM commercial real estate courses include management and leasing of office buildings, shopping centers, and retail properties. Additional courses cover asset management, legal issues, risk management, business ethics, human resource management, financial analysis, valuation strategies for real estate assets, creating and managing the real estate management company, and business development. IREM courses are available in a classroom setting and a home-study format; some are offered online.

IREM publishes a comprehensive series of professional books, monographs, forms, and research studies as well as the leading real estate management periodical, the *Journal of Property Management (JPM®)*.

In 1945, IREM set standards under which certain firms could be recognized as Accredited Management Organizations (AMO®). Holders of the AMO® designation have met the IREM standards of education, experience, integrity, and fiscal stability.

The IREM Foundation has several scholarship programs to assist real estate managers with tuition for attending IREM courses and for college scholarships. Approximately 100 local IREM chapters are found in the U.S., Canada, Asia, and Europe. Each conducts regular meetings, provides mini-seminars, and serves the interests of the real estate management profession.

International Real Estate Management

IREM is actively involved in real estate management around the world. Its first course offered outside of North America was shopping center management and leasing in Singapore in 1989. In the mid-1990s, IREM first offered courses in Central and Eastern Europe; by the late 1990s into the 21st century, it offered courses in South America, Western Europe, China, Japan, and South Korea. IREM assisted an emerging real estate industry in Central and Eastern Europe in developing its real estate management profession. IREM has CERTIFIED PROPERTY MANAGERS® managing properties on every continent.

For foreign countries, IREM has a distinct advantage over other real estate management associations because it offers courses and publishes books on all types of commercial properties. Most foreign countries have a primary need for residential or commercial real estate management education. In some countries where the majority of the population lives in government housing, the real estate management industry needs courses and publications on managing and leasing commercial properties.

International Council of Shopping Centers (ICSC)

ICSC was formed in 1956 to serve the shopping center industry. ICSC awards four professional designations to shopping center professionals in North America:

- Certified Shopping Center Manager (CSM)
- Certified Marketing Director (CMD)
- Certified Leasing Specialist (CLS)
- Certified Retail Property Executive (CRX)

In the late 1990s, ICSC developed two designations to recognize professional achievement in shopping center management and marketing outside of North America: the Accredited Shopping Center Manager (ASM) and Accredited Marketing Director (AMD) .

Designations

The objectives of the CSM program are to accomplish the following:

1. Establish and advance high standards in shopping center management.
2. Recognize managers who meet these professional standards.
3. Encourage others to train for careers in shopping center management.
4. Establish and maintain educational standards for the profession.

The CSM exam is a comprehensive test covering five areas: (1) shopping center management, operations, and construction; (2) leasing and development; (3) shopping center accounting, finance, record keeping, retailing, and merchandising; (4) marketing, promotions and community relations; and (5) insurance and law.

The CMD program, formerly the Accredited Shopping Center Promotion Director (ASPD) program, are to accomplish the following:

1. Establish high professional standards in the marketing activities of shopping centers.
2. Give industry-wide recognition to marketing/promotion directors who achieve professional standing.
3. Establish educational standards for the profession.
4. Encourage others to train for careers in shopping center marketing.

The CMD examination is a multiple-choice written test that covers five areas of shopping center marketing: (1) the marketing plan; (2) product development/center merchandising; (3) retailing/store merchandising; (4) media planning and public relations; and (5) administration.

The CLS designation was established in 1994. This designation recognizes shopping center leasing professionals. It also establishes guidelines for this segment of the shopping center industry. The objectives of the CLS program are as follows:

1. Raise the professional standard and improve

the practice of shopping center leasing by giving special recognition to those properly qualified professionals with responsibility for leasing shopping centers, negotiating as an agent for space in shopping centers, or representing tenants in the process of leasing space in shopping centers who, by meeting prescribed qualifications of experience and/or education and by passing a written examination, have demonstrated a high level of competence for the designation of CLS.

2. Instill knowledge of the principles and practices of leasing, and encourage an ethical code of conduct.
3. Establish education and/or experience criteria to qualify for this designation now and in the future.
4. Encourage others to train for careers in shopping center leasing.
5. Foster cooperation and a better understanding among the property owners, managers, tenants, and lenders involved in the leasing process.
6. Encourage shopping center leasing specialists in a continuing program of professional development.
7. Advise and participate in such seminars, meetings, and educational programs as may be necessary to foster these objectives.

The CLS exam consists of multiple-choice questions that cover seven areas of shopping center leasing: (1) trade areas analysis, (2) leasing fundamentals, (3) legal, (4) construction, (5) retailing, (6) financing, and (7) operations/marketing and promotions.

The CRX designation was developed in 2014 for shopping center professionals and is a global mark of professional achievement. ICSC descriptions of the program is, "the CRX defines the responsibilities, role, and abilities of a professional engaging in retail property executive leadership position including experts in asset management, development, redevelopment, finance, accounting, leasing, revenue generation, retailing, marketing, communications, legal, compliance, property, and facilities." The CRX exam includes questions in the aforementioned subjects.

ICSC offers extensive educational programs at the regional and national level. ICSC offers the University of Shopping Centers a week-long education program with concurrent education classes, the School of Retail Real Estate Professionals, and special seminars. ICSC also offers Idea Exchanges, one-, two- and three-day seminars on specialized topics offered throughout the country. The annual ICSC RECON, The Global Retail Real Estate Convention is a four-day program featuring speakers, a trade show, exhibits, and a leasing mall. The leasing mall provides developers, brokers, and retailers outstanding opportunities to meet and "make business deals." Appointments with retailers are made weeks in advance to discuss leasing space in specific shopping centers or other retail properties. The leasing mall is so successful that a mini-version is held at regional conferences around the country. ICSC also offers several one-week courses on shopping management, advanced shopping center management, marketing, and promotions. Specialty short courses of note are on temporary tenants (pop-up tenants), security, and legal issues. ICSC publishes books, technical reports, legal reports, and specialized bulletins.

ICSC has also developed International Design and Development Awards. This program was established in 1977 to recognize exceptional shopping center developments that have solved a variety of problems. The award honors shopping center owners, developers, architects, and managers.

An ICSC international conference is held in Western Europe and Asia. ICSC offers seminars on development, leasing, management, and marketing in Asia, South America, and Central America. Shopping center professionals throughout the world have been awarded professional designations by ICSC.

Building Owners and Managers Association (BOMA)

In 1907, a group of 75 office building managers formed the National Association of Building Owners and Managers, later known as the *Building Owners and Managers Association (BOMA)*. The organization held its first convention in Chicago in 1908. The program for the inaugural event included topics such as ventilation, economy in electric lighting, varnishes, cleaning problems, and division of costs of services in a building—topics that are still relevant today. That convention was the first time commercial real estate managers had met nationally to share ideas and exchange information.

In 1920, the association published the industry's first major research report on office building operating expenses—the annual Experience Exchange Report (EER). The EER analyzes the income and expenses of more than 3,000 office buildings across the U.S. and Canada, providing a standard of performance comparison for all office buildings. The report is the leading reference guide for office building operation. BOMA publishes five books on measuring buildings and tenant's space and periodically updates the most recent publication.

In 1915, BOMA published and continues to revise the industry stand for measuring office building, *Office Buildings: Standard Methods of Measurement.* BOMA and the Society of Industrial and Office Parks (SIOR) jointly published the *Industrial Buildings: Standard Method of Measurement, Mixed Use Properties: Standards Methods of Measurement, Multi-Use Residential Buildings: Standard Methods of Measurement and Retail Buildings: Standard Method of Measurement.* BOMA also publishes several books on office building management and leasing.

In 2009, BOMA established the BOMA 360 designation designed for commercial real estate professionals that recognizes all-around excellence in building operations and management. The curriculum includes:

1. Operations and management
2. Security and Safety
3. Training and Education
4. Energy
5. Environmental and sustainability
6. Tenant relations

BOMA has an association in every major metropolitan area and in many smaller cities throughout the U.S. The associations hold monthly meetings, lobby on behalf of the industry, and conduct mini-seminars. BOMA conducts an annual winter business meeting and an annual convention and office building show.

BOMA offers several education programs including Foundation of Real Estate Managers, an entry-level course, BOMA Office Measurement Standards Seminars and asset management courses for real estate managers. Their asset management curriculum includes the following topics:

1. Measuring financial returns
2. Leasing analysis, valuation, negotiations and approval
3. Portfolio management and capital markets
4. Value creation strategies at the property level

BOMI Institute

In 1970, the *BOMI Institute* was formed to provide office building managers with the knowledge to maintain their buildings' operations at peak efficiency. In 1973, the Institute developed the Real Property Administrator (RPA) program and designation. Eight years later, the Systems Maintenance Technician (SMT) and Systems Maintenance Administrators (SMA) programs and designations were developed. In 1988, BOMI developed a program and designation for facilities managers, Facilities Management Administration (FMA). To earn the RPA a candidate must meet a minimum real estate management experience requirement and complete several required and elective courses and an ethics seminar.

The FMA designation and program were developed to educate facility managers on the design and operations of building systems. Several courses are required to earn the FMA designation. BOMI's ethics course, *Good Business Seminar,* is required to earn the designation.

The SMT program trains building maintenance personnel on effective management of energy-efficient and environmentally sound building systems. The programs offer two levels of building operations proficiency. BOMI's ethics course is a requirement to earn the SMT and SMA designations.

PROFESSIONAL DESIGNATIONS

The real estate industry places great emphasis on professional designations. Today, many institutional decision makers hold professional designations, and they are familiar with the stringent requirements to become a CPM, CSM, RPA, and other commercial real estate designations. Asset managers frequently request that the real estate manager, who will manage their buildings, hold one of the aforementioned designations. Similarly, lenders and institutional owners often want to know the qualifications of a real estate manager when evaluating which company will be awarded a real estate management account. They know that the quality of management will make the difference between a property that is operated as a first-class property and one that has chronic problems. They also know the importance of the real estate manager in enhancing value. An owner may prefer to have a CSM or a CPM to manage a shopping center or mall and an RPA or a CPM to manage an office building or industrial property.

Professional designations offer tremendous benefits to the real estate manager. The recognition of such designations places the real estate manager in an elite group of professionals in the real estate community. The educational requirements to obtain the designations give the real estate manager the knowledge and practical skills needed to succeed.

Many real estate managers who hold one or several designations will attest to the fact that the greatest benefit to belonging to IREM, BOMA, or ICSC is the networking opportunities and sharing of information. These professional real estate management associations provide forums to meet other industry professionals to discuss common property and industry challenges and opportunities. Real estate management is one of a few real estate professions in which people are willing to share information. Many real estate managers find serving on a committee of one of these professional associations an invaluable experience. Serving as an officer of a chapter of IREM or of an association of BOMA or on a national committee of one of these three professional associations develops leadership skills and provides industry recognition. Many of the most successful real estate managers attribute a good portion of their career growth to their membership and involvement in one or more of these professional associations. Taking advantage of the benefits offered by IREM, ICSC, BOMA, and BOMI enables a real estate manager to manage, market, and lease a property owner's real estate business better.

CHAPTER

2

The Business Plan

Few things in real estate management are more daunting than the preparation of a business plan. However, when done properly, the business plan will point to the proper future direction of the property and the gathering and analysis of the information will provide the basis for going forward. A *business plan* is a formal statement of business goals, reasons they are attainable, and plans for reaching them. There are many reasons to prepare a business plan which include:

- The Acquisition of a new property
- The takeover of a new management account
- Changes in the market or trade area
- Changes in ownership
- Providing a basis for budget preparation
- Making a presentation to obtain a new management account
- Applying for financing
- Making a buy, sell, or hold decision
- Develop a plan to enhance the income and value of the property
- Annual review of the property

Many real estate management companies develop a business plan annually for each property they manage. The initial plan will require extensive research and analysis and subsequent annual plans will update the initial plan and address issues that are not meeting their objectives. The economy, the real estate market, new competition, *demographics* and *psychographics* changes in the trade area of a shopping center, changes in the property owner's financial situation and/or goals and objectives for the property, and significant occupancy changes are just a few of issues that can justify or require an updated or complete new business plan to be developed.

While the basic business plan will be almost the same in all of the situations, the conclusions may be different depending on the purpose of the plan and the owner's goals and objectives for the real estate asset. It must also be noted that this chapter will provide a very complete plan for a complex property, but quite often, a much lesser plan will suffice for the annual budgeting plan and/or the analysis of a sub portion of the property operations.

While there are generally accepted guidelines for the proper preparation of a business plan, it's important to take into consideration for whom the plan is being prepared for and what their parameters may be. A plan prepared for a buyer of a property who intends to pay cash for the property will not need analysis of the various types of loans that may be available and their impact on the cash flow of the property. A local buyer of a property may be quite familiar with the market and not desire additional market information.

The Business Plan should be an unbiased assessment of the property, it's strengths, weaknesses, goals, and a plan for achieving the owner's objectives. Typically, an owner will have an *exit strategy* which could be a short term, long term, and specified hold period. A business plan and/or annual updates to the business plan helps maneuver through changes in assumptions along the way, and to achieve the ultimate goal at the end of the hold period.

If one is preparing a business plan for a potential new client, considerable effort should be placed in showing the capabilities and prior accomplishments of the real estate management company. It should also be noted that if the competition for a new property is a large national real estate management company, they may do a full-scale business plan with professional back up and a complete analysis. While that may be a major job for a smaller real estate management company, it is essential that you do your best to match or exceed the professionalism of your competition.

In preparing a business plan for the purpose of obtaining a new client or account, it is important to identify the principals of the company and their backgrounds and accomplishments; particularly those involving management of other real estate holdings that are similar in nature to the type of property that is the subject property of the business plan. It is also important to identify the person who will be charged with implementing the plan and his or her qualifications and accomplishments as well.

The best preparation for putting together an effective business plan is to assume nothing and go in without preconceived conclusions and let the information point one in the proper direction. The person for whom the business plan is being prepared for may have set forth a preconceived plan and indicated that this is the desired direction for the business plan. The client would expect that and the writer of the business plan should take that direction into consideration, but the writer should also let the information lead in the logical direction. If the logical direction differs from the pre-conceived plan, the writer should then present both options to the client as alternative approaches.

As an example, two young entrepreneurs decided to invest in a shopping center for the first time and brought in an experienced real estate real estate management company to prepare a business plan and budget for their proposed acquisition. After five days of intensive analysis together going over the property, the real estate manager indicated that the property was not a good one for them to purchase, and that they should "walk away" from the deal even if it meant losing the deposit money. As one would expect, the young clients were very upset and indicated they had not hired the real estate manager to make a buy/sell decision for them, but rather to do an analysis as to what was likely to happen once they purchased the property. The real estate manger once again prepared the reports and budgets as requested, and again explained that this was not likely to be a good acquisition and they should not make the purchase. The resulting analysis showed a very poor performance for the property. Although the real estate manager presented an accurate analysis of the property, the clients were disappointed and the relationship did not end on a positive note. Two years later, the property had still not been sold and the young clients sent the real estate manager a "thank you" for steering them in the right direction. While we always want the client to be pleased with our work, we are also obligated to use our backgrounds and experience to gather all relevant information and analyze that information to form the basis for the future direction of the property; no matter the final conclusion.

As real estate managers, we want to please, but more importantly, we want to provide meaningful and accurate guidance. When coming to a conclusion that does not fit the goals of the client, the analyst must go to extreme steps to justify the recommended solution, but also be prepared for an unhappy client, even if it is the right decision. Sometimes we come to conclusions that do not fit the goal of the client, the analyst should be prepared to present those conclusions. Creating trust and rapport sometimes involves talking a client out of a sale, even if it might cost an account or sale.

The following outline is one of the most complete and organized guidelines for preparing a detailed business plan (or sometimes referred to as the management plan) and comes from a prior IREM publication:

- Title page
- Table of contents
- Letter of transmittal
- Executive summary
- Identification of the client and property ownership
- The purpose of the study and client objectives
- Time frame of the study

- Basic assumptions and limiting conditions
- General environment
- Identification of the property
- Description of land and leasehold interest
- Description of improvements
- Current economic/fiscal condition of the property
- Description of current management
- Analysis and statement of the problem (if there is one)
- Methodology
- Supply/demand and absorption analysis
- Market rent levels
- Range of possible solutions
- Analysis and testing of solutions
- Recommended solution
- Supporting material
- Certification and disclosures
- Qualifications of analyst
- Definition of basic terminology
- Appearance and style
- Cash flow analysis
- Comparison grid

This chapter follows this outline and explains the information to be provided and analyzed in each of these sections. Prior to doing the budget or a plan for a smaller part of the property, the annual business plan is not likely to be this extensive, but it must still be complete for the job being analyzed.

It is critical to note that the final presentation of the business plan must be clear and concise, have a professional look, must be accurate and objective, and details supporting any conclusions or recommendations but be provided. Before it's shared with the client, the business plan should be reviewed by at least one company executive or senior staff member who was not involved in the preparation of the plan to make sure that it properly represents the company, and that there are no typos or errors that could distract from an otherwise excellent presentation.

Most companies have a business plan template, but do not rely solely on the templated information. A proper business plan must be customized to the subject property and include information and make recommendations that are specific for that property. For example, if the business plan is being prepared for a 10-story office building, market data for surrounding industrial property may have no relevance to the subject property and should not be included in the plan. Obviously, the pages of the business plan should be numbered and great care should be taken that it's paginated appropriately with the table of contents. For electronic files, be sure that links to pages are inserted properly.

It is very possible to complete a lot of work and expense going forward only to discover that it is the wrong approach for that property. As an example, a shopping center had a vacancy created by a local pharmacist. The owner concluded that smaller local pharmacists were no longer available and immediately ordered the space to be divided for other small businesses. About halfway through remodel, a local broker came to them with a regional pharmacy chain that showed interest in the space and, ultimately leased the space even though it was smaller than their typical location. A market survey and analysis of the market would have turned up the fact that this market was well underserved by the lack of a pharmacy. A sophisticated leasing agent would have discovered this and likely would have contacted the chain stores about the location—even though it was smaller than their usual footprint. The proper analysis of the market place and the property's position in that market place will likely lead to better decisions and less wasted funds than proceeding without a proper business plan.

TITLE PAGE

The title page is the first thing the client will see when they start to read the plan. The client may spell out how they want the title page to appear, but if not, that page should identify the property that is the subject of the plan along with its street address. The title page should provide the current date of the plan, show a current picture of the property (either an aerial or satellite photo that also focuses on the property's trade area or micro market), and possibly include a short description of the property below the picture. It should also have and a "Presented to" listing the client and the current address, and should include the name of the person who prepared the report along with his or her current address, phone number, and e-mail address. This is not the place for a company slogan or other marking information. Be very careful with the photo and make sure it is a current one rather than a "file" photo. A file photo might have older tenants, the property may have been remodeled, or other obvious changes may have been made since that photo was taken.

TABLE OF CONTENTS

The table of contents is a very important part of the business plan. Any items that may be relevant to just that property should be listed separately. For instance, a property might have restrictions imposed by a *planned unit development (PUD)* agreement or underlying *covenants, conditions, and restrictions (CC&Rs)* or even governmental restrictions. Any major element of the analysis can have a separate section in the business plan.

The table of contents may also be compartmentalized into sub sections such as:

- Introduction to the business plan
- Property description
- Problem identification
- Market information
- Identification and analysis of possible solutions
- Appendix

These or any other logical sub sections will help to focus attention of the related areas of that particular section. The table of contents should be used as the guideline for the report, but the page numbers should be added only after the final report is complete to be sure that the numbering is accurate.

LETTER OF TRANSMITTAL

The letter of transmittal should be addressed to the person who requested the business plan, or if they designate a specific receiver, to that person with all of the information properly spelled, the title correct, and the company name correct. The purpose of this transmittal is to get the report to the correct person and should not discuss the conclusions and/or promote the person or company who prepared the report. Marketing information will be included later in the business plan. Company letterhead should be used, the letter of transmittal should be signed (either on hard copy or e-signature), and should also include direct phone numbers and e-mail addresses.

EXECUTIVE SUMMARY

The executive summary is expected to be just that—a summary of the plan. This section generally is composed of four subsections as follows:

1. Issues and concerns (current or those identified in the original acquisition plan)
2. Alternative courses of action
3. Evaluation of alternatives
4. Recommended course of action

This is the last section of the report to be prepared, just before the final table of contents as it is a reflection of the entire plan. It should outline the problems and reasonable alternative solutions, and provide the final recommended solution. It should be remembered that one of the proposed solutions is to "do nothing"—meaning to continue operating the property as it has been operated with no capital improvements. In most cases, the "do nothing" approach will lead to an under-performing property, but that should emphasize the need for the recommended solution.

The executive summary should include a brief financial analysis, with a realization that the full financial analysis is included in the business plan. The executive summary should give the reader a good overview of the report and a clear direction for the property if the plan is followed. It is likely that the client will share the report with other experts, accountants, contractors, etc. upon which the client relies. For this reason, don't assume in the executive summary that everyone will already have knowledge of the property. Some of the client's experts may not be familiar with, or have ever seen, the property.

The executive summary should be able to stand on it's own, but with much less back up than contained in the complete business plan. The plan should not be minimized, nor should a negative point of view be given. If a realistic business plan cannot be provided because of market conditions, or the cost of implementing a positive plan would be prohibitive, the recommended course of action could be to sell the property, rather than trying to turn the property around. Some clients are just not equipped to handle a major remodel or a complete releasing or repositioning plan of a property, and if that is the best approach, a recommendation of selling the property is most likely a very good one.

In general, it is important to remember the goals and objectives of the owner when recommending a course of action. The owner of the property might be a good owner/operator of an income-producing property, but may not have the time or inclination to get involved in a time-consuming rehab, renovation, or releasing of a property. The plan should be realistic and upbeat. If this plan is for a new account, the real estate manager should try and convey its excitement and optimism to work on the account.

IDENTIFICATION OF THE CLIENT AND PROPERTY OWNERSHIP

This is where the client is identified and, if available, the type of ownership. If partners are involved, they should also be listed. However, it is not unusual for the actual client to be a trustee for owners who do not care to be identified or a partnership where one or more of the partners do not wish to be identified. In that case, the trustee would be identified and it would be noted that the trustee is acting on behalf of an unidentified client and/or there are additional partners that wish to remain anonymous.

The business plan is developed to meet the goals and objectives of the property owner. These goals should be stated in the plan, so the recommended solutions can be directed to those aims. It is possible that the property is owned by a family trust with growth in mind, or it could be a trust whose main interest is in preservation of capital and/or cash flow. In general, working with a trustee is a rare situation.

PURPOSE OF THE STUDY AND CLIENT OBJECTIVES

While this is closely related to the identification of the client, this section of the business plan is to indicate the purpose of the study. Is it to solve a specific problem, such as a persistent vacancy? Is it to lower rental rates? The nature of the problem should be clearly stated. This section should be used to clearly state the objectives of the owners relative to the solution of the problem. Does the owner want to fix the problem and sell the property? Does the owner intend to hold the property for the long term and fix the problem in order to improve the income and value?

If the owners have set a specific goal, such as 95 percent occupancy at a given rental rate within five years, that should be specifically stated. The writer of the plan may not agree with the goals and objectives of the owner, and should state any disagreements as a way to clarify them. Once the owner has stated the goals and objectives and they have been discussed and evaluated, the business plan must reflect them. The information provided will either support the timeline of the goals and objectives, or provide data for why the goals and objectives are unlikely to be achieved in the desired timeline.

TIME FRAME OF THE STUDY

Generally, it is fairly easy to set a time frame for the study—it's always better to agree to a deadline that the real estate manager will be able to beat. When do you expect to get started on the preparation and when do you think you will finish the report? A recommendation should be made as to when the project should start. If for some reason, the job will not be able to start by the recommended time, it may be necessary to revisit some of the data to be sure that all data (such as appraisals, market leasing comps, etc.) and conclusions are still valid and that the desired outcome is still likely. Be sure to ask the client how much time they need to review it. The plan should be first presented in person, and the clients will want time to review it on their own. This is a great opportunity to ask how long they need before you follow up. It is quite possible that the client will provide the time frame for the actual commencement of the plan and the desired dates of completion. If the market is changing and those changes may impact the implementation and/or timing of the plan, that should be clearly stated so the readers understand there may be an urgency to the implementation of the plan.

BASIC ASSUMPTIONS AND LIMITING CONDITIONS

Unless you plan to go through every lease and financial document provided by the client, one must assume that the information provided is accurate and will partially be used to form the final conclusions. If the property is very unique, there may be very few comparables and the writer of the plan will make assumptions based on his or her knowledge of the market. Those assumptions should be clearly stated. It is possible that the client does not desire to divulge certain information to the author of the plan for the purposes of this report and that should be noted as a limiting condition.

It is also possible that there may be underlying restrictions by other tenants in the building, co-owners of the properties, *restrictive easements,* covenants, conditions, and restrictions (CC&Rs), *utility easements,* zoning and lease restrictions, such as *exclusives,* cancellations rights, *options,* etc. that may prevent an otherwise logical plan to go forward. Anything that is used to reach your conclusions and recommendations that you cannot verify by an outside source should be listed as an assumption, which would be based on your previous experience.

GENERAL ENVIRONMENT

The environment to be covered in this section is the immediate environment of the property. This would include the region in which the property is located as well as the neighborhood, trade area for a shopping center, or the market or micro market for an office building or an industrial property. If the property is a shopping center, it will be defined by identifying its trade area along with demographic and psychographics reports, but there must be an objective basis for the area being selected.

Maps should be included that locate the region within the state or county, and a map of the region itself with boundaries clearly defined. Quite often, the market or business area for an office or industrial building has already been defined by the local brokerage community. It is best to work within the parameters set by the brokerage community and determine how the area will impact the building and how it will compete within that environment.

If the region or neighborhood is evolving or changing, those changes should also be referenced in this section to ensure that the impact of the local market is properly represented. For example, if a major office tenant is relocating out of the area and vacancy rates are expected to significantly increase throughout the next six to 12 months, that anticipated impact should be noted. If there are any environmental conditions in and around the trade area or market, they should be mentioned and their possible impact on the subject property explained, such as a nearby contaminated river or building.

This section should include information on the services in the area including:

- Work pool education
- Transportation
- Development trends (past, current, and future)
- Cultural venues
- Climate conditions
- Rate of growth and forecast for future growth (why that growth is likely)

IDENTIFICATION OF PROPERTY

The property should be clearly defined with a full street address and a word picture of the property.

For example, a grocery-anchored neighborhood shopping center located at the southwest corner of Main Street and Tracey Avenue in the city of Sunnymeade. The property is situated on nine-level acres with entrances on both streets and a street light at the front of the property. The buildings are nine years old, well maintained with modern designs. The property is anchored by a Food City Supermarket of 49,000 square feet and a Morgan's Drug store of 17,000 square feet and has 12 restaurants and shop tenants.

The parking arrangements should be described as to adequacy and appearance. If there is a parking structure, it should be described and signage and lighting should be described and evaluated. The property's landscaping should be fully described and evaluated as to maintenance and safety concerns with sight lines for traffic being evaluated. There should be many pictures of the subject property including views down both streets.

DESCRIPTION OF LAND AND LEASEHOLD INTEREST

The description should include the size of the property (land and building), configuration or shape, current zoning, zoning of immediate surrounding dwellings, and any applicable restrictions/easements. For example, the site is nine-level acres and is rectangle in shape with 1,136 feet of frontage on Main Street and 345 feet of frontage on Tracey Avenue. The site provides for ample shop front spaces and parking for all units. The zoning is C-4, general commercial and the property is in compliance with that zoning with no variances. The property is held in *fee simple* and is subject to the leases of the tenants of the property, including leases from the anchor tenants. Development and future operations should be mentioned due to PUD permits which controls some of the future leasing of the property, but is not overly restrictive. Answering the following list of questions will help to describe the leasing restrictions:

- How does the subject property fit in with the surrounding area?
- What types of properties are located on the other three corners, and are they consistent with the subject property?
- Is the site fully served by the local municipal utilities and is not lacking any required services?
- Where are utility easements located and are they restrictive to the future of the site?
- What is the condition of the property?
- Are the property consistent with the zoning in the area?
- Where is the surrounding residential area, and is it made up of single family homes and/or apartment buildings?

It should be noted if the subject property's development and condition is consistent with the other properties in the area. It should be stated if the subject property is currently developed to the highest and best use for the site. If it is not, most likely a major renovation and/or change of use may be the recommended solution. It is also important to indicate if the local area is on the decline or if it's an emerging area. This can have a major impact on the recommended solution.

DESCRIPTION OF IMPROVEMENTS

Describe the square footage of the built-out portion of the property and outline the various types of units, such an anchor tenants, in-line shops, pad tenants, or (in the case of office use) the number of floor and any major tenants. If it is an office building, any commercial uses such as a roof-top restaurant, basement night club, and/or ground floor retail should be mentioned and their impact on the subject property should be evaluated.

The type of construction should be mentioned, such as wood frame, steel frame, or block construction, etc. The type of roofing and its condition, along with the type of landscaping and its condition should also be noted. The shape of the building may be an important factor in the recommended solution. If the building has an inefficient shape or parts of the buildings are either obstructed or difficult to access, these must be considered when coming up with the recommended solution.

If there is *deferred maintenance,* areas of concern should be identified here so that they may be further discussed and addressed in other areas of the report to include the section on analysis and statement of the problem, as well as the final recommendations.

If any of the parking is paid, it should be noted. The air conditioning system should be mentioned and it should be stated if the units are serviced by the owner or the tenants. This section should contain ample photographs of the exterior of the buildings as well as a significant number of pictures of interiors of major retail tenants. Street views of the properties should also be included and well labeled.

Much of the information for this section will be gathered by visiting the property; however, if a set of plans are available, it would be helpful to review the plans, look for differences in the site and the plans, and be on the lookout for areas that may have been modified from the original design, and evaluate the impact of those changes on the subject property. Any environmental conditions that exist on the site or any studies, evaluations, or possible problems should be identified and their impact on the property evaluated. If there are environmental programs underway, they should also be identified and any impact that they may have spelled out as well.

CURRENT ECONOMIC/FISCAL CONDITION OF THE PROPERTY

The fiscal condition of the property is most likely one of the most important aspects of the business plan as any proposed plan will likely need to be financed, and if the conditions are not right, it may prove difficult to proceed with any plan. This section should include full mortgage information starting with the amount of the original loan, current balance, payments and the term including balloon payments, any early call information, and/or any payoff penalties.

It should also be noted if the loan is in *default*. A full rent roll of the property should be included with any vacancies shown on the rent roll as vacant, not just left off the roll. The rent roll should include the following:

- Tenant name, (the one you would find on the tenant space, not the corporate entity name)
- Square footage
- Term of the lease with starting and ending dates
- Rental amount along with any increases during the term
- Contributions to the *common area maintenance (CAM)* or *pass-through charges*
- Contributions to marketing efforts
- Contributions to taxes and insurance
- Any options (early termination, renewal, expansion and first-right options) and rental terms for exercising the options

This section should also include three years of income and expenses for the property, as well as an analysis if the income and expenses are high, low, or in line with similar properties. If expenses are inordinately high or low, an explanation should be provided to help the reader put the information into context. In addition to stating that expenses are high or low, the supporting back-up materials should be stated, such as the *experience exchange reports* of IREM or materials provided by other trade associations to back up these opinions. If the analyst manages other properties in the area, those properties numbers can be used as comparison figures, providing that the owners have no objections.

The following list of financial questions should be answered to help form an opinion on the health of the property:

- Is the net income sufficient to support the debt and provide for the timely payment of reasonable expenses?
- Is the property financially able to support future plans and improvements?
- Are there any early due dates or balloon payments on the loan that could have a negative impact on the property?
- Should a cash reserve be implemented in anticipation of future vacancy?
- Is the subject property in a negative cash-flow position? If so, are the owners in a position to continue to support the negative cash flow until that situation can be corrected?

This section of the business plan is a good place to give an opinion as to the current value of the property and, therefore, the owner's equity. Most analysts are not qualified to provide an appraisal, but with proper courses and training, analysts can give their opinion as to the value, which is all that is needed for the sake of the business plan. If the market is positive for future growth, or if the market is declining and future growth is unlikely, that should be stated in this section along with any supporting information.

DESCRIPTION OF CURRENT MANAGEMENT

This section of the business plan will describe the management staffing and which services are contracted. Often, the real estate management company preparing the plan is also the managing and leasing agent for the property. If the real estate management company is assuming the management and leasing of the property, they may or may not want to comment on the work of the prior real estate management company.

This area can be a delicate one, especially if the owners are managing the property or the real estate management company is a captive of the owners. The analysis of the management must be objective, fair, and most importantly, be backed with actual facts that support the final analysis. Include the certifications and awards received by the personnel of the real estate management company. For instance, the Accredited Management Organization® (AMO®) designation from IREM. Members of staff may have earned and received professional designations such as the Certified Property Manager® (CPM®), also awarded by IREM, Real Property Administrator (RPA) awarded by BOMA or the Certified Shopping Center Manager (CSM) awarded by ICSC.

If the business plan is being prepared by a consultant who will have limited involvement in implementing the plan, an interview should be conducted with the head of the real estate management company. Every effort should be made to fairly evaluate how the subject property is being handled and what problems the real estate manager sees and how he or she sees them being resolved. This interview will most certainly require the approval of the client. It would be helpful to get the client's assessment of the real estate real estate management company before interviewing the real estate management company personnel to put the interview into context.

The real estate management company should be fully described as well as its relationship with the owners. Any contracts should be analyzed and attached to the report in the appendix. The term of the agreement should be analyzed, and if there are any variances with the local market, they should be noted. The staffing and experience of the current real estate management company should be analyzed and evaluated relative to the job currently being done on the property.

Is the management doing a credible job or is management a part of the existing problem? If management is part of the problem, a very objective analysis must be completed with facts to back up the conclusion. The current managements schedules for property visitations, monthly reporting, decision making, and accomplishments for the property should be noted and evaluated.

Problems areas should be clearly defined and examples, where available, should be part of the appendix of the business plan. If the current management is part of the problem, or contributes to most of the problem, that opinion should be clearly stated and not just referenced in any sort of a veiled way.

If available, review policies, procedures, and schedules of the existing management team and report on their contribution to either the success of the programs or their contribution to the problem. To the degree that the current management's policies, procedures and/or reporting are part of the problem, copies of those documents should be included in the appendix.

ANALYSIS AND STATEMENT OF THE PROBLEM

The analysis and statement of the problem is the main objective of the business plan. It is critical to identify the main problem or problems with the property, as this will form the basis for any solutions that are recommended. Are the problems global, regional, statewide, local, neighborhood related, or a combination of any? Clear reasoning must be provided for selecting the problem or problems that have been identified and minimize those areas that are symptoms of the problem, rather than the real problem.

If rents too low because the property owner and property managers are not current with market conditions, or if it's due to a very poor marketing program or deferred maintenance, the reasoning should be explained in detail. Relate your identification of the problem to the owner's goals and how solving the problem is going to further those goals. If there are multiple problems, there should be multiple solutions. If the explanation of the problem(s) runs two or three pages, it is a good idea to end the section with a brief summary of the analysis.

METHODOLOGY

The methodology section of the business plan explains how the situation will be analyzed, identifies the problem or problems, and formulates a solution that will help the property owner reach his or her goals. The approach should be outlined as follows:

- Review the owners objectives.
- Perform a physical inspection of the property.
- Prepare a detailed inspection report with recommendation and probable costs.
- Review current management policies and procedures.
- Analyze the economic and fiscal condition of the property.
- Identify and review all exterior market variables.
- Present findings of facts.
- Identify a range of possible solutions.
- Provide a suggested time frame for completion.
- Test all of the possible solutions and include a source and use a schedule for any capital to be raised and spent in each solution.
- Make a final recommendation based on the best results.

A statement as to the highest and best use for the property should be included as the basis for going forward with the proposed solution.

SUPPLY/DEMAND AND ABSORPTION ANALYSIS

The supply/demand and absorption analysis is one of the most critical elements of the plan. With a rare exception, the solution to the problem will be helped by a strong market and hampered in a weak market. Supply and demand will determine the properties strength in the existing market and proper projections will show the necessary strength to carry out the proposed plan. It's important to analyze the overall use and zoning patterns in the immediate area.

For a shopping center, it's important to understand the demographics of the area including population, income, family make up, average ages, and the direction that the demographics are heading. Psychographics are also of importance. It is important to not only know the income levels, but also where those incomes come are derived.

A lower income or even lower/middle income market is more than likely to support Class B or C office buildings and will likely not be attractive to an Class A office building. Industrial properties are less likely to be swayed by the income levels in the area, but will be interested in the work force and how that potential work force will impact their need to have a strong source of employees.

For the most part, office buildings are heavily impacted by location, image, branding, and proximity to supporting industries. Once the market and trade area have been defined, a complete inventory of competitive properties should be compiled. Each property should be visited and analyzed for rental rates, bill back costs, vacancy factors, current leasing effort, and condition of the property. One should take a lot of pictures during the tour of the properties, including inside stores and/or offices if possible.

Local brokers and/or appraisers are excellent sources of much of this information and if their information is used, they should receive proper credit in the business plan. Providing information to brokers and appraisers when asked will likely pay big dividends when you are looking for comparable information. Many brokers prepare and share figures on absorption and leasing rates, vacancy rates, and market rates. Those that are not provided by the brokers will require the writer to call and interview the real estate managers or leasing agents of competitive properties to gather the information. It is suggested that the call be straight forward to the building manager or leasing agent, tell them you are doing a market survey, and offer to share the final result if they will share with you. Most real estate managers and leasing agents in commercial property operations will share information if one is open with them and willing to reciprocate.

This market information must then be put in a format that allows the writer to compare the subject building with the market and determine its relative strength in today's market, and how it should fare in the market going forward. IREM has created a *comparison grid* to be used in setting rents, which is discussed later in this chapter.

Be sure to check with the building department to see what properties are on the drawing boards and when they may come on line. Today's market may look quite good for the subject property, but one new project in the market could change everything. It's important to stay up to date with local and financial news to glean information on what developments are planned and how likely they are to be built. Attendance and involvement with the local Chamber of Commerce or following the public hearings of both the local Planning Commission and Town/City Council are almost always a great source of information as to what is planned in the community and involvement in such organizations as Rotary can provide excellent contacts as well as making a contribution to the community. Such articles are excellent materials as back up for your business plan.

This market information is then used to determine how well the property is likely to perform as the proposed solution is put into operation. If the market is becoming weaker in the coming months, it will be more difficult to support an aggressive improvement program or the program may well be quite workable, but more expensive due to the weaker market. Always identify "revenue-generating" projects so the owner understands some improvements are directly tied to opportunities to increase rental rates and/or occupancy, as opposed to deferred or cosmetic improvements indirectly tied to revenue. All of the variables must be explained in the analysis and proposed solution. Back up of all of the market information must be included in the appendix as source materials.

MARKET RENT LEVELS

The most effective tool for establishing market rent levels is the comp grid established by IREM as an effective tool to be used as the basis for establishing market rent levels for all types of commercial properties. The comp grid should cover 10 or more items of comparison including age of the property, general condition of the property, amenities, cotenant, location, traffic, etc. Be very careful to choose truly comparable properties. While that is easier in larger markets, if one has to select comparables that are not right on target, then rent levels should be adjusted accordingly.

If the comparables are better than the subject property, adjust the rents down. If the comparables are not as good as the subject property, adjust rents upward. The key is to bring the comparables in line with the subject property—not the other way around. In both cases, it's important to be objective in setting the rents based on the gathered information. It is also critical to know if any of the comparable properties are offering above market incentives to bring in new tenants. Aggressive tenant improvement allowances can show increased rents in a comparable, which results in a lesser net rent for that property.

Free rent and/or provisions to allow the tenant to cancel in less than the full term of the lease can also have an impact on the rent levels in the market. It is important to know what the actual allowances are rather than what may be quoted as allowances. As part of the market rent levels analysis, identify the properties niche in the overall market. Is it a high-end shopping center because of fashion tenants? Is it a C office building because of its age, condition, and/or location that has passed its prime? Again, this classification must be justified by the information gathered in the study phase of the analysis.

A map of the area should be provided with each of the properties identified relative to the subject property. It is very helpful to include pictures of the comparable properties along with the pertinent information of each of the properties. Interviews with the real estate managers of the comparable properties can be very helpful, as well as local appraisers who are aware of the overall market place. These sources should be referenced in the plan.

If there is a property in the general area of the subject that is not a good comparable, it should be referenced and the reasons given as to why it is not a comparable.

Once this information is collected and analyzed, the recommended rents for the subject property should be given along with a word description of how those numbers were determined and what those rents will mean relative to the problem that is the subject of the report. It is possible to recommend a lower rent than the subject market rent to assist in solving a leasing problem or getting to an appropriate level of occupancy for refinancing purposes, etc. Whatever the final conclusion, the information in this section must back up and support that approach.

RANGE OF POSSIBLE SOLUTIONS

Below is a list of likely solutions to various problems within income-producing properties that could potentially be mentioned in this section of the business plan:

- Curing the physical deterioration and deferred maintenance
- Addition or reconfiguration of new space or amenities
- Staff reorganization
- Modernization (to overcome *functional obsolescence*)
- Updating worn fixtures or overgrown, sparse landscaping
- Reposition to meet a new market niche
- Implementation of a more aggressive marketing plan
- Pursuit of alternative financing, lender forbearance, or any combination of financial repositioning issues
- Adding addition buildings

It is possible that because of inability of the client to either refinance or bring additional monies to the table, that doing nothing is the only solution. However, generally, there are at least three or four possible solutions that range from the "do-nothing" approach to a comprehensive repositioning, with a change of the physical plant, and an upgrading of the tenant mix—both of which would require a substantial investment of time and monies by the client. Somewhere in between these two approaches may be the best solution for this property.

Each of the alternatives should be listed along with the operation and financial analysis to provide the plan for this approach, along with the resulting cost, time frame for completion, and ultimate benefit. Each of the alternatives should be a clear alternative and not just a slight variation from the previous one. It's important to not offer too many alternatives which may confuse the situation. If you considered some alternatives and reject others, it may be helpful to mention them and the reasons why they were rejected.

ANALYSIS AND TESTING OF SOLUTIONS

Each alternative in your range of solutions must be tested and should have at least a three-year budget. If the solution will take longer, the budget should extend out to the conclusion of that likely solution. Each budget should reflect the changes and income and expenses, including capital expenses to support the requirements of the solution. It is not necessary to use all of the tests of a solution, such as *return on investment (ROI), cash-on-cash return, net present value (NPV), internal rate of return (IRR), or payback period,* but the ones used should be fully explained and reasons should be given as to why the other alternatives were not used—otherwise, it may be assumed they were forgotten or that the writer was not even aware of those tests. It must also be noted that the payback period always translates into a rate of return and that should be noted. A five-year payback is equivalent to a 20 percent return and a 10-year return is equivalent to a 10 percent return. These returns cannot stand alone and should be measured against other returns and evaluated as to being either good or bad for the property, and why.

This section should include a full narrative of each of the alternative solutions which should tie in the with the budgets and the financial analysis. A matrix should be created that compares the salient points of each alternative solution and the resulting benefit.

Finally, the method of financing each of the alternatives should be shown with the amounts to be borrowed, the likely term and interest rates, and any special terms such as early call dates, step ups in payments, and/or escrowing of taxes and insurance. If there would be any penalties on existing financing, that too should be shown along with the likely cost of those penalties.

Part of the analysis will include an estimate as to the increased value of the property for each solution. While most writers of business plans are not appraisers, most will have sufficient training to issue an "opinion as to value." Market capitalization rates (CAP rate) must be used and that information will be gathered from recent sales in the market place. A map showing the property's location and selling CAP rates should be shown. Those will be averaged and if need be, adjusted, and the final CAP rate will be used in the solutions. The CAP rate on a given property may be substantially different than the average of the market place, due to being a troubled property, or alternatively might be a very low CAP due to the property being an outstanding and completely up-to-date property. These anomalies should be shown, explained, and adjusted out of the figures to provide a realistic market CAP rate. A narrative explaining the process would be part of this section of the business plan.

RECOMMENDED SOLUTION

The recommended solution is the ultimate purpose of the entire business plan. The recommended solution should be fleshed out with considerably more detail compared to the "range of solutions" and "analysis and testing of solutions" sections. First, it should be stated that this recommended solution either does or does not meet with the client's goals. If it does not meet the client's goals and objectives, the reasons should be clearly stated. The writer should be confident that this is the best solution for the property, and be prepared to defend the solution for the greater good of the property.

If a solution does not fit the owner's goals, expect to have an extremely strong case as to why something other than the owner's goals is the best way to proceed. The obvious answer is that the recommended solution is going to solve the problem stated earlier in the business plan, and that none of the other solutions meet the client's goals and solve the problem. Obviously, the various financial tests would have provided the selected direction; however, these should be sound reasons for the recommended solution in addition to the financial analysis.

If the recommended solution is a remodel of the office lobby and common hallways, a picture of one or two buildings' upgraded lobbies and hallways should be included so the reader can easily picture the final recommended approach. It is not enough just to paint a word picture, but to include photos as well where appropriate.

The time frame of how and when changes will be implemented will be essential as this will become the future operating plan for the property. The explanation should include any perceived risks and exposures that could hamper the plan. A specific recommendation as to how the plan will be funded is a must. A description of the marketing plan and leasing plan should be included with an explanation as to why this approach will be necessary to attain the desired results. The plan should include an anticipated commencement date and a date of completion. The testing of the plan should be referred to in this section and anything else that was considered. Finally, this section should include an explanation of how the recommended solution will best address the issues, concerns, and problems presented in the business plan, as well as the goals of the client.

SUPPORTING MATERIAL

While it has been suggested that some supporting materials be presented in the section of the report, most of the supporting materials are presented in the appendix. All materials should be of high quality and fully referenced within the body of the business plan. The supporting materials should appear in the appendix in the order that they appear in the plan.

It should be clear as to how the plan is numbered and it should be easy to reference the materials in the appendix without confusion. Every exhibit, chart, or map should be clearly identified. Only data that supports the business plan should be included.

CERTIFICATION AND DISCLOSURES

The certification and disclosures section of the business plan should list the various sources of information used to gather all of the content and opinions. It is not important for the writer to be the "expert" in all areas of the backup materials, but that expert sources were contacted for gathering the information. A long list of sources for the business plan is a good indication of the resourcefulness and hard work of the writer to trace down and gather the necessary information. This is also the place for any disclosures that may be pertinent to the client and/or the property in the context of the plan.

QUALIFICATIONS OF THE ANALYST

It is likely that many people other than the client will read the report, and it is important that they know the qualifications of the analyst. This is not the place for a formal resume, but rather a narrative on your experience and accomplishments. A good start for this section is to state the date you entered the business, the company you worked for, and any significant accomplishments of you and/or the company during your tenure.

In narrative form, bring the reader up to date with where you have worked and any significant work and accomplishments, especially relevant to the problems detailed in the business plan. Education that is relevant to your duties, as well as special courses offered by trade association, such as IREM should be listed to show both the expertise and dedication to the profession.

Any specific accomplishments relative to the problems involved should also be mentioned. This is the place for facts about such experiences—not speculation on performance. State the direct involvement and the results obtained.

DEFINITION OF TERMINOLOGY

Some of the people that will read this business plan might not be familiar with real estate terminology, therefore, it's necessary to define the terms of art that may not be common to all readers. Almost every trade book has a glossary of relevant terms that can be used as the source of the information. When citing the definition of a term that is being used, be sure to site the source as well. If you must cite a definition without a specific source, it is satisfactory to indicate that it is common usage within the industry, but that should be used very sparingly.

APPEARANCE AND STYLE

The business plan is going to be your introduction to many of the client's experts and support personnel. Make sure that the presentation is professional, logical, and well organized. Many clients will prefer an electronic copy of the report while others may prefer a hard copy—some might request both formats.

Spiral binding is a good option for a hard copy of the business plan, as it is neat and easy to read through as well as being easy to go back and forth from appendix to the basic material. Don't use a binder as they can easily come apart and they do not have as neat of an appearance compared to the spiral binding.

Think through the entire business plan before starting to put it all together. Use tabs for each section so that it is easy for anyone to go directly to any part of the plan without having to hunt through the entire plan. If you think you want the company logo on every page, then give some thought to how much space it will require.

Recheck everything at least twice before finalizing the plan. When doing so, re-read the entire plan and recheck the math. Where a chart or summary is presented in more than one place, be sure it is the same in all places. Once you are satisfied that the plan is ready to go to the client, have another person proofread the entire plan to be sure there are no typos, errors in grammar, spelling, or mathematical errors. This is also helpful if the plan has been compiled by multiple parties to ensure the flow is consistent (project name, ownerships name, etc.) and seamless. The proofreader should make sure that the presentation is logical, in line with the company policies, and has a consistent writing style.

It is not necessary that the analyst write the entire plan, but rather can be the point person with various staff personnel writing sections within their expertise. Obviously, the budgeting portion of the plan can be developed by the real estate manager and be written by the accounting department as they have previous budgets and work with them every day. They can be directed as to how many years you will want to present and how you want the information presented. Once they have completed this task, the analyst can review it, make any desired changes, and include it in the business plan.

The accounting department is also a good source of a five-year occupancy projection, showing each tenant and when their leases expire, if there are options, and where the rents may be in that time frame. The same personnel would do the tenant roster showing all spaces, rents, lease terms, percentage rent rates, and if applicable, deposits and contributions to building operating costs, taxes, and insurance.

If the firm has a leasing staff within the company, they would be a good choice for gathering and reviewing the demographic and psychographic information, along with making projections as to where the market is going into the future. The leasing staff analyze the various units within the property and assign values to each space as well as the likely future of those spaces.

In the past, very deep spaces were quite common for shopping centers, especially in smaller shopping centers. As tenants moved to smaller spaces, those very deep spaces became a problem and various solutions were brought about to resolve the issues. With the advent of big box tenants and discounters, the smaller centers were able to use deeper spaces and this changed the desirability of those spaces, and made much of that deeper space usable again. These are the types of trends that leasing personnel should be more aware of. However, consider that the leasing personnel are doing their best job when they are out leasing space, so their time should be used wisely with most of it leasing property rather than writing reports. Even if one is using an outside leasing agent, most will be happy to provide management with the required information, especially if the format is presented by electronic means and they have to fill in the blanks.

The sections on the real estate management company and it's personnel can well be written by a senior executive of the company. This person will also be fully aware of what is coming up and what may be good information for the presentation without giving away any company secrets in the process.

The financing section will require the help of a mortgage broker and/or lending agent with a bank or real estate company. Various types of financing have their advantages and all relevant types of financing those should be considered. If one particular financing strategy stands out as the best for this property, it should be listed in the business plan. Proper credit should be given to any person or company that provides the general information on financing that ultimately gets incorporated into the business plan.

The timing of the information flow becomes critical, especially when working with various individuals who will provide and analyze the information. The due date to the client is critical. He or she has set the due date for a reason and likely has other staff members and/or outside experts that will be waiting for the business plan, so that they can evaluate the recommendations.

The last thing one wants to do it is be late with the presentation. It is best to develop a timeline for the plan and assign different sections to members of the firm, such as management, leasing, and accounting personnel. Although it is seldom a problem, one should also be cautioned about being too early with a presentation. Take the time given to make sure the report is everything you want it to be. Trying to finish a few days early will give the analyst a few days to review the plan and tweak it before it goes out.

Give each of the contributors a realistic deadline for their materials and get them to "buy in" to the deadline. Their deadline should be about five working days before you absolutely have to have the materials, as you will still have to put it all together and make sure it all makes sense before finalizing the report. It is not good enough to set a deadline for the contributors and then just wait for the materials to arrive. It is good planning to check with each of the contributors along the way to be sure they are on target and fully understanding what you need and when it is needed.

As soon as you receive the materials from each contributor, it should be reviewed to be sure that it is complete. Do not wait until the final day of putting the report together to review the materials, as few of your contributors will have the time to go back, review their materials, and make changes to fit your deadline. Hopefully, when you have completed your first draft of the business plan, you will have time to send the completed plan to each of the contributors for review. The contributors should provide opinions on if material is being properly used, and if they agree on the conclusions drawn from those materials. This review by contributors is in addition to an overall review by a senior member of the company, which should occur prior to sending it the report to the client.

WHAT TO DO WHEN WRITING THE BUSINESS PLAN

- Properly identify the client with proper spelling of his or her name, company name, title, and proper address.
- Make sure the photograph on the cover is recent and in high quality.
- Be creative with your writing, but keep it professional.
- Show the correct date on the cover of the report, which should be the date the report is due.
- Set a time frame for the report as some of the information may have a fairly short shelf life.
- Assign page numbers to the entire report. A separate set of numbers for the appendix is acceptable.
- Make sure the table of contents is in proper order and that the page numbers correspond with the correct pages.
- Address the letter of transmittal to the client or the person designated by the client to receive the business plan. Include the direct phone number and e-mail address.

- Make sure the executive summary is a clear summary of the entire plan and is in complete agreement with overall materials presented.
- The executive summary should be able to stand alone, but with fewer materials.
- Accurately show who the client is, unless otherwise instructed.
- If the client asks you to use a specific name, trustee, or representative, that is what should be used.
- Be sure the purpose of the report is made clear and that is properly referred to throughout the entire plan.
- Clearly state the goals of the client.
- If your recommendation does not fit the goals of the client, explain why.
- Where you have provided assumptions, state that they are assumptions and why you have used them instead of reference materials.
- Identify sources of back-up materials.
- Be clear as to the neighborhood or market and all of supporting back-up materials.
- Provide maps, charts, and graphs to back up your conclusions.
- Give a clear opinion about the future of the subject property.
- Clearly identify the property, including street address and a general physical description.
- State the ownership of the property, any restrictions on its use such as CC&Rs, PUD guidelines, leasehold interests, etc.
- State the highest and best use of the site.
- Describe the improvements in an objective way including sub units, mechanical systems, landscape systems, etc.
- Provide income and expense analysis for at least three years (or more if the solution is going to take more than three years).
- Explain why expenses are either high or low and supply objective criteria for those opinions.
- Describe the current management in very objective terms and indicate if they are part of the problem and if so, why.
- Attach supporting materials if they are relevant to the conclusion.
- Clearly identify the problem or problems and relate them to the client's objectives.
- Explain your methodology in the preparation of the plan.
- Provide a supply/demand analysis and provide back up for the figures.
- Use a comparison grid to recommend the market rent levels with back up for your conclusions.
- Provide a range of solutions to the problem or problems including any solutions you considered, but did not include and why they were omitted.
- Provide financial analysis of each of the alternative solutions and then provide a matrix comparing the various possible solutions.
- Make a strong case for the recommended solution and refer to the tests to justify your recommendation.
- Provide supporting materials such as maps, graphs, charts, newspaper articles, and outside reports to back up the conclusions in the plan.
- Provide certification and disclosures and sign and date this section.
- Give credit to anyone that contributed information to the plan.
- State your qualifications for preparing the plan, but do not overstate your background or accomplishments.
- When you include a glossary, remember that some of the people that will read this plan might not be completely familiar with your industry.
- Use high-quality paper, covers, photographs, and professional binding.
- All charts, graphs, maps, summaries, etc. should be in color and should be properly framed for a professional look.

WHAT NOT TO DO WHEN WRITING THE BUSINESS PLAN

- Don't use a loose leaf binder as they tend to look a little sloppy and pages can easily get out of line.
- Don't use an older photo on the cover as things might have changed since that photo was taken.
- Steer away from sub sections unless they are needed to clarify the information.

- Don't summarize the report on the letter of transmittal that is the purpose of the executive summary.
- Don't combine the letter of transmittal with the executive summary—they serve two different purposes.
- Don't apologize or minimize the plan.
- Don't take for granted the client's knowledge of the property, remember others may read the plan that are not as familiar as the client may be.
- Don't propose an unrealistic time frame for the solution to be put in place and to work to the client's goals.
- Don't set the trade area or market any larger than is realistic.
- Don't present any back up materials without explaining how they impact the subject property and the solution.
- Don't use the words "it is obvious," explain everything.
- Don't forget to include information on current financing and how it must be dealt with for the recommended solution.
- Don't base your opinion on what someone may tell you, it should be on your own observations.
- Don't contradict yourself from one section to another.
- Don't be too brief in your explanations or analysis in the desire to keep the plan short.
- Don't omit grids and graphs to save space.
- Don't list so many alternative solutions that the plan becomes difficult to understand.
- Don't assume any of the information in the plan—everything must have a firm basis.
- Don't go against the client's goals without a very solid substantiation reason for that position.
- Don't add materials just to bulk up the plan.
- Don't include your opinion of your performance when addressing your qualifications—focus on explaining your experience and qualifications.
- Don't include letters of recommendation.

CONCLUSION

Writing a business plan is much like preparing a budget for the first time and can seem like an almost impossible task. Reading a final business plan can be overwhelming with all of the charts, summaries, photos, maps, and many sections that must all come together. The gathering of information can seem to be an insurmountable task, but once you get started, the pieces will fall into place. It has been said in the past "that the longest journey begins with a single step." That is the approach that one must take when commencing beginning a larger task such as writing a comprehensive business plan—just get started.

SECTION

II

Commercial Property Types

CHAPTER

3

Shopping Center Management

Shopping center management and leasing is generally more complex compared to other types of commercial properties. It's important to select retailers who serve the shopping center's customer base and complement the center's existing uses.

Further, the real estate manager and leasing agent must assist retailers with their efforts to generate strong sales by providing a safe, clean environment for the shoppers, selecting a strong tenant mix, and participating in marketing programs that target the *demographics* and *psychographics* of the shopping center's trade area.

Real Estate managers must be knowledgeable in many disciplines including security, contract law, evaluating prospective retailers, retailing concepts, accounting and financial reporting, marketing, social media, and community relations, evaluating demographics and psychographics, developing the right tenant mix, and managing maintenance.

Additionally, the real estate manager must be able to evaluate if the merchant can generate sufficient sales to pay the rent and contribute to the tenant mix of the shopping center. If the answer is yes, the shopping center manager may be asked to negotiate a rent-relief program for the tenant. If the answer is no, the shopping center manager may be directed by the property owner to negotiate a lease cancellation.

All of this is done within a market place that goes from very strong, favoring the property owner, to very weak which favors the tenant. The real estate manager must try to optimize the shopping center's position in a fluctuating marketplace and within a very competitive shopping center and retail marketplace.

CLASSIFICATIONS OF SHOPPING CENTERS

Shopping center classifications have traditionally been based on the size of the shopping center and the types of major retailers that anchor it. The size of the shopping center is determined by the amount of *gross leasable area (GLA)*—the area designed to be occupied by the retailers. All other areas in the shopping center are referred to as *common areas.* Today, shopping centers are also classified by the type and price points of the merchandise sold (e.g., *power shopping centers* or *outlet malls*) and the experience provided by a shopping center (e.g., *lifestyle* or *entertainment shopping centers*).

The following sections describe the major classifications of shopping centers as defined by GLA, major retailers, merchandise, and price points. There are two basic types of shopping centers: (1) malls and (2) strip centers. A mall is two rows of store facing one another and separated by a walkway. A mall can be an enclosed mall or an open-air mall. The other type of shopping center is the *strip shopping center* which contains a row of stores facing a parking lot. The row of stores can be in a straight line, L shape (or reverse L shape), or a U shape.

Neighborhood Shopping Centers

Neighborhood shopping centers range from 50,000 to 150,000 square feet of GLA and are usually anchored by a supermarket and drug store. Tenants in neighborhood shopping centers primarily offer convenience goods, services, and food. Some neighborhood shopping centers may have a drugstore, dollar store, or home improvement center as a major retailer. Small shops are generally service retailers such as laundromats, dry cleaners, insurance, real estate offices, and food services.

Some neighborhood centers feature local fashion shops. It is also not unusual to see a veterinary clinic, a doctor's office, or a dental office—rent prices are often less compared to medical or office buildings, plus there is usually more foot traffic. The neighborhood shopping center usually has one to three pads or outparcels—plots of land within the parking lot that are leased or sold to a retailer and typically occupied by restaurants or banks.

Neighborhood centers can come in many shapes and layouts, but they are generally located on busy intersections or major roads. The anchor tenant or tenants are most often near the center of the project with the small shops extending out on both sides of the anchors, or the anchors are on either end of the center with the shop tenants in between. Some neighborhood centers will have outlot or pads along the street and some will have shops facing a side street. Some neighborhood shopping centers are U shaped with the anchor tenant or tenants at the base of the U and the small shops extending out from there. Having the anchor tenant at one end and the shops extending out from there can make it very difficult for the shops that are the greatest distance from the anchor tenant. Some neighborhood centers have tried having offices on the second floor of the center, but quite often the parking problems between office and retail have created sufficient problems to minimize this practice.

In smaller cities, it is not uncommon to find second-floor office space as the shopping center may be the only commercial venue in town. There are ways of minimizing the conflict between office uses and retail. One solution is to have the offices facing what would be the back of the center with parking in that area. Another solution is to have a multigrade center with the lower grade serving the retail portion and the higher grade serving the office and with entrances on what would be the back of the center and both would have parking at their entrances.

Community Shopping Centers

Community shopping centers range from 150,000 to 400,000 square feet of GLA and are anchored by one or a combination of the following: supermarket, drugstore, discount fashion store, home improvement center, dollar store, and junior department store. The small shops are a combination of convenience and service stores, restaurants, and general merchandise as well as fashion stores. Community shopping centers are larger and cover more acreage than neighborhood centers. They often have three or four anchor stores and are located around the site to help direct traffic to the smaller merchants, while facilitating parking for all stores by creating shopping zones within the center.

Community shopping centers also have pads and outlot locations with restaurants, banks, and book stores, etc. The fashion merchants will generally want to be close to any fashion anchors, and services will generally be in lesser locations as they often do not need foot traffic to be successful. These centers can be long and narrow or can be L or U shaped or have two or three groupings of stores. Every effort is made to ensure that all have good visibility and that the traffic patterns are easy to use.

Regional Shopping Centers

Regional shopping centers range from 400,000 to 1 million square feet of GLA. Anchored by at least one full-line department store and tenanted predominately by fashion, gift, and general merchandise stores and restaurants. Originally, malls were developed as open-air malls, but most of these were converted to climate-controlled enclosed malls in the late 1970s through the 1980s. From the 1970s to the 1990s, almost all malls developed were enclosed malls. Another type of anchor retailer—the multiscreen theater—was added to many malls in the late 1980s. In the 1990s, large discount retailers became acceptable anchors for malls, and open-air regional malls were once again developed. In the past several years, the addition of discount department stores were added to the mix of regional shopping centers. Those stores will likely include Target and Walmart.

The regional shopping center is generally a mall type center with parking all around the exterior of the shops and a pedestrian mall down the middle.

The mall may be one straight pedestrian walkway known as a dumbbell design or may go off at angles or even be in the shape of a cross, but access and visibility are major concerns. The anchor tenants are usually at the ends of the walkways. These centers will almost always have outlot or pad locations and may even have outside groups of buildings with services and smaller merchants.

In a few markets where B malls have failed, they have been de-malled and converted to power centers or hybrid shopping centers with two types of shopping centers. These redevelopments may include apartments on the periphery of the site. Though the mall could no longer compete with larger and malls and other types of shopping centers, the site is usually excellent for other uses.

Super Regional Shopping Centers

Super regional shopping centers have in excess of one million square feet of GLA. They are usually anchored by four or more full-line department stores, major discount retailers, and/or a multi-screen theater, and have more than 100 small shops like those in a regional mall. The only differences between a regional and a super regional shopping center are the size and number of anchor retailers and shop tenants. The layouts are very similar to regional shopping centers and often are designed as multi-level malls. Some of these centers come with two or three floors, split-level parking areas, and outlot or pad locations. Many will have open-air buildings adjacent to the mall areas with big-box stores in that area of the shopping center. Entertainment has become an important part of super regional shopping centers with theaters, skating rinks, aquariums, and food courts.

Specialty and Festival Shopping Centers

Specialty or *festival (theme) shopping centers* typically range in size from 50,000 to 300,000 square feet of GLA. These are conversions of an existing non-retail facility (known as *adaptive use*), or they are developed around an architectural theme, such as an old world or a nautical motif. Festival or specialty shopping centers are tourist oriented. For example, Ghirardelli Square in San Francisco is a specialty shopping center that was converted from an old chocolate factory. Faneuil Hall in Boston, originally warehouses, is an example of a festival market place.

Specialty shopping centers usually do not have a major retailer—restaurants or various food services frequently serve as the main attraction. Specialty and boutique stores, such as a music-box store or a leather goods shop, are typical retailers in these shopping centers. Such stores require a tremendous amount of traffic to survive because their merchandise appeals to a limited number of people, and most of the items are not necessities but rather impulse purchases. The shape of these properties tends to be varied. Many are in the shape of a village and face mainly into the center of the property. Some face water ways and then have wandering streets to add charm. Many are very similar to the mall concept, but have much more ambiance and are designed to provide the customer with entertainment. It is not unusual for this type of center to have residential and/or a hotel above the retail shops. Developers have gone to great lengths to be sure there is adequate parking for both the residential and commercial elements of this type of shopping center. There are also specialty shopping centers devoted exclusively to restaurants and some that are devoted exclusively to a theme such as weddings—these both tend to be smaller shopping centers and located mostly in major metropolitan areas.

Outlet, Off-Price, and Discount Shopping Centers

Outlet, off-price, and *discount shopping centers* are generally classified as one type of shopping center, but each category is slightly different. Outlet retailers sell merchandise in their retail stores, but at a bargain price. Off-price retailers sell branded merchandise at less than traditional retail prices. The discount retailer sells merchandise at less than traditional prices; however, the merchandise is not necessarily branded.

These shopping centers range in size from that of neighborhood shopping centers to regional malls. They do not have traditional anchor retailers, and the collection of named outlet stores often serves as the main customer draw. The rest of the shopping center is leased by retailers who also sell mostly discounted or off-price merchandise and food service retailers. Originally, these shopping centers were located well away from traditional shopping centers to avoid conflicts and to keep their occupancy costs lower—a necessity for these retailers who operate their businesses at lower margins.

Many of these centers are now located closer to the traditional retailers and other types of shopping centers. A lower rental rate is also achieved if the developer limits the shopping center's amenities. Although these centers were originally developed with a minimum of amenities, the more recent developments are adding more amenities in an effort to draw more shoppers. These properties tend to be either long and one-shop deep back from the street, or grouped in such a way as to have parking in the middle of the shops that all face the center of the property.

Power Shopping Centers

Power shopping centers were first developed in the 1980s. The anchors or major retailers are heavy promotional and price-promotional retailers, ranging in size from 15,000 to more than 100,000 square feet. They include high-volume electronic stores, home improvement centers, sporting good stores, discount apparel, import stores, warehouse clubs, and other specialty shops. These shopping centers originally included small shop retailers that did not achieve their anticipated sales because cross shopping among the stores was limited.

The second generation of power shopping centers eliminated shop space, but included pad and outparcel retailers and power centers ranging from 250,000 to 750,000 square feet. The most recent change in this category is the *power town.* These are power shopping centers with an expanded tenant mix that may include a theater, higher parking ratios, and more customer amenities. The power town is usually larger than a power center, which often maxes out at 800,000 square feet. The tenant mix includes specialty-store space (as much as 25 percent) and at least three or more big-box anchors. An upscale trade area and highway visibility are also essential.

Lifestyle Shopping Centers

The *lifestyle shopping center* is a return to the downtown shopping area of the 1940s and 1950s with an open-air, street-scape design. Many lifestyle shopping centers range from 250,000 to more than 500,000 square feet and are designed with a street grid similar to that of a small downtown. Four generations of lifestyle shopping centers were created during the 1990s. The first was occupied by upscale fashion retailers, boutique stores, table service restaurants, and state-of-the-art multi screen theaters. The second generation included boutique hotels and two to three levels of multifamily residential housing on top of the ground-floor retail space. The third generation included department stores and larger specialty shops that were usually designed with a smaller format than stores in regional malls. The fourth generation of lifestyle centers are attached to a mall. The lifestyle center is referred to the tail of the mall. The mall is usually enclosed and the lifestyle portion is open-air.

Entertainment Shopping Centers

Entertainment shopping centers developed nationally in the 1990s. They were anchored by large multi-screen stadium-seating theaters and theme-oriented retailers and restaurants. The also had trendy fashion retailers that targeted the younger generation. After the turn of the century, new and expanded entertainment shopping centers added discount retailers, specialty department stores, and new entertainment—including amusement park rides. Entertainment shopping centers typically range from 200,000 to over 500,000 square feet. They are now being referred to as "shoppertainment." The Irvine Spectrum in Irvine, California, one of the first entertainment shopping centers, continues to evolve, adding specialty anchor retailers and a variety of entertainment.

Hybrid Shopping Centers

It is not unusual today to see shopping centers with many of the previously mentioned elements combined into one shopping area. *Hybrid shopping centers* include one large development with a big-box element, entertainment district, restaurant row, and neighborhood center within the complex. The entertainment element is an island in the middle of the U shape and is surrounded by all of the other shops. The center is built in a U shape with the parking in the middle and the shops facing inwards. Because of the size of the center, more than 1,000,000 square feet, the center provides a shuttle within the property to make it easier for the customer to shop the entire center.

The hybrid shopping center may be a combination of a power center and neighborhood center, or any combination of shopping centers. Most suburban cities that lost their downtown are encouraging developers to build town centers. These are usually hybrid centers with residential above the ground-floor retail. The overall mix of these centers includes discount stores such as big-box stores, multiplex theaters, supermarkets, drug stores, and a smaller mix of services and merchants. To date, these centers have been built in larger metropolitan areas as they require substantial traffic.

Downtown Shopping Districts

The proliferation of mall development from the 1960s to the 1980s caused the demise of many downtowns. Since the late 1980s, many municipalities are encouraging and working with developers to revitalize downtown areas to create shopping districts similar to malls. Municipal governments and redevelopment agencies assisted in assembling land, provided low-cost loans, built parking structures, helped in abating or deferring real estate taxes, provided infrastructure at no cost to the project, and even helped with ongoing maintenance costs. Downtown revitalization has had mixed results throughout the country, but some downtowns have experienced remarkable turnarounds. The trend of urban living has accelerated the revitalization of downtowns.

Neighborhood Retailing

Retail streets in neighborhoods are the heart of many neighborhoods. Many major metropolitan cities and suburban cities across the country have great retail neighborhood streets with exceptional local retailers and restaurants mixed with national retailers. These streets include Newberry Street in Boston, State Street in Chicago, 4th Street in Berkeley, Colorado Blvd. in Pasadena, and Fillmore Street or Valencia Street in San Francisco. Great neighborhood retail streets draw shoppers and visitors from outside the neighborhood. They are places to shop, dine, meet friends, and be seen.

CREATING THE BEST TENANT MIX

A shopping center's tenant mix is more critical to its success than it is for office buildings, medical office buildings, or industrial parks. Tenant mix must be based on the demographics and psychographics (the study of how people live and spend their money) of the trade area. The retailers' sales are the validation of the proper tenant mix.

Tenant Mix Guidelines

Helpful guidelines are available to determine the best mix for every shopping center. If customers in the trade area are affluent, the shops are more likely to cater to the preferences of people with higher incomes. If the trade area consists of families at the lower end of the income spectrum, the successful shops are more likely to carry popular price merchandise. In recent years, traditional concepts of tenant mix have changed. At one time, it was unthinkable to put higher-end retailers with an anchor retailer that sells popular price merchandise or to put discounters with traditional retailers. Now developers and shopping center owners are looking at the overall trade area and trying to meet the needs of the largest number of consumers.

Assuming sufficient numbers of shoppers are present to support the concepts, mixing various economic levels of goods can work as well. It is not unusual for smaller shops to be grouped around the anchor tenants that reflect their price points on the merchandise. The shopping center is zoned with high-end merchandise in one zone and most likely at the other end of the property a moderately priced zone. Most shopping centers are tenanted with retailers with similar price points.

Sources such as the *Survey of Buying Power*, published annually by the *Sales and Marketing Management Magazine,* detail how people spend their money in every major metropolitan area of the country. Evaluating such information helps develop a tenant mix. If, for example, a study of supermarket sales shows higher-than-average figures, an opportunity may exist for another supermarket. Studying the average sales per square foot of existing supermarkets can indicate whether a new store in this category will be successful. Many cities and counties keep track of retail sales in their communities and have those sales figures available for the public. These figures can be very helpful in determining what the sales are in the area, if they are increasing or decreasing, and if they indicate there may be additional areas of opportunity for retail shops in the area.

Multiplying the number of people in the trade area by the average purchases per person produces the potential sales in the area. The sales of the existing market can then be estimated. Sales tax figures can also be used to determine if the area has potential for a new supermarket and for various categories of merchandise.

Studying how people in the trade area spend their money reveals sales percentages in various uses, such as apparel, shoes, and restaurants. These percentages are then modified based on the competition and type of shopping center involved. Every category of merchandise can be evaluated in the same way. The sales potentials indicated by this type of study are meant to be a guideline and not an absolute figure. Analyzing the area's growth rates, traffic patterns, and quality of existing competition provides additional indicators for probable success.

The real estate manager's experience and general expertise play an important part in determining tenant mix. Overall, the goal is to mix goods and services to encourage impulse shopping while the customer is looking for something specific. Hair salons and barbershops do not usually need a high-traffic location because they are a destination-type retailer. A gourmet candy store or a jewelry store are usually located in a high-traffic location so a large number of customers can buy on impulse. These two types of retailers are often found in the center courts of malls.

Evaluation of Prospective Retailers

The shopping center manager can use sales comparison figures to evaluate prospective retailers. For example, in a negotiation with two prospective menswear stores, assume Prospect 1 is negotiating for lower rent and Prospect 2 seems willing to accept the terms. Prospect 1 has another shop averaging $400 per square foot in sales and believes she will do at least that volume at the proposed shopping center.

Prospect 2 believes he will average sales of $150 per square foot, but will pay the asking rent of $18 per square foot per year. Menswear stores generally pay about five percent of sales. Prospect 1 would pay a total rent of $20 per square foot based on her sales, if the rent were five percent of gross sales, a very comfortable rent-to-sales ratio. Prospect 2 would produce rent of only $7.50 per square foot based on projected sales, but the minimum rent is $18 and the ratio of rent-to-sales is 12 percent. All things being equal, Prospect 1 would make the better long-term retailer.

(NOTE: Rent-to-sales ratio is determined by dividing the retailer's sales into its rent. When a retailer's rent-to-sales ratio exceeds 12 to 15 percent, the retailer may not be generating a profit and may become a candidate for rent collection problems and possible failure.)

Potential Problem Retailers

When establishing a tenant mix, the shopping center real estate manager should avoid leasing to retailers who might cause problems. The manager should structure the retailer's lease to prevent or minimize the possibility of problems occurring, or provide the real estate manager with the right to cancel the lease if the problem persists.

Several property uses can create problems. The shopping center manager should carefully evaluate whether those uses should be included in the shopping center's tenant mix. The following sections list retailers that can cause problems for a shopping center and suggested lease modifications to alleviate the problems.

Location of Bars, Pubs, and Cocktail Lounges

Opinions are mixed on whether bars, pubs, and cocktail lounges should be in a shopping center. Some of the major retailers' leases in neighborhood and community shopping centers restrict these businesses from the shopping center or restrict their location within a specific distance from the major retailers' premises. Rowdy behavior in the parking lot might create a negative image for the shopping center. Another concern is litter accumulating late at night and into the early morning. If the real estate manager decides to enter into a lease with a tavern, the lease restrictions may require the tavern to have a uniformed security officer on site during specific hours, and may even require the tenant to police the parking lot on a regular basis to clean up any litter left by unruly customers in the late night hours.

Issues with Hazardous Waste

Hazardous waste can create issues for shopping centers especially when it comes to general disposal. For example, dry cleaning services can create hazardous waste from the chemicals used to clean clothes. Use of modern cleaning equipment may mitigate this potential concern. Some shopping center managers require dry cleaning operators to carry insurance to cover hazardous waste clean-up costs and will have specific provisions as to the disposal of the chemicals, to be sure they are not poured down the sewers or poured out behind the store in flower beds.

Another concern of dealing with hazardous waste is with automobile services. The lease should require the proper use and disposal of hazardous substances. Storage of automobile batteries can leak acid which can permeate the concrete they are sitting on. The disposal of oil from oil changes is critical, and again, the property owner does not want it dumped in the sewers or on the shopping center's grounds.

Offices in Shopping Centers

Some offices find shopping centers to be an attractive alternative to a typical office building. The shopping center provides office tenants with good exposure, rental rates comparable to or lower than those of most comparable office buildings, more amenities, and abundant free parking. Real estate managers should be concerned with long-term parking requirements. Some major retail leases restrict office uses within a specific distance of their premises. The lease for the office tenant should designate the areas in which employees may park, which must be away from the retail store fronts.

Miscellaneous Businesses

Specific parking areas are required for trade schools to avoid congestion in front of retail shops. While trade schools supply a continuous supply of potential customers, they also have substantial parking requirements and for longer periods of time. However, this type of tenant can be an excellent use for a difficult space in the center and with proper lease provisions can be a logical use for out of the way and poorly shaped spaces.

Most retailers do not create a problem for the customers or adjacent retailers. When a problem does arise, it can ruin a shopping center's image, create tension among retailers, and take a long time to correct. The real estate manager can alleviate potential problems by anticipating these concerns and addressing them in retailers' leases. A dance studio or karate shop next to a book shop may create problems between the uses. A second-hand book store or used clothing store may cause image problems with the new merchandise stores and especially with upscale merchants. Many leases have a provision for fines for employees that park in other than the designated parking. Some centers will provide limited parking in front of specific stores, with a 30-minute parking limit, but often, the center management will not agree to police the limits.

Temporary Tenants or Pop-Up Businesses

Temporary tenants have become an important part of the tenant mix and income stream for many shopping centers, especially malls. A temporary tenant program in a regional or super regional mall can generate significant annual income—often well in excess of one million dollars a year, while such a program in a strip shopping center can generate several thousand dollars. Many large regional and super regional malls have one person whose sole responsibility is leasing to and working with temporary tenants. These tenants can often become permanent tenants if they are successful in the center, however, the real estate manager should make sure that these businesses do not directly conflict with existing tenants by selling the same merchandise.

Temporary Tenant Leasing Program

Temporary tenant leasing programs have evolved from just filling space into a specialty leasing program. They now evaluate prospective retailers using criteria that are similar to those used to evaluate permanent retailers: merchandise, price points, intended design of the space, and/or display of the product, ability to staff the store during required operating hours, and ability to pay rent and run the store.

A temporary tenant or specialty leasing program provides opportunities to expand the shopping center's tenant mix by bringing unique and sometimes seasonal tenants into the shopping center. This allows the leasing agent to quickly bring new merchandise and products into the center. Many temporary tenants pay higher rent per square foot and have higher sales per square foot than permanent retailers. This is due to their much smaller space during the peak selling periods. One of the objectives of a temporary tenant program is to expand some of the retailers into permanent occupants. If a temporary tenant is not well known to the center management and/or does not have an excellent credit history, it is not unusual for that tenant to pay all of the rent and charges up front, plus a substantial deposit to cover any damage, etc.

Kiosks, Carts, and Other Uses

Temporary or specialty retailers have uses for kiosks, wall shops, or barricade shops in front of boarded or unoccupied spaces. Kiosks, also known as *Retail Merchandising Units (RMUs),* are designed for optimum, visually appealing display merchandise storage. RMUs and carts are customized to the architectural design and theme of the mall, entertainment, or lifestyle shopping center.

The developer or owner of the shopping center or mall provides the RMUs and carts. They give the shopping center a chance to try new retailer concepts and to offer prospective retailers an opportunity to test a concept or unique product while occupying space in a productive fashion. Parking lots are another temporary or specialty option that can be used for car sales, pumpkin and Christmas tree lots, fireworks stands, and farmers markets. Large vacant spaces can accommodate furniture sales and auto displays and sales.

More than half of the retailers that use temporary or specialty shops are local businesses. Leasing agents can find prospects by attending arts and crafts shows, flea markets, farmers markets, visiting other malls, and placing ads in the local newspapers. Existing permanent retailers are another source of prospects; they may want to operate a complimentary or totally different retail concept in a RMU or a cart. This is also a great way for existing businesses to test a new concept or a specific line of merchandise for their stores.

Licensing Agreements

Temporary and specialty occupancies are typically based on a licensing agreement rather than a lease. A *licensing agreement* provides the retailer the right to use space, but it does not create an owner-tenant relationship. This means the user of the space does not have all the protection of state owner-tenant laws. Many of the same issues found in a lease are included in the license agreement: use, hours of operations, payment dates, noise restrictions, sign restrictions, footprint of location, and security deposits. Other issues included are the right to relocate the retailer and criteria for the visual display of merchandise.

The shopping center management should ensure that temporary and specialty retailers do not unfairly compete with year-round retailers. Permanent retailers are often given the first opportunity to lease the vacant spaces, RMUs, and carts. Real estate managers should make them aware that the temporary tenants expand the tenant mix of the shopping center, extend people's shopping time, and provide additional customer draw. If there is any question as to a temporary tenant being a problem for an existing tenant, either the use should be denied or should be discussed with the existing tenant before a final decision is made.

Strip shopping centers have few opportunities to add temporary tenants. Some of the temporary tenants for malls and strip centers are costume stores the month before Halloween, tax preparation service from January through April or May, farmer's markets one day a week in the parking lot, and auto or RV sale in the parking lots. It is also typical that malls will add kiosks during the Christmas season for temporary tenants.

THE SHOPPING CENTER MANUAL

To protect retailers from unpleasant surprises, as part of the introductory program, they should receive a statement showing their rents and information on payment procedures (i.e., common area maintenance, taxes, utility billings, insurance, and merchant's association, or marketing fund dues). This information should be included in a welcoming booklet or shopping center manual.

The shopping center manual can be mailed or e-mailed but delivering it in person gives the shopping center manager and the retailer an opportunity to get better acquainted and continue their relationship. This is a good time to answer any questions the tenant may have and leave a business card. Insist that tenants call anytime if they have questions.

Essential Information

In addition to details on the merchant's rents and other charges, the shopping center manual should inform retailers where to pay rent and merchant's association or marketing fund dues, whom to call for emergency repairs in the common areas, the fact that the tenant is responsible for interior maintenance, where employees are to park their cars, and if the center has security how to call them if needed.

Typically, the mall's security staff does not operate inside the retailers' premises, and that fact should be explained in the shopping center manual. The waste removal system should be explained along with any recycling programs that may exist.

Most centers have a center wide waste removal program, but wet garbage for restaurants is most often handled by the individual restaurants. Some major tenants also have their own relationship with the waste disposal company and many do their own recycling programs.

Warranties on Equipment

The shopping center manuals include information on warranties for equipment the retailer is required to maintain, especially for a new project. Newer shopping centers and malls should inform the tenant about the warranty on the basic construction and on the air-conditioner compressor. While the warranty on most construction is one year in most jurisdictions, the air conditioning units may have a five-year warranty on the compressor. The merchant may not be aware of these warranties and could incur unnecessary expenses as a result. The air-conditioning systems are often quite complex, and the shopping center manual is a good way to inform merchants how to operate the system.

Shopping Center Plot Plan

The shopping center manual includes a shopping center plot plan with items of interest clearly marked. Those items may include the following: emergency shutoffs for electrical power; gas and water meters; location of roof ladders; sprinkler system risers and controls; multiple user grease traps; fire hydrants; sump pumps; and electrical and elevator rooms. It should also provide contact information for the persons who have keys to these areas for emergency access. If there is not an office on site, generally one of the merchants in the center will have a key to the roof ladders and equipment rooms or one of the trusted contractors for the sweeping or landscaping. Generally, any use of these keys must first be cleared with the management office.

The plot plan should show emergency escape routes, and the shopping center manual should include other emergency information, such as how to call the police and/or fire department and where emergency equipment is located. Emergency procedures are often included in the shopping center manual or in a separate emergency procedures manual. For more information on developing an emergency procedures manual, IREM has published the book, *Before and After Disaster Strikes,* which provides a thorough outline of what to expect before, during, and after man made and/or natural disasters.

RETAINING RETAIL TENANTS

Relations between real estate managers and tenants are more critical in shopping centers than in most other properties. A real estate manager must be concerned with the best tenant mix and, within that mix, must find the best operator for each retail category. Retailers need a successful, well-operated shopping center in which to do business. The real estate manager needs effective, professional stores in order to run a successful shopping center.

Real estate managers must make every effort to create an environment where retailers have the opportunity to maximize their sales. A successful business contributes to the success of the shopping center, not only with rent payment, but also by drawing traffic to the surrounding stores. The loss of a good retail store has a negative impact on the other retailers as well as on the buying public.

Establishing the Relationship

Relationships with retailers should start with the initial meetings and continue throughout retailers' tenancy. The property owner's representatives—the leasing agent, shopping center manager, maintenance personnel, marketing staff, and administrative personnel—must be aware of the importance of the real estate manager/tenant relationship. Every effort should be made to establish a "first-name" relationship. Meeting the property owner and returning all phone calls in a timely fashion will go a long way in maintaining a good relationship.

Knowledgeable Leasing Agents

Without a doubt, the leasing agent must be knowledgeable and helpful. A professional approach as well as direct, honest answers will go a long way toward building a strong relationship with tenants. The leasing agent must be well informed about the shopping center; desired terms of any lease agreement; uses and merchandise lines that are being sought for the shopping center; and completely honest in what is presented. It is much better in the long run to undersell the prospect than to oversell. Overselling may convince someone to sign a lease, but in the long run it is very likely to cause disappointment and resentment.

Once the lease is signed, if possible, the leasing agent should personally introduce the tenant to the real estate manager to avoid communication gaps. The leasing agent should follow up with an e-mail to the new tenant providing the contact information for the real estate manager. After the lease has been signed, it is not unusual for the leasing agent to concentrate on working with new prospects, but should the tenant call the leasing agent for help or clarification, every effort should be made to help the tenant out—even if it is only to tell them who to call to resolve their issues.

Knowledgeable Real Estate Managers

The leasing, management, and maintenance has a direct affect on the retailer. Retailers often overstate that impact and use it as an excuse for their non-performance of the lease. Hence, it's important to establish a positive relationship with retailers from the initial contact.

When meeting with the new tenant, answer any questions and provide information on what will happen from that point on. Many shopping centers have a tenant package that includes signage requirements, construction requirements, the name and contact information for the property contractor, as well as qualified contractors in the area for the tenant. The package generally includes phone numbers for the local building department for permits as well as utility contacts.

Be prepared to explain the retailer's next steps and provide guidance, advising the retailer of critical construction and grand opening information. This is an ideal time to provide the shopping center manual which includes operating information on the property. The meeting should be followed with a letter outlining what was discussed. It is also helpful to send a letter to all other retailers in the shopping center introducing them to new retailers and suggesting that they stop by and get acquainted. The real estate manager must also be fully aware of the lease provisions of this specific shopping center and be able to state the business reasons for those provisions. It not enough to say "it is in the lease," but it's important to provide the solid business reasoning for the questioned provisions.

Construction Management

While some national chain retailers are quite familiar with construction management, the local merchant typically has little experience in that area. If retailers have improvements to construct, they will be grateful for information on the following:

- How to obtain building permits
- Where to obtain temporary power for construction
- How to get the store sign approved
- How to contact marketing personnel
- How to get mail started at the store
- Whom to contact for security, phone, and utility services
- How to handle trash pickup

During the construction process, it is helpful to stop by and ask how things are going. If the tenant has a problem with city hall or a contractor, the real estate manager may have contacts with the building department that can help solve the problem. The best interest of the shopping center is to be sure the tenant completes construction and opens as soon as possible.

CREATING SOLID COMMUNICATION

Tenants appreciate a small gift and congratulations when their store opens. Some shopping centers will provide a small grand opening ad for the new merchant to introduce them into the market place. Before the tenant opens for business, conduct a walk-through of the premises.

The purpose is to complete a "punch list" of items that need to be corrected. The tenant should sign the list and then corrections should be made as quickly as possible, so they are not an ongoing problem for the tenant.

Once the merchant is operating, it's a good practice to stop by and visit periodically—ideally every few months. The purpose of these visits is to promote communication and to allow the merchant to bring problems and situations to the real estate manager's attention. Therefore, refrain from using this time to complain about late rents, poor sales, or parking violations. Identifying and solving tenants' problems early prevents major disasters and maintains positive relations. Tenants commonly complain that they only see the real estate manager when something is wrong or when it is time to renew the lease.

To ensure good communication, all phone calls and e-mails should be returned promptly. Problems often arise that need immediate attention, and a quick response can prevent hard feelings and small problems from becoming big problems. It's important to think about ways to communicate in shopping centers that have 24-hour businesses. It's essential to have an after-hours communications available for these retailers.

Recognizing Positive News for Businesses

When a merchant reports a particularly good sales month, a letter of congratulations or stopping by the store to issue the congratulations in person, is a good public relations tool. An attractive window display is another opportunity to compliment the merchant on a job well done. Tenants often point out problems in the common areas that might have been missed. Every effort should be made to thank the tenant for this extra effort. When businesses are involved in community projects, seize the opportunity to recognize their efforts with a letter of recognition, or better yet, a special breakfast or lunch.

Gathering information for a Newsletter

The real estate manager and marketing director should communicate regularly with the retailers to keep them informed of upcoming events. A monthly e-mailed newsletter is a great way to keep the lines of communication strong. The newsletter can contain information about new tenants in the shopping center, new store managers, shopping center sales comparisons by category, the leading store in each category, upcoming events, copy deadlines, and other miscellaneous information about the shopping center. Retailers can be encouraged to submit information about their stores and their employees. Newsletters are most effective in larger malls and specialty retailing environments.

Larger shopping centers, the newsletter could contain a marketing calendar which lists the advertising and marketing events throughout the year. The calendar could provide the dates of each event, a brief description, deadlines for ad copy, and a projected budget for each event. These calendars should be delivered before the end of the year so the tenants can plan accordingly.

An advertising section in the newsletter can inform the tenants of media publishing dates and media contacts at the local newspaper or radio station. It may list all upcoming events and the marketing fund or merchant association's plans for supporting the events with print or electronic media advertising. When a shopping center advertising section is being developed, it's important to contact some of the tenants personally and encourage them to participate. While they may be aware of the written notices, additional encouragement is often necessary and quite helpful.

Understanding Responsibilities

It's essential to have a complete understanding of the property's lease documents and the terms of each retailer's lease. A misunderstanding of responsibilities may leave the tenant thinking that the real estate manager is trying to avoid legal obligations.

Tenants must understand the differences between their expenses and which items are the shopping center's expenses. The lease documents, especially the construction exhibits, should explain in detail who is responsible for what. Even when the leases and construction documents are quite clear on the tenant's responsibilities, there can always be misunderstandings and a careful thoughtful approach is likely to help maintain a good property owner/tenant relationship.

Initial Condition of Retail Space

One area that can cause problems for retailer relations is the condition of the space when it is turned over to the retailer. Several arrangements are possible in the construction of the premises:

1. The retailer provides all improvements in a pad location.
2. The retailer takes the existing premises "as is."
3. The property owner completes the space, except for floor covering and interior partitions.

4. The property owner provides a turnkey store that has all improvements, except for trade fixtures and interior decor.

In cases in which an existing vacancy has substantial improvements, the retailer may be required to pay for those existing improvements, also known as *key money*. While this is not a common situation, it may be prevalent in successful regional and super regional malls. The more precise the lease and construction exhibits, the less likely there will be future disputes. Also, if an existing vacancy has equipment left behind by the last tenant, be sure to clear the title to that equipment before making an arrangement with new tenants.

Shopping Center Repairs

If there are major repairs for the property, it is important to inform the retailers ahead of time to give them a chance to explain if there are potential problems with the timing of the repairs and to reschedule if necessary. For example, major parking lot repairs may disrupt a merchant's sales event. Roof work often requires that large sections of the parking lot be roped off, causing parking problems. The work can be quite noisy and may cause problems within the store.

In some cases, tenants may have suggestions to help minimize the disruption of the work. Anchor tenants, in particular, are quite experienced in these larger projects and can often be helpful in finding good contractors or in suggesting procedures to make it easier on all of the tenants. It must also be noted that some anchor tenants have pre approval rights for larger projects or projects with costs above a specific amount in the shopping centers.

Organizing Repairs for Tenants

Retailers are usually responsible for maintaining the premises, which generally includes exterior doors, glass, and utility lines serving the premises—even if they are outside the retailer's premises. Pad retailers usually handle their own roof repairs. In-line retailers pay for their share of roof repairs, but the real estate manager is responsible for the work. While it is rare, there are some leases where the tenant can have the roof repaired at the property owner's expense—a situation that should be avoided if possible. The lease will explain who has maintenance responsibilities for different elements of the shopping centers.

Most shopping center leases require retailers to maintain the premises at their own expense. It is not advisable to perform or contract for repairs for which a retailer is responsible and then bill the repairs back to the retailer. A better practice would be to provide tenants with a list of maintenance contractors that they may choose for work on their premises.

There are exceptions to the caution against performing maintenance in the retailer's premises. For example, to ensure the roof-mounted air conditioners are properly maintained and to prevent excess traffic on the roof, having one contractor or the shopping center's maintenance personnel maintain them is often desirable. If possible, contract for the maintenance of the heating and air-conditioning unit but have the contractor bill the tenants directly.

If the real estate management firm provides maintenance services through its own maintenance company, a profit is allowable, but the total cost of the service should be competitive in the marketplace, and the retailer is entitled to know the basis of the billings. Be certain that the price from the subsidiary company is competitive and the service standards are no less than the standards maintained by other maintenance firms. Always inform the property owner and be sure to receive prior approval.

If general repairs are provided to the tenants for a fee, the best policy is for all work to be performed based on a written request from the tenant and the cost known ahead of time, if at all possible. The billing should be detailed and reflect the original request. If additional work is required, it should be discussed with the tenant before proceeding, and authorized in writing. It is best to inform the tenant that the maintenance company is either owned by or a division of the real estate management company.

Monitoring Opening and Closing Hours

The observance of uniform business hours by all or most retailers is a major component in creating a synergy in a shopping center. Shoppers expect all merchants to be open during shopping center hours as required in the lease. The lease will state which hours may be maintained by the tenant for each day of the week and which holidays the tenant is not required to be open.

Malls hours are typically 9:00 a.m. to 9:00 p.m. Monday through Saturday and 11:00 a.m. to 7:00 p.m. on Sundays. Department stores that have entrances directly from the parking lot into their stores may maintain longer hours. A theater in a mall and most restaurants, also maintains extended hours. The hours are extended during the Christmas and holiday season for the entire shopping center. Entertainment, outlet, and lifestyle shopping center hours are similar to those of a mall. The hours of a strip shopping center are typically 10:00 a.m. to 8:00 p.m. Monday through Friday. On Saturdays, 10:00 a.m. to 6:00 p.m., and noon to 5:00 p.m. on Sundays.

If the shopping center has an on-site real estate manager, maintenance personnel, or security staff, an individual may be assigned to complete a form that lists each store's opening and closing hours. When a retailer violates its lease requirement, the real estate manager should discuss the purpose of uniform hours and the negative impact opening late or closing early has on the store and the entire shopping center. If the tenant continues to violate the prescribed hours, contact the store's district manager or owner. Some leases call for a fine if a retailer violates the opening or closing hours.

Handling Tenant Requests

Tenant requests should always be handled in a timely and courteous fashion. If a request cannot be fulfilled, then it should be explained to the tenant along with a suggestion for a contractor or a solution to the problem. Some retail managers do not understand the lease provisions, and they do not appreciate learning that they are responsible for solving the problems—as well as paying for them. Again, a sympathetic approach along with helpful suggestions and patient discussion will most often get the situation resolved without destroying the relationship.

Requests such as a dirty sidewalk in front of a retail store or burned-out lights in the parking lot can be a source of irritation to tenants, or worse, can result in loss of business. If the solution takes four or five days, the merchant can easily assume that the management does not care—unless the real estate manager explains the delay and when the problem will be solved. Merchants appreciate a follow-up phone call to see that everything is accomplished. Every effort must be made to resolve problems as soon as possible, so they do not escalate out of proportion. Additionally, it is just good business to respond as quickly as possible and not have to readdress the issue two or three times to get a final resolution.

Handling Complaints and Disputes

When it is necessary to bring an infraction or default to the retailer's attention, the tenant should be given the benefit of the doubt—at least the first time. The tenant may not have understood the situation, the store manager may not have reviewed the lease, or perhaps circumstances were beyond their control. For example, if the lease does not allow retailers to park in front of their stores, referring to the employee parking provision is generally not productive. It is more beneficial to tell retailers that the reason for employee parking requirements is to allow two to four customers per hour the convenience of parking close to the store which should help sales for all of the businesses.

Retailers often ask for favors that go beyond the lease requirements. Rather than responding with a flat "no," reply sympathetically. When complaints are ignored, tenants build up resentment and feel that the real estate manager does not care or considers them unimportant. Instead, see to it that the work is done promptly, or deny the request in a courteous and timely fashion. It is not a good idea to do "favors" for a merchant just to foster good relations.

When disputes arise between retailers, especially disputes relating to lease requirements, step in to mediate the dispute. Feuding retailers have a way of polarizing the other retailers, which may cause anti-management sentiment. Make every effort to maintain open, business-like communication with all retailers. Even when a tenant is difficult, the best long-term interest is to remain calm and move any disagreements in a positive direction. Starting a discussion with "I understand your frustration" or "it appears there is a misunderstanding" can help diffuse a difficult situation.

MARKETING SHOPPING CENTERS

Most shopping centers can benefit from a coordinated marketing program. The larger the shopping center, the more resources are available and the broader the base of retailers to support its marketing program. This section presents the three ways shopping centers are currently marketed: (1) marketing funds, (2) merchant's associations, and (3) owner-sponsored programs. Although shopping centers may have different formats for their marketing programs, they address the same marketing issues, such as effective use of funds, marketing events, grand openings, and customer surveys.

Of the three approaches to shopping center marketing, marketing funds are the most common even though merchant's associations were the first to develop. Owner-sponsored programs are usually the least desirable of the three choices. The lease agreement states which approach the shopping center will use to market and promote the shopping center.

Marketing Fund

The preferred method of marketing shopping centers is the marketing fund. In the late 1970s, the owners of a number of regional and super regional malls set up an advertising or marketing fund in lieu of a merchant's association. Almost all malls and shopping centers, that have a marketing program, use a marketing fund.

Each tenant's lease requires a contribution of dues based on their square footage. The shopping center develops and administers the program with limited input from the retailers and in the best interests of all the tenants. This eliminates monthly meetings and the need to deal with the diverse requests and opinions of the retailers that are associated with tenants' associations.

Marketing fund programs should be balanced throughout the year and offer maximum benefits to as many retailers as possible. This approach works well in regional and super regional malls as well as in outlet, entertainment, and lifestyle shopping centers, but it can be more difficult to administer in smaller shopping centers. Usually, smaller shopping centers do not have a marketing fund of merchants' association.

Tenant Advisory Committee

Instead of merchant meetings, an advisory committee is selected from among the retailers. The shopping center marketing director should meet with this group periodically—usually quarterly or semi-annually. The advisory committee provides guidance and ideas for developing a marketing program, but the real estate manager and marketing director determine the marketing plan.

In new shopping centers, meetings may be held as often as once a month, but once the shopping center is established, the meetings can be reduced to two to four times a year. The decisions reached in these meetings should be reported to all the retailers in the e-mail newsletter describing the programs planned. Merchants that are not a part of the advisory committee should feel they are a part of the process, and their ideas and thoughts should receive careful consideration. There may be an annual meeting of the merchants to describe the upcoming year's marketing program. It's important to plan marketing events that meet with the approval the shopping center's tenants. If the tenants feel that a particular program or advertising approach is not working, it should be evaluated and changes should be made to make it more acceptable.

Structure of Dues for Marketing Fund

The lease generally explains the amount of dues, which widely but generally range from $2.00 per square foot per year to $5.00 or more per square foot per year in specialty shopping centers. The dues are paid monthly, and the shopping center manager has the responsibility for collection of the retailers' dues. The lease is the authority for the payment of dues, and that is the responsibility of the shopping center.

Major retailers usually negotiate whether they will participate in the marketing fund, and if they do, they generally negotiate their dues at a lower rate per square foot than smaller retailers' dues. Most of the major retailers have aggressive marketing programs on their own and do not feel they benefit that much from the individual shopping centers programs, but will support the marketing effort. The lease should allow the dues to be increased annually—either by a fixed dollar, percentage increase, or based on the *consumer price index (CPI).* The main purpose of the increase is to protect the purchasing power of the association or marketing fund.

Traditional Merchant's Association

During the early years of the shopping center industry, the merchant's association was the primary marketing and promotions vehicle. However, few merchant's associations still exist today.

Structure of Merchant's Association

These associations are created by shopping center owners or developers as nonprofit corporations. Nonprofit status gives the association effective buying power because nonprofits do not pay taxes, and as a corporation, the association's liability is limited. The retailers' leases are the basis for the merchant's association. Leases should have a provision that the retailer agrees to belong to the association, pay the dues outlined in the leases, and participate in a specific number of shopping center advertising programs each year.

The shopping center property owner should contribute an amount equivalent to between 25 and 33 percent of the money collected from the retailers toward the programs. Some owners have argued that they should not have to pay dues for the marketing of the center as it is for the benefit of the tenants only; however, both the owner and the tenants would benefit by a good marketing effort. The property owner should participate in the cost of those programs as well as lend support in administrative chores. The greater the tenants sales, the greater the opportunity for the owner to collect percentage rent. In addition, the greater the tenants' sales, the higher base rent the owner can charge.

Three approaches to membership are common:

1. Mandatory membership in the association as a lease requirement (most effective)
2. Lease provision that requires a retailer to join the association if 80 percent of the retailers belong (less effective)
3. Voluntary membership (least effective)

The association is governed with bylaws prepared by the shopping center owners and administered by a board of directors, who are elected by the retailers. The property owner always has a permanent seat on the board of directors and has veto rights over programs in the common areas that the owner deems undesirable for the shopping center. The bylaws should be fair to the retailers, and they should be encouraged to participate in the decision-making process. Major retailers often refuse to join a merchants' association and thus cause a split between large and small retailers. This is one reason for setting the participation level at 80 percent rather than 100 percent.

Structure of Dues for Merchant's Association

As with a marketing fund, dues are paid quarterly or monthly, and the real estate manager is responsible for collecting these dues. If the treasurer of the merchant's association is responsible for collecting retailers for dues, negative feelings can arise between retailers and that can be harmful to the association. Some merchant's associations want to collect their own dues and should be allowed to do so, but when difficulties occur, the real estate manager should step in to preserve good relationships among the tenants.

Merchant's Association Monthly Meetings

The merchant's association meeting is one of the most critical elements of the program. The association generally meets monthly to plan programs and discuss issues of mutual interest. The shopping center marketing director and board of directors will work together to carry out the bulk of the business; however, the board should keep the retailers informed by means of a monthly newsletter, e-mail, or posted on the shopping center's website. The real estate manager should always be available for discussions regarding the marketing program or other items of mutual interest.

Administration of Merchant's Association

In large shopping centers, a full-time, professional marketing director administers the merchant's association. The International Council of Shopping Centers (ICSC) has a program for training and certifying marketing directors. The professional designation is Certified Marketing Director (CMD), which recognizes a high level of experience, education, and training in that field.

The bylaws of the association should give the shopping center manager the right and obligation to hire, terminate, and oversee the marketing director. The marketing director's cost may be part of the property owner's contribution to the association—if the property owner makes a contribution. The marketing director or the real estate manager will function as the owner's representative on the board. The marketing director will develop the marketing program and administer the program with the board.

If a small shopping center has a merchant's association, it may handle marketing and advertising in various ways because funds are limited. The shopping center can hire a part-time marketing director for an hourly or a monthly fee, or it can retain the services of a public relations, marketing company, or the merchants may implement the program.

The least effective approach is for the retailers to run the association. This method of administration if most often used in neighborhood shopping centers. This arrangement does not usually work well because merchants lack experience in shopping center advertising and marketing, and often are too busy to devote much time to further activities. However, when retailers are in charge, the real estate manager generally prepares and mails minutes, meeting notices, annual calendars, and other administrative materials so the tenants can concentrate on advertising and marketing.

In the early days of shopping centers, neighborhood and community centers had a merchant's association but since the mid 1980s few of these centers have a merchant's association or a marketing fund.

Owner-Sponsored Program

A third marketing approach is for the shopping center owner to advertise and promote the shopping center independently with no support or involvement from the tenants. For a shopping center in which retailers seem unwilling to cooperate in advertising and marketing, this may be the only choice. In such cases, the shopping center sets up the program, implements it, and pays the costs. Even with this approach, it is still a good idea to talk with the tenants to be sure what is being done is well received by them.

One effective owner-sponsored advertising program is a weekly ad that uses a standard format but features different retailers or events each week. If funds are not available for a weekly effort, they should be scheduled as funds allow. This keeps the shopping center's name in front of the public and attracts prospective retailers. In this case, the real estate manager arranges for shopping-center-wide sales, civic programs, or paid events throughout the year. Car dealers, RV dealers, and even some large sporting goods stores will pay to use the parking lot for marketing their product—and as long as it does not compete with existing retailers and does not take up too much parking.

Use of Funds

It is difficult to have an effective marketing fund or merchant's association without a contribution from the property owner. Owners usually contribute between 25 and 33 percent of the amount the association or marketing fund collected from the retailers. Regional and super regional malls have annual budgets that allow for TV advertising, shuttle buses, ads in tourist publications, national celebrity visits, full-scale theme productions, extensive community involvement activities, direct mail brochures, and extensive holiday decorations. Smaller shopping centers cannot generate the income for such a broad approach and must use their funds carefully.

Regardless of the size of the shopping center, the funds are generally allocated throughout the year based on the shopping center's sales distribution. The largest expenditures are reserved for November and December, when most shopping centers receive 20 to 25 percent or more of the year's business. Most shopping centers allocate the least funds to February because it is typically the month with the lowest sales. Small shopping centers that have coordinated marketing programs generally have direct mail programs and coupon advertising.

PLANNING FOR GRAND OPENINGS

A new shopping center must take customers away from existing shopping centers or other retail venues, so it is critical to let the customers in the trade area know that a new shopping experience is available and give them reason to visit the shopping center. Major differences exist between opening a small shopping center and opening a large regional or super regional mall.

Grand Openings for Smaller Shopping Centers

A grand opening for a smaller shopping center is generally a two- or three-day event. It should be planned in conjunction with the opening of the major retailers or anchor tenants. It should not take place until at least one of the major or anchor retailers is opening or has opened—and preferably when all major anchors are open. The more shops that participate at the grand opening, the more effective the event will be. However, a successful grand opening prior to full occupancy may enhance the leasing of the shopping center.

A good grand opening time would be when the anchor retailers are open for business and approximately 70 percent of the small shops are open and operating. However, a shopping center may be developed in phases and all anchors may not be in the first phase.

Prior to the grand opening date, the marketing director or real estate manager should prepare and release publicity for any significant activity. Good publicity events include the initial announcement of the project, ground-breaking ceremony, signing of new retailers, addition of significant architectural features, naming of the shopping center real estate manager and managers of the anchors, and other small shops, charity events, and store opening dates.

Advertising Grand Opening Events

While smaller shopping centers typically do not allow for signage in the parking lot, the grand opening is a good time for banners on lamp posts and possibly even on the facades of the buildings. The banners should not remain on display for more than 30 days past the grand opening date.

Smaller shopping centers might use a direct mail piece to the local community, which involves each of the retailers preparing an ad for the mailer. Successful ads offer specials, such as 50 percent off a specific item or a two-for-one sale. Smaller retailers usually do not do as well if their ad is institutional in approach, or gives only the name of the shop and a description of the merchandise. The shopping center owner often subsidizes the initial direct mailings, but that is not always the case. Some owners subsidize 25 to 50 percent of the overall cost of the mailer. The size of the trade area helps determine the best number of mailers for a specific shopping center.

Grand Opening Activities and Events

Many shopping centers have prize drawings in connection with the grand opening. Customers usually register at one of the shops at the shopping center. The marketing director conducts the drawing and notifies the winners of their prizes. Having an actual drawing on site and awarding the prize will draw significant traffic. Gift certificates are generally good prizes because the winners can buy what they want, and it guarantees that the money is spent in the shopping center stores. One grand prize, such as a destination trip, or smaller prizes, such as DVD players, TVs, or dinner for two, are also great attention getters.

Shopping centers might give away small, inexpensive promotional items bearing the shopping center logo on canvas shopping bags, magnets, or water bottles. These may be distributed on the first day only, or they may be given to customers who make a minimum purchase on the grand opening day.

A formal ribbon cutting usually generates good publicity—especially if the mayor and/or other local dignitaries attend. When planning the grand opening, the real estate manager should avoid art shows, automobile shows, and recreational vehicle (RV) shows because they take up parking space needed for the grand opening.

Logistics of a Grand Opening Event

Prior to the grand opening, all involved parties should make every effort to have the buildings ready. Seating, trash cans, landscaping, shopping center parking, and lighting must be in place. In addition, construction materials should be removed and any other hazards should be eliminated because their presence might leave a bad first impression on the customers. Because almost every new shopping center will draw a good crowd for the grand opening, there should be extra maintenance personnel on hand to keep the trash cans emptied and papers removed from the sidewalks and mall. Additionally, extra security should be on hand to give directions and direct customers to the desired stores and to make sure that nothing gets out of hand to start the center off on a with a negative image.

Grand Openings for Malls, Life Style Centers, and Outlet Centers

Regional or super regional malls, and large life style centers and outlet malls have extensive grand opening budgets, and the event may stretch over several weeks and begin well in advance of the mall opening. Public relations efforts begin when the mall or shopping center is first announced.

One successful approach is to have a speaker available to visit civic groups, neighborhood groups, and other interested parties during construction to show them the plans for the shopping center and to discuss the tenant mix and the grand opening events. The speaker might also solicit ideas and opinions from the group members. These presentations can provide the developer with excellent insight into the public perception of the project and allow for changes in the planned programs to make them more meaningful to the shoppers.

An on-site office is typically established early in the construction process. While this office often serves as the construction office, it also serves leasing agents, the on-site real estate manager, and a public information representative who can answer questions and act as liaison between the neighborhood, specific tenants, and the media.

The planning process for a larger grand opening begins up to a year before the opening. The developer often chooses the real estate manager and the marketing director a year in advance so they can be part of the planning process and establish relationships within the community. The marketing director prepares the marketing plan for the grand opening and the first year. Each merchant receives a copy when signing the lease. National chain stores and anchor retailers have the resources to plan their own events and activities for the grand opening. The marketing director should be in touch with the marketing personnel to coordinate the shopping center's activities with the major retailers' activities.

Advertising Grand Opening Events

Because of the large trade area of a malls, life style centers, and outlet malls, the advertising plan should include direct mail, newspapers, radio, and possibly TV, and billboards. The specific media mix depends on the money available, competition, and customers targeted.

Grand Opening Activities and Events

Grand opening activities should be spectacular and varied since these malls and centers have ample budgets for these events. The pre-grand opening activities generally include a press party. Media representatives are invited for a tour and receive a press kit with all pertinent information.

The night before the opening, a black tie party and/or dinner is held for the retailers, civic officials, contractors, and possibly the public. Many larger centers have this event as part of a fundraiser for a local charity—thereby doing the community a good service and gaining extra publicity in the process.

This is a chance to thank everyone involved and to provide a preview of the finished product. Another alternative or additional program might be a charitable ball or event the night before the opening to which retailers, civic leaders, and contractors are invited. Giveaway programs can include cars, major vacation packages, and/or large cash prizes. The more creative the grand opening is, the more likely it is to make the local news. Sales specials in all the stores may last for the first week or two, and an ongoing program of events may last for months. Many stores hold promotional activities beyond those planned by the shopping center, giving the shoppers a greater selection of amusements and shopping opportunities.

Just as it is for smaller shopping centers, it's important to increase security and janitorial personnel. A security problem, a dirty mall, or parking lot may drive away many prospective customers. Remember the adage, "You never get a second chance to make a first impression."

CUSTOMER SURVEYS

A critical aspect of any shopping center's success is properly serving its customer base. The customer survey provides a way to determine shoppers' perceptions of the center and to invite suggestions for improvement.

Meeting the Customers' Wants and Needs

Shopping centers are working harder to tailor their marketing and tenant mix to the specifics of their trade area. As previously mentioned, it is not unusual for discount merchants to be in traditional mid-price malls and even more upscale malls as demanded by the trade area. We are seeing a broader range of tenants in the mix of shopping centers, such as art galleries, car dealerships, doctors and dentists, supermarkets, and/or mini markets are coming back into malls and power centers.

Additionally, the marketing efforts now include free Wi-Fi in the centers as well as comfortable seating where the customer can plug in their mobile device. Some centers now have plug in devices in the parking lot for electrical and hybrid automobiles. For example, a shopping center in Southern California is offering same-day delivery and gift wrapping. Many centers have even created their own "apps" with directories to the stores, special sales, or marketing events.

Developing Specific Goals

Before conducting a customer survey, management must develop specific goals. Is the purpose to evaluate the maintenance, cleanliness, tenant mix, or success of the shopping center? Is it to define tenant mix and determine what the consumer thinks is missing? Or is it to measure the impact of outside events, such as teenage cruising, major street work, or the opening of a competing shopping center? Once goals are defined, the survey must be carefully crafted to ensure that the responses will provide the necessary information.

Survey Types

Surveys can take many forms and can be conducted

on site, in focus groups, or through phone interviews. Visiting civic clubs and neighborhood groups for discussions can be very productive and provide opportunities for dialogue rather than just having participants fill in blanks on a form. Professional marketing organizations have the background and experience to design the survey, formulate the correct questions, recommend polling methods, and determine the proper number of customers to contact.

At the other end of the spectrum, an owner or real estate manager of a strip shopping center can use a simple customer survey to determine the desired information. Surveys can be used to evaluate maintenance and management as well as to inquire about shopping frequency, the means of transportation to the shopping center, which stores were visited, customer preferences, family demographics, and other information of interest.

Questionnaires can be distributed by all retailers or be mailed to the trade area or residents of particular zip codes. The intent of the survey, degree of any problems to be resolved, outside or out-of-pocket costs, and the time frame in which the information is desired are factors that influence the type of survey used. The survey can be paid for by the shopping center owner, the merchants' association, marketing fund, or the cost can be shared by the owner and the shopping center's marketing fund. The owner may want to use some of the information in its marketing and leasing program. If the results of the survey are used for leasing or are provided to prospects, they should include a disclaimer on the accuracy of the information and how it was obtained. Quite often, the shopping center will offer a prize for those who participate by way of a drawing for a TV, computer, for those who take part.

Most store owners and managers spend up to 70 hours a week in their stores, talking with hundreds of customers. Hence, a merchant survey can yield valuable information about shopping center maintenance, customer preferences, effective advertising media, lighting, security problems, and even problems with other retailers. Real estate managers must exercise care when evaluating merchant responses because they can be self serving.

COMMUNITY SERVICES

Shopping centers frequently use vacant or unproductive areas to offer a variety of community services from which the shopping center, its retailers, and the public can benefit. The shopping center must be aware of state laws that govern the public's right to use private property such as shopping center common areas.

Community Room

A *community room* is a large room, sometimes a converted vacant space, offered as a free meeting place for community groups and for a small fee to businesses. It gives the shopping center a chance to provide a service to the community, promote positive public relations, and generate additional traffic to the shopping center.

Community rooms are usually found in malls located in an area that would be difficult or impossible to lease and away from the store fronts and traffic areas. The facility is promoted through news releases to the media, direct mail invitations to community groups, information provided to retailers, and brief statements regarding the facility in the shopping center's advertisements.

Real estate managers must develop guidelines for the use of the community room in order to allow maximum use by the greatest number of organizations and to maintain control over all aspects of the room's use. The guidelines limit the times a group can schedule the room to prevent some groups from monopolizing it. A group might be allowed to reserve the room at least seven days, but no more than 90 days in advance, and for a maximum of five days within any month.

If the community room is located in a mall, the use may be limited to mall hours. If the room has direct access from the parking lot or if security guards or maintenance personnel are available, they can provide access to the room beyond business hours.

Community groups should be required to clean the room after using it and should not be allowed to affix any materials to the walls. A cork or white board may be provided for the group to post messages during their meeting. Public address systems or materials disturbing to shoppers are not allowed, and the real estate manager must always retain the right to reclaim the room, within a reasonable time frame for other uses.

Maintenance or security personnel are given the room's daily schedule and are made responsible for unlocking and locking the room for each group. If the community room is located in a shopping center without on-site personnel, a key to the room may be left with one of the retailers. The groups can be instructed where to pick up and return the key and how to secure the room. The mall's janitorial staff or a maintenance contractor should check and clean the room daily.

The shopping center manager can promote the mall to the captive audience in the community room by posting in the room a list of the retailers, a separate listing of the restaurants, including those that deliver, photos and ads of past and current events, and a calendar of upcoming marketing and merchandising events. Organizations using the community room may be required to sign a license agreement or a *hold harmless agreement.* Some malls have had requirements that users of the community room have liability insurance, but this has proven to be overly limiting as many smaller groups do not have such insurance.

Community Booth

The real estate manager must check with legal counsel on the rights provided by each state regarding the public's access and right to use public property for noncommercial uses. Some malls across the country have created booths where individuals or organizations can disseminate information. Some mall owners address this issue by building community booths in the common areas of their shopping centers as public forum facilities for individuals or groups. These booths are usually located against a blank wall in an area with ample pedestrian traffic. In most malls, community booths are booked every weekend and, in others, they are booked throughout the year.

The mall management must provide rules and regulations for the orderly and nondiscriminatory use of the community booth. The guidelines should include how an individual or organization applies to use the mall's community booth. The application process may require that the booth be reserved a minimum number of days prior to use. The application may ask for the name, address, and telephone number of the organization or individual sponsoring the activity as well as names of the participants. The guidelines may prohibit the sale of merchandise or services and limit the activities to the community booth. Signs may be restricted to a specific size. Individuals and organizations are responsible for cleaning the area inside and outside the booth. Public address systems or voice-amplifying devices should be prohibited and the organizers are prohibited from leaving the booth and confronting customers.

The mall manager must stay current with the changing laws regarding the public's right to use private property, particularly shopping centers, as a forum to disseminate information to the public. The International Council of Shopping Centers (ICSC) is the best source of information on this issue. If the shopping center manager follows the appropriate guidelines, the community booth can provide a public service to the community without creating problems for the shopping center.

Information Booth

The information booth is an area in a mall and larger shopping center that can provide customers with general information regarding the mall and its retailers. The staff of the information booth can also provide operational support for the mall's management and marketing staff. Information booths are usually found in larger shopping centers, primarily malls, lifestyle, and outlet shopping centers, that have budgets to support this service as well as substantial daily traffic.

The information booth can provide the customer with a variety of services, including information on mall hours, store locations, purchase gift certificates, and upcoming events. Information booth staff can also collect lost-and-found items, assist lost children or parents, issue wheelchairs, and rent strollers. A listing of positions available in the stores can be kept or posted at the booth. The information booth staff can receive emergency calls to the management office and answer questions regarding the mall. The staff may also serve as dispatchers for the mall's security and maintenance personnel.

The information booth can be a convenient place to sell mall gift certificates that are valid in any mall store. Certificates can be sold in dollar increments or for a specific amount. In either case, they should state that they are valid only at the mall.

The information booth's staff should be trained to handle emergencies, ranging from helping customers find their parked cars to initiating a response to a bomb threat. The booth should have a procedures manual that lists emergency phone numbers, details the dress code, and explains how to deal with the public and customers who are upset. The information booth personnel should also have very clear rules for what they can handle and what should be passed up to management to handle.

VACANT SPACES

Vacancies in shopping centers are generally unlighted and give the appearance of a blank wall instead of a prospering business with interesting displays and activities. Vacancies also create pocket areas of little or no traffic and cause retailers in nearby spaces to lose some of the benefits of the shopping center environment. Each additional vacant space multiplies this loss. The creative use of vacant spaces can help improve the image of the shopping center and offer community service opportunities.

Merchandising Vacant Space

Vacancies can be viewed as opportunities to help existing retailers merchandise their stores and to create goodwill in the community. The temporary tenant program can also be used to keep activity in these spaces, and it may well lead to a permanent tenant. These goals can be accomplished at very little expense.

The shopping center manager should consider offering the vacant space or spaces to retailers in the shopping center to display their merchandise. The retailers can decorate the show windows and have their merchandise displayed in another area of the shopping center. This offer is contingent upon the retailer's moving out of the vacancy on short notice, keeping the premises clean, abiding by the sign criteria, and relieving the shopping center manager of all responsibility for missing or stolen items. The tenant should enter into a license agreement covering these and other obligations and should be encouraged not to display expensive items that are likely to be targets for theft. Retailers are selected to display their merchandise in the vacancies based on which retailers can best utilize the space, who needs the most assistance, and where the retailer's space is located in relationship to the vacancy. Retailers may be offered the space on a rotating basis or for longer-term use.

Community Use of Vacant Space

An alternative to merchandising vacant spaces is to allow community groups the opportunity to use the vacancies. If the spaces are expected to be vacant for a short period, they can be offered to groups for a specific short-term purpose, such as a haunted house the week before Halloween, a collection area for Christmas and holiday toys, or a drop-off point for a food drive. Organizations may use the space for their membership drive or to register children for sporting activities, such as Little League sign-ups. Other organizations such as Girl Scouts, Boy Scouts, and 4-H clubs can use the vacancies to display their activities and promote their organizations.

If the shopping center is distressed with vacancies anticipated for an extended period, these spaces may be offered to community organizations on a long-term basis. Space may be offered to a community college or high school adult education program as a classroom or to the chamber of commerce for a temporary office. The shopping center manager must retain the right to relocate these organizations to another vacancy or to terminate their occupancy with sufficient notice to enable the organization to complete its function or find another location.

Another use is to convert a vacancy into a community room. Even if the shopping center already has a community room, a second may be considered if demand justifies its use. If the community room is for temporary use, the shopping center manager should not allow organizations to reserve the room more than two months in advance unless they have a very short cancellation provision. Community groups should also enter into a license agreement for the use of the vacancy.

Charging for Vacant Space

The real estate manager must decide whether to charge for the use of the vacancy. When the space is offered to community groups, it should be provided at no charge. If the community group uses the space on a long-term basis, the group should be responsible for the utility costs. When retailers use the space to display their merchandise, the space should be provided free of all charges. How will prospective retailers know that the vacancies are available to lease when they are temporarily occupied? This concern can be alleviated by maintaining a "For Lease" sign in front of the shopping center and a small "For Lease" sign located on the premises where it does not detract from the window display.

If the vacancies are spaces that have never been occupied, the real estate manager must weigh the cost to finish these spaces against the previously mentioned benefits. The cost to finish vacancies in a regional mall can be considerable. Many regional malls lease their spaces in almost completely unfinished conditions.

If the regional mall has a high percentage of vacancies, the real estate manager should consider selecting spaces in key areas of the mall that will have a severe negative impact if they remain vacant. Allowing long-term temporary retailers the right to occupy vacant space may be necessary to create a flow of traffic to areas of the mall that have few retailers. The shopping center manager must reserve the right in the license agreement to relocate the temporary retailer.

Sponsorship Programs

It's common that a major corporation may sponsor the mall's center court. This area of the mall may be named for the corporation—just as ballparks are named for sponsoring corporations. For instance, a corporation may sponsor the children's play area in the mall. A soft-drink company may have the exclusive right to provide its vending machines in strategic locations. Some sponsors provide *in-kind gifts* to defray the cost of a merchandising or marketing event.

SHOPPING CENTER SECURITY

The security needs and the programs to monitor shopping centers vary according to size. In many cases, the real estate manager can get the local police to drive through a few times each day and night, rather than have on-site security.

Conducting a Security Audit

The first step in developing a security program is to conduct a security audit by surveying the neighborhood and researching actual or potential security issues at the shopping center. Find out the type and frequency of criminal activities in the neighborhood. Note whether these incidents are problems within the shopping center, and ask for recommendations from an officer as to the appropriate action to take. Find out how often the police patrol the area and the shopping center, and if needed, how this frequency may be increased.

A physical inspection of the shopping center should be conducted for possible problem areas. Since good lighting is one of the best deterrents to crime, poorly lit areas are a major concern. Check for overgrown landscape areas where someone could hide to either break into a building or to accost customers and/or retailers.

Electrical, utility, and storage rooms can be sources of danger if they are not properly secured. All exterior roof ladders should be secured with a panel blocking the rungs of the ladder and the panel should be secured with a padlock. A visit with retailers to find out what they observe at odd hours helps increase the chance of detecting potential problems early and taking preventive steps.

Employee parking areas can be trouble spots. Shopping centers commonly require employees to park in back or remote areas of the parking lot. Monitor the shoppers use of the parking lot because it may not be necessary to have employees park behind the shopping center or a remote area. The local police may be willing to make additional patrols, or shopping center security can be scheduled to make additional checks and escort employees to their cars during late hours. These areas should have very good parking lot lighting.

Employing Security Guards

A key decision in developing a security program is deciding whether the shopping center needs security guards. Smaller shopping centers typically do not have a need for security guards, while large shopping centers and malls may need to develop security guard programs. A major decision in developing such a program is whether the shopping center or mall should hire the guards as employees of the mall or contract with an outside security guard company—both systems have advantages.

Hiring In-House Security Guards

The first advantage to an in-house guard staff is that the real estate manager has greater control over the security guard program, including selection and supervision of the guards. If the guards are employees of the shopping center, they know they will not be transferred to another property. This can build allegiance to the job and result in a lower turnover. In-house security guards also have a better opportunity to become familiar with the layout of the mall and to know the store managers and employees.

Employees also get an opportunity to get to know many of the customers and become familiar with teenagers that may become problems for the center and spend a little more time with them. Finally, the cost per guard may be less because the profit margin of the security guard company is saved.

Working with a Security Guard Company

Contracting with a security guard company also has distinct advantages. First, the company provides an expertise that the real estate manager may not have, and it is more likely to be current on the laws of citizen's arrest, detainment, curfews, and other law-enforcement regulations. Hiring an outside company also relieves the real estate manager of hiring, training, and terminating security personnel.

A security company has additional personnel to substitute for those who are ill or on vacation, and it can provide additional security guards during peak shopping center traffic periods and special events. Additionally, the security guard company generally has the capability to deliver guards on very short notice, should the situation arise. Finally, if a security guard is involved in an incident that ends in litigation, the security guard company's insurance carrier can defend the shopping center ownership and the real estate management company.

Armed or Unarmed Guards on the Property

Another question to decide is whether a security guard should be armed. Most security guards do not receive firearm training, and few are qualified to handle a situation that requires the display and possible use of a firearm. Armed security can give shoppers the impression that the shopping center or mall is a dangerous place.

Malls typically do not have armed security guards. If a shopping center has become a place where gangs hang out or there has been an inordinate amount of crime, an armed presence may be necessary. This decision should be given considerable research and discussions with security experts. The local police should generally handle emergencies requiring the use of firearms. If the mall is in an area where guards must be armed, the shopping center manager should work with the local police department to select a security guard company.

Security Guard Uniforms

Whether to outfit the security guards in a police-type or blazer uniform is another decision for the real estate manager. If a need to show force is likely, security guards should be in police-type uniforms. However, if the security guard's main responsibility is to serve a public relations function, blazer uniforms may be more appropriate.

Regardless of the type of uniform, it must be easily identifiable. All security personnel should wear name badges so they are easy to identify when investigating any problems that come up on the property.

Training Security Guards

If the security guards are employees of the shopping center, the real estate manager should develop an ongoing training program for the security force. Each new guard must become familiar with the property and receive a security guard's procedure manual. Regular training sessions should be conducted. At these sessions, the real estate manager reviews the security procedures for upcoming events, and the security guard supervisor discusses how to handle specific situations. Police and fire department representatives should be encouraged to attend some of these sessions and give their input as to the best procedures for various situations. The security guards should be encouraged to take an active role in these sessions and to discuss problems and offer suggestions.

The real estate manager should review the equipment the security force needs. Each security guard should receive a manual that covers possible situations the guard might encounter. At the end of each shift, the guard should give a report detailing any confrontations, how the situation was handled, and which topics should be discussed at the next meeting.

Parapolice Programs

Some cities offer *parapolice programs* that allow the city or the police guild to assign uniformed off-duty officers to patrol at the shopping center's expense. The advantage to the city is that it has more officers on patrol at no additional cost. A parapolice program costs more than contracting with a security guard company, but the police officers are trained professionals. As an alternative, it's possible for a mall to hire an off-duty police officer as the "chief of security" on a part-time basis, and the rest of the security staff can function as employees of the mall.

Relationships with Emergency Departments

A shopping center cannot afford inadequate security, and establishing a good relationship with emergency departments can help keep the security program cost effective. The shopping center should develop a working relationship with the community's police and fire departments and ask them to appoint liaisons to the shopping center or mall who report all incidents. The departments can be invited to use the shopping center after hours to practice emergencies and training.

Some regional malls are located near a sheriff or police department substation. As a result, the sheriff or police frequently cruise the parking lot and are visible within the shopping center. Some shopping centers have provided the police department space for a substation.

In response to customer concerns about crime in the mall, it's possible to develop a brochure outlining shopper safety and crime statistics for the area, along with safety tips and information on how to contact mall security and report a crime.

Security in Neighborhood and Community Shopping Centers

Strip and neighborhood shopping centers seldom have security problems other than minor vandalism in the parking lot and graffiti. Security problems that do occur usually result from one (or a combination) of the following three factors:

1. The shopping center is located in a high-crime area.
2. A rash of burglaries occurs in a short period as the burglars move from one area of the community to another.
3. A retailer or restaurant is attracting problematic clientele.

When no security problems, other than minor vandalism are present, the real estate manger can ask retailers and maintenance personnel to report suspicious people and loiterers. It's important to develop a rapport with the police precinct and request that officers periodically drive through the shopping center.

Graffiti should be removed or painted over immediately. Failure to do so will encourage more vandalism. If graffiti is an ongoing problem, try to determine when it occurs. Ask the police to drive through the shopping center during those hours. If that does not solve the problem, a private security patrol may be necessary during the period of the day or at night when the problems occur. Some city police departments now have effective graffiti details that can help identify offenders and obtain restitution.

Good lighting in the common areas is a deterrent to vandalism and other security problems. Problems occurring in the evenings or early morning hours indicate that the shopping center may need to give extra attention to lighting. Visiting the shopping center in the evening, walking throughout the parking lot, behind the shopping center, and on all sidewalks will help the determine if any areas need better lighting.

Community Mall Security

Enclosed community malls usually do not need security guards on duty 24 hours a day. Their security needs are similar to those of non-enclosed neighborhood shopping centers—with the exception that malls host marketing activities throughout the year and can attract more shoppers. If these situations warrant on-site security guards, create schedules based on the traffic and activities in the mall.

A security program may be needed during high traffic hours such as after school and on weekends. Combining the maintenance and janitorial staff with the security schedule provides on-site personnel 24 hours a day. For example, after mall hours, the night janitorial staff can clean the common areas and maintenance personnel can start their shift when the night janitorial crew leaves.

Develop a security program by first analyzing the hours the guards that are needed for each day of the week. Then, additional guards are scheduled for peak selling seasons and special events. The cost of the guard service is determined by multiplying the number of hours by the hourly rate.

Typically, the community mall security guard schedule provides guards during the peak mall traffic times each day of the week. Additional guards are on duty on New Year's Eve and Halloween—the two holidays when vandalism is more likely to occur. Extra security for the Christmas and holiday season usually starts the Friday after Thanksgiving. Traditionally, that Friday is the busiest shopping day of the year, otherwise known as "Black Friday," which means additional security is necessary during the Thanksgiving weekend. Many malls extend their hours the two weekends before the Christmas and holiday season, and the security schedule reflects the longer Saturday and Sunday mall hours.

Regional and Super Regional Mall Security

Regional and super regional malls usually schedule guards 24 hours a day or beginning an hour before and ending an hour after operating hours with the mall completely locked down during off hours. If the mall has two common area maintenance budgets, a mall and a parking lot budget, then separate security budgets are developed for each area. If one budget were to be used for both areas, the costs might be allocated unfairly because one area would be likely to need more security than the other would.

OPERATING AGREEMENTS FOR SHOPPING CENTERS

Two agreements provide restrictions, rights, and obligations to the shopping center owner and the tenants: (1) the reciprocal easement agreement and (2) the common area agreement.

Reciprocal Easement Agreement

The *reciprocal easement agreement (REA)* is made between the shopping center owner and the major retailers. It describes the property, defines the common area, and establishes the rights and obligations of each party. This agreement usually appoints the shopping center owner as supervisor of the common area who establishes the maintenance standards. The major retailers have the right to approve changes or additions to the common area as well as to remove the shopping center manager from the position of supervisor if the common area maintenance does not meet the agreement's standards.

These rights might also include the major retailers' approval of the shopping center remodeling plans. When a major retailer owns its building and the adjacent parking areas, this agreement provides crossover rights to use each other's common areas. Occasionally, the lender is a party to these agreements. This agreement may prohibit changes to the parking lot, other common areas, or additional development without the anchor tenants' approval. The anchor tenants want to protect their parking field and prevent buildings from obstructing their sight lines for the street.

Common Area Agreement Provisions

A *common area agreement* is made between the shopping center owner, owners of other parcels within the shopping center, and the anchor tenants regarding how the common areas will be managed and whether the approval of the anchor tenants is needed to expand the shopping center or make changes to the common areas—including the layout of the parking lot. The following are common provisions to a common area agreement:

- Maintenance standards
- Lighting
- Property taxes
- Maintenance director
- Reimbursement of maintenance costs
- Billing for expenses
- Effect of sale by shopping center owner
- Default in payment of expenses
- Lien for expenses or property taxes
- Right to maintain parcel separately
- Responsibilities if there is no maintenance director
- Sale and lease back of the major retailer's parcel
- General provisions
- Sale and sale-leaseback purchaser

Operating agreements can easily be violated. For example, the REA may restrict temporary tenants from using the common areas. Adding a pad or outparcel tenant to the common area may violate the common area agreement. Violations can be costly to the shopping center owner and possibly the real estate management company. It's important to meet with the shopping center owner to determine if the property has either of these agreements. If so, request a copy of the agreement to determine each party's rights and obligations as they affect the operation, development, and leasing of the property. If the shopping center owner is not familiar with the agreements, the owner's attorney should review and summarize the rights and obligations of the signatory parties.

Common Area Billings

Common area billings may cause problems between the real estate manager and the tenants if they are not handled properly. The costs may seem high relative to the work the tenants sees on a daily basis. To avoid potential disputes, ensure that billings are accurate, services are competitively priced, and retailers receive sufficient explanation to understand the expenses involved in the billings.

Experienced retailers may go to great lengths to negotiate limits on common area costs and/or exclusions to the billings, only to find those limits and exclusions are ignored in the billings. Such errors are most likely oversights, but they can promote an atmosphere of doubt and mistrust. It to build a model of each common area lease provision for each tenant and then to ensure that each billing adheres to that model.

It's important to review all billings before they are sent to the tenants. Once a retailer receives a few common area bills that are easy to understand, future bills may be viewed in a more positive light. *Common area maintenance (CAM)* and other operating expenses are billed to the tenants monthly based on an estimate budget. The monthly bills do not vary. When the year is completed, the real estate management company reconciles the budget to the actual expenses and either bills the tenant if the budget was exceeded, or gives the tenant a refund on future rent if the expenses were under budget. Unless required by the lease, copies of the actual invoices need not be sent to the retailers.

Finally, a timely billing is helpful to all concerned and reconciling the expenses to the budget should be completed within a couple months of the year end. There are probably more misunderstanding over common area billings than any other issue between owners and tenants.

Parking Requirements

A shopping center's size is determined primarily by the *gross leaseable area (GLA)* the developer can build on a parcel of land. Developers usually build the maximum GLA allowable; however, the amount of buildable GLA is restricted by the *parking area ratio* (the number of parking stalls per GLA) required by the municipality, and by any parking requirements in the anchor tenants' leases. Turning regular-sized parking stalls into compact parking spaces yields more parking spaces and more buildable GLA, while also providing more efficient use of the parking area. Generally, the number of compact parking spaces are determined by the local authorities and often by the anchor tenants in the common area agreement, REA, or the lease.

A shopping center should evaluate the shopping center's parking lot for potential hidden value. If the number of parking stalls exceeds the recommendations of the Urban Land Institute's (ULI) *Parking Requirements for Shopping Centers,* explore the possibility of reducing the ratio of parking stalls per GLA, while remaining in compliance with the parking requirements of the municipality and the anchor tenant leases. Such a reduction can provide additional building opportunities and generate further income for the shopping center, thereby enhancing its value. It should be noted, however, that the local municipalities will determine the parking requirements no matter what is recommended by the ULI studies. An example is creating a pad or outparcel in the parking lot and leasing or selling it to a bank or restaurant.

Capitalizing the income stream from a grounds lease will significantly increase the value of the shopping center. One should be cautioned that building a new pad our out parcel can result in visibility to some shops being reduced and that may cause problems with that tenant. Great care should be taken in the placement of new pads or out parcels. These can easily cause traffic-flow problems, such as a new fast food operation with an outside pick-up window and backing up traffic in the center during their peak traffic times.

DETERMINING PERCENTAGE RENT

Rent paid above the minimum rent is referred to as *percentage rent* or *overage rent.* The percentage rate for any retailer is stated in the lease agreement and is based on the profit margin of that type of business. Percentage rent rates are applied to gross sales, less sales tax, and any negotiated exclusions. The additional rent is based on a percentage of the retailer's sales above a predetermined amount. If the location in the shopping center does not benefit the retailer's sales, no percentage rent is owed. A retailer's payment of percentage rent recognizes the increased sales achieved by the development of the retail environment, and the property owner should benefit if it results in retailers achieving higher sales.

Percentage Rates

Supermarkets have a very low-profit margin, and they pay the lowest percentage rental rate in the industry, usually between 1 to 1.5 percent of sales. Most retail soft goods, shoe stores, restaurants, and specialty stores are in the midrange of profit margins, and typically pay from 5 to 7 percent of gross sales. Service retailers, such as beauty shops and barbershops, have a higher profit margin and typically pay 7 to 10 percent of sales. The best source for reasonable percentage rent rates are the existing leases and sharing such information with fellow shopping center managers to determine industry standards.

Breakpoints

On the first of each month, the retailer typically pays minimum rent and any percentage rent due above the minimum as required by the lease . Shopping center retailers typically pay either a minimum rent or a percentage of their sales—whichever is greater. The point at which a retailer is obligated to pay percentage rent is known as the *breakpoint*. A breakpoint can be *natural* or *artificial*. The natural breakpoint is determined by dividing the minimum rent by the agreed percentage rent rate. An artificial breakpoint is negotiated and is either higher or lower than the natural breakpoint. It if is lower, it benefits the property owner, and if it is higher, it benefits the tenant. (More information on these concepts and formulas, along with examples of calculating breakpoints are explained in Chapter 14.)

Major retailer report their sales and pay the percentage rent they owe annually. Smaller shop retailers and restaurants should report their sales and pay percentage rent monthly. After the year ends, the retailer's sales are adjusted based on the retailer's annual sales, which evens out the year's seasonal highs and lows. Even though a retailer may pay percentage rent in April and December, the annual sales may be below the annual breakpoint. If that is case, the shopping center owner refunds the percentage rent paid. Another approach is the tenants do not pay percentage during the year until their sales to date exceed the breakpoint. There are a few leases where the smaller tenant pays any percentage rent due monthly or quarterly and there is no year-end adjustment. That is not really fair to the tenant as it does not recognize the lower sales months and, therefore, makes his or her rent higher for the entire year.

Negotiating Percentage Rent Rates

Percentage rent calculations vary. The breakpoint can be negotiated higher or lower. One percentage rate can be used to determine the breakpoint and another can be used for sales above the breakpoint. A declining rate may be used, or the retailer may have the right to deduct taxes, insurance, and common area costs from percentage rent owed. This is not a common provision in leases, but some tenants had such rights in older leases.

Negotiating Lower Breakpoints

The retailer may demand a higher level of interior improvements to the store than the property owner is willing to provide, and the retailer may be unwilling to pay a higher rent to offset the cost of the improvements. The property owner may then propose that the breakpoint be lowered to offset the additional investment.

Negotiating Higher Breakpoints

A retailer may be forced to pay market rent and spend additional funds for a space that needs improvement. As an inducement, the property owner might agree to move the natural breakpoint higher to allow the retailer to recapture the additional cost to improve the premises. Retailers that are trendy with high sales and are in demand by shopping center owners and developers may negotiate an artificial breakpoint above the natural breakpoint.

Higher Percentage Rate to Breakpoint and Lower Percentage Rate Thereafter

Sometimes the shopping center owner and the retailer cannot agree on the rate for the percentage rent. The retailer might want five percent and the real estate manager owner might request six percent. A compromise is six percent to the breakpoint and five percent thereafter ($12,000 minimum rent divided by the six percent rate = $200,000 natural breakpoint; $12,000 minimum rent divided by the five percent rate = $240,000 natural breakpoint).

Deductions from Percentage Rent

While it is rare today to allow a retailer to deduct expense items such as real estate taxes and insurance from percentage rent due, known as *recapture,* some major retailers request the right to do so and some older leases still have those provisions.

REQUESTING AND ANALYZING RETAIL SALES

Retailers' sales reports are collected and analyzed for several reasons. The sales report determines if the retailer owes percentage rent and indicates whether the retailer is successful or a potential rent-collection problem. A retailer's performance is included in evaluating whether to renew the retailer's lease. When all the sales reports are combined, the real estate manager can analyze the performance of specific business categories as well as the entire shopping center. This analysis can point out weak areas in the tenant mix and can be used when developing the shopping center's leasing plan. Individual tenant's sales are confidential and not disclosed.

The sales for the shopping center or mall can also be a very effective marketing tool. The leasing agents can quote the sales per square foot for the entire center and for categories of tenants. If an anchor retailer's sales are superior, the leasing agent will discuss the sales with the store manager. The leasing agent may find out that sales are in the top 10 percent for chain's region or ranks number two in the state. For example, the shopping center's restaurants or jewelry stores sales may be twice that of national averages for their category. This information will get the attention of other restaurant operators and retailers.

Many retailers benchmark their projected sales to the sales of a specific retailer in the shopping center or mall. That retailer may give the leasing agent permission to disclose that their sales are in the top quartile for their chain, or its sales exceed a specific high sales per square foot. There is no better leasing tool than the success stories of retailers and restaurants in a shopping center and mall.

Evaluating the Shopping Center's Sales

Sales figures can be used to not only evaluate each retailer, but also to evaluate the shopping center as a whole, and to measure the success of various merchandise categories. Each category is totaled, averages are established, and each retailer in the category is compared with the whole. Comparisons can be made on sales per square foot as well as on sales increases or decreases.

It's important to not reveal individual retailer's sales figures to others in this process. If a category has three or fewer retailers, revealing the total sales would automatically provide each retailer with the sales of the others. For that reason, calculating category breakdowns is very difficult in neighborhood shopping centers and even some community shopping centers. The sales analysis in such shopping centers are limited to confidential individual retailer and shopping center analysis. If the shopping center is in a state where sales taxes are collected, sales tax figures can be used to measure the market share of an individual shopping center on an ongoing basis.

Pay close attention to sales when the shopping center has been remodeled or expanded or when it has added a major retailer and the existing retailer's sales do not increase. Even if nothing seems to be amiss, auditing a retailer who is close to the breakpoint may reveal enough additional sales to require the retailer to pay percentage rents.

Shopping centers and malls are evaluated by their sales per square foot. Retailers and other uses prefer to locate in shopping centers and malls whose sales out perform industry averages. The rent that property owners can charge retailers and restaurants is based on their anticipated and actual sales. These businesses cannot afford to pay rent as a percentage of their sales greater than a predetermined amount. Tenants include all rental charges such as base rent, common area charges, taxes, and insurance as rent. Retailers often refer to these collective charges as occupancy costs.

Analyzing Sales of Regional Shopping Centers and Malls

Sales analysis in a larger shopping center is a significant management tool shopping that can be provided to the retailers on a monthly basis. This summary enables retailers to compare and evaluate their performance based on that of other retailers in the shopping center. The sales reports are gathered and placed in predetermined categories such as apparel, gifts, shoes, food, and so on.

Each tenant is assigned a letter known only to management, and its sales are then compared on the basis of sales-per-square-foot and percentage of change. The numbers are compared to the same month in the previous year and to sales in the area for a comparison in the marketplace. These figures are frequently used to evaluate an area in a shopping center, a merchandise category, or specific sizes of stores. Sales figures often reveal certain areas of the shopping center that are stronger than others, which is helpful in locating specific retailers or uses. It is best to give immediate feedback by compiling this information and sharing it with the retailers each month.

Each merchandise category is analyzed to see how retailers are performing compared to others in the category. The sales are reduced to sales per square foot and listed by a predetermined code to ensure that no retailer's sales can be directly identified. The sales are then compared for the same period in the previous year and stated as a percentage of increase or decrease. The entire category is compared in the same way so the tenants and management can determine how well the specific tenant is doing in relation to the other retailers in that category. The shopping center can use this information in discussions with retailers about improving sales and for overall feedback. It can be very helpful to visit each tenant and provide them with the monthly analysis and discuss the results with the store manager and/or owner to determine what has gone well and where there are problems. The information is also useful in analyzing tenant mix.

Sales Analysis for Small Shopping Centers

In a small shopping center or an office setting with a few ground-floor retailers, analyzing sales by merchandise categories is not practical. Instead, the retailers' sales figures are compared in two ways: (1) to the individual retailer's figures from the previous year and (2) to sales per square foot of similar retailers.

The sales analysis report is also used to determine individual sales per square foot as well as the entire shopping center's sales per square foot. Comparing a retailer's sales per square foot to those of a merchant in a different category is usually not valid because different retailers produce substantially different sales results—even when both are quite successful.

The sales increase (or decrease) can be compared to sales reports for the city or county to see if the shopping center is holding its market share over time. General sales information can become a component of the leasing and marketing data. Retailers and restaurant operators want to be in shopping centers and malls where the tenants sales exceed national averages. If a shopping center has a supermarket or department store with exceptionally high sales, the leasing agent may state the supermarket or department stores sales are in the top 90 percent of that store. Store managers are usually willing to provide such information. Retailers like to benchmark their sales to specific retailers or categories of retailers when determining the projected sales for a new location.

Comparative Sales Analysis for Individual Retailers

This report gives information to retailers about their progress in comparison with other retailers within the shopping center that are in the same category. In the compilation of sales data, the shopping center must ensure that sufficient retailers are in a category so that an individual retailer's sales are not revealed.

The report covers the current month as well as the year-to-date figures.

Evaluating Existing Retailers

Each retailer's sales should be compared with national averages and with similar uses within the shopping center. Comparing the retailer with the category reveals whether the retailer is doing well, average, or poorly. It's important to also consider store size, specific type of merchandise, time of year, and any store changes. Once the sales figures are gathered, schedule a meeting with each retailer to discuss the results.

Projecting Retailer Sales Using Less Than a Year of Sales

In several instances, shopping center managers are required to project retailer sales with less than a full year of sales figures. For example, when calculating the annual budget or updating a cash flow forecast, the manager may want to include percentage rent in the estimate. When working on a lease renewal, lease cancellation, or mid-lease negotiation, the manager may need to project retailer sales.

With a full year of a retailer's sales, projecting the following year is fairly easy. If a tenant had sales of $627,000 in one year, and a projection for next year is needed, the manager looks at the market, competition, retailer's operations, and recent sales trends and applies an applicable percentage to the $627,000 of sales. For example, when applying a three-percent increase, the sales for the coming year would be $645,810.

The main issue in projecting retailer sales with less than a full year of experience is that retailers do not normally have the same sales percentages each month. If the sales were equal every month, take the first six months of the year, double that, and come up with the likely sales for the year. Service retailers are more likely to have fairly even sales spread throughout the year, but retailers that sell clothing, gifts, shoes, and other soft and hard goods may have disproportionate amount of sales during specific periods, such as back-to-school time, Valentine's Day, Mother's Day, and the Christmas and holiday season. Because of this, it's important to look more closely at the percentage spread during the year and use those figures to extrapolate the sales. It is fairly easy to determine the average percentage of each tenant's sales during the year and use those percentages to estimate a future year's sales.

Using Color-Coded Sales Analysis

Color coding a shopping center's plot plan shows where the best sales are and what is selling the best. Retailer sales are typically divided by sales levels: $1,000 per square foot and higher, $500 to $999 per square foot, less than $500 per square foot, and so forth. A color is assigned to each level, and the colors are then transferred to the appropriate locations on the shopping center's plot plan. Which locations generate the highest and lowest levels of sales becomes obvious. Since different store categories produce different sales, the type of store must be considered to determine the relevance of the figures, but this approach can quickly identify weak areas in the shopping center as well as in the merchandise mix. Some property owners add a separate category and color for retailers on rent relief.

Another use for color coding is to determine the occupancy costs of each retailer in the shopping center. The occupancy costs a measurement of the tenant's rent and all other charges as a percentage of their sales. Generally, retailers with occupancy costs in excess of 15 to 17 percent are candidates for future rent collection problems. Regional and national chains are not likely to have a rent payment problem with sales in these ranges, but they will express concern for the profitability of their store and may ask for a reduction in their rent, negotiate a lower rent at renewal, or not renew their lease. Using a figure of 17 percent, mark every space in the shopping center where a retailer has an occupancy cost of 17 percent or more. Then, compare the result to the color-coded sales map to determine where the problems are. While a specific retailer with high-occupancy costs may not be a problem because the store recently opened has high mark-ups, or has other sources of income, the exercise can be worthwhile and revealing.

Collecting Sales Reports

Collecting sales reports can be a difficult process, but to obtain an accurate sales report analysis, each retailer must report its sales on time. The typical retail lease provision requires shop retailers to report their sales between the 20th and the 30th of the month following the sales period. Even national retailers report sales monthly. Anchor retailers usually negotiate the right to report sales annually.

Collecting sales reports begins by explaining the requirements of the sales reporting provision in the retailer's lease to the retailer. An administrative staff member at the shopping center management office is usually assigned to collect the sales reports. If a retailer refuses to report sales, the real estate manager gets involved.

The first step in collecting delinquent sales reports is a phone call to the tenant. If the property has an on-site real estate manager, a personal visit is more effective. If the phone call and visit produce no results, and if the store is part of a chain, the district manager should be called. A letter can be sent to the retailer following the conversation. Continual nonreporting of sales figures may indicate that a retailer's sales are above the breakpoint and the retailer owes percentage rent. It may also indicate that the retailer knows that he or she does not owe any percentage rent and, therefore, does not feel the need to report the sales. If continued prodding does not get the retailer to report the sales on time, then consider the retailer for a sales audit.

The retailer's handbook or manual, developed and provided by the shopping center manager, should contain an explanation of the sales reporting procedure. The lease may provide for a penalty of double the base rent if a retailer fails to report its sales on time. The penalty for late sales reporting should be enforced, but only after several attempts to get the retailer to comply without threats. If the current lease does not provide a penalty, one should be included in the lease at renewal time. The ultimate step in collecting late sales reports is to place the retailer in default of its lease and seek legal action, but no one really wants it to go that far.

AUDITING RETAILERS' SALES

Leases with retailers and some service retailers call for minimum rent versus a percentage of sales, whichever is greater. Retailers that have a percentage rent provision in their leases should be considered for a sales audit. It is not necessary to audit every tenant. Many tenants' sales will never exceed their breakpoint that is necessary for them to pay percentage rent. Some owners believe that 10 percent of the tenants should be audited each year, while most owners will analyze each tenant's sales and determine if any tenants should be audited each year.

Choosing which Retailers to Audit

The shopping center manager analyzes which retailers to audit based on several factors. The first is whether the retailer is paying percentage or overage rent. Every retailer paying percentage rent is a candidate for an audit. Retailers may not be calculating their sales correctly through error, or they may be understating sales to avoid paying additional percentage rent.

When retailers' sales are within 20 percent of their breakpoints, or exceed their breakpoint, the possibility of sales audits should be analyzed. Tenants who are paying percentage rent may be under reporting their sales to keep from paying additional percentage rent. Most retailers whose sales are less than 80 percent of their breakpoint are not likely to be submitting incorrect sales reports. It is also quite likely that the person filling out the percentage rent reports for the retailer does not fully understand the lease provisions and is under reporting the sales without knowing it. The error should always be treated as just that—until or unless there is proof that the tenant is deliberately under reporting the sales.

In many shopping centers, no retailers are candidates for audits. This can occur when all the retailers' sales are low or when the minimum rent is so high that the retailers' breakpoints are elevated so none of them are likely to reach its breakpoint during the initial term of the lease. The shopping center manager reviews retailers who are likely candidates for an audit and selects retailers to audit based on the following criteria:

1. Which retailer is likely to be understating sales?
2. Whose business appears to be increasing although sales figures show very little growth from prior years?
3. When was each retailer last audited?
4. Which retailers owed percentage rent during their last audit?

It should also be noted that sales audits can be expensive and disruptive to the merchant. They should only be conducted by qualified personnel and, of course, must be kept confidential.

Defining Audit Procedures

Prior to selecting retailers for audits, designate an auditor from a national or a local accounting firm that specializes in conducting retailer audits. Firms that do not specialize in conducting tenant's sales audit are likely to charge considerably more than accounting firms that have a division dedicated to these types of audit. It is always best to obtain a couple of auditing quotes.

After carefully selecting the retailers to audit, send a letter to each tenant being audited. The letter requests the retailer to have the following records available: sales journal, general ledger, profit and loss statements, bank statements, sales tax returns, federal income tax returns, and all records necessary to substantiate deductions from reportable sales.

After the retailer receives its letter, the auditor calls the tenant and schedules the audit. The auditor sends the store representative a checklist of items to provide for the audit. Prior to the audit, the real estate manager meets with the retailer to explain the purpose of the assessment and to emphasize that the audit is a routine procedure. After the audit is completed, the auditor should meet with the retailer and review the results. If the audit shows that the retailer owes percentage rent, the parties follow the lease provision that states when the percentage rent is due. The owner pays for the cost of the audit unless the tenant's sales are misreported by a specific amount stated in the lease—that amount is typically two percent.

Retailer Audits of Billbacks

Many commercial tenants no longer blindly accept the shopping center manager's operating expense billback charges—tenants carefully scrutinize their own occupancy costs. Their base rent is a known dollar amount, as are pre-negotiated periodic rent increases. The unknown components of a retailer's occupancy cost are the property's operating expenses that will be billed to the retailer.

Retailer audits of billback expenses have the potential for developing trust or distrust between the retailer and the manager and/or owners of the property. If the real estate manager is caught intentionally overbilling the tenant, the tenant will most likely lose trust with the real estate manager. When the audit discovers inaccurate billings or honest errors, the tenant may always question the accuracy, but not the honesty of the real estate manager and/or the owners of the shopping center.

A good shopping center manager/tenant relationship can be ruined by an overly aggressive auditor who unfairly interprets or misinterprets the billback lease provisions and recommends that the retailer withhold payment to the real estate manager until the disputed issue is resolved. This can affect either party's decision regarding a lease renewal. Many anchor tenants will review a bill, pay all items that are not in dispute, and then withhold the disputed funds until they have been satisfied that they are due. This is a fair approach for both sides.

Billback Formats

Operating expense billbacks are presented in

different formats for shopping centers. The billback operating expenses for office and medical office buildings are grouped together and billed to the tenants in one budget, referred to as the building's *operating expenses.*

Strip shopping centers have one operating expense budget, referred to as *common area maintenance (CAM),* that is billed to the retailers along with several additional individual charges, such as real estate taxes, insurance, merchant's association, or marketing fund dues, HVAC maintenance, and other possible charges.

An enclosed mall has the same billback charges, along with two operating expense budgets: (1) the enclosed mall common areas and (2) the exterior common areas. If the mall has a food court, a separate food court operating or CAM budget is used. Separate billings are necessary because not all retailers may pay for each expense. For instance, if the supermarket owns its building, the taxing authority bills it separately for real estate taxes. The rest of the shopping center receives one or more real estate tax bills, which is prorated among the other retailers. Anchor retailers usually pay directly for trash removal, but the shopping center manager bills the other retailers for shared trash receptacles—if the trash removal company does not bill them directly. In a mall non-food court, tenants do not pay for the cost to maintain the common eating area for the food court. A pad tenant on the parking lot of a mall will pay parking or common area expenses but not mall common area expenses.

Each separate billable expense may have a different denominator for calculating a retailer's prorated share. The *denominator* is the sum of the square footage of the premises of all the retailers that are billed for a particular expense. Retailer charges are a significant portion of the retailer's occupancy cost. There are exceptions to the common area billings. Some merchants have their own water meters and trash removal services, some pay directly for their own insurance coverages, and some have their own fire alarm systems. Each of these exceptions requires the owner to have a different denominator or expense pool for those expenses involved.

FIXED COMMON AREA EXPENSES

Another approach in determining billback expenses is the "flat" or "fixed" common area billing. Because common area expenses have been a contentious area of the owner/tenant relationship in shopping centers, some shopping center owners have changed their system to fixed billing regardless of the actual cost of the CAM. This amount may be negotiated along with other issues that are negotiated before the lease is signed. Also negotiated is an annual percentage increase, such as the fixed CAM will increase five percent annually—effective the beginning of each calendar year. Both the owner and the tenant are taking a chance that the actual expense will be close to the amount billed and they do not have to worry about detailed billings and disputes at year end.

A variation on this approach is a fixed billing for those charges that are predictable, but actual billing on those items that they cannot control, such as snow removal. It is expected that owners will be realistic and reasonable in their billings for the fixed items, and for sophisticated tenants, it is not much of a problem in that they have many locations that are able to estimate the costs themselves. The smaller, less-experienced retailer is less inclined to know those costs, and if they want to be in that shopping center, they are more or less required to accept the charges.

Property Owner's Obligations

An important reason retailers audit billback charges is that the shopping center manager has an obligation to account to the retailer when handling that party's funds. The possibility for error is always present when one party handles another's funds. Unfortunately, some property owners intentionally charge items to the CAM account that are not common area expenses. The cost to clean and wash the windows on vacant spaces in a shopping center is an example of an expense that is not a common area expense and should not be a billback expense. Charging retailers for such expenses is inappropriate.

Shopping center managers have an obligation to bill retailers in accordance with the lease provisions. Even if the real estate manager disagrees with the billback lease provisions, the manager must follow the letter of the lease. Older leases, especially for major retailers, often have restrictions that prevent the real estate manager from billing these retailers for their full pro rata shares of all the *pass-through operating expenses.* This situation frequently occurs when the developer is anxious to make a deal and the cost of a concession places a limit on the amount of the pass-through expenses the retailer is obligated to pay. During lease negotiations, such concessions may seem relatively unimportant. However, billing back all the expenses that are allowable in the lease is important to the cash flow and value of the property. The real estate manager wants to bill all recoverable charges to the retailers. The collection of these charges will increase the property's net operating income and cash flow, thus, increasing its value. The difference between collecting 100 percent of the CAM and other pass-through charges and the actual amount collected is known a "leakage."

Billback Lease Provisions

The best way to avoid misunderstandings regarding retailer billback charges is to have clear and unambiguous lease provisions. There is no substitute for lease provisions that clearly delineate which charges are billable to retailers.

A lease form is not always up to date with the industry unless it is revised every few years. The revisions include modifying the billback provisions to include any charges that have become acceptable in the industry. For example, many years back management fees of the shopping center were not a billback item. Today, those charges are quite common in retail leases. Roof maintenance and possibly replacement was generally a owner expense a few years ago, and today, most new leases include this as a billable item to the tenants. If the expense is great, such as a major parking lot repair or replacement, the cost is amortized over the useful life of the item or a reasonable time period.

Retailer Audit Lease Provisions

The retailer should have the right to audit the real estate manager's billback expenses; however, that right should have limits.

Audit Areas

Retailers may request to audit five primary areas:

1. Calculation of the retailer's pro rata share of the billback charges
2. Expenses that are allowable billback charges
3. *Consumer price index (CPI)* adjustment to the base rent, flat CAM billings, and marketing contributions
4. Accuracy of the calculation of the square footage of the premises
5. Any billings from the shopping center manager to the retailer

Audit Restrictions

The lease provisions for tenants auditing the owner should include the following audit restrictions:

1. Advance notice. The retailer should be required to provide the real estate manager with at least a 30-day advance notice of an audit.
2. Location of the audit. The real estate manager should determine whether the audit will take place at the main office or at the property, if the property has an on-site management office.
3. Time if the audit. The audit must be conducted during normal business hours.
4. Frequency of the audit. Each billing year may be audited only once.
5. Timing of the audit. The audit may only be performed within 120 days from the date the real estate manager mailed the year-end billback reconciliations or adjustments to the retailer.
6. Period to be audited. The audit may only be for the most recently completed billing year.
7. Loss of audit privileges. The retailer may not conduct an audit if it is in default of its lease.
8. Cost of the audit. The retailer is responsible for the cost of the audit out-of-pocket expenses,

such as reproducing copies of invoices.

9. Confidentiality. The retailer and the retailer's auditor and/or audit firm must keep the results of the audit confidential. The real estate manager does not discuss with the other retailers the results of its audits of other retailers' sales.
10. Copy of audit. The retailer must provide a copy of the audit to the real estate manager.
11. Prohibit contingent audits. Some include a statement in the lease that prohibits the auditor from charging a contingency fee. An audit should be an unbiased review of the billback charges. If the auditor's fee is based on a percentage of any savings to the retailer, the auditor may be biased in favor of the retailer.
12. Witholding rent. The tenant may not withhold rent prior to or during the audit period.
13. Disputes. If there is a dispute between the shopping center owner and the tenant over whether certain expenses should be a billback charge, a third accountant selected by both parties will decide on the issues in dispute.

Retailer Audit Methods

Retailers use two methods to audit billback charges. Some large national retailers have in-house audit teams. Most retailers use a third-party accounting firm to conduct audits. Some auditing firms offer to audit the retailer's billback charges on a contingency basis—usually 50 percent of the savings they find. Some firms may overanalyze minor issues, and the retailer may withhold the entire billback charges until a small expense is resolved. The shopping center manager, out of frustration, may decide not to challenge a legitimate small expense that is questioned just to receive the balance of the billback expenses.

Retailer audits can be a burden on the real estate manager or the real estate management firm's staff, and may result in disputes over ambiguous wording in the lease. The best way to prevent this from occurring is to have a lease that clearly defines billback expenses and explains how the retailer's pro rata share is determined and to charge only expenses allowed in the lease to the billback budgets.

DETERMINING SQUARE FOOTAGE FOR RETAIL SPACE

Without a doubt, the square footage of a tenant's space is critical. The rents are set by the square footage, along with the common area billings, marketing monies, and even the tenant's success of sales.

There are many disputes between owners and tenants over the actual square footage of the tenants space. The only guidance on how to measure tenant's retail space is published by the Building Owners and Manager's Association (BOMA). That standard explains that the number of square feet in a ground-floor store area shall be computed by measuring from the building line in the case of street frontages, inner surface of the other outer building walls, inner surface of corridor and other permanent partitions, and to the center of other partitions that separate the premises from adjoining shop areas. No deductions shall be made for vestibules inside the building line or for columns or projections necessary to the building. No addition shall be made for bay windows extending outside the building line. While it is not set forth by any specific authority, another way of measuring retail space is to measure the outside of all outside walls and center line of any demising walls, with no deductions for supporting posts, entrances, or showcases.

Mezzanines may or may not be included in the square footages. It is always a good idea for the owner to spell out in the lease just how the spaces was measured and to include language in which the owner and tenant agree. The owner has an obligation to determine the square footage as accurately as is reasonable. If available, the measurement of the space by a *computer-aided design (CAD)* is the most effective and accurate approach. A sophisticated tenant is likely to measure the space on their own before agreeing to any square footage.

Space Planning for Shopping Centers

Anchor and national tenants have a formula for their space needs and usually know what they want and do not need the services of a owner space planner. However, new retailers have little or no idea what is the right square footage and/or layout for their proposed store or know how to plan for maximum efficiency. Basically, if new tenants take on too much space, they will be carrying a heavier burden of costs for rent, common area costs, taxes, and even employees and stock. As a result, it is prudent to have a list of a couple of retail space planners who can be recommended to tenants who may need help planning their store.

PERFORMING A RETAILER VISUAL AUDIT

In addition to being fully versed in all aspects of property operations, the real estate manager must know the factors that determine the viability of retail operations. To help retailers maximize their potential, the real estate manager must understand the elements of a successful retail store. It's important to have a basic understanding of stocking, merchandising, personnel needs, signage, merchandise turns, markdown policies, window display, store arrangement, and advertising. Armed with such basic knowledge and the tenant's monthly sales reports, the real estate manager should be in a good position to provide assistance and make informed decisions. Visiting retail shops, studying sales reports, and tracking rental payment histories can help the real estate manager recognize tenants who may be having problems, which can often lead to delinquent rent payment.

Visual Merchandising

"Just looking" is smart shopping, and any effort that enables the customer to see more is likely to produce additional sales. For many merchandise categories, the customer must have a chance to see the merchandise offered before deciding on a purchase. Merchandise is often sold to the customer who is "just looking."

Windows should convey what the store carries. Complicated windows are likely to be distracting. Props and window displays that conceal the shop's interior are outdated. The usual recommendation is to change windows and major display areas every two weeks. Some window signage may be desirable; some store names show better on windows than on blade signs. However, establishing a standard for such signage and maintaining some degree of uniformity in the shopping center is vital. Less merchandise in a window display is better than a clutter display. Most window displays have a merchandise and a color theme.

Slow-Selling Merchandise

The most troublesome issue facing store management is the need to quickly identify and deal with slow-selling merchandise. Store management must establish limiting-time standards based on acceptable stock turn rates.

Markdowns are unavoidable. However, strong psychological barriers keep retailers from expeditiously taking markdowns. The magnitude of the problem is considerable. The proportion of inventory that must be reduced to be sold increases each year. Therefore, retailers must set and implement standards. The result will be significant profit increase.

The following questions focus on important aspects of dealing with slow-selling merchandise:

- Is merchandise marked down after a specific number of weeks? The most practical and effective approach to a markdown program is to establish and implement standards based on the number of weeks on sale.
- Are the markdowns adequate? After the first markdown, follow-up markdowns should be taken until the merchandise is sold.
- Are follow-up markdowns taken? The markdown frequency in season is at four-week intervals to allow the typical customer two visits.

Professional Personal Retail Selling

The typical retail specialty store can increase sales significantly by providing employees with a basic training program in professional retail selling.

In the past few decades, personal retail selling diminished primarily because of the heavy demand for merchandise and the rapid growth of super stores as well as discount and warehouse stores. Through reduced staffing, large retailers have realized significant expense savings; however, small specialty stores must still maintain minimum sales staffs. This gives small shops the opportunity to gain a competitive edge by utilizing professional personal selling.

The following guidelines describe proven selling techniques for a wide variety of retail operations. In using these guidelines, the retailer must determine which procedures would be most effective for the needs, characteristics, and personality of the particular store. Although each shop differs in its merchandise, presentation, price lines, and salespeople, many of the guidelines are applicable to all professional retailers. The suggested techniques reflect these premises:

1. Every customer should be greeted within half a minute of entering the shop.
2. Every entering customer should be approached while in the shop.
3. Sales personnel should be on the selling floor except when it is necessary to be behind the service desk.
4. Sales personnel should always use professional approaches with customers.

Guidelines for Sales Personnel

The customer who enters a retail store to look at the merchandise is sometimes searching for a specific item. In most instances, however, the customer enters the shop to see what is new and makes most buying decisions while in the store.

Showing only low-ticket merchandise in the belief that the customer wants to spend as little as possible is a disservice. In specialty stores that usually carry more expensive items, most customers are interested in unique merchandise. For many busy customers, shopping is not primarily a recreation—it's a necessary chore. Thus, the customer feels a sense of accomplishment in finding and purchasing desirable merchandise. In sharp contrast to other forms of selling, the function of the retail salesperson is less to "sell" the customer and more to "show" the customer. To encourage customers to remain in the store as long as possible, it is valuable for retail salespeople to engage in conversation with customers. This creates an opportunity to show the customer more, respond to questions, and counter objections.

The salesperson must recognize the difference between being aggressive and being assertive. Aggressive behavior inhibits customer rapport, whereas assertive behavior indicates competence, knowledge, and professionalism, thereby promoting consumer confidence.

Seminars for Retailers

A shopping center's base rent is in part determined by the potential or actual sales volume of the retailers. A shopping center in which most retailers' sales volume greatly exceeds the national average can justify charging a higher base rent than a shopping center in which the retailers' sales are at or below the national average.

The higher the retailers' sales volume, the higher the rental rates they can command on vacancies and during lease renewals. When a retailer exceeds its breakpoint for paying percentage rent, additional rent in the form of percentage rent or overage rent will be paid. When retailers' sales are stronger, the likelihood of retailer failure is less. Costs associated with retailer failure are lost rent, commission expense, possible tenant improvement allowance, and marketing costs.

Retailer failures are of major concern to the shopping center manager because they give the shopping center a reputation as a location in which businesses have difficulty being successful. Statistics prove that the most likely retailer to fail is the small, independent business, and the first year is the most critical period. According to a Dunn & Bradstreet report, more than half of the businesses that failed had operated for less than six years. Twenty-nine percent of the failures occurred in the first two years of business. During the next three years, 28 percent of the remaining businesses failed. Only 20 percent of the failures occurred after the 10th year in business. The shopping center manager can help retailers maximize their sales by sponsoring retailing seminars designed to improve business and merchandising skills and to improve sales volume. Such programs are of particular importance in distressed shopping centers and in areas with weak economies.

Developing a Seminar Program

The seminar program, usually for larger shopping centers and malls, should be designed around the needs of the shopping center's retailers. Those who need the most assistance are the local merchants who, unlike managers of regional and national chain stores, do not have the same opportunity to attend professional retailing seminars. They also do not have the benefits of the retailing expertise of a large, sophisticated chain.

It's a good practice to offer seminars to retailers free of charge. For example, the local police department can present information on shoplifting. The Small Business Administration (SBA) can provide speakers on specific topics ranging from budgeting to market research. Lenders are generally willing to present seminars on cash management and financing. The display manager of a department store may be willing to teach a seminar on window displays. A professor from the local university might speak on motivational-sales training. The cost of these one- to two-hour seminars is nominal and paid by the owner of the shopping center. This is an investment in the shopping center's most valuable asset—its tenants.

Retail consultants can present classes on specific retailing subjects and meet with the retailers on an individual basis. The shopping center owner usually pays any consultant fees. Occasionally the merchants' association or marketing fund shares the expense, but their budgets usually cannot afford the cost. The retailers are never charged for the general seminar or the individual sessions with the consultant. If the retailer requests additional individual consulting, that is at the retailer's expense.

Topics for group sessions might include: in-store promotions, visual merchandising, personnel management, retail salesmanship, customer policies, return policies, sales forecasting, inventory planning, and stock pricing.

Promoting the Program

Even though the retail program is free to the tenant, many retailers must be convinced to attend. Small retailers often have limited time available, believe the program will not be worthwhile, or believe they know all there is to know about their business. The seminar should be publicized to all retailers; a bulletin and/or an e-mail with pertinent information is a first step toward gaining their interest. The real estate manager should meet with each merchant to discuss the program and the benefits of participating. If the real estate manager is assisting a retailer with a rent deferment program, financial assistance should be contingent upon the retailer's participation in the program.

It's important to attend the seminars and the individual consulting sessions to gain a better understanding of retailing and its challenges, learn to distinguish a poor retailer from a good one, and gain insight into an individual retailer's strengths and weaknesses.

EXPANDING A STORE SIZE

When retailers experience success, they find that their existing spaces are not large enough, and they want to expand their stores. If a retailer's sales have not yet reached the breakpoint that produces percentage rent for the shopping center owners, the negotiation and outcome almost always result in net benefits to the shopping center. Generally, the considerations are how much the expansion will cost and what the base rent and terms will be on the space being added. On the other hand, when an existing retailer is currently paying percentage rent and wants to expand, the property ownership can end up with large expansion costs and lose the existing percentage rent because the retailer will have a higher breakpoint.

For example, consider the case of a specialty supermarket that currently has 25,000 square feet. The basic rental is $4.50 per square foot per year because the lease was entered into several years ago; the percentage rental rate is 1.5 percent above the natural breakpoint; the current annual sales are $9,270,000 per year, producing percentage rents of $26,550. A vacant shop next to the supermarket has 5,000 square feet that is currently on the market for $12 per square foot. The supermarket agrees to take it over at that rate and wants the property owner to pay a third of the remodeling costs to combine the two stores—estimated at $50,000. The supermarket is willing to pay an additional rental of 12 percent on the up-front costs. With the current lease, the economics of the rents are as follows:

Current base rental	$112,500
Percentage rental	+ 26,500
Total rental	**$139,000**

Proposed lease economics:	
Base rental existing unit	$112,500
Base rental expanded space	60,000
Turn-on improvement moneys	+ 6,000
Total rental	**$178,500**

With the original lease terms, the natural breakpoint for percentage rent was $7,500,000, and the current sales level produced percentage rents of $26,500. With the new lease terms, the natural breakpoint will be $11,900,000. The net effect of this expansion is the loss of $26,500 of rental income, plus any percentage rents that would have been paid as the retailer's sales increased. Unless the sales increase to a point of approximately $13,500,000, the property owner will, in effect, pay for part of the retailer's expansion with no offsetting income.

There are two basic approaches in negotiating this situation so the property owner comes out whole: (1) retain the existing breakpoint or (2) increase the breakpoint but keep the existing percentage. In either case, you can expect the retailer to resist, but that is normal in negotiations. The tenant might argue that the property owner should share some of the expense because they now have the potential for more sales, more traffic to support the other retailers, and ultimately, more percentage rent if the plan is successful.

Retain Existing Breakpoint

It makes the most sense to retain the existing breakpoint of $7,500,000, which then becomes an artificial breakpoint—one that is negotiated. With this approach, the property owner's position has not lessened with the expansion. The property owner will get full return on the expanded space and expenses involved. The retailer is likely to feel penalized because it will be paying rent and return on the new space. Moreover, as sales increase, the tenant will also be paying percentage rent on the increased sales, which the new base rentals should cover. If the existing breakpoint were retained the under the expanded operation, the income would be as follows:

Base rental old store	$112,500
Base rental expansion	60,000
Return on construction	6,000
Percentage on existing sales	+ 26,500
Total rental	**$205,000**

Additionally, the property owner has the potential for more percentage rent on sales between $9,266,667 and the new natural breakpoint of $11,900,000, or sales of $2,633,333, which would produce an additional $39,500 at 1.5 percent of sales. The reason the retailer may not want to agree to this approach is obvious.

Increase Breakpoint: Keep Existing Percentage

The second approach—which would be less desirable from the real estate manager's point of view, but more acceptable to the retailer—would be to increase the breakpoint but retain the current level of percentage rent and add it to the rental factor. The total rental to the property owner before considering sales would be the same at $205,000, with the advantage that the $26,500 of percentage rent would be converted to minimum rent, which helps with financing and establishing the value of the shopping center.

If sales went up substantially to more than the $11,866,667 figure, the property owner would see some additional percentage rent. However, if sales stayed below the new breakpoint, there would be no additional percentage rent, but the property owner would have an expanded and, presumably, stronger anchor draw to the shopping center.

The tenant would almost invariably take the position that this expansion would increase sales, and therefore the property owner would undoubtedly realize a return on the moneys invested. However, the possibility exists that the tenant is already at its optimum size and any increase may not produce an increase in sales. The retailer will most likely argue strongly for increasing the breakpoint rather than retaining the existing percentage rent breakpoint. The result would depend on the strength of each of the parties to the negotiation.

Negotiating Other Changes

In addition to the basic rent issues involved during a negotiation such as this is a good time to completely review the lease and terms to determine whether other changes should be made. Older supermarket and drugstore leases often require the property owner to pay for roof maintenance and the insurance on the building, as well as to agree to limits on CAM charges. This is often a good time to try to get the lease on a fully net basis—especially if the lease term is to be extended at the time the expansion takes place.

Some trade-offs may be necessary in this process. In a case in which the property owner expanded and extended the lease for a supermarket, the owner was able to make the lease fully net when it was not before. However, she had to put a new roof on the retailer's space. The retailer argued, and rightly so, that the existing roof was 18 years old and had a recent history of leaks. If the retailer was to assume full responsibility for the roof, it wanted to be sure the roof was in good shape when the retailer took it over. The real estate manager had successfully negotiated expansions that showed an excellent return just by netting out the taxes, insurance, and maintenance provisions.

The main point is for the negotiator to fully understand the ramifications of the economics of the expansion and to calculate the actual and likely outcomes of the deal. The negotiator must not place too much reliance on getting a return on investment from a large increase in the retailer's sales that may or may not materialize.

FINANCIALLY TROUBLED RETAILERS

When retailers experience problems, the shopping center experiences troubles as well. Merchant failures can give a shopping center a negative image among existing and potential retailers as well as customers. When retailer failures occur in conjunction with a soft-leasing market, shopping centers are in serious trouble. Faced with the potential deterioration of a shopping center, it's important to search for practical, short-term solutions that will enable the shopping center to endure the difficult economic period. Solutions to this problem can include monetary and nonmonetary assistance to the financially troubled retailer.

Symptoms of Potential Failure

The most obvious symptom of potential failure is late rent payment, but it's possible to obtain early indications of this by monitoring a retailer's sales. If the retailer's sales are appreciably below national averages, the retailer is probably operating the business at a loss. The retailer's sales should also be compared with prior periods to determine sales trends. If the sales are consistently declining, the retailer is likely to experience financial difficulties immediately or in the near future.

Other symptoms of potential retailer failure are reductions in inventory, failure to maintain the shopping center's hours, reductions in the staffing level, cutbacks in advertising, and lower merchandise levels and turnover. When retailers have financial problems, they may be unable to purchase new inventory, which will continue to decrease sales. Retailers may respond to financial difficulties by attempting to reduce operating expenses. Reductions in store hours, staffing, and advertising generate immediate cost savings but often result in a continuing sales decline.

A more effective means of monitoring retailers' operations is to develop a good rapport with them so they will inform the manager of potential problems.

Analyzing Other Variables

The shopping center manager must analyze the impact of various factors on the shopping center before deciding whether to offer a retailer monetary relief. The most important consideration is the condition of the leasing market. Does the shopping center have existing vacancies and, if so, how long will it take to lease them? If any retailers fail, how long will it take to re-lease their spaces? In estimating the time it will take to re-lease a space, analyze the space in terms of its desirability, adjacent retailers, and visibility from common areas and fronting streets. It's important to have a strong understanding of the leasing market as well as the strength and weakness of the other retailers in the shopping center.

Once the vacancy period for the space is estimated, consider the effect a vacancy might have on the shopping center's tenant mix. If a retailer moves out, will the shopping center's ability to draw customers be significantly weakened? What effect would one retailer failure, or several retailer failures, have on the leasing program? In a soft leasing market, finding replacement retailers is difficult, and the difficulty is compounded when potential retailers notice vacancies and retailer failures in the shopping center. A further consideration is if the shopping center is developing a poor reputation among the retailers in the community.

The retailer may no longer be an asset to the shopping center. Another issue is the cost of replacing a retailer, which includes: loss of rent, rental concessions in the form of free rent or tenant allowances, remodeling costs, leasing commissions, possible legal fees, and lower percentage rents from other retailers resulting from reduced sales of retailers affected by the vacancy. Still, another consideration is the financial position of the shopping center—at least partial rent payment may be essential for the normal operation.

If the cost to replace the troubled retailer is too high, or if the retailer is having difficulties but deserves assistance because of prior contributions to the shopping center, a temporary rent relief program should be considered.

Rent Relief

Rent relief is designed to help a retailer overcome financial difficulty. Commonly used rent relief programs include deferred rent, percentage rent only, waived rent, and use of the security deposit.

- **Deferred rent:** The tenant's current rent and an agreed amount of future rent are reduced, and repayment is deferred to a later date. For example, a retailer's rent might be reduced from $2,000 per month to $1,500 per month for six months and then increased by $500 per month after six months. Delinquent rent can also be deferred to a later date. Charging interest on the deferred rent is not preferable because it hinders the retailer's recovery.
- **Percentage rent only:** The retailer's minimum base rent is eliminated for a specific period, and monthly rental payments are based on a percentage of the retailer's sales. The percentage used can be a rate already established in the lease or a renegotiated rate, which generally is higher.
- **Waived rent:** Past, present, or future rent is waived entirely. All or a portion of each month's rent may be waived for a time.
- **Use of security deposit:** All or a portion of the security deposit may be applied to rent owed or to future rent. Little is sacrificed with this method because the security deposit would be applied to delinquent rent or future rents if the retailer vacated before the lease expired.

A condition of a rent relief program may be that the retailer spend a percentage of the waived or deferred rent on additional advertising or inventory.

In some cases, tenants might tell other retailers in the shopping center about the rent relief they are receiving. If this happens, it's likely that other requests for rent assistance will come from other tenants. In there situations, tenants should be informed that each situation is analyzed individually. Since the property owner is the sole arbiter in granting a retailer's request, it's a good idea to run a credit and asset check on the retailer's accounts to determine the nature of the financial health before having a discussion with a retailer and owner regarding possible rent relief.

Lease Provisions in Rental Concessions

When offering a rental concession to an existing retailer, it's possible to reopen lease negotiations. The lease may have one or more provisions detrimental to the shopping center, and the offer of rent relief can be contingent upon the retailer's agreeing to modify or eliminate such provisions. Often, this approach will be sufficient to discourage a merchant from pursuing rent relief. The lease provisions that might be revised or eliminated include:

- **Options:** Eliminate the option or tie the rental rate in the option period to the adjustment in the CPI, prevailing rents in the market place, or other predetermined increase.
- **Restrictions:** Eliminate the provision allowing retailers to approve the shopping center's remodeling or expansion plans or to prohibit specific uses.
- **Exclusive:** The retailer's lease may prohibit similar uses within the shopping center. Such restrictions should be eliminated.
- **Use:** Placing more restrictions on the retailer's use may be desirable.
- **Assignment/subletting:** Assignment or subletting should be subject to the shopping center owner's prior written approval.
- **Marketing fund or merchants' association:** Membership in the merchants' association or marketing fund contribution should be mandatory.
- **Signage:** Conforming to the shopping center's sign criteria should be required.
- **Store hours:** The retailer should be required to maintain the same business hours as the rest of the shopping center.
- **Cancellation clause:** The owner may obtain the right to cancel the lease if the retailer's sales do not meet or exceed an agreed minimum amount over a specific period of time.
- **Termination of rent relief:** If a retailer tells others about the rent relief or is delinquent in the lowered rental, the relief program is terminated and all moneys are due under the original terms of the lease.

An amendment to the lease is required to formalize any modifications. If a portion of the deferred rental payment is due after the lease expires, the retailer should sign a *promissory note* for that amount.

Offering a retailer rent relief may be a distasteful solution to some owners, but sometimes it may be the only way to save a shopping center's most valuable asset—its tenants. If a shopping center is distressed or has a high vacancy, collecting partial rent is better than collecting no rent at all.

Nonmonetary Assistance

Nonmonetary programs can be alternatives to monetary relief, or they can be used in conjunction with a rent-relief program. First, consider how to help the retailer reduce operating expenses without affecting sales. Reducing the retailer's square footage will reduce base rent, pro rata tenant charges, utility costs, and possibly the size of the retailer's staff. If the retailer's sales do not depend on walk-by traffic, the retailer could be relocated to a less desirable area of the shopping center where the rent is lower. This solution is practical only if the retailer's fixturization costs are nominal. A hair salon could not afford to relocate because of the expense of the plumbing for its fixtures, but a gift shop could easily relocate.

Expanding the retailer's use provision may be beneficial. If the retailer is the only restaurant in the shopping center, the retailer's use provision could be broadened to include other food-related items. The real estate manager must be certain, however, that this will not have a negative effect on the present or future tenant mix of the shopping center or on the sales of other retailers. If the retailer's problem stems primarily from mismanagement, a new operator may be able to turn the business around. Thus, permitting a lease assignment may be a simple solution.

Many small retailers do not have strong backgrounds in retailing and do not have the opportunity to seek professional retailing instruction. Consequently, the merchant's employees do not usually receive the necessary sales training. The real estate manager should consider asking the shopping center owner to hire a retail consultant to provide seminars and individual consultations for retailers and their employees. These programs should not only be motivational training sessions, but they should also provide insight into the development of a merchandising plan, markdown policies, in-store signage, displays, budgeting, selling techniques, and other important retailing concepts and principles. The retailers benefit by acquiring valuable retailing techniques, and their employees receive professional sales training.

Most owners who have provided this service to their retailers consider the expense an investment in the financial strength of the shopping center. Through strong sales, they can expect higher base and percentage rent and fewer, if any, tenant failures.

Lease Termination

When the probability of a retailer's recovering from financial problems is slim, even though the owner has assisted with rent relief, nonmonetary assistance, or a combination of the two, seeking a termination of the lease may be best. Terminating the lease enables the owner to regain possession of the premises and place the space back on the market. The lease can be terminated by mutual consent or by eviction if the retailer is in default of its lease.

A mutual lease termination may be offered to the retailer for financial consideration. The real estate manager should request a current financial statement from the retailer before agreeing to the lease cancellation. If the retailer is a corporation and the lease has personal guarantees, a financial statement should be requested of the corporation and the guarantors. If both parties' financial statements are weak, a mutual cancellation with no cancellation payment or with a nominal payment to the property owner may be most practical. This enables the owner to seek a tenant that will be an asset to the shopping center.

While some believe that it is useless to incur the cost of taking a retailer to court for back or future rent if the retailer has no assets, others file a judgment and wait for the day when the retailer gains financial stability. If the retailer's financial statement is healthy, negotiate a lease buyout on the part of the retailer or enforce the lease, including the payment of rent and other tenant charges, until the space is re-leased. Establishing a standard operating procedure is impossible in this area. Analyze each case individually and with flexibility.

Always request a financial statement for the business and the owner of the business. If the tenant has other businesses, those financial statements should also be requested—those businesses may be profitable and pay the rent for the store in the subject property. It's possible that the owner may want concessions from the tenant for providing rent relief, such as modifying or eliminated onerous lease provisions—they should be addressed in the amendment.

TRADE ASSOCIATIONS AND INDUSTRY RECOGNITION

It's only through experience, training, and education that real estate managers can we build a base of information and experiences to help decide how to handle any given situation. When it comes to shopping centers, there are many different elements that make it a complex task to manage. Of course, experience is one of the best tools in our day-to-day problem solving; however, in addition to this, there are two trade associations that support the shopping center management field: (1) the Institute of

Real Estate Management (IREM) and (2) the International Council of Shopping Centers (ICSC).

Institute of Real Estate Management (IREM)

IREM is the oldest trade association involved in the management of shopping centers, in addition to office buildings, industrial buildings, residential housing and condominiums. IREM offers specific courses in shopping center management and leasing and offers the professional designation of Certified Property Manager® (CPM®). That certification, while not property specific, can be in the field of shopping centers or any of the other properties covered by the Institute. By attaining the CPM designation, you tell employers, property owners, and fellow managers that you have taken the time and effort to establish yourself through education and experience as a professional in the field.

IREM also publishes many books, reports, statistical data, and updates for the entire industry which is available to both members of the organization and non-members. IREM has chapters in most major cities where candidates and CPM Members get together to share information and educate themselves in the latest in their chosen fields.

International Council of Shopping Centers (ICSC)

ICSC is the largest trade association devoted to shopping center development, leasing, management, marketing, construction, financing and redevelopment. The ICSC offers a broad range of classes in all aspects of shopping center operations and offers five professional designations:

- CRX: Executive Leadership designation
- CSM: Certified Shopping Center Manager designation
- CMD: Certified Marketing Director designation
- CLS: Certified Leasing Specialist designation
- CDP: Certified Development, Design, and Construction Professional designation

Each of these designations requires a minimum level of experience in the field and the passing of a specific exam for that designation. In addition, ICSC also publishes many books, newsletters, reports, and industry updates for their members.

Developing a Resource Library

A resource library on retailing can be developed at the real estate management office or at the on-site management office. The SBA and many leading banks have publications, pamphlets, and books for the small business. Many books and reports on the subject of retailing that can be very helpful.

Subscribing to the leading retail trade journals is an excellent way to collect information for the library as a way to stay up to date on current trends in retailing. Included among these publications are *Retailing Today,* and *Chain Store Age Executive,* published by Lebhar-Friedman, Inc. The *Journal of Property Management (JPM®),* published by IREM is also a good publication that often features topics on retail.

CHAPTER 4

Office Building Management

Whether the office building market is stable or volatile, there are always changes that impact the management and leasing of office buildings. With so many new innovations in technology and an increased awareness of environmental concerns, the *smart building* (or green building) has become a goal that many new office buildings strive to attain.

New concepts such as *hoteling* or the increasing number of employees telecommuting have assisted in shrinking the average number of square feet needed per employee. There is a continuing trend for unassigned work stations. Some of the companies are doing away with space wasting conference rooms and letting the break rooms serve as conference rooms.

Milllennials and Gen Z are impacting the office markets and will continue to do so as they become a larger portion of the work force. They want functional, fun, and trendy work spaces. New office buildings and the remodeling of older buildings see a trend toward open spaces to foster collaborative work where the employees can easily interact. These generations are interested in amenities such as workout rooms and recreational areas.

The office market is one of the most cyclical markets in commercial real estate. When the economy is strong, companies expand and employment increases. In recent years, the office market has become sophisticated and competitive, requiring a more experienced and responsive management approach. A high-rise office building is a complex entity with many interrelated systems, as well as many occupants and visitors with varying needs that the skillful real estate manager must integrate. It is quite possible for a mid- or high-rise office building to have a ground floor of retail space, a basement night club, or entertainment center and a roof top restaurant all of which complicate the operations of the building. In some ways, an office building owner has more maintenance responsibilities than the shopping center and multi-tenant industrial property owner.

Security and safety have moved more to the forefront of the building operations. Emergency procedures are more involved because of the many people concentrated in a vertical tower. Most high-rise office buildings have comprehensive emergency procedures plans and in many cities, must do a fire or emergency drill with full evacuation one or more times per year.

Parking is of great concern for office building tenants and the cost of building parking garages is especially expensive—especially in urban areas making paid parking a must. Yet, many cities are encouraging developers to build buildings with limited parking while employers are encouraging their employees to take public transportation. Very few suburban office buildings have the need for paid parking, and most need large parking areas because of limited to no public transportation in the area.

The general movement and foot traffic of people in and out of office buildings are major real estate management concerns, especially with some office and medical office buildings requiring a controlled security entrance. Mechanical, safety, and energy conservation systems are highly technical and require highly trained employees or outside contractors. These systems are quite often expensive, but over time most of these programs will result in lower operating expenses and enhance the market ability of the building.

Although management practices and problem solving are similar for all types of office buildings, the categories used as industry standards can be helpful:

- Garden buildings (one to two stories)
- Low-rise office buildings (three to four stories)
- Mid-rise office buildings (five to 10 stories)
- High-rise office buildings (11 or more stories)

The description of these types of buildings varies from area to area. These categories are used in this chapter when discussing management differences in each type of building.

MANAGEMENT STAFFING

A major consideration in determining management staffing is deciding whether or not to employ an on-site manager. The primary criteria in determining this are the building's size and the number of tenants.

Deciding Not to Have an On-Site Real Estate Manager

Garden and low-rise office buildings are usually managed from a central office away from the project. Two issues must be addressed when managing office buildings without an on-site real estate manager: (1) the number of buildings one person can manage and (2) the provision for immediate response.

The first issue is the number of office buildings one person can manage. Several variables must be considered before answering this question. One major variable is the level of service the real estate manager and the real estate management company offer. One person can manage more properties if management provides only the minimal services of rent collection and responding to maintenance calls, rather than a comprehensive real estate management program designed to enhance value. The following lists some other variables to consider:

- Location of each property
- Condition of the property
- Age of the building
- Size of each building
- Number of tenants in each building
- Level of administrative support available to the real estate manager

For low-rise office buildings ranging from 40,000 to 80,000 square feet and within driving distance from the central real estate management office, one real estate manager can usually manage five to eight buildings at a high level of service, and eight to 12 buildings at a medium level of service.

The second issue is how management can provide the required response if the real estate manager is not available, or if the property is more than 30 minutes from the office. It may be practical to have an arrangement with a tenant in the building who can provide keys to utility rooms and respond to maintenance emergencies. Occasionally, this tenant may open a vacant space for a prospective tenant or respond immediately to any maintenance problem. Exercise caution, however, that the duties assigned to this person do not require a real estate license. As an exception to this rule. The owner of a 45,000-square-foot, one-story garden office building with small offices, and a fairly high turnover and occupancy rate, wanted more service for the building and felt an on-site presence would improve the lease. The third-party real estate manager hired a smaller real estate management company to have their office in the building and to handle the day-to-day operations. While this resulted in a little higher management cost to the building, it also contributed to higher occupancy, happier tenants, and a better bottom line for the building owners. This also resolved the issue of the on-site person being able to lease space by having a real estate license.

Deciding to Have an On-Site Real Estate Manager

Mid- and high-rise office buildings are usually staffed with on-site managers and administrative personnel, and depending on the size of the building, on-site maintenance staff. On-site real estate managers, or general managers, should be considered for office buildings exceeding 100,000 square feet. The square footage guidelines are one of several factors used to determine if a building needs and can support an on-site manager. One approach may be to employ an on-site manager of a small building to manage other office buildings.

High-rise office buildings are usually staffed with an on-site manager, an assistant manager, and an administrative assistant. A tenant relations coordinator, tenant improvement construction supervisor, and chief engineer may be added to the staff.

Deciding Not to Have On-Site Staff

Another, but less common, approach to office building management is the centralized approach, which has no on-site staff—except a building engineer or engineers and day porters. All systems are automated, and any problems are reported to a central office that responds by electronic means to the building engineer or the appropriate subcontractor with a requirement to respond within a given amount of time. The engineer or the subcontractor notifies the central office electronically when the problem is solved. So far, this approach has not been adopted by a large segment of the high-rise office building management industry, but has obvious attractions in the form of cost savings. This approach could be much more effective for a company that may have four or five high-rise buildings within a very short distance of each other.

SPACE MEASUREMENT

Measuring space in office buildings is a critical step in the overall management, operations, and leasing process. The more the same standards are used, the easier it is to make valid comparisons between buildings and to reduce possible future disputes between property owners and tenants.

The Building Owners and Managers Association (BOMA) has established the industry standards for measuring space in office buildings. These standards are periodically revised.

The American National Standards Institute (ANSI) has approved BOMA's standard method for measuring floor area in an office building as the industry standard. BOMA's publication, *Standard Method for Measuring Floor Areas in Office Buildings* describes the standards with illustrations. Leases often refer to the "BOMA Standard" for measuring the lease premises.

A major change in the last two revisions is that the rentable/usable ratio (R/U factor) for a building is calculated on the entire building and not on a floor-by-floor basis. This allows space that benefits all the building occupants, such as conference rooms, lunchrooms, and entrance lobbies, to be allocated to the entire building when calculating the rentable/usable ratio for every tenant. The new concepts defined by BOMA in *Standard Method for Measuring Floor Areas in Office Buildings* are as follows:

- ***Floor rentable area*** is determined by subtracting the area of the major vertical penetrations on a floor from the gross measured area of that floor. No deduction is made for columns and projections necessary to the building. Spaces outside the exterior walls, such as balconies, terraces, or corridors are excluded. Building rentable area equals the sum of all floor rentable areas.
- ***Floor usable area*** is computed by measuring the area enclosed between the finished surface of the office area side of corridors and the dominate portion and/or major vertical penetrations.
- ***Building common areas*** provide services to building tenants but are not included in the office area or store area of any specific tenant. They are considered part of floor usable area. No deduction is made for columns and projections necessary to the building. Where alcoves, recessed entrances, or similar deviations from the corridor line are present, floor usable area is computed as if the deviations were not present.

This revised standard constitutes a clarification of the prior method. Other methods to measure office space are used, but they are limited to a few specific regions. Spaces are most commonly measured by a *computer-aided design (CAD)* program because the level of accuracy ensures agreement between owner and tenant and avoids problems that occurred in the past.

Knowing the rentable and usable square feet of competing buildings enables a manager of an office or medical office building to identify the market rental rates for his or her building, and be aware on the building's position in the market.

SPACE PLANNING

It's important to note that the amount of square feet per employee has declined considerably since the 1990s, and it continues to decline. Some tenants have offset the reduction of space per employee by adding more employee amenities to their space plan. For years, space planning was just for efficient operations, but now it is also used to recruit and retain employees. Space planning continues to evolve as business' operations evolve, and with new technology and new generations entering the workforce, needs and preferences will continue to change.

Space planning is an important part of the construction process especially for tenants who not sure of how much space they need to operate their business, or how to plan their space layout for efficient use. CAD programs make space planning much easier and less expensive. The final space plan allows for an easy transition to working drawings for the actual construction. The building manager will select a space planner and offer space-planning services to prospective tenants who express a serious interest in the building. This service is often a component of the marketing of an office building.

Selecting a Space Planner

When interviewing and selecting a space planner, consider the following factors:

- How many millions of square feet has the space planner designed?
- Does the space planner understand marketing?
- What types of spaces has the designer planned? (e.g., general offices, law offices, or medical and dental spaces.)
- Is the space planner aware of the trends in the space-planning industry?

An efficient space planner should be aware of the property owner's tenant improvement budget. The discussion with the potential lessee should include telling them what they are likely to get for the allowance and what the tenant allowance will provide. For example, if the tenant asks for a relight (a glass wall used to allow light to enter an area), an experienced space planner would explain that a relight may cost a tenant up to five times the cost of studs, drywall, and paint. Once a lease is signed, at the tenant's expense, the space planner can offer design services and any extras beyond what the property owner agreed to provide.

Establishing Building Standards

Before any tenants move into a new office build, or the building is under construction, the property owner and real estate manager develop *building standards* that specify the quantity and quality of materials to be used in finishing the interiors of the tenants' leased premises. Ownership and management must establish building standards for the finishing of the tenants' premises before a space plan can be prepared for an individual prospective tenant.

Building standards form the basis for the specifics of the *tenant improvement allowance*. Tenant improvements are such important aspects of a lease that they are negotiated in detail, and the agreement regarding them is documented separately in a work letter. The *work letter* also relies on development of a preliminary space plan that is satisfactory to both the building owner and tenant. The standards must be reasonable and should allow a tenant to have a reasonably attractive, efficient, and complete space within the limits of the standards. If every prospect finds they have to spend substantial additional dollars just to have a workable space, they are likely to look elsewhere. The following information, provides guidelines and standards to consider in developing a well-executed space plan:

- **Walls and partitions.** Building standards are needed for both demising walls that define the tenant's suite and interior partitions that delineate individual spaces within the suite.

- **Doors, frames, and hardware.** The building standard should specify the type, quality, and finishes of corridor and interior doors (including door dimensions and thickness), lock sets, latch sets, door knobs, hinges, and framing. Identification of acceptable access control devices and the manner in which they will be installed is also appropriate. These devices may be a tenant-preferred option.
- **Ceilings.** Most ceilings in office suites are suspended from the building structure. Two basic types of suspended ceilings exist—one uses a T-bar to support acoustical tiles and the other uses a concealed spline to support mineral tiles.
- **Lighting.** The type of fixture as well as the orientation may also be specified.
- **Heating, ventilation, and air-conditioning (HVAC).** The HVAC system designed for an office suite is often set up in separately controlled zones. Building standards should state how HVAC will be provided to the tenant's space (e.g., overhead ductwork and vents, wall-mounted units in private exterior offices, or both). The standards include the number and type of vents and other components and the number and placement of thermostatic controls. Building standards must also state how air-conditioning zones will be allocated on building floors and whether the base pattern will be modified to accommodate individual tenants. Very small tenant spaces tend to complicate the assignment of zones within an office building. On the other hand, very small spaces can often be easily leased and for more per square foot than the average of the building. Though not ideal, some of these spaces may share a zone.
- **Electrical and telecommunications.** With increasing use of technology, the numbers of electrical and telephone outlets needed in office suites have also increased. Types of special cabling, including fiber optics, should be addressed along with appropriate housings (e.g., conduit). The electrical standards should state the amount of power provided to each floor. In addition, the standards should describe how individual tenants' special power needs will be accommodated.
- **Wall coverings.** Office walls may be finished in a variety of ways. Paint is a very common building standard finish because it is inexpensive, easy to apply, and easy to change. A standard is often established offering a range of perhaps a dozen colors in light to medium tones that yield a flat (no glare) surface finish. Other interior finishes may be offered on a shared-cost basis or at the tenant's expense. Wallpaper, vinyl wall covering, or wood paneling may be used instead of paint but it is more expensive.
- **Floor covering.** Floor coverings need to be durable and easily maintained because they endure more wear and tear than any other component of an office building. Two standard floor coverings used in offices are carpeting and resilient flooring known as vinyl composition tile (VCT). Building standards should be developed for both types of flooring. Although carpeting may be desirable for most areas, resilient flooring is most appropriate for kitchens or storage areas.
- **Window coverings.** Window coverings are more than just a building standards item; it is usually specified to achieve a uniform appearance when viewed from the exterior of the building and/or across interior office areas. Window coverings may be a component of the buildings energy efficiency. Several alternatives are available, including draperies and various horizontal and vertical window blinds. If the tenant wants window coverings that may be different from the building standard, they are often installed inside the standard window coverings for the building, so the outside of the building has a uniform look.
- **Fire preparedness.** Fire sprinklers are installed in a fixed pattern and mounted in the finished ceiling. They are usually installed before tenant space is finished for occupancy for the first time. The cost of moving sprinklers is substantial and should be considered in developing building standards. Fire exit signs need a secure storage area for media used for daily backup of a network or computer. Building standards should at least anticipate such requirements and be prepared to handle them appropriately.
- **Signage.** An even larger issue for ground floor retail tenants is signage. Local ordinances may specify size limitations for signs and address their installation on the exterior of a building. Some jurisdictions prohibit signs that are perpendicular

to the building wall. Building standards may set specifications for applications of signage to plate-glass windows, attachments to the exterior of the building, sign dimensions (maximum width and height), and use of neon signs. These standards are important to maintaining the appearance of the building. For instance, a Class A office building with numerous small retailers will be diminished in value if retailers' signage gives the building a tacky appearance. Obviously, the retail component of any office building will have a different sign criteria than that of the office tenants. For larger buildings, consider the possibility that a substantial national or even local tenant will want to lease a substantial portion of the building—they will then want their name on the outside of the building. Generally, the owner will get paid extra for these rights and will control the size, location, and make up of the exterior sign. Sometimes a tenant leasing a substantial portion of the building will negotiate for signage rights without a fee.

Many years ago, tenants were offered a tenant allowance based on the number of outlets, doors, lineal feet of partition walls, etc, per thousands of square feet leased. Today, the common method is to offer an allowance based on a dollar per square foot leased. For instance, the tenant allowance is $50 per square feet leased. This is a much simpler method for real estate managers to explain, and an easier method for tenants to understand. Tenants may upgrade any of the owner's building standards that do not impact the appearance of the building, and the operations of the building at the tenant's cost or the tenant may negotiate owner-paid upgrades.

BILLING BACK OPERATING EXPENSES

The process of billing back operating expenses to tenants is difficult, and owners are always trying to improve the process by enhancing their ability to recover from the tenants all the expenses allowable in the lease. No matter which method they use in accounting for and billing building escalation expenses, the property owner and/or manager of the building must carefully adhere to the lease provisions. Typically, the costs to operate the building, including maintenance, repairs, and some capital improvements such as replacing floor and wall covering in common areas, covering and management fees, utilities, real estate taxes, and insurance, are billed to the tenants.

Briefly tracing the history of office building leases helps set the stage for how things are done today. Originally, office space leases were *gross leases.* The tenant paid one amount each month for the rent, and the building owner bore all the building's operating costs. Throughout the years, some expenses escalated substantially, and owners sought protection from them. As an example, consider a medical office building facility in the late 1960s that was on a gross lease to a group of doctors. Within four years of the signing of the 15-year fixed-rent lease, the taxes increased to the point of exceeding rent, making the building worthless during the term of that lease. This situation prompted owners on future leases to bill taxes back to tenants in addition to rents. The same situation occurred with insurance premiums and eventually with maintenance. As these expenses escalated, building owners looked for ways to bill tenants for the expenses, protect the value of the building, and place the burden of increasing costs on the actual users of the facility.

Today, property owners prefer to bill tenants their share of the building's operating expenses by utilizing the *triple-net lease.* Two other approaches are the *base-year approach* and the *expense-stop method.*

Triple-Net Lease Approach

The tenant pays rent and its full share of the taxes, insurance, and operating costs of the building. This method is growing in use.

In general, the marketplace dictates the method to be used. Tenants consider "total occupancy costs" and have little interest in the labels that owners place on the various components. If the market for comparable lease space is $40 per square foot per year, and triple-net charges are $15 per square foot per year, the property owner, leasing agent, and real estate manager states their rents are $40 per square foot. Although this is accurate, the tenant will also consider the occupancy costs which includes base rent and *pass-through charges*. The tenant's occupancy costs are $55 per square foot.

Base-Year Approach

Another, but less common, approach is the base-year method. The tenant pays its pro rata expenses above its base year. For instance, if the expenses for a tenant's base year is $15 per square foot, the tenant's prorated share of the operating expenses are more than $15 per square foot for each of the subsequent lease years. During the term of the lease, the property owner pays the expenses up to the amount established in the base year.

Some tenants attempt to establish the base year as being the year after they move in instead of the actual year they move in the building. This provision can have a twofold effect on the building's income: (1) It delays any opportunity for reimbursement for increased operating expenses for one year, and (2) it is likely to set the base year at a higher level due to inflation.

If expenses go above the base-year amount in future years, the tenant is expected to reimburse the property owner for its pro rata share of the increases. If future expenses are below the base year, there is no reduction in the rent unless the tenant made that a lease requirement.

The base-year approach works reasonably well for owners and tenants, but some problems may arise that bring this approach into question. The base year works when the building is full and operating at normal levels of occupancy (i.e., 95 to 100 percent). In such cases, the expenses are fairly stable and generally do not fluctuate much from year to year. However, during a lease-up, the base-year expenses for the initial tenants can be quite low. For example, janitorial expenses are based on actual occupancy; elevators often have "light-load" credits in early years; and buildings in their first year may have some warranties for the first year, which keeps repairs and maintenance low. If the occupancy is low, management fees as well as gas, electric, water, and sewer charges are generally lower. Taxes are often based on an incomplete building for the first year, and insurance premiums may also be lower in the first year and increase as the building fit-up is completed. This can subject the initial occupants to large increases in future years under the base-year method. The same scenario can occur in a building with low occupancy.

To avoid setting a very low base and setting the tenants up for high escalations in the future, the property owner may gross up the building's operating expenses to a 95 to 100 percent occupancy. *Grossing-up* is increasing all expenses to what they would be if the building were fully operating at a 95- to 100-percent occupancy.

Expense-Stop Approach

Another method which was established in the 1980s is the *expense-stop clause* to the methods of billing back operating costs. Under this theory, the costs for operating the building at 95 or 100 percent occupancy were calculated and broken down to a square footage basis. To illustrate, suppose that the amount came to $14.00 per square foot per year. That amount was then built into the rents: The property owner was responsible for the first $14.00 of expenses per square foot in each lease year (which should always be the calendar year), and the tenant would pay for any increases above that level for each year of the lease. The theory of this approach is that the owner would take special care to be sure that the expense-stop amount used was an accurate reflection of the expected cost to operate the building at full or near-full occupancy. Originally, the target for the stop clause was 95 percent occupancy, as was the target for the grossed-up expenses; however, the more commonly used figure is 100 percent.

The expense-stop approach is not without its problems. The total rent available to any owner in a given marketplace is based on the market itself. Only so much rent or occupancy cost can be attained in the market, and that amount has little to do with how much the building owner needs to cover expenses, the mortgage, and potentially a profit. However, the experienced tenant watches the stop clause very carefully to be sure it represents a reasonable level of expenses for the type of building. Obviously, the stop-clause number could be a real benefit for the property owner or for the tenant, depending on where it is set and what the actual costs are. This approach is no longer a common method of billing tenants a share of the building's operating expenses.

EXAMPLES OF LEASE PROVISIONS

The following are examples of lease provisions for a base-year lease (Exhibit 4.1), an expense-stop lease (Exhibit 4.2), and triple-net lease (Exhibit 4.3), along with an example of how operating expenses may be defined in a lease (Exhibit 4.4).

EXHIBIT 4.1

Sample Base-Year Lease Provision

BASIC COST ADJUSTMENT—During each calendar year, or portion thereof, following calendar year **[insert year here]** and falling within the Lease Term, Tenant shall pay to Landlord, as Additional Base Rent hereunder, the sum of Tenant's pro rata share of the amount, if any, by which Taxes (hereinafter defined) for the applicable calendar year exceed Taxes for the Base Year (hereinafter defined) plus Tenant's pro rata share of the amount, if any, by which Expenses (hereinafter defined) for the applicable calendar year exceed Expenses for the Base Year. For purposes hereof, the "Base Year" shall mean the calendar year **[insert year here]**. Tenant's pro rata share of increases in Taxes and Tenant's pro rata share of increases in Operating Expenses shall be computed separately and independently of each other prior to being added together to determine the Excess. In the event that Taxes and/or Expenses, as the case may be, in any calendar year decrease below the amount of Taxes or Expenses for the Base Year, Tenant's pro rata share of Taxes and/or Expenses, as the case may be, for such calendar year shall be deemed to be $0, it being understood that Tenant shall not be entitled to any credit or offset if Taxes and/or Expenses decrease below the corresponding amount for the Base Year. Prior to the Commencement date and prior to January 1 of each calendar year during the Lease Term following year **[insert year here]**, or as soon thereafter as practical, Landlord shall make a good faith effort to estimate the Excess for the applicable calendar year. On or before the first day of each month during such calendar year, Tenant shall pay Landlord, as Additional Base Rent, a monthly installment equal to one twelfth of Tenant's pro rata share of Landlord's estimate of the Excess. Landlord shall have the right from time to time during any such calendar year to revise the estimate of the excess for such year and to provide Tenant with a revised statement therefore, together with, if requested by Tenant, reasonable backup information upon which such revision is based, and thereafter the amount Tenant shall pay each month shall be based upon such revised estimate. If Landlord does not provide Tenant with an estimate of the Excess by January 1 of any calendar year, Tenant shall continue to pay a monthly installment based on the previous year's estimate until such time as Landlord provides Tenant with an estimate of the Excess for the current year. Upon receipt of such current year's estimate, an adjustment shall be made for any month during the current year with respect to which Tenant paid monthly installments of Additional Base Rent based on the previous year's estimate of the operating expenses. Tenant shall pay Landlord for any underpayment within thirty (30) days following demand therefore by Landlord. Any overpayment shall, at Tenant's option, be refunded to Tenant or credited against the installment of Base Rent and Additional Base Rent due for the month immediately following the furnishing of such estimate. Any amounts paid by Tenant based on any estimate shall be subject to adjustment pursuant to **Paragraph A** (Exhibit 4.4), when actual operating costs are determined for such calendar year.

EXHIBIT 4.2

Sample Expense-Stop Lease Provision

Tenant's Base Rent shall include a component of expense representing the Landlord's basic cost of operating the building above the amount of **[insert dollar amount here]** per square foot per year. During each calendar year, or portion thereof, commencing on the first day of the Lease Term and falling within the Lease Term, Tenant shall pay to Landlord as Additional Base Rental hereunder the sum of Tenant's pro rata share of the amount, if any, by which Taxes, Insurance, and Operating Expenses (hereinafter defined) for the applicable calendar year exceed **[insert dollar amount here]** per square foot per year. Tenant's pro rata share of increases in Taxes and Tenant's pro rata share of increases in Operating Expenses and Insurance premiums shall be computed together to determine the Excess. In the event that Taxes, Insurance, and/or Expenses, as the case may be, in any calendar year decrease below the **[insert dollar amount here]** level, it is understood that Tenant shall not be entitled to any credit or offset. Prior to the Commencement date and prior to January 1 of each calendar year during the Lease Term, or as soon thereafter as practical, Landlord shall make a good faith effort to estimate the Excess for the applicable calendar year. On or before the first day of each month during such calendar year, Tenant shall pay Landlord, as Additional Base Rent, a monthly installment equal to one twelfth of Tenant's pro rata share of Landlord's estimate of the Excess. Landlord shall have the right from time to time during any such calendar year to revise the estimate of the Excess for such year and provide Tenant with a revised statement therefore, together with, if requested by Tenant, reasonable backup information upon which such revision is based, and thereafter the amount Tenant shall pay each month shall be based upon such revised estimate. If Landlord does not provide Tenant with an estimate of the Excess by January 1 of any calendar year, Tenant shall continue to pay a monthly installment based on the previous year's estimate until such time as Landlord provides Tenant with an estimate of the Excess for the current year. Upon receipt of such current year's estimate, an adjustment shall be made for any month during the current year with respect to which Tenant paid monthly installments of Additional Base Rent based on the previous year's estimate of the operating expenses. Tenant shall pay Landlord for any underpayment within thirty (30) days following demand therefore by Landlord. Any overpayment shall, at Landlord's option, be refunded to Tenant or credited against the installment of Base Rent and Additional Base Rent due for the month immediately following the furnishing of such estimate. Any amounts paid by Tenant based on any estimate shall be subject to adjustment pursuant to the Lease Agreement when actual operating costs are determined for such calendar year.

EXHIBIT 4.3

Sample Triple-Net Lease Provision

BASIC COST REIMBURSEMENT—During each calendar year or portion thereof falling within the Lease Term, Tenant shall pay to Landlord, as Additional Base Rent hereunder, the sum of Tenant's pro rata share of all expenses, including real estate taxes and insurance premiums for the operation of said building (hereinafter defined) for the applicable calendar year. Tenant's pro rata share of taxes and operating expenses shall be computed separately and independently of each other prior to being added together to determine total expenses. Prior to the Commencement date and prior to January 1 of each calendar year during the Lease Term or as soon thereafter as practical, Landlord shall make a good faith effort to estimate the operating expenses for the coming calendar year. On or before the first day of each month during such calendar year, Tenant shall pay Landlord, as Additional Base Rent, a monthly installment equal to one-twelfth of Tenant's pro rata share of Landlord's estimate of the operating expenses. Landlord shall have the right from time to time during any

(Continuted on next page.)

EXHIBIT 4.3 *(CONTINUED)*

such calendar year to revise the estimate of the operating costs for such year and provide Tenant with a revised statement therefore, together with, if requested by Tenant, reasonable backup information upon which such revision is based, and thereafter the amount Tenant shall pay each month shall be based upon such revised estimate. If Landlord does not provide Tenant with an estimate of the operating expenses by January 1 of any calendar year, Tenant shall continue to pay a monthly installment based on the previous year's estimate until such time as Landlord provides Tenant with an estimate of the operating expenses for the current year. Upon receipt of such current year's estimate, an adjustment shall be made for any month during the current year with respect to which Tenant paid monthly installments of Additional Base Rent based on the previous year's estimate of the operating expenses. Tenant shall pay Landlord for any underpayment within thirty (30) days following demand therefore by Landlord. Any overpayment shall, at Tenant's option, be refunded to Tenant or credited against the installment of Base Rent and Additional Base Rent due for the month immediately following the furnishing of such estimate. Any amounts paid by Tenant based on any estimate shall be subject to adjustment pursuant to **Paragraph A** (Exhibit 4.4), when actual operating costs are determined for such calendar year.

EXHIBIT 4.4

Paragraphs A–E apply to the following three sample lease provisions: Base-year lease (Exhibit 4.1), Expense-stop lease (Exhibit 4.2), and Triple-net lease (Exhibit 4.3).

A. Operating Expense Reconciliation: As soon as is practical following the end of each calendar year during the Lease Term, Landlord shall furnish to Tenant a statement of Landlord's actual operating expenses and the actual amounts due for the previous calendar year. If for any calendar year the Additional Base Rent collected for the prior year, as a result of Landlord's estimate of Operating Expenses, is in excess of Tenant's actual pro rata share of the operating expenses for such prior year, then Landlord shall refund to Tenant any overpayment (or, at Landlord's option, apply such amount against Additional Base Rent due or to become due hereunder). Likewise, Tenant shall pay to Landlord, within thirty (30) days following demand therefore by Landlord, any underpayment with respect to the prior year, whether or not the Lease has terminated prior to receipt by Landlord of a statement for such underpayment, it being understood that this clause shall survive the expiration of the lease.

B. Operating expenses for the building shall include, but not be limited to: Payroll expenses for any and all services provided for the operation of the building, disability benefits, pensions, hospitalization, retirement plans, group insurance, or any other similar or like expenses incurred under the provisions of any collective bargaining agreement; provided, however, that if such persons are not employed full time in connection with the Building and the Property, such labor costs shall be prorated, and provided further that wages, salaries, and other compensation for employees above the position of the onsite Real Estate Manager and for any corporate employees of Landlord or Landlord's trustees or agent shall be excluded.

C. Operating expenses: All management fees (not to exceed the fees then being charged by landlords of comparable class buildings in the vicinity of the Building for comparable services), the cost of maintaining

(Continuted on next page.)

a management office at the Building, and all fees for legal and accounting services relating to the Building and Property. All rental and/or purchase costs of materials, supplies, hand tools, and equipment used in the operation, repair, replacement, and maintenance and the control of access to the Building and the Property. All amounts charged to Landlord by contractors and/or suppliers for services, materials, equipment, and supplies furnished in connection with the operation, security, repair, maintenance, replacement of, and control of access to any part of the Building, or the Property generally, including the heating, air-conditioning, ventilating, plumbing, electrical, elevator, and other systems.

All premiums and deductibles paid by Landlord for fire and extended coverage insurance, earthquake and extended coverage insurance, liability and extended coverage insurance, rental loss insurance, elevator insurance, boiler insurance, and other insurance customarily carried from time to time by landlords of comparable office buildings or required to be carried by Landlord's lender.

Charges for all utilities, including but not limited to water, electricity, gas, and sewer, but excluding those charges for which individual tenants are responsible. All landscape maintenance expenses and costs of repairing, resurfacing, or striping of the parking areas of the Property, if any. If any resurfacing of parking areas occurs and is of such a magnitude of expense as to constitute a capital expenditure under sound accounting principles, then the cost of such resurfacing shall be amortized into annual operating expenses over the useful life of such resurfacing.

Costs of all maintenance service agreements, including those for equipment, alarm service, window cleaning, drapery or vertical-blind cleaning, janitorial services, security services, pest control, uniform supply, landscaping, music, and any parking equipment. Costs of all other repairs, replacements, and general maintenance of the Property and Building neither specified above nor directly billed to tenants.

The amortized cost of capital improvements made to the Building or the Property that are primarily to reduce operating expense costs or otherwise to improve the operating efficiency of the Property or Building or that are required to comply with any laws, rules, or regulations of any governmental authority enacted after the Commencement date or any changes in the existing laws, rules, or regulations of any governmental authority enacted after the Commencement date, the cost of such items to be amortized over the useful life thereof. Such amortization shall be in accordance with generally accepted accounting principles (GAAP) and shall include interest at the actual rate incurred by Landlord. Notwithstanding the foregoing, the portion of the annual amortized costs to be included in operating expenses in any calendar year with respect to a capital improvement that is intended to reduce expenses or improve the operating efficiency of the Property or Building shall equal the lesser of (1) such annual amortized costs; and (2) the actual annual amortized reduction in expenses for that portion of the useful life of the capital improvement that falls within the lease term.

D. Taxes: Taxes shall mean all real estate taxes and assessments on the Property, the Building, or the Premises; taxes and assessments levied in substitution or supplementation, in whole or in part, of such taxes; all personal property taxes for the Building's personal property, including license expenses; all franchise fees; all taxes imposed on services of Landlord's agents and employees; and all sales, use, or other taxes, excluding state and/or federal income taxes.

E. Occupancy: Notwithstanding any language in the Lease seemingly to the contrary, if the Building is not fully occupied during any calendar year, or portion of a calendar year, of the Lease term, actual operating expenses for purposes of this Lease shall be determined as if the Building had been fully occupied during such year or portion of a year.

GROSSING UP OPERATING EXPENSES

The operating expenses charged to a tenant are based on the method for billing pass-through expenses that is agreed upon in the lease. The gross-up provision allows the landlord to gross up operating expenses that are affected by the building occupancy, which may include utilities, service contracts, janitorial costs, management fees, and property taxes.

It is common to gross up operating expenses in office and medical office buildings, but the concept is often misunderstood. Some tenants believe that the landlord is padding expenses when the building's pass-through charges are grossed up, although the purpose of grossing up the operating expenses is to have the tenants pay their fair pro rata share. The following list is an example of why gross up is a fair approach:

- The example office building is 100,000 square feet.
- A tenant occupies 10,000 square feet in that building.
- The tenant pays a 10 percent pro rata share of the operating expenses.
- Janitorial costs are $1 per square foot.
- The cost for janitorial services at 100% building occupancy would be $100,000.
- The cost for janitorial services for the 10,000-square-foot space would be $10,000 (10,000 square feet × $1 per square foot).
- The building is only 50 percent occupied.
- The cost for janitorial services for the half-occupied building is $50,000 (50,000 square feet × $1 per square foot).
- If the tenant is charged the pro rata share of 10%, the charge is only $5,000 ($50,000 × .10) for janitorial services, while the actual cost to clean the tenant's premises is $10,000.
- When operating expenses are grossed up to 100% occupancy, the cost for janitorial services is stated at $100,000 (100,000 square feet × $1 per square foot) and the tenant is billed $10,000 (10,000 square feet × $1), which is the actual janitorial cost for the tenant's space regardless of the building's occupancy level.

A gross up benefits tenants who have a base-year lease. Since these tenants pay their share of the increases after the base year, they benefit from higher operating expenses during that base year. Since they must pay their pro rata share of operating expenses above the base-year expenses, higher operating expenses during the base year mean less of an increase in operating expenses for the following years.

Tenants will want the operating expenses grossed up to 100 percent occupancy during their base year when they have a base year operating expense pass-through provision—meaning that tenants pay their pro rata share of all expenses above their base year, which is usually the year they take occupancy of their premises.

If the building is not fully assessed for real estate taxes because it is new, the tax assessment for the first year may be based on a partially built building and the real estate taxes will need to be grossed up. If the building has low occupancy, a tax appeal may earn a lower assessment; again, the real estate taxes will need to be grossed up.

If the tenant's lease is not a base-year lease, the tenant may negotiate for the gross up to be at 95 percent building occupancy since a building is seldom fully occupied at all times and a five percent vacancy factor is the standard vacancy rate used for a building's pro forma. However, the difference between 95 and 100 percent is nominal. It is easier and there is less chance of a mathematical error if 100 percent is used.

Higher base-year operating expenses benefit tenants with a base-year lease, but they also benefit landlords who use other methods of billing operating expenses. The purpose of this provision should not be to bill the tenant for the maximum tenant charges allowed, but to charge tenants for their fair share of the building operation costs.

Gross-Up Summary

In an office building lease, the gross-up provision fills a legitimate function in the fair and reasonable allocation of operating expenses to the tenants. With the exception of the base-year approach to the allocation of building expenses, the gross-up process does not benefit the tenants, but it does not penalize them either. If the gross-up provision is used to establish a more reasonable base for the allocation of expenses, it can be a distinct benefit to the tenants. In all cases except the base-year approach, the gross-up provisions benefit the property owner in providing a more fair and equitable reimbursement of expenses.

OFFICE BUILDING GRAND OPENING

The grand opening can be as important for an office building as it is for a shopping center, but the audience is different. The grand opening of a shopping center is targeted to the shopper, while the grand opening of an office building is targeted to the tenants, prospects, and the brokerage community. Generally, the purposes of the grand opening of an office building are:

- To make the existing tenants feel good about their decision to move into the building
- To enhance the building's image in the business community and among office building brokers
- To attract prospective tenants
- To thank the contractors, architects, leasing agents, and others who played a role in the development and success of the building

A well-planned grand opening can also enhance the public's perception of the new building. Office buildings are generally not as controversial as a new shopping center, but any new commercial building may have some community opposition. The grand opening is an opportunity to minimize some of that opposition. Holding a charitable event as a grand opening program is generally an effective public relations approach. A charitable organization in the community that sponsors an annual event could hold its event in the building at no cost to the organization, and a contribution from the developer will benefit everyone.

Another event that can create goodwill for an office building is a party or reception in the lobby on the night before the opening. Guests can include brokers, tenants, prospective tenants, contractors, the press, civic officials, and neighborhood leaders. Any handouts should emphasize the positive aspects of the building and the ways it will be an asset to the community. Leasing agents, the real estate manager, and the staff should be on hand to answer questions and help create good relationships with all involved. Another approach is to coordinate the building's open house with several tenants' open houses.

BUILDING MAINTENANCE

The office building owner assumes more maintenance responsibilities compared to the owner of a shopping center or an industrial property. Typically, the building owner provides janitorial service five nights a week. Electricity, plumbing, HVAC, general maintenance, and light bulb replacement are also the building owner's responsibility. The tenant may be responsible for the maintenance of the carpeting and window coverings. Some office buildings have the electricity separately metered as some tenants use much more electricity compared to others.

In small buildings, the maintenance services are usually contracted because the building cannot support an on-site maintenance person. The following lists some alternatives:

- Work with a maintenance company that offers roving personnel
- Have a maintenance person, possibly a retiree, work a few hours a day cleaning the parking lot and handling minor maintenance problems
- Ask a janitorial company to provide light maintenance services
- Contract the work by job assignment

Mid- and high-rise office buildings have several on-site maintenance employees. A day porter is responsible for keeping the common areas clean during the building's normal operating hours, especially the rest rooms, and possibly handling minor maintenance. One or several building engineers handle the majority of the building's maintenance. Elevator maintenance, fire sprinkler inspections, major plumbing, and electrical maintenance are contracted. HVAC maintenance can be handled in several ways. The maintenance staff may be responsible for first-echelon maintenance with the balance of the maintenance contracted, the entire HVAC maintenance may be contracted, or it may be handled by the on-site staff.

MOVE-INS AND MOVE-OUTS

Relocation is a major disruption for a business and a major frustration for its employees. If handled properly, the actual move in or out of the office building can be a smooth transition. Otherwise, the disturbance can cause problems for everyone and sour the manager-tenant relationship. Once the tenant makes the decision to move into or out of the building, the real estate manager should meet with the tenant's office manager to discuss the move. The following checklist of important points to discuss can be helpful:

- Date and time of the move
- Number of personnel involved
- Size and number of moving trucks
- Specific elevator(s) needed
- Assignment of loading docks, if appropriate
- Assignment of staging areas
- Requirements for protecting the floor covering, walls, and elevator cabs
- Special cleanup after the move is completed
- Insurance requirements for the movers
- Repairs if needed as a result of the move

If the process is not controlled, the move may tie up parking, and the movers may command the elevators. The building's rules and regulations should address move-ins and move-outs and give the real estate manager control over the hours during which the move can be accomplished and the facilities the tenant will use in the process. The tenant is required to request a specific time for moving. Based on other building activities, the real estate manager will prepare a convenient schedule for all involved.

If the building doesn't have a freight elevator, a specific elevator should be assigned; padding blankets should be installed to protect the elevator. The common areas in the building may need special coverings placed over the carpeting and tile flooring. Temporary storage of furniture in the common areas is prohibited. If the building doesn't have a loading dock, an area in the parking lot may need to be roped off for the moving trucks. The moving company and the vendors assisting in the move are required to submit certificates of insurance that include the building owner and the real estate management company as additional insureds. A coordination meeting in advance of the move involving all personnel including a tenant representative, office maintenance staff, manager of the office building, and movers should all be represented.

If the move occurs on a weekend or in the evening, the elevator company should be notified and requested to have a maintenance person on call in case the elevator breaks down. If a major tenant is moving, a member of the building staff should be available during the entire move. A move involving an area of 30,000 square feet or more can take an entire weekend, and building personnel should be assigned shifts.

SECURITY

Security concerns have heightened in recent years in all types of buildings because of the potential for terrorist acts. Some high-rise buildings now restrict access to the building to tenants' employees, authorized vendors of building owner and tenants, visitors approved by tenants. Everyone is required to have proper identification.

Security Personnel

Garden, low-rise, and some mid-rise buildings in the suburbs and urban areas seldom need security guards on site. A private security company can be employed to randomly drive by the property several times a night. Janitors can be utilized to watch for problems. The exterior doors can be locked at a specified hour. Access after hours may be by a coded card or other device that registers the individual in and out of the building. Employees in the building should be instructed to report suspicious people in or near the building. Individual units should not be left open and unattended by the janitor staff or maintenance personnel assuming that the building is locked and the individual units are secure.

High-rise buildings usually have either a security guard in the lobby 24 hours a day or from around 5:00 p.m. until late in the evening. Janitorial personnel are in the building after the security guard locks the building and they can allow people access to the building. People entering or leaving the building after 5:00 p.m. and before 7:00 a.m. and on weekends and holidays must sign in and out at the lobby desk and indicate the tenant they are visiting. Some buildings require everyone to sign in and out regardless of the time of the day or evening, while other buildings will not allow a visitor access to the area beyond the guard station without a tenant confirming the visitor is meeting them. Employees must show their building identification cards. The elevator can be programmed so the visitor has access only to a specific floor. To minimize theft of business equipment, a tenant should have a pass to remove equipment from the building. Many buildings with 24-hour lobby guards do not have tenant directories because the guard provides directory service. Additional information on security is provided in *Chapter 17: Safety, Security, and Emergency Procedures.*

KEY CONTROL

Key control is critical to the security of the office building. A qualified locksmith should design and record the building's key system. Generally, a grand master key opens all locks in the building. From the grand master (which is never issued), submaster keys can be made for janitor closets, meter rooms, and individual floors. Each tenant's suite key is coded and marked "do not duplicate." Master keys should be numbered and should be issued only to individuals who need them and have signed for them. This list should be as limited as possible, keeping in mind the operating efficiency of the building.

When a tenant moves out, the lock cylinder should be changed to ensure security for the next occupant. The real estate manager can easily accomplish this by keeping four or five cylinders that have been set up for the system and rotating them throughout the building. If a tenant fires an employee and wants the locks changed, the building's locksmith should make the change at the tenant's cost. This is the only way to preserve the original lock system in the building.

When a master key is lost or stolen, the building should be rekeyed as soon as possible. In the meantime, a security guard may need to be stationed in the building. If a security officer or janitor lost the keys, that contractor should pay the cost of rekeying the building. If an investor in a unit in an office condominium evicts a tenant or changes tenants, it is the investor's responsibility to rekey the unit, conforming to the master key, or to take the risk of leaving the original lock in place for a new tenant. Access cards are becoming popular because they are more cost effective and can be replaced at a lower expense than a key. Most office buildings are smaller building and do not need security guards. Security can be a large operating expense in larger office buildings. Real estate managers should consult with firms that provide security equipment and security companies to develop appropriate security for the building when their buildings need security. When appropriate, building management should communicate with the local police regarding security and incidents in the immediate area of the building.

TENANT RETENTION PROGRAM

Tenant retention has always been an important component of building management. A commercial building's most valuable asset is its income stream—the rent paid by the building's tenants. When a building's income stream suffers from low occupancy, the building's value is diminished. After a tenant has moved into a building, keeping the tenant is easier and less expensive than replacing the tenant. Consider the potential costs of losing a tenant:

1. Vacancy can easily result in several months to a year or more of lost rents.
2. A leasing commission is typically required for a new tenant.
3. Tenant improvement costs can be substantial.

Whether the leasing market for office space is strong or weak, leasing agents regularly attempt to lure tenants from other buildings. They consider tenants in any office building as prospects for the building or buildings they are leasing. The best and most effective way to counter such efforts to interest tenants in moving is an effective tenant-retention program.

A tenant-retention program for an office building has several components. Though the real estate manager is responsible for developing and implementing the program, he or she needs the cooperation of the building's staff and contractors for the program to be successful. The components of the tenant retention plan include the following 10 items:

1. Excellent treatment of the tenant while he or she is a prospect
2. Handling of the lease negotiations, space planning, and space build-out in a professional and courteous fashion
3. Move-in process should be organized and helpful for the tenant to get relocated with as little hassle as possible
4. Building operations including maintenance, security, and parking contracts should be very transparent and very responsive, keeping the service to the tenant in mind
5. Accurate and timely tenant billings and a willingness to explain any questions to the tenants in a cooperative and helpful manner
6. Frequent communication between the building management and the tenants—not just a visit when something is wrong
7. Tenant's occupancy cost—do your best to make your building competitive—not the lowest price for services, but the optimum price
8. Building improvements—keep the building up to date and well maintained
9. Enhancement of the building's tenant mix—work on getting the best possible tenants in the building and where possible—tenants that will be of benefit to the other tenants
10. Building amenities, services, and programs for the tenants and their employees—try to add things that will be helpful to the tenants such as snack and lunch bars, dry cleaning drops offs, ATMs in the lobby, etc.

Understanding what alienates tenants enables the real estate manager to be proactive in retaining them.

Lease Negotiations

A tenant-retention program starts with the tenant's first communication with the building's staff—usually when the tenant is first contacted to lease space in the building. This is a period of "courting" the tenant. Once the "courting" period is over, the real estate manager or leasing agent negotiates the business terms of the lease, and the tenant or the tenant's attorney negotiates the lease provisions. These negotiations may take a few hours, or they may require weeks or even months.

Before introducing the tenant to the real estate manager, the leasing agent should complete all of the lease documents and inform the tenant of all of its responsibilities. For the leasing agent to complete his or her tasks and then leave the tenant to find the next contact is not adequate. Rather, the leasing agent should introduce the tenant to the real estate manager in person or by conference call (a letter or e-mail is impersonal and is not the best approach) so there is no gap in the communication between the tenant and building management.

The real estate manager should become the source of information and support for the tenant in finalizing the space plan for the premises and commencing construction of the tenant improvements. The real estate manager's helpfulness may be limited to explaining how building out the space can be handled, but even that can be of great assistance to a tenant faced with a multitude of concerns. Moat tenants are not aware of the time involved to develop space plans and construction drawings; the municipality's review and approval of the construction drawings; the time to bid the tenant improvement work; and then to construct the space. Often, the unknown factor is the time it takes the municipality to review and approve the construction drawings.

After the premises are completed, the real estate manager schedules a walk-through with the tenant and the contractor. Construction items that are not completed to the tenant's or the real estate manager's satisfaction are placed on a *punch list*. If such items are not completed shortly after the tenant takes possession of the premises, they will become a source of aggravation for the tenant. The real estate manager must follow up with the contractor to ensure that all of the items on the punch list are completed, while also making sure to visit with tenants to ensure they are satisfied with the results.

Lease Renewals

The first step in the lease-renewal process is to determine if the owner prefers to offer the tenant a lease renewal. There might be better options for the owner than to simply renew the tenant's lease. There may be better users for the building or tenants who are able to pay higher rents. The real estate manager needs to analyze the benefits of whether or not to renewing the tenant's lease. Too often, lease renewals are taken for granted without considering other options.

If it is determined that it is best to renew the tenant's lease, initiate this discussion at least six months prior to lease expiration. The goal of the initial contact should be to determine the tenant's desire regarding the lease and to inform the tenant about current rates and terms. Tenants often do not realize how the market has changed since they signed their leases. Renewing a lease for a lesser amount then the market rate shows that the property owner recognizes the value of the tenant. However, that is not advised when owners are concerned with capitalization of income to set sale prices and financing levels. Under these circumstances, striving for the market rate is a good idea.

An advantage to renewing a tenant is there will not be lost rent due to vacancy, and the leasing commission, if there is one, will generally be less than that for acquiring a new tenant. The cost of keeping an existing tenant usually much less than half the cost of acquiring a new tenant. Tenants who occupy large spaces should have their leases renewed a year before they expire.

Positive Communication

Timely return of all phone calls and e-mails is the first step toward establishing and maintaining good owner/tenant communications. The real estate manager and tenant often have different hours. If the real estate manager cannot return the call immediately, the administrative assistant or assistant manager should call the tenant back to let him or her know when the real estate manager will be available or see if anything can be done in the interim. The real estate manager must be available 24 hours a day, seven days a week to cover emergencies. Since problems do not limit themselves to business hours, the lines of communication must be open at all times. This can be achieved with the help of maintenance personnel or an answering service.

If major repairs are planned for the property, the tenants should be notified at least two weeks in advance. The real estate manager does not need to ask a tenant's permission to schedule repair work. However, advance notice, especially where a large repair job is concerned, can prevent major disruptions to the tenant's business. Breaking up a large repair into smaller jobs may also reduce inconvenience to the tenant. If the tenant's position is not considered, a large repair job can disrupt a planned event that cannot be changed.

Personal visits are the best method of communication with the tenant. Most real estate managers are not "on-site" managers and are not usually visible on the property. Therefore, visiting the tenants on a regular basis is advisable. At least one visit per quarter is suggested when properties are running well. In troubled properties or new properties with the usual start-up problems, more frequent visits should be made. Quite often, a tenant may be aware of a problem but be too busy to alert the real estate manager; a visit from the real estate manager gives the tenant the opportunity to convey the message and to discuss any other items of mutual interest. This also enables the real estate manager to head off a potential problem at its earliest stage of development.

Many buildings provide a monthly or quarterly e-newsletter. The newsletter is an excellent way to communicate with the tenants and their employees on a host of issues. The e-newsletter may inform the tenant of businesses that have recently signed leases and when they will open, of the accomplishments of the building's recycling program, or of information regarding the building's emergency procedures. It may also acknowledge tenants and individual employees for their accomplishments, promote the activities of businesses in the building, and discuss activities in the community. It is also possible to have a Facebook page for the building and post all of the information on that profile as well as interesting photos, latest in new tenants, etc.

Building Improvements

A tenant retention program includes improvements to the building, enhancements to the building's tenant mix, amenities added to the building, and services to the tenant's employees.

Building improvements include modernizing the elevators and mechanical systems and upgrading the common areas. The building's tenant mix can be enriched by adding tenants that provide a service to the other tenants or add prestige to the building. A deli, gift shop, hair salon, health club, bank, stock brokerage firm, restaurant, health club, or other retail service provides conveniences to the existing tenants and their employees. A prestigious law firm enhances the image of an office building just as a well-respected medical practice enhances the image of a medical office building. A lunchroom with vending machines, a conference room, and outdoor patio areas are just a few examples of amenities that can be incorporated into a building. Many garden style and low-rise office buildings with outdoor surface parking are adding covered areas of parking and charging extra for that, and are finding a good market for the service.

Most employees spend more time in their work environment than in any other place except their homes. The real estate manager can develop a tenant-retention program that makes the office building a pleasant, enjoyable, and sometimes fun-filled place to work. Management can offer tenants several services to help "deinstitutionalize" a building. A food drive or toy collection can build community spirit, or a series of monthly luncheon speakers can provide education and entertainment.

Tenant Improvements

Tenant improvement work is an ongoing process in most office buildings. It is critical that all work is completed in a timely fashion to meet the tenant's needs and at a competitive cost. The strength of the leasing market generally determines the amount of tenant improvement work the property owner must offer. In a weak market, such as during the *Great Recession*, property owners often provided *turnkey tenant improvements* for desirable tenants. A turnkey improvement provides the tenant with a complete build-out of the premises to the tenant's specification at the property owner's expense.

It's important that the building manager is in tune with the tenant's expectations of what is included in a turnkey improvement. Some tenants are able to demand larger tenant improvement allowances as inducements to occupy space in a building. In a strong market, a property owner may attempt to lease space "as is" or with a limited tenant improvement allowance and the tenant pays for additional tenant improvements. Often, when a tenant renews the lease, the property owner will paint and carpet an existing space as an inducement for the tenant to sign a lease. In a condominium-type office building, the real estate manager is likely to be involved in the tenant improvement process as a consultant or as a construction manager for a fee for the owner of the condominium unit.

Providing Tenant Improvements

Tenant improvements are market driven. They can range from a basic level of improvements, such as painting the walls and cleaning the carpets, to turnkey improvements. A common approach is to provide tenants with an allowance based on a dollar per square foot of spaced leased. For instance, the tenant will receive $50 per square foot for each square foot leased. Another approach would be to provide tenants with a fixed dollar amount of improvements. For example, the tenant will receive $70,000 toward building out its premises.

When the tenant's improvement allowance is not sufficient to build out the premises per the tenant's specification, either the tenant pays the difference at the time the premises are built out or the property owner pays the cost of the over-standard improvements and amortizes the cost over the term of the lease and increasing the tenant's rent to pay these costs. Generally, when the owner provides the improvements and charges for them, the extra charge will include an interest fee. This approach has an added benefit in that it increases the *net operating income (NOI)* and, therefore, the value of the building. Some investors will read the tenant's leases carefully and not include the amortization of the tenant improvements in the building income to determine the value of the building.

Determining Tenant Improvement Costs

For minor tenant improvements, unit prices can be used to determine costs. The real estate manager will obtain from contractors the cost to provide specific improvements. A contractor may provide unit prices, such as $350 for a two-by-four-foot light fixture, partition walls at $60 per linear foot, floor tile at $15 per square foot, and carpeting at $45 per square yard and the cost for other improvements. From this listing, the real estate manager can calculate the cost of the improvements while negotiating the lease. This approach is used for small jobs to obtain an estimate of the cost of the tenant improvements.

The alternative is to bid the work for each job. This approach generally assures the best price, but it can quite often delay the completion of the job. Contractors should be screened and selected based on experience with office buildings, reputation, financial stability, and reliability in finishing the work on time. When bidding the job, contractors need to have complete plans. For a realistic bid, the process must be open and honest. If one contractor's bid is used to establish prices for another, contractors will soon lose interest in providing costly bids that have no chance of being accepted.

All contracts should be written. They should include an outside finish date with a penalty if the date is not met. Payment should be made on a progress basis, and 10 percent retention should be held to cover contingencies and to get past the lien dates. Labor and material lien releases should be obtained before the contractor is paid. All work should carry a warranty, which in most areas lasts one year.

Allowing Tenants to Contract for Construction

Some owners will allow a tenant to contract for its tenant improvements. Many owners prefer to have their building manager contract for the tenant improvements to ensure the quality of the construction and the integrity of the building and its mechanical systems. An unqualified contractor, or one who isn't familiar with the building, can disturb the HVAC and electrical systems. On the other hand, exceptions may be necessary for experienced tenants with special wants or needs.

Obviously, the experience of the contractor in dealing with sophisticated office buildings and their system would make a difference in allowing an outside contractor. The property owner would require that he or she approves the tenant's contractor, or may have a list of preferred contractors the tenant must chose from to build out the tenant improvements. All work would have to be approved by the real estate manager and would have to comply with local building ordinances and permits.

Allowing the tenant to perform or contract for improvements is the exception. However, the tenant may negotiate this right. Major tenants may require the right to perform their own improvements. Sometimes allowing the tenant to contract the improvements will expedite the work. An owner of a small office building may allow the tenants to contract nonstructural improvements. Medical tenants may be allowed to contract for the installation of their expensive medical equipment.

The real estate manager should place restrictions and requirements on the tenant and its contractor. The real estate manager or building owner's representative should review and approve the plans. If the tenant is contracting for improvements, the building owner should be protected from liens. Each state has methods of protecting the owner, and the real estate manager should apply these methods whenever tenants are contracting work on the premises.

Establishing Contractor Requirements

All contractors must be licensed and bonded. They must be required to have insurance naming the building owner and the real estate management company as additional insureds or named insureds. The real estate manager should go through any sensitive areas with the contractor before construction begins to minimize problems during the process.

Core drilling should not be allowed during the building's regular hours. Parking, unloading, use of the building's elevator, and requirements for union employees should be discussed with the contractor. A consent to an *alteration provision* is signed by the tenant before the work commences. This agreement sets forth what the tenant is allowed to do in the space, when the work can be performed, the requirements stated above and who, if anyone, must inspect the work before the building owner approves it.

Building Operations

Daily building management activities can also be part of the tenant-retention program. Many real estate managers provide a letter of introduction as soon as the lease is signed and enclose a "Tenant Manual or Handbook and Emergency Procedures" booklet. The tenant manual informs the tenant of building activities and rules and regulations that will affect business. The tenant manual provides information on tenant directory listings, signage, after-hours HVAC, maintenance of the premises, alterations to the premises, payment of rent, and many other issues.

The tenant manual also includes a section on emergency procedures. Since the major San Francisco earthquake in 1989, the bombing of the World Trade Center in New York in 1993, the destruction of the World Trade Center in 2001, and the devastation of hurricane Katrina in 2005, the threat of terrorism tenants are more concerned than ever about being prepared for an emergency or a disaster. Management should review the emergency procedures booklet with the tenant and schedule regular practice evacuations for mid- and high-rise buildings. Such planning helps the tenant and the tenant's employees build confidence that the building's management has prepared for a natural disaster or a manmade emergency. (Chapter 17 discusses the development of emergency procedures.)

Tenant Billings

The tenant's occupancy costs are components of a tenant-retention plan that are frequently overlooked. The tenant's occupancy costs include base rent and *pass-through operating expenses*. The real estate manager should keep expenses as low as possible while maintaining the property consistent with the goals and objectives of the property owner.

Billing tenants for building operating expenses can be the source of problems between building owners and tenants. Tenants often do not understand just what is involved, so the costs frequently seem quite high. For this reason, the real estate manager must make sure the billings are accurate, timely, and understandable. Tenants often go to great lengths to negotiate operating expense lease provisions. When these provisions are missed or ignored in the billings, tenants are irritated.

Building a model of the lease provisions for the operating expense billing for each tenant can ensure that management complies with all exclusions and/or special provisions. The billing should give sufficient detail so the tenant can readily determine what was spent, when it was spent, and how the tenant's share was computed. It is not sufficient to send a billing showing the amount the tenant owes with no indication that the tenant is paying the amount stated under the terms of the lease. Copies of individual bills need not be provided to the tenants, but they should receive enough detail to fully understand the charges. This attention to detail will speed up the process and help maintain a good relationship.

Tenant Surveys

Periodically surveying the tenants to determine their opinion of the building's services is one of the best and quickest ways to evaluate a building's tenant-retention program. Management can accomplish this by including a questionnaire with the monthly billing (if the tenant is billed monthly), sending an online questionnaire, or visiting the tenants on a regular basis to see how they are doing and to learn if they have special needs management can address.

COMPARING LEASING PROPOSALS BETWEEN OWNER AND TENANT

Sometimes both the owner and the tenant are considering more than one proposal and making the final decision almost always comes down to final costs. Obviously, the owner and the tenant have different views on the costs of the lease and we will look at those two points of view. A shopping center has the additional consideration of percentage rents and a more critical concern with tenant mix, but other than comparing proposals for all types of commercial properties are basically the same. We use the shopping center example here as many office buildings and even some industrial properties have retail and restaurant tenants that will have percentage leases. Once the issues of tenant mix and tenant credit are covered, the final analysis comes down to the financial terms of the lease. We will use a small office building with an available space of 1,200 square feet and a proposed rent of $20.00 per square foot per year. The same figures could apply to a shopping center or even an industrial complex.

For example, the tenant would like an allowance of $5 per square foot and would agree to a 5 percentage rental provision and a triple-net lease. An established delicatessen/sandwich shop approaches the owner with an offer (A) to lease the space for $18 per square foot, triple net, five-year lease with a five-year option. The tenant requests an improvement allowance of $5 per square foot. This tenant has two other locations and is averaging $450 per square foot sales in both of his other locations, one of which is in an office building.

A local businesswoman also makes an offer (B) for the same space hoping to put in a delicatessen. This will be her first delicatessen, but she does operate a catering service. She is willing to accept the $20 per square foot rent, she would like an allowance of $2 per square foot for improvements. She will sign a five-year lease on a triple-net basis and she will accept a 5 percentage rent level. She estimates her sales at $300 per square foot.

The financial terms of (A) are as follows:

- Base rent 1,200 sq.ft. × $18.00 = $21,600
- Improvements 1,200 sq.ft. × $5 ÷ 5 yrs = $1,200 per year
- Net rent $21,600 – $1,200 = $20,400
- Percentage rent:

  21,600 ÷ .05 = $432,000 breakpoint
  1,200 × $450 = $540,000 estimated sales
  $540,000 – $432,000 = $108,000 × .05 =
  $5,400 + the base rent of $20,400 = $25,800
  Total rent: $25,800

The financial terms of (B) are as follows:

- Base rent 1,200 sq.ft. × $20.00 = $24,000
- Improvements 1,200 × $2.00 ÷ 5 yrs = $480 per year
- Net rent $24,000 – $1,200 = $23,520
- Percentage rent:

  $24,000 ÷ .05 = $480,000 breakpoint
  1,200 sq.ft. × $300 estimated sales = $360,000 which is below the break point; so no additional rent
  Total rent: $23,520

The owner is likely to accept the men's delicatessen/sandwich offer even at the lower rental rate because the potential rent is higher with a tenant that has a track record. If the owner did not have the delicatessen/sandwich shop proposal on the table, the owner might accept the delicatessen proposal as it meets the center's terms, but because it is an inexperienced tenant, the odds of success may be lower than desired.

The proposed tenant, on the other hand, may have a second offer, referred to as (C). This proposal is for a store of 1,400 square feet, triple net, $20.00 per sq.ft., but the owner has allowed for $3.00 per square foot allowance, a five-year lease with a 6 percentage rent provision. She estimates her sales at $300 per square foot.

The economics of the second deal (C) are as follows:

- Base rent 1,400 sq.ft. × $20.00 = $28,000
- Improvements 1,400 sq.ft. × $3.00 ÷ 5 yrs = $840 per year
- Net rent $28,000 – $840 = $27,160
- Percentage rent:

  $28,000 ÷ .06 = $466,667 breakpoint
  1,400 sq.ft. × $300 = $420,000 estimated sales
  That is below the breakpoint, so no percentage rent will be due
  Total rent: $27,160

In this case, she is will be renting more space than she needs and this will result in higher CAM charges as well as a high rental. If there are no other mitigating circumstances, she is likely to go with the smaller store. The decision is being made on first year, cash only and not *time value of money*. The larger square footage is more cash due to the square footage and may not be the most profitable as the more precise calculation would be to determine the net effective rent on per square foot basis of all three potential leases.

An office tenant and owner have a slightly different consideration and that is the load factor—or rentable verses usable square footage. Also, the percentage rental factor does not come into the considerations. The rentable square footage includes the tenant's share of the common areas of the building, and the usable square footage includes only the space under the direct control of the tenant. For purposes of this example, only rents are considered and not tenant improvements, but the calculation would be the same as it was for the shopping center example:

Consider the following example:

> Building A is 55,000 square feet, including a load factor of 10%. The annual rent is $19.50 per square foot of rentable space. Building B is 70,000 square feet and does not have a load factor, which means the rentable and usable square footage are the same. Building B annual rent is $21.00 per square foot of the usable space. Using rents as the only factor, which of the above two buildings would be the best (meaning lowest cost) for a tenant prospect?
>
> Leasing 1,000 square feet in Building A means paying rent on 1,100 square feet (the 10% load factor) multiplied by the rental rate of $19.50 per square foot. The rent for this space in Building A would be $21,450 per year or $21.45 per usable square foot. The rent in Building B would be $21,000 as there is no load factor, and it is simply the square footage multiplied the usable square footage of 1,000 square feet. Based on rents only, Builiding B would be the better choice for the tenant.

MANAGEMENT AND OPERATION ISSUES

The next sections explore creative ways real estate managers can enhance the services that office buildings can offer its tenants and increase the building's income.

Retail Tenants in an Office Building

Retail tenants can provide services to other tenants in the building, pay percentage rent, establish an identity for the building, and become an amenity for the building's marketing and leasing program. A strong retail component—especially in a larger office building—acts as a service to the office occupants as well as an additional draw for the public at large.

A well-known popular restaurant can often enhance the image of an office building. The availability of services for the offices is a plus in the leasing effort. Services such as dry cleaning stations, delis, copying and printing services, and gift shops add to the convenience of the office location.

The real estate manager must analyze a prospective retail or service tenant more carefully than an office tenant to ensure compatibility with the other tenants and with the building. A merchant who sells inferior merchandise or provides poor service will harm the building's reputation and annoy tenants. The retail lease in an office building must include provisions found in shopping center leases such as hours of operation, percentage rent, sales reporting, sales audit, and a very restrictive use provision. Operational issues include trash removal, deliveries, pest control, noise, odor abatement, janitorial service, after-hours entry, signage, supplementary HVAC, and over-standard utility usage.

Rent Out the Rooftop

The leasing of space for antennas is an excellent source of income for office buildings. The primary requirements for the office building to pursue this income source are a flat roof (a pitched roof can work, but it complicates the situation), and a roof that can withstand the weight of the units, although the newer units are becoming smaller and lighter as the technology improves. The taller the building the better, but current technology allows the antennas to work well on mid-rise as well as high-rise buildings.

Each antenna should be placed in a manner that allows as many antennas on the roof as is practical. Only industry professionals should install the antennas, and building representatives must supervise the installation. Any modifications of the roofing should be at the expense of the lessee, and building management or a structural engineer must approve all work.

In some cases, the antenna on the roof is not the only space the user requires. Typically, the user also needs cabling to the antenna and a small leased space or a space in the storeroom or maintenance area to locate power equipment. Many real estate managers manage the antennas in-house. Some larger buildings with multiple antennas hire a professional to manage the antenna program. The tenant should sign a *hold-harmless* and *indemnification agreement* protecting the building owner and real estate management company against damage or injury caused by the antenna or its installation.

The income from antennas can range from a few hundred dollars a month to several thousand dollars a month and more. Even a rental of $200 per month translates into $2,400 per year, and capitalized at 10 percent, that increases the building's value by $24,000. Multiply that number by several antennas and the results are significant, especially with a lower capitalization rate.

Condominium Office Buildings

In the United States, some small office condominium properties are successful because they are built to serve businesses that have small office requirements, are not inclined to grow, and want to have an investment in their office space. However, the main problems with office condominiums of any size are that they have no room for expansion for any one tenant and dealing with a unit owner that does not abide by the rules and regulations of the building can be very difficult.

The original sale documents must set forth the use restrictions and must provide for a real estate manager to oversee the property. In addition to his or her regular duties as real estate manager, the manager may also have opportunities to oversee construction for outside owners, find tenants for them, and help them handle administrative tasks. For the prospective developer, the attraction to selling the units as compared to leasing them is the instant return on the investment.

Building Storage

Basements, attics, and dead corners of the building and parking garages are great locations for storage areas in any building. Storage rates can range from 25 percent to 60 percent of base rents, with higher rates charged for the convenience of having the storage space in the same building as the tenant's office.

The build-out can be as simple as cubicles divided by a two-by-four inch stud open wall with a heavy mesh screen separating the units. The owner provides each unit with lights and a door, and the tenant uses its own padlock. Storage can add income and value to the building while offering a convenience to the tenants.

Parking Management

Office building parking varies from free, open parking for many suburban office buildings to parking for a fee in the garages of downtown office buildings and some suburban buildings. The basic parking policy of all office buildings is to provide convenient parking for tenants' customers and visitors and to eliminate unauthorized parking. This can be achieved by providing 20-minute and two-hour visitors' parking in stalls close to the building entrance.

Free Parking

Preventing unauthorized parking in a suburban office building's free lot can be difficult. An inexpensive approach is to give all the employees of building tenants parking stickers to affix to a car's rear bumper or rearview mirror. A more effective but more costly approach is to control employee parking with a card gate. With either approach, management must post signs at parking lot entrances warning against unauthorized parking. Overnight parking is typically prohibited, and most free lots are legally posted so the real estate manager can have abandoned or illegally parked cars towed.

Paid and Permit Parking

Most downtown office buildings and some suburban office buildings provide paid parking. Most owners contract with a parking garage operator to manage the building's parking. The building owner receives a percentage of the income, and the garage operator pays all the expenses from its share of the income. The owner's percentage varies from 60 percent to 85 percent, depending upon potential income. For example, the owner's percentage may start at 60 percent and increase five percent for every $60,000 of income above a fixed-base income level. Another approach is to pay the operator a management fee in lieu of a percentage of the income. A third approach is for the building owner to operate the parking garage.

Paid and permit parking can be controlled by parking attendants, electronic system or by a card system. If parking is for tenants only, a card system is more cost-effective than paying attendants to cover normal business hours.

Lots that have all-day, in-and-out paid parking are staffed or the tenant pay by inserting a credit card or cash in a parking machine and indicate the stall number where they parked. The parking lot is periodically visited by a person who monitors the parking lot or garage . If employees pay to park, they are generally assigned to a specific area but not to a specific space. This approach allows for more paid parking and reduces the problem of one person parking in the assigned space of another.

If an office building does not have adequate parking for its employees and visitors, leasing nearby parking can be explored. A church, lodge, or theater might not use its parking lot on weekdays, or a nearby shopping center might have abundant parking.

Transportation Management Plans

Municipalities are concerned with the impact a building has on traffic. Some municipalities require developers and property owners to create and submit a *transportation management plan (TMP)* for the building. The purpose of the plan is to minimize traffic in and around the building in accordance with the overall transportation plan of the city or county where the building will be located. As a condition of obtaining the building permits, the developer must agree to develop a TMP for the building and to provide the management necessary to implement and carry out the plan.

The TMP includes, but is not limited to, sending out questionnaires to all tenants' employees asking the form of transportation they use traveling to work and whether car pools or public transportation are feasible alternatives. The questionnaire asks employers to consider flex times so all employees will not be on the road at peak traffic hours.

The plan may encourage the use of bicycles by providing a safe storage cage for them. On one property, the safe area was a cage built of cyclone fencing and kept padlocked. Within the cage were individual bicycle racks where employees used their own locks to secure their bicycles. Employees also had a key to the cage, so two levels of protection were present. In another project, bicycles were protected with individual fiberglass bicycle storage modules and the building owner provided the keys to the employees. The tenants' employees signed a use agreement and paid a refundable deposit for each key.

As part of a TMP program, tenants might be able to purchase discount bus passes, making the bus ride more attractive. Reduced tickets can be distributed to employees who agree to use the bus to and from work. Typically, the property owner obtains bus schedules and makes them available to all employees by having them at a central location or by giving them to each office manager to distribute. The lobby of the office building may have an area for displaying the city's bus routes and other public transportation facilities. If an employee agrees to use public transportation, a provision of the plan may provide employees access to transportation for emergencies on a limited basis and special transportation to or from home if needed due to extenuating circumstances.

Another facet of the plan is an owner-sponsored program to encourage ride sharing. Additionally, the building owner can set up a preferential parking area for van pool or carpooling programs. In an office building, the city may require the building owner to offer carpool employees a lower rate for parking in the building lot or garage.

Because of the complexity of these issues, some leases have added a provision to ensure that the building owner has tenant cooperation and is able to pass the cost of the program back to the tenants through the common area billings or *pass-through operating expenses.*

Conference Rooms

A building conference room that is available to the occupants can be an excellent leasing tool. Many occupants do not want to pay monthly rent and costs on a room that is seldom used. However, they are often willing to pay for the use of the room on an as-needed basis, or it can be factored into the overall rental rate and offered as a building service.

The management office coordinates the scheduling of the room. The room should be fully equipped with conference tables, chairs, easel, whiteboard, plug-in phone, speaker phones, audio and visual equipment, coffee area, and a podium. Not all buildings benefit from having a conference room for their occupants. If the room is not used regularly or is not perceived as a positive leasing tool, the space should be converted to rentable area.

Lost and Found

People often lose personal items in office buildings. A lost-and-found policy should be established and made known to the occupants. A method of identifying missing property should be established and records should be kept of what is found and who claimed it. In large buildings, this activity may be handled by security, and in small buildings, the management office or the maintenance personnel may handle it. The tenant manual or handbook should include a section outlining the building's lost-and-found procedures.

PROFESSIONAL ASSOCIATIONS

Three professional associations provide education and information to the office building industry.

1. Building Owners and Managers Association (BOMA) is dedicated primarily to office buildings; it has chapters in major cities throughout the United States. BOMA provides education and publications and lobbies on behalf of the office building industry.
2. The Building Owners and Managers Institute (BOMI) awards the Real Property Administrator (RPA) designation and presents classes in various aspects of office building operations.
3. The Institute of Real Estate Management (IREM) has been a leader in office building management for many years. IREM awards the Certified Property Manager (CPM®) designation and the Accredited Management Organization (AMO®) designation. IREM sponsors classes in office building management and leasing as well as other classes in the areas of commercial and residential property management. The services offered by BOMA and IREM are reviewed in *Chapter 1: Introduction.*

CHAPTER

5

Medical Office Building and Clinical Facilities Management

Healthcare is a multi-trillion dollar industry. For years, this industry operated with sole physician practices similar to a cottage industry. Hospitals served a defined community and it seemed that they did not cross into other hospitals territories. The healthcare industry is experiencing an evolution on how healthcare is delivered due to federal regulations that have provided opportunities for millions of uninsured people to obtain insurance. The number of senior citizens continues to increase in our society. While the industry is growing, there is downward pressure on medical service fees and from the federal government and insurance companies. These are a few of the changes in society and the healthcare industry that are having a significant impact on medical professionals and how the operate their practices.

New medical delivery models are being developed with an emphasis on the right care and treatment at the appropriate location, in a facility best suited to deliver the service, and provided by the right team of medical professionals at an efficient cost with an optimum clinical outcome. The need for medical services to be clustered around hospitals has changed. Hospitals are moving services out into the community. They have acquired medical groups, both primary care and specialty groups, and opened clinics throughout the community staffed by these medical professionals. These clinics offer urgent care, primary care, physical therapy and medical specialists.

As the medical-delivery system changes, real estate managers, leasing agents, and owners of medical office buildings (MOBs) need to anticipate how these and future changes will impact the supply-demand equation for space in their MOBs. These changes will determine who occupies MOBs in the future, where new MOBs are located, which older MOBs will become obsolete, and who owns and operates these buildings—a number of the fundamentals of managing MOBs will need to change and adapt.

The development, leasing, and management of MOBs are a specialty niche within the commercial real estate industry. However, few commercial real estate management firms specialize in managing and leasing MOBs for the reasons discussed in this chapter. The real estate manager will encounter unique issues managing MOBs because of the different types of medical services provided, the large number of patients (most of them ill), visitors at MOBs, and the respective regulations that require certain building standards to be met through groups, such as the Joint Commission on Accreditation of Healthcare Organizations (JCAHO) and Center for Medicaid and Medicare Service (CMS). Few leasing agents will specialize in leasing MOBs. Recognizing the differences between leasing traditional office buildings and leasing MOBs allows owners, leasing agents, and real estate managers of MOBs to create and implement successful leasing and marketing programs.

LEASING MEDICAL OFFICE BUILDINGS

While many similarities exist between leasing MOBs and other office buildings, the differences are also significant. MOBs are typically more costly to develop than office buildings. They take longer to lease up and *tenant improvement (TI)* costs can be two to five times greater than the typical office building's TI costs. Because of the high cost of TIs, lease terms with medical professionals are typically 10 years or more with options. Historically, tenant turnover has been low. When hospitals purchase a medical group or solo physician practice, there is a greater chance their lease will not be renewed. Existing medical practices will evaluate the efficiencies of their space as a major factor in deciding whether to renew their lease or relocate. Some medical groups will find operational efficiencies and significant cost savings by merging with another medical group. The leasing team needs to monitor which medical groups are merging and inquire of their space needs.

Criteria for a Successful Leasing Program

When planning a MOB, a developer must carefully consider several important criteria that ultimately affect the success of the leasing program: location, healthcare providers not currently in the market, area payer mix, current area medical tenant mix, and market rental rates. Payer mix is the demographic profile of people with insurance, what types of insurance and what it covers, those that pay with cash, and the services which the area population has received. Healthcare also performs analysis that looks at the age, gender, etc., and determine what types of services they will statistically need, identify those providers (doctors) who currently provide those services in the market, and determine what the potential is for future patient care and the related growth.

Location

A major difference in leasing MOBs is the importance of location. Whether an office tenant is located in a downtown or suburban building and whether it is on 2nd Avenue or 14th Street is seldom significant to a tenant's operations. However, whether they are across the street from a hospital or a mile or more away from it has been important to most physicians' profitability.

Healthcare can be delivered in non-traditional space, such as shopping centers, grocery, large box retail and pharmacy, and urban office buildings. For example, Walmart, which has a pharmacy is seriously looking at urgent care/minute clinics as a compliment or possibly a feeder to their pharmacy. CVS and Walgreens are experimenting with in-store "walk-in" clinics staffed by nurse practitioners or physicians assistants.

Location is one of the most important factors for a physician or other medical professional when choosing where to practice. Since medical professionals' income is related to the number of patients they can see in a day, less time spent commuting results in more income generated. Therefore, planning for a MOB must take into account a location's proximity to the hospital or hospitals and/or its proximity to the medical professionals' patients or potential patients.

Other important location considerations when planning and leasing MOBs include the following:

- Convenience: Many people who work downtown prefer to have their doctor and dentist located in the city. This arrangement enables patients to minimize time away from work.
- Market to a particular group of people: A doctor or dentist may target an area with a specific employment base because employees with good medical and dental coverage often reside in particular areas of a city.
- Prestige: A new MOB with a contemporary design usually offers amenities not found in older MOBs. High-income medical specialists such as plastic surgeons may use the prestige and image of a modern building when marketing their practice.

Hospital-Owned Medical Office Buildings

An alternative to an independently owned MOB is one that is part of a hospital campus or a MOB that is owned by a hospital and is in close proximity to it. Hospitals lease space on their campuses or develop MOBs at very competitive rates to attract physicians to affiliate with them. Hospitals are often more concerned with recruiting physicians to affiliate with them than they are with a return on their real estate investment.

STARK laws do not allow healthcare organizations to offer below market/non-arm's length leases to physicians as an inducement to lease space from them if there is any referral from the tenants to the healthcare organization. The regulations are more commonly referred to as "STARK" law compliance.

Investor-Owned Medical Office Buildings on Hospital Campuses

Many hospitals will lease land on their campus to developers and *real estate investment trusts (REITs)* to build MOBs. The hospitals gain the benefits of having a MOB on their campus, while maintaining control of how the land is used that will attract physicians without the necessary capital investment and risk inherent in development. The ground lease typically will include parameters on the size of the building and the tenants that the building owner can lease to, which drives tenants that are supportive to the hospital.

Hospital-Owned Clinics

Many hospitals are developing or contracting with a developer to create clinics in the suburbs, and to staff these clinics with physicians and medical specialists who are their employees. These clinics complement the hospitals ambulatory care strategy and are feeders to the hospitals while increasing their presence in the community.

Investor-Owned Medical Office Buildings

Many MOBs are located near a hospital and some are owned and managed by the medical practitioners who occupy them. Such practitioners often assign the management of the building to their administrative staff or they contract with a real estate management company to manage and lease the building. The MOBs that are not owned by medical professionals are either self-managed or managed by a real estate management firm.

Tenant Mix

Tenant mix and tenant synergism are important to the success of many MOBs. The synergism in a MOB is the referral system that can be developed among the physicians and other medical professionals. Many specialists depend on referrals from primary care physicians or other specialists.

Ground-floor tenants that are important to the building's tenant mix include a pharmacy, restaurant, coffee shop, medical and dental laboratories, physical, therapy dialysis, and prosthesis supplier. Physical therapy and dialysis are both good first-floor tenants due to patients that may have ambulatory limitations, the noise of the physical therapy equipment, and the amount of water used in dialysis and the potential for leaks that could work their way down the building if located on higher floors.

If the building is located in a dense urban area, the ground floor may have retailers and restaurants similar to tenants in multiuse buildings with office or residential space above ground-floor retail space. If the location is in the retail core of a central business district, retailers and restaurants are potential tenants. If the location is in an area with several hospitals and residential developments within walking distance, potential ground-floor tenants include quick-service restaurants, and service tenants such as dry cleaning, convenience items, and small gift shops. A variety of ground-floor tenants increases the value of the building for the medical professionals. The amount of space on the ground floor that is leased to nonmedical uses will depend on the location of the building and the types of property uses in the area. Some areas will not support nonmedical uses on the ground floor.

A good mix of primary care physicians and specialists will provide a strong base for referrals within the building and sustain the building for many years. In addition, since physicians and other medical professionals are reluctant to move practices due to the high cost of medical or dental TIs, a MOB tenant basis is usually more stable than that of an office building.

Evaluation of Prospective Tenants

All commercial tenants are evaluated on three criteria: (1) financial status, (2) success of their business and/or their expertise, and (3) general use. Each property type places a different emphasis on each criterion.

These criteria are helpful in evaluating a prospective medical tenant, but with a different emphasis and with one additional aspect. Though financial status is an important criterion for all property types, it is less important in leasing medical office space because it is the rare exception when a physician or dentist fails. A medical professional starting a practice needs a business loan for equipment, TI, and operating capital. The requirements of the tenant's practice, such as special medical equipment and power needs, must be considered. Among the criteria the hospital may use to evaluate prospects are the type of practice and the contribution the practice will make to the success of the hospital.

An additional facet of identifying a solid tenant mix in a MOB is the synergy created between the physician practices and referrals. The micro medical community created within the building drives income to the adjoining practices and provides a single location for the patient to attend to all of their medical diagnostic and care requirements.

Pharmacy

Of all possible tenants, a successful pharmacy that is responsive to the needs of the medical professionals in the building is one of the best amenities a MOB can offer. Pharmacies usually pay higher rent, provide a building identity, and offer a valuable service to the medical practices and their patients.

Typically, an independent pharmacy ranges from 1,200 to 2,000 square feet. A national or regional drug store chain may lease substantially more space if the building is located in a heavily populated area or an area with several MOBs. The size depends on the selection and quantities of nonprescription items carried. A pharmacy should orient its merchandise to the needs of the medical practices, their staffs, and the patients.

A pharmacy as a retail tenant in a MOB creates special management considerations, including pick-up deliveries, pest control, trash and medical waste removal, and exterior and interior building signage. Many pharmacies have "pick-up" windows for prescriptions, or early morning pick-ups by couriers to multiple prescription deliveries to senior care, nursing, or skilled care multi-unit facilities where an on-site pharmacy is not present.

The tenant may insist on providing its own janitorial service because of the amount and variety of drugs on the premises. If the tenant's premises are separately metered, the building's *pass-through charges* to the tenant must be adjusted.

Rental Rates

An important criterion for the success of any income-producing property is establishing the correct or market rental rate or rates for a building. Income properties are not leased at pro forma rates, but rather at market rates. The procedures for conducting market surveys, evaluating the surveys, establishing a market range of rates for a building, and pricing each space are thoroughly discussed in *Chapter 7: Developing the Marketing Plan.* Two additional factors must be considered when developing the market rental rates for a proposed MOB.

First, most physicians do not operate in a real estate business environment, and they are not always current with real estate values and market rental rates. Many physicians—especially those whose present rent is considerably below market—must be educated to the market rental rates and the value of their new location. Value would be location to other practices that can provide referrals, such as a hospital—especially if the practice admits numerous patients and the physicians make continuous rounds.

Medical professionals may not be familiar with pass-through building expenses, after-hours, over-standard utility charges, and other special charges. It is usually best to explain these occupancy costs to the prospective tenant when discussing or negotiating the building's rental rate.

The second factor to consider in developing market rental rates is that many hospitals have strict guidelines from regulatory agencies on how they set rents. All must be equalized so as not to give unfair advantage to one physician or practice. Hospitals that lease medical space on their campuses or own MOBs near the hospital campus may lease space at very competitive rates to attract physicians to affiliate with the hospital. A component of the market survey for a MOB must include surveying the rental rates, concessions, operating expense pass-through charges, and TI allowances hospitals offer on space they own along with MOBs that are privately owned.

The Leasing Program

Medical professionals seldom lease large space; most medical and dental suites vary from 1,200 to 5,000 square feet. Hence, few opportunities exist to earn a large commission on one lease.

The process of completing a medical office lease often takes longer than completing other types of office leases. Many medical tenants are group practices, and decisions are often made only at the physicians' or executive team monthly meetings. They may discuss possible relocation during several meetings before arriving at a decision. Most tenants of MOBs engage an attorney to negotiate the lease provisions. In addition, some medical practices are part of a larger medical group, or are owned by the local hospital (health system), which adds another level of decision makers to the process.

When establishing the leasing program, the property owner and the real estate manager must consider many issues: who will do the leasing and where, how the brokerage community can be involved, and how they will handle referrals.

Leasing Office

An on-site management and leasing office is standard for large buildings, but it's a luxury for smaller buildings. If the building does not have an on-site leasing agent, but has an on-site real estate manager or property administrator, that person can assist the leasing agent by showing available space to walk-in prospects and arranging meetings between them and the leasing agent.

Leasing Strategies

Office building leasing agents occasionally represent a medical tenant, and a few will pursue the exclusive listing of a MOB. Many leasing agents do not have the experience, knowledge, contacts, or the desire to lease MOBs. There are some office building agents who will add either representing medical professionals or listing MOBs to their practice.

An alternative to working with an office building leasing agent is an investment broker whose client base is predominantly physicians. Many communities have a few independent investment brokers who represent medical professionals in their real estate investments. These brokers can be connected in the medical community, and they are aware of which physicians and group practices are looking for additional space, adding physicians, or splitting up.

Another approach to leasing MOBs is to hire an in-house leasing agent who devotes all or a portion of his or her time to leasing the MOB. This person is usually compensated with a base salary and an incentive for each executed lease. Most MOBs are not of sufficient size for an in-house leasing agent.

A final option is to assign the leasing responsibility to the real estate or property manager. Real estate managers can effectively lease the last 10 to 20 percent of a new building or re-lease existing vacancies in a building, but they seldom have the time to lease a building with excessive vacant space. The real estate manager or in-house leasing agents can handle lease renewals effectively because they have the opportunity to develop a relationship with the tenants and understand their needs.

Working with the Brokerage Community

The brokerage community, an important element in an office building's marketing plan, is not nearly as active as co-brokering leases for MOBs. Many commercial brokerage firms do not have a leasing agent who specializes in MOBs because this specialty market has limited space and prospects in comparison to the traditional office, industrial, or retail markets. A couple of firms may have one or two leasing agents who will add this specialty to their office leasing practice.

Since medical space is a submarket, many office building leasing agents are not familiar with rental rates, TI requirements and allowances, and concessions for medical space. However, the real estate manager or leasing agent of a MOB can develop an effective flow of communication with the office building brokerage community by establishing a working relationship with several leasing agents.

Sending quarterly e-mail updates to each office building leasing agent summarizing the building's occupancy and vacancy status, and listing each vacant space and its asking rate keeps brokers aware of the leasing opportunities in the building. This information is essential because MOBs often experience market conditions that are different from those of the office building market. For instance, the office building market may be soft and have a 10 percent vacancy rate while the MOB market may be strong and have a four percent vacancy rate. The developer and/or owner of MOB may not be willing or required to offer an extensive concession package.

Medical space is likely to have a higher base rent due to the higher cost of finishing out the space and higher building operating costs. Reassure the leasing agents that their position in the transaction and their commission will be protected if they follow the building's procedure for registering a prospective tenant. Since most office building leasing agents do not lease MOBs, offering a commission rate greater than those for office buildings attracts their attention.

For example, when a MOB lost a tenant that occupied 30 percent of the building, the owner of the MOB offered the brokerage community a commission 25 percent greater than that of most office buildings. This incentive commission was highlighted in the building's leasing flyer, and e-mails were sent to all the office building leasing agents in the county. Several leasing agents called the manager of the MOB inquiring about the building's vacant spaces, their rental rates, and the terms of the incentive commission. The incentive commission got the brokerage community's attention, and the vacated space was re-leased within six months.

Leasing Referrals

Medical professionals frequently consult with other medical professionals, and medical tenants often refer other medical professionals to the building's manager. The building manager might consider developing a referral program that offers tenants a fee or gift for referring prospects who sign a lease. Check the real estate laws and healthcare laws such as the *Health Insurance Portability and Accountability Act (HIPAA)* to ensure a fee or incentive gift provided to a non-real estate licensee or a medical professional is appropriate, ethical, and legal.

Cold Calling

Cold calling, one of the basic leasing techniques for office buildings, industrial properties, and shopping centers, can have mixed results in leasing MOBs. Physicians seldom have time to meet with an unexpected salesperson. The business or practice manager of the medical practice is often too busy for unannounced calls. These calls do allow the leasing agent the opportunity to leave marketing materials for the medical professional and the business manager. Cold calling by telephone to the physician's business manager is a good follow-up to sending mailers and Internet communications.

Leasing Meetings

Regularly scheduled leasing meetings are an important component of a leasing program. During the lease-up of a new building, the meetings should be held weekly or biweekly. A monthly leasing meeting is usually adequate for an existing building with a normal vacancy rate. An effective meeting must have an agenda and a leader. Agenda items include the inventory of space to lease, status of leases in process, a discussion of deal points, prospective tenants, results of recent marketing, advertising, and promotional activities, and plans for additional activities.

The leasing agents submit a leasing report at each meeting. The typical report lists space available, space leased, lease rates, TI expenses, a list of the deals in progress, a list of prospective tenants, and a comparison of the amount of TI dollars that was budgeted and the amount that is remaining. If any tenants have lease restrictions, such as exclusives, first right of refusal, options, space pockets, and so on, these should be on a separate report that members of the leasing team reviews at each meeting. A floor plan of each floor designating the vacancies and each tenant's space is attached to the report. This report is called a stacking plan. A leasing control book with the same information can be provided at the meeting.

Leasing Control Book

A leasing control book consists of floor plans of each floor and lease restrictions. A floor plan is prepared and regularly updated for each floor. The occupied space is crosshatched and the vacant areas unmarked. Such floor plans provide the leasing team with a quick, easy reference when they discuss specific prospective tenants and the building's marketing plan. The control book also includes a listing of lease restrictions. They are usually imposed on the property owner, and if violated, they can be costly. These restrictions include tenants' options, expansion rights such as first right of refusal for additional space, space pockets, exclusives, and occupancy limitations (e.g., minimum percentage of the building that must be leased to physicians). These restrictions are listed together on one master page and on each pertinent floor plan. A summary of the asking rents, pass-through charges, and other tenant expenses are included.

Lease Negotiations

As previously mentioned, leasing space to a physician or medical group often takes longer than leasing space to an office, industrial, or retail tenant. A physician's time is more limited than the average businessperson's, and the process from the initial contact to showing space, lease negotiations, and space planning can take longer than leasing for another use. When the tenant is a medical group, the decision to relocate or expand a practice is a group decision. Each member of the group or a majority of the group must be sold on the new space. The group's business meeting may be held weekly or monthly, and the leasing decision may be delayed until the next meeting. Physicians and medical groups are likely to use an attorney to negotiate the lease, which adds another player to the lease transaction.

Several lease provisions of particular importance to medical professionals and owners of MOBs are essential components of the lease negotiations. Each provision should be aligned with a priority of importance and economic value by the building owner, which will assist in negotiating those respective points with a potential tenant. Those provisions are discussed in the next sections. Several other lease provisions are discussed in *Chapter 10: Negotiating the Commercial Lease.*

Right to Cancel

A solo or two-physician practice may insist on the right to cancel the lease if a physician becomes disabled or dies. A sole-practicing physician is concerned that death or disability would eliminate the practice and burden his or her estate or family members with a lease obligation. A two-physician practice may be concerned that the space would be too large for the surviving physician. Many owners of MOBs are willing to accommodate this request. The property owner should request at least a 90-day advance notice of the cancellation by the physician's estate or the surviving partner. An owner who has invested considerable funds into TIs may require a cancellation fee. Typically, the fee is the unamortized portion of the TIs, the cost of a commission to re-lease the space, and a specified number of months' rent.

An alternative would be to have the physician take out a life insurance policy with proceeds paid to the property owner equal to the previously mentioned costs. Another option for the estate of the deceased physician or a physician who becomes disabled is to sell the practice. To keep the option of selling the practice open, a physician or a physician's estate will want to negotiate the right but *not* the obligation to cancel or assign the lease.

A viable alternative to closing a medical or dental practice is for the medical or dental professional or its estate to sell the practice. If this were to occur the medical professional acquiring the practice may want to extend the lease term. This is usually the best alternative for the tenants and the owner.

Assignment

Physicians—especially those who are in the later years of their practices—may want the right to assign the lease if they sell the practice. The standard commercial lease's requirement for assignment would apply to a lease with a physician. The property owner must be certain that the assignee has the ability to continue the practice successfully and to fulfill all the tenant's lease obligations—especially the payment of rent.

A group practice may want the right to release and add physicians as signatories to the lease. For instance, one physician may retire from a practice and sell her share to another physician. The retiring physician will want to be released from any lease obligations. If the replacement practice is successful and has an acceptable net worth, replacing one guarantee with another should not create problems for the property owner. Consideration should be given to the acquiring physician or medical group and their ability to continue to offer like or similar services and to avoid an expansion.

Occupancy Restrictions

Some medical tenants, such as pharmacies, medical labs, and specialties may request that the property owner lease no less than a certain percentage of the building to physicians. Conceding to this request may be necessary to obtain specific tenants, such as a pharmacy. These tenants are concerned that if the building is tenanted predominantly by such professionals as dentists and counselors, they will not receive sufficient referrals. The pharmacy may depend on physicians in the building for most of its business, and the medical labs and physicians with specialties may need a percentage of their business to come from referrals from physicians in the building.

The property owner should avoid such lease restrictions whenever possible, but if granting such a restriction is necessary, the lease should state the limits of the tenant's damages should the restriction be violated. For instance, the pharmacy rent might convert from a minimum base rent versus a percentage of sales to percentage rent only. Other tenants with such a lease provision might receive a reduced rent. The tenant should not be entitled to monetary damages. When the lease restriction is no longer being violated the tenant loses the concessions.

Exclusives

Specialists such as plastic surgeons, imaging firms, and physical therapists may ask for an *exclusive*—a right granted to the tenant that restricts the owner from leasing space to tenants that provide similar services. They base their request on the need for referrals within the building. An imaging firm will request an exclusive because of the high cost to purchase MRIs and other imaging equipment. From a practical perspective, it is not likely the building will lease to a second imaging firm. Property owners must carefully consider each request for an exclusive. Having several exclusives in a building limits the number of potential tenants. An unintentional violation of a tenant's exclusive can be costly to the building owner.

Two types of tenants that may justifiably request an exclusive are a pharmacy and a tenant that spends significant amounts of money for specialized equipment. If a building does not have good walk-by traffic, a pharmacy's business will depend on the patients of the physicians in the building. Granting a limited exclusive may be the only way to attract a pharmacy to lease space in the building. The exclusive should not apply to physicians providing medication to their patients. Other medical tenants that may request an exclusive are specialists. When a radiology group spends millions of dollars on specialty equipment, the physicians want to be sure they will have the sole opportunity to solicit referrals from the physicians in the building. When a medical professional such as a plastic surgeon or a physical therapist is starting a new practice, he or she may want to limit the competition in the building. Are existing tenants excluded in the exclusive provision?

An existing tenant's use provision may be broad and the tenant may add a service that violates another tenant's exclusive. When an exclusive is being negotiated, the leasing team needs to review existing tenant's use provisions.

An alternative to providing an exclusive for the full term of the lease is to provide an exclusive for the first year or two. This allows the physician or therapist time to develop a relationship with the physicians in the building and to solicit referrals. If an exclusive must be given, the provision should state the remedy the tenant has if the exclusive is violated. The remedy should *not* include monetary damages. The tenant may be offered a rent reduction or the right to cancel the lease if the lease violation cannot be corrected during a specific period. However, the best policy is not to grant exclusives, and if that is not practical, limit the number of exclusives provided. Exclusivity may come with rent premium if market conditions permit, as it limits the potential pool of tenants the building owner may attract.

Other Provisions

When presenting a suite in a MOB to a tenant, the real estate manager should discuss the building's policy on such important issues as placement of lab pick-up boxes, delivery, and acceptance of packages by building personnel, over-standard utilities, after-hours utility use, and after-hours building access. The handling of hazardous and medical wastes is a serious matter that the lease must address. If the prospective tenant is a retailer, such as a pharmacy, restaurant, or gift shop, the lease may include the following retail lease provisions: percentage rent, sales reporting, sales audit, hours of operation, continuous operation provision, signage (including window signage), no going-out-of-business sale, merchandise delivery, trash removal, and pest control.

The lease should address special requirements of the tenant's use and occupancy of the premises. These may include the following:

1. Special plumbing and electrical requirements
2. Requirements for proper installation, insulation, and filtering for electronic, electromagnetic, and X-ray equipment
3. Floor load or capacity to accommodate heavy equipment, such as medical records storage systems for practices that have not converted to electronic records
4. Elimination of noise or unpleasant odors
5. Accommodating vibrating equipment
6. Storage and removal of medical waste
7. Area for medical gases such as oxygen, nitrogen, and nitrous oxide
8. Emergency generator for medical professionals who perform surgery or have patients receiving treatment on special medical equipment, such as a dialysis machine
9. Storage of flammables and combustibles
10. Fire-resistant construction and/or automatic fire-extinguishing systems for spaces such as surgery rooms
11. Dedicated parking for physicians
12. If applicable, determine who takes responsibility for on-going care and record keeping of building systems encompassed in meeting the requirements of the varying regulatory compliance agencies, such as Joint Commission and Center for Medicaid and Medicaid Services

MARKETING MATERIALS

The marketing effort requires the development of brochures, flyers, and newsletters that create interest in the MOB and aid in its promotion.

Brochures

Four-color multi-page brochures present a prestigious image for a new building. Brochures should present all the features of the building, sample floor plates, locator map, photographs or elevation rendering of the building, description of the area, locations of hospitals and clinics in the area, and description of the building and the development team. Brochures are typically used for new MOBs and most existing buildings have an electronic flyer.

Flyers

A one-page glossy flyer is usually sufficient to promote an existing building. These flyers will have a photo or rendering of the building along with its name and address on one page. The other page will have a sample floor plate, possibly a small locator map highlighting the building's proximity to hospitals and freeways, a list of the building's tenants who serve physicians and their patients (e.g., pharmacy, medical and dental labs), and information regarding the leasing agent. These flyers can be produced with desktop publishing software and sent by e-mail. A few hard copies are printed and available for walk-in prospects.

Newsletters

A newsletter targeted to the medical and brokerage community is an effective way to promote a building. A list of physicians in the area can be obtained from the local medical/dental association's directories. Copies of the newsletter may be e-mailed to the hospital administrator and medical equipment supplier. These newsletters are especially effective during the construction and initial lease-up of a building. Stories are written on four major themes: (1) construction progress, (2) leasing progress, (3) profiles of new tenants, and (3) ongoing management and tenant relation issues.

The construction theme highlights the stages of construction—from breaking ground to the grand opening—with photographs and stories. Photos of unusual features of tenants' suites under construction are eye-catchers, and stories can describe special building materials, the construction timeline, and the procedures for building tenants' suites.

The leasing theme highlights specific leases signed, tenants' arrivals, and a statement of the percentage and the amount of space leased and occupied. Brief articles might also highlight a physician or medical group's practice or contribution to the community.

The newsletter can easily become a real estate manager's marketing tool for re-leasing the building and a component of the building's tenant retention program. Once the building is completed, the newsletter can present management issues, such as a review of the building's life-safety system and recycling program.

ADVERTISING

Real estate managers can use several methods of advertising to promote new and existing MOBs. Real estate managers advertise based upon the size, location, current market conditions, and marketing budget for all space—not just new buildings or construction. In many instances, the older the building, or if a building has recently been repositioned, a large advertising campaign will occur to promote the building.

Direct Mailing

A list of physicians, medical groups, and dentists can be obtained from local medical and dental associations. Brochures, flyers, and newsletters can be efficiently e-mailed to a MOB's primary group of prospective tenants.

Media Advertising

Many physicians support the performing arts. Metropolitan areas often have a magazine publisher that announces symphony, opera, and theater programs. Advertising in these programs can be a cost-effective way to reach the building's target audience in a prestigious publication. Other effective publications for ads are the annual directory and newsletters of the local or state medical and dental associations, as well as the monthly publications of prominent athletic clubs and business journals.

Signage

During the early stages of the development of a new or renovated MOB, a planned and coordinated signage program should start when the building's permits are obtained and the construction loan for the building is committed. If a "Coming Soon" sign is placed on the site too early, and the development of the building is delayed, the community will think the proposed building will never be built. This is especially true if the sign displays a building construction commencement or completion date that has not been met.

The initial construction sign might include a large photo of the rendering of the building and the names of the development team members: developer, general contractor, important subcontractors, lender, and property management firm. The leasing company and the leasing agent's name and phone number should be prominent on the sign. The names of tenants who have signed leases can be added to the sign or placed on an adjacent sign. A sign placed prominently on the building can give a running progress of the construction by saying, "Six months to complete," then "Five months to complete," and so on. The sign can also provide a running account of the percentage of building completion. Using the sign creates interest in the general community and informs prospective tenants who are delaying lease negotiations that time is running out for the best selection of floor area locations.

While the building is under construction and during the initial lease-up, a "For Lease" banner might be hung across the top of the building and "For Lease" paper window signs might be placed around the building. If the building has an on-site leasing agent or real estate manager, the sign should state "Leasing representative on site." A monument sign with the building's name, address, and leasing information with a phone number and e-mail address should be placed in front of the building. The building's directory may include a section on the top or bottom devoted to leasing information, with leasing listed under the letter "L" and under the management office's listing.

Existing buildings also require an effective leasing sign as part of an overall marketing plan to retain existing tenants attract physicians to the building.

PUBLIC RELATIONS (PR)

Several events can be used as public relations (PR) stories during construction, such as announcing plans to develop the building, grand opening, selection of a leasing agent, appointment of a real estate manager, and leases signed. Other stories can feature unique building designs, the demand for medical space (especially if the office building market is soft), a profile of the developer, or a profile of a unique medical practice with state-of-the-art equipment. An appropriate photo should accompany PR stories. The leasing agent might consider inviting the real estate or business editor of a local newspaper or business journal to lunch to discuss the history of the site and the development plans as well as to schedule a tour of the site or building.

Promotional Events

For new development, one of the first promotional events is a ground-breaking ceremony with dignitaries such as the mayor or city council members, the hospital administrator, prominent citizens, and other business leaders in the neighborhood. Hard-hat tours during construction for leasing agents, the media, prospective tenants, and dignitaries provide an excellent means to get attention for the building. A pre-opening party for tenants, prospective tenants, and selected members of the medical and business community is a way to present the "new" building. Management could also schedule the grand opening with the tenants' open houses as a major coordinated event. Since many physicians and medical groups depend on referrals, they may want the medical community to visit their new facilities. The real estate manager or the leasing agent might provide a presentation of the new building to community groups such as the Chamber of Commerce, business and social groups, and homeowners' associations.

Developing Relationships with Hospitals

Hospitals depend on physicians for patient referrals. They are constantly soliciting physicians to affiliate with them. When a physician agrees to affiliate with a hospital, he or she may need medical office space. The real estate manager should develop a rapport with the hospital administrator. The leasing agent or real estate manager of a MOB should keep the hospital administrator or physician relationship recruitment manager aware of space available in the building. "Space available" flyers should be sent to the administrator with a request to post a copy on the bulletin board in the physician's lounge.

REAL ESTATE MANAGEMENT

A growing number of investment groups and *real estate investments trusts (REITs)* specialize in investing in larger MOBs. Such firms often use third-party management firms to manage buildings they own in areas where they do not have sufficient buildings to warrant providing their own property management services. Smaller MOBs are owned by local investors or medical professionals. The great majority of MOBs are smaller, providing management and leasing opportunities for real estate management companies.

Seldom is the MOB market large enough for a real estate management firm to manage only MOBs. MOB management is often considered a second niche for a typical real estate management firm. Opportunities may exist to provide outsourcing services such as facility management to hospitals and other medical institutions that own MOBs. These services can range from full real estate management and leasing services to a menu of services from which the outsource client may chose. The services may include the following:

1. Conducting market surveys and recommending building rental rates
2. Locating sites and negotiating contracts for clinics
3. Renewing existing tenants' leases
4. Developing a tenant-retention program
5. Auditing leases to ensure tenants are billed correctly for all charges
6. Providing facility management services for the hospital's clinics
7. Reviewing service contracts
8. Performing governmental compliance surveys
9. Developing emergency procedures
10. Performing a security audit

Medical Building Features

Even though janitorial services, emergency procedures, and TIs are found in all office buildings, those issues take on an added dimension and complexity for MOBs. A MOB may have some or all of the following features not commonly found in the typical office building:

1. One extra-large elevator to accommodate a gurney
2. Specialized medical equipment that requires reinforced floors to accommodate the weight
3. Shielding for X-ray equipment
4. Large signage area in the garage and the building's common areas to accommodate sight-impaired patients
5. Directories in the main lobby and at each suite's entryway with both the medical or dental practice's name and each physician's or dentist's name clearly displayed
6. Directories at each elevator lobby and down lengthy corridors
7. Patient drop-off and pickup areas in front of the building and/or in the parking area
8. Emergency power for physicians performing surgery and for patient equipment (e.g., dialysis machines)
9. "Physicians only" parking spaces in the garage or parking lot
10. Storage area for medical waste containers and lab sample containers
11. Enclosed and secured storage areas for files, supplies, and medications
12. Wide halls to accommodate stretchers and gurneys
13. Railings in hallways at the height of the gurneys to protect the walls
14. Enhanced building security system
15. Additional entry doors that open automatically for wheelchairs
16. Nonskid entry lobby and corridor flooring
17. Waiting area in the building lobby
18. Lobby area wheelchair storage closet or alcove
19. Higher quality of *heating, ventilation, and air-conditioning (HVAC)* equipment

Medical Office Space Planning

Medical professionals are searching for operational efficiencies and exploring ways to reduce their occupancy costs. Increased efficiency is among the selling points used to convince a medical professional or medical group to relocate to a particular MOB. A component of an efficient medical practice is a well-planned space design. The number and layout of exam rooms, design of the support staff's work areas, and comfortable waiting area directly impact the number of patients that can be seen, efficiency of the staff, and patients' comfort and trust.

The new space plan may be designed for a more efficient layout for special equipment. The back of the house or business facilities, such as the business office, staff lounge, restrooms, storage area, and equipment room must also be efficiently designed into the space. Private offices for each physician are no longer common. More efficient operations result in less waiting time for each patient allowing for smaller waiting rooms. Electronic records have eliminated the need for large record storage areas. MOB space planners are designing spaces that efficiently support new technology and new methods of patient treatment.

Interview several space planners and architects who specialize in space planning for medical professionals. Some physicians and other medical professionals will have a space planner they prefer, while others will have limited understanding of the space-planning process. After selecting space-planning firms, the real estate manager will have one or several space planners to refer to prospective tenants. The building provides an allowance for space planning based on cost per square foot or on a fixed dollar amount that may be deducted from the TI allowance provided to build out the space. Another approach is to provide preliminary space planning free as part of the building's marketing program. Medical professionals' needs may include services related to space planning, such as the selection and layout of furniture and equipment, selection of colors and materials, signage throughout the suite, artwork, and telephone and computer systems. Meet with the prospective tenant to assess these needs and direct the design assessment and process.

The Space-Planning Design Team

The tenant may assemble the design team or rely on the real estate manager to do so. The team may consist only of the real estate manager and the medical professional who decide what modifications are necessary in an existing suite, or it may be a full design team. Minor alterations to an existing suite would be least expensive for the building owner and the medical professional. The full design team approach is more expensive for everyone; however, medical professionals seldom move, so the extra expense may be warranted.

Constructing an office is a long-term investment, and the costs can be amortized over several years. A full design team consists of (1) the tenant; (2) possibly the tenant's representative, who could be the office manager and/or the leasing agent; (3) possibly a family member of the tenant; (4) real estate manager; (5) architect or space planner; (6) interior designer; (7) TI contractor, and (8) the tenant's medical equipment representative. Some team members can serve multiple roles. For instance, the space planner may also provide design services.

The Space-Planning Process

The space-planning process requires an understanding of the needs of the medical professional. The space planner and the medical professional meet to discuss the space requirements of the practice and how the medical professional operates his or her practice and the medical equipment requirements. One of the objectives of the meeting is to review how the space can be efficiently designed to be cost effective to build, increase efficiencies in the operations for the medical practice, and reduce the medical practice's overhead. The space-planning and construction process includes the following phases:

1. Programming
2. Schematic design

3. Design development
4. Construction documents
5. Bidding and negotiations
6. Construction
7. Move-in

First, the space planner assesses the needs of the medical professional and develops a schematic design based on those needs. After refinement, a final design is developed and construction documents are prepared for bidding. Once the contract is created with the selected contractor to make TIs, the construction commences. Space planners may also provide interior design services, which include selecting colors, materials, furniture, and furniture layout. If the space planner is aligned with an architectural firm, project management may also be offered.

The entire process, from the first space-planning interview to the move-in usually takes two to six months. The space-planning process is often the first opportunity for the tenant to work with the real estate manager and the building's consultants. A qualified and responsive design team provides the new tenant with a positive initial impression of the building and its staff. This is the first step in establishing a cooperative and pleasant long-term relationship between the tenant and the building's staff.

Tenant Improvements (TIs)

The build-out of the TIs can be an exciting time for medical professionals and their staff, or it can be a disastrous experience with change orders, cost overruns, construction delays, and unfulfilled expectations. The foundation for a positive experience is good communication. The real estate manager, tenant, architect, space planner, and TI contractor must be clear on the scope of the TIs, cost, and construction timeline. A strong team relationship must exist among the real estate manager, contractor, medical professional, and consultants. Good communication and teamwork eliminate surprises, unnecessary delays, and unauthorized cost overruns.

Cost Estimates for Tenant Improvements (TIs)

There a number of construction execution delivery models included spec/build where architectural/engineering plans are fully developed, bid, and performed by a qualified contractor. Design build is an alliance between the architect and general contractor that is interactive and driven by the overall technical requirements and scope of the project, and can provide overall cost savings. Architectural services in the design build model are generally self performed or contracted by the general contractor with mechanical, electrical, and plumbing drawings developed and prepared by the respective mechanical sub-contractor.

Most TIs are contracted on a cost-plus fixed fee. An alternative is actual cost and a fixed fee with a guaranteed maximum price. Another option is a guaranteed maximum price with any savings shared between the contractor and the party paying for the improvements—usually the tenant.

The contractor develops a preliminary budget when schematic plans are completed. The contractor then meets with the tenant and the architect or space planner to review the cost and discuss value engineering options and cost reduction opportunities. The primary purpose of this meeting is to control cost. Most medical professionals and their business managers are not aware of construction costs. They are often surprised by the costs to build the suite to their expectations. At this time, the contractor solicits input from the mechanical, plumbing, electrical, and other specialty subcontractors. This meeting allows the medical professional and his or her architect, space planner, and interior designer to plan and build an efficient office at a pre-established cost.

The TI cost for a medical suite can be three to five times the cost for a typical office suite. The increased costs are due to building several small examining rooms with sinks, several restrooms, and cabinets in every room as well as possibly providing more extensive HVAC duct work, special utility requirements, and shielding in the walls for X-ray equipment.

The cost to build out a medical suite may exceed the building's allowance. Medical professionals are often required to pay a substantial portion of their TIs. Real estate managers should require tenants to sign off on plans for their spaces so the tenants can be held accountable if something is installed in the wrong place.

Construction Schedule

After all parties have reviewed and modified the schematic plans and the cost estimates, construction plans are prepared and final bids are obtained, reviewed, and approved. The construction plans are submitted to the city's building department. The time it takes for the plans to be approved will vary depending upon the staffing of the building department and the department's work loan. A building permit can take a couple of weeks to a couple of months to be issued by the city's building department. The general contractor or architect should inquire of the building department how long it will take to obtain a building permit. The time to obtain the building period must be added to the timeline to complete the construction of the TIs.

A construction schedule is prepared that incorporates the delivery and installation of medical and office equipment and the tenant's move-in. Construction meetings are recommended to ensure electrical and plumbing are in the right places—especially before the drywall is installed. The municipality's building department will inspect different phases of the job and issue a certificate of occupancy.

After the work has been completed, the real estate manager, contractor, and space planner walk the space with the tenant and develop a construction *punch list.* At that time, the real estate manager should also obtain the builder's warranties and explain them to the tenant. Typically, the construction of a medical office suite takes two to four months, depending on the size, scope, and complexity of the work. Occasionally, state regulatory agencies must provide pre- and/or post-construction approvals and inspections.

Contractor Rules and Regulations

TI construction can be a major disturbance to adjacent tenants and patients. The real estate manager should develop rules and regulations for TI contractors. A sample list of rules and regulations a real estate manager might use during construction is shown in Exhibit 5.1.

EXHIBIT 5.1

BROADWAY MEDICAL CENTER

Sample Rules and Regulations during Construction

Physicians treat patients throughout the day. Our goal is to keep the disruption and noise to a minimum. It is imperative that all comply with the following rules:

1. NO SMOKING in the building or garage areas.
2. NO RADIOS in the work area.
3. NO TRANSFER OR DELIVERY of construction materials through the lobby entrances.
4. NO PARKING in the three-minute parking areas intended for patient load/unload zones on Broadway.
5. NO PARKING/NO ACCESSING PARKING TO A & B GARAGE LEVELS.
6. NO PROPPING OR JAMMING of normally locked doors. Contact building management for access.
7. DAILY MAINTENANCE of construction area and delivery areas on C level of the parking garage is expected.

EXHIBIT 5.1 *(CONTINUED)*

8. DUMPSTERS must be brought into C level for construction trash. NO TRASH MAY BE STOCKPILED in the vacant spaces.
9. NO CORE DRILLING OR ROTO HAMMERING between 8:00 a.m. and 8:00 p.m.
10. NEGATIVE AIR PRESSURE shall be implemented before and maintained throughout the construction build-out.
11. SEGREGATION of construction dust and maintaining appropriate negative air pressure may require temporary construction walls/doors.
12. OBNOXIOUS ODORS, which include paint and glue, must be isolated within the construction area through proper ventilation or such work must be completed after building hours by arrangement with the building management.
13. When doing work that affects the FIRE ALARM SYSTEM of the building:
    - NOTIFY building management and SIGN IN prior to onset of work.
    - COMPLETE work that affects the fire alarm system NO LATER THAN 2:30 p.m.
    - NOTIFY building management and SIGN OUT following completion of work.
    - EXPECT TO STAY on the job until building management can confirm that the building's fire alarm system is clear.
14. TESTING/INSPECTIONS of the alarm system will be conducted, at contractor's cost, by ABC Equipment Company, which will require coordination through building management three to four business days prior to your inspection.
15. The building management office must approve CHANGE ORDERS.
16. MATERIAL SAFETY DATA SHEETS (MSDS) must be submitted to the building manager for all hazardous material, including nature of the material and when it will be used.
17. DAMAGE caused by contractor/subcontractors and/or deliveries must be repaired.
18. COMPLETED CONSTRUCTION MUST BE APPROVED by the building management.
19. Contractors and sub-contractors shall use DESIGNATED LAVATORY FACILTIES.
20. IDENTIFICATION BADGES should be worn by all contractors, sub-contractors, and suppliers.
21. DESIGNATED PARKING AREAS should be used by all contractors, sub-contractors, and suppliers.

Financing Medical Practices

Almost every community has a bank or banks with loan officers who specialize in providing financial services for medical professionals. These services can include business and personal loans and company banking. Real estate managers who manage medical office buildings should consider developing a relationship with lenders who specialize in financial services to medical practitioners. A physician new to the area or one establishing a practice may not be aware of the lenders in the community who specialize in accommodating their financial needs.

Medical practitioners are usually considered a low-credit risk because few physicians default on their loans. If their practices are not successful, they can maintain good earnings by teaching or by working for a hospital, medical group, or HMO. Loans for physicians and medical groups are usually for establishing a practice, purchasing new equipment, or financing TIs for existing or additional space or new premises. When a physician purchases new medical technology, he or she may need to pay for part or all of the equipment before it is delivered. Long lead times for delivery can take more than 30 days; the staff may require an additional 30 days to become familiar with the use of the equipment and to schedule appointments; and 30 to 60 days may elapse after an appointment before the physician receives payment for services. Three to five months may pass before income is received from use of the equipment.

The gap between the time the equipment is purchased and the time revenue is received must be considered when the physician discusses financing new equipment. Banks may prefer to loan TI funds directly to the physician instead of to the building owner if they specialize in loans to the healthcare industry rather than to developers or real estate loans. In addition, the lender may prefer to handle all the physician's financing needs, including his or her personal banking. The loan is often at a preferred interest rate because of the security of the loan and the low physician default rate. This is especially true when the loan is to a medical group of three or more physicians.

The physician or physicians may fully or partially, personally or corporately, guarantee the loan. The lender may collateralize the loan through an assignment of the physician's receivables. Another form of collateralization requires the physician to name the bank as the beneficiary on the physician's disability and/or life insurance policy.

Relocating a Medical Practice

Moving a practice is a major undertaking for a physician or a medical group and its staff. Medical practices seldom move, and the physicians and their staffs may have limited experience in moving. The real estate manager should be aware of the challenges the medical practice may encounter and be available to offer assistance.

The first question to ask the physician(s) or a medical group considering the relocation is the reason for the move. The following lists some common reasons for relocating a medical practice:

- It has outgrown its present space
- Seeking a more efficient space and building
- Relocation to be closer to a hospital
- Seeking an upgrade from its present facility
- It may be entering a new market or opening a satellite office

The next issue in relocating a medical practice is determining where to move. If the practice is concerned with operating more efficiently, a location closer to the hospitals or one closer to its patient base with convenient access to parking, and an improved space layout will be among its top concerns. If the practice depends on referrals, the physicians will want the new location to have physicians who are likely to provide them with referrals. If having an up-to-date image is important, a new building with amenities, such as an impressive lobby and common areas, pharmacy, medical lab, on-site parking, a better tenant mix for referrals will be essential. Another consideration may be convenience for the patients: location, travel time to the building, and parking.

The third concern is the layout and design of the facilities, how the staff will function in the new layout, and whether the building or the physician will be responsible for the space-planning costs. Financing the move, the cost of TIs, and the purchase of new furniture and equipment is often the responsibility of the medical professional. The medical professional must develop a *pro forma statement* to analyze the practice's monthly income and expense in the new location. A move frequently increases the profitability of the practice.

If the medical practice has a business or practice manager, he or she will be responsible for the analysis and planning of the move. In a solo practice, the physician(s) or nurse(s) may assume these responsibilities; however, they will find it difficult to coordinate the move while also fulfilling their other responsibilities. Patients must be notified of the move and given directions to the new location. Physicians and medical groups who provide referrals must be notified of the new location. A moving company must be selected, and the real estate manager will need to assist in coordinating the move.

Contingent plans must be prepared for the unexpected. The real estate manager should be aware of the challenges and frustrations encountered by the entire staff of a medical practice during a move. By understanding what is involved in a medical practice's relocation, develop a working rapport before the tenant moves into the building, thereby establishing a positive long-term relationship.

Janitorial Service

Managers of MOBs recognize that there are similarities and differences between establishing and implementing a janitorial program. Physicians' suites often have several small rooms outfitted with large equipment. Janitors who work in MOBs receive special health and safety training. They must be able to identify chemicals by the symbols on a container's label. They may be required to wear gloves when handling trash, especially biohazardous trash or infectious waste. Keep a log of all the janitorial and other maintenance requests and complaints.

Special Cleaning Services

Some medical professionals may request and pay extra for higher-level cleaning services than the typical building standards. The request may be to periodically hire another company to detail their office and equipment. If this request is granted, the service must be coordinated with the work of the building's janitorial service and after-hours entry to the building must be arranged. Some MOBs allow the tenants to contract directly for their janitorial service from a list of two or three firms approved by the building management. Terminal cleaning or the clean-up of bodily fluids requires special training and equipment. It's important to understand the frequency and scope of any terminal cleaning requirements and desired response time for clean-ups when selecting a janitorial service provider.

Medical Waste

Medical professionals are instructed to place biohazardous waste in separate containers that are picked up and disposed of by a company specializing in medical waste disposal. The building may have a storage room where each tenant places its containers of medical waste. Each tenant contracts for the pickup of its medical waste, or the building contracts for the service and includes the cost in the pass-through charges to the tenants or bills each tenant separately based on the size of its medical waste container. A firm licensed to dispose of biohazardous and infectious waste removes the tenants' medical waste, while the building's janitorial company disposes of all other waste and trash in the building. The service also needs the ability to clean-up medical bio-substances in the common area on short notice. On-site containment, clean-up, disposal, and appropriate reporting and follow-up equipment/supplies should be stocked.

Mismanagement in handling and disposing of medical waste can result in serious accidents and liability to the building owner, the property management firm, or the janitorial company. The care, custody, and control of medical waste should be placed upon the tenant and document through the lease.

Managing Parking Areas

A parking area for medical professionals must be designed to consider the special needs of patients and physicians. The physicians' parking area should be separate from staff and patient parking and should be close to the building or garage elevators. Medical professionals prefer assigned and reserved parking. This reduces the time it takes them to enter and leave the parking area or garage.

Parking areas for MOBs are larger than those for other office buildings. A MOB parking area has a higher turnover than that of a regular office building. An area should be dedicated for patient drop-off and pickup as well as for cab drivers. If the parking area is covered, or if it is a multi-level garage, the service entrance should have sufficient height for delivery vehicles and possibly trash removal trucks if they must enter the garage.

Many visitors are senior citizens and people with restricted mobility or impaired sight. The parking area may need large, easy-to-read signage, and wider parking stalls to accommodate people with walkers and/or wheelchairs. Each floor might be color coded for visitors' ease in locating their vehicles.

If a fee is charged for parking, the first 10 or 15 minutes may be free for patient drop-off and pickup. Tenants may want to offer validations for the first 30 or 60 minutes.

Security for Medical Offices

The combination of the amount of traffic through a MOB and the drugs kept in the offices creates potential for incidents. Periodic security seminars are usually conducted by the police department, which might include such topics as personal awareness, office safety, and watch programs for office tenants. After-hours building access is another security issue for many medical professionals who might need access. There should be a standard in place for how the building is accessed after hours.

Emergency Procedures

Chapter 17: Safety, Security, and Emergency Procedures provides a comprehensive discussion on developing and implementing emergency procedures for every type of commercial property. The following procedures supplement that information and apply to developing and implementing emergency procedures in MOBs, which often requires evacuating elderly and non-ambulatory patients as well as outpatient surgery patients.

Meet with the local fire department to coordinate an evacuation plan and arrange a meeting with the tenants and the fire department. The fire department will provide suggestions on when and how to properly evacuate the building. Fire departments in different cities endorse various methods for evacuating a building. Exhibit 5.2 illustrates a questionnaire that surveys the tenants' needs during an emergency and requests their work schedules.

EXHIBIT 5.2

BROADWAY MEDICAL CENTER
MEMO

DATE: January 2, 20XX

TO: Drs. Smith and Adams

FROM: Valerie Jackson, Building Manager

RE: EMERGENCY PROCEDURES AND INTERNAL PLANS: CONSIDERATIONS FOR EACH TENANT

To ensure quick, efficient response in the event of an emergency in the Broadway Medical Center, building management must be aware of special considerations that may be unique to your patients or staff. Please complete and return this survey to the management office by February 12, 20XX. We will then schedule the next emergency-preparedness planning meeting. Thank you for your participation.

NAME OF PRACTICE: ____

DATE ____________

Please list the names and contact information of at least two key people from your office who will be responsible for the emergency plans for your premises:

1.____

2.____

If you have decided to interface with another office on your floor for preparedness planning, please list its name: ____

EXHIBIT 5.2 *(CONTINUED)*

EMERGENCY INFORMATION SURVEY

1. Are you likely to have patients under anesthesia? Yes ____ No ____
2. Are you likely to have patients connected to equipment that would need to be transported when moving them? Yes ____ No ____ If so, list the equipment: ______________________________
3. Range of ages of patients: __________
4. Do you have special formalized guidelines that affect your emergency requirements? Yes ____ No ____ If so, please describe: ______________________________
5. Do you have certain surgery days? Yes ____ No ____ If yes, which days: ______________
6. Number of staff required to assist patients unable to evacuate on their own: ____
7. Do you need wheelchairs/gurneys for evacuating patients? Yes ____ No ____ If so, how many? ______ How many do you have available? __________
8. Do you have staff members who are disabled? Yes ____ No ____ If so, describe their specific needs: ______________________
9. Do you have combustible materials on your premises? Yes ____ No ____ If so, describe: ______________________________
10. Other considerations: ______________________________
11. Please complete the schedule below:

Day	Office Hours	Number of Staff on Site	Number of Patients on Site
REGULAR SCHEDULE			
Monday			
Tuesday			
Wednesday			
Thursday			
Friday			
Saturday			
Sunday			
HOLIDAY SCHEDULE			
New Year's Day			
Martin Luther King			
Presidents' Day			
Memorial Day			
Fourth of July			
Labor Day			
Thanksgiving			
Christmas			
Other : ________			
Other : ________			

Real estate managers of MOBs often meet on a regular basis to discuss security and related issues. Representatives of the local hospitals and police departments may attend some of these meetings. The police departments can provide recent crime statistics for the area along with security tips. If your facility is critical in nature, discuss the need to position your property higher on the priority listing for restoration of services and access with local utility providers and emergency response agencies. For instance, documentation of periodic fire alarm drills is a regulatory requirement for some medical practices.

CONCLUSION

The need for operational efficiencies is changing how healthcare is being delivered. Hospitals acquiring medical groups and competing directly with physicians is changing the dynamics of the medical profession. If the trend of hospitals acquiring medical groups continues, the majority of physicians will be employees of hospitals. What will happen to much of the space in MOBs these physicians occupied? These and many other changes in the healthcare industry, along with unanticipated changes in the future, will impact the investment in MOBs. What will be the demand for smaller and older MOBs near hospitals? Will these buildings be leased to different users? Will there be a higher and better use for their site?

The healthcare industry is changing and evolving, and these changes will continue to impact the management, operations, and leasing of every MOB and the entire industry. Some MOBs will benefit from these changes while other will not be able to accommodate the changes in healthcare delivery. Real estate managers and property owners need to monitor how these and other changes are effecting how healthcare is delivered. They need to evaluate how their building(s) can be positioned to benefit from these changes or how these changes can be mitigated. They may determine there are better uses for the building or the site than the existing building. Change will continue to be the operative word for the MOB industry.

CHAPTER

6

Industrial Real Estate Management

Industrial properties have evolved from utilitarian manufacturing buildings to modern, master-planned commercial developments with strict architectural guidelines and common area agreements to assure high levels of maintenance, signage and storage control, and parking and landscape requirements. The modern industrial community has become so attractive that many manufacturing and distribution companies now have their headquarters on site rather than in an expensive class "A" office downtown building. It is not only less expensive for them, but much more convenient to have all of their operations in one building and one site.

Industrial properties vary in function and size and may include such uses as a 1,000-square-foot storage warehouse, an incubator building with many small start-up businesses, a multi-tenanted industrial park encompassing hundreds of acres, research and development parks, and a large single-tenant building. It is not unusual today to see what looks like a campus setting to actually be a large master-planned industrial park.

TYPES OF INDUSTRIAL PROPERTIES

The Urban Land Institute (ULI) and The National Association of Industrial and Office Parks identifies three major types of industrial properties and six sub-sections. Each type of industrial property is discussed in the following sections.

Major Types of Industrial Properties

There are four major types of industrial properties as defined by the Urban Land Institute: (1) industrial areas, (2) industrial parks, (3) planned industrial districts, and (4) planned employment centers. The evolution of the industrial property industry is evident in the definitions of these four types of properties.

Industrial Areas

In older, heavily urbanized areas, large concentrations of freestanding factories, warehouses, and supply yards are frequently found intermixed with commercial and service establishments. Industrial areas are characterized by multi-level masonry construction with a higher level of sight coverage.

Properties in these areas usually have limited management requirements and *triple-net leases (NNN)*. A triple-net lease (NNN) requires the tenant to pay a prorated share of the real estate taxes, insurance, and maintenance for the building.

Many of these industrial areas have evolved throughout the years to become surrounded by communities that eventually become redeveloped into shopping centers, housing, and other community assets, with the industrial tenants and/or owners moving further away from major cities and into the suburbs. For example, just south of San Francisco is a large steel industrial operation that was closed but has now been developed into a large and attractive office complex.

Industrial Parks

The next phase in the evolution of industrial properties was the *industrial park*. Industrial parks were the first assemblage of individual buildings in a planned development. The industrial park has also been known as the business park, office park, and research and development park.

The business park or office park was introduced in part to indicate a variety of industrial and related service activities, but also to de-emphasize the industrial character of many of the occupants. Regardless, the presumption is that the industrial park is a project that has been planned and developed as an optimal environment for industrial occupants.

Planned Industrial Districts

The next stage in the evolution was the master-planned development with restrictions on the design, use, and occupancy of the industrial buildings. A *planned industrial district* may be further described as a suitably located tract of land subdivided and promoted for industrial use by a sponsoring managerial organization. In this sense, "industrial district" connotes a restricted use of improved land and the presence of proprietors who devote themselves to the area's planning and development.

Planned Employment Centers

The final stage in the evolution of industrial properties is the *planned employment center.* The planned employment center includes a variety of offices and service uses to serve the industrial businesses in the master-planned area and in the community at large. The planned employment center is a multiuse district to provide for employment needs of urban areas. It should be self sufficient to the degree that basic employee requirements are provided within its boundaries and are carefully designed to provide an optimal environment for a wide range of commercial and industrial needs. It should be fully integrated with the larger community of which it is a part.

Sub-Sections of the Major Types of Industrial Property

In the book, *Guide to Classifying Industrial Property,* the Urban Land Institute further categorizes industrial properties into the following sub-sections. The National Association of Industrial and Office Properties (NAIOP) has also categorized the industrial buildings in a similar fashion as follows:

Warehouse Distribution

Being the largest category, warehouse distribution encompasses general purpose warehouse, bulk warehouse, heavy distribution, refrigerated distribution, truck terminal, trans-shipment, and rack-supported warehouse. These buildings have ceiling heights of approximately 12 to 32 feet with an office component. Ceiling heights in Industrial buildings are becoming higher to meet the demands of the market.

Manufacturing

The manufacturing classification of industrial properties covers general purpose industrial uses, such as assembly and repair-related processes. It can be of almost any size, but generally has ceiling heights of 10 to 32 feet, along with an office component.

Flex

The third classification is flex warehouse spaces. It covers areas of research and development (R&D), along with offices, retail showrooms, storage areas, data call centers, and service centers. In general, flex warehouse spaces will likely have ceiling heights of 10 to 32 feet.

Multi tenant

Multi-tenant properties are smaller—generally no more than 120,000 square feet. They are often configured in L and U shapes, and they have multiple tenants. Generally, these tenant spaces range between 5,000 and 15,000 square feet. These properties are quite often the locations of start-up companies.

Freight Forwarding

The freight-forwarding warehouse category covers all areas of transportation, including road, rail, water, and air. It is further sub-classified as *intramodal,* which involves truck-to-truck transport, and *intermodal,* which largely involves other means of transportation, such as airplanes and trucks. Obviously, these uses will have a great interest in being close to freeways, maybe shipping and possibly air transportation.

Data Switch Center

Data switch centers encompass two facility types: (1) a data warehouse and (2) a switch center. While they are quite similar in nature, the data warehouse has a higher need for more energy usage. In the future, this type of facility will become much more common.

MEASURING INDUSTRIAL SPACE

Space measurement can become an issue if the property owner does not provide the tenant with specific information on how the space was measured. The most accurate measurements are done by a *computer aided design (CAD)* program. However, the property owners of many older buildings do not have the advantage of such a system. While re-measuring an older building can be expensive, it has the potential for eliminating a costly dispute with a tenant once the lease is signed. Many older building were built from specific plans, but the final square footage figures are often not accurate due to changes in the construction. These changes can create new square footage or eliminate square footage that was on the original plans. It's important to remember that every calculation in the lease agreement hinges on the square footage of the building. If the calculation is wrong, the rents will be wrong, and common area bill backs will also be wrong.

The most commonly used standard is found in BOMA/NAIOP *Industrial Floor Measurement Standard 2012*. The standard offers two approaches for establishing the rentable area in industrial buildings: method A and method B.

Method A: Exterior Wall Methodology

The *exterior wall methodology*, known as "method A," is used to determine the rentable area in industrial buildings. In a single-floor building, the rentable area is the gross building area. The *gross building area* is the area between the exterior walls on all four sides extending from the ground to the roof line. Fully enclosed accessory buildings such as power plants, repair shops, garages, warehouses, laboratories, and other structures are considered part of the plan—provided they are used primarily for such industrial activities and are included in the total floor area.

In multiple-occupancy floor areas, the rentable area is reserved for the exclusive use of the tenant plus a proportionate share of the building common areas. Method A is by far the most common approach to the measurement of space in the operation of industrial properties.

Method B: Drip-Line Methodology

The *drip-line methodology*, referred to as method B, is measured by the point lying beyond the exterior wall lying within the same vertical plane as the outside edge of an overhang or portion of the building roof system—hence, the "drip line."

In multiple-occupancy floors or buildings, the rentable area is the tenant's area plus a proportionate share of the building common areas. The mezzanine area and exclusions are treated the same in both approaches:

- Mezzanine floors may or may not be included in the floor area depending on the definition and local conditions. Generally, if the mezzanine is finished for offices or work areas and/or is air conditioned, it is considered part of the leasable area.
- Exclusions from floor areas generally include canopies and covered staging platforms; unenclosed connecting links; unenclosed exterior staircases or fire escapes; exterior steps and landings (if outside the measure line); and unenclosed shipping/receiving platforms beyond the measure line.

Regardless of the methodology used to measure the industrial space, the end result should be an accurate measurement and the tenant should understand how it was done. There should also be an agreement via lease language on the square footage of the leased space.

EVALUATING THE NEEDS OF INDUSTRIAL TENANTS

Industrial tenants have a wide variety of space needs, ranging from incubator space of less than 1,000 square feet to hundreds of thousands of square feet for manufacturing and distribution. The following lists what the real estate manager must assess when determining tenants' space requirements:

- Zoning classifications
- Size and configuration of the building
- Outside storage and parking
- Fire sprinkler system
- General utility capacity for larger manufacturing companies
- Amount of floor area, column spacing, floor load capacities

- Ceiling heights are increasing and of great interest to many industrial tenants
- Ratio of warehouse space to office space
- Truck loading facilities, rail spur, and access to the airport, freeway, and shipping ports
- Truck turn around space is quite important to many industrial tenants

SELF-SERVICE STORAGE

Many self-service storage facilities are developed on industrial-zoned properties. A self-storage facility is a rental property with individual storage units, each with its own door. The tenant normally provides the lock, keeps the key, and handles the goods to be stored. The flexible design of the buildings often allows them to accommodate odd-shaped parcels to be built under freeways or to be used as a buffer between heavier industrial uses and office or residential areas. Many of these self-storage facilities also have exterior, uncovered storage for boats, RVs, and specialty trailers.

Significant development changes have occurred since the self-storage concept originated more than 40 years ago. Self-storage facilities were first developed in the 1960s to meet the storage needs of businesses and residents. The original concept was to provide less-costly storage space that was managed much like apartment buildings. Today, such facilities commonly have a small office for daytime leasing and management activities.

For self-storage leasing, break-ins are a common concern. An electronic sensing alarm system connected to a direct-dial system to alert a central station or the police is a good way to maintain security. This system can be tied to a card-operated entry system to allow for late-hour entry, or the entire system can be closed at a given hour and secured by the system.

Retail and self storage have proven to be a good combination in some circumstances. A store located on a busy street can generate income and high traffic on the front of the property, while storage facilities occupy the less expensive back areas.

MANAGEMENT RESPONSIBILITIES

The industrial tenant focuses on such features as location—including access to the highway system and other forms of transportation—labor pool, prevailing wages, site zoning, availability of common carriers, ceiling heights, loading facilities, floor load capacities, clear span areas within the buildings, utility needs, and other physical requirements. The effective real estate manager works to meet these needs while maintaining an environment that is pleasing to existing tenants, prospective tenants, and the surrounding neighborhood. The management of industrial property ranges from a single-tenant building with a triple-net lease to the multiuse industrial development.

The management responsibilities for a building with a triple-net tenant consist primarily of collecting rent, monitoring the tenant's lease requirements,insuring the building, paying real estate taxes, ensuring building maintenance standards, and communicating with the tenant. Generally, the real estate manager regularly walks the building to be sure the tenant is complying with lease requirements. It is a good idea to schedule an annual inspection of the building so the real estate manager can see electrical rooms, air conditioning towers, basement sump pumps, and roofs, etc. to be sure the entire building is being properly maintained. It is not that unusual for a tenant to cut back on maintenance as it nears the end of the lease term. This is a good time for the real estate manager to meet with the tenant.

The multiuse planned industrial development. This development—typically occupied by industrial, office, and retail tenants—is more management intensive. These projects are staffed with an on-site manager, an administrative support person, and maintenance personnel. Their responsibilities include lease administration, CAM, limited exterior building maintenance, tenant improvement construction, establishing a tenant-retention program, developing emergency procedures, marketing and public relations efforts, and coordinating leasing activities with the brokerage community.

Insurance

The insurance requirements for industrial tenants vary depending on whether the building is occupied by a single tenant or by multiple tenants. Most single-tenant buildings are leased on a triple-net basis. The tenant is required to obtain an insurance policy with specific minimum limits of coverage with the property owner and the real estate management firm. Tenants must provide the property owner with evidence of insurance that conforms to the insurance requirements in the lease. Tenants in multitenant buildings reimburse the owner for their pro rata cost of the insurance.

While most property owners require tenants to have at least $2 million in liability coverage, dangerous industrial uses and other uses warrant a higher limit. Property owners are increasing the liability insurance required by all tenants. The property owner's insurance agent can provide advice and recommendations on the amount of insurance tenants should carry.

Taxes

Tenants commonly pay the pro rata share of real estate taxes for their premises. For a single-use building, the bill may go directly to the tenant, although many owners prefer to pay the bills and collect from the tenant to be sure the taxes are paid on time. In the latter case, the tenants are required to pay the property owner for the real estate taxes a week before they are due to the municipality. In multiple occupancy buildings, the property owner pays the tax bill, allocates it per the leases, and generally collects it with the monthly budgeted pass-through expenses.

Single-Use Buildings

The single-use industrial building may be leased to the tenant on an absolute net basis with the tenant being fully responsible for repair or replacement of all parts of the building. A triple net lease requires the tenant to pay for the real estate taxes, insurance, and the maintenance. The tenant will usually perform the maintenance. Even in this situation, the real estate manager must set some standards, such as a quarterly air-conditioning service, periodic painting of the exterior, and an annual roof inspection. The real estate manager must visit the property regularly to be sure the work is being performed and the tenant is fulfilling the lease responsibilities.

A thorough inspection of the property should be conducted within six months prior to the lease expiration, and the tenant should be informed of all maintenance needs. When the tenant vacates, the real estate manager conducts a final inspection or walk-through with the tenant. The security deposit is not released until all maintenance is completed. Maintenance issues at the end of a long-term lease can be heavily contested if a tenant believes it is not responsible for the repair and/or replacement of specific items. A clear lease document and regular inspections will minimize these problems.

Multi-tenant Buildings

Maintenance responsibility for multi-tenant buildings is usually divided between the property owner and the tenants. The real estate manager must carefully review the tenant's lease to identify areas of responsibility. The tenant is usually responsible for the maintenance of the premises and mechanical equipment. Typically, the owner is responsible for the maintenance of the roof, common areas, and the structural components detailed in the lease. Common area agreements often require the owner to repaint the exterior of the buildings on a prearranged basis at the tenant's expense.

Planned Industrial Developments

When the property is a planned industrial development with many different uses, the maintenance responsibilities vary depending upon the needs of the tenants as they are reflected in the maintenance provision of the lease. Although the maintenance of the building's interior is the responsibility of the tenant, in some situations the property owner is responsible for providing janitorial services. The real estate manager assumes responsibility for maintenance of the HVAC units and requires tenants to reimburse the owner for this expense. Specific maintenance specifications should be made based on the type of equipment to be used in the space. This ensures that the units are in good condition when tenants vacate. Tenants are billed quarterly or semiannually for their pro rata share of the HVAC maintenance, or they can pay the bills as the maintenance occurs.

Common area maintenance for industrial properties is handled similar to shopping centers; that is, the real estate manager maintains the common areas and bills the tenants for this cost. The real estate manager develops an annual budget, bills the tenants monthly for their pro rata share, and adjusts the billing to the actual expenses at the end of the budgeted period. Depending upon the lease, roof and structural maintenance may be an expense of the property owner, or they may be included in the CAM expense.

TENANT SERVICES

The maintenance management program helps tenants with their maintenance responsibilities. The real estate manager interviews and evaluates several service contractors, such as janitorial, window washing, and carpet cleaning, and provides the list to the tenants. The list should include at least three contractors for each area of maintenance with no preference stated. They may be preferred maintenance contractors the tenant may be allowed to select any contractor of their choice.

Multi-tenant industrial developments provide an opportunity for businesses to promote their services and products within the development. For example, a real estate manager of a 500,000-square-foot multi-tenant industrial development in the northwest conducts an annual trade fair where tenants display their products and services and the property owner provides refreshments and entertainment. This event gives tenants additional business opportunities and creates camaraderie within the development. A monthly or quarterly open house at the on-site management office gives the management staff a chance to develop rapport with the tenants and to meet the tenants' employees.

Construction Management

Large industrial developments, especially those with incubator space, have considerable ongoing tenant improvement construction. The real estate manager develops a construction management program to meet the improvement requirements of new tenants, as well as the expansion and remodeling needs of existing tenants.

The first step in developing a construction management program is to obtain the "as-built" plans for the development. If as-built plans are not available, the property owner may request the real estate manager to contract with a firm to create a survey of the properties that can be used to market and lease the property. The next step is to compile a list including the general contractor and all subcontractors who have worked on the project. Space planners are interviewed, and one is selected to work with prospective tenants. Space planners prepare the design of the premises, and if they are qualified, the working drawings to obtain the construction permit from the municipality and for the general contractor to begin construction of the *tenant improvements (TIs).*

Several general contractors should be interviewed, and at least three should be selected to bid on TIs. Contractors' insurance companies must provide evidence of worker's compensation and liability insurance and include the property owner and real estate management company as named insureds on their insurance policies. The evidence of the proper levels of liability insurance must be provided prior to work being performed—except in emergencies.

Each general contractor is requested to bid each job. If the work does not require extensive remodeling or build-outs, the real estate manager may use construction unit pricing. Under unit pricing, the real estate manager acquires bids on specific construction activities, such as installing an electrical outlet or building a wall, and then contracts for the work based on unit prices. The bids are usually good for a year. This method is often used when a tenant renews and the property owner makes minor improvements to the premises. Unit pricing eliminates the need to bid for small jobs.

The real estate manager or the maintenance supervisor conducts a final walk-through with the contractor and the tenant before the tenant moves into the space. There is some benefit to using the same contractor for all of the tenant improvement work in the building, but one must be cautioned to have either a unit pricing guideline or an agreed-upon range of prices—in some cases, contractors can slowly increase prices. Another approach is to bid one or two jobs per year and compare that to what the existing contractor is charging to keep the prices in line.

A construction management program facilitates the marketing and leasing program, meets the existing tenants' construction needs, and provides a construction supervision or coordination fee for the real estate management company. Certain tenants representing larger companies will have their own construction crews for the TIs and as long as the specifications are clear. However, tenants of smaller companies will most likely not have the capability to coordinate their own TIs. In this case, the real estate manager may be assigned the supervision of the TIs.

Exterior Signage

The control of exterior signs is as important in industrial properties as it is in all other commercial properties. The property owner should establish and enforce reasonable sign criteria for the property that are consistent with the signage requirements of the city or county. The sign criteria should be included as an exhibit in the lease. Multi-tenant facilities are not likely to have larger signs for the individual tenants. All signage should be approved by the property owner's management team.

Exterior Storage

Control of exterior storage is critical to the operation of industrial properties. It is not unusual to see delivery pallets, 55-gallon drums, or even truck trailers stored outside the tenants' premises. Such items are unsightly, take up valuable parking space, and are potential fire hazards. A recommended approach to storage control is to include the development's storage rules and regulations in the lease as part of the overall rules and regulations for the property. If exterior storage is allowed, it should be fenced in such a way as to mask what is behind it. Another alternative is to have an exterior common storage area on the property for storage and charge for its use.

Security

A security audit and, if necessary, a security program are integral components of a property's emergency procedure plan. The real estate manager conducts a security audit and takes preventive measures to minimize problems. Since there are usually no interior common areas, security problems would most likely occur in the parking lot or on the tenant's premises.

Parking lot security starts with good lighting. Administrative and maintenance personnel must be alert for loiterers and anything that appears unusual. Tenants should be reminded to report suspicious people on or near the development to the management office or the police. In the evenings, a drive-by security patrol can check for unlocked doors, abandoned cars, and loiterers.

If a security problem exists, the real estate manager can hire on-site guards, erect a fence with limited or guarded access around the project, and install surveillance equipment. The police can be encouraged to drive through the development and meet with tenants to review security procedures for their premises. Seldom do industrial properties need security personnel.

Environmental Concerns

An industrial tenant that manufactures or processes chemicals on the premises might produce materials that pollute the ground, air, or water. The real estate manager must inquire as to how the property is to be used, what environmental concerns the proposed use may present, and how the property owner is to be protected from damage and potential liability—both during the lease term and after the lease term ends. The real estate manager should regularly conduct a visual environmental audit to ensure no issues exist that might cause the property owner problems during the lease term or after the tenants have vacated the building.

One such audit in a small industrial park found automobile batteries stored on a concrete floor. The batteries were leaking acid through the concrete, and the acid was seeping into the ground. Other audits found a cleaning plant dumping used cleaning solvents on the ground outside the rear door of the premises, a photo-processing plant flushing used chemicals down the toilet, and a painting contractor discarding used paint solvents into the ground in an outside storage area. These are examples of tenants that may cause environmental damage through spills and improper disposal of their hazardous materials. If the lease does not include proper protection for the property owner, the owner might be held accountable for the actions of the tenants long after the tenants have moved away.

Other environmental issues include controlling the use of utilities and maximizing their useage. Rooftop solar energy sources are commonly being considered by industrial tenants as well as water usage and low consumption lighting, motors and air conditioning. A recent study published by the National Association of Industrial and Office Parks showed that industrial buildings with a green footprint obtained better rental rates in conservative areas of the country.

SUSTAINABILITY IN INDUSTRIAL PROPERTIES

Sustainability programs for industrial properties present both opportunities and challenges. Working with industrial tenants—who often have control over their space to a greater degree than tenants in other commercial property types—on sustainability and resource efficiency can be challenging because they may have energy-intensive business operations, often around the clock. Benchmarking energy and water use can be difficult because many tenants view utility data as proprietary business information. Tenants also may not understand the utility cost savings benefits possible through resource efficiency. Education on your sustainability program and its benefits is critical.

Other tenants may desire sustainable space and properties because their companies have corporate sustainability initiatives, or they work with a large company that requires sustainability among their suppliers. These tenants often seek LEED certified industrial properties, which are becoming much more common, or they will fit out their spaces with sustainable, energy- and water-efficient features.

Common sustainability initiatives at industrial properties include LED lighting retrofits, installation of lighting controls, such as motion detectors and sweep lighting, installation of high-efficiency water fixtures, waste recycling programs, and drought-resistant landscaping, as well as landscaping and hardscapes that manage water runoff. The large flat roofs of many industrial properties are also prime candidates for rooftop solar arrays that can generate on-site power. Newly constructed industrial properties often incorporate sustainable features such as recycled and low-emitting building materials, building envelopes that improve indoor thermal comfort, more daylighting than in conventional industrial properties from previous generations, and highly efficient, properly sized HVAC systems.

CONCLUSION

With the evolution of industrial properties from free-standing masonry buildings with triple-net tenants to multi-tenant developments, industrial real estate management entails many of the management responsibilities of office and retail properties, especially as the properties grow in size and complexity.

SECTION III

Marketing and Leasing

CHAPTER 7

Developing a Marketing and Leasing Plan

Marketing and leasing is such a critical component of a property's business plan. Leasing space is the critical activity that validates the development of a project and the investment in a building. The success of a commercial development is dependent upon the initial lease-up of the building, while the success of an existing building is dependent upon a successful ongoing leasing program. In fact, the goal of every real estate manager and leasing agent is to develop a cost effective and efficient leasing program to meet or exceed the goals and objectives of the property owner.

The major components that contribute to a successful leasing program include (1) the building's location; (2) the building's design and features; (3) the owner's understanding of the market (4) the owner's willingness to do market deals; (5) the market conditions; (6) the development and implementation of an effective marketing and leasing program; and (7) selection of the right marketing and leasing team members. The success of these seven factors is ultimately apparent in the building's cash flow and value.

DEVELOPING THE LEASING AGREEMENT

Before embarking on an extensive effort to develop a marketing and leasing program for a building, the real estate management company needs to enter into a leasing agreement with the property owner. The leasing agreement will provide the real estate management company or brokerage firm with the authorization to market and lease the property. The agreement will also state the rights and obligations of the leasing company and the owner of the property.

It's likely that the property is being managed by the real estate management company. If so, a leasing section will either be included in the management agreement or there will be a separate agreement. If the property is *not* managed by the real estate management company, a separate leasing agreement needs to be negotiated and signed by the property owner, along with an executive of the real estate management company or brokerage company.

Some items in the leasing agreement must be negotiated. The most critical and negotiable issue is the term or length of the leasing agreement. The leasing team will need sufficient time to develop a marketing program, implement it, contact prospects and negotiate the lease. A year is considered the minimum time to accomplish the aforementioned marketing and leasing activities—longer is better.

TYPES OF LEASE LISTING AGREEMENTS

There are three common types of lease listing agreements: (1) the exclusive right to lease, (2) exclusive agency, (3) and open listing.

Exclusive Right-to-Lease Listing Agreement

The exclusive right-to-lease listing agreement is the most common agreement used by property owners when they contract with a broker or real estate management company to lease their building. It is also the agreement preferred by brokerage firms and real estate management companies because it provides the real estate management or brokerage firm the exclusive right to lease the building. If another leasing agent brings a tenant to the building and a lease is signed, the listing broker will still be paid a *commission*. Usually, the listing leasing agent will enter into an agreement with the tenant's broker or leasing agent to share the commission. Even if the owner, or anyone else, finds a prospect and a lease is entered into with that prospect, the listing broker is nevertheless paid a commission. When another broker or party brings a prospect to a building, the building listing broker will be the lead in the leasing process.

Since the building's listing agents invest a considerable amount of their time, expense, and expertise, that had been developed over years of marketing and leasing buildings, they want to be sure that they will be paid a commission—or a portion of the commission—regardless of who brings a prospect to the building and finalizes a lease. They do not want to be competing, but cooperating with the brokerage community to find tenants for the building. The advantage of this type of agreement to the owner is the assurance that the leasing agent(s) or real estate manager(s) are committed to spending the necessary time marketing and leasing the property.

Exclusive Agency Lease Listing Agreement

The exclusive agency listing agreement is similar to the exclusive right listing agreement, except in this situation, the owner is responsible for finding a tenant. If the owner finds the tenant, a commission is not paid to the listing firm. Owners benefit from this arrangement by not having to pay commission if they find a tenant. The disadvantage, however, is that leasing agents are more likely to believe that owners are competing with them to find tenants for the building. A dispute over who first contacted a tenant or how the tenant became aware of the building can easily develop.

When an exclusive agency listing agreement is used, it is in the interest of both parties to have an addendum to the agreement that lists which prospective tenants the owner is working with or intends to contact. The addendum may state that the broker will not be paid a commission if any of the specified prospects enters into a lease with the owner. An alternative to not paying the brokerage firm for tenants is for the owner to pay a partial commission to the brokerage firm for those tenants.

The owner must be careful not to compete or give the perception of competing with the brokerage firm. The brokerage firm will want to have its "For Lease" sign on the property and be the only party to list the property with commercial multiple listing services online. The firm will also want to receive all inquiries from prospects and other leasing agents. It is important for owners to recognize these preferences and comply with all reasonable requests so that there are no conflicts between owners and their broker(s).

For example, a grocery-anchored shopping center developer is likely to have a strong relationship with supermarkets and exclude these tenants from the leasing agreement. When a lease is entered into with a supermarket, the listing leasing agent may not pay a commission. Usually, the supermarket or other major tenants have entered into a lease with the developer before the start of construction and possibly before the developer selected a leasing agent. Developers will not start construction of a grocery-anchored shopping center until there is a lease with the supermarket. There is usually sufficient amount of space remaining for the leasing agent or real estate manager to lease, which makes the marketing and leasing effort and time worthwhile.

Open Lease Listing Agreement

Open lease listing agreements do not provide the leasing firm with the exclusive right to lease the building. The property owner will pay a commission to any broker who brings a prospect who enters into a lease. In theory, this type of agreement will encourage all leasing agents to "work" the property, searching for tenants for the building.

In reality, though, few if any leasing agents will market a building under an open-listing agreement. If leasing agents invest their time in marketing a building, they want the assurance that they will be paid a commission when a lease is executed. Leasing agents would not know if the list of tenants have been contacted by other leasing agents or the property owner. Other leasing agents may claim these prospects are their clients.

FINALIZING THE LEASING AGREEMENT

Once the owner and the brokerage firm have agreed upon the type of listing arrangement, a leasing agreement needs to be executed by both parties. The agreement will formalize in writing each party's rights and obligations, as well as the broker's compensation.

The leasing agreement is usually provided by the brokerage firm. Most brokerage firms have developed their own agreement, and in some markets, a commercial multiple listing service will provide an agreement for its members. Few owners—usually only those who have a large portfolio of properties—have their own leasing agreement.

The leasing agreement should be carefully reviewed by each party. Many of the provisions are standard for all types of agreements, and there is little to negotiate in these provisions. There are others provisions, though, that need careful scrutiny and may require negotiations. A discussion of many of the issues and provisions in a leasing agreement, from both the owner's and the broker's perspectives, is provided below.

Leasing Agreement Issues and Provisions

1. **Parties to the Agreement.** The owner and the broker are named.
2. **Exclusive Agreement.** The brokerage firm is appointed as the exclusive leasing agent for the property. The issue to discuss is whether the broker is granted the exclusive right to lease the property or an exclusive agency.
3. **Description of the Property.** This provision describes and provides the property's legal address. If the agreement is for a specific space or spaces in the building, this agreement will describe those areas. A *metes and bounds* description may be necessary for a parcel of land, such as a pad or an out parcel. A site plan of the property may be an addendum to the agreement.
4. **Leasing Agreement Term.** The length of the agreement and its commencement and expiration dates are stated. The brokerage firm usually prefers at least a one-year agreement, which will enable the firm to develop and implement a marketing plan, contact prospective tenants, show space, and negotiate leases. An agreement less than a year does not provide the marketing and leasing team with sufficient time to develop and implement their plan. Most agreements will provide both parties with a 30-day written cancellation right—with or without cause.
5. **Registration of Prospects.** This registration provision will usually state that the broker and the owner agree on a registration list. When an agreement is cancelled (or expires and is not renewed) the broker and owner may establish such a list. It is to the broker's advantage to register a list of prospects with the owner so that, if a lease is entered into with any of those listed, the broker will receive a commission. Brokers benefit from making sure that every prospect they contact or show space to is included on the leasing report(s).

   The owner, on the other hand, is concerned that the broker will provide a list including prospects who do not yet have a serious interest in the building. The owner wants to protect against future disputes, and so wants only those prospects actually involved in lease negotiations on the list. If another broker represents a listed prospect in the future, and a lease is entered into, the owner does not want two brokers claiming a commission for the same prospect.

   One method to settle any possible disputes over which prospects should be included on the list is to review the last few leasing reports and include only those prospects who have shown serious interest or are in lease negotiations. A time frame for executing the lease will also be stated, and those deals not completed within the given limits will be taken off the broker's list. The opportunity for the leasing agent to earn commissions for these prospects will then expire. The leasing agent will want a six-month period (or longer) to complete a lease with a prospect while the owner may negotiate for a 30- or 120-day period.

6. **Commissions.** This provision states the commission rate and the commission payment schedule. The agreement may exclude from the commission calculations of income derived from the following: parking, percentage rent, *consumer price index (CPI)* increases, pass-through operating expense charges, over-standard or after-hours utility charges, late payments and fees, security deposits, payment for over-standard improvements, etc. The agreement also may state that commissions are paid only on base or minimum rent.

   A negotiable issue is whether or not the broker is to be paid a commission if the tenant expands or renews the lease. The broker brought the tenant to the building and therefore should be paid a commission on all transactions between the tenant and owner. The owner paid the broker for the initial transaction, so any subsequent transactions—such as expansion and lease renewal—should be strictly between the owner and the tenant. Additionally, any subsequent transactions are likely to occur several years after the initial lease is executed, and the broker is no longer involved with the property. The owner is usually in a strong negotiating position on this issue, and will often prevail.

   Some brokerage firms' agreements will state that, if the owner intends to sell the property during the lease listing agreement, the leasing broker will receive the exclusive right to sell the property. Most owners will not agree to this request—they may believe another broker is more qualified to sell the property; they may want to sell the property themselves; commit to doing something in the future; or have not yet decided what is best. This is another issue that brokers are usually willing to exclude from their leasing agreements.

7. **Cooperating Brokers.** The owner authorizes the broker to cooperate with other brokers, and the broker agrees to market the property and cooperate with other brokers.

8. **Rent Schedule.** Some lease listing agreements state either the anticipated asking rental rate or the anticipated deal-making rental rate. These rates are derived from a conversation between the broker and the owner about the market rate for the building. The agreement may also state other lease terms, such as the minimum and maximum lease length and the tenant charges. Many agreements will not include this section.

9. **Advertising.** The owner authorizes the broker to advertise the property and list it with commercial multiple online listing services. The owner will want full approval of all ads. The issue to negotiate is who pays for this advertising.

10. **Signs.** The broker is authorized to place "For Lease" signs on the property. The cost of these signs is usually the broker's expense.

11. **Leasing Meetings and Reports.** The broker will meet with the owner a specific number of times to discuss the marketing plan and leasing progress. If the building is in initial lease-up, or if there is excessive vacancy, the owner may want to meet with the broker weekly or bi-weekly. If a building has limited space to lease, a monthly meeting will usually suffice. If the owner's office is not near the property or the broker's office, the meeting can be in the form of a conference call. A few days prior to the meeting, the broker should provide the owner with a leasing status report, which may be formatted as an addendum to the agreement.

12. **Property Disclosure.** The owner agrees to fully disclose to the broker and prospects all known information regarding zoning, land restrictions, existing lease restrictions, and environmental and hazardous issues affecting the property.

13. **Security Deposits.** The broker is authorized to accept deposits from prospects on behalf of

the owner. If the deposit is nonrefundable, the broker will want to negotiate to keep a portion—possibly half—of the money in case the tenant does not complete the transaction and forfeits the deposit.

14. **Dual Agency.** The agreement may state that the owner chooses to allow the broker to act as a dual agent, representing both the owner and the tenant in a lease transaction. The owner may not agree to this provision, however, believing that the broker may not serve the best interest of the owner when acting for both parties. If the parties decide on a dual-agency agreement, the broker will agree not to disclose confidential information of either party. Some states require that the broker provide the owner with a pamphlet on the law of real estate agency. In these states, the agreement will affirm that the owner acknowledges receiving and reading the pamphlet.

15. **Lease Form.** The parties agree that either the owner will provide the lease agreement or that the brokerage firm will provide its standard agreement, which the owner must approve. A few areas also have commercial multiple listing services that provide their standard lease agreement for their members to use. Many brokerage and real estate management firms do not have a lease agreement and the owner must provide it. The lease agreement is between the owner and the tenant, while the leasing agreement is between the owner and the brokerage firm. There is no industry standard lease agreement.

16. **Referrals.** The owner agrees to immediately refer all inquiries to the broker.

17. **Right to Reject Prospects.** The owner reserves the right, in his or her sole and absolute discretion, to reject any prospective tenant or any proposed lease terms presented by any broker. The owner is not obligated to pay a commission on any rejected prospects.

18. **Assignment.** Often, the owner enters into a leasing agreement because of his or her relationship with a leasing agent. If the agreement is assigned, the owner may want the option to cancel the agreement.

19. **Sale of Property.** The leasing agreement is usually cancelled upon sale of the property. The broker asks that, in the event of a sale, the owner will attempt to get the purchaser to agree to continue listing the property with the broker.

20. **Disputes.** The parties agree on how a dispute will be settled. Often, the parties will agree to binding arbitration, with the prevailing party being reimbursed for costs. If the issue in dispute can not be arbitrated, or the parties have not agreed to arbitration, the prevailing party is reimbursed for its legal fees as well as costs.

21. **Nondiscrimination.** The owner and the broker agree to comply with all applicable antidiscrimination regulations and laws.

22. **Governing Law.** This agreement is governed by the laws of the state in which the property is located.

23. **Indemnity.** There is usually a mutual *indemnity provision.* The owner agrees to indemnify the broker for his or her performance, except for willful acts, gross negligence, and false and misleading representation. The broker agrees to indemnify the owner for any claims brought by a third party caused by the gross negligence of the broker. There are many different versions of this provision, but the language used may need to be reviewed by the firm's attorney.

24. **Competition.** The owner may want to include a provision stating that the broker will not lease any property in direct competition with the owner's property. However, such a request may not be in the owner's best interest because it will likely exclude many of the larger brokerage firms. If the brokerage firm is leasing a property that is in competition with the owner's property, the two parties should first resolve whether or not the properties are in direct competition, and

then decide how the owner's property can be marketed and leased without a conflict of interest. Seldom do both buildings have identical features, location, and available space size, so they can be marketed by the same broker without conflict. Often, marketing two similar buildings in close proximity to each other enables the leasing agent to devote more time and marketing expense to each building.

25. Confidentiality. The broker agrees to keep all information provided by the owner confidential, except for that which the owner authorizes for use in the property's marketing and leasing efforts. The owner may also require that the broker keep all data regarding existing and future tenants confidential. The owner does not want the building's tenants' information used in the brokerage firm's leasing database, such as the tenant's lease expiration, in any other listing that the firm might develop to market and lease other properties or find tenant representation.
26. Independent Contractor. The agreement will state that the broker and the leasing agent are independent contractors, and not employees of the owner.
27. Insurance. The brokerage or real estate management firm must carry professional liability insurance.
28. Right to Reject Prospects. The owner has the right to reject any prospect and not be obligated to pay the broker a commission.
29. Lien Law. In specific situations, some states provide the broker with the right to file a *lien* on the property for commission that is owed and not paid. This provision makes reference to that law.
30. Notices. This provision states where notices will be sent for each party, as well as the delivery method.
31. Entire Agreement. This provision states that the listing agreement constitutes the entire agreement, supersedes any prior written or oral agreements, and is the prevailing agreement.
32. Exhibits. The agreement may refer to exhibits such as site plans, commission schedules, etc.

The next issue is the commission rate. There is no standard industry commission rate or schedule, and commissions are negotiable. The agreement must state how the commission will be calculated: a percentage of the rents, fixed fee, dollar amount per square foot, or any formula agreed upon by the owner and the real estate management company. It should also state how the commission would be shared on a co-broker deal. The payment schedule is the next concern. Will the commission be paid entirely when the lease is executed or paid over time?

The agreement should state whether a commission is paid when the tenant renews, expands, or exercises an option. Brokers often believe they should be paid each time a tenant renews and expands because they introduced the tenant to the property. However, many property owners refuse to pay a commission on renewals and expansions because they paid the broker for bringing the tenant to the building, and any changes to the tenant's occupancy are negotiated by the owner or the real estate manager.

THE MARKETING DEVELOPMENT TEAM

The marketing team is responsible for developing the marketing strategy and the marketing materials for the building. The leasing team will use the marketing materials while implementing the marketing strategy. Usually, the marketing team does not include everyone on the leasing team. Either the real estate manager or a leasing agent will head the marketing team. Larger firms may have marketing or support personnel assigned only to developing marketing materials. Most firms will assign this responsibility to the real estate manager or leasing agent supported by administrative staff with skills needed to develop these materials. An alternative is to contract out the development of the marketing materials. Time always seems to be of the essence when developing marketing materials. Marketing materials that may be needed are discussed further in this chapter.

THE MARKETING BUDGET

The marketing budget can be a predetermined dollar expense or developed while the marketing and leasing plan is being developed. The marketing and leasing teams will develop a budget for their components of the marketing and leasing plan. There are several possible marketing costs including designing the materials and possibly a logo for the building, producing hard and/or electronic copies of brochures and handout materials, advertising, signage, services of a public relations firm, demographic and psychographic reports, and direct mailing costs. The budgets for existing buildings are usually nominal. The budget for a new building, depending on its size, may be substantial.

After a budget is developed, the real estate management company's executive along with the person responsible for marketing and leasing the property will determine which, if any, of the expenses they believe they should incur. The real estate management firm's executive will meet with the property owner to discuss and determine who will pay for which expense. The amount of the potential commission that may be earned is often a consideration in these discussions.

There is no rule of thumb on the amount of a marketing budget and who pays for which expenses. The recommended marketing budget is not a percentage of the building's projected rents over a specific time or a dollar per square foot of the building area. The marketing budget is based on what the marketing and leasing teams believe, as a result of their analysis, of the building's market position, amount of space to lease, and the attributes and deficiencies of the building. The marketing team and the real estate manager meets with the property owner to discuss their recommendations and the property owners determine if all, or a portion of, the recommended plan is approved.

Geographic Information Systems (GIS)

GIS technology has become one of the better tools to determine the growth of markets. While the overall concept of GIS is extremely complex, it allows the integration of database information, such as various census tract demographics, with the physical map of the area. The real estate manager can use this technology to map income levels and other trends on a map of the area. Various studies have found this approach much better than the previous approach of treating the study of the demographics and their application to a map as two separate functions. The technology is expanding and adding new dimensions rapidly. When performing any market survey in the future, the real estate manager should consider how he or she might benefit by using GIS technology.

BUILDING ANALYSIS

The marketing team needs to understand the building position in the market. How does it compete with its competition? The first step to accomplish this is to have a thorough understanding of the building. The marketing team should know the building better than the owner. What are the building's attributes and deficiencies? What do tenant like and dislike about the building and its location? Which features will be emphasize in the marketing materials and which deficiencies must the leasing team be prepared to address. A building analysis is discussed in chapter 9.

TENANT MIX

Tenant mix is the synergism created by the right grouping of tenants in a building or a shopping center. In a shopping center, the strength of the synergism created by several merchants is a primary factor in determining each tenant's success, thus, the success of the shopping center. The correct tenant mix in a shopping center maximizes each tenant's sales potential and the shopping center's percentage rent potential. For instance, regional malls are tenanted primarily by fashion department stores and fashion, jewelry, gift shops, and restaurants.

A neighborhood shopping center anchored by a supermarket and drugstore will be occupied primarily by service and food tenants that serve the customers' daily needs.

Another aspect of tenant mix is the placement of tenants. Some businesses thrive in a space with high traffic and high visibility. For instance, a jewelry store and a high-end chocolate store is an ideal center court tenant in a mall. A pharmacy is usually an excellent ground floor tenant for a medical office building and should have street-level exposure.

When a leasing team develops a leasing plan, it compiles a list of ideal tenants and assigns each a location in the building. When negotiating a lease with potential tenants, the leasing agent attempts to convince why they should locate in a particular location. Seldom is every tenant located on the first proposed leasing plan, but that plan is the starting place for locating tenants.

Shopping Center Tenant Mix

Once the real estate manager has completed an in-depth market survey, the shopping center tenant mix starts to take form. Generally, the purpose of the tenant mix is to provide a broad range of goods and services consistent with the needs and preferences of customers within the trade area and those who shop at the shopping center. A good tenant mix creates a synergy among retailers, restaurants, and service tenants, which will yield higher total sales for individual tenants than they could achieve on their own. The rent a shopping center can charge tenants is directly related to the sales of the tenants. Retailers and restaurants know that the rent they can afford cannot exceed a certain percentage of their annual sales. It is encumbered on the marketing and leasing team to create the best tenant mix possible for the shopping center that will provide the best opportunity for the tenants to generate superior sales.

Each type of shopping center has a different tenant mix because it meets or serves different customer wants and needs and different trade areas. A neighborhood shopping center anchored by a supermarket provides for the daily household needs of its customers. A gourmet supermarket would not be a good location in a moderate-income neighborhood, nor would a discount shoe store be in an affluent suburb. If the market and drugstore are properly selected for the trade area and the other stores complement the anchor tenants in services, merchandise, and price points of product, the tenant mix will be compatible with the purpose of the particular shopping center and with the demographics and psychographics of the trade area.

A *neighborhood shopping center* usually has service tenants. Typical tenants for a neighborhood shopping center include cleaners, shoe repair, florist, bank, savings and loan, real estate office, card and gift shop, pet stores, fast food, quick service and table service restaurant, delicatessen, pizza parlor, ice cream parlor, hobby shop, wine and liquor store, health spa, hardware store, medical professional, dollar store, and perhaps limited discount or specialty fashion and jewelry stores.

The *community shopping center* generally has a fashion focus in addition to the service tenants found in the neighborhood shopping center. It is usually anchored by two or three major tenants—including a junior department store, discount fashion store, and other box stores such as a large pet supply store or a bed and bath store—and draws from a wider trade area than a neighborhood shopping center. Because of the fashion draw of the community shopping center, apparel shops, jewelry stores, and shoe stores may be found in this type of shopping center. Community shopping centers also provide for the daily needs of their trade areas, so supermarkets, drugstores, dollar stores, and home improvement stores are additional anchors.

The *regional* and *super regional malls* are fashion oriented due to the anchor department store. Saks or Neiman Marcus would probably be an anchor in a regional mall serving a high-income area and Sears or Walmart would probably be an anchor in a middle-income area. The emphasis in regional and super regional malls is on fashion, with scores of clothing and shoe stores. Food is always a good draw, and because of the traffic generated, small specialty shops can do very well. Non-traditional major retailers have become acceptable anchor tenants, such as warehouse and discount box stores.

The *festival or theme shopping center* is oriented to the tourist and, to a lesser degree, to nearby workers. The shopping center itself is a draw, and the merchandise is more "one of a kind" than merchandise found in traditional shops. For example, music box shops, teddy bear shops, or kite shops do not usually survive in a neighborhood or community shopping center, but they can thrive in a specialty shopping center. Restaurants are the traditional anchors for festival or theme shopping centers. Some smaller theme shopping centers specialize in very specific uses such as restaurants only, automobile service and support, home decorating and furnishings. These shopping centers usually require the support of a very large trade area.

Discount, outlet, and *off-price shopping centers* are referred to as "value shopping centers," and they have tenants selling in all three areas. Maintaining the value image is important, but ensuring that merchants actually sell at a discount can be difficult. "Fashion for less" is the main attraction of this type of shopping center, with other merchandise lines filling out the balance of the mix. Restaurants, again, are an important part of the tenant mix, as are linens, shoes, jewelry, children's wear, and gifts.

Lifestyle shopping centers were first developed in the 1990s. Originally, they were not anchored in the traditional sense by a department store or junior department store. The tenant mix is generally made up of very strong national tenants in the areas of fashion, home decorating, upscale services, table service restaurants, specialty food, and entertainment. These shopping centers are focused on lifestyle, convenience, and meeting the current needs of the modern-day shopper.

A *power shopping center* is a large shopping center anchored by medium- to large-box stores. Box stores are usually large concrete constructed buildings each occupied by one retailer. Box retailers are warehouse stores such as Costco, super hardware stores such as Lowes and Home Depot, discount retailers such as Target, Walmart, Ross and Marshalls, book stores, pet supplies, home accessories and more. Power shopping centers often have pad tenants. There is little cross shopping in a power center so there typically are no small shop tenants.

After the ideal tenant mix is designed for the shopping center, the marketing and leasing team determines the best locations for the desired retailers, restaurants, and service tenants. For example, women's fashion retailers are not placed together in one area of the mall—they are strategically spread throughout the mall so the shopper walks by several other stores. If a mall is anchored by high-end fashion retailers, they will be placed closer to that anchor store. End-cap locations in strip shopping centers may be leased to drive-through businesses such as Starbucks or banks. The ideal tenant mix and the placement of tenants are by design. The marketing and leasing team decides which tenant to seek and where to place them. Sometimes the tenant may prefer another location and negotiations will determine which space the tenant leases.

Office Building Tenant Mix

The tenant mix is not as critical to the success of an office as it is to the success of a shopping center. However, office building tenants can enhance the reputation of the building and its marketing and leasing program and provide amenities to the tenants in the building.

In marketing the office building, the real estate manager can use the presence of respected and established tenants to great advantage. For example, an office building tenanted primarily by Fortune 500 companies enjoys a reputation of success and prosperity, as does a building tenanted by leading law firms and financial institutions. An office building located in the state capital may have several government agencies as tenants, which lends a sense of stability and strength to the tenant mix. A building's tenant mix may include services to the business community. A restaurant, bank, escrow office, stockbroker, printer, health club, business dinning club, and gift shop are amenities that should be marketed as additional services in the building.

A building's tenant mix is also reflected in its population level. A building with mostly professional offices usually has a low-population count, while one tenanted with service companies has a high density of employees. The population count in the building may be an indicator of a particular service or specialty food tenant that may do well in the building. An office with a national or international insurance company is likely to attract smaller insurance agency that write policies for the national or international firm. A building near a court house may include law firms, just like a building located in the retail component area of downtown will have desirable location with shops and restaurants within walking distance of the building. An indicator of the type of tenants who are likely candidates for a building are the types of tenants in nearby buildings.

Medical Office Building Tenant Mix

The tenant mix or tenant profile of a medical office building is a positive feature in marketing and leasing. The key to a good tenant mix in a medical office building is consistent referrals among the medical professionals within the building. Location near a pharmacy is a major convenience for physicians and their patients. A general practitioner will refer to specialists such as cardiologists or obstetricians for consultation and referral. Medical groups such as radiology labs and physical therapists need referrals from primary care physicians and specialists in the building. When a medical office building has a referral network within the building, other medical professionals will want to locate their practice in the building.

Industrial Park Tenant Mix

The industrial park is least affected by the tenant mix but, like the office building, it does benefit from well-known tenants. Larger industrial parks may develop pads or out parcels for restaurants, and market space to tenants that will provide services to other tenants in the park such as a deli. If an industrial park is near a major manufacturer, or can attract a major manufacturer, that tenant may attract its suppliers to locate in the park.

Planned industrial developments may include areas for businesses that service the employees of the industrial tenants. Major industrial parks may include fast-food, quick-service, full-service restaurants, a medical facility, business services, hotels, and retail facilities. Smaller industrial parks frequently develop a similar tenant mix on a smaller scale. Supporting uses within, or adjacent to, an industrial park provide important services to the park's tenants and their employees. The tenant mix in an industrial park should be one of the features in the marketing materials for the project. The location of the industrial park and access to freeways are a determining factor for many of the non-traditional industrial tenants mentioned above.

MARKETING

In the late 1890s, the owner of a soap factory in England made a statement regarding his advertising that has become one of the most famous quotes of our time. He said, "50 percent of my advertising is wasted; I just don't which 50 percent." This section provides dozens of methods to market a building. Many of them will not be needed or be effective for every building. The property type and the amount of existing and anticipated vacant space are factors in determining the selection of marketing materials and techniques used to effectively lease a building.

Leasing Package

The leasing package is helpful for brokers and prospective tenants. Brokers use it to keep current on the property. Prospective tenants become aware of a property by visiting the area, receiving a leasing package from the leasing agent for the property, checking online commercial real estate sites or working with a broker.

Today, most marketing materials for re-leasing space consist of e-mail brochures sent to the brokerage community and prospects. One-page flyers are still developed as handouts and are sent to targeted specific users. The cost of these materials is relatively nominal and is measured by the cost of the software program and the time to develop and distribute the materials.

Three approaches are common to presenting a leasing package to prospective tenants:

1. Provide sufficient but limited information to pique the prospect's interest. If the prospect shows continued interest, the full leasing package is provided.
2. Provide the entire package to each prospect. There are no additional costs to e-mail larger marketing packages. The question is, will the prospect read the larger packet or does that even matter?
3. A hybrid approach is to e-mail the complete package to those prospects that have a high probability of leasing space and e-mail the limited package to all other prospects.

Whatever approach is used, all materials should be professionally prepared to reflect the quality of the building. The leasing package is designed to present the property in its best light and to answer pertinent questions. Any information that conveys the message of service and quality and distinguishes the building from the competition should be included in the leasing package.

Marketing Online

E-mailing marketing materials to other brokers is the most common way to market properties. Regional and national commercial multiple-listing services enable brokers to list properties with photos and detailed descriptions of the properties. Brokerage firms have their own websites that list their properties, while some larger properties have their own websites that include a list of spaces for lease.

Shopping Center Leasing Package

The leasing package for a retail tenant should include general information of interest to all retailers, but it should also be tailored to the specific retailer. A balance is necessary between e-mailing too much material, which is likely to go unread, and sending too little information, which keeps the prospect from reaching any conclusions. The basic leasing package may contain a list of tenants, a plot plan, an area map, an aerial photograph of the site, demographic and psychographic profiles of the trade area, comments on the shopping center's sales (without giving specific tenants' sales), and if the shopping center or mall has a marketing fund.

Transmittal Letter

The *transmittal letter,* which is usually e-mailed, is a critical part of the leasing package. Neither prospective tenants nor leasing agents—especially those for large chains who receive a great number of leasing packages—have time to read long letters. Therefore, the letter or e-mail should be brief, professionally prepared, and addressed to an individual by name. The letter should also explain the benefits of leasing space in the shopping center. Computer technology can easily personalize letters to address the specific features of the location and the specific requirements of the tenant. For example, a cover letter e-mailed to ice cream parlors could mention the number of schools within walking distance of the shopping center along with the number of families in the trade area of the shopping center.

Tenant List

Prospective tenants are interested in the shopping center's existing and future tenants. Some merchants follow other merchants into new locations because experience tells them they will do well next to, or near, a given merchant. Listing the merchant's trade name as well as what is sold is helpful: for example, "Lucky Market, a discount grocer." The list of tenants should never imply that a tenant has signed a lease for the subject shopping center when the tenant is only in the negotiating stage. Prudent owners do not reveal the name of a prospective tenant if the lease has not been executed. The list may include a disclaimer stating there is no assurance these tenants will remain in occupancy.

Plot Plan

The plot plan should be prepared specifically for leasing. If it was prepared for a different purpose, it should be modified for inclusion in the leasing package. The engineering plot plan may suffice, but it is not attractive. Showing tenants' names in the locations they occupy is helpful. A prospect may want to be next to the dress store or, conversely, may not want to be next to the pet store or the anchor tenant. A disclaimer should be included stating that the property owner does not guarantee information provided by other sources, such as traffic counts obtained from the city, information that is subject to change; and that the site plan and list of tenants can change.

Lease Outline Drawing

A *lease outline drawing (LOD)* is similar to a space plan for an office building except it is a drawing of the perimeter without the prior tenant's improvements except for restrooms. Since each retailer have their own format, existing improvements seldom have any value to the next retailer. The exception may be a restaurant operator who may be able to use some (or all) of the prior restaurants fixtures and equipment. The equipment and fixtures would not be on the LOD; however, the space for the kitchen and other rooms may be on the LOD.

Map of the Area

The area map should show freeways and major roads. Important items should be clearly labeled for quick identification by the reader. If the location is not in an area readily known to many retailers, an area map is helpful.

Aerial Photograph

Experienced retailers are interested in the trade area. An aerial photograph quickly tells retailers the housing density in the area, road patterns, and shopping center's proximity to its competition. Aerial photographs are available rather inexpensively online. When using an aerial photo, however, be sure it is up to date and includes the most recent residential areas and roads.

Location of Other Retailers

Most retailers want to know where major retailers and possibly similar stores are located in the area. A map with the logos of these stores inserted at their locations provide a picture of the retailing strength of the area. The logos of the tenants may be added to the aerial map. Many retailers like to be in close proximity to specific retailers who have the same or a similar customer base.

Demographics and Psychographics

Complete *demographic* and *psychographic* packages are available from several companies specializing in such information. The real estate manager informs the demographic company of the shopping center's cross streets and the area of demographic interest, such as a three- or five-mile radius. Knowing the demographics and psychographics helps the prospective tenant decide if the population in the area represents the store's customer base.

Shopping Center's Sales

A tenant views a retail location on the basis of its potential sales. Rent is a function of sales. For this reason, it is important to show the tenant a strong sales potential, if it really exists. Care must be taken to keep the confidentiality of an individual merchant's or restaurant's sales in the shopping center—unless that merchant gives specific approval to reveal them. However, general indications can be given. For example, "The shopping center sales average in excess of $780 per square foot; sales are up 9 percent for the most recent 12-month period; the restaurants are averaging sales of $885 per square foot; the supermarket is number one in its division." Any positive sales information is of interest to the knowledgeable merchant or restaurant operator.

Traffic Counts

The amount of traffic passing the shopping center is very important. Traffic counts are measured based on average daily automobile traffic passing the shopping center. These figures are generally available from city, county, or state traffic agencies for little or no cost.

Comparing the automobile traffic counts on the shopping center's street with other streets in the area is important because their relative counts are significant; however, measuring the increase or decrease in traffic counts is also important because that may affect the shopping center's location. Sometimes the street with the second-best traffic count may be a better location because it has less congestion at peak hours.

Automobile traffic on a street may move too fast to be of help to the shopping center. If traffic is one way and in the direction of work, that may pose a problem for some uses. Many retailers, such as wine and liquor stores, along with restaurants prefer homebound traffic. Many regional shopping centers have built-in car counters at each entrance to provide daily traffic counts into the mall. Multiplying the number of cars by the average number of persons provides daily customer traffic counts. Technology is available that will take pedestrian counts for specific areas within a mall or specialty shopping center by any time interval. If the intersection has a signal, known as a hard corner, this should be mentioned. The signal slows traffic and thousands of cars each day must stop in front or near the shopping center.

Marketing Fund's Calendar of Events

A coordinated advertising and promotion program is developed for malls, life style shopping centers, specialty shopping centers, and outlet shopping centers. A professionally prepared calendar of events shows the prospect that the shopping center management is concerned about the tenants' success and makes a coordinated, ongoing effort to generate traffic, which should translate into higher sales for everyone. Photographs of successful merchandising, sales, or promotional events can capture a prospective tenant's interest.

Developing a Database

Many successful shopping center leasing agents developed a database of retailers, restaurant, and service tenants. The database is constantly evolving with new names and contacts numbers.

Office Building and Industrial Property Leasing Packages

Leasing packages for office buildings and industrial properties have similarities and differences to those for shopping centers. Following is a review of information that can be included for both property types:

Brochure

Electronic and hardcopy brochures can be a simple one-page, two-color handout or an elaborate, multicolor presentation. They should include a photo or rendering of the building, location map, list of the building's features, and leasing agent's contact information.

Building Photo

Color photos of the exterior and interior features of the building are of great assistance to an out-of-town company or prospect that must convince others in the company of their building selection.

View Photo

Views are desirable features of an office building—especially water views. Photos taken from several floors can give different view perspectives. Some developers will use a drone to take photos from different floor levels before a building is developed. Check with the municipality regarding rules and laws regarding the use of drones.

Floor Plan

A floor plan showing common areas, the space plan of vacated and existed tenants, and window modules is used for office buildings. A plan showing office and warehouse space is used for industrial properties. Floor plans showing the actual configuration of current vacancies can be helpful when the prospect is not able to visualize the space.

Transportation

A map indicating public transportation stations, routes, freeways, and major arterials is useful for prospective tenants of both industrial and office properties. The industrial user may need additional information on air, water, rail, and truck transportation.

Employment and Housing

The cost and availability of skilled, unskilled, union, and nonunion labor may be a major concern to industrial users. In addition, the cost of rental housing and the price of homes are concerns for some businesses.

Building Services and Features

A list of tenants in the building that provide services to other tenants, such as a stockbroker, bank, restaurant, and gift shop, highlight the amenities in an office building leasing package. Special features, such as impressive large lobby with seating areas, life safety, common areas, conference room, lunch room, and covered parking are excellent selling points.

Area Amenities

A map of the immediate area listing restaurants, financial institutions, governmental offices, court house, significant retailers, health clubs, public transportation stops, and freeway access indicates the amenities of the area and the benefits to be located in the area. The amenities on the map will vary depending on the property type.

List of Tenants

Fortune 500 companies, well-known law firms, businesses, technology companies, restaurants, and health clubs can add prestige to the building. The leasing package should include their names.

Prospecting for Tenants

Prospecting for commercial tenants is a never-ending responsibility that takes the leasing agent down many paths—often with uncertain results. However, most leasing agents indicate that, in spite of the uncertainties, they are most successful when they actively prospect—no matter what the particular activity may be.

Following is a review of prospecting techniques for shopping centers, office, medical office buildings, and industrial properties:

The Leasing Sign

It is generally agreed that one of the most effective leasing tools is a sign on the property. The sign should be in good condition and professionally designed and fabricated to reflect well on the project. It should be easy to read from the street. The sign should feature the leasing agent's name, phone, and e-mail numbers in large print. If the project is new, the leasing sign should include the name of the developer—particularly if the developer is known for quality projects. Some leasing agents like to indicate the square footage of space available, others believe that can limit the inquiries, and tenants quite often are not sure of their space needs.

There are companies that will provide heavy weight paper stock for lease signs with colorful graphics that cover all, or a portion of, the retail property's vacant spaces window. These signs are colorful and draw attention to the space. Many of the large malls will use these signs on the vacancies. They can also be used to announce a new retailer or restaurant for the vacancy. There are wrap-around signs that include very colorful photos of one or two people shopping, and a large for lease sign with the pertinent leasing information. Many prospects will not search online for space available, and they may enjoy driving an area looking for space available becoming familiar with the neighborhood.

Direct Mail vs. E-mail

A direct-mail program to selected prospects is not as popular, but is still an effective marketing solution. Mailing should be targeted to specific tenants in a specific area—even those who are not in the market for space would aware of the project and might discuss it with someone who does have an interest. Extensive direct mailings will incur better responses. For direct-mail campaigns, an overall response of one to two percent is considered good.

Compared to direct mailing, e-mail is more cost effective due lack of postage costs. The costs would be more directed to the time put into design or purchasing specific e-mail lists. However, the likelihood of e-mail messages being treated as spam or immediately deleted are strong.

Therefore the wording, timing, and overall design should be strategically considered before an e-mail campaign begins. A good amount of time and consideration should be spent on developing and producing e-mail content.

Cold Calling and Canvassing

Calling on potential tenants in their places of business can be very time consuming, but it is still considered a very productive prospecting activity. When the leasing agent contacts tenants with a specific use, that is called *cold calling*. When the leasing agent contacts all the tenants in a building, regardless of their use, that is called *canvassing*. Each of these methods for contacting tenants can provide overall knowledge of an area. As an additional benefit, each can identify prospects for other properties the leasing agent represents.

For each canvassing trip, a goal of a specific number of calls should be determined. Business cards and information sheets should be distributed freely. It is wise not to try to accomplish too much in the first visit. If the decision maker is not in, the leasing agent will speak with the manager, executive administrative assistant, or receptionist. Be sure to leave the information and request that it be passed on to the decision maker. Later, the leasing agent will make a follow-up call to be sure the decision maker received the information.

Telephone Canvassing

The telephone can be an effective, time-saving leasing tool because it allows the leasing agent to contact many prospects in a single day. As in canvassing, specific goals are necessary. The purpose of the call is to learn whether the business owner is in the market for additional space, to find out when his or her lease expires, and to obtain permission to e-mail a brochure or schedule a follow-up visit.

Billboards

Larger shopping centers, specialty centers, and major commercial projects with large trade areas may benefit from a "coming soon" billboard campaign. Measuring the impact of billboards can be difficult, but they can be useful marketing tools in some situations—though they are seldom used.

Project Signs

New projects often have a large project sign with a color rendering that includes the names of the developer, leasing agent, architect, general contractor, and lender. The leasing agent's company, phone number, and e-mail address are placed strategically on the sign.

Various Print Advertisements

For every profession, there is a trade journal. Advertising a property in a trade journal can be an effective way to reach a specific category of tenants. Local chapters of professional associations may allow advertising in their monthly or quarterly newsletters.

Larger display ads are used to announce the grand opening or remodeling of major buildings, major lease-up activities, or major tenants who have just executed leases in the building.

Placing ads in the weekly business newspaper or business magazine in the community is another a direct way to reach businesses.

Publicity

Publicity has credibility well beyond that of advertising. The leasing agent should develop a publicity program to cover the entire leasing effort. A creative leasing agent can find many legitimate publicity opportunities, including the following:

- Unique building features
- Remodeling or repositioning a building
- Energy-saving features
- Design features
- Ground-breaking ceremony
- Placement of the corner stone

- Signing of well-known tenants
- Signing of anchor tenants
- Impressive levels of lease-up
- Announcing the building or shopping center manager
- A new store manager
- Sending announcements via press releases
- Grand opening
- A celebrity appearance at the property or one of its stores or restaurants.

A public relations (PR) agency can assure maximum coverage of the property. If public relations is handled in-house, a rapport with the media should be developed in advance. The real estate manager should introduce him or herself to the real estate editors of the local newspapers and develop a working rapport with them. They may offer to be real estate source for the editors and writers.

Social Media and Online Presence

Social media is the most cost-effective marketing and networking tool available to real estate managers. LinkedIn, Facebook, and Twitter, to name a few, are the top social media methods for allowing companies to reach the public. It's important to stay focused when using social media and to ensure professionalism—but also remembering that everything placed online is there forever. Prospective tenants will review everything that a company or individual has ever published on any form of social media.

Social is best used in sharing successes and making announcements promoting the properties, as opposed to giving a blatant sales pitch. Craft your marketing effort so that it encourages prospective tenants to communicate. It is important to understand that social media is not a direct advertisement, but a method of direct communication with one's prospective tenants. The general public want to see a vacant space that is available, read about a job opportunity, or even see the new landscape or common area improvements that were made to a building. This is what is interesting in social media and it is also what gets re-tweeted, liked, shared, or pinned because it provides people with a new, unique opportunity to tell the story and be noticed.

It's important that once the online presence is established that it's also maintained and regularly managed. The Institute of Real Estate Management (IREM) offers an eBook titled, *Social Media for Real Estate Managers* that serves as a great resource in creating business pages through social media sites like Facebook, LinkedIn, or Twitter. The eBook also provides assistance for establishing and maintaining a social media presence, especially for those new to this process.

Other ways to have a strong online presence are also through blogs, forums, or even wikis. These platforms allow for information and knowledge sharing and have the potential to reach far larger audiences than traditional forms of marketing.

Civic and Business Meetings

Being active in local civic and business organizations offers another means to broadcast the leasing message and to meet prospective tenants. Such meetings offer opportunities for the real estate manager or leasing agent to tell the building's story and to listen to what others are doing in the business and civic areas.

Broker's Associations

Many areas of the country have broker's associations. They may be local independent associations or a chapter of national professional commercial property associations. These associations are a great place to network. Some of these associations have monthly meetings where brokers present their listings.

Open House

Hosting an open house for the brokerage community and another for the business community to show off a new or remodeled building is a means to bring prospects to the site. Events for an open house include ground breaking, topping off, grand opening, and remodeling. The best way to attract brokers is to hold the open house from mid-afternoon to just after dinner time. This allows brokers to attend who want to be home with the family for dinner or have an evening event.

Employment Ads

Checking employment ads can indicate which companies are expanding and may be in need of additional space. The retail and service business ads may indicate which businesses may be planning to open another store, significantly increase their market penetration, and new businesses that have entered the market.

Business Directories

Business and trade associations such as the chamber of commerce, the local economic development council, and the downtown business association have directories that provide excellent leasing leads and opportunities for a leasing ad.

Community Charitable Events

Encouraging a community organization to hold a benefit black-tie party at the mall or on the top floor of an office building before its grand opening brings community and business leaders to the property and generates excellent publicity.

Monitoring Government Contracts

When the government awards a contract to a manufacturer, the Boeing Company for example, the manufacturer and its suppliers may need additional office and/or industrial space.

Government's Space Requirements

The General Services Administration (GSA) sends out information that list its space requirements. Property owners can be included on the e-mail list by contacting the local GSA office. State and local municipalities may have similar mailings for their space needs.

Model Office and Vacant Spaces

Furnishing a model office and inviting brokers to tour the building can help market its unique features. Many real estate managers believe they should not just clean vacant commercial spaces but also paint the premises and possibly replace the floor covering.

Developing Contacts at a Hospital

Medical office buildings and office buildings with medical space should be marketed to hospital administrators. Hospitals encourage doctors to affiliate with them, and those doctors often need medical office space. Hospital personnel responsible for recruiting doctors to affiliate with the hospital need to know what spaces are available for new physicians to the area.

Medical Office Building E-mail Lists and Medical Journal Ads

The e-mail list of the county's medical society may be available for purchase. Another means of direct contact with the medical profession is to advertise in local and regional medical journals. In the Seattle area, for example, the local journal is the *King County Medical Society Bulletin,* and the regional journal is the *Western Journal of Medicine.* The best position for the ads is the back cover or the inside cover pages.

Luncheon for Managers of Medical Practices

To present a new medical office building, the property owner may have the real estate manager host a luncheon for the business managers of medical practices. A real estate manager responsible for the leasing of a new 125,000 square foot medical office building hosted, on behalf of the developer, a series of luncheons for the managers of medical practices in the area.

There were four luncheons in one of the best hotels in the city near the medical community, each with a speaker on a topic of interest to medical group managers, such as refinancing a medical practice and the new space plans for more efficient operations.

Medical Group Managers Associations

The Medical Group Managers Association is an association of medical group managers that are headquartered in Denver. They have local chapters across the United States. These chapters have local and regional meetings, which may be a good opportunity to network with the managers of medical practices.

Networking

Networking is simply developing and sharing contacts. Staying active with real estate and business community and having a finger on the pulse of the market is an important component to the marketing and leasing of commercial buildings.

Brokers' Tours

Scheduling a tour of the building with individual brokerage companies is an excellent opportunity to develop a rapport with them and discuss the building with small groups of leasing agents. Providing snacks, a box lunch, or breakfast is greatly appreciated by the leasing agents.

Managers and Leasing Agents of Other Projects

Building a network with real estate managers and leasing agents of competitive projects is worthwhile. Sharing data can produce valuable information on prospective tenants for everyone. There may be opportunities to refer prospects whose space needs cannot be met in your building to nearby buildings. When the competition is fully leased, they are no longer your competitor.

Suppliers

Suppliers of goods or services often have a vested interest in new tenants who could be new customers. For example, a supplier of restaurant equipment may provide leads to the real estate manager on existing restaurant operators who are interested in opening another restaurant. A manufacturer or producer of ice cream could be helpful in locating an operator who would then provide another retail outlet for the ice cream. Suppliers can be helpful for many kinds of businesses.

Building Tenants

Existing tenants are good sources of new tenants. The real estate manager should keep tenants aware of vacancies. They may be in need of expansion space, or they may know of businesses who would be interested in the building. The competition is always canvassing a building's tenants, and so should the building's real estate manager.

Sources of Retail Prospects

Several useful prospecting resources are available for leasing shopping centers and retail properties.

1. Chamber of commerce: Prospective tenants sometimes stop by the chamber office for information on the community, and they note any leasing opportunities that are registered at the chamber.
2. Redevelopment agencies, economic development agencies, and downtown associations: An active source of finding prospective tenants is agencies and associations. One of their functions is to market the benefits of its area to create interest.
3. Other shopping centers: The leasing agent should regularly visit other shopping centers and retail areas looking for new tenants, new uses, and new ideas.
4. Monitoring tenants' ads: Advertisements on radio and television or in the magazines and newspapers provide a viable list of desirable tenants. Those who advertise warrant special attention in leasing efforts.
5. Classified ads: The real estate manager and leasing agent should read the classified ads for retailers that are looking for managers or additional help because they could be in the market for expansion space.
6. Local and area directories and newsletters: Many local directories and newsletters supply excellent information.
7. Shopping center conventions: The International Council of Shopping Centers' (ICSC) hosts an annual convention where developers, brokers, and retailers rent booths to display their shopping centers, space they have listed, tenants they represent, or their merchandise or products. It is not necessary to have a booth to attend, or to be successful locating prospective tenants. The real estate manager or leasing agent can make many contacts with retailers by visiting their booths, and in advance, schedule meetings with them during the convention.
8. Deal-making sessions and idea exchanges: ICSC conducts deal-making sessions through the year in different regional areas. These idea exchanges are two-day conferences held in every region of

the country and attended by brokers, developers, real estate managers, and retailers. They often include a much smaller version of a leasing mall.

9. **Shopping center trade journals and other publications:** Various trade journals and publications related to the retail industry will provide a good source of information for finding prospective tenants.

CONCLUSION

Not every business is a potential tenant for a commercial building because each business has its unique space and location requirements, and some retail tenants have co-tenancy requirements. A marketing and leasing plan is developed to target a specific group of prospects for the building. There are many techniques and marketing materials that can be used to market and lease a building. The marketing and leasing teams will determine the target market for a building and develop the most effective marketing and leasing plan to reach these prospects to achieve the leasing goals of the property's owner.

CHAPTER

8

Preparing to Lease a Building

Understanding the goals and objectives of the property owner are essential for preparing to lease a building. After a thorough discussion with the property owner, the real estate manager assembles a leasing team comprising of professionals from many disciplines who will be responsible for implementing the diverse and specialized activities needed to complete a lease transaction. While assembling the leasing team and its consultants, the real estate manager should gather information on the building, its market, and competition to develop a leasing and negotiating strategy. This chapter explains the intricate details or activities involved in coordinating the leasing of a building.

THE OWNER'S GOALS AND OBJECTIVES

Properties are managed and leased based on the property owner's goals and objectives, which are usually centered on increased cash flow and enhancing the value of a building. While these are typical goals for any investment, the property owner may have other specific issues or "pressure points" which will influence the leasing and negotiating strategies. For instance, the property ownership may want to increase the percentage of credit tenants which is likely to lower the building's cap rate to determine the value of the building. Another goal may be to incorporate long-term leases for the security of a continual income stream. The property owner may want to sell the building and not invest in long-term capital improvements, but focus on leasing the building to full occupancy.

In some cases, credit worthiness of prospective tenants may not be a concern of some owners who plan to sell the building in the near term. While in other cases, a property owner may want to own the building for long-term appreciation and might be more willing to invest capital in building improvements.

There are a number of these "pressure points" that property owners might have. Other examples include partnership disputes that might accelerate the need to sell the property. A property owner may have loan requirements that require the property to maintain a *net operating income (NOI)* of no less than a specific amount, and when the NOI falls below the specific level, the partners must contribute capital to partially pay down the loan. The property may be experiencing *negative cash flow* and *capital call* (also known as cash call), which is putting pressure on the partners. Some partners may not be in a position to contribute their share of the capital calls. These pressure points, which are often not evident to the real estate community, can alter the goals and objectives of the property ownership.

Changing the goals and objectives may change the negotiating position of the real estate manager and the property owners. For instance, a property with negative cash flow and partners struggling to fund the short fall may not be in a position to offer significant or any tenant improvement allowance. This is likely to change the negotiating posture of the real estate manager on some issues and lease provisions.

The property ownership may have different goals for each building they own and different objectives for negotiating with each prospective tenant. The ownership of a *lifestyle shopping center* may be willing to offer a significant tenant improvement allowance for an international fashion retailer whose sales far exceed those of other fashion retailers. A restaurant in a mid- to high-rise office building is a great amenity for the building and its tenants. The ownership may offer very favorably rental terms to one of the best restaurants in the area. The property may have a high occupancy and the property ownership is willing to be aggressive, and lead the market, with its rental rate and lack of concessions on future leases.

Understanding the Property

The real estate manager and/or leasing agent must develop a thorough understanding of the subject property. It's important to assess the property's strengths and weaknesses. After studying the market and the competition, the real estate manager can position the property in the market and highlight the property's strengths and be prepared to address its weaknesses or deficiencies. Recommended improvements may be necessary to improve the building's position in the market.

In order to determine the building's position in the market, the real estate manager must conduct a *market survey* and analysis of each competing building. After completing this analysis, the building can be evaluated based on the competition and position in the market. When this is done, the correct rental rates can be established for the building. A thorough market survey will provided accurate market data and enable the real estate manager to determine accurate rental rates for the property.

Once rental rates for each space have been established, they will serve as budgetary goals for lease negotiations. For a retail tenant, this goal might be $45 per square foot minimum rent, triple-net charges, a five-year lease with no options, an improvement allowance of $10 per square foot, and a percentage rent provision of five percent. These provisions are generally spelled out in a leasing plan for the coming year.

ASSEMBLING THE LEASING TEAM

Leasing space requires the expertise of several professionals from different disciplines in the real estate industry working together to achieve their client's leasing goals and objectives. Owners assemble leasing teams to find tenants for their buildings, while tenants assemble leasing teams to find space to operate their businesses. These teams must work together to complete a lease or deal.

The owner's team will include leasing agents, administrative support, an attorney, space planner, tenant improvement contractors, the building's real estate manager, engineer, and possibly the building's lender and other professionals.

Many players are involved directly and indirectly in the lease negotiation. Some players—such as the real estate manager, the property's leasing agent, and the tenant's representative—are often directly involved in the entire negotiation. The property owner and the tenant may not be directly involved in the negotiations, but they decide whether to accept or reject the lease terms and provisions. Seldom is an attorney involved in negotiating the deal's business terms—e.g., rent and possible concessions. However, attorneys may be involved in negotiating the lease provisions, available for consultation on specific provisions and issues, or they might not be involved in the deal at all.

One responsibility of the person in charge of leasing a property is to keep all the players involved in the deal. A deal that appears to be proceeding to closure can come to a complete standstill if one or more players do not complete their responsibilities. The longer it takes to completing a deal, the greater the chance it will collapse—as time is usually of the essence and alternatives are always being considered. Each player in the deal must recognize his or her role and be willing to move the deal along to its completion.

The number of players on the tenant's team will vary depending on whether the tenant is a local business or a national company. A local business will hire a leasing agent, an attorney, and may require the services of a space planner, designer, and possibly a general contractor. Regional and national companies have real estate representatives, site selection committees, construction coordinators, lease administrative personnel, and they often contract with local leasing agents to find several alternative locations to consider.

Rhythm of the Deal

An interesting or creative perspective on the "deal" is each deal has a rhythm and each player is like a musician playing in an orchestra. The leader of the transaction is the "conductor." While the conductor of the orchestra calls on each musician at the right moment to play their instrument, so does the real estate manager by assembling a team of professionals with different skills to provide their expertise in analyzing a component of the transaction at the appropriate time. Every transaction needs a conductor. The real estate manager leads a team just as the orchestra conductor leads the orchestra. Just as there is a rhythm to a song, there is a rhythm to a lease transaction.

Property Owner

The property owner will provide the parameters for each lease term that it either wants or needs. The property owner's role is to analyze the terms of the potential deal, the use of the space, and the negotiated lease provisions, and to make the final decision as to whether to accept or reject the lease. The decision may take many turns while the lease terms and provisions are negotiated. Each party submits offers and counter-offers. The property owner should rely on the real estate manager or leasing agent's advice as to the market rental rate for the property, market concessions, and other deal terms.

The property owner needs to be responsive to all lease proposals and counter-offers. Everyone in the deal must have a sense of urgency in completing the deal to avoid the other party losing interest or finding another alternative. However, at times a delay in responding to an offer or a counter-offer is part of the lease-negotiation strategy.

The Real Estate Manager

The real estate manager is responsible to the property owner either in the role of leasing agent for the building or in supporting the building's leasing agent. The real estate manager's role includes keeping the property owner educated on the market, the rental rates of competing buildings, and providing recommendations for the rental rates and possible concessions. This includes educating the property owner as to the building's position in the market, and if necessary, alternatives to improving the building's market position. If the real estate manager is also responsible for leasing, the role discussed for the leasing agent also applies to the real estate manager. If the real estate manager serves in a support role, he or she should evaluate prospective tenants and offer an opinion as to the benefits and possible objections to the specific tenant or its use. The real estate manager should review negotiated lease terms and provisions and evaluate their impact on the operations of the property.

The real estate manager's most important role is to be the leader of the transaction delegating responsibilities to the other team members, creating action activities and time lines for each team member, and following up with them to ensure they are timely in meeting their commitments.

THE LEASING AGENTS

Many leasing agents specialize as either a property owner or a tenant agent. Some leasing agents will have both property owners and tenants as clients, but they usually spend the majority of their time representing one or the other to avoid conflicts of interest.

The Property Owner Leasing Agent

Most property owners do not have a leasing team or the time to lease properties themselves, so they contract with a brokerage firm to lease their buildings. Some will use the building's real estate manager to lease the building. An exception would be large developers and *real estate investment trusts (REITs)* with in-house leasing departments.

One of the advantages of contracting with a brokerage firm is its leasing agents are "in play" at all times, looking for prospects, networking with other leasing agents (from their own firm as well as from competing firms), and becoming aware of deals that have taken place. They are constantly monitoring changes to the market conditions.

Leasing agents do not receive a salary and work for commission. They are highly motivated to complete deals because they are usually the only member of the leasing team who are compensated only after a deal is completed. All the other members of the leasing team either receive a salary, an hourly fee, or paid based on a negotiated contract.

The Tenant Leasing Agent

Many businesses are represented by leasing agents in their search for space. The tenant's leasing agent, referred to as a "tenant rep," provides a valuable service. Tenants are not in the real estate business, and they seldom have more than a cursory knowledge of the commercial real estate market. They often do not have the time or interest to educate themselves on market conditions, nor do they have the resources or the contacts to know the terms of comparable deals. The tenant rep fills this gap by providing a wealth of knowledge about the market along with the ability to select and analyze buildings that meet certain space and location needs. This allows a tenant to focus on business operations, knowing that a real estate professional is looking for space that will meet the specified business requirements on the best possible terms.

Leasing agents have an influence over which buildings their tenants select and play an important role in the lease transaction. Though tenant brokers are not on the building's leasing team, they are a player in the lease transaction and can facilitate the completion of the deal. They will work with the building's leasing agent to ensure the members of their leasing team are completing the responsibilities. The leasing agents for the owner and the tenant are partners in a moment of time to complete the deal—even though they are negotiating against each other. It is important to note that tenant rep brokers are almost always paid for by the building owner. Even though this fee is usually paid for out of the deal, tenants are still able to achieve an overall savings by utilizing a tenant rep broker, and they benefit from the knowledge and advice of their broker.

The Tenant's In-House Leasing Representative

Some national businesses, especially retailers and restaurant chains, have their own in-house real estate representative. These businesses are highly specialized and have very specific needs. The in-house real estate professionals have a unique understanding of their firm's real estate requirements, and as such, are responsible for either managing the leasing process or for working directly with owners or their leasing agents to locate and negotiate leases.

When managing the leasing function, the in-house leasing personnel hires brokerage firms to find locations; work with an in-house attorney or law firms to review the lease document; coordinate the build-out of the premises; and negotiate the lease. In some situations, in-house leasing personnel will work directly with the property owner to negotiate the lease.

The Property Owner's In-House Leasing Agent

Though the great majority of property owners use brokerage firms to lease their properties, there is some benefit from having an in-house leasing team. The in-house leasing agent often leads the leasing effort and is often part of the owner's team, developing or acquiring properties. This allows the benefit of focusing only on leasing the employer's properties, giving the in-house agent a better understanding than an independent leasing agent would have of the owner's goals and objectives for each property. They are able to focus all efforts on leasing the properties. Many REITs and large commercial property development firms have an in-house leasing team. For instance, developers and owners of regional malls will almost always have their own leasing team. Owners of regional and super-regional malls and their leasing team are able to network with all the national retailers and most of the regional retailers. They do deals with these retailers directly. Grocery-anchored shopping center REITs that have a large concentration of properties in a metropolitan area will also employ an in-house leasing agent(s).

The Asset Manager

An *asset manager* is responsible for the management and overall performance of an investment, which involves enhancing the property's cash flow and value by developing and executing a long-term strategy consistent with the owner's goals and objectives. In the real estate industry, asset managers are usually employed by financial institutions, REITs, real estate funds, and many corporations that have large real estate holdings. They select and hire the property's leasing agent, real estate manager, and other real estate professionals.

The asset manager is responsible for carrying out the strategy and monitoring the performance of a portfolio of properties, and for supervising the leasing of the properties in their portfolio. They make leasing decisions in their role as the owner's representative. There is a risk element in every transaction, and the asset manager measures that risk against the value the lease brings to the property.

The Administrative Assistant

The administrative assistant supports the real estate manager or leasing agent. The administrative assistant's most important responsibility is to keep the deal moving by providing support to the real estate manager or leasing agent and to prepare lease documents and support materials.

Prospective Tenant

The prospective tenant has final authority to accept or reject an offer or counter-offer. The role of the prospect is similar to that of the property owner. The prospect must rely on the advice of his or her leasing representative regarding the market rental rate for the property and space under consideration. Unlike the property owner, who is likely to be actively involved in real estate, prospective tenants are not real estate professionals and they may have only a vague understanding of the market. They place a heavy reliance on the advice of their leasing agent.

Attorneys

Attorneys are charged with protecting their client's interests. A good attorney recognizes a client's need to make a deal while providing advice on negotiating lease provisions. Since the lease is a legal document with rights and obligations for the owner and the tenant, attorneys protect clients' interests by negotiating the lease in their clients' best interests. The parties to any transaction should know and understand the responsibilities of the attorney. The attorney's role can be misunderstood by leasing agents and occasionally by owners and tenants if the property owner does not clarify their role to the leasing agent, real estate manager, and the attorney.

The Architect

Architects have the assignment of designing buildings that will maximize the efficiency of a site, which translates into designing buildings with the greatest amount of income-producing space within the budget.

The architect needs to be an active member of the leasing team. The owner and leasing agent must work with the building design to lease the space as configured by the architect. From a leasing perspective, the primary role of the architect is to design a building that will be accepted in the market and meet the space requirements of its targeted tenants.

An architect is also a valuable member of the leasing team when a building is being renovated. The architect can redesign space that is difficult to lease because it no longer meets the space requirements of today's tenants. This eliminates *obsolescence* in the building, and once again, maximizes the site's efficiency and revenue-generating potential.

The Construction Manager

Large office buildings, medical office buildings, and business parks will often have an on-site *construction manager*. This person works with the prospective tenant, the space planner, the interior designer, and the general contractor. When a lease is executed, the construction manager will contract for the build out of the premises and supervise the general contractor, ensuring that the premises are built on time and in keeping with the lease requirements. The construction manager has an important role coordinating the activity of the space planner and general contractor who builds out the space. Meeting the construction timeline is an important component to the leasing process, especially for tenants who need to open and operate their businesses by a specific date. Retail properties do not need construction managers to coordinate the tenant's improvements because retail tenants have a designer and contractors who buildings out all of their locations.

SPACE PLANNING

Space planning is an important component of the leasing process. The space planner acts as a valuable member of the leasing team by helping tenants to understand their space needs. Sophisticated tenants quite often have their own space planners and have a good idea of what they need before they start the leasing process. However, smaller or independent tenants generally have less understanding of their real space needs, and assistance from the owner can help finalize a lease.

The space planner's job is to work with tenants to produce viable space plans for their occupancy in the building, keeping within the financial constraints of the owner's and each tenant's budget. Sometimes the space planner is a member of the architect team that designed the building, but usually the space planner has its own firm.

General Contractor

A *general contractor* is hired by the owner of all property types to build out the premises per the architect's specifications. The general contractor also liaisons with the city to file plans and receive permits, and they are often called upon to "value engineer" the build-out within the owner's and tenant's budgets.

Retail tenants usually have dedicated contractors who build out all their stores and provide pre negotiated cost estimates.

The Interior Designer

Office and medical tenants may use the services of an interior designer. The criteria for selecting an interior designer are similar to choosing a space planner. It is important that the interior designer understands the prospective tenant's budget and what amount, if any, the owner is contributing to the design of the space. Interior designers must be aware of, and keep to, the timeline to complete their portion of the process to have the tenant's space ready by a targeted date.

The Lender

A lender can influence the leasing of a building if the building's loan has specific lease requirements. The developer's and sometimes the owner's lender may place restrictions on the terms of a lease. The following lists several criteria that the lenders use when underwriting loans—some can be turned into lease-term restrictions that are placed on the property:

- Minimum lease rates
- Percentage of *common area maintenance (CAM)* and building *operating expenses* that are reimbursed by the tenants
- Minimum length of the lease
- Required periodical rent step-ups
- Staggered lease expiration dates
- *Loan-to-value ratios (LTVs)*
- Loan's expiration (retail anchor tenant leases and other anchor tenant leases may be required to expire no sooner than a year after the loan matures)
- Quality of the tenant
- Contribution the tenant(s)—especially the retail tenant—makes to the building
- Credit rating of the tenants

The lender is also concerned with onerous lease provisions that might interrupt the property's income flow; lease termination rights, co-tenancy provisions, operating covenants of anchor stores, and other lease encumbrances. Some loans will not allow the owner to enter into a lease with rental rates that are below a predetermined amount without the lender's approval.

The Mall Marketing Director

Most properties and property owners do not have a sufficient amount of properties to afford a marketing director. However, all malls have a marketing director who is responsible for advertising and promotions of the mall targeted to the shopper. They can also be a member of the leasing team knowing which retailers are needed for the mall, etc.

The main role of the mall marketing director is to develop an effective marketing strategy and successfully execute its advertising and promotional programs for the shoppers and the community. This person also has the responsibility of continually evaluating the mall's tenant mix and making recommendations to improve the tenant mix based on categories of merchants and restaurants that might need upgrading, and which existing tenants should be replaced due to poor performance.

The mall marketing director should have a prominent position on the leasing team especially since they will be the most familiar with the mall's trade area, customer profile, dynamics of its tenant mix, and the strengths and weakness of competing malls and shopping centers.

THE MARKET SURVEY

The greatest influence the real estate manager has on the value of a property is to influence the income side of the income-expense equation. Opportunities exist to improve the value of property by reducing operating expenses, but more significant opportunities exist to increase the property's income.

An essential element in maximizing the property's income is maintaining the building's rental rates at their market value. To do this, the real estate manager must be knowledgeable about market conditions. This information can be gathered through a *market survey*. Trends can be identified when the surveys are conducted on a regular basis.

Market surveys are also used in managing and financing the property and in the acquisition process. The surveys enable the real estate manager to project rental rates, concessions, and lease-up or a building's absorption rate, all of which are essential to developing the income components of a budget. Market surveys are needed when developing or refinancing a building. They are also needed to satisfy the due diligence requirement when analyzing a building for purchase or sale. Accurate information and a correct analysis of the information are essential to meeting the objectives of the market survey.

Determining the Market

The first step in conducting a market survey is to define the area to be surveyed. Determining the boundary of commercial properties is not difficult when the real estate manager is active in the area, however, being new to the area, a more detailed analysis is necessary. It is impossible to place a mileage ring around the property to determine its market area. The boundaries are formed by man-made barriers such as freeways, changes of property use, or locations of competing buildings. It's easier to determine the market area when there are natural barriers, such as a river or mountain area.

The market's size is another variable in defining its boundary. For instance, the market for a Class A office building in a city's central business district (CBD) may be a less than one mile in each direction, while the market for a regional mall in the same city may cover the entire county. The boundaries of the shopping center's trade area encompass the area in which most of its customers live or work. For example, when determining market rates for a grocery-anchored shopping center, the real estate manager should survey all shopping centers anchored by one or more major tenants located in the shopping center's trade area. Surveying small, unanchored strip shopping centers or enclosed malls is not necessary because they are not in direct competition with the grocery-anchored shopping center. If the trade area does not have sufficient competing shopping centers to provide a valid comparison, the real estate manager should then survey grocery-anchored shopping centers in a similar trade area outside the subject shopping center's trade area.

Office buildings are classified as Class A, B, or C buildings and are located downtown, in a secondary business district in a city , or in the suburbs. To establish the boundaries of the area to be surveyed, the real estate manager must first identify the classification of the office building and then determine which buildings are its competition. Suburban buildings typically do not compete directly with downtown office buildings because most tenants choose among buildings in one particular area.

The method used in determining the area to survey for industrial properties is similar to the method used for office building surveys. However, factors such as labor pool, freeway access, and location to critical infrastructure can influence a trade area.

Conducting the Survey

An effective means for gathering market information is contacting leasing agents and real estate managers in the marketplace and inquiring about their "asking" and "deal-making" rates, the concessions they make, and their vacancies. Internet real estate listing sites provide a list of properties for lease, the size of each vacancy, their asking rental rates, and the name and contact information of the listing brokers. This is good information and provides a list of buildings with space for lease that may not otherwise be found. The leasing agents for each building on the list that is competition for the building being leased should be contacted to discuss the buildings' deal making rate.

Conducting the market survey is not difficult or time-consuming. Depending on the size of the market, the initial survey may take a day or day and a half. Subsequent surveys will take considerable less time. The initial survey takes longer because the boundaries of the market must be defined, competing properties within the boundaries must be located, and the person responsible for leasing each property must be identified.

Market Survey Form

The real estate manager should develop a market survey form to record the rental information and features of the subject properties and the competition. The information on the survey form will vary according to property type. Exhibits 8.1, 8.2, and 8.3 are market survey forms for shopping centers, office buildings, and industrial properties, respectively. They request information on location, building features, condition of the property, deal-making rates, tenant charges, concessions, and vacancies. The forms are discussed in detail later in this chapter.

Competing Property Identification

The best way to locate competing properties is to drive the area within the boundaries of the micro market or trade area. When the real estate manager locates a competing building, he or she should inspect it and complete a market survey form for the property. Competing properties are marked on a map that is updated for subsequent surveys. A tour of each competing building is necessary to determine the condition of each building and how they compare to the building being leased. While inspecting the properties, the real estate manager can find the name and phone number of the leasing agent on the directory of the office building or on a sign on the property. With the market area identified and the form in hand, the real estate manager is prepared to conduct the survey.

Visual Inspection

Each competing property and their current vacancies must be visited to learn how it compares with the subject property. The building's leasing agent can provide the rental data, but only a visual inspection will disclose the building's features and the condition of the property and vacancies. Ideally, the real estate manager tours the vacancies, but in practice, building managers do not give tours to their competitors. Most buildings do not have an on-site

EXHIBIT 8.1

Market Survey—Shopping Centers

CENTER DATA					MAJORS		RENTAL INFORMATION									CONDITION						
CENTER	AGE	NUMBER SHOPS	SOFT	PARKING LOT	MAJORS	VACANCY	ASKING RENTS	DEAL MAKING RENTS	%	TAX	INS	CAM	CPI	HVAC	OTHER	P/L	BLDG	AREA	ACCESS	TENANTS	VISIBILITY	COMMENTS

EXHIBIT 8.2

Market Survey—Office Buildings

BUILDING DATA				RENTAL INFORMATION					BUILDING SERVICES							
OFFICE BLDG	AGE	STORIES	VACANCY	ASKING RENT	DEAL MAKING RENT	OPERATING EXPENSES	CPI	OTHER	PARKING	ON-SITE MGT-MAINT	JANITOR	SECUR	ELEV	HVAC/HR	LIFE SAFETY	OTHER

EXHIBIT 8.3

Market Survey—Industrial Properties

	Property Date				Majors	Rental Info								
Property	Zoning	Age	Sq. Ft.	No. of Bldgs	Major Tenants	Vacancy	Asking Rates	Deal-making Rates	Tax	Ins	CAM	CPI	HVAC	Other

Condition					Features							
Parking Lot	Bldg	Area	Access	Type Const	Sprinklers	Util	Ceiling Heights	% Ofc Space	Truck Loading Facilities	Rail Spur	HVAC	Misc

building manager or leasing agent. Plus, they will be reluctant to drive to the property to show vacancies to a non-prospective tenant. For shopping centers, the real estate manager can see through the window of the vacancies and pace off the frontage of the vacancies and the side of the building to determine its size. This cannot be done for office buildings and industrial properties. Office building features, such as life-safety systems, energy conservation features, and security programs may not be observed during a property inspection. These features are obtained by contacting the building's real estate manager or leasing agent.

Real Estate Manager Interview

Once the building's features and property conditions are noted, the real estate manager schedules an appointment or phone call with the building's real estate manager or leasing agent to review the property's rental information. If the building's leasing contact information is not listed on site, the real estate manager can ask one of the tenants for this information.

Most real estate managers and leasing agents are willing to share their information with one another. One way to elicit market information from a competitor is to share specific rental information on one's own property. The real estate manager should be prepared to briefly discuss the size of the building, its location, rental information, and vacancies. Explain the asking rate and deal-making rate and the concessions necessary to make a deal. For example, "My building is asking $38.00 per square foot, but we will make a deal at $36.00 with one month free rent for each year of the lease." Obtaining the deal-making rates is essential. If only the asking rates are requested, the survey data will be distorted, and the conclusion may be incorrect. Free rent, tenant improvement allowance, moving allowances, and other concessions affect the face rate that is charged. Face rate is the rent paid without deduction for concessions. For instance, a rental rate at $18 per square foot for five years with six months' free rent has a face rate of $18, and an effective rate of $16.20 per square foot. The effective rate takes into account the free rent and other concessions.

Tenant charges also affect the rental rate. Are the office building operating expenses established from a base year? If so, what is the base year? Is a stop clause used? If so, what is the dollar amount of the expense stop? Base-year and stop clauses are discussed in *Chapter 14: Financial Analysis for Real estate Manager*. Other charges to consider are common area maintenance, real estate taxes, insurance, and merchants' association or marketing fund dues. Tenants will include the *pass-through charges* along with the base rental rate to calculate their occupancy costs. They will compare competing buildings based on their occupancy cost—not just the base rental rate.

The last information to obtain is the vacancy rate or the amount of vacant square footage. For some properties, this information can be obtained by walking the property. For others, such as office buildings, the information must be provided by the real estate manager or leasing agent. The listing sites online may be helpful in determining vacancy rates because all the vacancies for a building are usually included on each building's listing. Lastly, a few of the regional, national, and international real estate brokerages track market data and research departments will typically share this information freely.

After the market information is obtained and the information is entered on the market survey form, the real estate manager can compare the subject property with the competition, determine the property's position in the market, establish its market rental rates and concessions (if necessary), and project the property's lease-up.

Frequency of Survey

The frequency of the market survey depends on several variables, but it must be conducted as often as necessary to remain current with market conditions. The following lists when the market survey is necessary:

- Recommending rental rates for the marketing and leasing of a building
- Developing the property's annual management or business plan
- Projecting the lease-up of a new or renovated building
- Estimating income for the budget
- Assuming a new management or leasing account
- Establishing or adjusting market rental rates

Evaluating the Market Survey

Properly evaluated, the market survey clarifies the position of the subject property in the market and ranks the property with the competition within its specific classification. The survey compares building features and indicates areas in which the subject building excels and those in which it is deficient. This information can be used to identify areas of the building that need better maintenance or that require capital improvements to maintain or upgrade the building's position in the market.

In evaluating the information from the market survey, the real estate manager must recognize that a classification of properties does not have just one market rental rate, but rather a range of rates. For instance, the Class A office space in a city's central business district (CBD) may range from $40 to $52 per square foot annually.

The variance within the range of rental rates in a market depends on several factors. An important factor is the building's location. A Class A building adjacent to a rapid transit station may command a higher rate than a building several blocks away. Another variable is location within the building. A space with a view commands higher rents than one without a view. A corner location in the central court of a mall rents for considerably more per square foot than an in-line location with less exposure and foot traffic.

The size of the space is another variable when evaluating the survey. Small spaces rent for more per square foot than larger spaces when everything else is equal. In a shopping center, deep spaces usually lease for less per square foot than shallow spaces. End cap spaces with a drive-up window in a strip shopping center rent for more per square foot than in-line spaces. Corner locations in an office building are more valuable than an in-line location. Other variables include the following:

- Prestigious address of an office building
- Strong major tenant in a shopping center
- Unique design of an office building
- Cost of the pass-through expenses to the tenants
- Immediate neighborhood of the building
- Quality of the building's management
- Condition of the property
- Services the tenants receive
- Features or amenities of the building
- Amenities in the immediate area, such as restaurants, retailing, public transportation
- Truck-yard size or number of loading doors for an industrial building
- Green building features

When determining the subject property's position in the range of market rental rates, the real estate manager compares all of these variables with the competition.

The real estate manager rates each building based on a visit to the building as well as general knowledge of the area. Even though evaluating buildings is more of an art than a science, an accurate analysis of the market and the market rental rates for each building is essential for the real estate manager to establish the building's position in the market, its rental rates, and possible concessions. An experienced real estate manager will fairly quickly develop the art of evaluating and comparing buildings.

Formal Market Survey Analysis

The market survey analysis is a report that provides a complete picture of the market area. It is used to compare the subject property to its competition in order to establish the property's market rental rate.

The market analysis includes general information on the competition, demographics, psychographics, traffic patterns, and other issues that have a direct impact on the subject property. The survey also includes an objective analysis of the property so it can easily be measured and evaluated in the market place. An analysis of comparable buildings includes all comparable properties that are in the trade area or that have an impact on the subject property.

Shopping Center Market Survey

The shopping center market survey form (Exhibit 8.1) includes information on the property, the major tenants, rental information, and the physical condition of the property. The following is an explanation of the items in the shopping center survey. Some of the information cannot fit on the form and should be listed on a separate page and attached to it.

- Name of each shopping center surveyed with the name of the subject property first
- Estimated age of property
- Number of all shop spaces (occupied and vacant)
- Number of square feet of the gross leasable area (GLA)
- Number of parking stalls (important only if the shopping center does not have sufficient parking)
- List of the major and important tenants
- Vacancy number and size of each vacancy, i.e., one at 1,200 sq. ft., two at 1,800 sq. ft., one at 2.800 sq. ft. and dimensions of each space
- Asking rental rate
- Deal making rental rate
- Percentage rent provision in use (yes or no)
- Cost per square foot for real estate taxes

- Cost per square foot for insurance
- Cost per square foot for common area maintenance (CAM)
- Consumer Price Index (CPI) adjustment in tenant's lease (yes or no)
- Tenant pays for the maintenance of the heating, ventilating, and air-conditioning (HVAC) unit (yes or no)
- Other tenant charges (merchants' association, marketing funds dues, mandatory advertising)
- Physical condition of the parking lot (P/L) (good or poor)
- Physical condition of the building (good or poor)
- Surrounding area
- Access to the shopping center
- List of tenants (attach to form)
- Visibility of the shopping center relative to traffic and easy identification
- General comments

Office Building Market Surveys

Many of the items from the shopping center market survey are included in the office building survey (Exhibit 8.2). The following lists additional considerations:

- Frequency of janitorial service provided
- Operating expense provisions
- Security on site (full time, part time, drive by, or none)
- Number of elevators
- Availability of and rate for after-hours HVAC
- Life safety features
- Distance from convenient public transportation
- Distance from restaurants
- Distance from shopping
- Other community amenities
- Number of elevators
- Design and impact of the lobby

Industrial Property Market Survey

The industrial park market survey (Exhibit 8.3) is similar to the other two forms and is self-explanatory:

- Distances to freeways and major artery
- Building features such as utility capacity, dock high loading, storage area, sprinklers'
- Type of construction, ceiling heights, clear span, amount office space, etc.

Using Market Survey Information

The real estate manager must share the market survey information with the leasing agent and property owner as soon as possible to determine the building's rental rates and any concessions. Rental rates must be adjusted to reflect current market conditions and to maintain the building's competitiveness.

Although property owners are usually aware of market conditions, they may have a misconception of their property's position in the market and the range of market rates. The market survey keeps the owner aware of the property's correct position in the market and the range of market rates.

Ideally, the real estate manager arranges for a meeting with the owner to review the survey and establish the rental rates and concessions. If the owner is out of the area, the real estate manager can include the survey with the monthly management report or send it as a separate report. The real estate manager should include recommended rental rates and concessions. An owner who is aware of market conditions and deals being made in the market is in a better position to evaluate the deals the real estate manager or leasing agent presents.

Additional Market Information

Additional sources of information can be consulted in developing a market survey. Most major commercial brokerage firms produce quarterly or annual market surveys they release to the media and industry journals.

The leading commercial brokerage firms often hold annual breakfast or luncheon meetings to report on the market in their areas. The real estate or business sections of local business magazines and newspapers frequently report on the real estate market. All of these sources may have an online presence and can be readily obtained.

ANALYZING THE BUILDING

The real estate manager and the leasing agent must have a thorough understanding of the building they are leasing. They need to know the building's attributes and deficiencies. They must know operational issues, the building's tenant mix, and information about the area. They must be prepared to answer questions for prospective tenants and their leasing representative. Listed below is basic information needed to be prepared to present a building to a prospective tenant and/or its leasing representative.

Understanding the Shopping Center

Shopping centers have two customers, the shoppers and the tenants. Before retailer or restaurant operators will consider locating in a shopping center, they need to know if their customer base is representative in the trade area of the shopping center. The real estate manager will need to obtain current demographics and psychographics of the trade area.

The retailers and restaurant operators will need to know what major retailers and competitors are located in the trade area. The sales of the shopping center and general sales information of the tenants in the shopping center is of importance to the prospective tenant. This information helps them project their sales if they locate in the shopping center.

A shopping center's sales can be used as a selling tool to attract specific tenants. The real estate manager should know each tenant's sales history in their shopping center, and be prepared to use that information in the leasing effort. Individual tenants' sales are confidential and should not be discussed.

Real estate managers must be in a position to talk about the shopping center's overall sales record, and prepared to discuss in more general terms the sales of specific lines of merchandise and anchor tenant performance (without giving specific sales figures). For instance, the real estate manager should know the sales per square foot and the total sales for the shopping center. If the shopping center or mall has several tenants in one category of merchandise, such as gifts, jewelry, fast food, women's wear, or shoes, the sales per square foot for that category should be calculated and the range for the highest-and-lowest tenant's sales per square foot in that category should also be calculated. The real estate manager can share that women's wear is averaging more than $650 per square foot and has increased sales at the rate of 11.3 percent throughout the previous year. In a regional or super-regional mall, lifestyle, and outlet shopping centers the owner should know the sales per square foot of all tenants and all categories of merchandise.

Real estate managers should not divulge individual tenants' sales. However, success stories may be shared as long as a specific merchant's sales are not revealed. A property owner might indicate that a supermarket tenant's sales are in excess of $1,200 per square foot, or that the tenant's sales are the highest in that division or store chain.

Even if a category of merchandise is weak, there is likely to be one merchant doing well. Without mentioning the name of the business, it may be revealed that one merchant is well above the others. It is also satisfactory to share that a given apparel store or food court tenant is the number-one producer in that shopping center—as long as the actual sales are not disclosed.

Some municipalities provide traffic counts on specific streets and intersections. This provides information on the number of people who pass by the shopping center daily. Many malls, outlet centers, and life style centers have traffic counters in different areas of the shopping center or mall and in the parking lot.

The real estate manager and leasing agent must know the breakdown of the common area maintenance charges, the real estate taxes, insurance, and possibly other changes, such as marketing fund dues, HVAC maintenance, and other charges.

The size of the shopping center, the number of parking stalls, and the size of each major tenant should be known. Some shopping centers and malls have built-in leasing problems based on the property's size and shape, and the leasing team needs to be aware of them and address how they will be marketed in the marketing and leasing plan.

Understanding the Office Buildings

The leasing teams needs to understand the operations of the office building. What type of HVAC system and the type of elevators? What are the buildings hours and how is the building accessed after hours. What is the life-safety system and does the building have security guards. If so, how do people access the building?

The leasing team needs to know the building size, the size of each floor plate, and the building's load factor. The load factor is needed to calculate each space's rentable area. The parking ratio also needs to be determined.

Building Design

The design of an office building is a key component in determining the types of tenants who are interested in the space. The floor plate is one feature that plays a significant role in determining who these tenants will be. To state it simplistically, large floor plates attract larger tenants and small floor plates attract smaller tenants. The depth from the building core to the curtain wall also determines the size of tenants. Once the floor plate has been established, limitations on the size and shape of individual spaces have also been determined.

Window mullions will also have an impact on the size and configuration of the spaces and offices within a building. A law office will often want a large number of private offices, and window-mullion spacing is a significant factor in determining the exact sizes of these offices. There are ways of building space that does not match the window mullions, but these layouts are often awkward and more expensive to build compared to construction that works with the mullion spacing. If a building's floor plate is not a square or rectangle, it can create some space-planning challenges.

The leasing team must know the method the tenant's pass through or building operating expenses are calculated. They need to know the breakdown of the building's operating expenses.

The owner is typically responsibility to build out the tenant's improvements. The real estate manager must determine the timeline to build out a space. How long will it take to have a space plan drawn and approved by the tenant, construction drawn prepared, and the time it takes to obtain a building permit, construct the premises, and receive the final inspection and certificate of occupancy?

Understanding Industrial Properties

Zoning is the big issue for industrial buildings and tenants. Additional issues to consider include floor loads, clear span ceilings, ceiling heights, high-pile storage ability, utilities, loading docks, truck court size, truck turning radius, dock configuration, rail spur, if the building has fire sprinklers and what type, exterior-storage area, the available labor pool, and transportation systems in the area. Oftentimes, certain types of industries will be clustered together. Take, for instance, the flower district in New York City. Most of the supporting business are located nearby, and a wholesale flower business would not want to locate away from this district. Many industries are geographically located in a certain area—even if zoning would let them go somewhere else.

Pricing Each Space in a Building

Once the market survey has been completed and analyzed, the competition toured and studied, the building analysis completed and the building positioned in the market, the real estate manager is ready and prepared to analyze each space and recommend its rental rate. A building will not have one rental rate, but a range of rental rates. Each space does not have the same value to prospective tenants. Center court spaces in a mall are small spaces in a high traffic and valuable area, and have the highest rent per square foot. A ground-floor space in an office building in the retail core of a strong downtown, such as San Francisco or Seattle will lease for much higher rent then the rest of the building. If the building was located outside the retail core, the same space will lease for much lower rent. These are simple examples why some space lease for higher or lower rent than other space in the same building, and why comparable buildings a few blocks apart may lease for different rates.

The real estate manager should present its market survey and recommended rental rates and concessions if needed to the property owner, discuss the market data, and provide recommended rental rates for each space. The property owner is now prepared to accept the rental rates recommended or discuss why he or she believes a different rate or rates for the building is its market rate(s).

INFORMING THE PROPERTY OWNER OF MARKET CONDITIONS

Property owners who live in the area where their property is located will be more knowledgeable of the market conditions, verses property owners who do not live in the area. It is the real estate manager's responsibility to inform the property owner of the market conditions, how its building is positioned in the market, and recommend rental rates and lease concessions if necessary.

The first step to educating the property owner of the market is to tour the property owner around the trade area of the shopping center or micro market of the office building or industrial property. During the tour, the real estate manager should take the property owner to the competing buildings and walk each building. During the inspection of the competing building, the real estate managers should point out the building's advantages and deficiencies and how it compares to the property owner's building. This tour will provide the property owner with an understanding of the market and the buildings its property will compete with for tenants. The property owner will then be aware of how its building is positioned in the market.

The real estate manager has several opportunities to provide the property owner with market information. The business plan the real estate manager developed for the property will have a section on the marketing and leasing plan. This section will include a market survey, a discussion on the market, and possibly recent deals in the market. Next, each monthly management report prepared for the property owner will have a section on marketing and leasing. This section will discuss all leasing activities, the status of each prospective tenant, along with other marketing and leasing activities for that month. Periodically, this section will have an updated market survey and each report has a summary discussion of the market conditions. The real estate manager should send the property owner's articles on the market along with the surveys and reports prepared by local and national brokerage firms and real estate consulting firms. These reports are usually reported on in the local newspaper and business journal. These reports can easily be e-mailed to the property owner on a fairly regular basis. Depending on the property owner's schedule, a regularly scheduled phone call should be arranged to discuss the market and leasing activities along with other property issues.

BREAK-EVEN ANALYSIS

How does a real estate manager, leasing agent, or property owner know if a proposed lease is a good deal or a bad deal? The economics of a lease is one method to determine if the proposed lease is merely acceptable, a good deal, or if it should be rejected. A method to determine the economic benefits of a proposed lease is to perform a *break-even analysis*. The break-even rent is the point at which income covers the property's operating costs plus debt service. When a deal is presented to the property owner, an analysis should be included showing the proposed lease profit or loss. The real estate manager can determine the break-even rental rate for the property and then compare it with the proposal.

The break-even analysis amortizes the income, commission, and tenant improvements over the life of the lease and includes the building's operating expenses. These figures are then converted to a dollar-per-square-foot-per-year amount to arrive at the dollar per-square-foot profit or loss before and after debt service. Depreciation and amortization of the loan and *time value of money* are not considered.

The following is an example of a break-even analysis: A lease is proposed for 2,000 square feet of space in an office building for five years, with three months' free rent, one year and nine months at $15 per square foot, two years at $17 per square foot, and the fifth year at $19 per square foot. The property owner's contribution towards tenant improvements (TI) is $15,000. The building has an operating expense stop clause of $5 per square foot. The lease commission is five percent of the base-rental income over the term of the lease, payable half on lease execution and half when the tenant takes occupancy and commences paying base rent.

Terms

Space: 2,000 sq. ft.
Rent: 3 months free, 1 year 9 months at $15/sq. ft., 2 years at $17/sq. ft., and 1 year at $19/sq. ft.
TI: $15,000
Stop expense: $5/sq. ft.
Commission: 5% of gross income

1. Determine rent over five years, average annual rent, and average annual rent per square foot.

Year 1: 3 months free = 0
9 months (2,000 sq. ft. × $15/sq. ft. ÷ 12 mos. = $2,500/mo. × 9 mo.) = 22,500
Year 2: 2,000 sq. ft. × $15 = 30,000
Year 3: 2,000 sq. ft. × $17 = 34,000
Year 4: 2,000 sq. ft. × $17 = 34,000
Year 5: 2,000 sq. ft. × $19 = 38,000

Rent over 5 years: $158,500
Average annual rent: $31,700
($158,500 ÷ 5 years)
Average annual rent per square foot (Also known as *effective rent*):
$15.85 ($31,700 ÷ 2,000 sq. ft.)

2. Determine owner's non-reimbursable operating expenses.

The lease states the owners will pay the first $5 per square foot of operating expenses over the life of the lease. The tenant will pay all increases in operating expenses.

3. Determine base commission, annual commission averaged over 5 years, and the commission per square foot per year.

Gross income: $158,500
Commission rate: .05
Commission: $7,925
Divided by five years: 5
Average annual commission: $1,585
Divided by 2,000 sq. ft.: 2,000
Commission/sq. ft./yr.: $ .79

4. Determine tenant improvement (TI) cost per square foot per year.

TI: $15,000
Divided by five years: 5
TI cost/yr.: $3,000
Divided by sq. ft.: 2,000
Cost/sq. ft./yr.: $1.50

5. Determine debt service.

Obtain annual debt service from the owner and divide that amount by the square footage of the rentable or usable area of the building, depending upon how the building is leased. Assuming the debt service in this example is $400,000 per year and the rentable area of the building is 55,000 square feet, compute the following:

Annual Rate/Sq. Ft.
Base income: $15.85/sq. ft.
Less: Operating expenses: (5.00)
Lease commission: (.79)
Tenant improvements: (1.50)
Profit (or loss) before debt service: $8.56
Less: Debt service: (7.27)
Net profit (or loss): $1.29/sq. ft.

The profit of $1.29 per square foot times the 2,000 square feet provides a total dollar profit of $2,580 per year or $12,900 for five years.

Armed with this information, the real estate manager and the property owner can determine whether this is a good or bad financial deal. Each time a lease is presented to the owner, a *break-even analysis* should accompany the deal. If the net amount is a loss, the real estate manager compares the loss with the cost of not making the deal. The cost of not making the deal is the cost of additional lost rent added to the break-even analysis that is projected for the next deal. The next deal is a best estimate of how long the space will remain vacant, how much rent can be collected, and how much tenant improvements will cost.

During a soft market, the owner is sometimes better off accepting a low net profit or even a small loss than gambling on finding another tenant for the space at a higher rate. Giving four months' free rent may be better than waiting for a more lucrative deal. If there is no backup prospective tenant and another deal is unlikely in the next few months, giving free rent is losing nothing because the space would be vacant and nonproductive anyway. The phrase "it is better to collect rent than dust" was common during the soft office building market of the mid-1980s and again in the first decade of the 2000s. This phrase suggests that it is often better to accept a lease during a weak market or a building with leasing problems with a low profit, or even net loss than to allow the space to sit vacant for an extended period and incur a greater loss. If the deal or lease will have a net loss, it may be prudent to negotiate for a shorter lease term with the hope that the market will improve in a few years and the renewal lease rate will be substantially higher.

There are other factors to consider when evaluating if a lease is best for the building. A property owner of a large shopping center may be willing to accept a low profit or even a loss to attract one of the best fashion retailers in the world. The property owner knows that having this retailer will attract other superior retailers and they are likely to pay additional rent to be near this retailer.

LEASING REPORTS

The building's income stream is almost always the owner's most important issue. A property owner who is not aware of the activities of the leasing and marketing team can easily become discouraged with the team and may eventually change leasing personnel and even the real estate management company. Depending on the amount of vacant space in a building, the owner will want to receive a leasing report possibly weekly to monthly. During the lease-up of a new or renovated building, the report may be provided to the owner weekly.

Regular leasing reports and meetings can accomplish several objectives:

1. Keep the property owner informed of the leasing team's activities.
2. Keep the property owner aware of changes in the market rental rates.
3. Enable the property owner and leasing team to adjust the property's rental rates and concessions to reflect changes in the market.
4. Review the marketing and leasing activities since the previous leasing meeting.
5. Review the prospects listed in the leasing report.
6. Review proposals and counter proposals.
7. Enable the property owner to tell if the leasing team is still providing the effort needed to lease the building, or if the team has lost interest in the leasing of the buildings.

The leasing report provides a short comprehensive summary of the leasing activities and status of each prospect, as outlined in Exhibit 8.4.

The owner's leasing report may include the following information:

- A description of the market conditions for the subject property type
- A list of leasing deals and their terms that have been recently completed in the market
- The amount of space that was available to lease

EXHIBIT 8.4

Leasing Prospects Report

PROJECT NAME: COLLEGE PLAZA
MONTH: MARCH 2000

DATE PREPARED: MARCH 30, 2000
PREPARED BY: JOAN JONES

SUITE #	USEABLE SQ.FT.	DATE SHOWN SPACE	PROSPECTIVE TENANT	TYPE OF BUSINESS	NAME OF CONTACT	CURRENT LOCATION	PHONE #	SOURCE	TERM YRS	RENT QUOTED	TI WORK EST	FREE RENT	BROKER COMM	STATUS REMARKS
A-12	1,400	3-23	Anita Cross	Health food	Anita	Highland St.	786-5312	C	5	$22.00	?	?	$4,200	4
A-14	1,400	3-23	Little Nickel Ads	Ads	Sandy	6th Avenue	881-4646	A	5	$22.00	?	?	$4,200	4
B-2	1,500	2-3	Crystal Jewelers	Jewelry	George	None	985-3568	A	7	$25.50	2.000	2MOS	$4,500	0
B-4	2,800	2-15	Cards Galore	Cards & gifts	Mary	West Mall	773-7766	C	10	$22.50	0	1MO	$8,400	1
B-6	1,400	1-6	Tanning/Toning	Tan/Tone	Karen	Main St.	898-6868	B	3	$21.00	0	1MO	$4,200	2
B-10	2,800	12-10	Pizza/Pizza	Restaurant	Mario	Broadway	689-6896	D	10	$22.00	0	0	$8,400	3
A-16	1,800	2-15	Sandwich Shop	Fast Food	Jim	None	785-1234	E	7	$21.00	0	0	$5,400	6

STATUS LEGEND:

0 - LEASE COMPLETED
1 - LEASE OUT FOR SIGNATURE
2 - LEASE UNDER NEGOTIATION
3 - GENERAL TERMS DISCUSSION
4 - PRELIMINARY PROJECT TALKS
5 - PROBLEM IN TALKS
6 - NO DEAL LIKELY

SOURCE LEGEND: (How prospect found out about building)

A - DRIVE-BY
B - NEWSPAPER ADVERTISING
C - COLD CALL BY PROPERTY STAFF
D - DIRECT MAILING
E - BROKER
F - OTHER

in the building at the beginning of the leasing assignment

- The amount of space that has been leased
- The amount of space that is available
- The average rent achieved on the space leased in the building
- The square footage of tenants' spaces expiring this year and each of the next five years
- The amount of TI dollars budgeted for the building
- The amount of TI dollars paid to date
- The amount of TI dollars remaining and offered to prospects
- Each prospect, listed with the following:
  - o Name
  - o Use
  - o Square footage requirements
  - o Required occupancy date
  - o The status of the deal (e.g., inquiry, space shown to prospects, letter of intent, lease being drafted, lease out for signature, as well as the square footage of each deal and the cumulative square footage of all the deals in each status category)
  - o Terms of the deal (e.g., rental rate, concessions, TI allowance, length of the lease)
- Each prospect's rating, on a scale of 1–5 or 1–10, for likelihood of completing a deal
- Exceptions to lease terms or provisions (e.g. exclusives, caps on pass-through charges)
- Name of the tenant's leasing agent
- A section for notes on the development progress of each deal

LEASING MEETINGS

Leasing meetings are important to allow the leasing team and the owner to engage in a dialog of the status of all current activities of the marketing and leasing program. Leasing meetings are usually held monthly unless the building has a large vacancy. If the meetings are held too infrequently, communication breaks down. The meetings can be in person, via audio, or visual conferencing.

The leasing personnel should e-mail the owner with an updated leasing report prior to the meeting. The report must be tailored to the property. The leasing prospect report in Exhibit 8.4 outlines the status of each prospect. A supplementary report may be included to show the amount of space available; leases out for signature; spaces occupied and vacant; tenants' move-ins and move-outs during the previous month; the amount of tenant improvements per tenant and a total for all tenants; the commission paid and budgeted to date; and the average rent per square foot achieved to date. A map or floor plan of the property is color-coded for occupied spaces, spaces leased but not occupied, leases out for signature, and leases in serious negotiations.

If the property owner is an absentee owner or asset manager who visits the property infrequently the real estate manager should include a thorough leasing report in the building's monthly management report. In addition, the real estate manager and leasing personnel should call the owner or asset manager periodically to review the property's leasing status (Exhibit 8.5).

EXHIBIT 8.5

Lease Status Checklist

Tenant: ______________________

	Date: Lessor	Date: Lessee
1. Lease prepared	________	________
2. Leases sent to lessee	________	________
3. Properly signed	________	________
4. Initialed changes	________	________
5. Guaranty signed	________	________
6. Lease notarized	________	________
7. Financial statement	________	________
8. Corporate resolution	________	________
9. Security deposit	________	________

Comments:
____
____
____
____

The person who negotiates a lease is responsible for its proper preparation. The lease status checklist form lists the items that must be provided by the lessor or the lessee. The date is indicated when each item is completed. This form ensures that each lease is properly prepared.

EXECUTED LEASE DISTRIBUTION

	Date
1. Fully executed lease	________
2. Copy to tenant	________
3. Copy to landlord	________
4. Copy to building manager	________
5. Copy to management company file	________
6. Copy to lender	________
7. Copy of construction exhibit to contractor	________
8. Other:____________________	________

The executed lease distribution form is used to keep track of who received copies of the executed lease. The date the lease is executed is recorded on the top line and the date is recorded after each party receives a lessee copy.

RESPONDING TO A REQUEST FOR PROPOSAL

When a tenant's leasing agent is analyzing several buildings for its client it may send each building's real estate manager or leasing agent a *request for proposal (RFP).* The RFP will list many of the issues that are important and some critical to the tenant's business and its operations. The RFP will indicate the tenant's space needs, generally including the desired area, the size of the building, any special building requirements, and the requested lease term. RFPs allows the tenant's leasing agents to compare, on a spread sheet, several buildings under consideration. The leasing agent or real estate manager for the building, with the advice of the owner, will promptly respond to the RFP. The leasing team should have information that is likely to be included in an RFP readily available. This will enable them to promptly respond to the RFP. Listed below are several issues that may be included in a RFP. Each tenant will add issues that are specific to their business and its operations. It is unlikely that all these issues will appear in a RFP:

1. Building name
2. Building address
3. Property owner's name and address
4. Tenant's name and address (provided by the tenant's leasing agent)
5. Building size
6. Space requirements (size and possibly configuration provided by tenant's leasing agent)
7. Building load factor (office and medical office buildings)
8. Lease terms (length of lease and options provided by the tenant's leasing agent)
9. Tenant's use (provided by the tenant's leasing agent)
10. Exclusives and/or other lease restrictions (provided by the tenant's leasing agent)
11. Base rent
12. Tenant charges
13. Security deposit
14. Rent commencement date
15. Tenant improvement allowance
16. Space planning allowance
17. Time to obtain the building permit and build out the tenant improvements
18. Time to build out the premises
19. Tenant expansion options (provided by the tenant's leasing agent)
20. Lease cancellation rights
21. Employee parking
22. Assignment and subleasing
23. Signage
24. Tenant's insurance requirement
25. Relocation requirements
26. Hazardous substance (identifying existing hazardous substance on the property)
27. Building services (office buildings and medical office buildings)
28. Building hours
29. After hour HVAC charges (office buildings and medical office buildings)
30. Building security
31. Building amenities
32. Area amenities
33. Public transportation
34. Structural defects
35. ADA and other code compliance
36. List of current tenants
37. Commission (provided by tenant's leasing agent)
38. Response time (provided by tenant's leasing agent)
39. Signature and date

THE LETTER OF INTENT

The *letter of intent (LOI)* is a document provided by either the owner or the tenant to the other party as an offer of the business terms of a lease agreement. An LOI indicates that the parties are both interested and willing to pursue negotiations in good faith. It is a good tool for both the owner and the tenant to show interest without being bound until all of the terms are negotiated and agreed upon. The following issues are common in an LOI:

1. Premises (address)
2. Size of premises
3. Use
4. Term (may include options)
5. Base rent
6. Percentage rent (retailers and restaurant tenants)
7. Tenant charges (taxes, insurance, maintenance, etc.)
8. Commencement date
9. Rent commencement date
10. Security deposit
11. Compliance with law (building is in compliance with all laws and regulations)
12. Condition of premises (how the premises are being delivered to the tenant)
13. Tenant improvement allowance
14. Insurance
15. Financial contingency
16. Parking
17. Maintenance responsibilities of the premises
18. Signage
19. Broker representation
20. Expiration date of the LOI
21. Non-binding agreement
22. Signature block

THE LEASE

Typically, the owner will provide the lease for the building, which is usually developed with the help of the legal team. Some areas, such as Seattle and Los Angeles, have real estate associations or commercial multiple listing services that have developed a lease or leases from their members to provide their clients. Larger institutions, real estate partnership, and developers will likely have their own master leases that contain generic lease provisions, but are also particular to their business needs. The real estate manager and the lease agents should have a working knowledge of the lease and be prepared to either negotiate lease provisions or advise the owner regarding changes and additions that the tenant's leasing representative or attorney is requesting. Leases are always evolving and it is in the owner's best interest to update its lease every few years—or more frequently if necessary. *Chapter 10: Negotiating the Commercial Lease* provides a thorough discussion on scores of lease provision, why they are important to the owner, and in some cases, the tenant and how to compromise on many lease provision.

The Green Lease

Environmental issues are at the forefront of our society, governmental agencies, and many businesses. It is wise to advise the owner to incorporate sustainable practices in the building's lease. These leases are referred to as a *green lease.* A green lease is a typical commercial lease with additional provisions added to address environmental and sustainability issues.

The green lease provides a way for owners and tenants to communicate and meet shared environmental standards, which may include developing a recycling program, improving a building's indoor environment, increasing purchases of environmentally friendly cleaning products and materials, improving energy efficiency, and reducing water consumption and waste. Green leases are increasingly being seen as not only a social responsibility, but also as a smart alternative to improve efficiency and reduce costs and operating expenses for the owner and tenant alike.

The owner's efforts to green a building and negotiate green leases are often rewarded by an increased ability to attract and retain socially conscious tenants. Owners also benefit from green leases because they set the foundation for tenant behavior, and can ensure that all tenants take an active role in the property's green efforts.

Green leases are a benefit to tenants as well. They can reduce a tenant's occupancy costs by improving efficiency and reducing costs for items such as water and energy. Sustainable practices are becoming an increasingly important consideration for employees, and environmentally friendly policies often help tenant businesses to attract and retain talent.

Ultimately, green leases offer a win-win situation for owners and tenants. A wealth of information about green leases and strategies for sustainability in commercial real estate is available from real estate associations and governmental agencies.

Lease Preparation

Someone is assigned the responsibility of preparing the lease documents. The responsibility may be delegated to the owner's attorney, the real estate manager, the leasing agent, or an administrative assistant. The owner will provide its lease form or use one provided by the real estate management or leasing company. Real estate professionals are not attorneys and do not draft leases or lease provisions, but complete information needed in the lease document. Rewriting of lease provisions and creating new lease provisions is the responsibility of the owner's attorney. Sometimes the tenant's attorney may provide the wording for modifying or creating a new lease provision. It is important that the lease document is prepared promptly, reviewed by the appropriate team members, and promptly provided to the tenant or its representative.

LEASE RESTRICTIONS

Almost every commercial property has built-in lease restrictions established by city or county authorities and are placed on the property by tenants during lease negotiations. Municipalities establish restrictions that are usually related to zoning and allowed uses or types of businesses.

Lease restrictions are negotiated between the owner and the tenant. Lease restrictions may include exclusives, options to extend a lease, option to expand, option to purchase the building, the number and placement of pad buildings in the parking lot of shopping centers, and prohibit specific businesses that has customers that need long-term parking in a shopping center. Lease restrictions may prevent leasing to specific uses. A supermarket may have a provision in its lease that prohibits the owner from leasing to a theater or a school because their customers use parking long term. A lease restriction may provide a tenant with a right to expand into a designated area and before the space can be leased to another tenant, the other tenant has the first right to lease the space. A lease restriction that is common for retail properties and can be negotiated on other types of commercial properties is an exclusive. An *exclusive* provides a tenant with the sole right to provide a product or service. If a tenant in a shopping center has an exclusive for a Mexican restaurant, the property cannot be leased to a restaurant who serves Mexican food as their primary business—or even as additional items to another formatted restaurant without violating the tenant with the exclusive lease. An office tenant may have an exclusive as the only bank or savings and loan in a building.

All the leases for a building need to be carefully abstracted or summarized and a report listing each restriction prepared for the real estate manager, property owner, and leasing agent. Each party involved in leasing should be thoroughly familiar with each lease restriction. If any of these lease restrictions become an issue in negotiations, it is much better to quote a restriction beyond the owner's control than to just say "no."

WORKING WITH THE BROKERAGE COMMUNITY

The marketing and leasing plan should including working with the brokerage community. Many tenants appoint a broker as their exclusive leasing representative for locating space and negotiating the lease. The real estate manager must recognize that brokers have tremendous influence over the tenants they represent. They can influence and select which buildings the tenant will visit and, of course, they have a major influence over which building the tenant selects. Alienating a broker or the brokerage community can result in some prospective tenants not being shown a property and lost deals. Throughout the lease negotiations, the real estate manager should emphasize the importance of the tenant's broker's role.

Communication

The real estate manager can communicate in many ways to the brokerage community that its cooperation is encouraged. Personal contact with the brokers is the best method to communicate information concerning available space. Regularly taking brokers to breakfast or lunch is an excellent way to develop a working relationship.

Membership in professional organizations, such as the Institute of Real Estate Management (IREM), International Council of Shopping Centers (ICSC), Certified Commercial Investment Manager (CCIM), the National Association of Industrial and Office Parks (NAIOP), and the Society of Industrial and Office Realtors (SIOR), provide other opportunities to network with brokers.

The real estate manager can arrange to make presentations to leasing agents at brokerage firms that have weekly sales and leasing meetings. A brokerage firm either specializes in leasing one type of property, such as office buildings, or has several divisions specializing in specific property types.

The real estate manager should request a meeting with the division that leases the property type he or she represents. It's important to provide marketing materials, brochures, plot plans, photos, and aerials as handouts of the properties he or she manages and leases. It is always wise to bring snacks or other food to the broker's meetings when presenting properties you are leasing.

Continuous follow-up is necessary to keep properties in front of the brokerage community. The real estate manager can develop an e-mail describing the property, space for lease, pertinent information of the property and the area, photos of the property, rental rates, and lease terms. The property's e-mail is sent to all brokers or brokers who specialize in this property type periodically.

COMMISSIONS

Leasing agents working for brokerage firms are paid a commission for each space they lease. Typically, owners pay the *commission*. Therefore, structuring the commission schedule is one of the most critical elements in a marketing and leasing program. The commission schedule must be carefully considered to provide the proper incentives to the leasing agent and to be a fair expense of the project.

There are no standard commissions. Commissions are negotiable. The rate of commission is dependent upon several factors and may include all (or some) of the factors below:

- Size of the space being leased
- Length of the lease
- Gross or net income the owner earned during part or all of the lease term
- Expertise of the real estate manager or leasing agent
- Condition of the market
- Difficulty of the leasing assignment
- Relationship between the owner and the leasing agent
- The importance of the leasing assignment to the brokerage firm
- Property and investment issues the owner is dealing with
- The occupancy of the property
- The need for a specific tenant
- Real estate management or leasing company's cost of doing business
- Amount the property owner is willing to pay

There are many different formulas to determine commissions. *Commissions* may be a percentage of the base rent collected during the term of the lease or a period of the term of the lease. They may be based on a dollar per square feet of space leased by the tenant. Commissions may be a fixed-dollar amount for a space. There may be incentive commissions based on exceeding a targeted amount of space leased in a specific period. An incentive commission may be increasing the percentage used to calculate the commission, the dollar per square foot used to calculate a commission, a fixed-dollar amount, or a significant gift such as a trip to a resort. After establishing the commission formula the owner needs to determine the payment schedule of the commission. Commissions are paid at specific times such as when the lease is signed, the tenant occupies the premises, or when rent commences—after a number of months the tenant has occupied the premises or monthly as the rent is paid. There is no standard method to pay commissions. Examples of different commission formulas are provided in *Chapter 14: Financial Analysis for Real estate Managers.*

APPRAISING PROSPECTIVE TENANTS

The real estate manger needs to have in place a process to evaluate every prospective tenant. There are two components to evaluating prospective tenants: (1) The perspective's financial statement and credit history is evaluated for all types of tenants, and (2) the type of property and the specific use and tenant.

Owners considering a tenant prospect should ascertain the tenant's credit standing and net worth. In the case of a retail or restaurant tenant, the owner also has an interest in a the tenant's reputation as a merchant or restaurant operator and the tenant's history in the retail business, merchandise or menu, price points, level of service, sales of existing stores, and projected sales.

A credit check is straightforward and usually very inexpensive. Typically, an owner is not looking for perfect credit, but wants someone with a good history of paying bills and meeting financial obligations. Major red flags include judgments and collections. Credit checks are most often performed after the lease terms have been agreed upon, but if the lease is very complicated or for a unique space, the credit check may be done before negotiations begin. This circumvents spending significant amounts of time to finalize complicated arrangements, only to discover that the tenant prospect has a poor history of paying bills.

It is also extremely important to get a credit history on the entity actually signing the lease. A husband and wife may have an excellent credit history, but indicate that they want the lease in the name of a family-held corporation. In such a case, the couple's personal credit does not support a family corporation unless they sign a lease guarantee. As another example, it is not unusual for national retail tenants to separately incorporate individual stores and—without a corporate guarantee from the parent company—such a lease has no financial backing beyond that of the individual location.

The financial statement of the tenant is another item that is important to the owner. A financial statement is always helpful; it should be signed and reasonably current. The building owner wants the tenant to have sufficient capital to meet the lease obligations, even in difficult times. Seeing ownership of real estate on the financial statement is always reassuring because a tenant is less likely to leave without notice if he or she owns property.

Liquidity commensurate with the obligation undertaken and a reasonable debt-to-equity ratio are other positive factors. Setting a minimum net worth is not productive. It is better to evaluate each prospect in light of the space being leased, history of the tenant, probable investment by the property owner, risk involved, and condition of the building in the marketplace. In some cases, small or start-up prospects are asked to prepare a qualification package or business plan to help them think through the process and costs of a new business (Exhibit 8.6).

It is not necessary that all tenant prospects have a high net worth. Many small office space users and small retailers have a limited net worth that is sufficient to support their business. For example, a shoe store of 800 square feet can be opened with a reasonable fixturization cost. On the other hand, a frozen yogurt store or beauty shop requires a fairly large cost in fixtures and build-out, and the owner would want evidence of a higher net worth to support the lease. Each lease proposal and tenant prospect should be evaluated individually, ensuring

EXHIBIT 8.6

Prospective Lessee Qualifications

Complete in full and submit to:

This form does not obligate either party to the performance of a contract for leasehold property. It is purely for information and does not constitute an offer to lease property or any negotiation for such a purpose.

Name: ______________________ Home Phone: ______________

Residence Address: Business Phone: ______________

______________________ Social Security #: ______________

____

Own _____ or Rent _____ If rented, monthly rent: __________

Name and address of landlord: ______________________

____

____

Which shopping center are you interested in? ______________________

What kind of business do you propose to run there? ______________________

____

Present business or profession: ______________________

Salary (annual) __________ Will this income continue? __________

Other income (annual) __________

May we contact your present employer? Yes ____ No ____

Shall we contact you first?: Yes ____ No ____

Employer's Name and address ______________________

____

Phone number: ______________________

Business Experience—Retail: Describe fully the business operations and your roles; indicate dates:

____

____

____

____

EXHIBIT 8.6 *(CONTINUED)*

Other Work Experience: Describe fully the business operations and your roles; indicate dates:

____

If you have other businesses, please provide pertinent operating statements for the last twenty-four months where possible.

Will you have a continuing role in these businesses? If so, what will that role be?

____

How will you operate your new business at our property? Who will manage? How many employees will you need?

____

EXHIBIT 8.6 *(CONTINUED)*

If your business is a partnership or a joint venture, describe its legal and financial structure and submit copies of all appropriate legal documents.

____

____

____

____

____

____

____

If your business involves a franchise, supply a copy of the agreement, information on how the purchase is being financed and financial and business report on the franchisor.

What improvements do you plan to make to the premises (fixtures, carpet, etc.) and at what cost? How will improvements be financed?

____

____

____

____

____

____

____

Describe your anticipated start-up operating expenses at the new location and list amounts (include inventory, supplies, initial payroll costs, insurance, etc.)

____ $________________

____ $________________

____ $________________

____ $________________

____ $________________

____ $________________

____ $________________

____ $________________

EXHIBIT 8.6 *(CONTINUED)*

How will you finance your start-up expenses?

____

____

____

Analysis of projected income from operations at the new location for the first two years (complete where applicable).

Revenues		
Gross sales	$__________	$__________
Cost of goods sold	__________	__________
Gross margin	__________	__________
Other revenues (specify)	__________	__________
TOTAL REVENUES	$__________	$__________
Expenses		
Salaries and wages	$__________	$__________
Payroll taxes	__________	__________
Compensation insurance	__________	__________
Utilities (electricity, water, telephone)	__________	__________
Repairs and maintenance	__________	__________
Janitorial services, laundry	__________	__________
Supplies	__________	__________
Advertising and promotion	__________	__________
Rent and related costs	__________	__________
Insurance (fire, liability, plate glass)	__________	__________
Management fee	__________	__________
Real estate taxes	__________	__________
Personal property taxes	__________	__________
Financial expenses (include principal payments)	__________	__________
Total expenses	$__________	$__________
Net Operating Income (cash)	$__________	$__________

EXHIBIT 8.6 *(CONTINUED)*

If you project a loss in net operating income, explain how it will be financed and supply supporting material.

Current Financial Statement

I. Personal: Where a partnership, joint venture or corporation is involved, the appropriate financial statement should be supplied.

II. Business: If several businesses are involved, supply separate individual financial statements where possible.

Indicate sources and amounts of income other than that from business described herein.

Please include a means of verification of all items on the attached financial statement: i.e., account number, tax bills and returns, inventories, etc.

EXHIBIT 8.6 *(CONTINUED)*

FINANCIAL CONDITION AS OF ___________ 20___

Name(s)	
Residence Address	Telephone Number
Business Address	Telephone Number

MARITAL STATUS:

☐ MARRIED ☐ SEPARATED ☐ UNMARRIED

If you check either of the first two boxes, are any of the assets listed community property? ☐ Yes ☐ No

If the answer is "Yes," list spouse's name if not listed above:________________

ASSETS		AMOUNT	LIABILITES		AMOUNT
CASH			NOTES PAYABLE TO BANKS		
				(Itemize, Schedule 6)	
STOCKS AND BONDS	Listed (Schedule 1)		OTHER NOES AND ACCOUNTS PAYABLE	Real Estate Loans (Schedule 2)	
	Unlisted (Schedule 1)			Sales Contracts & Sec. Agrmts. (Sch. 5)	
				Loans on Life Insurance Policies (Sch. 4)	
REAL ESTATE	Improved (Schedule 2)				
	Unimproved (Schedule 2)		TAXES PAYABLE	Current Year's Income Taxes Unpaid	
	Trust Deeds & Mortgages (Schedule 3)			Prior Year's Income Taxes Unpaid	
				Real Estate Taxes Unpaid	
LIFE INSURANCE	Cash Surrender Value (Schedule 4)				
			OTHER LIABILITES	Unpaid Interest	
ACCOUNTS AND NOTES RECEIVABLE	Relatives and Friends (Schedule 5)			Others (Itemize, Schedule 5)	
	Collectible (Schedule 5)				
	Doubtful (Schedule 5				
OTHER PERSONAL PROPERTY	Automobile			TOTAL LIABILITIES	
	Other (Itemize, Schedule 5)			NET WORTH	
	TOTAL			TOTAL	

ANNUAL INCOME	(REFER TO FEDERAL INCOME TAX RETURNS FOR PREVIOUS YEAR)	ANNUAL EXPENDITURES	AMOUNT
SALARY OR WAGES		PROPERTY TAXES AND ASSESSMENTS	
DIVIDENDS AND INTEREST		FEDERAL AND STATE INCOME TAXES	
RENTALS (GROSS)		REAL ESTATE LOAN PAYMENTS	
BUSINESS OR PROFESSIONAL INCOME (NET)		PAYMENTS ON CONTRACTS AND OTHER NOTES	
OTHER INCOME (DESCRIBE) (Income from alimony,		INSURANCE PREMIUMS	
child support, or maintenance payments need not		ESTIMATED LIVING EXPENSES	
be disclosed)		OTHER	
TOTAL INCOME		TOTAL EXPENDITURES	

Give details of any contingent liability as endorser or guarantor, or on suits or judgments pending. (If necessary, use separate sheet.)

____

____

HAVE YOUR INCOME TAX RETURNS EVER BEEN QUESTIONED BY ANY GOVERNMENTAL AUTHORITY? ______ (If so, explain)

____

HAVE YOU EVER GONE THROUGH BANKRUPTCY? (Explain)

____

HAVE YOU FILED HOMESTEAD? (Explain)

____

EXHIBIT 8.6 *(CONTINUED)*

Additional Bank References

Name: ______________________ Acct # ____________

Bank: ______________________ Phone: ____________

Address: ______________________

____

I hereby authorize the bank to release information confirming my account to Company.

Signature: ______________________

Name: ______________________ Acct # ____________

Bank: ______________________ Phone: ____________

Address: ______________________

____

I hereby authorize the bank to release information confirming my account to Company.

Signature: ______________________

Name: ______________________ Acct # ____________

Bank: ______________________ Phone: ____________

Address: ______________________

____

I hereby authorize the bank to release information confirming my account to Company.

Signature: ______________________

that the proper financial tools are in place to meet the obligations of the particular arrangement.

Tax returns are a great supplemental tool to verify the financial statements and to evaluate the company's ability to remain profitable.

Appraising Prospective Tenants

Proper evaluation of prospective tenants is almost as important as setting the rents at the right levels. If qualifications are too restrictive, some excellent tenant prospects will be lost. On the other hand, if care is not taken, the real estate manager may be faced with rent collection problems and needless evictions. In very tough leasing markets when tenants are hard to come by, financial requirements may be relaxed and a chance can be taken on a weaker tenant.

Tenant Concerns

In offices and industrial properties, the use of the space is seldom the reason a tenant is turned down, although, tenant mix is taken into consideration. Consider a manufacturing industrial tenant in a business park as an example. A prospective tenant may want to employ too many people in the space or might generate too much noise. Generally, however, office and industrial tenants are evaluated with emphasis on their financial statements rather than on their uses. Exceptions could include an office or industrial tenant that uses hazardous chemicals or taboo businesses such as drug cultivation.

In shopping centers, the real estate manager not only reviews a tenant's financial statement and credit checks, but also looks at the tenant as a merchant and analyzes how the business fits the shopping center's tenant mix. For most uses, these considerations are equal to or greater than the financial considerations.

The real estate manager must evaluate the tenant's ability as a merchant. What are the tenant's current sales? Does the tenant have a good reputation in the community? In retail, It can be harmful to the other merchants if a tenant does not maintain the shopping center's hours, sells shoddy merchandise, or offers misleading sales.

The process of appraising prospective tenants is based on many factors, including the following:

- Tenant's financial strength
- Tenant's ability as a merchant
- Amount the owner has to spend on improvements particular use
- Number of vacancies available on the property
- Number of vacancies available in the general marketing area

The goal is to obtain the best possible tenant under the existing circumstances, thus, minimizing the risks of tenant failure and maximizing occupancy and rental income for the property.

CHAPTER

9

Preparing for Lease Negotiations

The party best prepared to negotiate a commercial lease has a distinct advantage over the other party. Preparation can best be described with one word—knowledge. Knowledge is power in the negotiating process, and one should be as well prepared as possible when entering into a lease negotiation.

Often in negotiations, and many other aspects in life, people will defer to the most knowledgeable person. To best serve a client, the real estate manager and/or leasing agent must be fully prepared to negotiate the commercial lease. This chapter discusses many issues to consider when preparing to negotiate a commercial lease with a special focus on the players in lease negotiations. The real estate manager often serves a dual role as the building manager and the leasing agent. Sometimes these two roles are separated between the real estate manager and a leasing agent. For the following discussion, it is assumed that the real estate manager is also the building's leasing agent and will be referred to as the leasing agent.

GOALS AND OBJECTIVES OF THE PROPERTY OWNER AND TENANT

It is best to review the current goals and objectives with the property ownership before entering into lease negotiations. The property ownership's leasing goals may have changed since the last discussion and there could be new factors to consider that could impact the negotiations. For example, property ownership could be planning to make significant improvements to common areas that would positively impact the desirability of the property and command a higher rental rate, or they may have developed a new strategy for the property.

The subject property may be one of several properties in a real estate portfolio and the short- or long-term goals for the portfolio may have changed—thereby altering the objectives for the property. Some larger retail tenants may have recently renewed their leases, firming the property's ownership negotiating stance on all monetary provisions—especially for base rent and *tenant improvement (TI)* allowances.

The property ownership may have recently encountered "pressure points" that need to be addressed, which may alter the negotiating strategy for the property. As an example, the property's loan may require the ownership to pay down the mortgage if the property's *net operating income (NOI)* falls below a specific dollar amount. The potential income from the lease that is to be negotiated may be critical to maintaining the property's NOI above the lender's threshold for requiring that the partnership pay down the loan. Another example is the need or desire to sell the property. The ownership may not be as aggressive negotiating non-monetary lease provisions and directs the negotiating team to focus on revenue issues, while being willing to offer additional TIs to achieve a higher base rent. Any new factors affecting the property from the ownership's perspective must be thoroughly understood and be reflected in the lease negotiations.

In addition to understanding the ownership's perspective, it is also imperative that the leasing agent also understand how the co-location of tenants within a property or area can create an environment that supports the growth and wellbeing of all the businesses or can cause business to struggle and ultimately fail—both of which ultimately impact the NOI and the value of the property. Who the prospective tenant is may alter the negotiating position on several lease provisions. For instance, the ownership of a regional mall is likely to offer concessions to one of the best woman fashion retailers knowing that the retailer will draw other prominent fashion retailers to the mall. The ownership of a high-rise office building is aware that a four-star restaurant on the top floor or on the ground floor will add prestige and a great amenity to the building, and thus, would be willing to offer a very attractive TI allowance package to have this restaurant in the building.

A credit tenant will bring more value to a building than a noncredit tenant. A building is valued based on its income stream or NOI. The income, or base rent, of a credit tenant has greater value (and less risk) than the same amount of rent from a non-credit tenant. Who the prospective tenant is may alter the property ownership's stance on base rent, concessions, term of the lease, and renewal options. A retail property may be losing market share, and for defensive reasons, may need a particular retailer and is willing to offer a "sweet-heart" deal during negotiations for the right retailer.

The location of the space being considered may alter the ownership's negotiating posture. If a prospective tenant is willing to take a less desirable space, especially one that has been vacant for some time, the ownership may be willing to offer concessions not available for other spaces in the building. Conversely, the ownership may harden its negotiating position on the best space or spaces in the building—especially for a retail property where high visibility is often one of the most critical factors in site selection and the willingness of the tenant to pay a premium rental rate.

Before starting negotiations with a prospective tenant or its representative, it is best to discuss with the property ownership the negotiation goals for this particular prospective tenant. Once issues have been agreed upon during negotiations, it is difficult to walk back from them. If this happens, the negotiating team is likely to lose credibility.

Ideally, the leasing agent should be aware of the goals and objectives of the prospective tenant—although this may not always be possible. Some prospective tenants will be reluctant to share their goals and objections for fear of placing themselves in a weaker negotiating position. Many of the prospective tenant's goals will, however, be aligned with those of the property ownership. For instance, a retailer or restaurant may want to be in a particular shopping center because all the retailers in the shopping center significantly outperform the national sales average for their category of business. In this case, the property ownership is in a strong negotiating position.

If a prospect has many similar options to locate their offices, the property ownership may be in a weaker negotiating position. The leasing agent should attempt to discover the perspective tenant's goals, which often are difficult and sometimes impossible to determine. Developing an understanding and appreciation of the property ownership's goals and objectives, as well as those of the prospective tenant—at least as much as they are willing to share—is the first step in preparing to negotiate a lease.

THE PULSE OF THE DEAL

Every lease transaction, or "deal," takes on an often precarious and sometimes fragile life of its own. Any number of events can slow a deal, create barriers to completing negotiations, and make it difficult, if not impossible, for owners and tenants to complete a lease transaction. Every deal has a "pulse" that must be maintained by all the key players. Any player in the deal can slow its pulse and unintentionally place the deal at risk of failing. If the pulse of the deal is allowed to stop, for even a short time, it may not be revived. If the pulse stops for an extended time, it is almost never revived.

Key Players in the Deal

A lease transaction can have just a couple or several key players. For the most part, the property owner and the potential tenant are the key players in the deal—and occasionally the only players. But they typically call upon the expertise of several professionals, led by their leasing agents, to complete the leasing process.

Each key player in the leasing process has a responsibility to keep the lease transaction moving towards a completed lease and at the pace established by that player's client. Most owners assign the responsibility to leasing professionals for developing and implementing a marketing and leasing plan for their buildings. These professionals may be employees of the owner, but typically they are professionals working for commercial real estate firms.

Tenants also may look for space and negotiate a lease independently. Large corporations often have a real estate division that handles their real estate transactions. Most tenants, however, use the services of a commercial real estate brokerage firm's leasing agent. The respective leasing agents, representing the owner's search for tenants, and the tenant's search for a location usually take charge of the "deal."

Leasing agents play a critical role in the success of their clients' business—the building. The owner's leasing agent is assigned the responsibility of developing and implementing the building's marketing and leasing plan. This plan, similar to the marketing and sales plan of most businesses, will ultimately determine the success of the owner's business—the building. The leasing agent has a wealth of knowledge concerning market conditions, including rental rates, concessions, building's *pass-through charges,* recent deals in the area, building's vacancies, and the strengths and weaknesses of competing buildings.

The leasing agent's advice and recommendations are important during the initial lease-up of a building and its ongoing leasing. The owner depends on the leasing agent to maintain a high occupancy at a competitive rate. The leasing agent is the owner's primary source for market information and recommendations on negotiating the business terms of each lease negotiations. Many leasing agents will also be prepared to negotiate all the lease provisions.

The Leaders in the Deal

Each of the players in the transaction fulfills a critical role in bringing the deal to completion. Yet, every transaction needs a leader to ensure that all the players are performing their tasks in a timely manner and no one is slowing the leasing process. One of the key players in the deal needs to take charge of the deal flow and maintain the pulse of the deal. This person is the owner's leasing agent and often both the owner's and the tenant's leasing agents share this responsibility. The owner's and/or the tenant's leasing agent assumes a leadership role in keeping all the players focused on completing their part of the deal. Ideally, the two leasing agents work in tandem to keep the pulse of the deal beating to a successful conclusion. Each player in the deal is working on several transactions or deals concurrently, and it is easy for one or more of them to lose track of the pulse of a specific deal by focusing their attention on other lease transactions.

The leasing representative (or representatives) in charge of the deal creates a timeline with targeted goals for each player to ensure that all are aware of their deadlines and that the pulse of the deal maintains its rhythm. Though leasing agents should lead the deal process, the ultimate responsibility for the deal flow rests with the owner and the tenant.

The Timeline of the Deal

Leasing agents have always said that it takes longer to do a deal than in the past. The lease document is always evolving, becoming longer in length with new provisions designed to offer new protections or address new issues that develop in an ever-changing marketplace. The hazardous substance provision did not exist until the mid 1980s, and now it takes up two pages of the lease and—depending on the tenant's use—can be one of the most contested and longest provisions.

A lease transaction, starting with the leasing agent's initial search for tenants and ending with the tenant occupying the premises, typically takes months and sometimes over a year to complete and can vary greatly depending on the property type (office, retail, or industrial). The tenant's leasing agent may spend weeks searching for several locations that meet the tenant's needs. Then, the tenant will require a few days or weeks to visit and analyze alternative locations. If the tenant is located in another city or state, it may take even longer before the tenant visits the building. A space planner for an office building requires about a week to interview the tenant and understand the tenant's business, as well as a week or two to prepare the space layout or test fit. Office tenants need to know if their operations will efficiently "fit" into the available space. Property owners seldom, if ever, provide space-planning services for national/regional retailers or industrial users. These tenants have a prototype or several prototype plans that will be used for different spaces which can avoid the time needed to create a layout or test fit.

A TI contractor needs a couple of weeks to price the cost of the build-out. The premises must be built out based on the timeline for the tenant's move-in date. If tenants are relocating from another space, they will be in a difficult position if their new space is not completed on time, so constraints can become critical during a negotiation process. The property owner needs the space built out and occupied as soon as possible to generate rent from the premises. If the space is not delivered on time, the tenant may require the owner to pay a penalty for the delay. Retailers typically lease space in as-is condition, and the owner may be required to demo existing improvements or the owner may provide a TI allowance.

Retailers may have a preferred contractor who builds out all their stores in a region. This can prove challenging if their contractor is not familiar with the local building code authority. If a tenant intends to use a non-local contractor and the build-out time is short, suggest that the tenant engage the services of a local architect or contractor to expedite the process. Many retailers open stores only during specific periods of the year, and if their space is not ready during one of those windows, they will delay their move-in and store opening to avoid opening during the "wrong" time of the year—also known as "blackout periods." This issue is an important component in the timeline for prospective retailers.

While it takes just a few hours to draft a lease, it can take months for the attorneys, leasing agents, tenant(s), and property owner to negotiate the document. During this period, the key players in the transaction are working on other transactions and their priorities will vary; however, the key players may not share the same priorities. The leader must keep each player focused and adhering to the timeline.

Once the lease has been executed, it typically takes a month or longer to have the TI plans and construction drawings reviewed and approved by the local building department (generally the city or the county) and a building permit issued. Depending on the extent of the build-out—which can range from cleaning or replacing the carpet, painting the walls, removing all existing improvements, and building out the premises to the specifications of the new tenant—the TI contractor may need a few weeks or several months to build out the premises. The sooner the lease negotiations are completed and the lease is executed by the owner and tenant, the sooner the build-out process commences and the tenant can occupy the premises.

PREPARING THE TEAM PLAYERS TO NEGOTIATE

Even though there are two parties to a lease arrangement, the team that negotiates the agreement may include several people on both sides. The owner is likely to be represented by a leasing agent. The real estate manager may serve as the leasing agent or will act in a supporting role to the leasing agent. If the owner is an institution, there will often be an asset manager representing the property ownership. Many owners will also include legal representation in the lease negotiations. The tenant will likely have a leasing agent and an attorney. In the case of larger retailer, the tenants will have store-operating personnel involved in the lease negotiations.

The Owner's Leasing Agent

As mentioned previously, the owner must have full knowledge of the property. In that same vein, the leasing agent must also fully understand the property and the owner's goals and objectives for the property, as well as for the particular negotiation. This agent should have a firm grasp of the overall direction of the property, be familiar with the trade area or the micro-market in which it is located, have researched competitive buildings along with their strengths and weaknesses, and offer a good perspective on prospective tenants and what they are looking for in the negotiations.

The leasing agent will use its resources in the real estate community to find out the general terms of recent deals in the market, such as rental rate, triple net (or some variety of a net lease), TI allowances, and *common area maintenance (CAM)* charges. Other general terms consider whether parking should be included or available for a fee, if any free rent was provided as a concession, along with any other amenities that may have been part of those deals.

The leasing agent may have the authority to accept specific terms if they are within preset guidelines from the owner. It will be the responsibility of this agent to bring to the owner the various proposals that come out of the negotiations, and to recommend the best course of action if they are not within the initial agreed-upon guidelines.

Chapter 8: Preparing to Lease a Building, discusses several issues that the leasing agent must have full knowledge of before entering lease negotiations.

The Tenant's Leasing Representative

The tenant is likely to be represented by a leasing agent. Though the owner and the tenant each have their leasing agent, the objectives of the two leasing agents are similar. Each leasing agent desires to complete the "deal"—a lease that will meet the goals and objectives of its client. The leasing agent will negotiate the best "deal" possible for its client. If each party is to achieve their goals and objects, they will need to find common ground. Each party will need to offer concessions to achieve concessions from the other party. Leasing agents for each party are partners in a moment of time to complete the deal—even though they are negotiating against each other.

The Real Estate Manager

If the real estate manager is not serving as the leasing agent, he or she may not always be a party to the negotiations, but should nevertheless have input concerning the desirability of the particular prospective tenant and any potential problems that may arise. The real estate manager may have known the tenant from another building, and be familiar with any issue with the tenant, such as rent collections, poor operations, or other lease violations.

There could also be factors with the building that impact the overall lease negotiations with specific tenants. For example, if a potential tenant of an office building has unique weight requirements resulting from an extensive fire-proof filing systems or a vault, the real estate manager may be in a position to recommend one location over another due to structural integrity of the building. Or, if a first-floor retail space is being considered by a potential restaurant business, it may be necessary to explore the availability of specific locations to accommodate the venting needs associated with the hood system. In this situation, completing with the negotiations only to find out that the proposed hood vent would require a large venting chase in the middle of the upstairs tenant's CEO's office, would not be a good situation. These types of complications should be explained to the leasing personnel so they can be considered in the negotiations and/or final approval of a tenant.

If the property is a shopping center or other type of retail property, provide the tenant with a unique perspective as to the property's tenant mix, along with the contribution different uses and specific prospective tenants may provide to enhance the tenant mix of the property. Provide valuable perspectives on the tenant mix for other property types as well—especially for medical office buildings (MOBs) where referrals among medical professionals in the building are a valuable asset for a building. *Chapter 5: Medical Office Building and Clinical Facilities Management* provides more information on the different aspects of managing this property type.

The real estate manager can provide the leasing team with cost data for specific TIs, anticipated increase triple net charges, cost when offering specific concessions, and how specific prospective tenants operations may positively or negatively affect the operations of the building. For example, if a prospective user plans to construct a data center in a multi-tenant office building where full-service leases are generally negotiated, suggest that the data center be sub-metered so that the resulting electric charges can be billed back to the tenant. These discussions should take place before negotiations commence.

The Asset Manager

An asset manager generally represents institutional owners. When institutions own properties, the asset manager is assigned to make decisions for the ownership. The main difference between asset managers and individual owners is that the owners act on their own behalf, while asset managers act in a fiduciary capacity and must make prudent decisions for the property ownership. Although they have the same roles, the possible consequences for the two are substantially different. As a result, an entrepreneur owner is generally more flexible than an asset manager and can make decisions on the spot while the asset manager may need to receive the approval of a committee or a supervisor. It is helpful for the tenant representative to know the structure of the property ownership, as it can play a major role in the outcome of the negotiations.

The Attorney

The attorney also plays an important role in leasing. Typically, attorneys are involved in the transaction to ensure the lease language is in the best interest of the party being represented and to ensure that the language is legally correct as to form. Typically, the attorney's role is not to negotiate the business terms of the lease; however, there are many attorneys who do negotiate business terms as well as the non-monetary lease provisions. The owner should establish the attorney's role and make it clear to the leasing team, especially if the attorney is present at the negotiations. Most owners and prospective tenants want only one person negotiating on their behalf, and for that individual to consult with the other interested parties between negotiating sessions.

The main responsibility of the attorney is to evaluate the lease language and advise his or her client as to its possible legal and business consequences. Attorneys are protective of their clients and will forcefully advocate for their client during negotiations. The final decision on all issues is still up to the owner and the prospective tenant during negotiations.

Avoiding Deal Failures

There is an endless list of reasons why transactions never become deals. Some of these reasons are unavoidable, but many others could be prevented. Deals often fail due to needless factors such as poor communication between the parties involved, one party not responding in a timely manner, and people allowing their personalities or egos to get in the way of a successful transaction. The following list outlines a few of the most common explanations—both the inevitable and avoidable—for transactions failing to become deals:

Disagreements on Costs

One party might not be able to afford the deal—a legitimate reason why a transaction fails. Either the owner cannot or will not reduce the building's rent or provide the concessions the prospective tenant requires. The prospective tenant may not perceive the same value in the space that the owner does, or the tenant may not be able to afford the rent. The following list of questions will assist the leasing agent in finding out what rent each party can afford:

- Is the cost of TIs a concern for the owner and/or the prospective tenant?
- Is the owner willing to offer free rent that will reduce the effective rent for the tenant, thus, meeting the prospective tenant's rent budget?
- Is the tenant willing to accept a smaller TI allowance as a trade off for lower rent or possibly the opposite?

- Could the term be extending to allow a longer amortization of the TI allowance provided by the owner or the TI costs?

Before giving up on a deal, the leasing agent should explore every possible means to structure the business terms of the lease that will meet each party's goals and objectives.

Insufficient Knowledge of the Area

A owner or asset manager who does not live in the area may lack sufficient market expertise to recognize the right deal. Often, asset managers are responsible for a portfolio of properties located in several cities and they simply do not have the same market expertise for each market. This can easily occur when an asset manager or owner of an office building is evaluating an offer from a retail tenant for ground-floor space. The owner or asset manager may understand the office market, but may have limited knowledge of the retail market. Conversely, the prospective tenant may not be familiar with the market conditions especially if the tenant is entering a new market, and find the building's rental rates more than what it usually pays.

The real estate manager and the leasing agents for both parties can better educate their clients by providing market studies and terms of recent lease transactions to support the asking rent of either the owner or the prospective tenant.

Inaccurate Sales Projections

A retailer may be overly conservative in sales projections, and consequently pass on a good location. Many retailers will benchmark their projected sales for a location on the sales of specific retailers in the area. Leasing agents should attempt to obtain the sales of other retailers in the immediate area which will enable prospective retailers or restaurants to better project their sales for the subject property.

Retailers refer to their sales projections as a "sales call." Obtaining sales of retailers and restaurant that are not a part of the retail property may be difficult. Developing working relationships with other real estate managers in the area, leasing agents, property owners, retailers, and restaurant operators are an excellent source of the sales in the area. The sales information is usually not a specific dollar amount but a general number, such as a higher-end supermarket's sales exceeding $35 million or a cosmetics retailer sales that are more than $2,000.00 per square foot.

Unrealistic Goals

One party does not have an understanding of the market. The owner may perceive value in a building that the market doesn't reflect, or the owner may be stubborn in asking a rental rate that has no relationship to the market. On the other hand, prospective tenants are not real estate professionals and are usually not up to date on market conditions. Their frame of reference for rental rates may be the rate they are paying on a lease negotiated years ago or rates they are paying in another city that has no relations to the rental rates of the subject property. Rental rates quoted in a good market can easily cause "sticker shock" for prospects and for tenants renewing their lease. Be prepared to provide the tenant with current market data.

Incorrect Market Data

The tenant may have been provided inaccurate information about the city, property details, trade area's *demographics* and *psychographics*, or a host of other misinformation. It is best to have accurate information regarding the property, area, and economy available to be presented to the prospective tenant and prospect's leasing agent before lease negotiations.

Inflexible Lease Documents

A lease that is too one sided may be prohibitively onerous for the tenant. In a strong market, the owner may effectively use an aggressive lease, while in a weak market its lease may have to be converted to a "tenant friendly" lease. The challenge is not that the lease is too onerous for one party, but that the party who presented the lease form is too rigid in its negotiations of the lease document, and not willing to negotiate lease provisions that the other party cannot accept. Reasonable people can usually, but not always, find a way to restructure contentious lease provisions in such a way that both parties can "live with" the final lease document. The leasing agents should first determine which lease provisions are stumbling blocks to moving the negotiations forward. Once this information is obtained, the agents should ask each party why these particular lease provision(s) is objectionable and offer a compromise.

Uninvolved Decision Makers

The decision makers may not be party to the negotiations or be too far removed from the transaction resulting in the deal never getting approved. The leasing agent should attempt to discover which issues concern the decision maker the most and then provide the decision maker with information needed to make a decision. This data could involve market data, information about the property, the trade area or micro market, or the economy in the area that will relieve the concerns of the decision maker. Sometimes attorneys, in their zeal to protect their clients' interests, become a hindrance to completing the transaction. No attorney wants to be called a "deal killer."

The property owner must determine each player's role in negotiating the lease. Usually, the leasing agent will negotiate the business terms of the deal. The other lease provisions are then negotiated by either the leasing agent with the attorney, or just the attorney who negotiates on behalf of the client. When the leasing agent and the attorney are working in tandem negotiating the lease, the property owner has the best possible team negotiating the lease. The leasing agent understands the market and brings that knowledge to the table while and the attorney understands the legal implications of the lease language and the resulting impact upon his or her client.

Hidden Agendas

It's possible that one party may have a hidden agenda. If this is the case, the transaction is likely to fall apart somewhere during the negotiation process. An example would be if the tenant is using the negotiations for leverage to renew the lease in another building. It is difficult to determine if one party has a hidden agenda.

Lack of a Timely Response

The oldest adage in real estate is "time kills deals." A lack of a timely response from any party to the negotiations provides the prospective tenant with an opportunity to find alternative space, or the owner to find another prospective tenant with a more attractive offer. This is why the leaders in the transaction must be aware of the pulse of the deal and ensure that each player is fulfilling their responsibilities in a timely manner. A couple of examples are a space planner taking too much time to design the office space or a general contractor taking too long to provide a bid to build out the premises.

Personality Conflicts

Personalities can clash, and people may develop a dislike for one another that causes interest in completing the transaction to fade. In this situation, one or two people may need to be removed from the negotiations. They may continue to play an important role behind the screen advising their client, and the other players, on their negotiating team.

Simply put, an ego can kill a transaction. Everyone does not have the same experience and expertise, yet everyone in the transaction is important and should be respected for their role in the "deal." As the familiar saying goes, "what goes around comes around," and how people treat others will indeed effect how they themselves are treated in the future. Whenever possible, people will avoid dealing with those who have treated them unfairly.

Changing Goals and Objectives

A owner who moves the "goal posts" is not negotiating in good faith; and this will most likely cause a deal to collapse. A *letter of intent (LOI)* signed by the owner and the prospective tenant will outline the business terms of a proposed lease and reduce the possibility that one party will renege on the business terms of the LOI. Business terms may be renegotiated if other monetary and sometimes even non-monetary issues are presented after the LOI is signed. A LOI outlines the basic terms of the "deal" and usually what is left to negotiate are some of the other provisions in the lease since one party, usually the tenant, has never seen the lease document, the owner is presenting.

The tenant may find a better location or the landlord may find a tenant who either is a better fit for the building or will lease additional space. This seldom happens during negotiations. The LOI may state that each party is negotiating in good faith and, for a specific period of time, each party will refrain from negotiating for another space or another prospective tenant for that space.

Anticipating Deal Obstacles

It's important to plan for potential obstacles rather than being swamped by them during negotiations. It may be in the best interest of your client for you to coach the prospective tenant's leasing agent on non-confidential concerns of the property owner. For example, the leasing agent for a retailer may inform the owner's leasing agent that the client has blackout periods when they will not open a store. The lease needs to be negotiated and signed by a specific date for the tenant to build out their premises and be open before one of the blackout period commences. If not, the retailer will either not take the space and move on to another location, or will delay taking the space until after the blackout period, which results in a delay in payment of rent.

Many lease negotiations break down and the deal dies through no fault of either party. This can happen for a multitude of reasons; some beyond the control of either party. The most common reason is one party cannot afford or will not accept the terms that the other party is offering. The old adage, "sometimes the best deal is the one that did not happen," applies to some lease negotiations.

NEGOTIATING TIPS

The following lists several strategies that can improve the lease negotiating process:

Be Prepared

The leasing team should come to the table with as much practical knowledge as possible. The team should know who the tenant is. If the tenant is a public company, the available financial and operating information will be useful in understanding the strength of that tenant's position.

The leasing representative should know how its building rents and other charges compare to that of the competition and the building's position in the market. The tenant will want to know if the owner's *common area maintenance (CAM)* charges or pass-through operating expenses also known as *billback charges* are reasonable for the building and the market.

It behooves the leasing team to find out why tenants are looking for an additional location or moving from an existing space. If the tenant(s) have multiple locations, why does this particular location appeal to them? Will this location replace an existing location or are they looking to expand and open a new location?

In an office setting, the owner should also ascertain that the tenant fits into the building's tenant mix. Generally, with the exception of specialized buildings, a reasonably quiet tenant with operations that do not disrupt the building's other occupants will most likely be a fit. In the retail market, a more thorough analysis of the prospective tenant's use, merchandise, price points, advertising, and operations is needed to ensure the prospective tenant will enhance the tenant mix of a shopping center.

Finally, it is a good idea, before negotiations begin, to make sure that the other side has the authority to negotiate and accept compromises. It is quite frustrating to reach an agreement on a given point only to be told that the vice president (or anyone else who has to sign off on the decision) could not be convinced. An example is negotiating with a franchisee or licensee who does not have the franchise rights for a particular area or city.

Consider the Options

The owner should have a desired financial outcome for the lease negotiations, and should approach the negotiations with that goal in mind. It is wise for the leasing team to discuss a fallback position in case the negotiations do not allow for the deal they have in mind. Obviously, one of the fallback positions for either side is to walk away from the negotiations. A good negotiation is a series of ideas being presented and then accepted, rejected, or compromised. To maintain the pulse of the negotiations, it is a good idea to establish the items that everyone agrees with from the outset, and then deal with the areas of disagreement. No lease negotiation should be terminated at the early stages until both sides have been able to present their position and discuss and consider the alternatives presented by the other side.

Remember that there is nothing wrong with allowing the other party to "table" a point of discussion which is proving to be particularly difficult. This allows both sides to continue to move forward with negotiations on the rest of the document. You may find that there are very few points that require extensive discussion. If items remain to be resolved at the end of the negotiation session, suggest that the parties review that language internally and provide suggested compromises that can be discussed at a subsequent negotiation session. Be sure to set a date and time for the next discussion before the parties part; this will help keep the players focused on the deal and maintain the pulse of the negotiations.

Remaining open to alternative ideas can often be beneficial. A owner may have a need for a specific base rent and only be able to compromise on the TIs, or a tenant may be willing to pay for some of the improvements if the owner provides an option on favorable terms. The deal should be negotiated in its entirety rather than trying to piece together a lease arrangement one point at a time. If owners get their asking rent, they may give on the TIs; however, if the owner is being asked to compromise on concessions or TIs without knowing what rent the tenant will offer, it is difficult to reach an agreement.

Keep It Professional

Egos should be kept out of the negotiations. Posturing is not likely to help in the negotiating process, and may end what could have been a reasonable deal for both parties. It is helpful to keep in mind that one day the owner may be benefiting from a strong market, but the next time around it may switch to a tenant's market. For that reason alone, it is a good idea to treat the other side with respect and courtesy. It is not wise to indicate that the other party is being unreasonable by not coming up or down on the rental terms. This may apply to either side, so it is hard to place the blame. One side or the other may have reached the breaking point, and in such a case, even a few cents matter a great deal.

If negotiations do fall apart, there is a reasonable chance that the parties may meet again. It is therefore a good idea to end with a handshake and indicate a willingness to make another deal in the future. Closing doors on future connections makes no sense, especially in retail leasing where some owners and tenants make multiple deals.

Everyone who approaches a lease negotiation is interested in walking away with a lease. The exercise is not intended merely for educational purposes, but rather for concluding a satisfactory arrangement—a "win-win" deal that benefits both parties. Both sides should be looking for ways to make the negotiations work and work through any differences if at all possible. Taking time to understand why the other side has taken a specific position will often lead to an acceptable compromise. A good negotiation generally requires a lot of "what ifs" from both sides before the final arrangements are agreed upon.

Keep Records

Keep a journal record of each negotiation session to document what was covered and where possible problems and solutions exist. Quite often, a negotiation will take a turn with compromises, but then a break is taken and, when discussions resume, the specifics have been forgotten. It's helpful to recap discussions at the start of any new negotiations.

It is a good idea, after a negotiation session has ended, to send a memo to the other side recapping the day's discussions and the issues that are open for the next session. If there are misunderstandings, this provides an opportunity for them to be addressed so that both sides will be prepared to move forward when the negotiations resume.

Employ Effective Strategies

To begin with, both sides must be aware of the importance of issues and attempt to keep them in perspective when negotiating. It should be noted that all points in a negotiation are not equal. For example, the owner sets the rents to meet the market, generate income, and create value. The tenant may want the owner to extend the lease in exchange for a lower rent, but such terms would lock the owner into a lower rental rate for a longer period of time. Hence, the offer is not likely to be accepted, even though it seems reasonable to the tenant.

Be wary of the "let's-split-the-difference" approach to negotiating. It is too easy for one side or the other to set a ridiculous figure and then offer to split the difference. There is little doubt that some negotiations reach the point that the "split-the-difference" approach can be a reasonable one, but in general, it is not a valid approach for negotiations. Another negotiation ploy is to say something like, "I gave you four concessions so you owe me four concessions." However, not all concessions are equal.

When one side's negotiations do not seem reasonable, the other side should have no problem pointing out, in a courteous fashion, why that approach will not work. There is nothing wrong with either party explaining why a particular issue is more important to them and provides little room for flexibility. Often, the issues can be resolved to the satisfaction of both parties.

Expressing emotions during negotiations seldom leads to a lease deal. This is business—not to be taken personally—and it should be treated as such. A temper tantrum, storming out of a meeting, and name-calling are not good negotiating techniques. If emotions start to build up, it is a good idea to take a break and start again when reason has been restored. It is not likely that the other side is *trying* to incite anger, but sometimes unproductive things are said in the heat of the moment. Anger or an emotional outburst can easily bring negotiations to a halt and make the other party very reluctant to come back to the table.

Words are powerful, so choose them carefully in a negotiation. Owners typically are proud of their buildings and feel they do a good job with ownership and management. If a prospective tenant suggests that everything is not as presented, the owner is likely to get defensive. On the other side of the coin, most tenants are also proud of their business and reputation. An owner's suggestion that the tenant is less than the best may bring negotiations to a grinding halt.

Even when nothing negative is intended, both parties should keep in mind that words are powerful and should be used very carefully. This is one of the reasons that it is a good idea to have a leasing agent dealing with another leasing agent. If words are not well chosen, leasing agents are less likely to be offended; whereas the owner or tenant may take them much more personally.

It is also important to remember that silence is often a very effective tool. Will Rogers said, "Never miss a chance to shut up." This is often a good negotiating strategy. Just sitting quietly and letting the other side break the silence to start another approach or even offer suggestions or concessions may help move the discussion in a positive direction. Be sure to listen, really listen, to what the other side says and don't sit there simply thinking of your next response.

Ultimately, each negotiator must evaluate their techniques and approaches. Following any negotiation, the leasing team should evaluate what went well, what did not go well, and, more importantly, what can be done to improve future negotiations. Was the negotiator too passive, failing to lead the discussion, or aggressive to the point of turning the prospect off to the property? Was the leasing team unable to answer questions that were asked during the session? Did the prospect become upset during the session and, if so, could this be prevented in the future? There is no single way to negotiate, but team member assigned to negotiate should evaluate their own approach, try to learn from past negotiations, and refine the process to make future negotiations more productive for all parties involved.

Negotiations

The next step is negotiating the lease itself. These negotiations can be a very time-consuming process and require great attention to detail, especially for major shopping centers and high-rise office buildings that have long and complicated leases. While many lease negotiations last only a few days or weeks, complex lease negotiations can take months to complete.

Both parties must take great care to be sure that all of the terms and conditions of the lease are fully understood before agreeing to them. If there is doubt on either side, the item in question should be discussed until there is proper understanding. Neither side should be reluctant to bring up any issue regarding the lease. Most owners and tenants are not interested in taking advantage of the other side; they are just trying to protect their interests and must therefore understand what they are agreeing to. There are tens of thousands to millions of dollars involved over the term of a lease, so it is not surprising when the process takes a long time.

The real estate manager and leasing agent should thoroughly understand the lease document and how each provision affects the building, its operations, cash flow, and value. *Chapter 10: Negotiating the Commercial Lease* discusses scores of lease provisions and how to negotiate a compromise that will meet the objectives of the owner and the tenant. As previously mentioned, knowledge is power, and an understanding of the lease document places the real estate manager and/or leasing agent in a stronger negotiating position.

Final Approval

The final approval for a lease can take only a few hours, but it may require considerable time as well. Quite often, the leasing agents for the owner and the tenant negotiate the terms, and then the lease must go to their principals for final approval. Generally, when the process has been handled by qualified agents, the final approval is almost certain; but this is not always the case.

In most cases, the lease is negotiated, the tenant signs it, and the document is then sent to the owner for his or her signature. In most states, the lease is not legally executed until the tenant and the owner have signed it and the owner returns a copy signed by both parties to the tenant. The old adage "time kills deals" applies to negotiating and executing a lease.

In very rare occasions, the owner will have difficult space to lease or a highly desirable tenant—these are conditions that may prompt the owner to be the first to sign the lease. Generally, when a lease is presigned by the owner and sent to the tenant for a signature, the tenant is given a specific period of time to sign it before the offer expires. Owners do not want their signature on leases that are not fully executed out in the marketplace. They want to proceed with other negotiations if a particular deal is not going to be completed.

Tenants will have the same requirements for owners when the tenant is the first party to sign the lease. The tenant has the same concerns as the owner in having a signed lease out in the market. It will limit the tenant's options until it is either signed or rejected. In most jurisdictions, if tenants have signed the lease but not received a signed copy back, they are free to cancel the lease at any time prior to receiving the lease signed by the owner.

Optimizing the Negotiating Position

Lease negotiation is an art, not a science. Depending on the market conditions, either the owner or the tenant can be at a distinct advantage or disadvantage during the process. In a strong property ownership market, the tenant will have little room to negotiate because the owner will have many other options and won't have to work hard or give away concessions to sign leases. In a strong tenant market, however, the owner will be at a disadvantage and will almost surely be required to make concessions to secure a tenant.

All things considered, the person with the most knowledge of the market and the strongest understanding of the other side, and is best prepared to negotiate, will be in the optimal position to take advantage of the existing conditions and secure the best possible deal for its client in the market.

CHAPTER

10

Negotiating the Commercial Lease

A successful negotiation of a lease is one of the most important responsibilities for both parties involved in the process. The results of a lease negotiation have long-term effects on the owner's property as well as the tenant's business. The ideal outcome of lease negotiations is a win-win situation for both parties. This chapter explains the importance of the lease provision and how it impacts the owner's property and/or the tenant's business.

The person (or persons) responsible for negotiating the lease on behalf of the owner must understand how each lease provision impacts the cash flow and value of the property, as well as its tenant mix and daily operations. Owners want their commercial tenants to be successful. Successful tenants pay their rent on time, prefer to renew their leases and if they are retailers or restaurants, have a good chance of paying percentage rent in addition to their base rent.

A wise owner will understand how each lease provision impacts the operations and profitability of the tenant's business. Owners will want the best negotiated lease possible, while at the same time, not overburden tenants with a lease that restricts their ability to be successful. Since the owner and the tenant are obligated to fulfill their responsibilities described in the lease, they should both understand their rights and obligations in the lease and how the lease impacts them.

With a thorough understanding of the lease document, the leasing agent, real estate manager, attorney, owner, and tenant can negotiate each provision to achieve the best possible deal. The lease document is a lengthy and, for some people, an intimidating document; yet, reading the lease reveals that most of the provisions are relatively easy to understand. Those provisions that may seem a little complicated can be explained by an attorney, or by an experienced leasing agent or real estate manager.

This chapter is designed as a reference for professionals negotiating commercial leases. There is no standard commercial lease and many owners prefer a lease drafted for them by an attorney that addresses specific provisions that meet the owner's objectives. Other owners will use a lease that is widely used and accepted in the industry. Occasionally, an owner will use a tenant's lease which can usually be very one sided. While some institutional property owners, REITS, and developers, will have a lease drafted specifically for them that can be very onerous for the tenants. There are many different lease forms in the industry, but they all have many of the same provisions worded a little different to capture the philosophy of the owner, or the attorney drafting the lease.

THE LEASE FORM

If you were to ask most real estate managers and leasing agents if the lease is complicated, they are likely to say "yes." Many real estate professionals do not take the time to understand the lease, how each provision can impact the owner and the tenant, and how to negotiate the many lease provisions. People who believe the lease is complicated have not taken the time to understand the lease. Knowledge is power, and when we have the power of fully understanding the lease, we are in a much better negotiating position.

The party whose lease form is used starts the negotiations with a tremendous advantage. They have presented the other party with all the issues drafted to their advantage. The owner's lease form is almost always used when negotiating leases. Anchor retail tenants and governmental agencies are exceptions, and will typically insist on using their own lease form. Some national shop retail tenants and large office users will also attempt to have their lease form used. In these situations, the negotiating strength of the owner will determine which lease form is used. Regardless, every provision can be negotiated to the satisfaction of both parties. The outcome of the negotiations will depend on each party's negotiating strength, skill, understanding of the lease, prioritization of the transaction, and approach towards negotiating the lease. When all the parties to the lease negotiations work towards a win-win situation together, the results almost always end with an executed lease that will be beneficial to both parties.

Lease Net-Ness

The term net-ness describes the building expenses that the tenant pays. Leases are *gross, single-net, double-net, triple-net,* or *modified net.*

In a *gross lease,* the tenant pays base rent and is not billed for any tenant charges. In theory, these charges are included in the gross rent. In a single-net lease, the tenant pays base rent and real estate taxes. In a double-net lease (net-net lease), the tenant pays base rent, real estate taxes, and building insurance. In a triple-net lease (net-net-net lease), the tenant pays base rent, real estate taxes, building insurance, and maintenance. This lease is also referred to as a fully-net lease. You may see these various net options abbreviated as N, NN, or NNN which indicates a single-net, double-net, or triple-net lease.

A useful mnemonic device for recalling net-ness is the name TIM: in single-net leases, tenants pay the taxes (T); in double-net leases, tenants pay taxes and insurance (TI); in triple-net leases, tenants pay taxes, insurance, and maintenance (TIM).

Different geographic areas have different terms for exceptions to a triple-net lease, such as special net, true-net, absolute-net, or industrial-net leases. Reading the leases carefully and inquiring about the definition of terms is important. For example, a tenant may negotiate to have specific expenses excluded from the *pass-through charges* or *common area maintenance (CAM)* charges. A supermarket may negotiate to exclude security cost from the CAM, while another tenant may place a "cap" on the amount of liability insurance the tenant will reimburse the owner. The anchor tenant may negotiate to pay its pro-rating share of no more than five million dollars of liability insurance. When one party in the negotiations of a lease states the property's leases are triple-net, follow the advice President Ronald Regan used in negotiating with the Russians which is "trust but verify." The best advice is to carefully read the lease and always advise your client to have an attorney review and comment on the lease.

The real estate manager should be careful how lease terms are used. Some people refer to a lease as a "net lease" but really mean that the tenant pays base rent, taxes, insurance, and maintenance, while others use the textbook definition of a net lease to mean that the tenant pays only base rent and real estate taxes. When someone refers to the net-ness of a lease, that term should be clarified during lease negotiation or sale of a property to avoid misunderstandings, future problems, and possible litigation. Imagine an agent entering into a lease with a tenant using the term "net lease" to mean triple-net lease rather than single-net lease, while the tenant uses the textbook definition and expects to pay only rent and real estate taxes.

THE COMPONENTS OF A LEASE

No matter which lease form is used, to be valid, it must include six required components that are described and defined in very specific language. These required components are:

1. The parties to the lease
2. Description of the leased premises
3. Term (or duration) of the lease
4. Consideration of the rent and charges paid to the owner by the tenant

5. Description of the tenant's use of the premises
6. Rights and obligations of both parties.

These components may appear in a different order, but they must all be present for the lease to be valid. The first five components are typically found on the first page or two, and the sixth requirement is covered throughout the rest of the lease.

Although the lease may not include all of these lease provisions, those responsible for negotiating the lease should be aware of and understand all of the provisions in order to be most effective. A discussion of each of the typical lease provisions is provided below.

Table of Contents

The lease is a substantial document, typically in length between 25 and 50 (or more) pages. The lease often contains a table of contents for quick reference, which identifies the pages on which specific lease provisions appear.

Acceptance of Keys

This provision states that if the tenant gives the keys to the premises back to the owner or the owner's representative, the lease is not thereby cancelled. This is to prevent a tenant from claiming that, because the keys to the premises were given to the real estate manager or to maintenance personnel, the premises were surrendered to and accepted by the owner, and the tenant is no longer obligated to fulfill the terms and obligations of the lease.

Acceptance of Premises

Tenants have a specific time period—usually no more than one week after the premises are turned over to them—to notify the owner in writing of any construction defects. If the tenant does not notify the owner within the specified time period, that tenant has accepted the premises by default.

Tenants may negotiate for a longer notification time period and will also require that the owner correct any defects that are found as soon as possible. To avoid a conflict, the tenant and owner should complete a checklist inspection upon move-in and move-out, itemizing defects in the premises. When a tenant is using its contractor to construct its tenant improvements, the checklist inspection should be before the tenant improvements commence. Retail tenants and restaurant users almost always contract directly for their tenant improvements.

Advertising

Shopping center owners want all their tenants to advertise and promote their businesses in order to maximize sales potential. There are several benefits to the tenant and the owner when the tenant's sales are strong. First, better sales mean a more financially sound business. Second, there is a relationship between a tenant's sales and the rent they can (and will) pay. Retailers and restaurant operators typically want their rent to be within a percentage range of their sales, and higher sales mean they can afford to pay more rent. Third, the greater the retailer's sales, the greater the opportunity for that tenant to pay percentage rent which is often a component of retail leases. An advertising provision is seldom used in unanchored and multi-anchored strip shopping center leases, but it is often used in leases for regional malls as well as lifestyle, entertainment, outlet, and specialty shopping centers.

Originally, this advertising provision required tenants to spend a minimum percentage of their gross sales on advertising (usually two percent) and to provide evidence of that expenditure. But monitoring the amount a tenant spends on advertising is difficult for the owner.

As an alternative, the provision may require the tenant to advertise in a minimum number of the shopping center's advertising tabloids. If the tenant does not advertise a minimum number of times, the owner may place an ad giving the tenant's name and address, and the tenant will be responsible for reimbursing the owner for the cost of the ad. Tenants will negotiate for a minimum number of tabloids to advertise in, based on their advertising and merchandise plan.

Alterations

The owners of office and medical office buildings almost always coordinate the construction of their tenants' alterations. They want to maintain the integrity of their building's mechanical, electrical, and structural systems. They also want to ensure that all work in the building is of the same standards. If major tenants in an office or medical office building insist on performing their own alterations, the owner will place stringent requirements on the tenants and the contractors doing the work. On the other hand, owners of industrial properties and shopping centers will often allow their tenants to perform their own alterations. The lease should state whether or not the tenant may construct any improvements to the premises and should specifically reference structural vs. non-structural improvements. If the tenant is given permission to make improvements to their space, the owner will reserve the right to review and approve, in writing, any plans for alterations, additions, or other improvements and will also require that the tenants agrees to certain terms and regulations.

The following list summarizes the terms and regulations that are often required by owners when tenants are permitted to make improvements within their space:

Rules and Regulations for Tenant Improvement Work

1. The tenant may not make any alterations or improvements without owner's prior written permission.
2. All requests for additions or alterations must be in writing and must be accompanied by a drawing showing what is to be done.
3. All work must be performed with the proper building permit issued by the local authority.
4. All work must be done between the hours set by the owner.
5. The owner must preapprove any on-site staging.
6. Any core drilling must be preapproved by the owner and done within specified hours.
7. Any penetrations of the roof must be either done by the owner's contractor or supervised by the owner's contractor.
8. Any deliveries are to be done during specified hours, at a place designated by the owner.
9. Materials and/or trucks are not to block any tenant entrances, tenant storefronts, or prime parking spaces.
10. When elevators are involved, all deliveries must be assigned elevator times.
11. All contractors must carry evidence of liability insurance and a bond if working in a tenant's space, and they must name the owner and the owner's real estate management firm as additional insureds.
12. All work must be done by licensed contractors.
13. Contractors are to be liable to the building for utility costs during construction.
14. The tenant is responsible for all costs and will prevent any liens against the building and/or will immediately satisfy any liens that are filed.
15. The tenant is to maintain entrances to the construction site or staging area in a clean and safe manner at all times during the entire term of the construction project.
16. The tenant is responsible for any construction barricades and/or safety devices for the protection of the public during construction.
17. The owner and tenant are to have final inspection of all work, and the owner is to issue written approval when the job has been completed satisfactorily.
18. The owner is to be provided with a certificate of occupancy issued by the municipality.

Tenants are usually prohibited from doing work on the roof without the owner's prior written approval and supervision by the owner's representative and may be required to use the owner's roofing contractor to protect any warranties. Owners will also restrict tenants from core drilling or other construction activities that may be disruptive to other tenants, their visitors, and customers during normal business hours. Additionally, depending on whether the alterations add value for re-leasing the premises, owners may stipulate that the leased premises be restored to original condition at the tenant's sole expense when the premises are vacated or the lease expires. The cost to remove wiring and cabling can be expensive, and the owner will usually require the tenant to remove all wiring before vacating the premises.

The tenant may negotiate so that the costs of the owner's alterations are at fair market price. The fee that the owner adds to supervise the work be reasonable.

When a owner allows a tenant to perform their tenant improvements, there should be rules and regulations the tenant and its contractors must follow. These may be included in an exhibit to the lease or in a separate agreement between the owner and the tenant.

Arbitration

There are some owner-tenant conflicts that may be settled faster through *arbitration* than by going to court. This provision usually states which issues will be arbitrated and which will not. Owners prefer to deal with monetary default through the legal system; however, many nonmonetary default issues may be better handled through arbitration with people who understand real estate. The arbitration provision provides an alternative to going to court to settle a dispute. It's common when the owner and tenant do not agree on the market rent for either extending a lease or the rental rate for a predetermined period, such as the fifth year of a 10-year lease. The owner and the tenant will each select an arbitrator and the two arbitrators will select the third arbitrator. These three arbitrators will determine the new rent increase when it is based on the market rate.

Another arbitration method is the "baseball" arbitrator. Each party states what they believe is the market rate. Each party selects an arbitrator and the two arbitrators select a third arbitrator. The three arbitrators determine the market rate and whichever party is closest to the market rate becomes the new rental rate. This method forces each party to be realistic on the rate they believe is the market rate.

Other issues to address in this provision are the geographic area and the type and size of buildings that will be used as comparable to determine the market rate. The arbitrators are given two weeks to a month to provide their recommendations.

Assignment

The *assignment* provision is important to tenants because they often cannot sell their business unless the owner agrees to the lease assignment. Owners prefer to have the right, at their sole discretion, to approve tenant requests to assign or sublet a space. This ensures that the owner has the opportunity to run credit checks, background checks, review financials, etc. on the assignee so that they may confirm whether the assignee has the expertise and financial health to operate the business and pay the rent. The courts will require owners to be reasonable in their criteria to disapprove an assignment. Leases will also state that the owner must be reasonable in accepting or rejecting an assignment.

The owner who approves an assignment will want the assignment to be "without release"—meaning that the *assignor* (the tenant assigning the lease) must fulfill the obligations of the lease if the assignee defaults. Under an assignment without release, the owner can collect past due rent from the assignor if the assignee doesn't pay rent as required in the lease, or if the assignee is a retailer or operates a restaurant or service business and subsequently closes that business, under the continuous operations provision, the owner could require the assignor to step in to operate the business. This is an obvious hardship, especially if the assignor has moved on to another business or retired, and the assignor will therefore try to negotiate to an assignment with release.

An assignment "with release" frees the assignor from all future obligations of the lease. If the assignee defaults, the owner cannot look to the assignor to cure this default.

If the issue of assignment with or without release must be negotiated, the owner or tenant may offer an alternative that requires the assignor to guarantee the performance of the assignee for a limited time (e.g., for the first few years of the remaining term of the lease). If the assignee does not default in any obligation during the specified time period, the assignor is then released of all obligations under the lease.

Attorneys' Fees

All leases typically provide that the prevailing party in any legal action concerning the lease is entitled to reimbursement of reasonable legal fees.

Auction and Sale

This provision applies to shopping centers, other retail properties, and office buildings with a retail component. Because "going-out-of-business" signs, sales, or auctions can give the impression that the property is failing, owners include in the lease a provision stating that the tenant may not conduct a bankruptcy or going-out-of-business sale or auction—or post signs announcing such activities—without the prior written consent of the owner.

Auditing Rights

The tenant is given the right to audit the CAM charges and other pass-through charges, such as real estate taxes and insurance. Because the owner incurs expenses on behalf of the tenants, it is only fair that tenants have the right to audit the owner's pass-through charges and review the invoices to ensure that the charges are appropriate and reasonable. The owner typically places the following ten restrictions on that right:

1. The audit must commence within 90 days of the date the tenant receives the year-end adjustments.
2. The tenant can only audit the period of the most recent year-end adjustments.
3. The audit will be conducted in the place where the owner maintains the financial records and during normal business hours.
4. The results of the audit will be kept confidential.
5. The auditor will not be paid a contingent fee.
6. The auditor will be a certified public accountant (CPA).
7. The owner will receive a copy of the audit.
8. The tenant must not be in default of the lease during the audit.
9. If the owner disagrees with the results of the audit, another CPA who is mutually selected by the owner and the tenant will conduct the audit and those results will be binding.
10. The tenant may not withhold rent or other payments during the audit.

There are several issues listed above that the tenant may negotiate out of the audit provision, especially items five and six, as many tenant audit firms do not comply with these points.

The tenant may also negotiate if the CAM audit reveals a discrepancy in the amount being charged to the tenant in excess of a set percentage (for example, two to five percent). The owner would be required to reimburse the tenant for the tenant's reasonable cost to conduct the audit. This language discourages owners from inflating expenses.

Authority of Signatory

Each party should establish the authority of the individuals who represent the owner and the tenant. An entrepreneur signs the lease for a business as its owner. In the case of a *corporation*, an officer of the company may be a signatory on behalf of the corporation. However, the authority of that officer to commit the corporation to the lease should be officially documented. It is common for the owner to require a corporate resolution authorizing the corporate officer to sign the lease. The tenant may require the same of the owner. The corporate resolution should be appended to the lease as an exhibit.

Cancellation

Owners never want to offer tenants the right to cancel their lease. There are situations where a tenant may negotiate for a lease cancellation. When a lease cancellation is requested, it is usually by a retail tenant. During the *Great Recession* of 2008 through 2012, some retail tenants were able to negotiate a lease cancellation because the shopping center had an unacceptable vacancy rate and there were few retailers looking for space. With high vacancy, the reduction in the overall number of visitors to a shopping center reduces the potential income of the remaining tenants.

A retailer who is desired by all owners may be in a strong negotiating position to negotiate a lease cancellation. Owners resist giving a tenant a cancellation right, but some owners may be required to in order to obtain a specific retailer. If the right to cancel is given, both the owner and the tenant should be able to cancel the lease based on the same criteria. Typically, the provision allows the tenant the right to cancel the lease if the retailer's sales do not exceed a specific sales volume. For example, if the tenant's sales do not exceed one million dollars during any time during the first three years of the lease, the tenant has a one-time right to cancel the lease.

Owners should limit the right to cancel to a one-time right rather than an ongoing right, and should negotiate a mutual right of cancellation for both owner and tenant. If there are unamortized tenant improvements (TIs) or leasing *commissions* at the time of cancellation, the tenant should be obligated to reimburse the owner for those costs as a condition of the cancellation. After the tenant notifies the owner of their intent to cancel the lease, the tenant should be required to remain open for an additional four to six months. This period provides the owner with time to re-lease the space.

Commission

Owners recognize and respect the role leasing agents and real estate managers play in leasing a building. If brokerage services are used, the lease will reference the specific brokers involved and will often indicate which party the broker represented (owner or tenant). The lease may also reference the amount of the commission which is typically calculated as a percentage of the gross rent. However, sometimes the lease may only reference that the commission is paid pursuant to a separate agreement between the owner and the listing broker. The owner usually pays commissions. If the owner is responsible for paying the commissions, the tenant will want the lease to state that the tenant has no responsibility or liability to pay commission.

Common Area Maintenance (CAM) and Other Pass-Through Charges

Pass-through and CAM charges include several expense categories—maintenance, utilities, insurance, real estate taxes, security, management fees, etc. The method of billing these charges to tenants varies depending on the netness of the lease e.g., gross to triple-net lease and modified-net lease.

Lease Language

Owners do not want the lease to limit the expenses included in pass-through charges by stating that the tenant will pay "the following list of expenses." The tenant may interpret this to mean that any expenses incurred but not listed cannot be billed, and owners want to make sure they have the right to pass through to the tenant all legitimate expenses of maintaining and operating the premises. Owners, therefore, want the lease to state the basic pass-through expenses while allowing for additional expenses as needed. Representative lease language might be "the pass-through expenses or the CAM expenses shall include but are not limited to the following list"; and the provision could include an itemized list of typical expenses of the pass-through and CAM charges, as well as mentioning "such other necessary and/or related expenses as may be incurred."

Tenants naturally do not want their pass-through expenses to include items they believe are not operational expenses, such as commissions, costs to resolve tenant disputes, and tenant improvements. Owners will accept these exclusions.

One exclusion that is often negotiated is the cost of capital improvements. The owner wants to include capital improvements to upgrade the common areas—such new carpeting in the hallways of an office building—in the pass-through charges. The owner also wants to pass through to the tenants the cost for energy-saving equipment or other equipment that will reduce the building's operating costs. If the owner cannot recapture these costs, and the savings benefit only the tenants, there is limited or no incentive for the owner to incur these expenses. Tenants may negotiate for the cost of the equipment to be amortized over its useful life, while the owner might counter by financing the cost of the equipment and including the payment in the pass-through charges.

Leased or Leasable Square Footage

The formula for determining each tenant's pro rata share of the CAM and pass-through expenses can be based on "leasable square footage" or on "leased square footage." In the leasable square footage formula, the tenant's pro rata share is the percent that tenant's premises are to the entire square footage of the building. This is by far the most common formula used for calculating CAM and pass-through charges.

The leased square footage formula, on the other hand, measures the tenant's pro rata share against only the percentage of the space that actually is leased. When the formula for measuring space is based on leased space, the numerator is still the square footage of the tenant's premises, but the denominator is the *gross leasable area (GLA)* of the leased spaces only:

	Square Footage of Tenant's Space
÷	**GLA of Leased Spaces**
=	**Tenant's Pro Rata Share**

Consequently, the denominator changes every time a space is vacated or leased. As the amount of leased space decreases, the tenant's pro rata share gets larger. If half of a shopping center were vacant, a tenant's pro rata share would be half what it would be if the leasable square footage formula is used.

As an example to demonstrate the practical difference between these two formulas, consider a tenant who leases a 2,000-square-foot space in a shopping center. The GLA of the shopping center is 100,000 square feet, and the shopping center is only 80 percent occupied. Based on leasable square footage, this tenant would have a pro rata share of 2 percent (2,000 ÷ 100,000 = .02). However, using the leased space formula, this same tenant would be responsible for 2.5 percent of the charges (2,000 ÷ 80,000 = .025). With pass-through charges totaling $300,000 in the shopping center, the tenant's pro rata share would be $6,000 at the 2 percent rate ($300,000 × .02) and $7,500—a significantly higher amount—at the 2.5 rate ($300,000 × .025).

The owner's theory behind using leased square footage is the merchants in the shopping center are benefiting from the maintenance of the common areas, and therefore they should pay the total costs. However, merchants do not believe they should be charged for the costs attributed to vacant spaces. Tenants believe they are being unfairly penalized by having to pay a higher percentage of tenant charges simply because the owner is unable to lease the vacant space. Experienced tenants will not accept the "leased area" concept, and the "leasable area" concept is standard in the industry. The lease will state whether the leasable or leased area is used in the formula to calculate the tenant's prorate share of the building's operating expenses.

Management Fee or Administrative Fee

The building's management fee is a typical pass-through charge for all commercial buildings. Prior to the early 1980s, shopping center owners did not charge the management in CAM expanses, and instead charged an administrative fee based on a percentage of the CAM charges. This fee was usually 10 to 15 percent of the actual CAM expenses. In the early 1980s, shopping center developers and owners began charging a management fee instead of the administrative fee, which is often considerably greater than an administrative fee.

Some shopping center owners are very aggressive and attempt to negotiate for both a management fee and an administrative fee. These two fees are for the same service and tenants will negotiate to pay for only one of these fees.

When the management fee is agreed to as a pass-through charge, the tenant may negotiate a cap on the fee. The cap can be based on an agreed percentage of the building's gross income or a fixed-dollar amount. The tenant may negotiate that the fee will be based on a market fee.

Caps on Pass-Through Charges

Tenants may negotiate to place a cap or ceiling on the amount of the increase in their pass-through or CAM charges. A cap places a limit on the amount of the charges or on their annual increase. Owners will resist caps, because they believe that they operate their building efficiently and there are several expenses over which they have little or no control. If a cap must be negotiated, the owner may agree to cap the controllable charges to a specific percentage increase each year, such as five percent, but not to cap the uncontrollable charges, such as real estate taxes, insurance, utilities, snow removal, etc.

Fixed CAM Charges

Although it is not common, some shopping center owners bill tenants a flat CAM charge and do not make adjustments for the actual CAM expenses. This can eliminate any disputes over the charges, and guarantees a known cost for tenants. Yet, it is risky for both the owner and tenant because the expenses may exceed the flat charge or be overstated. Fixed CAM started with regional and super regional malls. When negotiating a flat rate, the prior year's CAM charges should be used as a base to determine the coming year's CAM expenses. These expenses need to be carefully reviewed to determine if there are any unusually high or low expenses—such as an abnormal snow fall—that might distort the figures.

Open and Enclosed Mall CAM Charges

The terms *mall* and *strip shopping center* are often used interchangeably, but there is a difference between these types of shopping centers. A strip shopping center is a row of stores facing a parking lot or the street. The row of stores may be a straight line, L shape or U shape. A mall has two rows of stores facing each other with a walkway between them. A mall has two and possibly three CAM budgets, each with a separate charge to the tenants—one for the parking lot and exterior areas, another for the mall common areas, and the third for the food court common area, if applicable. This permits the separation of pass-through expenses for tenant billings.

For example, tenants who do not front on the mall, such as pad site, pay their pro rata shares of the parking lot and exterior CAM expenses, but they are not billed for the interior mall CAM expenses. Only food court tenants pay towards the food court CAM. Anchor tenants will often negotiate to exclude charges associated with the mall's common area because they have entrances to their store from the parking lot, (and developers knows that anchors are crucial to the mall's development and success).

When an anchor is exempted from paying mall area CAM expenses, the owner wants the shop tenants to pick up the mall area CAM costs. Each shop tenant's proration is then based on the GLA of the tenant's premises, divided by the total square footage of all shop space for stores that front on the mall, excluding the square footage of the anchors. This allows the owner to pass through to the shop tenants the portion of the mall CAM the anchor tenants are not paying.

	GLA of Tenant's Space
÷	**GLA of Shop Space with Mall Frontage**
=	**Tenant's Pro Rata Share**

Thus, if a mall has 800,000 square feet of GLA, of which shop tenants occupy 200,000 square feet, anchor tenants have 575,000 square feet, and pad tenants occupy 25,000 square feet. The denominator for the shop tenants' proration formula would be 200,000 square feet. A shop tenant in a 2,000-square-foot space would pay one percent of the mall CAM costs (2,000 square feet ÷ 200,000 square feet = .01).

CAM and Operating Expense Pass-Through Insurance

The cost of insurance for office buildings and industrial properties is included in the operating expenses that are billed to the tenants. For shopping centers, the insurance included in CAM charges is for property damage to the common areas and for liability coverage if someone is injured in those areas. This portion of the insurance premium is excluded from the building insurance expense that is billed separately to the tenants. The premiums are divided this way because some tenants—i.e., those in freestanding buildings and sometimes the anchor tenants in shopping centers—are responsible for providing their own insurance coverage.

By allocating part of the premium for the insurance on the whole shopping center as a CAM expense, the owner ensures that those tenants who pay for maintenance of the common area also pay to insure it. The same situation prevails when anchor tenants own and insure their building, but pay a pro rata share of CAM expenses, which include insurance for the common area.

Maintenance Reserves

The maintenance *reserves clause* in this provision allows the owner to charge for a reserve for major maintenance needs that may arise in the future. For instance, if a parking lot needs to be resurfaced in five years, the owner may bill tenants their pro rata share of the cost monthly for the next 60 months. Major tenants do not pay towards this maintenance reserve, but pay their pro rata obligation of the total expense when it is incurred.

Office and medical office building owners may use maintenance reserves to replace items such as *heating, ventilation, and air-conditioning (HVAC)* system equipment, parking lot replacement or repairs, renovation to the lobby, or carpet in the common area. This allows the owner to collect in advance for major maintenance instead of either billing the tenants one large amount in the year the expense is incurred, or billing the tenants over the useful life of the equipment or improvements following the year when the expense is incurred. The lease must state the owner has the right to collect maintenance reserves before the owner can bill the tenants for this expense.

Tenants want to be certain that the owner uses the reserves for their intended purpose. This can be an issue when a property is sold and either the seller keeps the reserves or the buyer transfers the reserves to a personal account. If tenants agree to a maintenance reserve, they may require the owner to place those funds in a separate trust account and provide all tenants with an annual accounting of the maintenance reserves.

Gross Up Operating Expenses

The operating expenses charged to a tenant are based on the method for billing pass-through expenses that is agreed upon in the lease. The *gross-up provision* allows the owner to gross up operating expenses that are affected by the building occupancy, which may include utilities, service contracts whose cost are dependent upon the building's occupancy, such as janitorial, costs, management fees, and property taxes.

It is common to gross up operating expenses in office and medical office buildings, but the concept is often misunderstood. Some tenants believe that the owner is padding expenses when the building's pass-through charges are grossed up, although the purpose of grossing up the operating expenses is to have the tenants pay their fair pro rata share. Contained in the list below is an example of why gross up is a fair approach:

- The example office building is 100,000 square feet.
- A tenant occupies 10,000 square feet in that building.
- The tenant pays a 10 percent pro rata share of the operating expenses.
- Janitorial costs are $1 per square foot.
- The cost for janitorial services at 100 percent building occupancy would be $100,000.
- The cost for janitorial services for the 10,000-square-foot tenant would be $10,000 (10,000 square feet × $1 per square foot).
- The building is only 50 percent occupied.
- The cost for janitorial services for the half-occupied building is $50,000 (50,000 square feet × $1 per square foot).
- If the tenant is charged his pro rata share of 10 percent, the charge is only $5,000 ($50,000 ×

.10) for janitorial services, while the actual cost to clean the tenant's premises is $10,000.

- When operating expenses are grossed up to 100 percent occupancy, the cost for janitorial services is stated at $100,000 (100,000 square feet × $1 per square foot) and the tenant is billed $10,000 (10,000 square feet × $1), which is the actual janitorial cost for the tenant's space regardless of the building's occupancy level.

Tenants will want the operating expenses grossed up to 100 percent occupancy during their base year when they have a base-year operating expense pass-through provision—meaning that tenants pay their pro rate share of all expenses above their base year, which is usually the year they take occupancy of their premises. If the building is not fully assessed for real estate taxes because it is new, the tax assessment for the first year may be based on last year's assessment when the building was partially built and the real estate taxes will need to be grossed up.

If the building has low occupancy, a tax appeal may earn a lower assessment; again, the real estate taxes will need to be grossed up. The tenant may negotiate for the gross up to be at 95 percent building occupancy since a building is seldom fully occupied at all times and a five percent vacancy factor is the standard vacancy rate used for a building's pro forma. However, the difference between 95 and 100 percent is nominal. It is easier and there is less chance of a mathematical error if 100 percent is used and it is the most accurate.

A gross up benefits tenants who have a base-year lease. Since these tenants pay their share of the increases after the base year, they benefit from higher operating expenses during that base year. Since they must pay their pro rata share of operating expenses above the base-year expenses, higher operating expenses during the base year mean less of an increase in operating expenses for the following years.

Higher base-year operating expenses benefit tenants with a base-year lease, but they also benefit owners who use other methods of billing operating expenses. The purpose of this provision should not be to bill the tenant for the maximum tenant charges allowed, but to charge tenants for their fair share of the building operation costs.

This lease clause in the operating expense pass-through charges will state whether gross up is allowed, and if so, what occupancy percent is the building grossed up to.

Compliance with Governmental Requirements

The owner places the burden on tenants for compliance with governmental regulations that affect their occupancy. If a tenant does not comply, the owner retains the right to perform the work needed for compliance and bill the tenant.

Tenants will negotiate that the building meets all governmental regulations when they take occupancy; if not, the owner will promptly bring the building up to compliance at no cost to the tenants. The cost of future governmental regulations is a negotiable issue. If in healthcare, certain types of occupancies require regular maintenance of the fire/life safety systems, HVAC, etc., and that all records for these systems are kept current and on site. If the tenant is in a multi-tenant building, it may be difficult for them to perform that maintenance as it may affect other tenants. A second example is compliance with ADA requirements or at a least a statement by the owner that the property/building or premises is compliant at the time the lease is signed.

Condemnation and Eminent Domain

This provision addresses the government's right to take property for public use upon the payment of just compensation. Such a provision cancels the lease if all the premises are taken by *eminent domain*. In case of a partial taking, the owner and the tenant have a right to cancel the lease if more than a specific percentage (e.g., 20 percent of the premises or common area) is taken. Tenants should determine what percentage of their property's parking lot and other common areas can be taken without impacting their business. If more than that portion is taken, they will want the right to cancel their lease.

This provision provides the owner with the rights to the entire damages awarded or the total payment through eminent domain however, the tenant is allowed to file a claim with the condemning authority for compensation that may be recoverable due to a loss incurred based on damage to the tenant's business, or the removal of merchandise, furniture, trade fixtures, or equipment.

Continuous Operation

Shopping centers, other retail properties, and properties with a retail component are the property types that routinely require this provision. Shopping center owners require their tenants to remain open during the hours established for the shopping center because of each business's importance to the synergy of the property's tenant mix. More tenants being open means greater choices for shoppers, increase traffic to the property, the likely the tenants will generate greater sales, and a greater opportunity for the owner to collect percentage rent.

All the stores are required to maintain minimum store hours. Shoppers want to know when they are at the shopping center during its normal hours that all the stores will be open. The *continuous operation* provision requires tenants to maintain store hours as designated by the owner and prohibits them from closing their store for any length of time. It also requires the tenant to keep in stock, on the premises, a full and ample line of merchandise; to maintain an adequate sales force; and to occupy and use the entire premises.

A penalty is included for each violations of the continuous operations provision. If the tenant repeatedly violates this provision, the owner may want the right to cancel the lease, while the tenant may prefer a monetary penalty. Anchor tenants seldom agree to a continuous operation provision.

A form of a continuous operations or often referred to as "no-go-dark" clause is used in multi-tenant commercial office buildings as the same synergy of tenants and the support they provide as a group, or mini-eco system in the building contribute to the success of all of the tenants.

Co-Tenancy

A co-tenancy provision provides a right to one tenant based on another tenant's cessation of operations. Through this provision, tenants may ask to pay only percentage rent or to cancel the lease entirely if a named co-tenant or a named group of tenant leaves the shopping center or occupancy falls below a specific percentage. From a owner's perspective, this provision can have a domino effect on losing tenants and should be avoided. From a tenant's perspective, key tenants may be an important customer draw and, if they vacate, any resulting decline in sales and profits needs to be mitigated.

If a co-tenancy is granted, the owner negotiates for a time period (e.g., six months to one year) to replace the vacating tenant(s) before other tenant(s) may cancel their lease. An alternative to allowing tenants to close their store and cancel the lease is to allow them to pay reduced rent—or percentage rent and tenant charges only—until the space or spaces are re-leased. Another option requires tenants to show proof of declining sales (e.g., 10 percent or more) before they can exercise their co-tenancy provision rights. If a shopping center does not have traditional anchor tenants, such as many lifestyle centers, the tenant may negotiate for the right to cancel its specific tenant vacate for example if three of nine named tenants vacate the shopping center the tenant with the co-tenancy provision may cancel its lease.

A co-tenancy provision could be tied to the occupancy of a shopping center. If occupancy falls below an agreed percentage (e.g., 70 percent) tenants with co-tenancy provisions may exercise their co-tenancy rights. Under these conditions, a decline in the shopping center's occupancy rate may cause significant pressure on the owner to retain tenants who are having rent payment problems or whose leases owner would prefer not to renew. It's seldom that owners agree to a co-tenancy provision.

The owner will attempt to resist the request for a co-tenancy provision; however, if an important tenant is in the balance, the owner may not have a choice and consequently will provide a co-tenancy provision. In this case, the owner may negotiate for some of the issues discussed above.

Default By the Owner

Tenants negotiate for the right to cure a owner's default. Often, this default has to do with the owner not maintaining the building. Tenants want the right to subtract any costs they incur to cure a owner default from their rental payments. They may also negotiate the right to cancel the lease if the owner's default impacts their business. The owner wants sufficient time to cure a default and will resist giving tenants the right to cancel their lease.

Default By the Tenant

There are two types of defaults: (1) monetary and (2) nonmonetary. The lease states what comprises a monetary default (e.g., not paying rent and other charges) as well as what time frame the tenant has to cure the default. The time to cure a monetary default might be only a few days, while the period needed to cure a nonmonetary default (an industrial tenant not repairing damage they created to their premises) might be a week or a month. There may be varying time frames to cure nonmonetary defaults by the tenant driven by compliance with local, state, or federal requirements and mandates.

If the tenant does not cure a nonmonetary default in the allowed time period, and if the owner can cure it on behalf of the tenant (e.g., repairs to the building or premises that are the tenant's responsibility), the owner wants the right to cure the default and charge the tenant for that cost as additional rent. The tenant negotiates for a cure period that is as long as possible, as well as for what remedies the owner may execute in the case of a default.

Description of the Leased Premises

Each party wants to be sure that the other party has no doubt about which space they are negotiating for, and the lease must include a readily identifiable description of the leased premises. This explanation may take several different forms, such as a street address, description of the space, or legal description of the property. To be very clear, a copy of the *site plan* (for a shopping center or single-tenant industrial building) or a *floor plan* (for an office building, medical office building, or multi-tenant industrial property) with the space outlined and crosshatched is often attached to the lease as an exhibit.

The size of the space is usually stated in this provision. Space measurement is discussed in detail in *Chapter 8: Preparing to Lease a Building*. Regardless of the method agreed to by the owner and the tenant to measure the space, the square footage may be off by a few feet. The owner prefers that the lease states the space is "deemed" to be a specific square footage or is "approximately" so many square feet. If both parties agree to this wording, they are agreeing to the size of the space regardless of its actual size.

If an approximately square foot is not used and the actual size is used to determine the size of the premises, the lease may state the tenant may not object to the square footage stated in its lease after the tenant takes possession of the premises or occupies the premises. If the tenant disputes the square footage of the premises, it must do so before a specific time, usually before the tenant takes occupancy.

Entry by the Owner

The owner must retain the right to enter the office and medical office buildings at all reasonable times to inspect and provide essential services and clean the premises. For retail stores, tenants maintain and clean their premises and most owners do not want the right to enter a tenant's premises because of concerns regarding lost or stolen merchandise. They generally advise retail tenants to change the locks upon occupying the premises and owner entry in the case of an emergency would be by force.

Estoppel Certificate

An *estoppel certificate* is needed whenever a owner refinances or sells a property. A prospective buyer of income-producing property or a lender who is financing (or refinancing) a property will want to confirm each tenant's lease status and to verify the information provided by the owner.

The lease includes a provision that requires the tenant to execute an estoppel certificate—a statement by the tenant of the status of the lease—at the owner's request. The owner will require the tenant to sign the estoppel with a short time period, usually 10 to 14 days. If the tenant does not respond to this request, the owner is empowered to act as the tenant's attorney-in-fact in executing the estoppel certificate.

Estoppel certificates typically state that the lease is in full force and effect, and should include the date to which rents and other charges have been paid, along with the following information:

- Term of the lease
- Expiration date
- Amount of rent per the lease
- Amount of the security deposit
- Any delinquent or prepaid rent
- What options exist
- Whether or not all the owner's work has been performed
- Owner or tenant defaults
- Any lease modifications

Tenants may negotiate for additional time to allow their attorney to review the estoppel. Many lenders and buyers of property, as well as national tenants, request to use their own estoppel form instead of the owner's. It is not always practical for the owner to agree to this in advance, because a future lender or buyer may require a specific form.

Exclusive Use

An *exclusive use* provision grants the tenant the sole right to sell a specific product or provide a specific service. Because the exclusive prevents the owner from leasing to other tenants with similar product lines, owners are understandably reluctant to grant this provision and will review this provision very closely. Exclusives are found mainly in retail properties, but they are occasionally an issue when leasing office and medical office buildings as well.

In malls as well as in lifestyle, entertainment, and outlet shopping centers, most uses must be duplicated to provide consumers with a wide variety of merchandise, opportunities for comparison shopping, and entertainment. In neighborhood, community, and specialty shopping centers, most uses can be duplicated without harm to any of the merchants.

From an owner's perspective, exclusives place a limitation on their ability to lease a shopping center or other type of building by excluding tenants who provide the same merchandise or services as the tenant with the exclusive. Exclusives also put an administrative burden on owners and real estate management companies and, if violated, create potential liability. Even if owners do not intend to duplicate a use, it is best for them not to grant an exclusive, as it could undermine their efforts to create the optimum tenant mix.

Tenants may negotiate an exclusive for a multitude of reasons. The tenants might not want competition, or they might be trying to exclude a particular business from entering the location. Tenants might also provide a service that requires expensive equipment (such as a medical group that purchases MRI equipment), and want the opportunity for increased referral business to pay for and earn an acceptable return on the cost and operations of the equipment.

The general rule for the owner is to avoid exclusives. There are, however, a few exceptions when a owner may agree that an exclusive is warranted. If necessary, the owner may be able to grant an exclusive that will be less burdensome while still accomplishing the tenant's objectives. When exclusives must be granted, the following should be considered to include in the provision:

- **Exclusives should not apply to anchor tenants, their assignees, or their sub-lessees.** Anchor tenant use provisions have few, if any, restrictions. Anchor tenants add new lines of merchandise during their lease term, and some of that merchandise may conflict with another tenant's exclusive.

- **They should not apply to any existing tenants, their assignees, or their sub-lessees.** The use provisions of existing tenants may not prohibit them from selling a product that a new tenant has an exclusive right to sell.
- **Exclusives should not be transferable to a tenant's assignee or sub-lessee.** The tenant who is granted an exclusive should not be allowed to transfer this right to others. Tenants may object to this requirement because it may prevent them from selling their business.
- **Extensive limitation on the product sold or service provided should be applied.** For example, an exclusive use to operate a hair salon should not include the exclusive right to sell beauty products because several other types of stores sell such products.
- **Exclusives should exclude the incidental sale of the product by other tenants.** If an exclusive is provided to a candy store it is likely that other retailers, such as card shops, will sell a few candy items. The exclusive with the candy store will exclude stores that have incidental sales of candy or limit the size of the display area of the tenant.
- **They may be limited to a particular area.** For example, an exclusive might apply only to the north wing of a large shopping center. This will work only for a large shopping center or mall and for specific uses.
- **They may be contingent on the payment of percentage rent.** For instance, if retail or restaurant tenants do not pay percentage rent by the third calendar year of the lease, their exclusive rights are forfeited. Most tenants will not accept this requirement.
- **Exclusives may be offered for a specific period.** They might apply only to the first year of operations, providing tenants a chance to start their business without direct competition in the shopping center or office building. A physical therapist wanted an exclusive in a medical office building to generate referrals from the other medical professionals in the building. The owner provided the physical therapist with a one-year exclusive to develop a working relationship with the other medical professionals in the building.
- **Specific damages if the exclusive is violated must be included.** This is very important for owners. If specific damages are not included in the lease, the tenant may claim millions of dollars in loss of business, income, and value of the business. The tenant may have the right to cancel the lease or have the minimum rent eliminated, and the tenant would then pay only percentage rent along with the other tenant charges, or the tenant's minimum rent may be reduced. The base rent may be reduced by a percentage say 50 percent. Once the exclusive is no longer violated, the rent is per the original lease term.

Expansion Rights

Expansion rights occur when the tenant has a right to expand in the building, usually adjacent space, when it becomes available. Though it may seem like a fair request by the tenant, it can be problematic for the owner. The owner wants to remain able to lease the space to another tenant—possibly one who will occupy a large amount of space in the building and has better credit. A problem could also arise if the owner forgets the tenant's right and leases the space to another tenant.

If this provision is granted, it is usually to a large space use and often a national tenant. This provision is more common in an office building than other types of commercial properties. If this lease provision must be given, the owner is advised to place obligations and restrictions on the expansion right, such as the following:

- Designate the exact space for which the tenant has the first right of refusal.
- Increase the rent on the additional space to market rate.
- Stipulate that the tenant has a limited time frame after the space availability is announced to notify the owner of their intent to take the space.
- Require that the tenant must lease the space within a specific period.
- State that the tenant must not be in default.
- Provide the tenant with a one-time right.
- Stipulate who pays for the tenant improvements.
- Set forth the expiration date.

- Provide that if the expansion occurs with minimal term left on the lease, the term for current and expansion space will be extended for minimum amount of time—preferably three to five years.
- If the landlord violates the tenant's right, the tenant's remedy is stated.
- If the owner violates the tenant's right, the tenant's remedy is stated.

Failure to Deliver the Premises

In rare instances, the owner may not be able to deliver the premises to a tenant on the agreed upon lease commencement date. This may be due to a setback in the construction of a new building, a delay in the move-out of an existing tenant, a delay in obtaining a building permit for the tenant improvements, a holdup with building out the tenant improvements, or *force majeure.*

Because owners do not want to lose new tenants in these cases, they will insert the following stipulations into the lease:

1. The lease remains in force under such circumstances.
2. The owner cannot be held liable for any loss or damage.
3. The minimum rent and all tenant charges are waived until such time as the owner delivers possession of the premises to the tenant.
4. In the case of shopping center, tenants may extend the allotted time (usually 60 to 90 days) to install the fixtures required for the business.

In negotiating the lease term, either party may request that any delay in possession will extend the term of the lease for an amount of time equal to the period of delay.

A delay in the move-in date can cause havoc to a tenant's business. Some retailers will only open a new store during specific periods of the year, and typically avoid "blackout periods" (e.g., November, December, and January). If a window of opportunity is missed, the retailer may not open for three months or more. Under such circumstances, retailers negotiate for their lease commencement to be deferred to a specific date. Tenants may insist that, if the delay extends beyond a certain number of months, they have the right to cancel the lease.

When tenants give notice to their current owner that they will not renew their lease only to find out that their new space will not be ready for occupancy as planned, they may be left with nowhere to go when their lease expires. If the current owner has not yet re-leased their space, the lease may be allowed to continue on a month-to-month term; however, the tenant is then at the owner's mercy. In such situations, owners often charge 150 percent of the tenant's last month's rent—or even more.

Tenants may negotiate for their new owner to pay a penalty if the premises are not ready on the agreed date. This penalty could be tied to the additional rent these tenants will have to pay in their current building or to the cost of finding a temporary location. Seldom is the space not ready when a owner commits to a date; however, when this does occur, the disruption places financial and operational hardships on the tenant, and that tenant will want to be compensated.

Floor Area—Definition of Measurement

As discussed in Chapter 8, various organizations have published standard methods for measuring space and leases will often refer to these standards. A common office building standards is the published BOMA, *Standard Method for Measuring Floor Areas in Office Buildings.* BOMA also publishes a standard for measuring retail space which is *BOMA's Retail Buildings: Standard Methods of Measurements (ANSI/BOMA Z65.5-2010).* A common standard for measuring industrial space is the BOMA and SIOR *Industrial Floor Measurement Standard.*

Force Majeure

The force majeure provision relieves owners of liability or responsibility if they are delayed or hindered in, or prevented from, performing any act or obligation required by the lease because of strikes, lockouts, "acts of God," riots, failure of power, governmental laws or regulations, war, or other causes beyond their reasonable control. Any obligation so delayed is extended for a period equivalent to the period of the delay. The most likely delay on the owner's part arises during construction of the building or tenant improvements. Tenants may also negotiate for similar force majeure rights.

Go-Dark Provision

Major retail tenants will request a go-dark provision. This provision allows the tenant to close operations while continuing to pay rent (go dark). The tenant's position is that, as long as the owner receives rent payments in accordance with the lease, the tenant should have the right to close the store. The owner should argue that a major retail tenant has been given concessions—perhaps a prominent location, a long-term lease, or an attractive rental rate based on that tenant's customer drawing power. If this retail tenant's store closes, the shopping center may be devastated and the rest of the tenants may suffer. This can have a domino effect on the shopping center and negatively impact the owner's ability to receive percentage rent from multiple tenants. As tenant's sales decline, the rental rates the shopping center can attain also declines. There is a direct correlation between a retail or restaurants sales and rental rates.

The go-dark provision may be a determining factor in whether or not a lender will finance or refinance the property. If owners must give a tenant a go-dark provision, they will negotiate for required advance notice, reimbursement of unamortized tenant improvements and commission, and the right to recapture the premises and terminate the lease.

Tenants, on the other hand, may not want the owner to cancel the lease if they go dark. For anchor tenants, often the rent they pay is substantially below the market rate, allowing them to sublease the space at market rent and earn a profit. The spread between the rental rate the tenants is paying and the market rate usually increases the longer the lease is in effect. Tenants may offer the owner a *buy-out* based on the present value of the income stream for the remaining term including options. For a large tenant, this buy-out is likely to be in the hundreds of thousands of dollars or more.

Guaranty

Typically, the owner will require the lease to be guarantied by the owner of the company. Exceptions are for major corporations and governmental agencies. Tenants will want to limit their guarantee. The tenant may request for a rolling *guaranty*. For instance, the tenant may request a two-year rolling guaranty which means that at any point in time, the tenant guaranties only the next two years of the lease. If the owner must accept this request, the owner may counter that after receiving rent equal to its cost of tenant improvements and the commission the tenant's two-year rolling guaranty may take effect.

If the owner paid $75,000 in tenant improvements and commission, and the rent is $5,000 per month, it will take 15 months of rent for the owner to be reimbursed for these expenses. If the tenant vacates the premises any time after the 15 month with a two-year rolling guaranty the tenant is obligated to guaranty 24 months of rent from the time they stopped paying rent. A lease guaranty is generally attached as a separate document (Exhibit 10.1) to the lease and should be notarized.

Hazardous Substances

The hazardous substance provision is often the longest provision in the lease. Cleaning up a hazardous spill is very costly. In addition, a buyer may delay or cancel the purchase of a property, or a lender may delay or not finance a property, if a hazardous substance is present. However, some tenants must use hazardous materials in the operation of their business—photo processors, dry cleaners, automobile repair shops, and service stations are obvious examples—and their activities must be monitored. Many medical professionals handle hazardous medical waste. The owner's main concerns in regards to hazardous materials are illegal use and disposal, and who pays for governmental fines in the event of a spill or contamination. The tenant is required to:

- Comply with all governmental regulations regarding hazardous substances.

EXHIBIT 10.1

AGREEMENT OF PERSONAL GUARANTY
ATTACHED TO AND MADE PART OF THE LEASE AGREEMENT
DATED _______________, 20___ BETWEEN
__________________________________ ("LANDLORD") AND
___________________________ ("TENANT")

The undersigned "Guarantor," in consideration of the making of the foregoing Lease Agreement between Tenant and Landlord, does hereby unconditionally guarantee the payment of the rent by the Tenant and the performance by Tenant of all the financial duties and obligations under the Lease Agreement.

Guarantor also agrees that Landlord is not first required to enforce against Tenant or any other person any liability, obligation or duty guaranteed by this Agreement before seeking enforcement thereof against Guarantor. A lawsuit may be brought and maintained against the Guarantor by Landlord to enforce any liability, obligation or duty guaranteed by this Agreement without the necessity of joining the Tenant or any other person in the lawsuit.

It is expressly agreed and understood that Guarantor additionally and unconditionally guarantees the performance under the Lease of ______________________________________ (TENANT).

EXECUTED to be effective as of the ___________ day of _______________________, 20__.

GUARANTOR:

____

Name: ____

ADDRESS: _________________________________

____

PHONE NUMBER: ___________________________

EMAIL ADDRESS: ___________________________

- Allow the owner to inspect the premises.
- Provide the owner will required reporting of the use and disposal of hazardous materials.
- Pay for all cleanup costs, fees, and penalties imposed by any governmental authority.

If the tenant is a medical professional, that tenant will also be required to contract with a certified and licensed medical waste removal company. The tenant may negotiate for the owner to certify that the property has no known hazardous waste and, if it does, that the tenant is not responsible for its cleanup and relevant penalties.

Holdover

The holdover provision has important economic implications for both parties. Any *holdover tenancy* after the expiration or termination of a lease is construed to be a *month-to-month tenancy* subject to all the terms and conditions set forth in the lease. However, the minimum rent is increased for the holdover period—usually to 150 percent of the last month of the lease term. This increase is used as a motivating factor to encourage the tenant to vacate when the lease expires. The greater the rent increases during the holdover period, the greater the likelihood that the tenant will either agree to a lease renewal or vacate the premises.

The owner may even negotiate for a holdover rent of two to four times the last month's rent to motivate the departure of a tenant. This is especially helpful when the premises are leased to another tenant who expects to take occupancy by a specific date. The tenant may also be liable for any damages the owner suffers from the holdover. These damages may include the penalty the owner must pay to the tenant who has leased the space but cannot move in on the agreed upon date.

Tenants often hold over because the space they are moving into is not yet ready. It is to their benefit to negotiate for rent to increase only a nominal amount during the holdover period, for no changes to be made to the lease, and for no penalty to be charged.

Hours of Operation for HVAC Use

Though tenants usually have building access 24 hours a day, the hours of operation vary depending on the type of property. For office and medical office buildings the HVAC is operated during building hours stated in the lease, and the tenant is charged for any after-hours HVAC use. The lease will state the building's hours and whether there is a charge for after hours use of HVAC.

HVAC Maintenance

The owner typically maintains the HVAC systems in office and medical office buildings and these cost are generally included in the pass-through operating expenses (or in the base rent for gross leases). For this reason, this provision is usually not needed in office and medical office building leases, but is common in retail and industrial leases.

There are two approaches to maintaining the HVAC units for retail and industrial properties. The first is to have the tenants maintain their units and provide the owner with evidence of a maintenance contract. A possible problem with this method is tenants may have different standards of maintenance and several HVAC contractors will be walking the roof and leaving materials that may damage the roof.

The second and preferred method is for the owner to contract for the maintenance of all the HVAC units and bill the tenants for the cost. Because all work is contracted to one company, the real estate manager is usually able to negotiate a discounted service price. This ensures that HVAC units will be serviced properly and will be in good condition at the expiration of the tenant's lease and reduces foot traffic on the roof. An efficiently run HVAC unit and a discounted service fee result in direct savings for the tenant, and the life of the equipment is prolonged.

Tenants want this provision to state that the price of the service is at the market rate, and may want to negotiate who is responsible for the cost of major repairs and equipment replacement. They also may require that the equipment is inspected by a certified contractor, all necessary repairs are made, and faulty equipment is replaced before they assume responsibility for the cost to service and maintain the equipment. Additionally, tenants may negotiate out of being responsible for replacing equipment, especially if the unit is an older unit or a major replacement is needed during the last year of their lease.

If tenants install a supplemental HVAC unit, the owner will want them to pay for it and be responsible for the maintenance, repairs, and replacement.

Building Insurance

When the owner insures a building, tenants are responsible for reimbursing the owner's cost to insure the property. The owner does not want to limit the type or amount of insurance coverage that may be necessary. The lease may state that "insurance shall include all insurance premiums for fire, liability, rent loss, flood, earthquake, and any other insurance or *endorsement*, which may include an 'all-risk' endorsement or any other insurance that the owner or owner's lender deems necessary."

Some anchor tenants in shopping centers and industrial tenants in free-standing buildings may attempt to have specific coverage, such as earthquake (on the West Coast) and loss of rent insurance, excluded from their share of the insurance cost. They also may negotiate to cap the amount of liability insurance coverage. Though non-anchor tenants do not have the negotiating strength to obtain these exclusions, they may still attempt to place limitations on the type and limits of insurance coverage for which they agree to reimburse the owner.

The lease will also state that if the tenant's business causes the building's insurance premium to increase, the tenant will pay the increase.

Tenant Insurance

The owner wants to be certain that if any of a tenant's inventory, fixtures, or equipment is damaged, stolen, or destroyed, the tenant will have funds to replace those items, continue to operate the business, and pay rent. The *insurance provision* states that the tenant must carry insurance on the furniture, fixtures, equipment, and inventory of the business. Ground floor tenants in office buildings and retail and restaurant tenants in shopping centers may be required to have plate-glass coverage; particularly those with large storefront windows. The lease mandates that the tenant must have a minimum amount of liability insurance. The tenant is also required to have *business interruption insurance*.

The owner will require that the tenant provide evidence of such insurance and include the owner (and the owner's real estate management company) as a named insured on the policies. The lease should also allow the owner to provide coverage if the tenant does not obtain the required insurance, and to be reimbursed by the tenant for the cost.

Janitorial Services

The owner typically provides janitorial service for office and medical office buildings. The lease should state the frequency of janitorial service, list the days this service will be provided, and state that the owner will determine janitorial specifications. The tenant may request that the janitorial specifications are an exhibit to the lease, and that the owner not be allowed to change the specifications without the tenant's approval.

Key Money

A seldom-used lease provision that benefits the landlord is the *key money provision*. Under this provision, the tenant pays the landlord a fee—usually a substantial amount—for the right to lease space in a property. This provision is most often seen in retail properties, and might be used for a new shopping center expected to be a great success or for an existing retail property that is already extremely successful or in a phenomenal location.

The reason why some, retail properties may command key money is the retailers in the shopping center or on a specific street are achieving sales per square foot far in excess of the typical shopping center or street in the area and the industry. For example, if the sales in malls and on good retail streets in the metropolitan area average $500 per square foot and the retailers' sales in a particular mall or on a great street are in excess of $1,000 per square foot, some retailers may be willing to pay key money to located in that mall or on that street.

Property owners are rarely able to charge this fee. If the premises are in a highly desirable location, tenants assigning their lease to another tenant may be able to negotiate for key money from that tenant (the assignee). The tenant has no incentive to ask for key money it all goes to the owner. The tenant and the owner may negotiate to split the key money if the tenant is able to obtain it for a lease assignment. In reality, key money is very rare in the U.S. and most other countries.

Owner's and Tenant's Work

The lease usually includes a provision that states the condition of the premises when the owner delivers it to the tenant, and that the tenant agrees to accept the premises subject to completion of any owner's work. The owner's and tenant's work exhibit describes any owner's work to be completed as well as specifying what work the tenant will provide for the premises.

Late Charge

The late charge provision provides the owner the right to charge a *late fee* if the tenant does not pay rent by a predetermined date. If tenants are late in their payments, the owner has two primary means of recourse: (1) give the tenant a formal notice of default or (2) include a late charge and possible interest if permitted in the lease.

Tenants negotiate for the owner to give them written notice that the rent has not been received and to grant a grace period before the late charge is assessed. Tenants don't want to be assessed a late charge in the case of an accounting error or a late mail delivery. Owner's may charge a fixed late fee, plus a percentage of the unpaid rent balance to offset the additional cost of collecting the past due balance and compensate for not having the funds available to pay the mortgage, operating expenses, or re-investment.

The amount of the late charge should be stated (e.g., 12 percent of the amount past due); in no event should the percentage rate be more than the legal maximum allowed. If the owner uses the services of an attorney to collect delinquent rent, the attorney's fees should be a tenant expense in accordance with the terms of the lease.

Lease Commencement Versus Rental Commencement

It is not unusual for the lease and the rent to commence on different dates. For example, the lease may begin while a retail tenant is installing fixtures and merchandise, but the rent payments start at a later date.

Owners want their tenants to abide by the terms and conditions of the lease (such as tenant's insurance and parking provisions) while building out their premises or moving in. It is to the owner's advantage for both the lease and rent to commence as soon as possible, potentially as soon as the tenant improvements have been substantially completed by the owner or the tenant. Tenants may negotiate for rent to commence at a later date to either obtain additional time to build out their premises (retail tenants) or to have some free rent while they are open for business.

Liens and Encumbrances

If the tenant does not pay a contractor for tenant improvements or maintenance, that contractor may place a lien on the leased premises or the property. Such an encumbrance can delay or prevent the sale or refinancing of the property. To protect the owner's interests, the *liens and encumbrances* provision requires the tenant to keep the premises and the property free from any liens arising from work performed or contracted by the tenant. It also gives the owner the right to require the tenant to obtain payment or *performance bonds* in an amount equal to 1.5 times the total estimated cost of work, materials, labor, and supplies. Lien rights for the owner and tenant vary from state to state.

Maintenance of the Tenant's Premises

The lease should state which repair and maintenance items are the owner's responsibility, and which items are the tenant's responsibility. It is common in office and medical office buildings for the owner to maintain the tenant's premises. The cost of the maintenance, including janitorial service, is either built into the rent or is included in the building's pass-through operating expenses. Leases for these buildings may exclude specific maintenance, such as cleaning the carpet and window coverings.

In shopping centers and most industrial buildings, tenants are responsible for all repairs and maintenance to their premises. The tenant is usually responsible for all maintenance inside the leased premises, and the owner performs all maintenance outside those premises. The owner typically maintains the exterior walls, roof, foundation, structural portions of the building, and common area. The cost of repairing and maintaining these areas is usually included in the CAM charges.

If the tenant is responsible for, but fails to maintain the premises, the owner, after providing written notice to the tenant, has the option of performing the necessary work and charging the cost to the tenant as additional rent. Tenants are expected to repay the owner promptly, or risk being placed in *default*. Tenants negotiate for a reasonable time period to contract for the repairs after receiving written notice from the owner.

Marketing Fund or Merchants' Association

Only shopping centers and major retail properties require tenants to support the *marketing fund,* or much less commonly, the *merchant's association*. This provision states the minimum payment required, usually based on the tenant's square footage, and provides for an annual increase in funding.

The owner negotiates for tenants to be required to contribute to this fund, and will make participation mandatory. Anchor tenants may reject mandatory participation, but will often agree to contribute to the funding efforts. Tenants negotiate whether they must pay dues and, if so, the amount of annual fees, how increases are determined, and the amount that the owner must contribute to the fund. Owners often contribute between 20 and 25 percent of combined tenant contributions.

Marketing funds, which replaced the merchant's associations in the 1980s for most existing properties, are typical in mall, lifestyle, entertainment, outlet, and specialty shopping centers. They typically do not exist in neighborhood and community strip shopping centers and power shopping centers.

In shopping centers where marketing funds exist, tenants are required to pay a grand opening assessment, which is usually a dollar amount per square foot. Tenants who open for business within a year of the grand opening of the property are also assessed grand opening dues to offset the shopping center's initial marketing efforts. Some tenants will negotiate that a specific percentage of the merchants must be obligated to pay to the marketing fund for them to pay a marketing fee.

Medical Waste

Medical waste can be classified as hazardous materials (see *Hazardous Substances* on pages 17 and 19). If present, the lease must outline how medical waste will be disposed of and stipulate that the tenant is liable for any damages or fines resulting from its use, storage, or disposal.

Most Favored Tenant

The most favored tenant provision derives its name and function from the "favored nation" trade advantages that one country gives another. It is a provision that is neither well known nor often used in the industry, though it does occasionally appear in commercial leases prepared by tenants.

This provision grants a tenant all the concessions that other tenants have or will be granted. For example, if one tenant has a cap on real estate taxes and another does not pay CAM charges, a tenant whose lease includes a most favored tenant provision is automatically granted those concessions. Obviously this provision will not be found in a owner's lease form. Owners want to avoid granting this provision, which may appear in a tenant-generated lease form.

Options

Options provide benefits for tenants and potential obligations for owners. Although some owners and leasing agents offer options freely, many owners are understandably reluctant to grant them. Tenants, on the other hand, want to negotiate for as many options as possible. Several types of options can be incorporated into a lease and they are usually granted by the owner as specific concessions when necessary. The option(s) granted in a particular lease may relate to the lease term (extension or renewal of the lease), the premises (expansion of the tenant's space), or the lease itself (cancellation by the tenant).

Option to Extend

An option to extend grants the tenant the right to extend the lease term. Most owners prefer not to grant this option because many factors can work to their detriment during the term of the lease, thereby making an extension of the lease unfavorable. If, for example, rent is not paid on time, a retail tenant's sales are low, or a tenant causes problems for building management, the owner wants to be able to allow the lease to terminate at its expiration. The owner may also have a more desirable replacement tenant for the space and would be unable to lease it to the new tenant if the existing tenant exercises their option to extend.

Tenants should always negotiate for a renewal option. The option doesn't cost the tenant anything, and it provides the possibility of remaining in the premises beyond the lease expiration. If rent during the option period is pre-negotiated, the renewal rental rate may be lower than the market rental rate. If the pre-negotiated rental rate is higher than the market rate, the tenant could renegotiate for a lower renewal rate. Owners may agree to lower the rate, or they will be left with a vacancy. If a tenant wants to sell its business and the location of the premises is important to the success of the business, having one or several options may increase the value of the business. Conversely, if a tenant has only a few years left on their lease term with no option to extend, it may be more difficult to sell the business—especially if the tenant is a retailer or restaurant.

If the owner must grant an option to extend the lease, it should be contingent on several criteria, including the following:

1. The tenant must not be in default of the lease on the date the option is exercised and when the option period commences.
2. The tenant must provide notice that this option will be exercised within a specific time frame—e.g., no later than 120 days and no sooner than 180 days before the lease expires.
3. The option will be canceled if the tenant has a number of defaults, a major default, or if the lease has been assigned.
4. If possible, the option is contingent on the retail tenant paying percentage rent or exceeding a specific sales volume during the last two years of the lease.

The tenant may counter these requests as follows:

1. The tenant must have a reasonable time to cure a default before losing the right to extend the lease.
2. The time period to exercise the renewal option may be extended, and the tenant is granted a grace period.
3. Minor defaults do not void the option, the tenant will have reasonable time to cure the default, and the option is assignable with the lease (which is often necessary to sell the business).
4. If the tenant has a percentage rent provision, the option is not contingent on the tenant paying percentage rent. If the base rent is high, it may not be possible for the tenant's sales to exceed the *breakpoint* to pay percentage rent. If this issue becomes a deal breaker (though it is unlikely), the tenant may agree to lose this option if sales do not exceed a predetermined level that the tenant believes is easily achievable.
5. Tenants will resist the efforts to have the option cancel if the lease is assigned. If a tenant sells its business, having the lease assigned will prevent many tenants from selling their businesses.

The rent for the option period can be stated as a predetermined amount, adjusted to market rate, or stated as an increase based on the *consumer price index (CPI)*. The owner wants it to be no less than the rate paid during the last month of the prior lease term. If the rent is to be based on the current market rate, and that market rate is less than what the tenant is already paying, setting such a minimum protects the owner from undue financial loss. However, the tenant is still likely to renegotiate the rent down to the market rate in these situations.

If the rent in the option period is based on *market rent*, this provision should describe other comparable buildings as well as the size and location of the premises within the buildings that will be used to determine this amount. This protects both the owner and the tenant from an unnecessary dispute and possible arbitration.

Option to Expand

An option to expand the tenant's leased space may be related to specific space designated on the site plan (for a shopping center or an industrial park) or the floor plan (for an office building or medical office building). The right to expand to additional space gives the tenant flexibility in growing its business. However, this provision becomes an obstacle for property owners if they have other tenants in mind for the space into which the tenant has the right to expand.

If property owners must offer this concession, they prefer not to grant a first right of refusal to lease additional (usually contiguous) space, but rather a first right of offer or first right to negotiate.

A first right to negotiate gives the tenant the opportunity to negotiate for additional space before the owner negotiates with any other prospective tenant. If the owner offers this provision, it should state that, if both parties are unable to agree on the terms of the lease for the additional space within a specific time period (e.g., 10 days), the property owner may negotiate and enter into a lease with another tenant.

Option to Cancel

See the section on *Cancellation* located on pages 6–7 of this chapter.

Option to Purchase the Property

Giving tenants the option to purchase the property is very seldom. In these rare circumstances, the tenant has a limited time frame in which to notify the property owner and execute the sale. The price may be fixed, based on a formula, or determined by an appraisal. There are several issues to negotiate if the tenant receives this option: how an appraiser will be selected; whether this provision allows the first right of refusal or the first right to negotiate; how this right can be fortified; and when this right can be exercised.

Over Standard Utilities

The owner must have the right to charge the tenant for the consumption of utilities in excess of the standard amount consumed by the typical tenant. Some medical groups or physicians may have equipment that consumes excessive amounts of electricity. In shopping centers, hair salons, restaurants, and laundromats may consume excessive water. These tenants should be charged for their over standard utility consumption if the utility is not individually metered (meaning that the tenant places service in their name and makes payment directly to the utility provider). Some buildings have a single water, gas, or electric meter that brings service to the building. In those instances, it is helpful to have a submeter for each tenant suite that measures the utility consumption. If this is not practical, the lease should allow a charge for excessive utilities that are consumed so that the owner may recover those costs.

Tenants want to be sure they are being charged fairly for their consumption of over standard utilities. They may negotiate for a formula to be used in these calculations. They also want the additional amount paid to be credited to the overall utility charges.

Parking

Convenient parking is an important criterion for a successful shopping center. Parking stalls located closest to the stores can turn over eight or more times a day—i.e., if there is an average of one or two people per car entering the shopping center in an eight-hour period, 12 customers could have parked in a stall close to the stores. Consequently, when a tenant's employee parks all day in one of those stalls, many customers are deprived of this convenience.

The owner often requires tenant employees to park in a designated area. This prohibits their use of prime customer parking areas and grants the owner the right to fine tenants and/or tow employee cars for parking in the nonemployee parking spots.

Parties

It is important to know exactly who the tenant is—e.g., a corporation, a partnership, a *limited liability company (LLC),* a married couple, or an individual. If the lease is with a general partnership, all of the partners should sign it. If the tenant is a married individual, it is usually best to obtain each partner's signature. If only one of them signs, it is wise to obtain the advice of an attorney regarding spousal obligations.

The owner may want proof that the person signing the lease for a partnership or corporation is authorized to enter into the lease on behalf of that entity. The tenant may want similar proof that the owner's representative is authorized to enter into the lease on behalf of the owner. It should be noted that, in most states, minors may void a lease at their option, so it is important to proceed cautiously if the prospect's age is in question.

Percentage Rent

Retailers, restaurants, and some service tenants usually have a percentage rent provision in their lease. The typical retail lease provides for the tenant to pay either a minimum rent or a percentage of sales—whichever is greater. This provision requires tenants to submit monthly sales reports and an annual statement of sales signed by an officer of their company or a CPA.

Most leases have a fixed percentage rate for the entire term of the lease. Some owners with older leases receive a substantial amount of percentage rent from their tenants, whereas leases executed in the past five years have high breakpoints that mean tenants seldom achieve the sales volume to pay percentage rent. There is always the possibility a tenant may do exceptionally well and pay percentage rent. The percentage rate is based on the type of business and its profit margins.

Quiet Enjoyment

In the lease provision of *quiet enjoyment,* the property owner promises that during the term of the tenancy no one will disturb the tenant in the tenant's use and enjoyment of the premises. Quiet enjoyment includes the right to exclude others from the premises, the right to peace and quiet, the right to clean premises, and the right to basic services such as heat and hot water and, for high-rise buildings, elevator service. For example, the failure to provide heat would be a breach of the implied provision of quiet enjoyment because the lack of heat would interfere with the tenant's use of the premises. The tenant may want to negotiate to ensure that minor defaults do not void this provision.

Radius

To protect the opportunity to collect percentage rent and avoid diverting sales, retail owners often prohibit their tenants from opening another store nearby. The *radius provision* prohibits the tenant from opening a similar store within a specified distance, e.g., three to five miles for a strip shopping center and five to 15 miles for a regional mall. If the tenant opens a store within the radius restriction, that tenant may be required to add the sales from the new store to those of its store in the shopping center when calculating percentage rent. Another reason for the radius provision is to protect the traffic flow to the shopping center.

Tenants will usually accept this provision but negotiate the radius distance. They also do not want the owner to have the right to cancel the lease if they open a nearby store, and consequently bargain for a lesser penalty for violations. It also may be arranged that tenants are not in default of their lease if they acquire another business or chain store with a store within the specified radius.

Recapturing the Premises

Many owners object to a tenant earning a profit on their space because they assumed the original risk in developing or purchasing the building, and they are the ones who sustain losses during a soft market. The owner's right to recapture allows the owner to take back space the tenant wants to sublet or assign. The tenant may have entered into its lease when the market was depressed, and a few years later, rents increased substantially and the tenant sees an opportunity to assign or sublease all of a portion of its premises for a significant profit.

This provision may apply to shopping centers as well as office buildings. Anchor tenants who close their store in a shopping center might assign the lease. Since they are usually paying much less than market rent for the space, such an assignment or a sublet could yield a substantial profit.

Rather than recapturing the premises, the owner might allow the tenant to sublet or assign the space, provided that the profit is paid back to the owner. One drawback this creates is that the tenant may not be willing to charge higher rent without benefiting from the increase. An alternative is for the owner and the tenant to share the increased rent. If they do split the increased rent, it will be after deducting the costs to re-lease the space, including commissions, advertising fees, attorneys' costs, and TIs.

Reconstruction

After major damage to the building, the owner generally reserves the right to cancel leases and not rebuild if the destruction exceeds a certain percentage of the property. That percentage is determined on a project-by-project basis, but it is important that the specified percentage remain the same for all leases within a given property.

Tenants want the right to cancel their lease if the damaged or destroyed portion of the property impacts their business. Owners prefer to allow this only if there has been a substantial impact to a tenant's business. Tenants also want to negotiate the length of time the owner has to reconstruct the building before the tenant may cancel the lease. The tenant may negotiate that the building will be reconstructed to standards that are the same as, or better than, those in place before the damage.

Recycling

If the management of the building implements a recycling program, either voluntary or as required by the local municipality, tenants are required to participate in the program. A recycling program may be part of a green building program, and may reduce waste pickup and building operating costs. Depending on the market for recycled materials, selling these materials may earn a profit that can be credited to the building's pass-through charges. Tenants may negotiate to share in any savings generated from the recycling program by applying the revenue generated by selling recycle materials to the operating expenses that are passed on to the tenants.

More information about starting a recycling program can be found in *Chapter 16: Efficient and Cost-Effective Maintenance Programs.*

Relocation

The relocation provision grants the owner the right to relocate a tenant's premises. It is common in office buildings but not as common in shopping center leases. Office building owners don't want a tenant who occupies a smaller space to prevent a much larger tenant from moving into the building. The relocation provision, therefore, allows the owner to relocate the tenant to comparable space at the owner's cost.

Retail tenants are likely to negotiate this provision for several reasons: the importance of a specific location to a merchant in a shopping center, the differences in the rental rates for particular locations, and the costs of relocation. Many retail tenants do not accept a relocation provision because the location of their space is critical to their business.

However, relocation may be an important consideration in leases with temporary or seasonal tenants, for tenants located next to another tenant with the right to expand, for combining spaces to attract larger tenants, or in allowing the flexibility to recapture space when expanding or remodeling a shopping center.

If retail or office tenants accept a relocation provision, they want the owner to guarantee that they will not be moved to a less desirable space, or that in such an occurrence rent will be adjusted accordingly. Retail tenants may negotiate to limit relocation to a particular area in the shopping center. Retailers may also negotiate that they cannot be relocated during their best sales months, such as November and December. Owners will agree to pay for moving costs as well as for building out the new space to the tenant's existing specifications. Tenants may negotiate for the owner to pay for all relocation costs, including the cost to connect computers, new letterhead, relocation notices, etc. Tenants may also ask for their rent to be abated during the move, and possibly for a couple days after the move, so that they have time to set up their business.

Base Rent or Minimum Rent

The rent provision states that the tenant will pay to the owner, without notice or demand and without any deductions, a fixed annual minimum rent. This will be paid in monthly installments during the term of the lease—either on or before the first day of each month. If the lease commences on a date other than the first of the month, the monthly minimum rent is prorated for the first month. The minimum rent is usually the starting point for lease negotiations between the owner and the tenant.

If free rent is given to the tenant, the lease must be very specific as to whether or not all other charges (e.g., building operating expenses, pass-through and CAM charges, real estate taxes, insurance) are also free during that period. The best way to prevent any misunderstanding is to state the date on which each of these charges will commence.

All rents and tenant charges, except percentage rent, are due and payable monthly concurrent with the payment of minimum rent. Percentage rent is usually paid at the end of the month based on the prior month's sales. Collectively, these payments are defined as the tenant's *occupancy cost*.

Minimum Rent Adjustment

The minimum rent adjustment is one of the most negotiated lease provisions. The three related issues to negotiate are: (1) the method used to increase the rent; (2) the amount of each increase; and (3) the frequency of the increases. Owners want rent adjusted annually, while tenants negotiate for a flat rate during the entire term of the lease.

Market conditions are the determining factor in rent increases. This is another reason why owners—and especially tenants—should conduct (or have conducted for them by their leasing agent) a *market survey* before they negotiate a lease. This survey will provide not only market rental rates, but also market rent steps and building pass-through charges.

Rent Adjustment Documentation

Rent increases may be stated as part of the minimum rent provision or in a separate provision. Regardless of its presentation, the provision for increased rent includes several blanks for listing the adjusted (stepped-up) annual and monthly rental rates and the periods they cover. The specific increases may be an agreed-upon fixed amount (e.g., $1.00 per square foot per year) or a percentage increase.

Cost of Living Adjustment

Another approach—one that both owners and tenants believe to be fair—is based on the rise in the cost of living (i.e., the inflation rate measured in the CPI. The increase in minimum rent is based on the percentage increase in the CPI from one period to another. Owners want this *cost of living adjustment (COLA)* to be made annually, while tenants negotiate for longer periods (usually two to three years) between adjustments.

Owners generally believe that an annual CPI rent

adjustment protects the property's value from inflation and increased operating expenses that are not reimbursed by the tenants. However, retail tenants are usually concerned that the CPI increase may exceed the increase in their sales, and all tenants need to keep their rent increases to a manageable level. Some tenants believe that the CPI is not an accurate reflection of their increase sales or revenue. For these reasons, the minimum rent adjustment based on the CPI is negotiable.

In the early 1980s, the CPI increased more than 10 percent each year. To prevent double-digit minimum rent percentage increases in situations such as this, tenants attempt to negotiate a ceiling or cap on the CPI increase. For example, a tenant might agree to an annual CPI adjustment of no more than five percent. In conceding to a CPI cap, the owner will want to be ensured of receiving no less than an agreed upon minimum increase, and therefore will negotiate for a floor to the CPI. Thus, if the tenant requests a five-percent ceiling, the owner may insist on a three-percent floor. The lease in this situation might state, "The annual rental increase shall be based on the CPI but will be no greater than five percent and no less than three percent."

When the parties to a lease agree that the minimum rent adjustment is to be based on the CPI, several specific issues must be resolved and stated in the lease. These issues are detailed below.

Base Year

The first issue to resolve concerning CPI rent increases is a definition of the *base year*—the year from which the CPI increases will be measured. Owners prefer the base year to be the year the tenant takes occupancy. Tenants negotiate for the base year to be the year after they take occupancy of the premises. Often, the compromise is based on the time of the year the tenant takes occupancy of the premises to make the determination. For example, a tenant who takes occupancy in November may be granted the following year as the base year, but the tenant who takes possession of the premises in February will be encouraged to accept the year the lease begins as the base year.

Effective Date

Along the same line, the next issue to resolve is the date the CPI rent increase becomes effective. The CPI increase may begin on the anniversary of the rent commencement date or on January 1 following that date. Thus, if a lease commenced on July 1, 2016, the base period for rent adjustment would be the first year of the lease—from July 1, 2016 to June 30, 2017. However, if the lease states that the CPI adjustment will be implemented "on January 1 after the lease commencement," the first lease adjustment would be for the period from January 1, 2017 to December 31, 2017.

Geographic Price Index

A third issue to resolve is which geographic price index to use. The CPI—published monthly by the U.S. Department of Labor, Bureau of Labor Statistics includes the national average (for U.S. cities) as well as the averages for many (but not all) major metropolitan areas. (The CPI for a few cities is published bi-monthly; some in even-numbered months, others in the odd months,or semiannually.)

The owner is not able to compute the tenant's CPI-related rental increase until the CPI is published. The monthly reports are normally available three to four weeks after the adjusted month (i.e., the CPI for January is published around the end of February). For those metropolitan areas with CPIs that are published semiannually, the report may not be released until three or four months after the period ends. In areas with a CPI that is not reported monthly, the owner may prefer to use the U.S. city average to expedite the adjustment of tenants' minimum rents. For CPI increases, the owner may prefer to use "all U.S. cities and U.S. averages" while the tenant may prefer to use the "specific U.S. city and specific U.S. average." The tenant can minimize rent adjustments by searching recent CPI geographic history and negotiating to use the one with the smallest annual increases.

Adjustment Frequency

The frequency of minimum rent adjustments is another issue to resolve. Owners prefer annual adjustments, while tenants usually negotiate for less-frequent adjustments (e.g., every three years). Anchor retail tenants often negotiate for a fixed-rental increase every five years.

Full or Partial Adjustments

Also to be decided is whether the increase will be based on the full CPI (100 percent) or on a part of it. In a partial adjustment, the agreement may be to increase the minimum rent based on a particular percentage of the CPI increase (e.g., 67 percent). Thus, if the CPI increase is six percent, rent is increased four percent (.06 × .67 = .0402). However, if the change in the CPI is negative—i.e., a decrease from the prior period—the minimum rent is not reduced. The owner will not lower the rent in this situation because the building's operating costs do not decrease and the mortgage payment does not decline.

Rules and Regulations

The owner is responsible for operating the property in a manner that is generally beneficial to all the tenants, visitors, and customers. To achieve this, the owner usually sets rules for tenants and their operations that address issues of conformity and safety. Typically, these *rules and regulations* specify constraints on loading and unloading, shipping and deliveries, accumulation of garbage, maintenance of the environment (room temperature, use of loudspeakers, etc.), employee parking, use of the premises, placing notices on the property, and general housekeeping. Office buildings, medical office buildings, and multi-tenant industrial buildings provide extensive rules and regulations as an exhibit to the lease. Some shopping center leases insert these policies within several provisions throughout the lease while others have a rules and regulations exhibit.

Building rules and regulations are likely to stipulate environmentally friendly guidelines. Preferred parking for hybrid or alternative fuel vehicles, mandatory use of green cleaning products, bans on energy-intensive equipment (e.g., space heaters), and designated smoking areas that are removed from the building are just a few of the regulations that are becoming more popular.

The rules and regulations provision requires the tenant to comply with the owner's guidelines, and gives the owner the right to modify them as necessary. It also states that the owner is not responsible to the tenant for any nonperformance by other tenants, and that the rules and regulations are to be applied and enforced uniformly. The tenant wants the rules and regulations to be fair and reasonable, and may try to modify or negotiate some of them accordingly.

Sales Reports

If the lease has a percentage rent provision, it will also have a sales reporting provision. These reports are the only way the owner will know if the tenant owes percentage rent. Even if a retail lease does not have a percentage rent provision, the owner should negotiate for a sales reporting provision. This provision requires the tenant to submit sales reports monthly to the owner. It may include a financial penalty if the tenant does not submit the sales report on time.

The monthly sales report is the best way for the owner to know how a tenant is performing. The owner and the real estate manager may need this information to determine whether or not to renew the tenant's lease. Monthly sales reports also provide the owner with advance warning if the tenant is having financial problems. All tenants report their sales monthly, except anchor tenants, who report their sales annually. These sale reports enable the real estate manager to better analyze the performance of the shopping center as a whole and each of its tenant categories. However, it is usually more difficult for the real estate manager to collect sales report than rent.

There are two issues for tenants to negotiate in regards to this provision. The first is the necessity of the provision. If the tenant has no percentage rent provision, the tenant believes there should be no sales reporting. The second is the penalty for late submissions. Tenants want to avoid a fee if their sales reports are submitted late. If they are not successful with this request, they can negotiate for the penalty to be waived the first time they are late.

Gross Sales Definition

The percentage rent provision defines the gross sales to which the percentage rate will be applied and lists which items, if any, may be excluded from gross sales. Sales tax is one such exclusion; refunds and returns also may be deducted. Tenants seek to exclude as much as possible, while owners want to include as many items as they can in the definition of gross sales in order to maximize their opportunity to collect percentage rent.

Tenants may attempt to exclude discounted sales to their employees from their reported gross sales, and landlords may be willing to grant this with limitations—e.g., the lease may refer to "sales to employees at a discount, not to exceed two percent of the tenant's total gross sales." Tenants also negotiate to exclude items that are sold as a *loss leader,* such as lottery tickets. They may want to exclude income from repairs and vending machines, credit loss, etc.

The Owner's Auditing Rights

Some leases allow the owner to cancel the lease if the tenant deliberately understates sales. The percentage rent provision requires tenants to maintain sales records for a minimum of five years or longer, and grants the owner the right to audit the tenant's sales. The owner is responsible for the cost of the audit unless the tenant's reported sales are inaccurate by a certain percentage or more, usually two percent.

Owners want the right to audit not just the prior year's sales, but every year's sales. Tenants negotiate for the owner to be required to notify them of the audit within a specific period (e.g., within 60 days of the time their December sales reports are submitted). The audit should be for prior years only, and each year may be audited only once. The results of the audit are confidential.

The Security Deposit

A *security deposit* is an amount paid by a tenant to a owner, to be used as recourse if the tenant defaults on the lease. The purpose of a security deposit is to have funds available if the tenant defaults—it is not intended to be the last month's rent.

The tenant must also be sure that the security deposits are being handled in accordance with the lease provisions and returned promptly upon lease expiration, or sooner by joint agreement.

Anchor tenants and national tenants typically have established credit ratings, and they negotiate to omit the security deposit requirement. Local and regional tenants usually agree to pay a security deposit. In lieu of a specific deposit, the lease can require the tenant to provide a letter of credit valued at a certain amount.

The Amount of the Security Deposit

The amount of the security deposit is typically one month's base rent. During a soft market, a owner may waive the security deposit entirely. If the tenant's business is new or financially weak, however, the owner may negotiate for a security deposit equivalent to two or even three months' rent. The tenant prefers as little a security deposit as possible. If the tenant must pay more than the standard one-month's-rent deposit, the terms may be negotiated.

Tenants may request that, if their rent is paid on time for 12 consecutive months, the amount of the security deposit in excess of one month's rent will be refunded. The owner may agree to this, but stipulate that the tenant must redeposit that amount if subsequent rent payments are late.

Another approach for retail tenants is to have their excess security deposit refunded when their annual sales exceed a specific amount. If sales drop below the specified amount, they must increase the amount of their security deposit.

The Owner's Use of the Security Deposit

If tenants do not pay their monetary obligations under the terms of the lease, the security deposit may be used to cure the nonpayment, if provided for in the lease. The security deposit could also be used to reimburse the owner for any tenant-required repairs or maintenance that the tenant refuses to perform. The security deposit provision should require the tenant to reimburse (or restore) the full amount of the security deposit held by the owner if the deposit is used to cure a default by the tenant. Should the owner have the need to apply those funds to a delinquency or other default, the tenant should be immediately notified that they are being used and the reason for this use. A request for the tenant to replace those funds should be included.

Return of the Deposit After Lease Expiration

Depending on local laws, the security deposit provision usually concludes by stating that, if the tenant is not in default of the lease, the owner will return the security deposit without interest and within a set number of days after the expiration of the lease term. Tenants should negotiate a specific procedure and date for the security deposit to be released. Unless required by law, owners will not pay interest on a security deposit because of the amount of time needed to calculate this insignificant amount of interest.

Signs

An office tenant who leases a large amount of space may negotiate for the property's sole signage rights, desiring to be the only tenant allowed to place signs on the building's exterior. The owner often negotiates to allow other tenants the right to display their signs. If the market is strong, the owner may be able to negotiate a fee for the building's signage rights. Regarding signage on the building directory, the number of lines granted to a tenant and who pays for this cost are issues to be negotiated.

A tenant's signage provision (or a *sign restriction provision*) requires tenants to submit plans for their exterior signs for the owner's approval. These plans must be based on the property's sign criteria, which are included as an exhibit appended to the lease. The lease requires the sign to be installed and maintained by the tenant and will also require that the tenant obtain all necessary permits prior to installing the sign(s).

The Site Plan

A *site plan* showing the layout of the building is usually attached to the lease as an exhibit. The leased premises, including its dimensions, are identified on the site plan when the building is one story (crosshatched, outlined in red, or otherwise delineated). A ground lease may include a *metes and bounds* (boundary) description of the land parcel.

Owners are advised to include a disclaimer on the site plan and in the body of the lease, stating that the site plan is not drawn to scale and that the owner has the sole right to alter it without the tenant's approval. This disclaimer is very important to owners in case they want to expand the property. This situation is most common with shopping centers, where the owner wants the right to extend or add a building, create a separate parcel in the parking lot for a pad or outlot building, or remodel or rehabilitate the property without having to get each tenant's approval.

Adding a pad tenant on a ground lease will significantly increase the value of the shopping center. For example, if the annual ground rent is $80,000 and the shopping center is valued using a 10 percent cap rate, adding a pad tenant increases the property's value by $800,000. If the cap rate used is five percent, the value of the property increases by $1.6 million.

The site plan provision is also important for the tenant. In shopping centers, anchor tenants want to protect their sightline from the street and negotiate a "no build zone" to ensure that future construction does not obstruct their sightlines. Anchor tenants will often negotiate for a predetermined amount of parking to be available in a defined area. Non–anchor tenants may attempt similar negotiations for parking but, unless the retailer is highly sought after, the owner will not agree to this concession.

Storage

Exterior storage is unsightly, can lead to fires and vandalism, and can be a hazard to traffic on the property. The lease should be very specific as to whether or not exterior storage is allowed and, if so, what can be stored, where, and for how long. The parties to the lease also need to decide if storage areas need to be enclosed with a fence, wall, or landscape.

Store Hours

There have been many different methods to determine what the store hours should be for tenants in shopping centers and malls. The best method is having the owner establish the store hours and have them become a lease requirement. The typical store hours for a strip shopping center are 10:00 am to 9:00 p.m. Monday through Friday, 10:00 am to 7:00 am Saturdays and 11:00 am to 6:00 p.m. Sundays. Some landlords will extend the closing time an hour. These are minimum hours and tenants, such as a restaurant opening earlier for breakfast and remain open later for late dinners and drinks, may do so.

For enclosed malls, all the tenants must maintain the same hours with an occasional exception—although mall management will periodically close the mall for cleaning and security reasons. Some malls will open the common areas an hour or two early for mall walkers and deliveries to stores with no rear entrances. The typical mall hours are 10:00 am to 9:00 p.m., Monday to Saturday, and 10:00 am or 11:00 am to 7:0 p.m. on Sundays. Malls will often have extended hours during the Christmas season with many malls remaining open until midnight the week or two before Christmas.

If there is a theater in the mall with no outside entrance, the mall will remain open passed the time the theater closes. Anchor tenants usually have outside entrances so if they have a special sale beyond mall hours, and the entire mall is not participating in the event, the mall may be closed and shoppers will enter the anchor store directly from the parking lot. The owner will have the right to change the store hours and which days the shopping center or mall is closed—the lease will require that the tenants honor the revised minimum hours.

There are a few tenants who will negotiate to make changes to the store hours and days they are required to be open. Most banks are closed Saturdays around 2:00 p.m. and are not open on Sundays. A governmental agency is likely to be closed on Saturday and Sundays. Some medical tenants in a shopping center will not open on Sundays. These are case-by-case situations.

Taxes

The taxes for office and medical office buildings and multi-tenanted industrial properties are included in the pass-through operating expenses charged to the tenants—except for those tenants with gross leases. Typically tenants in shopping centers reimburse the owner for the property's real estate taxes and assessments. It is common for shopping center owners to estimate the amount of these charges, bill tenants monthly for the estimated costs (similar to the CAM charges), and adjust these payments based on the actual cost early the following year. Anchor tenants in shopping centers and industrial tenants in freestanding buildings often negotiate for the right to reimburse the owner for tax payments after the owner has provided them with a copy of the payment. This may mean that the owner fronts the tax payment for these tenants, or the tenant must reimburse the owner for the taxes a week before they are due.

Tenants are almost always responsible for taxes on over-standard improvements. If a building's tax assessment increases because of a tenant's over-standard improvements, that tenant is responsible for the increase. The tenant is likely to insist on receiving evidence that the improvements are what caused the tax assessment to increase.

A prudent real estate manager analyzes each successive assessment when it is received. If the analysis reveals that the property is over-assessed, the property manager may hire a consultant to appeal the assessment. If the appeal is successful, the savings will be passed on to the tenants. Because tenants are the beneficiaries of any tax savings, the owner wants them to pay for the analysis and appeal of the assessment. Tenants may negotiate to reimburse the cost of an appeal if it is successful, but this may discourage the owner from appealing. The lease may grant some tenants—usually major tenants and freestanding tenants—the right to directly contest real estate taxes on their premises, without owner approval.

Tenant Improvements

If no work is to be performed by the owner, the lease should indicate that the tenant is accepting the premises in "as-is" condition. If the owner is providing tenant improvements, they should be specifically described in an exhibit know as "Owner and Tenant Work." The exhibit should then indicate that anything not specifically included as owner work is to be paid for by the tenant.

Term or Duration of the Lease

A lease must have a finite term with fixed starting (commencement) and ending (termination) dates. For example, "The term of this lease shall be five years, beginning on November 1, 2018 and ending on October 31, 2023." The lease should not have an open expiration date—e.g., a date "to be agreed upon in the future."

Most owners want tenants to open for business as soon as possible, but are not concerned with the specific month this occurs. Some retail tenants have blackout dates when they will not open a store. Depending on the retailer, the blackout period can extend from November 1st to March 1st, or it may include several specific periods during the year.

There are a few issues to be raised regarding the expiration date. To manage occupancy levels and the building's income, owners do not want a large number of their leases expiring around the same time. The expiration dates should be staggered over different months and several years. Owners and tenants of shopping centers agree that leases should not expire just before or during the Christmas holiday season. Both parties want to have the benefit of an additional best-selling season. Since the majority of profits are earned by many retailers during the last six weeks of the year, they do not want the lease to expire during the year's last three months. Most retailers do not have their grand opening during the Christmas season, making it difficult for owners to lease vacant spaces during the last two months of the year. They may have temporary tenants lease space for the Christmas season.

Typical Lease Duration

The length of a lease varies depending upon several factors: property type, the amount of space being leased, whether the tenant is a national or local business, the amount of build-out that is being invested, etc. At one time, owners preferred shorter-term leases so that they could increase rents more frequently. They soon realized how costly it is to replace tenants, and that longer leases provide more stability and security. For these reasons, owners generally prefer longer-term leases.

Leases for industrial properties vary in duration depending on the size, costs of tenant improvements, and moving and setup. Office building leases for Class A buildings are usually five to seven years, while Class B or C buildings have three to five years. Tenants who take large spaces in office buildings prefer leases of 10 years or more. Medical office building spaces warrant longer leases (usually 10 years, often with options) because of the high cost to build out a medical and dental suite improvement, which can be two to five times the cost of building out a typical office suite.

The length of retail leases varies more than any other type of commercial property. National retailers usually negotiate for lease terms of seven to 11 years, and most local shop tenants negotiate for terms of three to five years. Retail tenants whose build-out costs are high (e.g., a restaurant) negotiate for longer leases—usually 10 to 20 years with multiple options. These tenants require longer lease terms to amortize the cost of their tenant improvements and fixtures; additionally, their loans to finance the purchase of equipment may be for periods longer than five years. Leases for pad and outlot tenants typically are for 20 to 30 years—often with multiple five-year lease options.

For years, anchor retail tenant leases were 30 years with six five-year options. Since the 1990s, however, many anchor tenants have negotiated 20-year leases with eight five-year options, allowing them to control the space for the same duration but with the right to terminate 10 years sooner. It is in the best interest for all tenants to negotiate for lease renewal options that will give them the option to extend their lease if they so choose.

Title to Improvements

This provision gives the owner title to the tenant's improvements it wants to remain on the premises when the lease expires. Some improvements have no value and are costly to remove and the owner will require the tenant to remove these improvements upon termination. The tenant may negotiate to remove and keep some of the tenant improvements but would also be required to restore the property. For example, a restaurant tenant would not be allowed to remove gas appliances without also properly capping the gas lines to prevent the risk of explosion.

Use of the Premises

The lease must state the tenant's use of the premises, and the use provision should be very specific about what business the tenant can conduct on the leased premises. The owner's control over the tenant mix of any property is based on the allowable use(s) in each tenant's lease. This is especially important for shopping centers and retail properties where the owner attempts to create the best tenant mix for all the tenants, property, and trade area.

The *use provision* in shopping center leases should limit the type of business the tenant may operate—and the products or services that can be sold—without being so restrictive that the tenant cannot operate successfully. For example, all types of shopping centers frequently have multiple restaurants, but this use should be tightly controlled.

If a shopping center has three restaurants, the owner does not want all three to serve the same type of food. To do so would dilute the sales of each restaurant, limit the variety of selection available to customers, and reduce or eliminate the potential for percentage rent. The likely result would be that one or all of the restaurants would go out of business.

The use provision in a restaurant lease states the type of food offered, whether alcoholic beverages may be served, and whether the food is eaten in the premises or not (i.e., carryout or drive-through). Such a lease provision might be phrased as follows: "Mexican restaurant with beer and wine for on-site consumption and takeout," or "Chinese restaurant with on-site consumption, takeout and delivery, and no hard liquor served." It is the exception to restrict carryout food.

Another way of limiting the use is to state what percentage of the store's entire sales a particular product may represent. An owner who believes that only one candy store can be successful at the shopping center will be rightly concerned when a lease proposal is received from a card and gift store chain with a national format that includes incidental sales of candy. In order to allow this store to operate and still protect the sales and potential percentage rent of a candy store, the use provision could limit the square footage of the card and gift store's candy display or limit the store's percentage of candy sales. For instance, "Sales of candy may not exceed six square feet of display area" or "Candy sales cannot exceed 15 percent of the tenant's total annual sales volume." It is easier to monitor and enforce a restriction based on square footage than one based on sales. Another approach is to state that candy sales must be incidental to the sales of cards and gifts.

Retail tenants usually negotiate for the right to add merchandise. One common way chain store leases do this is to state that tenants may add merchandise sold in their other stores. This provision creates a problem for the owner: The new merchandise may already be provided by another tenant and the market may not support both tenants selling this product. A more challenging situation arises when the owner has given another tenant the exclusive right to sell that product; if the chain store tenant then adds the product, the owner is in violation of the first tenant's exclusive provision.

If the shopping center or mall has a tenant, or multiple tenants with exclusives, the list of exclusives become an exhibit to the lease with a statement in the use provision prohibiting the tenant from selling the product or providing the services listed on the referenced exhibit.

Some anchor tenants will try to negotiate for a use that allows "any legal use." Property owners typically resist this because the tenant can provide almost any service and product with this use provision and possibly violate other tenants' exclusives, or damage the tenant mix in the shopping center.

In office buildings, a common mistake many owners make is to state that the use is "general business purposes." This allows the tenant to conduct any legal business in the premises. A four-person firm in a 1,500-square-feet space could become a 20-person answering service, thus, placing a burden on the building's parking and other facilities.

The use provision for industrial properties should also be specific to the tenant's intended use. The owner may be concerned that, if the use is changed, the new use will create a potential or possible hazardous waste situation.

An additional requirement for tenant uses in general is that the tenant's use must be legal. If the tenant's use of the premises is illegal (e.g., gambling in a state where gambling is prohibited), the lease is voidable and the owner should seek the advice of an attorney to determine if the lease may be cancelled by the owner. The use provision can also assist in establish a building as a green building, and the owner's and tenants' green practices. It sets the framework for green building operations and the importance of tenant cooperation. Use provisions for all building types should be specific regarding the tenant's use.

Utilities

The utilities provision requires tenants to pay, in a timely manner, all utilities that are billed directly to them for their premises. The provision also grants the owner the right to bill the tenant for a pro rata share of any utility that is not separately metered for each of the premises. Electricity and gas are commonly provided by private utility companies and metered directly to each retail and industrial tenant, but other arrangements may exist. The utility expense is included in most office and medical office building operating expenses (or in the rent if the lease is a gross lease), and are seldom billed individually to the office/medical office tenant.

The exception is when a tenant uses over standard utilities or has a submeter, the owner reads and then bills the tenant for their usage. Municipal or other governmental authorities typically bill for water charges. The water bill may include charges for sewage disposal based on water consumption and may also include other items such as stormwater fees. Many shopping centers have a common water meter that supplies water to the entire building. In order to bill back the water/sewer charges to the various tenants, that owner will either include this cost in the CAM expense or each tenant space will be placed on a submeter, and then be billed their share of the water usage.

Waste Disposal

Garbage pickup (trash disposal) may be considered as a utility, or it may be addressed separately. Disposal service may be contracted for the entire shopping center and charged in the CAM expenses, or individual tenants may contract for this service and pay the charges directly to the waste pickup service. Tenants want to be sure they are paying for their fair pro rata share of the waste disposal. If any tenants have more trash than is typical, those tenants should be billed for the extra trash they generate and the payments should be credited to the waste disposal bill.

For example, if waste disposal is charged to a shopping center's CAM expenses, but some tenants pay directly for their pickup service, an adjustment must be made to the CAM billings. In such circumstances, tenants who contract directly for trash disposal are charged only for disposing of debris in the common areas—a small amount since only a small portion of the CAM expense is for emptying common area trash receptacles. One of the best ways to handle this issue is to create a separate charge for those tenants who use the common pickup services, and to exclude this charge from the general CAM costs.

Tenants who generate trash posing potential disposal problems—e.g., food wastes from restaurants, animal excrement and other materials from pet stores—may be required to have special water-tight containers. Some waste materials are potentially hazardous (e.g., medical wastes, dry cleaning chemicals, photo processing agents), and this provision must address the proper disposal of such waste.

The trash removal expense for office and medical office buildings are included in the buildings operating expenses pass-through charges. Industrial tenants are usually billed separately for the trash pick–up.

Exhibits

Finally, several exhibits are attached to and incorporated into the lease. They are usually appended in the order in which they are referenced in the body of the lease, identified as Exhibit A, Exhibit B, etc. These attachments usually augment or clarify specific aspects of the lease or spell out relevant details. The most common lease exhibits are listed below:

- *Site Plan of the Property.* This exhibit depicts the layout of all the buildings and the boundaries of the property. There may be changes to the site plan in the future—the most common being changes to the parking lot to accommodate expansion of the main building, the addition of a pad or outlot building, or changes in configuration when a shopping center is remodeled. The site plan may include a disclaimer that allows the owner to make changes to it. The tenant negotiates what changes can occur in the common area, potentially an important issue for retail tenants.
- *Demising Plan of the Tenant's Premises.* The tenant's premises are marked on a layout of the building or the floor the tenant occupies where the tenant's leased space is located. They may be outlined in colored ink or crosshatched in red or blue. The same disclaimer that appears in the site plan exhibit should be included in this exhibit.
- *Description of the Owner's and Tenant's Work.* This exhibit, usually a standard form, lists the improvements to the premises that will be provided by the owner and by the tenant. Usually this document also includes specifications for particular work.
- *Corporate Resolution of the Tenant.* If the tenant is a corporation, a corporate resolution authorizing one or more individuals to sign the lease should be appended to the lease. The resolution, which should be signed by two officers of the corporation, states that the officers who signed the lease on behalf of the tenant have the authority to bind the corporation to the lease. The tenant may request the same guaranty from the owner.
- *Guaranty of the Lease.* The owner will typically require the lease be guarantied as discussed in the provision on lease guaranty.
- *Sign Criteria.* The sign criteria restricts the size, location, and materials used for fabricating the tenant's sign for shopping centers, industrial properties, and some office buildings. All exterior tenant signs must comply with the sign criteria in order for the property to maintain its image.

A Green Lease

Green leasing (also called energy-aligned leasing) seeks to advance sustainability and resource efficiency at a property through lease clauses or addenda. These clauses typically call for the landlord and tenant to exchange energy data for benchmarking and tracking purposes, collaborate on sustainability programs, and share the costs of building upgrades that result in efficiency gains and utility cost savings. Clauses may also specify tenant operational and behavioral requirements that maintain sustainable and efficient operations. For example, the lease may prohibit the use of space heaters or other energy-intense equipment that is not vital to business operations, or specify sustainable and efficient tenant improvement standards such as energy efficient lighting and ENERGY STAR kitchen appliances and office equipment.

Green leasing has gained some traction as a way to overcome barriers to sustainability and resource efficiency. However, the clauses associated with green leasing are still unfamiliar to many brokers and real estate attorneys, who may object to them. In order to initiate a green lease with a tenant, it is important to engage those tenants with an interest in or commitment to occupying sustainable real estate. It is also important to discuss green lease clauses early in the leasing process.

Sustainability Certifications

Sustainability certifications are available for new construction developments and existing properties. They sometimes come into play during the lease negotiation process, but are mainly focused on one area of operations—energy performance. Other certifications focus on the comprehensive sustainability performance of the property.

ENERGY STAR Certification

ENERGY STAR certification, granted by the U.S. Environmental Protection Agency, is available to office properties that are benchmarked with the free ENERGY STAR Portfolio Manager tool. If enough data is entered into Portfolio Manager, the software tool generates a 1 to 100 score that compares the property's energy performance to national averages from the Commercial Buildings Energy Consumption Survey (CBECS), a statistical study regularly performed by the U.S. government. An ENERGY STAR score below 50 means the property is performing worse than 50 percent of similar buildings nationwide, while a score above 50 means it's performing better than 50 percent of its peers. A score of 75 or higher means the property is a top performer, and it may be eligible for ENERGY STAR certification.

In order to obtain an ENERGY STAR score:

- All energy used by the property (e.g., electricity, gas, oil, steam, onsite renewable energy, etc.) must be entered into Portfolio Manager.
- There must be at least 12 full consecutive calendar months of energy data for all active meters and all fuel types.
- A property needs the following in order to obtain the ENERGY STAR certification. The certification award year is based on the date the certification is approved.
- A total score of 75 or above is required.
- At least 75% occupancy be be obtained throughout a 12-month assessment period.
- The data submission must be verified by a professional engineer or registered architect.

Leadership in Energy and Environmental Design (LEED)

LEED is a market leader in sustainability certifications and recognizes properties that meet a high threshold for sustainability performance. LEED certification applies to several different project types:

- Building Design and Construction (BD+C)—for new construction properties
- Interior Design and Construction (ID+C)—for building interiors including tenant spaces
- Building Operations and Maintenance (O+M)—for existing building operations
- Neighborhood Development (ND)—for new land development or redevelopments with a mix of properties and uses

LEED O+M for Existing Buildings is the certification type most concerned with commercial management because it focuses on the ongoing sustainability performance of the property. LEED O+M assesses properties around the following credit categories:

- Location and transportation

- Sustainable sites
- Energy and atmosphere
- Materials and resources
- Indoor environmental quality
- Innovation
- Regional priority

Properties can be certified at different levels: Certified, Silver, Gold, and Platinum.

IREM Certified Sustainable Property Certification

The IREM Certified Sustainable Property certification is an attainable, affordable, and meaningful sustainability recognition program for existing office properties, multifamily communities, and shopping centers. The certification is most appropriate for buildings when LEED certification is out of reach. It assesses sustainability performance in five categories: energy, water, health, recycling, and purchasing. IREM provides a certification checklist and a book of templates, checklists, and tools that make it possible for property staff to complete the certification process without having to engage an outside consultant.

WELL Building Standard

The WELL Building Standard® is an evidence-based system for measuring, certifying, and monitoring the performance of building features that impact health and wellbeing. WELL is administered by the International WELL Building Institute™ (IWBI)—a public benefit corporation whose mission is to improve human health and well-being through the built environment. WELL is third-party certified by Green Business Certification Inc. (GBCI), which administers LEED certification and LEED professional credentials. WELL Certification is available for new and existing buildings, new and existing interiors, and core and shell projects. There are three certification levels: Silver, Gold, and Platinum.

Green Globes

Green Globes® is a building rating system administered by the Green Building Initiative. The sustainability certification is available for a range of property types in the new construction, existing buildings, and interiors categories. Green Globes recognizes projects that meet at least 35% of the 1,000 available points in six assessment areas: energy, water, resources, emissions, indoor environment, and environmental management. There are four certification levels: One Green Globe, Two Green Globes, Three Green Globes, and Four Green Globes.

CHAPTER

11

Leasing Opportunities

There are greater opportunities to increase the cash flow and enhance the value of a building working the income side of the property's ledger than the expense side. Once a property has achieved stabilized management and operations, there are few, if any, opportunities to lower the operating expenses. While operating the property efficiently, the real estate manager should explore opportunities to increase the property's revenue. There are countless ongoing opportunities to increase the income of a building through creative leasing. This chapter explores several opportunities real estate managers have used to increase a building's cash flow and enhance its value.

LEASING WHEN NO VACANCIES EXIST

When a building achieves 100 percent occupancy, the tenancy could easily be to focus ones leasing effort on other properties and to ignore leasing at the subject property until a tenant's lease is up for renewal or a tenant is vacating its premises. A fully occupied property, however, is not the end of the leasing effort, but the beginning of a fine-tuning process that can add substantial cash flow and value to the building.

It's rare for a building to not have older leases with low rents, tenants who have too much or too little space, under-utilized space that can be converted to leasable area, or open space that can be converted to rent-producing storage areas. For these reasons, the real estate manager should continue leasing activities even when the building has no vacancies. A professional leasing sign should always be on the property. When prospects inquire about space, they should not be told, "We have nothing available." Rather, the real estate manager should discuss their needs to see if they might be potential replacement tenants and tell them when space might become available. If no space in the building will meet the prospects needs, the real estate manager may have other buildings with the right space available for the prospects. Regular visits with existing tenants reveal their needs, which may be for additional space, or the need to downsize or close the business. Any tenant who wants to increase or decrease its space is a potential opportunity to improve the income and value of the property.

The following cases are good examples of leasing opportunities when no vacancies exist:

- A small office building fully leased had a conference room of 500 square feet that was rented out approximately 10 times a year at $100 per day. The space was converted to an office and rented at $40 per square foot per year. The property owner realized a net gain of $18,800. At a cap rate of eight percent, an additional building value of $235,000 was created. The rent for the new office was $20,000—minus the rent for the conference room of $1,200 provided an increase of $18,800 and using an eight percent cap rate the increased values was $238,000.
- The same building had six small, enclosed areas under the stairwells. All were empty and dirty. They were cleaned, painted white, and offered as storage to tenants in the building at $100 per month—each totaling $600 per month or $7,200 annually. The added value to the building was in excess of $90,000 for an investment of less than $3,000.
- Another small office building had a hallway 10 feet wide by 30 feet long that was no longer in use. An enterprising young person rented the hallway for a snack bar at $30.00 per square foot; she received an allowance of $12,000 to install the plumbing. The added value to the building was

more than $112,500 for a space that appeared to have no value.

- A specialty sporting goods store had excessive space and the tenant struggled paying rent on the 5,000-square-foot shop. After some negotiations, the property owner split the store in half. The tenant was paying $20.00 per square foot per year, and the reduction in the rent space saved the tenant $50,000 plus lower *common area maintenance (CAM)* charges and utility costs. The tenant needed less inventory. The rent on the spaced carved out of the tenant's space was increased $5 for the new 2,500-square-foot store. The rent on the new space increased $12,500. This increased the cash flow and value of the building. The added value to the shopping center was $156,000 ($12,500 divide by the cap rate of eight percent). The cost to divide the space was approximately $98,000. The shopping center now has two strong tenants instead of one weak tenant, increased cash flow, and greater value.

There are plenty of stories told of abandoned elevator shafts being refinished as one-person offices or convenience item stands; storerooms being refinished into office space; breezeways being closed in for rentable space; basements and attics being converted to leasable area or storage space; three-story atriums being split into separate floors and leased; kiosks and carts being added to the mall; and shallow or wall shops being built in front of the blank walls of a department store on a mall and pad buildings being developed on the parking lot.

Opportunities to improve the income of the property are endless, and the real estate manager should not stop leasing activities just because the property is fully leased.

NEGOTIATING THE PAD OR OUTLOT DEAL

Pad or outlot parcels are highly sought in shopping centers and selective office and industrial parks. Pads are found in all types of shopping centers ranging from small unanchored strip shopping centers to super regional malls. Pad buildings are located in the parking lot close to the streets. An office or industrial park may include a pad building. The portion of the office or industrial park fronting a major thoroughfare may have sites ideal for a pad building. Almost all pad buildings are occupied by one tenant. A pad building occupied by two or more tenants is called a splitter pad building. Pad buildings are typically occupied by fast-food and sit-down restaurants, drive-through espresso stands, and banks. These tenants can afford higher occupancy costs in return for the location's high visibility, easy access, drive-through windows and surrounding parking. They are located on the street perimeter of the property providing excellent visibility and access from main roads. Pad tenants prefer to be located near a corner with a traffic light.

Pad deals can be very profitable. The addition of pads, also known as outlots, or out parcels, as they are called in different areas, offers an outstanding opportunity to enhance the cash flow and value of commercial properties.

PAD OR OUTLOT TRANSLATION

There are three types of pad deals: (1) the *ground lease,* (2) *build-to-suit*, and (3) sale of the site. A separate parcel is created for each pad so they can be sold or developed separately from the rest of the shopping center. The pad site will accommodate the pad building and required parking and landscaping. There is a cross easement between the shopping center and the pad parcel for customer access and parking.

The shopping center's common area agreement, which is signed by the developer and the anchor tenants, and the anchor tenant's leases will address the placement, size, and number of pad buildings that is allowed on the parking lot. Occasionally, other tenants' leases may have similar requirements for pad buildings on the site.

The ground lease is the most common pad deal. The developer or property owner created a separate parcel and leases the parcel, or land, to a tenant. The tenant enters into a long-term lease with multiple options and builds their prototype building.

The second option is a built-to-suit transaction. The owner may lease the land and the tenant builds their prototype building. The choice to develop the site, or use a build-to-suit arrangement, is quite similar to the ground lease. The exception is that either the owner will actually develop the building or the tenant will develop it and sell it back to the owner, and then lease back the building and land. In both situations, the lease will be *triple-net* and subject to the *common area agreement*. The tenant, especially banks, prefers to build their buildings because they can finance their building on more favorable terms that the developer, thus, lowers the cost to develop the building and lowers its occupancy costs.

The third option is the sale of the pad site. Because the pad site is one of a property's most valuable parcels, there is usually greater demand from tenants and investors for the site. The parcel of land and its development is subject to restrictions in any existing tenant's lease and the common area agreements.

Most developers prefer the ground lease and then the build-to-suit lease; the least preferred pad deal is the sale of the pad. Developers and shopping center investors prefer the long-term income stream for a credit tenant.

A pad building is typically occupied by one tenant. Another approach is the splitter building, which is a freestanding building on a parcel of land that is split into two or more spaces and leased like in-line spaces. The lease is a triple-net lease; however the owner is responsible for paying the taxes, insurance, and exterior maintenance costs and then billing the tenants their pro rata shares of the costs.

Pad deals are typically long-term leases due to the very specialized nature of the buildings, the cost of the buildings, and the tenant improvements. Whether the tenant or the property owner pays the cost of the building, a long-term lease is necessary to amortize the construction and the tenant improvement costs. The lease term is usually 20 to 30 years with multiple five-year options.

Creating a Pad Site

Another major consideration is the configuration of the pad itself. Two approaches are possible. The first, and best, is to create a legal separate parcel out of the parking lot. This provides the owner of the shopping center with the option of leasing or selling the parcel. Developers prefer to create a legal parcel for the pad and maintain flexibility to ground lease or sell the building.

Planning Issues

When adding pads to a project, the property owner or real estate manger must consider some important issues. Most pad tenants want direct access from the street rather than from within the project. The corner is typically the most valuable site for a pad, but it is also the most difficult to provide with direct street access. Some municipalities will not allow a curb cut within a presubscribed distance—say 150 feet from an intersection. If the pad will have a fast-food restaurant, espresso stand, or a bank with a drive-up window, allowance must be made for stacking traffic while customers wait for the drive-up window service. If this is not designed properly, the waiting traffic will block the entrance to the property and/or impair the traffic circulation within the project. Because the pad building is exposed from all sides, great care must be taken with the design of the building so that trash and delivery areas do not present an unsightly view to the street or to the interior of the property.

ADDING A PAD BUILDING TO AN EXISTING PROPERTY

When considering adding a pad to an existing shopping center, the property owner must review and research several major issues. Among them are the parking requirements of the municipalities, parking requirements of the anchor tenants, and restrictions in tenant leases prohibiting pad buildings in the parking lot. Other issues include the configuration of the pad and financing strategies.

Approval Issues

Anchor tenants' leases often address the placement,

size and number of pad buildings that may be developed in the parking lot. The addition of pads is of concern to major tenants because pads may impair the sight lines from the street and within the parking lot to the tenants' buildings, as well as contribute to congestion in the parking lot. Anchor tenants are protective of their parking field. They may prohibit pads buildings from the parking area in front of their store. They usually restrict the height and size of the pad building.

Municipalities have parking requirements for shopping centers. They are concerned that parking does not spill out of the parking lot onto residential streets. Municipalities will establish a parking index for shopping centers. The index is a required number of parking stalls per 1,000 square feet of *gross leasable area (GLA)*. For example, an index may state that there must be five parking stalls for every 1,000 square feet of gross leasable area. This is known as a five-to-one index or ratio. The shopping center must have five parking stalls for very 1,000 square feet of GLA.

Shopping centers are almost always developed with the maximum amount of GLA and no excessive parking stalls. The developer prefers to maximize the development and potential income of a site. If an owner of an existing shopping center wants to add a pad building to the shopping center, it must be determined if there are excess parking stall to accommodate the pad building. If this is not the case additional parking stalls must be created. The number of additional parking stalls must be determined. If the pad building is a 4,000-square-foot restaurant and the municipality's parking requirements are five parking stalls for every 1,000 square feet of GLA, an additional 20 stalls must be added to the shopping center. The pad building will be developed on existing parking stalls and these stalls need to be replaced.

Let's assume the 4,000-square-foot pad building and its walkway and landscaping will be placed on 12 parking stalls. The shopping center now needs to add 32 parking stalls, 20 parking stalls to accommodate the requirement for the building, and 12 parking stalls the building will be situated on.

If the shopping center has no additional parking stalls where can the required additional parking stalls are found? A parking consultant is hired to review the parking layout and determine if the lot can be reorganized more efficiently. There may be an opportunity to convert some full-size parking stalls to compact parking stalls. The consultant will check with the municipality's requirement regarding the percentage of parking stalls that may be compact parking stalls. Often, the area behind the buildings are not stripped for parking stalls and several new parking stalls can be created in these areas. If the required additional parking stalls can be found, the owner of the shopping center can complete the transaction with the tenant. If fewer than the required number of parking stall can be created, the real estate manager will determine the amount of additional GLA that can be created by the added parking stalls and seek a tenant of that size or smaller.

Creating a pad building will generate additional revenue and enhance the property's value. The cost to create a separate parcel and bring utilities to the site is usually nominal in relationship to the revenue and value created. As an example, if a pad parcel is ground leased at $70,000, with a management fee of four percent of the gross income and the site is valued at a five percent cap rate, the increased cash flow is $67,200 ($70,000 minus the management fee of $2,800) and the value enhancement is $1,344,00 ($67,200 divided by .05). The analysis of adding a pad site and building to a property is one of the best and cost-effective means to increase a property's revenue and value.

SUBLETTING AND ASSIGNMENT

Lease agreements are usually very clear about the terms and criteria that will be acceptable for the owner's approval of a sublease or an assignment. Most courts have held that the owner cannot prohibit subleasing or assigning but can set forth reasonable requirements for granting an approval. Property owners generally have a lease provision regarding subletting and/or assignment, and charge a fee for the handling of the transaction. (Assignments are discussed in more detail in *Chapter 10: Negotiating the Commercial Lease*.)

The lease term is an issue in subleases and assignments that can add value to the building. A lease assignment or sublease may be an opportunity to extend the lease term. If the lease is extended, the rent for the new term may be pre-negotiated or be market rent when the original term expires. This can save the down time the space would be available since the original tenant is unlikely to have renewed its lease.

Who receives the increase in rent the subleasee or assignee may pay? Owners will want any increase rent above the rent the sublessor or assignor is paying. If all the increase in rent goes to the owner, there is no incentive for the sublessor or assignor to charge more rent that he or she is paying. A fair compromise is the owner and the tenant will equally share any increase rent.

LEASE RENEWAL OPPORTUNITIES

The lease renewal is one of the most important transactions in commercial real estate, and yet it often does not get the attention it deserves from the owner or the tenant. Each party assumes that the other party would be eager to renew the lease and that they would agree upon an increased base rent. Both parties frequently leave the renewal until the last minute, taking for granted the other side's desire to extend the lease agreement. Sometimes each party simply assumes that the only necessity is for both parties to agree on the new rental rate.

Tenant Retention Program

The real estate manager and property owner's involvement with a lease renewal should start before the tenant and owner sign the initial lease. A lease renewal starts with the tenant retention program. The first phase of that program begins with the initial contact with a prospect for the building. This period, along with lease negotiations and move-in, gives the tenant an initial impression of the building, the owner, and the real estate manager. These perceptions will have a lasting effect. The building's tenant retention program establishes the foundation for the relationship between the tenant and the building's management and ownership. Components of a tenant retention program include making improvements to the building, enhancing the building's tenant mix, creating an environment for the tenants' business referrals, and de-institutionalizing a building with programs for tenants' employees.

PLANNING AHEAD

Instead of anticipating a casual meeting to discuss a lease renewal with the tenant, the owner should approach the lease renewal with the same diligence used in planning for and negotiating the original lease. To avoid possible negative outcomes that may accompany poor planning, the real estate manager should provide the owner with alternatives to renewing the lease, market rents, and possible lease concessions. Armed with this analysis, the owner should decide in advance of the lease expiration date—whether or not to negotiate a renewal. Renewal discussions should commence at least six months prior to the lease expiration. For tenants of larger companies, renewal discussions should start one to two years prior to the lease expiration. Some major businesses may not be willing to commit to a renewal that far in advance of the lease expiration.

If the owner decides not to renew the lease for a given tenant, that tenant should be notified as soon as possible to allow for other arrangements to be made. Likewise, if the tenant decides not to pursue the renewal, the owner should be given adequate notice to release the space.

PREPARING TO RENEW A LEASE

If both parties agree to renew the lease, the transaction itself should be completed months before the lease expires. Owners should include lease renewals in a building's marketing and leasing program.

Likewise, tenants would be wise to include lease renewal analyses in both their short- and long-term business plans, and as part of their growth strategies.

Assessment of the Building's Negotiating Strength

The real estate manager's first responsibility is to assess the building's negotiating strength. Factors to consider are the building's current and anticipated future occupancy status, position in the market, the general economic situation, status of the competition, and the property owner's motivation and financial ability to meet the market demands.

Occupancy Status

The building's occupancy status consists of the present occupancy or vacancy rates and an analysis of the leases that are expiring during the next five years. A lease expiration schedule is very helpful in providing an ongoing analysis for all building leases. This analysis includes each tenant's lease expiration date, the likelihood the tenant will renew the lease, and the tenant's future space needs.

By combining the analysis with the projected amount of new space that will be leased in the building during the same period, the real estate manager can give the property owner an estimate of the present and future occupancy or a vacancy status report. If a building has a high-occupancy rate, and this rate is likely to be maintained in the near future, the real estate manager should start negotiating from a position of strength.

Market Position

Next, the real estate manager evaluates the building's competitive position in the market. While the criteria the real estate manager considers will vary depending on whether the building is an office building, enclosed mall, or a single or multi-tenant industrial property, they will include some or all of the following: location; anchor tenant; amenities and features; image and business climate; retailers and restaurants sales; trade area; and demographics and psychographics. The subject building is compared with each of its competing buildings to establish its competitive ranking and market position. In studying the competition, the real estate manager must determine the competing buildings' rental rates, concession packages, and size and location of vacant spaces. When analyzing the market, it is best to check with the municipalities building department for proposed and soon-to-be-developed buildings. Some of these buildings may be competition to the subject property and could change the property's market position.

Economy

It is important to consider the area's general economy as well as the economy of the property's micro-market or trade area in assessing the building's negotiating position.

Property Owner's Motivation

The final consideration in evaluating the building's negotiating position is the building owner's motivation and ability to meet the demands of the market. Does the owner have the financial resources to compete with market deals? Are funds available for tenant improvements, lease concessions, or other out-of-pocket expenditures? An owner who is strapped for cash will not be able to offer some negotiating options, such as tenant improvement allowances, that may be needed during lease renewal discussions. This is known as a "pressure point" for the property owner. Another possible pressure point would be a loan that is coming due and requiring a specific *net operating income (NOI)* to be refinanced requiring the property owner to be more negotiable in the renewal terms.

Evaluation of Tenant's Desirability

Once the building's negotiating position has been determined, the next decision is whether the tenant should be offered a lease renewal. Most tenants are desirable tenants, and the building owner wants to retain them. However, there are a few good reasons not to renew, such as poor rent payment history or the need for the tenant's space to be combined with adjacent space for a larger user. The tenant's use may be a present or potential problem for the building. For example, an auto-body shop may present a potential for a hazardous chemical spill or unlawful disposal of hazardous waste. The leasing plan may be to upgrade from non-credit to credit-worthy tenants. Credit tenants will create additional value for a building. A building with credit tenants paying the same rent as non-credit tenants in a similar building in the immediate location will have greater value than the building with non-credit tenants. The revenue stream from credit tenant is more secure, and an investor will pay more for that secure revenue stream.

Shopping centers have additional reasons for not offering a tenant a lease renewal. A tenant's use may no longer be appropriate for the changing demographics or psychographics of the trade area. Remodeling or upgrading a shopping center can also affect its tenant mix.

A merchant's sales per square foot may be significantly lower than the sales for similar merchants in the shopping center or the national averages. The retailer's sales performance and overall operation of the store are crucial when evaluating a lease renewal. Shopping center managers always seek to improve the property's tenant mix by replacing weak tenants.

When the market is poor, it is difficult to apply strict criteria to lease renewals. Real estate managers and building owners often jokingly say that the only criterion in a soft market is the "mirror test." The real estate manager holds a mirror under the tenant's nose; if the mirror fogs up, the tenant's lease should be renewed. Regardless of the market and the building's economic conditions, the real estate manager and the property owner should have the necessary information available prior to the lease expiration.

Determination of Lease Renewal Terms

After analyzing the building's negotiating strengths and weaknesses and the tenant's desirability, the real estate manager must determine the terms of the lease renewal offer—if one will be made. The new terms will usually be limited to the new rental rate, but in a soft market, concessions such as free rent, refurbishment of the premises, and tenant improvements may be necessary. The real estate manager should develop a cost estimate for each of these concessions before discussing the alternatives with the property owner. This will enable the real estate manager and the property owner to know the range of the costs necessary to renew the tenant. A strategy for an initial lease renewal offer with different fallback positions can be developed, and different lease renewal proposals can be compared with the cost of not renewing the tenant. Costs of not renewing include loss of rent during the period it takes before a replacement tenant is paying rent, tenant improvement costs, a full commission, and other possible concessions. Typically, the cost to renew a tenant is a small fraction of leasing to a new tenant.

THE COST OF NOT RENEWING A LEASE

If the lease is not renewed, it may create a challenge for both the owner and the tenant. Knowing the costs of not renewing the lease is therefore important for both parties. There are both direct and non-direct monetary costs to be considered.

Direct Monetary Costs

There are many direct monetary costs that owners must face when a lease is not renewed. The most obvious of these is the loss of base rent, since new leases usually require vacancy prior to the lease's commencement. There is also the loss of percentage rent, or overage rent, paid by some retailers and service tenants.

An often overlooked cost is the loss of the building's *pass-through charges.* These charges, shared by most tenants per their lease arrangements, are an income component in the owner's operating budget and cash flow. If free rent is negotiated with a new tenant, another issue to resolve is whether or not pass-through charges will be reimbursed during the free-rent period. This is an issue that is often poorly documented in a lease and can lead to disputes between the owner and the tenant.

Another cost is that of *tenant improvement (TI)* expenses to rebuild the premises for a replacement tenant. New leases generally require more improvements than renewals. Retail and industrial properties are often re-leased in "as-is" condition, but if the market is soft, the replacement tenant may be offered a tenant *TI allowance.* Owners of office and medical office buildings, on the other hand, almost always provide improvements for new tenants. In a soft market these costs will be greater—easily in the tens or hundreds of thousands of dollars. A related cost to consider is the downtime as TIs are being constructed.

The cost of *concessions* for a new lease is also a factor. These are limited only by the imagination of the tenant and the owner, and can include lower rent; reduced, capped, or eliminated pass-through expenses; free or reduced parking rates; over-standard TIs; reimbursed moving expenses and relocation notifications; new signage; gifts; and any other negotiated concessions.

The final direct monetary cost for not renewing a lease is the commission paid to the leasing agent for a replacement tenant. In a soft market, the owner may pay a double commission to get the space leased. On the other hand, the commission for a lease renewal—if required at all—is usually considerably less than that for a new lease.

Non-Direct Monetary Costs

The non-direct monetary costs for owners when tenants do not renew their lease are also significant. The impact to the building and the other tenants is a major consideration.

Specific tenants often provide services that attract and retain other tenants (e.g., a restaurant or bank in an office building), and the loss of these key tenants may have a negative impact on the leasing of other space in the building. For example, a stock brokerage firm can be important to an office building's image. In a medical office building, a pharmacy is a significant addition, and some medical practices are an important source of referral business to other medical professionals. A shopping center is impacted when tenants with a good customer draw decide not to renew their lease. Too many vacancies in a shopping center can create a negative perception among its customers.' The non-direct cost of these tenants not renewing their leases may be that other tenants decide to leave—and the building's tenant mix is weakened.

In addition to the concern about losing the existing tenant, there may also be the unknown factor of whether or not the replacement tenant will be a good tenant and live up to the owner's expectations.

There are other possible costs to not renewing a tenant that seldom come into play; however, when they do, they can be very costly for the owner. The first is that, if the owner were to sell the building, vacancies could impact the building's selling price and how long it takes to sell. The second is that, occasionally, a building's lender will require the owner to pay a portion of the loan if the building's occupancy, gross income, or NOI falls below a predetermined amount. If the property is a shopping center with some tenants having a co-tenancy provision based on the occupancy of the shopping center—and the occupancy is just above that threshold for some tenants to cancel their leases—a lease may be renewed to prevent some tenants from exercising their co-tenancy provision.

The Tenant's Costs

Although the owner's cost of not renewing a lease can be significant, the tenant's cost of not doing so can be much greater. The real estate manager should estimate the cost for the tenant not to renew its lease. This analysis can strengthen the owner's negotiating position. A tenant's entire business may suffer if the lease renewal decision is not handled with foresight.

If location is important to the tenant's business, relocating to a less-desirable location can have a tremendous impact on its success and profits, as well as daily operations. Retail and service customers are not likely to patronize a business that relocates far away, and they can sometimes even be deterred by a move of just a few blocks. The tenant who relocates may also lose the customer draw provided by an anchor tenant or other key tenants in the area. For instance, a dry cleaner who is adjacent to a supermarket in a shopping center is likely to lose many customers in the process of moving a few blocks away to a small, unanchored strip shopping center. Will the customer base need to be rebuilt after the move? The tenant must consider whether or not a different location will impact employee retention or make it more difficult to recruit the best employees.

Another cost for the tenant not renewing a lease is the moving expense. This includes the cost of the physical move, the costs to connect computers and other equipment, and the cost to notify customers of the new location. Another relocating cost is printing new letterhead, business cards, and other marketing materials.

Finally, the tenant should consider the cost of building out the premises in a new location. Even if the new owner is contributing to the TIs, this contribution may not cover all the build-out costs. This can be a significant cost for any business—and especially for medical professionals and other tenants with high-fixturization costs.

Although it still may be worthwhile for a tenant to not renew a lease and move to a new location, these additional costs must be considered carefully in order to reach an informed decision about the lease renewal.

DOCUMENTING THE LEASE RENEWAL

After the lease renewal negotiations have concluded and both parties have agreed on the terms, the real estate manager prepares the lease renewal documents and must decide whether to prepare a lease addendum or a new lease.

A *lease addendum* (or *lease amendment*) usually only adjusts the rent and possibly provides concessions. This form is easy to prepare, and the tenant's attorney usually does not need to review the document. However, if the original lease is at least three years old, it will probably not include the latest state-of-the-art lease provisions. If an addendum is used to renew a lease, it should not state, "All terms and conditions shall remain the same except for a rent adjustment." The original lease may have included concessions, such as free rent and/or tenant allowances, and such language would extend those concessions to the renewal.

Preparation of a new lease is usually best; it gives the property owner the benefit of the most current industry lease provisions and the protection that goes along with them. A new lease form provides the opportunity to add provisions that address specific problems the real estate manager has experienced with the tenant. For example, the lease may stipulate a monetary penalty if the retail tenant fails to submit its sales reports on time and a similar penalty if an *estoppel certificate* is not signed and returned to the property owner within a specific time.

It's important to document a lease renewal with a new lease. If a tenant has renewed its lease two or three times using an addendum, another addendum will likely date the lease another three to five years. The tenant will have the advantage of a lease that is probably 10 to 15 years old. The property owner's lease should be reviewed periodically and new and modified provisions added to the lease document.

A renewal is often the most cost-effective deal that can be made in a building. There is no vacancy factor during the time between tenants, tenant improvements are usually considerably lower, free rent is often less or nonexistent, and the lease commission is often half that of a new lease.

POP-UP BUSINESSES IN SHOPPING CENTERS

A unique aspect of shopping centers is that vacancies are visible to everyone, and vacancies can have a negative impact on property income, the perception of tenant prospects, as well as businesses of the existing merchants, and on the public as well.

A pop-up business program for tenants may help a mall or strip shopping center avoid or overcome some of the negative effects of vacancies. Pop-up businesses, also known as *temporary tenants,* have become an important component of the leasing plan and a revenue source for malls. Strip shopping centers have limited opportunities to lease to temporary tenants, but when spaces are likely to be available for an extended period of time, the real estate manager should explore temporary uses of the space.

Malls and Small Pop-Up Businesses

The mall common area is an ideal place to locate retailers who sell unique and specialty products. They are willing to pay a premium rent for the opportunity to be located in a very high-traffic area during the best-selling period of the year. Some pop-up businesses will remain throughout the year.

In past years, the idea of a pop-up business was considered less than desirable in commercial properties. They were thought to give the property a poor image. However, property owners have come to realize having these small pop-up businesses can be beneficial—especially if the program is well managed. Most mall developers and their real estate managers have developed these programs to enhance the mall's tenant mix, provide for testing new retail concepts, and of course, occupying vacancies. Most regional and super-regional malls earn well in excess of one million dollars and some malls in excess of two millions dollars annually from their pop-up business programs.

Malls have the best opportunities and facilities to develop a seasonal and a year-round pop-up leasing program by leasing *kiosks* on the interior mall common area or in-iine vacant spaces—or until the spaces are leased to a permanent tenant. It's common for mall developers to assign the marketing and leasing of their pop-up lease program to a full-time leasing agent whose primary responsibility is to market, lease, and administer the pop-up lease program.

Strip Shopping Centers and Pop-Up Businesses

Strip shopping centers may lease in-line spaces and a small defined area in the parking lot to pop-up businesses. For example, Halloween costume stores will lease space for the month of October. Automobile and RV dealers may lease space in the parking lot for weekend blow-out sales. The real estate manager must be certain that the shopping center has plenty of spaces to accommodate the shoppers, and that no tenant's lease and the common area agreements between the anchor tenants and owner prohibit such use of the parking lot.

Operational Issues with Pop-Up Businesses

When entering into a license agreement with a pop-up business, the real estate manager should adhere to the principles of building a good tenant mix. The tenant should not conflict with any of the existing uses within the shopping center. For example, a sporting goods business wanted to use an empty store during the holiday season in December. The shopping center did not have a sporting goods store and the real estate manager knew the use would be a good complement to the existing tenant mix. Because the store was temporary, the real estate manager asked for a higher rent per square foot and full contributions to the *common area maintenance (CAM),* real estate tax, and insurance costs. The merchant did so well during the season that the real estate manager was able to negotiate a short-term lease to enable the tenant to evaluate a permanent location in the shopping center—eventually, the tenant leased a permanent space.

A pop-up business should be subject to all of the same restrictions that apply to a permanent business—it's not fair to burden them with rules and regulations and allow the short-term tenants to be free of them. One major exception is signage. A professionally prepared temporary sign is allowed because it is impossible to amortize the cost of most standard signs during the short occupancy period.

In addition to bringing in a line of merchandise that may ultimately complement the shopping center year round, the pop-up business often provides seasonal merchandise that would not otherwise be offered. Christmas trees on a vacant parcel attract customers that might not otherwise come to the shopping center.

Consideration must be given to the temporary tenant's impact on other tenants in the property. Each offer for a temporary space must be evaluated for its potential positive and negative impact on the shopping center. In all cases, the pop-up business should receive an agreement that allows for quick cancellation in case a permanent tenant is located and leases the space.

As mentioned, regional malls generate well over $1 million each year from pop-up businesses. Strip shopping centers can also generate several thousands of dollars from these programs.

POP-UP BUSINESSES FOR OFFICE AND INDUSTRIAL PROPERTIES

Even though pop-up tenants for shopping centers seems to be the most common way to fill vacant space, there is a new pop-up trend in office building space that started in New York in Midtown Manhattan. Due to the struggling economy in the wake of the Great Recession, many commercial tenants were leaving the area, downsizing their office space, or searching for less-costly rental prices. However, more tourists were still visiting New York and looking for places to stay overnight. In an effort to fill vacant office space, the pop-up hotel concept became a trend. Although it is still not a mainstream concept, real estate managers will continue to see increasingly creative uses for vacant office building space in the future.

For vacant industrial space, however, the trends in this market are more unique. Real estate managers are seeking interest from local artists who rent vacant space from old warehouses to be used for art shows and exhibits, while other industrial spaces can be used for local farmer's markets on weekends. These tenants are interested in large open areas that provide great windows for lighting. For these types of pop-up businesses, they are willing to pay fees at an hourly or daily rate. As more traffic is drawn to the area, tenants will become more interested in long-term leases.

MAINTAINING MARKET RENTS

If a property owner does not stay current with market rents, it is easy to lease space a few dollars per square foot below market. A two dollar under marker rate on a 3,000-square-foot space is a loss of $6,000 of rent and using an eight percent cap rate, the building's value is $75,000 less. If spaces continue to be leased below value, the loss in value compounds from space to space. The real estate manager conducts a market survey when he or she assumes the management of a property and periodically updates the survey. The analysis of the survey is presented to the property owner with recommended rental rates. When leases are renewed and spaces released, tenants are paying market rents.

Some property owners seek value in their buildings that the market does not perceive. They are too aggressive in their rental rates and spaces that become vacant will remain vacant until the rents are adjusted to market rents. The real estate manager's survey and analysis of the market, followed by a discussion with the property owner will provide the necessary market data for the property owners to establish market rents for the building.

TENANT BUY-OUTS

One of the great opportunities in leasing is a tenant *buy-out*. Some retailers are downsizing their space needs, and many older retail concepts are not able to compete in today's market. If such tenants occupy space at below-market rates, buying them out and re-leasing their spaces may make sense—especially if the property may be sold or refinanced in the near future. There are endless approaches to the terms of a buy-out of an existing tenant's lease. Before approaching a tenant with a buy-out offer, the real estate manager should find out if the tenant is willing to pay a fee to have its lease cancelled. There is no standard formula to determine the amount of a buy-out. If the tenant is unwilling to offer the property owner a buy-out, and if a buy-out makes economic sense, or if finding a stronger replacement tenant is advisable, an owner buy-out has two common approaches:

1. **Tenant's benefit**—Estimate the profit the tenant is taking from the store, multiply that by the years left in the lease, and suggest that the tenant can have the same profit without risk if the property owner buys out the lease. If the tenant's business is not doing well, that may not be a significant number. Of course, the owner has to be able to recapture the cost of the buy-out when the space is re-leased. A tenant may not be doing well or even losing money and would welcome an opportunity for a mutual lease cancellation. The question is, who pays whom to cancel the lease?
2. **Owner's benefit**—Consider the income from the existing tenant. For example, compare the tenant's 5,000 square feet at $12 per square foot with the current market value of the space split into two stores at $23.20 per square foot. The difference is $56,000 in rent or $700,000 in value if the increased income is capitalized at eight percent. If the cost of the division is $100,000, the owner could spend up to $600,000 buying out the tenant and still break even. Obviously, the offer would start substantially below that point and would consider other benefits and drawbacks of making the change. A property owner can accomplish a buy-out with a greater comfort level if the replacement tenants are committed before the deal is negotiated.

If a property owner negotiates a buy-out without a tenant in hand, the owner is safer to make the buy-out conditional on getting a suitable replacement, with a time limit for the tenant's benefit. The market can easily change midstream, and the anticipated profit can quickly become a painful loss.

Another consideration when estimating the cost of the buy-out is the expense of re-leasing the space, which may include a commission, no rent for a few or several months while the space is being built out, and tenant improvement costs. If a buy-out seems to make sense, but the owner does not have the cash, the tenant may still accept the offer and take the payment over time at a reasonable interest rate or at a slightly higher price.

Buy-outs, store splits, and recapture of under-utilized spaces can be very complicated. Such deals may require convincing tenants of their benefits, and they can demand a great deal of time to finalize. Once an agreement has been reached, it should immediately be documented and signed by the parties. Either party can easily back out of a verbal arrangement.

The real estate manager should analyze the benefits and cost of a buyout. The following questions will be a component of the analysis:

1. Is the existing tenant an asset to the property?
2. Is the tenant struggling or needing to downsize?
3. Is there a better tenant for the space?
4. How long will it take to release the space?
5. What is the cost to divide a space into two or more spaces. This cost may be surprising.
6. What additional rent can be charged for the space?
7. Will a tenant improvement allowance be necessary to release the space, and if so, what is the estimated cost of these improvements?
8. Is there a marketing cost?
9. What is the cost of the lease commission?
10. Will there be any other costs?

Compare the above costs to the cost, if any, to retain the tenant and include the lost non-monetary opportunity to replace the tenant. Develop and support your recommendation.

THE BENEFITS OF A STATE-OF-THE-ART LEASE

It is easy and convenient for a property owner to continue to use a lease form that is several years old. Leases evolve as the industry, laws, and governmental regulations change and new ones are enacted. One of the changes in leases over the past few decades are the expenses that are included in pass-through operating expenses that were not included. For years, capital improvements were not pass-through charges. Today, these expenses are a pass-through expense included in the CAM charges if they are included in the CAM lease provision. Capital improvements to the common area, such as replacing carpet and wall covering in hallways in office buildings are an acceptable pass-through expense. Replacing carpet in enclosed malls is an acceptable CAM expense. Upgrading mechanical equipment that will reduce energy usage is an acceptable pass-through charge.

Tenants will negotiate to amortize the cost of these improvements over their useful life. For years, shopping center owners charged an administrative fee as a percentage of the CAM cost instead of the management fee to CAM. The management fee is much greater than the administrative fee. It is currently standard for the management fee to be a CAM expense. The lease should be included in the pass-through reimbursements and CAM provisions. The reimbursement of these expenses will increase the property's cash flow and enhance its value. The real estate manager should encourage its clients to have their attorney periodically review its lease and propose updated changes.

LEASING OPPORTUNITIES

There are always leasing opportunities to explore for increasing a property's cash flow and value. The real estate manager should consider if any of the opportunities explained in this chapter are appropriate for the property or properties being managed. Every opportunity should be considered, and when appropriate, analyze and discuss with the property owner.

CHAPTER

12

Developing a Leasing Program

Real estate management provides a platform for developing several sources of income—management fees are the primary source. Real estate management is a very labor-intensive service business, and clients are demanding of the services they require of real estate managers. The fees to manage properties are often a low-profit margin. These fees alone may not cover all the company's expenses or generate a profit for the company. A firm's portfolio of properties provides several opportunities to provide additional services to clients while generating ancillary income. Adding transactions can significantly increase a firm's income and profit margins. Many firm's profits are derived from their ancillary services which includes transaction income. Leasing can be a very profitable source of income.

An equally or possibly more important reason to add leasing to the services a real estate management company offers is leasing is often the property owner's number-one concern. There are two means to increase the *net operating income (NOI)* of a property. First is through effective building operations. An effective maintenance management program will reduce operating expenses during the first year and minimize future increases of annual operating expenses. The second means to increase the NOI is by increasing income.

There are many more opportunities to increase the NOI through leasing than there are opportunities to increase the NOI through operating expense reduction. Once a property has an efficient and cost-effective maintenance management program, expenses cannot be lowered every year. There are numerous opportunities to increase income and a property's value by developing a comprehensive leasing plan. The market must be monitored to keep rents at market levels. For instance, vacancies can be leased more effectively to reduce downtime, while the tenant mix of a property can be enhanced. Lease renewals should not be automatic but analyzed as to whether or not to seeking a better tenant is a good idea. Non-credit tenants could be replaced with credit tenants in order to increase the value of the property. The real estate management company may assume this responsibility and bring additional value to its clients.

This chapter focuses primarily on developing a leasing capability within a real estate management company and training real estate managers to serve as leasing agents for properties they manage. Other complimentary transaction activities are discussed to broaden the menu of services that real estate management companies can offer clients, while generating new sources of revenue for the real estate management company. The number-one goal is to bring additional value to the clients, and when that is accomplished, the real estate management firm will generate additional income.

BENEFITS OF IN-HOUSE LEASING

One of the differences between commercial and residential real estate management is that commercial real estate managers often have the opportunity to lease industrial, retail, office, or medical office space, while residential real estate managers usually supervise the on-site leasing team.

Developing an in-house leasing capability for a commercial real estate management company has five benefits:

1. An effective leasing program enables the real estate management firm to better serve its clients and meet their goals and objectives. A survey of property owners by the Institute of Real Estate

Management (IREM) reported that five of the six most important responsibilities of the real estate manager are leasing-related tasks.

2. An effective leasing program is an important component of a real estate management firm's client-retention program. Some property owners prefer to assign the real estate management and leasing function to one firm.
3. The management company will have the opportunity to submit management proposals on properties for which the owner prefers to use one firm for managing and leasing properties.
4. Leasing allows commercial real estate managers the opportunity to increase their compensation by generating lease commissions.
5. Leasing gives commercial real estate managers the chance to increase their company's earnings by generating lease commissions.

The real estate management firm must consider several factors before entering the leasing arena. If a firm decides to offer leasing services, its leasing program must be planned, coordinated, and supervised to be effective. Inexperienced real estate managers will need training. Each real estate manager's portfolio must be analyzed to determine its leasing potential. The real estate manager must have sufficient time to fulfill all the management responsibilities and effectively implement a plan to lease the vacancies and handle renewals.

Some properties in the portfolio may be located in an area where the real estate manager may not be able to efficiently and effectively lease the property. The leasing task for some properties may be so time consuming that the real estate manager is not the right person to lease the property. It is best for the client and the real estate management firm not to lease these properties. The real estate management firm should only assume the marketing and leasing of properties it is confident it can provide a service equal, or superior to, that of other firms in the area. Assuming that the real estate management firm should lease every property in its management portfolio is not always prudent. "Impossible" leasing tasks can jeopardize a management account. A brokerage firm can more effectively lease some properties.

Proper incentives are one of the best methods to motivate performance. Commission splits between a real estate management firm and its real estate managers are typically different from those between a brokerage firm and its full-time leasing agents. The leasing agent's entire income depends on commissions. They receive no salary and very few of their expenses are reimbursed. On the other hand, a real estate manager has a good base salary, expense reimbursements, and usually a year-end performance bonus.

An important area that is easy to overlook is lease preparation and administration. Whose lease form will be used? Who will prepare or draft the lease and administer the leasing function? The next section reviews the process for establishing a leasing program in a real estate management company and providing real estate managers with the incentive to aggressively implement a marketing and leasing program for some of all of the properties in their portfolio.

Advantages of In-House Leasing to the Real Estate Management Team

Many commercial real estate management firms report that their management fees do not cover all their operating expenses. Leasing commission income and other income, such as tenant improvement supervision fees, commissions from sales, consulting, serving as an expert witness, and refinancing fees are essential to the commercial real estate management firm's profitability. Without these ancillary income sources, many firms would be unprofitable.

Another benefit of a leasing program is retention of good real estate managers who enjoy the challenge and the financial rewards of leasing. The opportunity to increase one's compensation by earning commission income plays an important role in a real estate manager's decision to stay with a firm or accept an opportunity with another firm. Commission splits between the real estate management firm and the real estate manager are an important component of the firm's employee-retention program.

Advantages of In-House Leasing to the Real Estate Manager

Leasing activities are important to the commercial real estate manager for several reasons. First, leasing represents an opportunity to increase the real estate manager's income. Real estate managers typically have the assurance of a regular paycheck but limited opportunities to earn significant performance income. A year-end incentive bonus based on the company's profitability and the real estate manager's performance is usually the only additional income available to most residential real estate managers. Commission income has the potential to be a major source of income for commercial real estate managers.

Real estate managers with firms that offer a good commission incentive can increase their annual income by 20 to 50 percent and occasionally even by a greater percentage. This is an excellent component of an employee-retention program. Several methods of sharing commissions between real estate management firms and real estate managers are possible. Commission splits are discussed later in this chapter.

Leasing provides additional challenges and broadens a real estate manager's knowledge and experience. Leasing activity is a welcome diversion from the challenges of dealing with tenants, maintenance problems, reviewing financial reports, and writing monthly management reports. Successfully leasing a property has a positive effect on a property's income, NOI, and value; it also creates a sense of pride in the real estate manager's performance. Few, if any, other activities make a property owner happier than signing leases—especially in a soft market.

Commission income positively affects the fees a real estate manager's portfolio generates, and it can make the difference in whether a real estate manager's portfolio is profitable. The executive of real estate management companies must recognize that some real estate managers prefer not to lease and others may not be effective at leasing. These real estate managers may be great real estate managers, but lack the aptitude or interest to lease. These real estate managers play an important role in the company and serving the company's clients. For instance, when a commercial real estate management firm in the northwest added leasing to its services, it decided to only hire future real estate mangers who had the skill, aptitude, and interest in managing and leasing the properties in their portfolio. This strategy was reflected in the firm's bottom line.

Advantages of In-House Leasing to Clients

The property owner derives several advantages when the real estate management company assigns the leasing to the real estate manager. When the real estate manager serves as the leasing agent, the owner needs to communicate with just one person regarding management and leasing activities. The owner has the advantage of talking to the real estate manager, who knows more about the property than anyone else.

If the property is a shopping center, the real estate manager knows the competition, the trade area's *demographics* and *psychographics*, the shopping center's strengths and weaknesses, and its tenant mix. With this information, the real estate manager can identify underrepresented businesses in the trade area and develop a marketing strategy to attract, contact, and lease to those businesses.

If the property is an office building, the real estate manager understands the micro-market and can assess the building's position in the market and relationship to the competition to determine which types of users are the best potential tenants.

TENANT RETENTION

Property owners are always concerned with keeping their buildings full and achieving the maximum income from their buildings. That can be achieved through an effective marketing and leasing program and a good tenant-retention program.

During a depressed commercial real estate market, an IREM study of property owners found that the management task that received the highest rating was tenant retention. But even in a strong, stabilized market, property owners are concerned with retaining their tenants because replacing tenants is more costly than keeping existing tenants. Following in importance after retaining tenants, property owners reported that negotiating leases and obtaining tenants were the next most important management tasks.

Five of the six top-rated real estate management tasks in the IREM study were focused on leasing or tenant-retention tasks. The study also asked real estate owners which trends affect real estate. Of the 63 trends listed, vacancy was rated highest. Clearly, the most important issue for property owners was keeping a building fully occupied. This is accomplished more through an effective leasing and tenant-retention program than through any other program undertaken by the real estate manager. Though this study has not recently been updated, it is safe to assume property owners have the same concerns especially during depressed markets such as the Great Recession.

Leasing Effort

Greater opportunities to enhance the value of a property are found by increasing a building's occupancy than by reducing operating expenses. Most property owners focus more on leasing progress than on management activities. A successful leasing program is the most effective component of a client-retention program. A property owner may overlook minor discrepancies in the financial reports or delays in completing management activities, but if the leasing program is unsuccessful, the property owner will give the leasing to another company, and the real estate management account may be in jeopardy.

The last 10 to 20 percent of a building is usually the most difficult space to lease in a building, and leasing it usually takes the longest time and the most effort. When the lease-up reaches this point, leasing agents for brokerage firms often turn their attention to another assignment where commissions are more likely to be earned. They may spend little time attempting to lease the remaining space in the building. However, the profit from a building with typical financing usually comes from the rents on the last 15 percent or less of the space leased. Leasing the last 10 to 15 percent of a building is critical to its cash flow. The real estate manager, who knows the building and the market, can take on the assignment of leasing the remaining vacant space to bring the building to 100-percent occupancy.

Leasing agents for brokerage firms are usually not interested in the assignment of re-leasing one or several small spaces in a building. Re-leasing one or two spaces in a shopping center—unless they are large spaces such as anchor spaces—is seldom an effective use of a retail leasing agent's time. If the real estate manager's workload allows time for leasing, he or she can effectively re-lease space in shopping centers, office buildings, medical office buildings, and industrial properties. The real estate manager is the best person to handle lease renewals. Seldom does the real estate manager have the time to handle the leasing of all the space for a new building. That responsibility is best performed by a full-time leasing agent or a couple of leasing agents.

TRAINING THE REAL ESTATE MANAGER FOR LEASING

The executive real estate manager should develop a leasing training program for inexperienced real estate managers and an ongoing training program for experienced real estate managers.

All real estate management associations have leasing seminars. IREM offers courses on marketing and leasing office buildings as well as shopping centers and retail properties. The courses are available in classroom, home study, and on-line formats. The International Council of Shopping Centers (ICSC) offers leasing classes at its Management Institute and University of Shopping Centers; it offers a leasing designation. Building Owners and Managers Institute (BOMI) offers a course on Marketing and Leasing Office Buildings. Each of these organizations has several publications on leasing commercial properties.

Some areas have commercial real estate listing services and many of these organizations offer commercial real estate classes including classes on lease.

EIGHT STEPS TO SUCCESSFUL LEASING

Successfully leasing a building involves the following eight steps:

1. Understanding the property owner's goals and objectives
2. Understanding the property and its position in the market
3. Understanding the market conditions
4. Being able to identify likely prospective tenants
5. Prospecting
6. Networking
7. Marketing
8. Understanding and negotiating the lease

Each step can be learned. Every real estate manager can be effective in leasing a building by following these eight steps.

Property Owner's Goals and Objectives

The real estate manager must first meet with the property owner and discuss the goals and objectives for the building. The most obvious goal would be to lease the property on the best terms in the shortest time. However, if the property ownership has limited funds (i.e., a negative cash flow, a limited positive cash flow, or limited resources), the leasing plan must also be tailored to achieve other goals and objectives.

For instance, if a property owner has limited or no funds for tenant improvements, one goal would be to lease space in "as-is" condition and to provide either additional free rent or a lower rental rate. In another situation, a property owner may intend to sell the building in 12 to 18 months and, to increase the NOI, might be willing to offer additional tenant improvements to tenants who pay a higher rental rate. Yet, another property owner or developer may need to attain a certain building occupancy level by a particular date to obtain financing. In some cases, if the building's occupancy falls below a certain level, the property owner may be required to pay down the loan balance. Such an owner may be willing to provide additional concessions to accelerate the building's lease-up.

The Property and its Position in the Market

The second step, understanding the property, seems simple. Who knows a property better than the real estate manager does? However, understanding a property from a marketing and leasing perspective is different from understanding the management and operations of the property. For instance, if the property is an office building, does the floor plate appeal to small or large users? If the property is a shopping center, which merchants would enhance the synergism of the shopping center's tenant mix? What are the property's attributes and deficiencies? How does the property compare to its competition?

Market Conditions

The real estate manager can better understand the market by conducting periodic surveys that indicate which buildings are the primary competition; where the majority of the vacancies in the area are located; what the other buildings' rental rates, tenant charges, and rental concessions are; and how the subject building compares with the competition. Using this information, the real estate manager can determine the building's position in the market and its market rental rates and can then price each space accordingly.

Prospective Tenants

After assembling the information from the first three steps, the real estate manager can determine which types of tenants are likely candidates for the property. Office building tenants typically relocate within three to five miles of the building they occupy. When an office building real estate manager knows the building's floor plate size and configuration, he or she can contact prospects and have these space requirements. The office building's classification,

Class A, B, or C, will also help define the target market for the building. The market survey for a shopping center indicates which retail and service uses are over- and under-represented in the trade area. The analysis of the property's tenant mix indicates which uses the shopping center needs. The trade area's demographics and psychographics are an indicator of which merchants and restaurants to pursue. The shopping center real estate manager can combine this information and the space requirements of different categories of retail tenants to develop a list of likely prospects for each vacant space.

Prospecting

Prospecting is the most time-consuming activity of the marketing and leasing program. Prospecting includes canvassing in person, by phone, and e-mail. Good signage, working the brokerage community, keeping in contact with the building's existing tenants, and being involved in the community are important components of the building's marketing and leasing program.

Networking

The brokerage community is a great source of prospects. Many commercial leasing agents represent tenants with the assignment to them one of multiple locations for their businesses. Networking with the commercial brokerage community, especially leasing agents who specialize in the property type and possibly geographic area, is a rich source of prospects.

Marketing

Seldom do commercial buildings have a marketing budget more than a few thousand dollars. The two most effective means to advertise a commercial building are placing a sign on the property and placing the property on commercial real estate internet listings. There are national internet listing sites and some areas have regional sites.

THE LEASE AND NEGOTIATIONS

Many real estate managers and leasing agents are initially intimidated by the building's lease. Typically, 20 to 60 pages with a small font can be imposing; however, nothing in a lease is too complicated for any real estate professional to understand. The real estate manager should develop a thorough knowledge of each lease provision by spending a couple of hours reviewing the lease with an experienced real estate manager or leasing agent. An attorney can explain a few provisions that seem complicated. Lease provisions are discussed in *Chapter 10: Negotiating the Commercial Lease.*

The majority of the leases the real estate manager negotiates are with small businesses. Some of these businesses handle their own lease negotiations, while a leasing agent or an attorney will represent others. If the real estate manager has completed the previously mentioned steps to successfully leasing a building, he or she is ready to negotiate a lease.

In reality, negotiations do not resemble a chess match with each player trying to defeat the other. The great majority of business people know that the best-negotiated deals are win-win situations. Each party usually gives a little in order to reach a compromise. If the parties are far apart in their positions regarding the business terms, either the tenant cannot afford the space or the property owner cannot afford the tenant.

To be successful at lease negotiations, the real estate manager must be knowledgeable about the market conditions and the property owner's goals and objectives. In addition, he or she should understand the lease, be flexible, and prepared to recommend to the property owner to walk away from a poor deal.

In-House Training

A series of in-house seminars can be developed and presented once a week or once a month for a fixed period, or they can be ongoing. The mini-seminars can include outside speakers, such as attorneys, leasing agents, tenants' in-house real estate representatives, space planners, and tenant improvement contractors, along with the firm's own experienced real estate managers. Sessions can be devoted to a variety of topics, including the following:

- Analyzing a specific property and its tenant mix
- Discussing a complicated deal
- Reviewing a challenging leasing situation
- Reporting on market conditions and activities
- Discussing how to negotiate lease provisions
- Reviewing each property's leasing status
- The space planning process
- The timeline to build out a space including:
  - Selecting the tenant improvement contractors
  - Space planning construction drawings
  - Permitting process
  - Construction and final inspection
  - Issuance of the *certificate of occupancy (C of O)*

FINDING TIME TO LEASE

The executive real estate manager who decides to enter into or expand the firm's leasing activities must make a commitment to allow real estate managers sufficient time from their management duties to market and lease their properties. When real estate managers do not have the leasing responsibility, frequently it is because the property owner assumes the real estate manager does not have time to lease. Real estate management activities can become all encompassing. Even the real estate manager may wonder how he or she will find the time to devote to leasing. The management of one large property, a portfolio of small and medium properties, or even the management of one small problem property, can undoubtedly become a career activity.

Five criteria determine whether the real estate manager has sufficient time to lease some or all of the properties he or she manages: portfolio size, the property's location, demands of the property owner and clients, availability of support staff, and the real estate manager's efficiency and expertise.

Portfolio Size

A real estate manager who is not involved in leasing can manage a larger portfolio than a real estate manager who assumes that responsibility. It is relatively easy to determine whether the portfolio will be more profitable if the real estate manager takes on the management of more properties without leasing responsibilities, as opposed to taking on fewer properties with leasing responsibilities.

The following is a hypothetical example:

Reducing a real estate manager's portfolio by one 100,000-square-foot shopping center reduces the management fee $70,000. This reduction in portfolio income could be offset by leasing more than 16,500 square feet of new space in the real estate manager's portfolio at $35 per square foot—assuming the leases are co-brokered and the real estate manager received one fifth of the commission. If lease renewals were added to the real estate manager's responsibilities, several thousands of dollars of additional commission income would be earned. Some real estate managers can handle lease renewals without a reduction in portfolio size. Others can assume the leasing of some of the properties in his or her portfolio without a reduction in portfolio size.

By counting the number and square footage of the vacant spaces in the real estate manager's entire portfolio and determining which spaces are likely to lease during the year, as well as which tenants are likely to renew their leases, the executive real estate manager can estimate the potential annual commission. The commission from one or two good-sized spaces can equal or exceed the entire annual management fee for the building. The real estate manager's leasing activities require no time from accounting personnel and little time from the administrative staff. The income earned from leasing commissions requires little time from the rest of the staff.

When comparing potential commission income to the reduction of the management fee income (resulting from reducing the size of the real estate manager's portfolio), the executive real estate manager must remember that the real estate management company is not losing the management fee income. Rather, it is shifting real estate management assignments or incurring additional costs of hiring another real estate manager to manage the one or two properties each real estate manager in the firm gives up to devote time to leasing. The cost of adding one more real estate manager, in this hypothetical situation, is usually less than the management fee from one to three properties, since the company's fixed costs are in place. Without the commitment from the executive real estate manager to avoid overloading the real estate managers' portfolio, the real estate managers will not have adequate time to develop and implement a successful marketing and leasing program.

Property Location

The next criterion in determining whether real estate managers have sufficient time for leasing is the location of the properties in the portfolio. Buildings that are a two-hour drive, or more, from the office steal valuable time from the real estate manager. Travel distance is an important factor when determining the portfolio of each real estate manager along with the firm's management portfolio.

Client or Property Demands

The client or property's demands on the real estate manager's time can be difficult to estimate. Some property owners want to be involved in almost every decision while others rely on the real estate manager's judgment and become involved only in major decisions. Problem properties command a disproportionate amount of the real estate manager's time. When a firm assumes the management of a problem property, the fees should reflect the additional time the real estate manager must devote to it. When a problem arises during the ongoing management of a property, the fee usually is not increased to reflect the extra time and effort necessary to solve the problem. A problem client will take a disproportionate amount of the real estate manager's time.

Support Staff

A critical criterion in determining whether the real estate managers have sufficient time for leasing activity is the number and type of support staff. How many real estate managers share an administrative assistant? If one administrative assistant works for five or six real estate managers, that person can provide only basic clerical support. The administrative assistant who works for two or three real estate managers can assume many of the real estate managerial responsibilities, such as handling maintenance calls and dealing with vendors and contractors. Such assistants assume the responsibilities of both an assistant real estate manager and an administrative assistant.

Relieving the real estate manager of some daily real estate management tasks is an excellent way to provide time for leasing activities. The executive real estate manager should compare the cost of additional administrative support to the potential to earn commission income. Hiring an assistant real estate manager to work with two or three real estate managers may be a cost-effective way to allow real estate managers time to lease their properties without reducing their portfolio size.

When analyzing the cost benefits to include leasing in a real estate manager's responsibility, other sources of income that may be included in the equation are commissions from selling and refinancing properties. Though real estate managers typically do not sell or finance properties on a regular basis, when they do, the commission is usually much greater than a property's one-year management fee. Selling and refinancing properties can be included in the firm's mini seminar topics.

Efficiency and Organization

The final criterion in assessing a real estate manager's time to conduct leasing activities is his or her efficiency and organization. An unorganized and non-proactive person will never survive as a real estate manager. To be successful at leasing, establish specific goals and make a personal commitment to leasing by taking care of management responsibilities. The goals may be the number of square feet of space that the real estate manager expects to lease each quarter and the number of renewals to negotiate annually. The commitment includes devoting a certain amount of time to leasing activities.

The real estate manager must first decide how much time to spend each day on leasing activities and then develop a daily plan. For example, a real estate manager may plan to spend two hours per day on leasing activities. Each day, the real estate manager plans to make a minimum number of cold calls, sends out e-mails, and makes a specific number of follow-up phone calls from messages sent the prior week. Combining time commitment with a well-conceived marketing and leasing plan will produce leasing deals.

Some real estate managers are not interested in leasing. They prefer real estate managerial, operational, and tenant-retention activities and are not comfortable in a "selling" environment. Such real estate managers are well suited to properties that require 100 percent of the real estate management's time, and therefore never provide leasing opportunities. The executive real estate manager will assign a different portfolio of properties to those real estate managers than the portfolio of properties assigned those who want to include leasing in their responsibilities. Another approach is to hire only real estate managers who are interested in leasing.

The real estate management firm's executive real estate managers have considerable control over the time the real estate managers have for leasing. The executive real estate manager is responsible for evaluating the potential income from entering the leasing field and other benefits to gain from providing leasing services to clients. If the conclusion is favorable, the executive real estate manager is responsible for creating an environment that allows the real estate manager's time to develop and implement successful leasing programs on the properties they manage.

SELECTING PROPERTIES TO LEASE

The property owner's objective, with few exceptions, is to lease the property at market rates as quickly as possible. This is obviously also the goal of the real estate management firm. To reach this mutual goal, the executive real estate manager must determine who is the most effective person to lease the property.

A careful selection of the properties managed that offer the best leasing opportunities is important to the commission potential in terms of the time expended for marketing and leasing, the maintenance of a good relationship with the property owner, and most importantly, accomplishing the owner's goals and objectives. It may be important to the client or to client relations that the real estate management assumes the leasing responsibility for a property with leasing problems.

COMMISSION SPLITS

An incentive plan for real estate managers is an important component of a real estate management firm's leasing program. As previously mentioned, a real estate manager has an active and hectic daily schedule, and he or she can easily fill the day with routine management tasks. An income-incentive program, usually in the form of commissions, provides additional motivation for the real estate manager to extend the workday, develop leasing expertise and skills, and aggressively pursue lease deals.

Commissions for leasing agents at brokerage firms were originally 50 percent of the commission paid to the brokerage firm (referred to as "the house"). The incentive commission schedule varies from firm to firm. Most brokerage firms increase the leasing agent's share of the commission as more commission income is earned in an effort to retain and attract the best agents. The agent's share of the commission may increase when the agent's "desk cost" is covered.

For instance, if the desk cost is $100,000, the agent receives 50 percent of the commissions earned until the house receives $100,000. The agent receives a larger share for all additional commissions earned. Some firms charge the broker a monthly fee and allow the broker to keep 80 to 100 percent of the commissions earned. Regardless of the commission split, all leasing agents have one thing in common—they do not receive a salary. The leasing agents also pay for all or most of their out-of-pocket expenses.

Since the real estate manager receives a good salary, providing a commission split to the real estate manager similar to that received by leasing agents is unrealistic. The split between the real estate management firm and real estate managers should reflect the importance of commission income to the firm and provide an additional and proper incentive to the real estate managers to aggressively implement leasing programs for properties in their portfolios. When determining commission splits, the executive real estate manager must address three issues: (1) what share of commissions the real estate managers will receive; (2) whether an incentive should be offered, and if so, the amount of the incentive; and (3) how a commission will be shared with a real estate manager who brings a tenant to a property managed by a co-real estate manager.

The real estate management industry has no standard commission splits. The commission splits discussed in this chapter have been successful for several companies and are intended to serve as a point of discussion for executive real estate managers and real estate managers.

Some firms pay their real estate managers a fixed-commission percentage, regardless of whether the commission is earned from new leases or renewal leases. Real estate managers may earn 10 to 30 percent of the commission paid to the firm.

Another approach is to offer a different commission split for new leases and renewals. There are two reasons for that approach:

1. The commission for new leases is often twice that for renewals. On a new lease, the real estate management firm earns more income and can share more of the income with the real estate managers.
2. It usually takes more time to market a space, find a prospect, and negotiate the lease for a new tenant than to renew an existing tenant's lease.

The real estate manager may have an incentive, in the form of a large share of the commission, if specific annual leasing goals are met. For instance, the real estate manager may earn 20 percent of the commission on renewing half of the tenants whose leases expire and 25 percent of the commission on the remaining lease renewals. A portfolio-specific leasing goal is established, and if the real estate manager exceeds the goal, the commission on new leases above the goal increases from 25 percent to 33 percent. The goal is based on the amount of vacant square footage in the real estate manager's portfolio and the probability of leasing the space.

The commission split for a ground lease, build-to-suit, or sale of a pad site or out parcel is equal to the commission splits of a new tenant. The commission splits offered to real estate managers vary in the industry. A nominal commission for the real estate manager of five to 10 percent of the total commission may not be just compensation for the extra time a real estate manager needs to devote to marketing and leasing. The executive must develop a commission split that provides sufficient incentives to the real estate manager. Such a program will maximize the income earned by the real estate managers and the real estate management company. As previously mentioned, commissions are an excellent means to retain real estate managers.

Leasing Non-Managed Properties

Occasionally, an opportunity may arise to lease a property the real estate management firm does not manage. The property owner may manage the property, but may not have the expertise or time to lease it. Usually, these are small properties with one or two vacancies. New leasing activities often lead to the property owner requesting the real estate management firm to handle the lease renewals. The relationship and trust that can build between the property owner and the real estate manager who handles the leasing can lead into acquiring the management of the property, the opportunity to represent the property owner in acquiring another building, or the sale listing for the property.

Tenant Representation

Occasionally, a real estate manager has an opportunity to represent an office or industrial tenant that is looking for an additional location or a retail tenant that needs several locations. If a prospective tenant's space needs cannot be met at one of the properties in the real estate management firm's portfolio, the real estate manager should attempt to represent the tenant and find the tenant space in another property. The commission may be based on the firm's standard splits, or it may be a higher commission split. The justification for a higher split is that the real estate manager is devoting time in addition to the time necessary to manage and lease the properties in the portfolio and the commission to be earned is not anticipated or budgeted.

A great source of tenant representation opportunities is contacting all the contractors and service providers with which the real estate management company works to learn what their space requirements are and whether the firm can represent them. The real estate management firm has been giving business to these firms for years, and they may want to express their appreciation by allowing the real estate management firm to represent them in fulfilling their space needs. These firms may not even know that the real estate management company with which they have done business for years also does leasing. A real estate management firm in the northwest contacted all the firms with which they did business. They found that a small security firm was looking for new office space, and it gave the assignment to the real estate management firm. A real estate management firm in Texas went through a similar exercise, and received an assignment to find 10,000 square feet of office space for an engineering firm with which they had provided business to for more than 10 years.

The real estate manager may be able to generate additional tenant representation leasing opportunities through his or her community and neighborhood activities. Often, a friend or neighbor needs representation in finding and negotiating an office space or a second retail location. Membership in business and civic organizations can provide such tenant representation opportunities.

Commission Overrides

Some property owners use a brokerage firm to lease their property but request that the real estate management firm supervise the leasing agent. The real estate management firm receives a leasing commission override for this service expressed in dollars per square foot or a percentage of the income earned from the lease. The real estate manager earns a share of the commission override.

Incentive Commissions

Many brokerage firms commonly pay incentive commissions. The justification for an increased commission split is to reward extraordinary performance and to retain top producers. The typical incentive is to increase the leasing agent's or real estate manager's share of the commission as the individual's productivity rises. Some brokerage firms and property owners with in-house leasing personnel increase the agent's share of the commission splits when the agent's commissions or number of square feet of space leased exceeds a predetermined amount. For example, after the brokerage firm's share of the commission earned by a leasing agent exceeds $75,000 or the property owner's leasing agent leases 40,000 square feet, the agent's share of the commission increases by 10 to 20 percent.

That procedure works well for brokerage firms because their agents, in theory, have the entire universe to lease. However, the real estate manager's leasing activity is usually limited to the properties he or she manages. An alternative to establishing an incentive based on a predetermined square footage of leased space or commission dollars earned for the firm is to establish incentive criteria based on exceeding the leasing projections established for each property in the annual management or business plan and budget. This is a fair approach for several reasons. Each real estate manager's portfolio has different amounts of vacant space with different degrees of probability of leasing the space. The incentive goal based on a fixed amount of square footage for all real estate managers excludes some real estate managers from achieving the goal while others may achieve the goal with little effort. The real estate manager and property owner have discussed which vacant spaces are likely to be leased during the next budgeted year. The real estate manager played a role in establishing the leasing goals. The incentive helps generate additional income for the real estate management firm, which bases its commission income projection on the space it expects to lease in each property it manages. The commission income from additional space leased will exceed the firm's budgeted commission income.

The executive real estate manager meets with each real estate manager, reviews the lease projections established by the property owner and real estate manager, and using these projections, establishes leasing goals. Once the real estate manager exceeds the goal (whether measured by dollars of commission earned or square footage of space leased), the real estate manager's share of the commission might increase by 10 to 20 percent of the commission the real estate management company earns. Once 50 to 100 percent of the projected renewal space has been renewed, the real estate manager's share of the commission split might increase by another five to 10 percent.

Commission Splits among Real Estate Managers

Occasionally, a real estate manager finds a tenant who wants to lease space in a building managed by one of the firm's other real estate managers. The real estate manager's share of the total commission, for example 25 percent, could be shared equally between the real estate manager of the property and the procuring real estate manager. The executive real estate manager should develop a commission split that encourages the real estate managers to exceed their leasing goals, maximize the firm's commission income potential, and keep the property fully occupied.

NEGOTIATING THE LEASING COMMISSION AGREEMENT

The property owner and the real estate management firm must enter into a leasing agreement when the firm is awarded the leasing. The following discussion reviews several of the provisions of a leasing agreement. In this discussion, the real estate manager is referred to as the leasing agent and the real estate management firm is referred to as the brokerage firm.

Few contracts are negotiated with more expectations and end with more disputes and unhappy parties than the leasing commission agreement. An unfortunate end to a relationship is unnecessary if the parties negotiate the contract completely so no room is left for misunderstanding.

The first step in engaging the services of a leasing agent is to be sure the person is experienced and active in the type of property involved and knows and understands that market. Some property owners avoid using an agent who is leasing a competing building in the area, but others believe the more space the agent controls in the immediate area, the greater the likelihood of acquiring leases.

The building owner or the leasing agent prepares the lease commission agreement. If the leasing agent's form is used, the real estate manager should evaluate it carefully and make changes where necessary to ensure that the property owner is responsible only for agreed-upon services. Some leasing agreements include commissions for sales, leases made by the owners, extensions of existing leases, and so on. If that is not the desire of the owner, such items must be eliminated.

Contract Period

The contract should be for a specified period, which will vary according to the assignment. If the agreement is for a single store or office, it can be for a shorter time. If, on the other hand, the contract is for a full lease-up of an office building, industrial park, or shopping center, the term of the contract is likely to be fairly long. In any case, the wording of the period of the agreement must be specific and not "until leased up" or "until terminated by either party." The agreement needs to be no less than six months and preferably for one year for the leasing agent to have sufficient time to market the property, show space to prospects, prepare *letters of intent (LOI)*, and negotiate the lease and have both parities execute the lease. The contract can always be extended, and it typically contains other cancellation provisions, which will be discussed later.

Property Leasing Parameters

The contract should list the legal name of the brokerage firm along with the legal name of the owner and the specific property or location to be leased. If the property is an entire office building, the building name should be indicated along with the approximate square footage of the space involved. Attaching a plot plan showing the areas to be leased is useful.

The specific asking rents may be indicated, along with the parameters for leasing (e.g., triple-net lease, base-year lease, five-year term, no options). The asking rent provision also generally indicates "and such other terms and conditions acceptable to the owner of the property."

Leasing Commissions

Commissions are fully negotiable. The contract should clearly state the leasing commissions and when it is paid. The different means to calculate commissions is discussed in *Chapter 14: Financial Analysis for Real Estate Managers.*

If the property owner has a negotiation underway at the time of signing the agreement, that negotiation should be excluded from the agreement in writing to prevent any misunderstanding later. If the owner will negotiate for the anchor tenants and/or the first-floor tenants in an office building, the contract should also state that exclusion to avoid future problems.

Most exclusive leasing agreements exclude commissions on common area costs, utility paybacks, tax and insurance reimbursements, and other extraneous items, but to be sure that both parties understand the deal, the agreement should spell out all of these matters. Typically, the initial leasing agent does not share in a commission on the tenant's future expansion or the exercise of an option. The commission agreement should specifically state these and any other exclusions.

Co-Brokering Commissions

The agreement should indicate the method of sharing commissions for a deal in which another leasing agent is involved. Most commission agreements require that the listing leasing agent cooperate fully with other brokers and that the commission be split between the leasing agents on terms satisfactory to the listing leasing agent. The agreement may also require that the commission be split equally between the leasing agents. In very difficult markets, the agreement may allow the outside leasing agent to receive a full commission and the listing agent to receive a half commission. This results in higher commission cost for the property owner, but it stimulates activity in the brokerage community. The agreement must address this issue. During strong markets, some leasing agents will not share their commissions with a co-broker.

Commission Payment Method

The exclusive authorization to lease defines when and how commissions are to be paid. No standard commissions or standard methods of payment exist. The following are alternative approaches:

- Half of commission due on signing of lease and half due on the commencement of the lease or when base rent commences
- One third due on signing of lease; one third due on commencement of lease; one third due six months after tenant opens for business
- Entire commission due on signing of lease (not common)
- Commission paid over the term of lease on a monthly or annual basis
- Based on the needs or preferences of the property owner
- Based on the needs or preferences of the real estate management or brokerage company

Stating the payment method in the agreement is important for both owner and agent. The agreement should specify who pays for marketing materials, such as brochures, signs on the property, leasing packages, and advertising. These items are fully negotiable and can cause disagreements during the term of the agreement if they are not fully addressed.

Leasing Reports

The agreement requires the agent to provide specific leasing reports. Depending on the leasing assignment, the reports may be provided as often as weekly or as seldom as once a month. In a lease-up situation, if the property owner is local the agent is likely to attend weekly meetings in the property owner's office to discuss the progress of the leasing as well as any problems or ideas. Agents prefer to know up front what the property owner requires in terms of meetings and reports so they can prepare their proposals with full knowledge of those expectations.

Lease Preparation

The agreement should state who will prepare the actual lease documents and who will sign them. It is unusual for an agent to sign an agreement on behalf of a property owner, but it does happen. If the property owner requests the leasing agent or real estate manager to sign the agreement, the authorization should be in writing for each lease. Time is of the essence and both parties agree to prepare documents, forward proposals, and react to and/or approve leases in a timely fashion. Some property owners allow the agent to approve leases that meet a given set of guidelines, and others prefer to give the final approval on all deals—even if they appear to be within preset guidelines.

Commission Agreement Termination

Property owners want the right to cancel the agreement if the property is sold with no further obligation for any deals not approved at the time of the sale. They also want the right to cancel the agreement if the agent is not producing the desired results.

Most agents want the right to follow up on existing deals and to receive a commission if they conclude the leases in a reasonable period after the end of the contract or after cancellation of the agreement. The actual period for the above issue is fully negotiable, but it should be realistic for both parties. At the end of the contract or upon cancellation, within a specified number of days, the agent generally provides a written list of prospects in negotiations or prospects they are in the process of presenting to the property owner. For example, the leasing agent has 120 days to reach a final deal on a lease out for signature. If a lease is completed within the 120-day period, the agent receives a commission; if the lease is not completed within the agreed period, the agent does not receive a commission. If the lease negotiations are complex, the period may need to be extended.

Other Provisions

Most contracts have provisions that do not allow discrimination, that indicate that the relationship is one of agent-owner or independent contractor-owner and not employee-employer, and that specific issues will use arbitration rather than legal action to resolve disputes. Generally, the contract is nontransferable.

The broker will insist on a *hold-harmless provision* for the use of information provided by the property owner that is deemed reliable. Both the property owner and the broker will hold each other harmless from the other's negligent acts. Each will also have liability insurance and name the other as an additional insured and the real estate management company may be required to have *errors and omission (E&O) insurance.*

LEASE ADMINISTRATION

The executive real estate manager must establish a lease administration program to support the marketing and leasing program. This program includes, preparing lease documents, developing marketing materials, and keeping a record of lease restrictions. Some areas have commercial real estate associations that offer a commercial multiple listing service and basic lease documents. If the real estate management firm belongs to this association, they have the right to use its lease forms. This is a great benefit the real estate management firm can offer its clients.

Some property owners prefer to have their attorney prepare each lease, while others allow the real estate management firm to fill in the blanks on the lease and, when necessary, discuss negotiated changes to the form's standard lease provisions with the attorney. If the real estate management firm prepares the lease, it is best to assign the lease preparation to one or two administrative personnel. Real estate managers are typically not attorneys and should not be drafting lease provisions that have been negotiated.

Each real estate manager is usually responsible for preparing marketing tools with assistance from the administrative staff. Marketing materials include brochures, flyers, internet marketing materials, demographic and psychographic reports, traffic counts, and housing and rental prices for retail properties, and so on. Additional information can be found in *Chapter 7: Developing a Marketing and Leasing Plan.* When lease restrictions are provided to a tenant (e.g., *exclusive*, *first right of refusal*), they should be summarized, placed in a leasing control book or electronic file, and distributed to the property owner, real estate manager, and administrative assistant.

LEASE TAKEOVER

The responsibility for leasing a property is exciting for the real estate manager, and it generates great expectations for the property owner. The real estate manager anticipates leasing space that has been vacant for some time. The property owner has confidence that a new marketing and leasing plan will lease the vacant space. The organization and efficiency of the real estate manager and the administrative staff during the leasing takeover directly affect the success of the marketing and leasing program.

When assuming the initial leasing responsibility, the real estate manager and support staff must accomplish many things simultaneously. First, the real estate manager must instill a sense of urgency to everyone involved. Before starting to present space and negotiate leases, the real estate manager must also perform several other tasks. The following sections describe many of those responsibilities.

Property Owner's Goals and Objectives

The real estate manager must meet with the property owners and become aware of their goals and objectives, which will determine the leasing strategy. Leasing the property at market rates as quickly as possible is the obvious goal of just about all property owners. To achieve this goal, the property owner must have available funds to compete in the market, especially if the market is soft. Funds will be needed for *tenant improvement (TI)* allowances and other out-of-pocket concessions as well as to support the building during periods when tenants are provided with free rent. If the property ownership has limited funds, the goal may be to offer fewer tenant allowances or to lease the space in as-is condition and to provide either additional free rent or a lower-base rent.

Agreement on Lease Terms

The real estate manager and property owner must agree on the market rental rates for the building. If the property owner believes space in the building is worth $35.00 per square foot, and the real estate manager's understanding of the building's position in the market will support only $29.00 per square foot, the two must discuss their differences and either resolve them or not enter into an agreement.

The real estate manager must believe that the building is marketable at the terms established and approved by the owner. These terms include asking and deal-making rates; periodic rental increases; the amount of concessions, such as free rent and TI allowances; and the length of the lease. The real estate manager should send the property owner an e-mail summarizing their meeting, and the proposed leasing rates and concessions package for the building.

Lease Form

Many institutional owners require that their lease form be used, while many small development firms, private investors, and pension-fund advisers usually do not have a standard lease form and will use either the building's existing lease form or the real estate management firm's lease form. If the real estate management firm is providing the lease form, the property owner should review and approve the form in writing. A good lease form that is property-specific is an excellent sales tool when marketing the real estate management firm. Some commercial real estate multiple listing services provide lease forms for its members.

Negotiating Lease Provisions

The property owner either authorizes the real estate manager to negotiate lease provisions or insists that an attorney assume this responsibility. Even when the real estate manager negotiates the lease provisions, occasionally situations will arise when the real estate manager will seek an attorney's advice. Will the property owner select the attorney, or will the real estate management firm use its preferred law firm? The ideal situation is for the real estate manager and the attorney to work together in the negotiations of the lease. The real estate managers provided a practitioners perspective on the lease while the attorney provided the legalese perspective.

The real estate manager should always advise clients to have a real estate attorney review each lease that has been negotiated by the property owner or the real estate manager. Some property owners will have their attorneys negotiate the lease while others prefer to have the real estate manager negotiate the lease, then turn it over to the attorney for final review and possibly negotiations.

Lease Approvals

The longer a prospective tenant's lease proposal receives no response, the greater the possibility the tenant will reconsider, withdraw the offer, and lease space in another building. The property ownership should appoint one of its representatives as the party who will review, approve, and sign leases. A real estate manager who receives a lease proposal should immediately review it with the property owner and follow up with a quick response to the prospective tenant—either accepting the terms or presenting a counteroffer. When all parties agree on the terms, the real estate manager should prepare and deliver a lease to the tenant for review and signature. The old adage that "time kills deals" applies to transactions in which one party or service provider does not have a sense of urgency to complete the deal.

Lease Restrictions

Lease restrictions are concessions provided to tenants that include exclusives, first rights of refusal, offer to lease additional space, cancellations rights, prohibitions from placing specific categories of tenants in a particular area of the property, space pocketing, and many more. Lease restrictions that impact the property's marketing and leasing program should be summarized and circulated to everyone on the leasing team.

Shopping centers often have *common area agreements* or *reciprocal easement agreements (REA)* signed by the property owner and major tenants with covenants that may affect the shopping center's leasing program. For instance, the common area agreement may prohibit construction of a building in the parking lot, such as a pad building for a bank or fast-food restaurant. If the property owner does not provide the real estate manager with a summary of these restrictions, the real estate manager or a lease administer must read and summarize each existing lease and review the common area agreements.

Property Inspection

Inspecting the property from a marketing perspective reveals its strengths and weaknesses and suggests improvements that would enhance its marketability. For instance, is the office building's lobby outdated, are the elevator cabs obsolete, and is the lighting level in the corridors too low?

Market Survey

A market survey accomplishes four purposes:

1. Reveals the market rental rates and possible concessions for each building in the area
2. Helps determine the market rates for the subject properties

3. Assists in comparing the subject building's strengths and weaknesses to its competition
4. Positions the property in its market

Without conducting a market survey and understanding the building's position in the market, the real estate manager will be hampered in developing a competitive leasing strategy. The marketing survey is an excellent sales tool to convince the property owner that the real estate manager and the real estate management firm are committed to devoting the time to effectively lease the property. It also educates the property owner to the market condition for the property's micro-market and the market rental rates for the property. *Chapter 8: Preparing to Lease a Building* discusses conducting a market survey and determining rental rates.

Developing Marketing Materials

The type of property and the amount of existing and anticipated vacant space determine the selection of marketing materials, which range from four-color, multipage brochures to two-color, one-page brochures or flyers. More commonly, software publishing programs enable the real estate management firm to produce quality-color marketing materials. The cost of such materials is relatively nominal.

Additional marketing information may include floor plans and plot plans; renderings and photos of the property; lease signs; a list of existing tenants and special building features; demographic and psychographic data; a list of area businesses and major employers; view photos for an office building; and aerial photos, traffic counts, and sales information for a shopping center or other retail property.

The real estate management or leasing agreement states whether the property owner or the real estate management firm is responsible for the cost of the marketing materials. If a brochure is not being created, the out-of-pocket cost of the marketing materials are usually nominal. The real estate manager or an administrative person in the firm will be responsible for preparing or gathering the marketing materials.

Internet Listings

National real estate Internet listing services list properties for sale and lease by geographic area and property type. Several areas of the country have regional Internet listing services. A few areas of the country have commercial multiple-listing services. Such services are invaluable in marketing commercial properties for sale or lease.

Meeting the Building's Tenants

The competition is always *canvassing* the subject property. The real estate manager should canvass the building by visiting the tenants to inform them that he or she is the new leasing agent, inquire into their current and future space needs, and ask if they know of any businesses interested in space in the building. Existing tenants are often sources of leasing leads. A short letter or e-mail and subsequent visits should follow these initial contacts.

Working the Brokerage Community

As soon as the real estate manager has the leasing listing and knows the building's lease terms, the real estate manager should make the brokerage community aware of the real estate management firm's listing and provide information about the building and its vacancies to the brokers. The real estate manager may give leasing agents tours of the building and place publicity notices in newspapers and business journals. The real estate manager might follow the lead of some brokerage firms and periodically e-mail their prospects and other leasing agents a list of all the properties they have for lease and for sale.

Lease Preparation

The firm with an exclusive leasing agreement on a property is usually responsible for preparing the leases. The real estate manager's administrative assistant often handles this task. This person will need the following:

- Supply of lease forms
- Correct landlord's signature block
- Lease with exhibits
- Site or plot plan

- Guarantee document
- Construction exhibit, also known as landlord's and tenant's work
- Sign criteria
- Sample lease provisions such as options and exclusives

Since time is of the essence, the real estate management firm's goal should be to have a lease prepared and mailed or delivered to the prospective tenant within a short time—e.g., within 48 or 24 hours after the lease terms are mutually agreed. Some property owners will have their attorney prepare the leases.

Leasing Meetings and Reports

To communicate the progress of the marketing and leasing program, the real estate manager should schedule monthly or bimonthly meetings with the property owner whenever feasible. If the property owner does not receive leasing updates, he or she may assume the real estate manager is neglecting the leasing effort, which may put the management and leasing account in jeopardy. If the property has a leasing problem, the meetings should be more frequent. If the property owner is not located in the area of the property, the leasing meetings can be conducted via phone conferences.

Issues discussed during the leasing meeting include monthly leasing reports, vacant spaces, prospects who were shown the property, the progress of lease negotiations, recently executed leases, spaces under construction, tenants who have moved out or moved in, leases that expire during the next 12 to 24 months, recent deals in other buildings, and general-market information. Periodic e-mail messages to the property owner on specific leasing activities are a great way to informally keep the property owner aware of the progress of the leasing plan and activities.

Proper Use of Retail Tenants' Sales

The primary reason to receive retail tenants' sales reports is to determine whether they owe *percentage rent,* also known as *overage rent.*

The second use of tenants' sales information is to detect early signs of a tenant with financial problems. A tenant whose business is faltering may become a rent collection problem and eventually will move out of the shopping center when its lease expires or will need to be replaced before that time. This information is used when developing a shopping center's tenant mix and leasing plan.

A third use of tenants' sales information is as a marketing tool. The sales statistics provide valuable information for the marketing and leasing program. First and foremost is whether the tenant is "right" for the shopping center. The tenant's sales for the current year are compared with its previous years' sales, sales for other tenants in the same line of business in the shopping center, and the sales of the entire shopping center. Comparing the current sales with sales during a previous period points to trends that can then be compared with the sales trends of other tenants. This information indicates whether the tenant's business is improving, exceeding the performance of other tenants, or lagging behind the shopping center's performance and industry standards.

The sales analysis of all tenants by business category indicates the strengths and weaknesses of the shopping center's tenant mix. Tenants' sales are studied on a sales-per-square-foot basis. An examination based solely on total sales for a store is relatively meaningless. A tenant occupying 1,000 square feet with sales of $500,000 is probably an excellent performer, but those sales would be poor for most tenants occupying 10,000 square feet. The shopping center's average sales per square foot and categories of tenants' sales per square foot are useful marketing tools when leasing a shopping center.

A prospective tenant will be more likely to lease space at a shopping center whose sales are above national averages. The rent a retail or service tenant can afford is directly related to its actual or potential sales volume. If the shopping center's sales are strong, a tenant will be willing and able to pay higher rent. The individual tenant's sales information is confidential; however, it should never be divulged. The shopping center or categorical statistics of tenants' average sales per square foot do not reveal any one tenant's figures. The sales reports also enable the real estate manager to analyze each tenant's performance and determine the strengths and weaknesses of the shopping center's tenant mix and leasing plan.

Managing Vacant Space

One component of the marketing and leasing program that is easy to overlook is managing vacant space. The first step in managing vacant space is ensuring that the space is always ready to present to a prospective tenant or a leasing agent.

During the construction phase, the real estate manager must develop a working relationship with the general contractor's superintendent. The real estate manager should explain why vacant space that is not under construction must be clean at all times. During the final stages of construction and during the subsequent tenant improvement construction period, construction workers may store materials in vacant spaces and use these areas as a place for their breaks. All stored material should be neatly stacked in one corner of the vacant space, and construction workers must properly dispose of their trash. The vacant spaces should be inspected periodically.

One of the first things a prospective tenant does when inspecting a vacant space in an office building is to walk up to and look out the window, so the windows and sills must be kept clean. When all the construction crews have completed their work, and tenant improvement work is not in progress, the real estate manager and maintenance personnel should inspect the vacancies at least monthly. It is embarrassing to take a prospective tenant into a vacant space and have to apologize for its condition. The condition of the vacant space is one of the first impressions the prospects have of the building and the operations of the property.

The next step in managing vacant space is to price each space according to its value. Ground-floor space, upper-floor space, and spaces with views, especially water views, have greater value in an office building. A prestigious location in an office building is important to some firms and not to others. A law firm may be willing to pay a premium to lease the top floor for its image—whereas a national insurance company may prefer to lease space on a lower floor at a lower rate.

Center court and point locations are usually 100-percent locations in a shopping center. Retail spaces with good visibility and shallow depths have greater value than deep spaces that are difficult to locate. Premium locations should be reserved for experienced and/or creditworthy tenants who will pay a premium rate, produce high sales, and offer a strong possibility of paying percentage rent. Location is critical to the success of some tenants, while it has limited value for others. Jewelry and specialty candy stores desire center court locations in a mall, while a rental formal wear store or shoe repair store may prefer a secondary location with much lower rent. Stores selling impulse items need good visibility and a great number of people passing by, whereas a destination tenant relies on advertising, referrals, and customer loyalty.

The real estate manager should not break up large blocks of space in an office building or several contiguous small shop spaces in a shopping center; such spaces should be held for large users if other space is available for small users. All or most of the other space in the building should be leased before these spaces. A tenant who wishes to lease a portion of such spaces should be placed at either end of the vacant area and contiguous space should be leased until all the space has been filled. When two tenants lease portions of a large block of space, they should be given adjacent space or space at opposite ends, so the remaining space is as large a block as possible.

In a soft market, it is tempting to offer every prospect any vacant space. Prospective tenants understand, however, when the real estate manager explains why the owner will not lease 3,000 square feet to a tenant on a vacant 15,000-square-foot floor in an office building if space is available on other floors. The property owner, real estate manager, and leasing agent must have the discipline and courage to direct prospective tenants away from large blocks of space or locations reserved for a more appropriate use.

Partnering with a Brokerage Firm

Sometimes it is in the best interests of the property owner for the real estate management firm to partner with a brokerage company that can bring expertise, presence, and a depth of resources that will enhance the leasing effort. An office building may have a large vacancy or a shopping center may have several vacancies, and the real estate manager may lack sufficient time to lease all of it. A partnership with a leasing firm might assign the marketing and prospecting responsibility to the leasing firm, while the supervision of the marketing effort, negotiating and drafting the lease, and communicating with the property owner remain with the real estate manager. A partnership with a leasing firm may also be useful in leasing a specialty building, such as a medical office building, for which few leasing professionals have the expertise and contacts to successfully lease the building. If a shopping center is in a rural area, a real estate manager may assign leasing to local retailers to a local brokerage firm, while the real estate manager remains responsible for leasing to regional and national retailers.

The real estate management firm and a leasing company can share the commissions in several ways. If the real estate manager supervises the leasing agent, the leasing agent usually receives all of the commission, and the property owner pays the real estate management firm a leasing commission override. Another approach is for the leasing company to receive the major share of the commission, e.g., 75 to 90 percent, while the real estate management firm receives the balance.

When both companies are prospecting for tenants, the commission may be shared 50/50 on all leases, or the firm that procures the tenant and negotiates the lease may receive a larger share of the commission, e.g., 75 percent, while the other firm receives the balance. Another approach is for the firm that procures the tenant and negotiates the lease to receive all of the commission. This approach could lead to competition between the firms and disputes over who first contacted a prospect. The best choice provides each firm with a portion of the commission for each lease.

Partnering with In-House Leasing Agents

If the real estate management firm has full-time leasing agents or real estate management is a division of a brokerage firm, the real estate manager and the leasing agent can jointly lease the property. The real estate manager has a relationship with the property owners, and knows the building and its tenants. The leasing agent devotes 100 percent of its time to leasing and has leasing contacts. They may share the commission by applying any of the commission splits previously discussed. The real estate manager may offer to share the lease renewal commission with the leasing agent as an incentive for the agent to become a member of the leasing team and share the commissions for new leasing.

It is critical to the success of the leasing program that the real estate manager and leasing agent work collaboratively to lease the property. The real estate manager must appreciate the role of the leasing agent and the leasing agent must appreciate the role of the real estate manager. If the leasing agent is in-house, the manager of the leasing division and the manager of the real estate management division must model the behavior they expect of their personnel.

ADDITIONAL TRANSACTION OPPORTUNITIES

Once leasing has been added to the services offered by real estate managers, the executive real estate manager should consider two additional transaction activities: sales and refinancing. These activities provide the firm's clients with valuable services, and they can generate far greater income than leasing activities. The biggest obstacle to adding these two services is the fear of the unknown. Most real estate managers have not been responsible for selling or refinancing properties, yet most have assisted in the due diligence necessary to sell or refinance a property.

One of the best ways to get involved in these two transaction activities is a joint venture with a sales broker and a mortgage broker. Each party contributes different skills to the venture.

The real estate manager has much to offer a broker. First, the real estate manager has a client that needs to sell or refinance its property. Next, no one knows the property better than the real estate manager does. The real estate manager will be asked to revise the current year's budget and to develop the next year's budget. He or she may tour prospective buyers, lenders, and their consultants through the property several times.

The real estate manager will be responsible for obtaining an *estoppel certificate* from each tenant and for copying leases as necessary. The real estate manager may have the relationship and the confidence of the client and is inviting the sales broker or mortgage broker into the transaction. The sales broker markets the property and negotiates the sale. The mortgage broker contacts lenders and negotiates a new loan for the property.

Each party plays an important role in completing the sale or refinance. One of the most important aspects of the entire process is having a relationship with the client to provide these services. The real estate management firm will share the sales fee with the sales broker and the refinance fee with the mortgage broker. Once the real estate manager is confident in his or her ability to market the property and complete the transaction without the need to joint venture with a broker or a mortgage broker, the real estate manager can handle the services alone, and the firm can receive the entire commission or fee. The real estate manager should receive a fair share of the commission or fee earned by the real estate management firm for his or her involvement in the transactions. Transactions are often hidden income that a real estate management company could earn by repositioning itself to include leasing, sales, and refinancing in its menu of services while bringing additional value to its clients.

SECTION

IV

Efficient and Effective Property Operations

CHAPTER

13

Administration and Record Keeping

All real estate managers need to prepare standard correspondence dealing with insurance, common area costs, lease infractions, lease renewals and modifications, environmental concerns, and a host of other issues. In addition, real estate managers require specific procedures to guide them as they deal with owners, tenants, the public, lenders, city officials, and contractors. The following lists the eight steps necessary to create an effective lease administration program:

1. Establish forms, procedures, filing systems, and operating systems to handle all likely administrative tasks in an effective and efficient way.
2. Evaluate each lease to be sure that it is complete and ready for input into the system.
3. Set in motion any requests for missing information to be sure it is obtained at the earliest possible time.
4. Have knowledgeable, trained personnel available to handle the input of the lease information.
5. Enforce measures for double checking the input. This generally means that one person handles the input and another checks the accuracy of the information.
6. Implement procedures to uniformly administer all elements of the lease during its term, from commencement through its final termination.
7. Employ spot-auditing procedures to ensure the quality of the administrative process.
8. Develop an internal mechanism to identify administrative problems and work towards solutions in the shortest time possible, consistently maintaining the quality of the operation.

PROCEDURES, FORMS, AND STANDARD LETTERS

Procedures, forms, and standard letters are integral parts of managing and leasing commercial properties. Daily interactions with tenants, clients, contractors, attorneys, accountants, leasing agents, city officials, and mortgage holders require that real estate managers conduct business in a consistent fashion.

Property owners, especially institutional owners, need confidence that their real estate management firms and real estate managers are professionally equipped to handle every situation effectively and efficiently. When interviewing real estate management firms, property owners often request a review of the firms' procedure manuals to ensure that a management firm's branch offices consistently follow established procedures and guidelines. Owners also want to know that the management firm has thoroughly analyzed its management, operations, and leasing responsibilities to maximize the potential of the property.

It is critical that all documents that are e-mailed to others and/or posted on outside sites are marked confidential and indicated that they are not to be shared with anyone else without written permission from the sender. An orderly compilation of the company's procedures, forms, and standard letters enhances the creditability of a management company's expertise. For example, if the procedure for approving invoices is not established throughout the company, property owners cannot be certain the real estate management company has accounting procedures and controls to handle and disburse their funds properly. Since rent collection is one of an owner's top priorities, the owner will have greater confidence in a management company that routinely follows specific steps or procedures to ensure that this important function is not neglected.

The preparation of the company's procedures requires management to evaluate carefully how they want to conduct their business. For example, entry-level real estate managers and administrative support personnel can use the procedures to ensure that they establish guidelines that anticipate most situations. The company's procedures also provide the firm with credibility. They should be used as marketing tools.

Real estate managers can create a new forms as each situation arises. Anyone with access to Microsoft Excel, Word, or a similar software program can create professional-looking forms with little effort. It is much easier and more productive, however, to find, use, or modify a form that other real estate managers have used. IREM also offers a variety of standard forms and checklists as one of its benefits of membership.

LEASE ABSTRACT

Once the management office receives an executed lease from the leasing agents, the lease is summarized so the salient points can be readily available to provide an abbreviated view of the lease to the real estate manager and the accounting department. The information needed for the day-to-day administration of the lease includes lease terms, tenant information, rental information, expense reimbursements, insurance requirements, and lease options. Software programs for commercial property management include a lease, abstract, or summary report. Although these reports differ in form and layout, they all contain the same basic information. Smaller shopping centers with shorter leases may use a two-page summary while large enclosed malls with food courts or high-rise office buildings might have lease summaries up to four pages.

The lease summary includes the tenant's name and leased premises address, legal notice address, rentable square footage, and the anticipated lease commencement and expiration dates. The summary notes the monthly and annual base rent and future base rent step-ups. Additionally, the summary indicates how the tenant is to be billed for operating expenses, *common area maintenance (CAM),* taxes, insurance, and other items. The summary also lists any security deposit requirements along with due date and late fee information. Additional information summarized includes any special rights or obligations provided for in the lease (relocation options, cancellation options, renewal options, *right-of-first refusal* or right-of-first offer options).

The real estate manager, administrative assistant, or the property accountant is assigned the responsibility of summarizing leases. If the administrative assistant is assigned this task, review it to ensure everything is complete and accurate. One person should summarize all leases for a building in order to become familiar with the property's standard lease form. Some firms prefer to have the property accountant summarize the lease because he or she will administer the tenant's billings and record the rental payments. In some firms the real estate manager summarizes the lease and the accounting department checks and confirms that the summary is an accurate reflection of the lease. In other cases, attorneys will also provide a redline lease which compares the tenant lease form to the standard lease form for easier review and summarizing. There is no right or wrong way for assigning who will summarize leases.

An error in summarizing a lease—for example, a missing *consumer price index (CPI)* increase or a missed rent step—can result in incorrect billings, so it's prudent to have a second person, such as the controller or real estate manager, check the income section of the lease summary by comparing rental increases, *operating expenses,* and CAM provisions to the lease. Some companies have separate lease administration and accounting/billing systems—two systems can be compared on a monthly basis to ensure accuracy.

DEFERRED CONDITIONS REPORT

While the lease summary is prepared, the deferred conditions summary is also prepared, which is a valuable tool in tracking future changes in the terms of the leases. The information is listed on the month and year of the change. The summaries are then read at the beginning of each month and the appropriate action is taken. If the action is taken by a property accountant, the real estate manager should also check the summaries monthly to be aware of the changes that should be made.

TENANT ROLL

In most circumstances, two tenant rolls must be prepared. The asset manager or property owner may have a very complete tenant roll that incorporates all changes in lease terms over the entire term of a lease. The real estate manager, however, generally needs a less-detailed tenant roster that includes the basic information needed for day-to-day operations. The tenant roll should be changed each time a change is made in the basic information and each roster should be dated to ensure that it is current. Each tenant roll should contain the following:

Listing of all spaces in the property in numerical order

- Names of the tenants
- Suite/unit numbers
- Square footage
- Lease commencement and expiration dates
- Current rentals
- Future rent steps
- Security deposits
- Percentage rent rates for retail tenants
- Expense reimbursement information
- Percentage share
- Expense stops (if applicable)
- Monthly billings
- Lease options

LEASE RESTRICTIONS SUMMARY

In a soft leasing market, offering concessions to attract good tenants is not unusual, and major tenants often negotiate concessions. City or county authorities frequently place restrictions on the types of tenants or uses that can occupy space in a shopping center. For these reasons, keeping a *lease restrictions summary*—a separate listing of all lease restrictions that may have a future impact on the leasing and management of the property—is important like the deferred conditions summary the list of restrictions. The real estate manager and leasing agent should check the list of restrictions each time a new lease is considered to be sure no violation of any restriction occurs. The list should be electronically available to the leasing agents, real estate managers, and owner to be sure that everyone in the loop is fully informed. Common restrictions include options to renew, first right of refusal, right to cancel, exclusives, and use restrictions.

Options to Renew

An *option to renew* is a right of the tenant and an obligation of the property owner. The listing of restrictions should include the tenant's option notification date and any other restrictions that might prevent the tenant from exercising the option. Other restrictions may include that tenant has not been in default during the lease term. A retail tenant's option may be contingent upon payment of percentage rent during the last two years of the current lease term. The option may also only be available if the tenant has reach a given level of sales for a specific period of time. To exercise the option, the tenant usually must notify the property owner, in writing, during a specific period—often not less than 120 days or more than 180 days prior to the lease expiration date. This information should be placed in the deferred conditions report 60 days prior to the notification date to put the real estate manager and/or the leasing agent on notice that the date is approaching. Renewal options will also define rental rate—whether it's market rate, a percent of market rate, or a set rental rate defined in the lease option.

Right-of-First Refusal

The *right-of-first refusal* is much like an option in that the holder of the right must be offered the space to lease or purchase before a transaction can be concluded with another party. This right is most often found in office buildings rather than shopping centers. Generally, the tenant has a limited window to exercise a right-of-first refusal and that should be listed in the summary. When a building has one or more tenants with rights-of-first refusal, the real estate manager should indicate which site or floor plan the tenants have those rights, and which spaces are encumbered by the restrictions.

Right-of-First Offer

A *right-of-first offer* is related to a right-of-first refusal, but the former is considered to favor the seller while the latter is considered to favor the rights holder. The lease may state that the space will be offered at market rent and the tenant may lease the space at that rate. If the tenant turns down the opportunity to lease the space, it no longer has expansion rights to the space and the leasing agent may negotiate with any prospect for the space.

Right to Cancel

While it is unusual, some tenants are granted the right to cancel a lease prior to the full term. This right is generally tied to sales performance for retailers, but for office tenants it is sometimes tied to contract negotiations. The window for cancellation and terms of the right, including any required termination fees due from the tenant, are listed in the summary. For example, a tenant may have the right to cancel the lease during the January immediately following the third calendar year of the lease if the tenant's sales do not exceed a stated sum during that year. If the right to cancel is given, either the property owner or the tenant should have the right to cancel.

Exclusives

An *exclusive* gives a tenant the sole and exclusive right to sell a particular product or to provide a particular service. This right is most often granted to major or anchor tenants and less often to large, strong national chains. If a tenant is granted an exclusive right, it should be listed in the summary and the exact language of the right should be included. The tenant may have the right to carry a specific type of merchandise, a specific brand, a limited shelf space of a given type of merchandise, etc. Before a new lease is accepted, these rights must be reviewed.

Use Restrictions

An anchor tenant in a shopping center or a pharmacy or a medical specialist in a medical office building may place *use restrictions* on the balance of the property. The restrictions may prohibit specific uses of the property or uses within a specified distance of the tenant's space.

For example, supermarkets often restrict other food operations by either indicating that they may not be in the shopping center or, if they are allowed, by requiring that their square footage be limited. Supermarkets also try to prohibit theaters or, if they are allowed, request they not closer than a specific distance from the front entrance to the supermarket—190 feet, for example.

The city or county may also set certain restrictions against uses in a shopping center. Through the *planned unit development (PUD)* restrictions, the city does not allow beauty parlors or theaters in one shopping center because both uses take up parking spaces in excess of the average for most retailers of a similar size. There might also be instances where office tenants may have use restrictions. For example, an office tenant may indicate other call centers may not be in the building due to high usage of parking, or perhaps a tenant doesn't want a competitor in the building. A summary of these restrictions should be available to the owners, real estate managers, leasing agents, accounting personnel, and possibly, legal counsel.

RENTAL RECORDS AND PERCENTAGE RENT

Getting the tenant set up on the rental records is an important task that lets accounting know what to bill and collect. Typically, the tenant record contains the following information:

- Legal and operating name of the tenant
- Premises address as well as billing address
- Suite/unit number
- Accounting system-assigned tenant number
- Square footage

- Current rental price
- Date of next rental increase
- Amount of security deposit
- Amount of current common area
- Tax, insurance, and marketing fund estimates
- Reporting requirements for percentage rents
- Information on late charges.

It's more common than not for management companies to send out rent statements via e-mail since it's "greener," saves money, and arrives to tenants quicker, which results in quicker rent payments. For *accrual accounting,* each item is posted as being a receivable at the first of the month, and it is then credited when payment is received. All items of income must be separated and accounted for individually so future inquiries on the account can be answered properly. This rental record is generally prepared from the lease summaries once they are completed for each new tenant. Prior to billing rents, a rent summary detailing rents and other charges to be billed by each tenant should be prepared by the accountant and reviewed and approved by the real estate manager to ensure that it's properly billed.

Percentage rents are most common in shopping centers, but office buildings with a retail and/or restaurant component and industrial parks with the same types of tenants also need to track sales and rents if their lease provisions include percentage rents.

Percentage Rental Lease Requirements

To track the various percentage rent lease provisions, the real estate manager prepares a summary showing every space in the shopping center (or office building or industrial park) and indicate the occupying tenant and any lease provisions regarding percentage rents. If the tenant's lease in a shopping center has no percentage rent requirements, this should be noted on the record. The record should include the name of the tenant, the agreed percentage rent rate, the frequency of reporting and payment, and any special considerations, such as deducting sales to employees, wholesale sales, or returns, to observe when calculating percentage rent is owed.

SALES REPORT FORM

Most tenants that represent major retailers do not need help preparing their percentage rental reports. However, the tenant of smaller businesses often does not fully understand the percentage rent provisions, so providing blank sales report forms are helpful. If monthly reporting is required, the tenant should receive about 14 blank monthly report forms at the start of each year. The forms should show how that tenant's percentage is calculated, when the forms should be returned, and to whom they should be sent. Even if the property owner does not provide such forms, the tenant has an obligation to submit them on a timely basis. The most effective way to be sure to collect all sales reports is by phone, e-mail, call, or personal visit.

Percentage rent provisions create the potential for additional moneys. They implicate an accounting function that involves analyzing the sales reports to determine if additional moneys are due, seeing that they get on the record, and finally, ensuring that the moneys owed are collected. The sales figures must be analyzed to determine how the tenants are doing and how the shopping center is doing. Sales reports are used in several ways to evaluate sales and aid in the management and marketing of the shopping center.

Monthly reports should show each tenant that is obligated to pay percentage rent, the cumulative sales by month, and a two- or three-month running comparison of the sales figures. The report can be used to quickly evaluate how the tenants are doing, but it is not of much help in analyzing the shopping center as a whole.

Reports for Small Commercial Properties

For small shopping centers or other commercial properties, a report can be prepared for management use showing the tenant's sales for the current month compared to the same month last year, the year-to-date sales for both years, and an analysis of the percentage rent potential. Management does not share this report with the merchants because the different uses are not easily compared in any meaningful way.

Reports for Large Commercial Properties

For regional, super regional, lifestyle, and outlet shopping centers, as well as other larger commercial properties, real estate management often compiles information by dividing the tenants into lines of merchandise (such as women's wear, men's wear, restaurants, gifts, shoes, etc.), calculating each tenant's sales per square foot, as well as the percentage increase or decrease, and then ranking all merchants without revealing any specific tenant's performance. The report is then given to all tenants (with each tenant represented as a letter or number to conceal its identity) so the tenants can compare their performance with that of the other retailers.

Shopping center management frequently calculates the tenant's sales per square foot and sets up meaningful clusters. For example, the clusters would range from less than $200 per square foot, $200 to $350 per square foot, $350 to $500 per square foot, $500 to $800 per square foot, and $800 per square foot and above. Management then plots the sales on a shopping center with different color codes to identify where the higher sales per square foot are located and, equally as important, where the lower sales per square foot are found. The information then serves as one tool for evaluating opportunities for improvement, changes in tenant mix, and/or the renewal of leases about to expire.

Most retail leases require the tenant to submit an *annual sales statement.* This report must be signed by an officer of the firm. Shop tenant submit their sales monthly while anchor tenants submit their sales annually.

SECURITY DEPOSIT LOG

With the exception of governmental agencies, large national tenants, credit worthy tenants, and major anchor tenants, most tenants are required to post a security deposit to assure the performance of the lease. The lease will often require that this be paid to the owner upon lease execution. The real estate manager must properly account for these deposits. Most owners are not required to put such deposits in a separate bank account or to pay interest to tenants as long as they hold the deposits. Nevertheless, a listing or log of the deposits should be maintained. The log is prepared at the time the lease summary is prepared, and it is updated anytime a change occurs. If the building is sold, the deposits must be transferred to the new owners.

OPERATING EXPENSE BILL BACKS

Tenant bill backs, also known as charge backs and *pass-through charges,* should be timely, fair, and accurate. A series of inaccurate bills to tenants will destroy tenant confidence in the real estate manager and the property owner. Slow billings can hurt a property's cash flow, and failure to collect moneys due can reduce the value of the property. The best way to ensure accurate billing for each tenant is to create a master schedule listing every tenant and the specific terms of their lease as it pertains to the common area billings. From that list, a sub list of each line item can be prepared and the proper allocations listed. With that in hand, the actual preparation of the bills becomes rather routine.

Many methods for billing operating expenses are available. Tenants can be billed on the basis of a *pro rata share* (in shopping centers the share can be based on leasable or leased area), a base year, a stop expense (common with office buildings), or a flat fee. Some tenants negotiate exceptions to the standard method of charging for the building's operating expenses.

Countless exceptions to the various methods of charging for CAM or operating expenses exist. Specific operating expense items may be deleted from a tenant's charges. For instance, a supermarket may negotiate to exclude security costs from its charges. A cap or ceiling on billable operating expenses may be negotiated, such as a three-percent limit on annual increases in office building operating expense charges. In some cases, a cap is placed on specific operating expense items. An industrial park tenant may pay its pro rata share of taxes and insurance but negotiate a four-percent cap on all other operating expenses. Leases may set a cap on controllable operating expenses only. Examples of *non-controllable expenses* (which are not capped) include utilities, taxes, insurance, and snow removal costs. Usually a major retail tenant will negotiate a pro rata share of CAM expenses that do not exceed one percent of its gross sales. The next three sections consider the treatment of bill backs for shopping centers, office buildings, and industrial properties.

Shopping Center CAM Charges and Bill Back Expenses

In a shopping center, *common areas* are areas where the tenants and their customers have common use. This area can also be described as all areas other than those areas where tenants have *exclusive use* (their premises). CAM charges are billed to tenants for the expenses associated with those areas.

Most shopping center leases provide tenants to pay their pro rata portion of the shopping center's operating costs, taxes, insurance, and maintenance. These costs are referred to in a number of ways: net expenses, bill back or charge back items, pass-through items, tenant charges, and CAM charges. With any change in occupancy or with a new tenant, the potential exists for error in the CAM billings, or worse, the potential failure to bill tenants.

Shopping centers frequently have two or three formulas for the distribution of CAM charges. For instance, taxes for the entire shopping center may be allocated to each parcel, but insurance may be allocated only on a portion of the shopping center because major tenants often insure their own buildings. For these reasons, the real estate manager must have a complete understanding of all individual lease terms as well as the shopping center's operations.

Common Area Maintenance (CAM) Costs

Even though the theory behind CAM charges is to bill the tenants for the cost of maintaining all of the common areas, the real estate manager can only bill a tenant for those expenses the lease allows. In summarizing the tenant's lease, determine which charges are billable, how the tenant's share is calculated, and how the tenant will reimburse these expenses. The tenants pay a pro rata share of the CAM expenses based on a formula that uses the square footage of their premises as the numerator and the square footage of the shopping center as the denominator. CAM billing would be easy to calculate if all tenants pay on the same basis.

Leased Square Footage

One rare exception is to calculate the tenant's share of CAM expenses using the leased square footage of the shopping center rather than the leasable square footage as the denominator. Leasable square footage includes all the occupied and vacant spaces in the denominator. Leased square footage includes only those spaces actually occupied or leased. If leased square footage is used to determine the denominator, the figure can change every month as the shopping center's occupancy changes.

Some property owners take the position that tenants should pay the total cost of maintaining the common areas since they and their customers are the only ones using the facilities. These owners do not allocate any of this cost to vacant spaces or require any contribution by the owner. The tenants, on the other hand, do not believe they should be penalized for the property owner's inability to lease the vacancies.

If a tenant occupies 2,000 square feet and the *gross leasable area (GLA)* is 100,000 square feet, the tenant's share of the CAM expenses based on the leasable square feet would be two percent. If the same tenant's lease required paying a pro rata share of CAM expenses of the leased square footage, and the shopping center had 20,000 square feet vacant, the tenant would pay 2.5 percent of the CAM budget—this is calculated using the 80,000 square feet occupied as the denominator and the tenant's 2,000 square feet as the numerator).

The leased square footage is used when the property owner is attempting to pass on all expenses, but most experienced tenants, their leasing agents, and attorneys will not accept leased square footage as the denominator. The majority of leases in shopping centers use leasable square footage to determine each tenant's share of CAM expenses.

Tenant Maintains Portion of Common Area

When a major tenant is concerned that a poorly maintained common area will have an adverse impact on its sales, they can exercise their right to maintain a portion of the common area. For example, if the management of a supermarket owns the building and land with a *reciprocal easement agreement (REA)* and he or she is not satisfied with the level of maintenance, it may exercise its right to maintain either the entire common area or just the part on the land that is owned. Some anchor tenants insist on maintaining their portion of the common areas, and in their effort to keep their operating costs down, they maintain them poorly. The majority of anchor or major tenants will allow the property owner to maintain the common areas.

Tenant Pays Less than Full Share

An example of another exception is presented when a tenant occupies 28 percent of the leasable area of the shopping center but negotiates to pay only a 25 percent share of the CAM costs. The shopping center owner must either pay the three-percent difference or, if the lease permits, pass that cost along to the remaining tenants. A fast-food tenant may be required to pay a premium on common area costs to cover increased common area expenses due to the nature of its operations. This premium is generally stated as a higher percentage of CAM cost—for example, the fast-food operator who occupies 2.5 percent of the shopping center but by agreement pays 3.5 percent of the costs. The excess should be credited against the expense balance of the other tenants, as they are presumably paying higher maintenance costs within their allocations.

Malls have several common area charges—an interior mall CAM, an exterior mall CAM, and a food court CAM. For malls, the anchor tenants usually do not pay for interior mall common area charges. The denominator for charging all the other tenants facing the mall excludes the square footage of the major retailers. They will pay their pro rata share of the exterior (parking lot) common area charges. The denominator for this CAM charge includes all the tenants and other major retailers.

Tenants Exempt from Certain Expenses

Major retailers create another exception to all tenants paying their pro rata CAM shares when the terms of their leases do not require them to pay a particular expense. They use their own lease forms when entering into agreements with property owners. For example, if the shopping center's security is a CAM expense, but the supermarket's lease form does not require payment for security, the real estate manager would bill the supermarket for its pro rata share of the CAM expenses less the security expense, which becomes an unreimbursed expense that the property owner absorbs. The expense is not added to the other tenants' CAM costs unless the exception is included in the other tenants' leases.

Individual and Central HVAC

Another exception to the simple pro rata share of the CAM billings occurs when the property owner is responsible for maintaining all but the major tenants' HVAC units as part of the CAM budget. In this case, remove HVAC maintenance from the CAM budget and establish a separate tenant charge for it. Only those tenants whose HVAC units are maintained by the property owner would be billed for the expense. If the property owner maintains the HVAC units on 30,000 square feet of tenant space, then a tenant in a 2,000-square-foot space would pay 6.67 percent of the owner's HVAC maintenance costs. If tenants do not have the same number or size of HVAC units, each would be billed for the cost of maintaining its unit(s).

Two choices are available for billing tenants for HVAC when the shopping center has a central plant. The plant can be set up as a profit shopping center, and the tenants can be billed an agreed rate to produce a profit. The owner would be responsible for repairs, replacements, and the basic costs of operating the system. If this approach is taken, the cost to the tenant should not exceed the cost the tenants would have if they owned and operated their own HVAC units.

The second approach is to include the cost to operate the HVAC central plant as part of the CAM charges. The tenants would receive HVAC service at the actual cost of the service and, of course, would share in the cost of all repairs, replacements, and day-to-day operations. In either case, a model should be established to determine which expenses will be included in each billing and how each tenant (or space) will be billed, including any negotiated exceptions or limits. Few shopping centers or malls have a central HVAC plant.

Enclosed Malls

An enclosed mall has two CAM budgets: (1) a parking lot budget paid by all the tenants on a pro rata basis, and (2) an enclosed mall budget paid only by those tenants in the mall. For example, a enclosed mall of 500,000 square feet has 450,000 square feet of tenant space in the mall and 50,000 square feet in buildings adjacent to the parking lot. The denominator for the enclosed mall CAM budget is 450,000 square feet, and the denominator for the parking lot CAM budget is 500,000 square feet. A tenant in the mall with 5,000 square feet would pay 1.11 percent of the mall CAM budget and one percent of the parking lot CAM budget. The theory behind the two formulas is that only those tenants that receive the benefits of the enclosed mall common area should be responsible for its expenses. The mall is also likely to have a food court CAM expense for those tenants operating in the food court.

Department stores are usually able to negotiate an important exception in their leases. Instead of paying pro rata shares of all enclosed mall CAM expenses, these tenants pay their full pro rata share of parking lot expenses but pay none of the enclosed mall CAM costs or only a nominal contribution toward them. Although most property owners and real estate managers do not agree, the major retailer's reasoning for not paying its pro rata share of the enclosed mall CAM expenses is that it receives no benefit from the mall since it has entrances from the parking lot. However, because their customers use the parking facilities, they are willing to pay their pro rata share.

When a major retailer is not required to contribute to the expenses of the mall CAM budget, the leases of the small shops must state that the denominator for these expenses will exclude the square footage of the major tenants. The cost of the mall CAM expense is then paid entirely by the small shops. If the small shops' leases do not exclude the square footage of the major tenants from the denominator, the property owner would not be reimbursed by them for the major tenants' pro rata share of the mall CAM expenses. In the previously mentioned example, if two major tenants occupied 300,000 feet and did not pay mall CAM costs, the denominator for the mall CAM budget would be 150,000 square feet. The tenant with 5,000 square feet would pay 3.33 percent of the mall CAM expenses instead of the 1.11 percent. If the major retailer makes a nominal contribution to the mall CAM budget, this amount is credited against the actual expenses before calculating each tenant's CAM share.

Common Area Bill Allocation

Common area billings can be complicated and confusing to the tenants and sometimes to the real estate management team. If bills are properly allocated and recorded, preparing accurate and timely common area billings is much easier. The real estate manager codes the bill to the proper account and forwards it to the accounting department for payment.

When preparing bills, the real estate manager should review each invoice to be sure it is being allocated to the correct property, coded accurately, and is a proper charge. It is quite possible that an item can be charged to the tenants under the lease provisions, but there may be good reasons for not billing it at that time, or not billing it at all. Only a real estate manager is likely to be aware of such situations. If copies of each invoice are kept with the bill, make copies to respond to a tenant's inquiry. Each month's total expenses provide the basis for an easy comparison to what was budgeted and provides year-to-date figures.

An analysis should list tenants by space number (not alphabetically) and provide a quick summary of how each tenant's charges are calculated. The denominator is the total square feet of all tenants who are charged for the expense. For instance, all tenants of a 550,000-square-foot mall may pay their pro rata shares of the shopping center's common area parking lot maintenance expense. The denominator is 550,000 square feet. Only those tenants on the mall portion of the shopping center (475,000 square feet) pay the common area mall maintenance expenses, resulting in a difference in the denominators for calculating each tenant's charges. Merchants' association or marketing fund dues are usually calculated on a dollar-per-square-foot basis. The HVAC charge is usually a fixed monthly or quarterly charge based on the size and number of the tenant's HVAC unit.

CAM Billing Policies

The property owner's right to be reimbursed for CAM expenses has a significant impact on the cash flow and the value of a shopping center. The real estate manager should be current with the trends in the industry with respect to CAM expenses and methods of billing tenants. The lease document used for new and renewing tenants should include provisions reflecting these trends. When shopping centers were first developed, tenants were billed their pro rata shares of CAM expenses based on each month's actual expenses. The shopping center industry changed to billing the tenants based on an estimate of the common area annual expenses.

CAM Estimates

In the 1960s, the shopping center industry began billing tenants based on an estimated budget. The real estate manager developed an annual budget and billed the tenant 1/12 of the budget each month. This eliminated the need to calculate the CAM expenses and bill each tenant monthly for its share of the actual expenses.

When CAM charges are billed on a monthly estimate, the real estate manager prepares a CAM budget for the upcoming calendar year and the current year estimates are adjusted to the actual expenses at the beginning of the following year—these calculations are detailed in year-end adjustments.

Occasionally, a major retailer will require their property owners to bill their portion of the CAM based on actual costs. In such situations, real estate managers should request that the major tenant accept an estimated monthly bill once they have confidence in the real estate management company's billing procedures.

Fixed CAM

In recent years, the concept of fixed CAM has become fairly common. Most owner-tenant disputes revolve around CAM issues—especially at the year-end reconciliation. Many owners have included a fixed CAM provision in their leases, which can take several different forms.

The most common is for property owner and tenant to agree upon a monthly figure that represents the tenant's share of CAM expenses with no adjustment at year end. Both owner and tenant take their chances that the costs will be in the range projected, and all disputes should be eliminated. In this situation, the CAM charge is increased annually based on an agreed percentage or fixed increase.

Another variation is fixed CAM for most CAM items, but not for those items that are difficult to control, such as taxes, insurance, or snow removal. The tenant pays its share of the actual cost of such items, but the balance of the costs are fixed.

Office Building Operating Expenses

Three common methods to bill office building tenants for their share of the building's operating expense, also known as *escalation expense,* are a *base-year expense* or on an *expense-stop method.*

Base-Year Method

A common method to bill office building tenants is the base-year method. The tenant is responsible for its pro rata share of the increase above the operating expenses over the base year expenses—typically the year the tenant's lease commences. For example, if a tenant occupied 5,000 square feet in a 100,000-square-foot building, and the operating expenses increased from $600,000 in its base year to $650,000 the following year, the tenant would pay $2,500 in escalation expenses. ($50,000 increase in operating expenses over the base year multiplied by five percent, the tenant's percentage share of the building.) If, during the tenant's third year of occupancy, the expenses increased to $689,000, the tenant's share of the escalation would be $4,450 (five percent of the $89,000 increase above the $600,000 base year).

In a soft leasing market, the tenant might be able to negotiate the base year to a later year in the lease. For instance, the tenant occupies the premises in the year 2017, but negotiates its base year to be 2018. The tenant would start paying operating expenses in 2019. If the market is strong, the owner might be able to negotiate the base year to precede the year the tenant occupies its premises. In that situation, the tenant would pay escalation charges during the first year of its occupancy. Many tenants negotiate a new base year when renewing their leases.

Expense-Stop Method

Another method of billing the tenants for operating expenses is the expense-stop method. The owner would pay the operating expenses to a predetermined dollar amount per square foot, and the tenants would pay everything above that amount. A tenant with 7,500 square feet in a building with a $6.00 "stop" and operating expenses of $6.65, would pay $4,875 in escalation charges (the tenant would pay $0.65 per square foot on 7,500 square feet). In theory, if all the tenants have the same stop, the property owner will always know its share of the operating expenses. Note that if expenses come in lower than the expense stop, the owner benefits as no credits are given to the tenants in this situation. In practice, many tenants negotiate a higher stop expense when renewing their leases.

Exceptions to Standard Billing Methods

Exceptions to an office building's standard method of billing escalation charges are similar to those reviewed in the preceding section on common area billings in shopping centers. An office building tenant may have a cap on its share of the increase in operating expenses or on specific expenses, such as maintenance. The tenant may feel that the property owner has little or no control over the cost of insurance, taxes, utilities, and snow removal but has direct control over maintenance expenses. (See Chapter 4: Office Building Management, for an explanation of the "gross-up" process.)

For many years, office building escalation charges were billed in the year after the expenses were incurred. For example, if a tenant's base year was 2015, the tenant would pay the 2016 increase in 2017. For current practice, the real estate manager estimates the building's operating expenses for 2016 based on the budgeted expenses and billed the tenants on a 1/12 basis monthly, commencing the beginning of the year. For the next year, the estimated bills would be reconciled to the actual expenses.

Industrial Property Building Expenses or Bill Back Charges

Industrial properties are usually billed on a base-year or triple net method. The base-year method is similar to the method used for office buildings. The *triple-net* method allows the property owner to bill all operating expenses to the tenant or tenants on a pro rata basis. The three net charges are taxes, insurance, and maintenance. When a tenant pays operating expenses on a triple-net basis, no exceptions are made to any of the charges.

YEAR-END ADJUSTMENTS

Commercial tenants are billed estimates for their agreed tenant charges—for example, CAM, other pass-through expenses, taxes, and insurance—based on operating expenses budgeted for the year. Each month the tenant is billed 1/12 of its pro rata share of the budget. Leases often will allow the owner to adjust the monthly estimates if operating expenses increase significantly over the budget (typically the result of non-controllable expense increases such as higher snow removal costs or large increases in taxes) The typical commercial lease states that the property owner will provide the tenants with a reconciliation of the estimated budget with the actual expenses as soon as practical in the following year. Some tenants negotiate a predetermined date by which the owner is obligated to provide the year-end adjustments.

The property owner should complete the reconciliation and notify the tenants of the adjustments as soon as possible. Tenants become irritated and lose confidence in the property owner and the real estate management company when they do not fulfill their obligations on a timely basis. It is difficult to expect tenants to fulfill their commitments if the real estate management company or the property owner does not. If the reconciliation results in the tenant owing significant charges, it's recommended to include a letter explaining the reason for this. An essential factor in administering tenant escalation clauses is effective tenant communication. Even some of the most sophisticated tenants may not understand all of the intricacies of these rent adjustments. A copy of the letter and reconciliation schedule should be placed in the tenant lease file.

Actual Expenses Exceed Estimated Expenses

When the actual expenses exceed the estimated expenses, the real estate manager determines amount to bill each tenant above their annual estimated pass-through payments.

Estimated Expenses Exceed Actual Expenses

If the estimated expenses exceed the actual expenses, the tenant should receive a refund. Before a refund is sent to the tenant or credited to the account, the property accountant should provide the real estate manager with a listing of each tenant's adjustments. The real estate manager and the property accountant should research the tenant's payment record for unpaid fees or charges, such as nonpayment of late charges, delinquent merchant's association marketing fund dues, or nonpayment of any other charges. This is an opportunity to clear up minor unpaid charges not worth collecting through protracted discussions with the tenant, legal action, or placing a tenant in default.

After any charges have been deducted from the refund, a refund check is sent or the amount is credited to the tenant's account along with an explanation for the adjustments. Although the method of handling the credit balance is up to the property owner, owners frequently ask for the real estate manager's recommendation—both refunding the amount and crediting the tenant's account have advantages.

Sending a Refund Check to the Tenant

Sending a check directly to the tenant is an acknowledgement that the money belongs to the tenant. A tenant rarely receives money from a property owner, and such a payment develops good owner-tenant relations. Sending a refund is an opportunity to also inform the tenant that the property owner, through the real estate management company, is operating the property with cost-effective procedures, evidenced by the refund check. Former tenants (assuming they were not in default upon lease expiration) would receive checks as no future charges on their account to apply a credit to.

Crediting the Tenant's Account

An advantage to crediting the tenant's future rent is that the owner has received a partial payment for the next rental payment and thus has use of the tenant's money for a longer time. One possible disadvantage is that the tenant may overlook the credit and make the customary rental payment, creating a credit on the books that must be communicated to the tenant.

BILLING TENANTS

One of the ongoing debates in commercial property management is whether to send tenants invoices for their rent and tenant charges. There are three basic approaches: (1) bill monthly, (2) do not bill at all, or (3) send 12 invoices at the end of the year for next year's billings.

All three of the these approaches can be successful, but the real estate management company must decide which approach meets the property owner's concerns and needs. Once the best option is determined, it will need to be incorporated into the tenants' accounting and reporting systems.

Monthly Billing

The following lists three reasons for monthly billing:

1. The tenant receives an invoice each month as a reminder that rent is due on the first of the next month. The invoice also states what each tenant's charges are, and any increase in the base rent due to a rent step-up or a CPI adjustment.
2. Tenants' billings are always current since the accounting reports are already programmed in the system. Late charges and other fees are easily included in the monthly invoice which prevents tenants from using the excuse that they do not have an invoice or they do not understand the charges.
3. The monthly invoices, e-mailed to the tenants, also provides the opportunity to include messages, such as welcoming new tenants to the building or reporting that the property's sales increased a specific percentage during the last month.

No Billing

Simply put, not sending tenants' bills saves time. Many real estate management companies that have switched from monthly tenant billing to no billing have found no change in their properties' receivables. Those tenants who have historically paid their rent on time continue to do so, and those tenants who have collection problems continue to be late.

Real estate managers who do not bill their tenants monthly contend that the tenants' lease states the monthly rent. They notify the tenants in December of their tenant charges (such as pass-through expenses, CAM, taxes, and insurance) for the coming year. Since tenants' rent payments are automated, they do not need monthly invoices, and they generally discard them. Late charges and other non-recurring fees are billed separately.

Billing One Year at a Time

The third approach to billing tenants is to e-mail 12 invoices at the end of the year—one for each month of the coming year. This approach accommodates the tenants who need an invoice for each month, and the tenants who do not need invoices receive them only once.

Since the invoices are automated, it makes it easier if a tenant's rent has a fixed step-up during the year—the base rent will increase for that month and each subsequent month.

Invoice Format

Sending the tenants invoices, whether monthly or once during the year, provides an opportunity to include a sales reporting form on the invoice for those tenants who have a percentage rent provision in their leases.

A rental invoice should list each of the tenant's charges and calculate the total rent due. This form is used for the hybrid approach of sending 12 invoices at the start of the year. The top portion is the actual invoice and the bottom portion is a sales report for the previous month. The tenant fills in only the gross sales for the reporting month and multiplies the agreed percentage rate times the reported sales. The percentage rent is subtracted from the base rent. The difference is the percentage rent owed. The lower portion of the form, along with a check for any percentage rent due, is mailed to the property owner.

Annual Sales Statement Format

The annual sales statement form is used when the tenant submits the certified annual gross sales statement. An advantage to including the annual sales statement is that the tenants have a form on which to submit their monthly sales. The form provides their sales breakpoint, percentage rent, and the address to which their report and percentage rent check should be mailed.

A disadvantage to this form is that the tenants' leases typically require them to submit their sales to the property owner by the 20th of the following month; for example, January sales reports are due by February 20. Thus, the tenant is sending the January sales report, which is determined in February, and any percentage rent due, with the March rent check. The tenant's sales report and percentage rent is received 10 days late (March 1 and not February 20). However, sales reports are more difficult to collect than rent. Since they seldom all arrive on the 20th of the month, receiving the report on the first of the next month instead of the preceding 20th of the month is acceptable to most property owners.

CAPITAL IMPROVEMENTS

A lease may include roof maintenance, exterior painting, replacement of existing capital improvements in the common area, and common area energy conservation improvements in a shopping center's common area maintenance expenses or in an office building's operating expenses. Some leases allow reserves for future replacements. If the parking lot will need a major resurfacing at a cost of $50,000 in five years, the real estate manager could include in the CAM budget a $10,000 reserve for each of the next five years. The real estate manager may establish a reserve of less than $10,000 per year when including the interest and are on the reserve fund more than five years.

Some property owners will not include the interest earned in the calculation to determine what to bill the CAM budget for each year, and allow the interest to be added to the reserve fund in case the cost of the job exceeds the estimated amount. If reserves are set aside as planned, when the maintenance is undertaken, the funds will be available, and the tenants will not be billed for a major expense all in one year. The lease should address the issue of reserves.

The amount to reserve can be set by first determining which maintenance or capital improvement items the lease allows as pass-through expenses, then anticipating what the cost of these items will be and when the expense will be incurred. Major tenants seldom contribute to a reserve, but they pay their pro rata shares of the expense when it is incurred if that is stipulated in their lease. In such a case, the amount to reserve would be determined by subtracting the major retailer's pro rata shares. If they are responsible for 75 percent of the CAM expenses, the owner would need to reserve $12,500 of the $50,000 parking lot resurfacing costs. The other tenants would be billed for their portions of the reserve over five years. When the work was completed, the major tenants would contribute their share of the expense, or $37,500.

If the property owner and real estate manager include reserves in the CAM or operating expense bill-back charges, they need to be careful that the amount of the reserves does not cause the total charges to be so high that the combined rent and charges are not higher than the market charges for the area, thus, reducing the property's competitive position. This can occur when too many future maintenance items are added to a reserve fund.

ADMINISTRATIVE FEES

Prior to the late 1980s, typical leases for shopping centers provided that each tenant would pay an administrative fee for the property owner's efforts and cost to administer the maintenance and operations of the common area. This fee was a percentage of the actual CAM expenses—usually between 10 and 15 percent for the shop and pad tenants and five to 10 percent for the anchor tenants. If the anchor tenant agrees to an administrative fee of five percent to 10 percent of the actual common area charges, it usually excludes utilities, insurance premiums, and major repairs from the fee. The administrative fee was in lieu of charging the tenants the property's management fee. Since then, most shopping center property owners have eliminated the administrative fee and replaced it with the property's management fee. The management fee is typically significantly larger than the administrative fee. Some owners will include both fees in the CAM lease provision. This is a controversial approach because both fees are for the same service, but anything negotiated by the parties with full disclosure is a legitimate approach. However, the owners who include both fees should have them clearly spelled out in the lease, and if tenants object, they should include their objection in the lease negotiations.

One of the most important aspects of common area costs and administrative fees is to keep them as competitive as possible. Common area costs are often thought of as a "pass-through costs," and the property owner may not be too concerned with them. However, it's important to look at "total occupancy costs" and use that figure, along with the base rent, to compare the total occupancy cost very carefully to other buildings. Rent and common area costs must be competitive, and the billings must be in keeping with what is happening in the marketplace.

Typically, the tax and insurance provisions do not state that an administrative fee can be added to these items. Some believe the administrative fee is justifiable on taxes and insurance premiums due to the time and effort the real estate manager expends on both.

The real estate manager must ensure that the taxes are assessed in accordance with the local statutes, reasonable in the marketplace, and properly allocated. The real estate manager must also check the assessment each year to be sure that it is appropriate and, if it is not, initiate and complete a tax appeal. Supplying copies of bills and breakdowns to tenants also requires time. Insurance requires bidding on the initial policies, administering the insurance, allocating the costs to the proper tenants, and working with tenants so they fully understand the billings. However, if the lease does not give the right to add on related administrative fees, a tenant is justified in refusing payment. In most leases, nothing implies the addition of an administration or supervision fee. Office buildings have included the building management fee in the building's escalation costs. Another supervision fee is not included because it is presumed that by including the management fees, all supervision costs have been covered.

Tenants' Right to Audit

The tenants' leases may provide them the right to audit the CAM expenses—many owners limit that right. The following lists the limitations and requirements generally included in the lease:

- Audit must be done within a certain period of time after the expenses have been reconciled and mailed to the tenants (typically 90 days)
- Audit is only for the most recent completed year
- Auditor must be a qualified accountant
- Accountant cannot be paid on a contingency basis
- Results of the audit must be confidential between the property owner and the tenant

ACCOUNTING CONSIDERATIONS

The following lists important questions to consider for administration and record keeping purposes:

- Will the property records be kept on a cash, accrual, or modified-accrual basis?
- How will the real estate manager deal with bank reconciliations and check requests?
- How will invoices be coded for proper accounting?
- What system does the property owner require for approval of expenses that are over budget or outside of the budget?

Accrual versus Cash Budget Entries

For many years, operating budgets and financials were prepared based on a cash system only, and clients converted this information to an accrual basis. In *cash-basis accounting,* income and expenses are recognized when money is received or paid. In *accrual-basis accounting,* income amounts are recognized when earned and expense amounts are recognized when incurred—whether the cash has been received, paid, or not paid.

Another option is a modified accrual system. Most institutional owners require accrual basis accounting reports. A *modified-accrual accounting* is a cash-basis system in which only large items, such as real estate taxes, insurance premiums, and major capital items are accrued. This system's goal is to incorporate the best of both systems.

The real estate manager and the client still need to know the cash position of the property. As a result, the real estate manager will first prepare the budget on a modified accrual or accrual basis and then convert that budget to a cash basis. The reverse situation also is not unusual.

The two most logical expense items to be entered on most budgets on an accrual basis are taxes and insurance. In many instances, these items are entered differently. In many jurisdictions, real estate taxes are paid in two installments during the year. On a cash basis, the two installments would be entered in the months in which they are actually paid (Exhibit 13.1). In California, for example, one entry would be made in April and the other in December. The insurance premium is generally prepaid in full once a year; this example uses the month of June.

To convert the tax entries to an accrual basis, the expenses are spread evenly over the year on a monthly basis, with an adjustment for the actual cash out of pocket in the months in which they are paid (i.e., April and December). The insurance, which is paid on an annual basis, is spread out over the year and adjusted in the month of June, showing the monthly accrual of $4,000 offset by the $48,000 in premium paid. If the premium is paid over a three-year period, the monthly accrual would be 1/36 of the total, and the adjustment in the month paid would be the total premium.

If the basic budget is prepared on an accrual basis, the monthly reports should also be prepared on the accrual basis. If this is not done, each monthly report will require an explanation of the variance between the cash and the accrual basis.

In general, most leases require CAM to be reconciled on an accrual basis. So, even if an owner requires cash basis financials, the real estate manager would still need to determine all adjustments required to convert the cash books to accrual books to properly calculate CAM.

EXHIBIT 13.1

Cash Versus Accrual Budget Entries

CASH FORMAT

ITEM	JAN	FEB	MAR	APR	MAY	JUNE	JULY	AUG	SEP	OCT	NOV	DEC	TOTAL
REAL ESTATE TAXES				48,600								48,600	97,200
INSURANCE						48,000							48,000
TOTAL	0	0	0	48,600	0	48,000	0	0	0	0	0	48,600	145,200
ACCRUAL FORMAT													
REAL ESTATE TAXES	8100	8100	8100	(40,500)	8100	8100	8100	8100	8100	8100	8100	(40,500)	0
INSURANCE	4000	4000	4000	4000	4000	(44,000)	4000	4000	4000	4000	4000	4000	0
TOTAL	12,100	12,100	12,100	(36,500)	12,100	(35,900)	12,100	12,100	12,100	12,100	12,100	(36,500)	0

Bank Reconciliation

A bank reconciliation is a critical financial tool for the property owner. The reconciliation brings all of the financial records together and verifies the accuracy and completeness of the real estate management firm's reports. It is best if the bank statement date and the date of the financial reports are the same, but that is not mandatory.

Many real estate management companies close their books on the 25th of the month in order to get monthly management reports to owners by the due date. They have the bank records closed on that date as well. In some companies, the accountant prepares the bank reconciliation and the real estate managers are responsible for reviewing it for reasonableness, including reviewing any reconciling items.

Check Requests

The real estate manager uses the check request form to instruct the accounting department to issue a check when an invoice is not available or is not appropriate to the transaction. A check request form is often used to return a security deposit to the tenant or as a down payment on a larger job when the invoice has not yet been prepared. This form provides the authorization for the accounting department to issue a check and creates the necessary documentation in the files as a backup. This entire process can be done electronically.

Coding Invoices

Coding invoices is a simple process; however, it can involve several employees or several departments, depending upon the size of the real estate management firm. The coding of invoices has important accounting implications.

Coding System

When setting up the coding system, the real estate manager must make a few decisions. First, who will be responsible for deciding which account an expense should be charged, and who actually codes the bill? Next, will a second person approve the expenditures? Will the property accountant be responsible for reviewing the accuracy of the codes? Finally, what format will be used to code the invoices?

Since the real estate manager is responsible for the operations of the property, he or she may personally code and approve all invoices. Real estate managers may also delegate the coding of the invoices to their assistants or operations managers. After the invoices are coded and approved, the real estate manager approves them for payment by initialing the appropriate form. When reviewing the invoice, the real estate manager should ensure that the property charged is correct, the description is informative, and the coding is consistent with where the expenditure was coded in the budget.

Each person who approves invoices should have monetary limits of approval. These limits should be based on the property owner's requirements or on the real estate management firm's policies. The property owner may require the real estate manager's supervisor to approve all invoices above an agreed amount, such as $10,000, or the property owner may want to approve such invoices. The real estate management firm may set approval limits based on the person's position within the company. Entry-level real estate managers, senior real estate managers, and those in upper management and executive positions may have different limits of approval.

Each invoice can be stamped with the appropriate approval code, or a preprinted code approval form can be attached to the invoice. Coding stamps or attachment sheets usually allow for approving an invoice and splitting the charges between two or more budgets, such as landscape supplies for CAM parking lot and mall expenses, or for splitting an invoice between two or more projects.

Accounting for Invoices

Once the real estate manager approves the invoice, it is forwarded to the accounting department for payment. The property accountant should review the coding to be sure it has the proper approvals, code is correct, extensions are correct, and the bill is an invoice and not a statement.

Occasionally, utility bills are sent to the accounting department for payment before the real estate manager's approval. This situation occurs if the real estate manager and the property accountant cannot process the invoice in sufficient time to meet the payment due date. A late utility bill payment could mean a late fee or a utility shut-off, both which should be avoided. When the time element is crucial, the real estate manager approves the bill after it has been processed for payment. If the billing is in error, there is usually time to revise the payment amount before it is paid, or an adjustment can be made to the next month's billing. Many owners maintain running spreadsheets on utility charges and track the usage and charges for each property on an ongoing basis.

Nonbudget/Over-Budget Expense Approval

The typical real estate management agreement requires the real estate manager to receive prior written approval for a non-budgeted expense over a predetermined amount. The form provides for a concise but brief explanation of the need for exceeding the budget or the spending limit. The real estate manager should discuss the approval form and receive verbal approval from the property owner before the form is mailed. The property owner signs the form and returns it to the real estate manager or sends an e-mail approving the expenditures. The form is filed in the property's file.

RENT COLLECTION

Rent collection is one of the real estate manager's activities more important responsibilities. Without an adequate and consistent income stream, few property owners can continue to implement a maintenance management program, invest in capital improvements, properly serve tenants, and pay the debt service on the property. Most, if not all, property owners require the real estate manager to make rent collection a first priority.

Delinquency Reports

Delinquency reports are essential tools for determining when rent collection procedures are necessary. An important issue to consider is the timing and frequency of delinquency reports.

One of the differences between commercial and residential property's rent collection is how rent is paid. Apartment residents usually pay their rent to an on-site resident manager, while commercial tenants send their rent checks through the mail. Sometimes rent may be mailed directly to the accounting department or to a lockbox account. However, if payment is sent to a lockbox account, it can result in further delays in confirming rent receipts. Most commercial tenants will pay their rent electronically. Because of delays in mail delivery, most commercial real estate management firms do not produce their first arrearage or delinquency reports until at least the fifth of the month. Real estate management firms select a fixed date for the first arrearage report. The earlier in the month the report is produced, the more effective the rent collection program will be.

Some real estate management firms produce a second arrearage report 10 to 15 days following the first report. Most accounting systems are set up to maintain a running accounting of collections and can be easily accessed by the real estate manager at any time. In most cases, real estate managers will run new updated reports and at month's end, a final report is included as part of the owner's monthly reports. This is normally a detailed report showing the total amount delinquent with sub-accounts showing each delinquent item and the amount due for each category.

The real estate manager should follow up with habitually delinquent tenants early in the month. It's recommended to obtain an *arrearage report* and contact tenants based on their preferred method of contact a minimum of three days before late fee grace period ends to give them the opportunity to pay their rent prior to late fee charges being assessed to their account. Even if the first arrearage report is not produced until the 10th of the month or later, the real estate manager knows which tenants are rent collection problems. Check with the property accountant right after the first of the month to determine if those tenants have paid their full rent. If the rent has not been received, immediately contact the tenant. This approach to rent collection eliminates the temptation to delay rent collection activities until an arrearage report has been prepared. It's important to contact delinquent tenants immediately.

Rent Collection Procedures

There are typically three reasons that tenants pay their rent late:

1. Cash flow problems with businesses
2. Poor bookkeeping procedures most often found with small businesses
3. Tenant's deliberate use of the property owner's money

If a tenant pays its rent three to four weeks late every month, the tenant has earned interest on or has had the use of the owner's funds. If the tenant has multiple locations, this can be a significant amount of money. In this case, aggressive and effective rent collection procedures should be put in place.

The first step in a rent collection program is to instill a sense of urgency in everyone involved in rent collection. The real estate manager can easily become engrossed in marketing and leasing, tenant relations, maintenance management, emergency procedures, or the "paperwork" of real estate management and not devote sufficient time to rent collection. A lax rent collection effort adversely affects the real estate management company and lowers management fees. Property owners will lose confidence in the real estate manager and the company, and the account will be in jeopardy. In addition, most management fees are based on a percentage of the collected income.

The next step in a rent collection procedure is to review each tenant's lease. Though most commercial leases call for rent to be due on the first of the month, they differ on when rent is considered late, when a late charge can be assessed, what procedures to use for assessing a late charge, and how to calculate a late charge. Real estate managers often implement the company's rent collection procedures and are surprised to find that tenants have an old lease form that varies from the current form and calls for rent to be due later in the month or does not provide for late charges.

Contacting Tenants

When contacting tenants, a personal visit is usually more effective; however, the quickest and most practical way is by phone. Otherwise, communication by e-mail is another option, but be sure that the e-mail is sent to the person responsible for rental payments. This often occurs with many regional and national tenants whose rent payment comes from the company's main office, usually located in another area of the country from the real estate management company.

When contacting a commercial tenant that sends its rent payment through the mail, never accuse the tenant of not paying rent. Rather, take a firm but polite approach and inform the tenant that the rent payment has not been received. The payment may currently be in transit, lost in the mail, misplaced, misrouted in the real estate management company's office, or credited to another tenant.

Late Charges

Reminding tenants of the late charge provisions in their leases and enforcing the provisions are important components in the rent collection procedure. Some commercial leases allow an automatic late charge assessment if rent is not received by a certain date. Others require a written notice to the tenants and a short time—usually three days—for the tenant to respond with a rent payment before a late charge is assessed. Most experienced tenants negotiate this provision in their leases.

Review the tenant's lease and follow the prescribed procedure for assessing a late charge. When a tenant is informed that a late charge will be assessed and the rent is not received by the required date, the late charge should be assessed immediately. If a threat is not carried through, the real estate manager's credibility on the issue will be lost.

Most tenants will pay their assessed late charges if that is a lease requirement. If they refuse to pay, the lease must be reviewed for further action. Most commercial leases consider late charges and other fees as additional rent and the remedies are the same as for nonpayment of rent, thus, allowing the real estate manager to deduct the charge from the tenant's security deposit, place the tenant in default of its lease, and commence eviction action.

Notice of Default in Payment of Rent

Notices of default can serve a very useful purpose in assuring compliance with various lease terms. Most well-drafted leases have default provisions that spell out the timing for payment of rent and the action that the property owner can take to gain compliance. Depending on the reasons for the default, the owner may consider several approaches.

Immediate Notice of Default

A notice of *default* is generally used after the real estate manager has tried to collect moneys or obtain the tenant's cooperation in correcting a problem within the premises, such as unauthorized signage or parking in customer spaces. Going directly to an attorney for legal action in the event of a breach of the lease is one option, but this solution is expensive and generally causes hard feelings on the part of the tenant.

Some leases require advance written notice before the property owner can take legal action. It's helpful to use a default letter template for initial default notice. If the tenant doesn't cure the default by the time provided in the letter, then refer the default to an attorney with the property owner's permissions. Real estate managers will also inform the tenant in advance if they are forced to get an attorney involved. This shows that the real estate manager is looking out for the tenant's best interest in giving them the heads up before getting an attorney involved.

The real estate manager must be fully aware of the timing allowed in the lease and properly state this information in the notice of default. If the lease allows tenants 30 days to cure a nonmonetary default and you give them only 10 days, the tenant can argue that proper notification has not been provided and, should the matter wind up in court, the tenant is likely to win.

Some leases require that notices of default be mailed to the tenant by certified mail—return receipt requested. Some indicate only that the notice must be mailed to a specific location in order to be valid. However, sending the notice by certified mail is a good idea because the return receipt provides evidence that the notice was received. This makes tenant denial difficult.

In cases in which the tenant tends to be lax in paying rent, but is not really a payment problem, personally hand the notice to the tenant. The personal touch and showing a little sympathy can go a long way in preserving a good relationship.

Before a notice of default in payment of rent is sent to the tenant and the guarantor, review the lease for the following:

1. Has the lease been assigned without release? If so, send a copy of the notice to the assignor after checking the notification provision of the assignment. Send a copy, if any, to the tenant and the guarantor.
2. What are the notification provisions in the lease regarding method, time, and party to receive notice?
3. When is rent due? Although most leases require rent payment on the first of the month, a few leases are negotiated for rent payment due later in the month.
4. What is the grace period for payment?
5. Is there a late charge provision? If so, is prior notice required before a late charge can be assessed?

After a notice of default is sent, set up a reminder for the date of compliance on your calendar file in your software program to allow for timely follow-up.

Alternatives to an Immediate Notice of Default

One alternative to placing the tenant in default is deducting the amount of the delinquent rents from the tenant's security deposit. The typical security deposit provision allows the property owner to use the deposit for damage to the premises caused by the tenant or its visitors, for nonpayment of rent, and for other charges. The tenant is notified through the mail—return receipt requested—that its security deposit has been reduced by the amount of the late charge. The tenant is then asked to forward a check to bring its security deposit back to the required amount. Since the tenant has not paid the late charge, it is not likely that the security deposit will be reimbursed. However, when the tenant vacates and all other lease obligations have been fulfilled, the tenant is refunded the security deposit less any delinquencies.

If the tenant is having cash-flow problems, the real estate manager, with their owner's approval, can take one approach or a combination of the following five approaches:

1. Demand that the rent be paid on time
2. Start eviction procedures per the property owner's rights in the lease
3. Develop a payment plan
4. Relocate the tenant to a less costly space
5. Offer monetary relief (rent relief).

Offering rent relief can take several forms: deferred rent, reduced rent, waived rent, or application of a portion or all of the security deposit towards the back or future rent. If a payment plan or rent relief is negotiated, an amendment to the lease should be prepared that should be executed by all parties to the lease. However, some real estate management companies do not want their real estate managers preparing lease documents and would rather have attorneys handle this process.

Another alternative to pursuing delinquent rent is to issue the tenant a notice to pay rent or quit. This notice provides the tenant the option to vacate the premises. The real estate manager should receive approval from the property owner—preferably in writing before issuing such a notice.

Some owners want an aggressive approach toward delinquencies, while others are more lenient. The real estate manager should understand these preferences and keep the owner informed about the company's rent collection procedures. When a rent collection procedure is agreed upon, the real estate manager must keep the owner informed of those tenants in arrears and the action taken to collect delinquent rent. Delinquencies are discussed in the real estate manager's monthly management report, and if rent collection becomes a problem, discussing the collection efforts and results monthly on the phone or in person may be necessary.

Rent Collection Procedures after Notice of Default

Once a notice is issued, the management staff can be assigned the responsibility of collecting the rent. Rent checks will be mailed or dropped off at the management office. In special situations, the real estate manager or assistant manager can visit the tenant to collect the rent.

Rent received after a notice of default is deposited daily. Good internal controls dictate that one person open the envelopes and makes a list of the checks received. A second person records the checks on a deposit slip and deposits the checks at a local bank. The deposit slip and the list of checks received can be faxed or e-mailed daily to the controller at the real estate management firm's main office.

The controller for the real estate management firm sweeps the account daily by transferring the money to the real estate management firm's main bank—or a bank designated by the property owner. If the on-site management office has a computer connected to the main office, an on-site staff person can post the rent collected and generate an arrearage report. If the on-site office does not have the ability to interface with the main office, the real estate manager or the assistant can check off from a list of tenants those who paid and those to contact for nonpayment. Many property owners can track their properties at will.

Collection Agencies

When a real estate manager is unsuccessful in collecting past due rent from a former tenant, the real estate manager may need to turn the matter over to a collection agency. Before this occurs, a collection agreement is negotiated between the real estate manager as agent for the property and the collection agency. The main points to negotiate include (1) how collected rent is apportioned between the property and the collection agency—for example, a 50/50 or 60/40 split; (2) whether the property is charged attorney or court fees; and (3) whether the real estate manager has the sole discretion in deciding whether to commence litigation. A *transmittal letter* or an e-mail to the collection agency authorizes the collection process to begin. Supporting information regarding the collection and the collection agency's form should be attached to the letter.

Forfeiting Security Deposits

The primary purpose of the security deposit is to reimburse the property owner for a tenant's monetary default. A security deposit can be used to repair damaged caused by a tenant and other non-rental issues. Some states require a separate bank account for security deposits; the owner or real estate manager must ensure their accounts and procedures comply with local codes. When applying the security deposit because of default or for any other reason, send a letter notifying the tenant why and how the property owner is using the security deposit and to replenish the security deposit account. The letter should be sent by registered mail and a copy of the letter, and the return receipt should be inserted in the tenant's lease file.

LEASE FILES

A standard procedure should be established for filing each tenant's lease and correspondence—this can be a paper file or an electronic file. This allows easy access to information for anyone in the real estate management company.

Two files should be maintained for each tenant: a vault file and a working copy. The vault or "gold" file is a signed original that is placed in a fireproof cabinet. It is not used for day-to-day operations. The working copy of the lease does not need to be an original. It is becoming more common now to have the operating leases set up as lease files electronically and can then be reviewed on the real estate manager's personal computer or tablet, as needed. When the building has an on-site manager, the working file is kept in his or her office; otherwise, it is kept at the main office. In larger offices, if paper copies are maintained, it is a good idea to keep only one project in a file drawer so there is little chance of mixing up files and/or losing a file by putting it in the wrong place.

INSURANCE

Owners and tenants have specific responsibilities with regard to insurance. The commercial lease governs those responsibilities.

Tenants' Insurance Certificates

The typical commercial lease requires the tenant to maintain specific types of insurance coverage with stated minimum limits. The tenant is also required to provide the property owner with evidence of the coverage, and the insurance policy must name the property owner and the real estate management company as additional insured.

The real estate management company is responsible for monitoring the tenants' lease obligations. The real estate manager or an administrative assistant requests a certificate of insurance from the tenant and ensures that each certificate states the proper type and amount of coverage and that the owner's name is correctly stated as an additional or named insured as well as the real estate management company. An insurance summary showing each tenant, lease requirements, and expiration date of the current certificate is helpful.

A follow-up electronic system similar to the deferred conditions report can be developed to list each tenant's insurance expiration date 60 days in advance.

The real estate manager's assistant sends a notice reminding the tenant of the insurance expiration date and requesting a new certificate for the renewed insurance. Keeping track of tenants' insurance can be even more time consuming and difficult than collecting rent.

Property Owner's Insurance

The property owner acquires the insurance for the property and bills the insurance expense to the tenants per the bill-back method allowed in the lease. The owner's insurance does not cover the tenants' improvements, stock, or fixtures.

The real estate manager must be alert to insurance coverage limits negotiated by tenants in their lease that may affect the owner's ability to fully recover the premiums. If both parties agree that the tenant will reimburse the property owner for a pro rata share of premiums for $1 million liability coverage, but the owner elects to carry $5 million in coverage, the owner will be liable for the premiums above the agreed amounts.

Insurance for Shopping Centers

If a major retail tenant and many pad or outlot tenants in shopping centers are required to provide fire and extended coverage insurance for their building, the rest of the tenants are billed for the property owner's fire and extended coverage for the buildings they occupied. When this situation exists, a different denominator is used for allocating common area insurance and building insurance for shopping centers. These distinctions are both important when purchasing the insurance coverage and when allocating the costs. Shopping center leases generally allow the property owner to bill the tenants on a full pro rata basis.

Most property owners include rental interruption insurance premiums as part of the bill backs under the insurance clause. National chains and major tenants may negotiate this provision out of the lease, believing that the owner should pay for the protection of its income stream—not the tenant who will be out of business during the interruption. Tenants also argue they have their own income streams to protect.

Insurance for Office Buildings and Industrial Properties

Insurance for office buildings and industrial properties is included in the building operating expenses and billed back to tenants, along with the other operating expenses of the buildings. One bill is sent to the tenants covering all of the expenses.

NOTICE OF NONRESPONSIBILITY

A notice of nonresponsibility form is used in some states to protect the property owner against liens from tenant-contracted work. These forms are available in each area with this protection and have specific requirements for that area. The form is posted in a conspicuous location on the premises, and it is officially recorded. Verifying this process is important because communities have widely varying requirements. Some municipalities require the form to be posted within a specific time of the start of construction to be valid.

REAL ESTATE TAXES

Most shopping centers, office buildings, and industrial properties have one real property tax bill for the entire property. The property owner pays the taxes and bills the tenants for their pro rata shares based on the total leasable area of the property. For example, in a property with 100,000 square feet of leasable area, a tenant occupying 2,500 square feet is responsible for 2.5 percent of the property tax bill.

In some shopping centers, there are exceptions to having one property tax bill covering the entire property. The real estate manager must be aware of these exceptions to be sure all property taxes are properly allocated and that the property owner is reimbursed. Major or outlot (pad) tenants may have their parcels segregated and may be billed separately for property taxes. Before starting any allocations, the real estate manager should obtain an assessor's map to determine how the property is segregated for tax purposes. The real estate manager should reconcile that map to the leases. A property tax record can then be prepared to allocate the costs properly.

A major retail tenant in a shopping center may have its building footprint and possibly its parking field on a separate parcel. The building and land will be separately accessed and receive a separate tax bill. The balance of the shopping center would receive a separate tax bill which would be allocated to the rest of the tenants. In a mall, the taxes on the enclosed structure are allocated only to the mall tenants, while taxes on the parking lot are allocated to all tenants. Because of these variations, the potential for misallocation is great.

Another variation on tax billings is the base-year tax approach. The theory of base-year billing is that the property owner sets the rents knowing the amount of the taxes in the year the tenant takes occupancy. The tenant's base year is stated in the lease. The base year is negotiable, but it is usually the year the tenant takes occupancy of the leased premises. If the taxes on the premises were $800 during the base year, the property owner would pay $800, and the tenant would pay the annual increase more than $800. For example, a lease is negotiated today, and the current taxes on the premises are $1,120. For this example, assume a five-percent per-year increase in taxes. The amount each party would pay on a five-year lease is shown in Exhibit 13.2. If a new lease is signed, the new base rent will reflect the current taxes on the new commencement date. The full pro rata bill back is much more common for shopping centers than the base-year approach, but base-year formulas still exist in older leases and, from time to time, in current negotiations. Office buildings and industrial properties may have the full bill back charge or a base-year formula.

TAX APPEALS

Real estate taxes represent a major expense of commercial properties. The tenants' leases need to be carefully summarized or abstracted to correctly bill each tenant for its share of the real estate taxes.

Importance of Tax Appeals

Because taxes are such a large portion of the operating expenses of commercial properties, it is prudent to analyze them on an annual basis to make sure they fairly represent the value of the building and are in line with comparable buildings in the area. Additionally, leases should be carefully evaluated to be sure those who will benefit from any reduction in taxes are also required to pay a pro rata share of the cost of any appeals made for that purpose.

EXHIBIT 13.2

Five-Year Allocation of Taxes Using Base Year Approach

	Taxes	Landlord Pays	Tenant Pays
Year 1	$1,120.00	$1,120	-0-
Year 2	$1,176.00	$1,120	$ 56.00
Year 3	$1,234.80	$1,120	$114.80
Year 4	$1,296.54	$1,120	$176.54
Year 5	$1,361.37	$1,120	$241.37

Cost of an Appeal

Many property owners face a dilemma in the area of real estate taxes. While many older commercial leases provide that each tenant must pay a pro rata share of the real estate taxes of the property, these leases often do not state who bears the cost of a tax appeal. Generally, in this situation, the property owner must bear the cost of the appeal, but the tenants will benefit if a savings results. A successful appeal to reduce property taxes will also reduce tenants' operating costs, which makes a building more competitive in the marketplace. Additionally, most building leases are structured so the property owner pays all the operating costs on the vacant spaces; therefore, the owner will receive a direct benefit by achieving a tax reduction.

Lease Language

The best lease provisions allow the property owner to pass the costs for appealing the taxes along to the tenants. A sample provision might be:

> *The term 'real estate taxes' shall also include all expenses, including attorney's and other consultants' fees reasonably incurred by the property owner in seeking reduction by the taxing authorities of real estate taxes applicable to the property.*

This statement places the burden of the cost of the appeal on those most likely to benefit from a tax reduction. If taxes are charged back based on base year and appeal won for that particular year, then the real estate manager needs to adjust the base year down to reflect the revised real estate tax expense for that year.

Appeal Hazards

Building owners and real estate managers should keep in mind that in most jurisdictions, appeals can result in tax increases as well as decreases. A careful evaluation of the taxes should be prepared prior to submitting them for appeal. If the taxes are based on a realistic property valuation and are in line with like properties in the area, the owners and/or real estate managers are probably advised to accept the current assessment.

Methods of Appeal

There are two methods of appeal for the commercial property owner: (1) perform the research, file the appeal, and attend the hearings without the use of outside experts or tax consultant companies; and (2) hire a company that handles tax appeals to evaluate a case and decide if an appeal is warranted.

If the necessary research shows that a reduction in taxes is warranted by the facts of the case, the first method has an excellent chance of being successful. Unfortunately, one ingredient often missing from this approach is a knowledge of the tax laws and procedures in the community—a critical factor in complicated cases.

In following with the second method, these companies are often headed by former tax officials who are familiar with many different applications of the tax laws. Many of these companies take cases on a contingency basis, getting their fees from successful appeals and getting nothing if the taxes are not reduced. The contingency fees may range from 30 to 50 percent of the savings, usually for the first year or two of savings only. Some companies, however, use different percentages over a longer period.

The owner of the property should choose a tax specialist who has a proven track record in the community, and who is familiar with the type of property in question. Additionally, the specialist should be experienced in dealing with the tax appeal board and should have a good working relationship with the taxing authorities. The process should not be confrontational because the economic facts should support a case for reduced taxes, or the appeal should not be filed.

Economics of an Appeal

The following example focuses on a shopping center of 32,322 square feet in a major metropolitan area. This property was developed in very good economic times and is located in a fairly affluent area. The shopping center is approximately six years old and, until a downturn in the economy, it enjoyed high rents and 100-percent occupancy. The developer sold the property for a substantial price, and the real estate taxes were quite high based on the property's net income and the selling price. In the previous two years, the asking rents had fallen significantly and occupancy levels had dropped dramatically. The shopping center had been unable to institute annual rent increases, even though the tenants' leases provided for them.

Original Tax Base

The following numbers are based on the actual income and expenses for the property at the time of the first assessment, and are representative for the period involved (final assessor valuations were slightly different due to rounding, allocations, etc.).

The original income and expenses for the shopping center follow:

Gross possible income (32,322 sq. ft. × $2.00/ sq. ft. × 12 mos.)	$775,728
Vacancy and collection	(31,030)
Operating expenses	(253,690)
Net operating income	$491,008

Capitalized at 8.5 percent indicated valuation of $5,776,565

This produced a tax bill of $51,715 for the first full year of operations. The tax to each tenant came to $1.60 per square foot per year. This was a fairly high rate for the marketplace, but it was based on a realistic value in line with similar properties in the area.

Tax History

This shopping center is a California property subject to Proposition 13, which limits the annual tax increases to two percent, unless the property is sold or improved. Neither of these events took place during the periods in question, so each year the taxes were raised by two percent, giving the following results:

Tax Years	Actual Tax Bill
2007–2008	$51,715
2008–2009	52,749
2009–2010	53,804
2010–2011	54,880
2011–2012	55,978
2012–2013	57,098
2013–2014-	58,240

The property has had a consistent 11 percent vacancy rate, or approximately 3,555 square feet. The same 3,555 square feet have not been vacant, but as one space was leased up, another fell into problems and was vacated. The new rent on vacated spaces has invariably been lower per square foot than the rent of the vacating tenants. Contract rental increases have been forgiven, and the asking rate for new space is now $15.60 per square foot per year, or $1.30 per foot per month—well below the asking rates prior to the downturn.

The Appeal

A careful review of the operating statements clearly indicated that the property was operating at a level considerably below that used to establish the original tax base, and the property owner made a decision to appeal the taxes on the property.

The financial analysis was as follows:

Gross possible income (32,322 sq. ft. × $1.30/ sq. ft. × 12 mos.)	$504,223
Vacancy and collection loss	(46,571)
Operating expenses	(235,126)
Net operating income	$222,526

This represents a decrease in net operating income of $268,482 after six years of successful operations. The downturn apparently was not caused by poor management or inadequate leasing efforts.

Using the same capitalization rate (8.5 percent) that was originally used to value the property, the value of the property is $4,512,978 or approximately $1,263,563 less than the value as initially determined. Because of the high vacancy factor, reduced rents, and depressed market, a tax specialist could make an argument for a higher capitalization rate (i.e., lower value), which would reduce the taxes even further. Management, however, decided to take a very conservative approach, believing that the assessor would be more open to a reasonable request than to one that pushed the limits on all fronts. The automatic two-percent increases on an annual basis were not based on valuation; rather, they were based on the legal maximum increase.

Appeal Results

By transferring the original mill rate to the new valuation, the assessor came up with the following tax billing:

New value $4,512,978 × .009 = $40,616

This appeal will decrease real estate taxes $17,623 in the current year, representing a savings for each tenant of approximately 61 cents per square foot of occupied space for the year. A tenant renting a 1,000-square-foot space will realize a savings of $610 on the tax bill, less the pro rata share of the cost of the appeal. The owner, who pays the taxes on the vacant space, will save approximately $1,900 this year, making the exercise valuable on that basis alone. Additionally, common area costs for the new tenants will be lower because of the appeal, making the space more attractive in the marketplace. This appeal was performed in-house, so the only cost was for the appeal itself and the drawing up of some documents to prove the case. No effort was made to charge off management time for the procedure; however, that would have been a reasonable charge against the total costs.

Because the appeal was based on lower occupancy and a difficult market, the owner will now be required to submit a tenant roster and an operating statement each year to justify the continued lower assessment. If the economic conditions improve, the assessment will be raised as the fortunes of the property improve.

If the owners had elected to use a consultant for the job, a fee of 35 to 40 percent of the savings would probably have been negotiated, but in some cases may actually start as low as 20 percent. A tenant with a 1,000-square-foot property would still have benefited by approximately $366 in the first year of the reduction.

Even if the appeal had been unsuccessful, the effort would have been worthwhile from a management perspective as long as taxes were not raised as a result. The filing of an appeal shows existing merchants that the property owner considered the matter and made a reasonable effort to reduce the taxes.

UTILITIES

If possible, management should avoid billing premises utilities back to tenants. If management has no choice because of the excess cost of retrofitting meters for each space, the next best choice is submetering to prevent any argument about each tenant's usage. Billing tenants separately for utilities cost is more common in shopping centers and industrial properties than office buildings.

In some states, the owner is not allowed to bill tenants for electricity on the submeter readings so that it is used to estimate the costs—the owner and tenant negotiated a per square foot charge for that service. It is difficult to allocate electricity costs between a 1,200-square-foot store open eight hours a day, six days a week, and a 2,300-square-foot diner open 14 hours a day, seven days a week. Consider also the problems in allocating water costs to five different tenants ranging in size from 900 square feet to 4,000 square feet and in use from a Laundromat to a variety store.

Tenants such as supermarkets and restaurants may want to control the lighting around their premises because their business hours extend beyond those of the shopping center. For example, if a supermarket is open 24 hours a day, the electricity to the light poles in the parking lot in front of it may be connected to the supermarket's electrical meter. In this situation, the real estate manager should remove the electricity cost from the CAM budget, create a separate billing for it, and bill all the tenants except the supermarket for their pro rata shares of the CAM electricity expense.

Another difficulty in allocating utility costs occurs when tenants have excessive usage. This situation can be resolved in several ways. The first is to bill the tenants whose use is excessive an over-standard utility charge and then credit the charge to the CAM budget. A consultant or utility company representative should determine the amount of over-standard utilities consumed by a particular tenant. A second solution is to remove the utility expense from the CAM budget and have a separate meter for the tenant with the excessive usage. This tenant is billed on its actual usage, and the other tenants are billed a pro rata share of the master-meter utility cost. The denominator for calculating these pro rata utility shares would be the square footage of all the tenants—except the one with the separate meter.

To bill tenants their cost of a master-metered utility, check to see which meter or system serves which spaces. This can be done by reviewing the original plans or, if necessary, by physically checking each space. Every tenant's usage must be determined because a pro rata square footage allocation is seldom an equitable approach to utility distribution. The local utility company can generally be of help in determining probable usage by each type of tenant in a shopping center, giving special consideration to minimum billings and peak demands. A model of utility use allocations should be prepared and monitored.

CASH FLOW STATEMENT

The monthly operating cash flow statement provides critical information for the financial analysis of the property for the prior month. Wide variances in individual expenses are quite possible, and such variances could have a severe impact on the property owner's cash flow. Some property owners believe a quarterly report is adequate, but most require a monthly report. Property owners often stipulate the final format of the report and may provide the chart of accounts so the real estate manager's numbers tie in with other reports to the owner.

Most statements are keyed to the budget that is prepared and approved prior to the commencement of the property's fiscal year. It is accepted practice to begin with the gross possible rent, or gross scheduled rent—the rent that would be collected with the property fully leased. The *effective income* is determined by subtracting the lost income from the anticipated vacancy and credit loss, which is either the actual number of vacancies, historical factor that appears to be reasonable in the marketplace, or projection of which spaces will be vacant and for how long during the budget period. The net figure is the total rent the owner can anticipate collecting. Some owners eliminate the gross rent calculation, but factoring in a figure for vacancy, credit loss, and collections is recommended.

Percentage rents, if any, are usually separated from base rents as an individual line item because they are subject to fluctuation. CAM, taxes, insurance, and utility recovery items are also generally segregated for easier tracking, but all bill-back items can be subtotaled. Miscellaneous income includes interest income, late charges, and so on. Total revenues are shown as a line item for easy review.

Expenses are almost always assigned to different operating budgets—based on who will finally pay the bills or how the bills will be treated from an accounting perspective.

Operating expenses are items subject to being billed back to the tenants. They are separated into categories detailed enough to allow the real estate manager to analyze them and simple enough for the tenant to understand. Major repairs may include those items that may be billed back over time, or they may be an arbitrary category created by the property owner to track larger expenses.

Total operating expenses are a line item combining all of the previously mentioned expense items. Total income less operating expenses equals net operating income. This figure is used to establish value through capitalization of the net operating income.

Owner's expenses are expenditures paid by the property owner and not billed back to the building occupants. This category does not include capital items or the costs of servicing the mortgage. Such costs are not considered to be "operating costs" and are, therefore, placed after net operating income (placed below the line).

Capital expenditures, such as replacement of major building components and leasing commissions, are shown below the line (after NOI) since they are almost always amortized over a period in excess of one year. These items are deducted from net operating income on the net cash flow statement.

If the property has a mortgage, the mortgage payment is deducted at this point, and the net result is cash flow after debt service.

This statement does not take into consideration the property owner's income tax position and/or cash distribution to the owner.

MARKETING BUDGET FOR SHOPPING CENTERS AND MALLS

Malls, outlet shopping centers, lifestyle shopping centers, and specialty shopping centers have a marketing budget. The property owner is responsible for developing and implementing the marketing program. Typically, the merchants are assessed dues based on a dollar amount per square foot per year. The property owner traditionally contributes 25 to 33 percent of the amount collected from the tenants.

TENANT REQUESTS

In the day-to-day management of properties, real estate managers receive many requests from tenants for information, answers, required services, and services management is not obligated to provide. A lease agreement sets forth the parameters of the relationship between real estate manager and tenant. Just to "follow the lease," should be easy, but the lease often is not clear on the specific limits of the obligations.

The nature of the relationship with the tenant is often affected by the approach the real estate manager takes. When responding to a tenant request, consider which of the two different relationships apply: (1) a fiduciary relationship or (2) a non-fiduciary relationship. If the request pertains to common areas, taxes, or insurance billings, real estate managers operate in a fiduciary capacity on behalf of the tenant, and they have a higher obligation to provide information and help assure the tenant that moneys are being spent responsibly. If the tenant is asking for a copy of the lease or for an interpretation of lease language, a real estate manager does not have a fiduciary obligation, but may want to be helpful to the tenant which encourages a good working relationship with the tenant.

Common Area Requests

Most tenants sign their lease with a general idea of the cost of the CAM, taxes, and insurance. Over time as these costs increase, tenants may request explanations from the real estate manager of these charges. It is best to explain the budget to the tenant and be willing to answer any question.

Complaints about Contractors

Tenants may complain about the work of contractors on the property. Some of the contractors come in at night to perform their services, and some come in very early in the morning before the property is open for business. Tenants can easily believe the contractor's job is not being done, and at times, they may be right. The real estate manager should discuss the tenant's issues and in a few situations suggest that the contractor's representative call on the tenant to discuss the problem in the presence of the real estate manager.-

Other Tenants' Billings

To the extent that one tenant's billing may affect another tenant, the second tenant has the right to know about it. If an anchor tenant occupies 32.5 percent of a shopping center and has negotiated a lease or common area agreement limiting its CAM contribution to 28 percent, a tenant that is paying the difference has a right to know. If the property owner is paying the difference, the real estate manager can demonstrate that to the tenant. Most owners and/or real estate managers keep allocation charts so they can show each tenant how the charges are allocated and give the tenant the opportunity to verify that the billings are accurate.

If one tenant has negotiated a concession in common area, tax, or insurance payments and the other tenants are not paying for that concession, the other tenants have no right to know about the lease negotiations. Nevertheless, if such concessions have been made, the property owner and/or the real estate manager must take great care in what they say to other tenants. Comments such as, "Every tenant is paying its fair share," would not be accurate if some tenants have received concessions.

It is not a good idea to tell the other tenants that no one has concessions when, in fact, they do—even if the concessions do not cost the other merchants anything. A good answer is each lease is negotiated separately and the outcome of the negotiations are based on several factors many unique to the specific tenant.

Contracts and Agreements

All contracts and service agreements for the common areas are made on behalf of the tenants. For that reason alone, every tenant has a right to see the contracts if they wish. If more than one property is on a contract, the property owner and/or real estate manager may not want anyone to see the information on other buildings. In such cases, each property should have its own contracts.

The real estate manager should let the tenants know that management is always interested in meeting with contractors they believe to be capable of performing building services. Management should always be happy to talk with potential contractors, take comparative bids on projects, and improve its position. If a tenant recommends a new contractor for common area work, interview that contractor to see if they are qualified and if so, solicit a bid at the appropriate time.

If contractors are owned by the property owner or the real estate management company, that fact should be available to the tenants so they do not discover it from a worker and feel that it is being hidden from them. Quite often, an employee of the owner and/or real estate manager can do many jobs more efficiently and for less money than an outside contractor could, but the tenants should know if the contractor is a captive company.

MISCELLANEOUS ADMINISTRATIVE ITEMS

This section presents forms, lease, provisions letters, and other useful information that did not fit logically anywhere else in this chapter. The entries are in alphabetical order.

Abandoning Tenant

When a tenant vacates the premises before the lease expires, the real estate manager must notify the tenant that it is still obligated to fulfill the lease terms. A letter to an abandoning tenant informs the tenant that it remains obligated for the rental payments. If the rent is not current, the letter includes a demand for rent. This letter can counter a tenant's potential claim that the property owner or real estate manager verbally agreed to cancel the lease.

Antenna and Satellite Disk

This income component involves leasing space on the roof for antennas and satellite disks. Depending on a user's need for the building's location and height, a property owner can charge an annual rent from a few thousand to a hundred thousand dollars for space for one antenna or satellite disk.

Many buildings can accommodate several antennas and disks. Considerations in installation include whether the roof can bear the weight of the antenna or disk, the appearance of one or multiple antennas or disks on the roof, interference that one antenna may create for another, maintenance requirements, and access to the roof.

The tenant's lease or a separate agreement is used for a tenant's use of the roof. The agreement will state that the tenant is responsible for the repairs and damage to their equipment and to the building if the damage is caused by the tenant, people servicing the equipment, or its equipment.

Assignment of Lease

When a lease is assigned, it is important to have all parties sign a document covering the salient points. The owner or its attorney preapproves the format. The assignment of lease includes all pertinent information in the lease, such as the names of the owner and tenant as well as the description of the premises. It indicates the effective date and states the disposition of the security deposit. Any unresolved issues, such as moneys due, year-end common area reconciliation, or changes in terms are included.

Most owners use an assignment without release—an assignment that does not release the assignor, the party assigning the lease, from his or her obligations under the lease. It protects the property owner if the assignee, the new tenant, defaults on the lease. In that situation, the assignor would be obligated for all future rents. If the assignment is for a retail space and the lease has a continuing operation clause, the assignor would be obligated to operate the business if the assignee failed to do so. Each party to the document should receive a signed original of the assignment.

Holdover Agreement

Commercial leases have a *holdover tenancy* provision stating that if a tenant does not renew its lease and remains in possession of the premises, the tenancy is on a month-to-month basis and the rent is increased—usually one and a half to four times the last month's rent.

Normally if a tenant subsequently renews their lease, any holdover rents charged may be waived. If a property owner and tenant have agreed to continue the tenancy on a month-to-month basis, a holdover agreement documents the understanding. This agreement states the rental rate and the notice necessary to terminate the lease.

Holiday Schedule

All tenants are notified if the building's management office is closed on a holiday. In most buildings, the real estate management office has a 24-hour answering service that contacts the real estate manager or engineer on call in the event a tenant calls. If the building has a guard station or an office building lobby guard, the station's phone number may be provided in the e-mail or letter. On-site maintenance personnel or roving guards may be reached through their pagers and cell phones.

Litigation Report

Occasionally, a property owner is involved in a legal dispute with a tenant or a visitor to the property. A dispute with a tenant is usually over unpaid rent. Frequently, the tenant has vacated the premises, and the real estate manager is taking legal action to collect past and future rent obligations. Owners want real estate managers to diligently collect all rent and other charges owed. It is futile, however, to expend the owner's funds to pursue a tenant who has no assets; most owners today want to approve any legal action prior to any moneys being expended.

Include the status of all litigation in the monthly management report or in a separate report. When the litigation report includes collection, the former tenant's assets should be stated. The report should state the probability of collecting all or a portion of the funds owing. It should include the attorney's cost to date and the estimated cost of resolving the litigation.

If the suit is an action taken by a party against the property owner, similar information is provided. In the case of a slip-and-fall suit, the property's insurance carrier usually defends the owner, and only a summary of the case is necessary.

Lobby/Mall Directory Listing

The lobby/mall directory listing authorization letter avoids any misunderstanding regarding how the tenant wants to be listed on the building's directory. This form is provided to the tenant and nothing should be ordered without a written order in hand.

Moving Notice

The real estate manager notifies the accounting department, the in-house maintenance staff, and anyone else that needs to know if a tenant is moving into or out of the building. The moving notice used for this purpose is also used as a check of the real estate management company's responsibilities.

Move-In

The date a tenant moves into the building triggers several events. The tenant must be billed for its rent and tenant charges. If the first month's rent has not been prepaid, it is due. If the tenant's insurance certificate and estoppel have not been received, the real estate manager or administrative assistant must follow up. Maintenance service contracts, such as janitorial service for office buildings and some industrial properties and HVAC service for retail and some industrial properties, will commence or the service will be upgraded when the tenant moves in. It's recommended that a move-in checklist be utilized to ensure everything is completed on a timely basis and nothing falls through the cracks.

Public relations releases may be mailed to the print media when a lease is executed and when a retail tenant takes occupancy. Some property owners send the tenant a welcome gift—usually a plant or flowers on the day the tenant opens for business.

The real estate manager must indicate to the accounting and administrative staff the day the tenant opens for business. The real estate manager must be in close communication with the tenant and the tenant improvement contractor to be certain of the exact date the space will be ready for occupancy.

Move-Out

The move-out notice is just as important as the move-in notice. Several events take place before, during, and after a tenant moves out of a building. When a tenant moves out, notify the cleaning company to discontinue cleaning the space (office building only), and remove the tenant's name from the directory. The security authorization card is immediately removed from the security file, and the tenant is no longer allowed in the building after hours. When a tenant vacates, either the lock set or the keying system for all doors in and to the premises are changed. The HVAC should also be adjusted for the unoccupied unit.

The premises must be inspected for damage and for abandoned personal property. It's recommended that this move-out inspection be done with a tenant representative so they are aware of any damages noted and can sign off on the inspection form. The moving notice should have a section for the tenant's move out, in which the real estate manager informs the accounting department what to do with the tenant's security deposit. If the tenant has damaged the premises, inform the accounting department to withhold a portion of the security deposit to repair the damage. Photos of the damage should be taken and stored in the tenant's file and copies sent to the tenant with the letter explaining why the tenant's security deposit has been reduced or not refunded. In addition, the security deposit should be reduced for any arrearage still owed. A forwarding address should also be obtained for future notices and billings. Next, the space must be cleaned, and depending upon the condition of the premises, painting and repairs may be necessary.

Newsletter

Every property can benefit from a newsletter. The primary purpose of a newsletter is to develop a friendly rapport with the tenants and their employees. The newsletter can also be a valuable communication tool. The newsletter can highlight new and existing tenants, provide security tips, highlight emergency procedures, promote upcoming events, and include announcements related to the building's operation staff.

It should be noted, however, that the ongoing effort to produce a newsletter on a regular schedule can be a very time-consuming task and difficult to manage during peak administrative activity. Due to this, some companies focus on e-mail to communicate ongoing information to their tenants.

Parking

Open parking allows flexibility, but when parking is limited, specific assignments are made. When parking spaces are assigned, a towing policy may be necessary. Some office properties will charge tenants and/or their employees for prime, reserved spots.

Assigned Parking

Assigned parking is common for office buildings but rare for shopping centers. Assigned spaces should be clearly numbered. The best place for the number is often at the rear of each space. When allocating spaces, the real estate manager should place the assigned area as close to the tenant's premises as is practical. If spaces are to be patrolled, a bumper sticker or a rear view mirror hanging placard will identify the user.

Towing Policy

Few actions upset tenants, visitors, or customers more than to return to the parking lot to find their cars gone. This makes the decision to tow illegally parked cars a difficult one for real estate managers. A towing policy must weigh the negative public relations that can be created when a tenant's or customer's vehicle is towed against the problems illegally parked cars can create. If a towing policy is implemented, it is essential that the real estate manager understand any community requirements on signage that will notify the driver that a towing policy is in effect.

Most parking violations involve tenants not parking in their assigned areas, abandoned vehicles, vehicles in reserved areas or drive lanes, and persons parking their vehicles on the property and going elsewhere. The real estate manager must control the use of the parking lot and garage to provide convenient parking for visitors or shoppers, access to reserved parking stalls, and clear drive lanes for delivery trucks and emergency vehicles.

The first step in developing a towing policy is to consult with the local municipality or police department regarding the rules for legally towing a vehicle. The real estate manager then establishes parking rules for the garage or parking lot, such as the following: short-term parking stalls, employees' parking areas, loading and unloading areas, and rules for overnight parking. Parking rules and regulations are included either in the tenants' leases or in the building's rules and regulations. The tenants' handbook should include information on employee parking, and if the property is a shopping center, the handbook can include a map indicating employee parking areas. Parking information can also be conveyed through the property's newsletter and e-mails.

The parking area must be properly posted. Signs usually state who can park on the lot, for what period of time, which company will tow unauthorized vehicles, and possibly the number of the municipality's ordinance that allows towing.

Appoint members of the staff who are the only persons authorized to have a vehicle towed. The persons selected must have a thorough understanding of the towing policy and good judgment to implement that policy.

When a vehicle is parked in an unauthorized zone, or is otherwise illegally parked, take one of several actions: attempt to find the driver of the vehicle, place a warning message on the vehicle, or tow the vehicle. In some cases, the vehicle's owner is a tenant who can be identified and notified to move the vehicle. Identification is simplified when employees are given a numbered parking sticker, all employees have provided the real estate manager with a description of their cars and license numbers, or the real estate manager or security person is familiar with the vehicles driven by tenants and their employees.

If a warning message is placed on the vehicle, the message should state that if the car is not moved by a certain time, e.g., 1 to 12 hours, the vehicle will be towed. Some municipalities require up to 72 hours' notice before towing abandoned vehicles. Care must be taken that the warning message is not glued to the windshield or left in a place that will obstruct the driver's vision. If a warning is posted on the windshield and the driver is unable to remove it and has an accident, the property owner or real estate management firm might be held liable.

If the decision is made to have a vehicle towed, the real estate management staff should expect to be visited by an unhappy and possibly belligerent tenant or customer. If this happens, explain politely but firmly why the property needs to enforce parking rules and what steps were made to notify the driver prior to the vehicle being towed. The violator must also be told how to regain possession of the vehicle, and should be advised that the real estate manager regretted the necessary action.

E-Mail Reminder

E-mail reminders are a fast and inexpensive way to bring issues to the attention of suppliers and tenants. Possible uses include reminding tenants that sales reports are missing or that insurance certificates are about to expire. E-mails must not be used to relate confidential information or to chastise the receiver. It is not a good tool to use if the tenant is in default or has violated property rules as anyone seeing the e-mail will be able to determine that the tenant has a problem.

Signage

The tenants' signs are among the first things a person notices when approaching a shopping center, industrial property, and sometimes an office building. These signs have an impact on the presentation of the property. A property without sign criteria usually ends up with many nonconforming signs made of several materials such as wood, plastic, or metal. Some tenants may even display homemade signs.

The property owner or real estate manager can control the appearance of signs by including sign criteria in each tenant's lease. The sign criteria should state the maximum size of the sign, type of materials that must be used to manufacture the sign, type of letters, and method of lighting. Shopping centers need sign criteria for storefront or window signs to prevent store owners from taping paper signs on the windows or across the front of entrances. In most office buildings, tenants' signs are limited to a directory listing and the company name on or adjacent to the tenant's entry door. The property owner provides these signs, and that allows the owner complete control over the signage.

Standard Transmittal

Real estate managers frequently e-mail documents (for example, leases, maintenance agreements, or contracts) to tenants or vendors for their electronic signature. A standard transmittal letter usually accompanies the PDF. The letter explains what the PDF is and what steps the tenant should take.

Tenant Handbook

The real estate manager should provide each tenant with a tenant handbook and emergency procedures. Both can be electronically transmitted. A cover letter should accompany the tenant information booklet, which tells tenants how to fulfill their responsibilities, e.g., rent payment, remodeling, and trash pick-up as well as the rules and regulations of the building. The emergency procedures portion of the booklet provides instructions for responding to a variety of emergencies. The package is provided or e-mailed to tenants before they take possession of their space.

Tenant Contact List

The real estate manager should have a tenant list for each property listing the tenant name and address, contact name and information including phone number and e-mail, home office listing, and emergency phone numbers. The most convenient and accessible tenant list would be electronic and can be on the real estate managers' computer or handheld tablet. As contacts may change, this information should be updated with the tenant on an ongoing basis—annually at a minimum.

Tenant Name Change

When a tenant changes its retail name, the real estate manager should be notified and, when appropriate, should be provided with a copy of the corporate resolution authorizing the name change. The tenant's account and lease must also reflect the name change.

Termination Agreement

Occasionally, a property owner and tenant will mutually agree to terminate the tenant's lease. This usually occurs when the tenant can no longer afford to pay the rent, and the owner has determined that the tenant does not have sufficient assets worthy of the expense of legal action. The property owner may have a new tenant in mind and negotiates a lease cancellation. The owner's main objective is to regain possession and re-lease the premises. The tenant agrees not to take legal action against the property owner for any alleged actions. Such a clause is intended to provide protection to the owner if the tenant attempts to sue based on a false claim, such as misrepresentation when the lease was signed.

Occasionally, a retail tenant that is failing claims the leasing agent or property owner made promises that have not been kept; e.g., the shopping center would have specific tenants or it would reach a certain occupancy level by a particular date. The tenant's claim is usually a ruse to get the property owner to agree to an early termination or an attempt to find a deep pocket to bail the tenant out of its financial problems.

Transmitting Signed Documents

When a lease is fully executed, the tenant receives a copy. Accompanying the tenant's paper copy of the lease is a letter welcoming the tenant to the property. The lease may be sent electronically with a welcoming e-mail. The communications with the tenant will include the names and phone numbers of the building manager, construction supervisor, and marketing director (if the property is a mall or lifestyle, specialty outlet shopping center). The document and letter are sent by certified mail with a return receipt requested. E-mails can be printed and stored in the tenant's electronic or paper file. It is important that management confirm receipt of the documents.

Utility Costs

If there is a choice, all utilities should be separately metered in shopping centers and industrial properties to avoid unfair pro rata charges and disputes between owners and tenants. However, during the development process, master-metering utilities is usually less expensive. When more than one tenant shares a meter, there is great potential for dispute. If possible, management should ask the utility company to estimate the amount each tenant would be billed if it were on a direct-bill basis. Generally, the utility company is aware of usage for similar businesses and will share information that provides a basis for the separate billing. One caution: Some leases call for pro rata square-foot billings—even on utilities. If a lease so requires, utilities should be billed accordingly.

Yield Analysis—New Lease

Exhibit 13.3 analyzes the economics of a new lease. Does the lease make economic sense? Does it meet the owner's minimum requirements? The top portion of the form summarizes pertinent lease information. The rental rate is an annual rate and may be for the first year only, or it may be an average of rents over the lease term. For consistency, operating expenses are calculated in the same manner as rent. Construction costs and leasing commissions are calculated over the term of the lease. The net income is divided by building costs or current value depending on the owner's instructions. The yield is then compared to pro forma figures to evaluate the proposed lease. Even if the net figure does not meet pro forma, the lease may be accepted for other reasons. The balance of the form considers debt service.

CONCLUSION

Real estate managers can easily devote all of their time to responsibilities that directly enhance the value of the property. Although the excitement of finalizing a lease is unmatched in real estate management, a good lease arrangement can be negated by a poor lease administration program.

EXHIBIT 13.3

Yield Analysis Form

Prepared By:____________________________
Property:_______________________________
Tenant:_________________________________
Lease Area (sq. ft.)_________________________
Building Area (sq. ft.)______________________

Date:__________________________________
Term of Lease:__________________________
Percentage Rent:________________________
Stops or Limits:_________________________
____

		Annual Per Sq. Ft.
A. Proposed tenant rental rate		$__________
B. Expenses (per square foot):		
1) Operating Cost	$______	
2) Construction cost to be paid by owner $___ –Term (years)	$______	
3) Leasing commission $___ –Term (yrs.)	$______	
Total Expenses (Sum of 1, 2, & 3)		$__________
C. Net Income (A less B)		$__________
D. Original cost of Building plus capital improvements (cash, mortage, closing costs, capital improvements)—Bldg Area		$__________
E. Current Value (most recent appraisal)—Building Area		$__________
F. EFFECTIVE YIELD: cost basis (C—D)		☐
G. CURRENT YIELD: (appraised value) C—E		☐
H. Debt Service (principal plus interest)		$__________
I. Net Income after Debt Service (C less H)		$__________
J. Current equity (D less mortgage)—Building Area		$__________
K. RETURN ON EQUITY (I—J)		☐

CHAPTER

14

Financial Analysis for Real Estate Managers

Advances in technology have enabled real estate professionals to perform more in-depth financial analysis of income-producing properties. Software programs and the ever-evolving electronic tablets have created an ease for real estate professionals to play "what-if" scenarios for rental rates that potentially increase or decrease, along with determining fluctuations in operating expenses, financing costs, equity contribution, and other variables.

Simply put, real estate management is a people business. The better people skills real estate managers have, the more likely they are to be effective in operating properties. Along with those skills, however, it's essential to have a basic knowledge of the mathematics involved in analyzing properties, negotiating lease deals, and keeping records. In fact, the real estate manager's relationship with property owners, office, industrial, and retail tenants depends heavily on his or her ability to understand and maintain proper accounting and reporting of a property's income and expenses. These skills have also become especially important due to institutions, property funds, foreign investors, and *real estate investment trusts (REITs)* as major holders of income-producing properties.

Areas that require specific math skills include basic rental computations, such as basic rents, rents per square foot, stair-stepped rents, and increases in rents based on percentages and *consumer price index (CPI)* changes; percentage rents for retail tenants; *floor-area ratios (FAR)* and parking ratios; *bill-backs* of operating costs for office buildings, industrial parks, or shopping centers; and evaluations of operating statements.

This chapter addresses the math requirements that come up most frequently in operating commercial properties. A financial calculator was used for many of the calculations. If the reader uses a standard calculator or specific software program, some answers may differ slightly due to the financial calculator's rounding.

FINANCIAL ANALYSIS FOR SHOPPING CENTERS

To make the calculations in this section more meaningful, they are based on the example of a neighborhood shopping center of 112,000 square feet shown in Exhibit 14.1. To the extent possible, these figures reflect current shopping centers and demonstrate the essential math applications.

Allowable Building Area

Most communities have maximum allowable building square footage on a given site. If the allowable ratio for common areas to building area is three feet of land for every square foot of building area, the property will need the following:

Building area	112,000 sq. ft.
Parking, sidewalk, landscaping, etc.	+336,000 sq. ft.
Total required	448,000 sq. ft.
or	
(43,560 sq. ft. in an acre)	10.2847 acres

If the site was less than 10.2847 acres, the developers would either have to get a variance from the city on the required parking spaces, or build less square footage. If the site were more than 10.3847 acres, but the developers only wanted to build 112,000 square feet at the time of development, they would need more land for future expansion plans. For the reverse problem, the number of square feet the shopping center could have if constructed on an

EXHIBIT 14.1

Neighborhood Shopping Center

Merchant	Square Footage	Minimum Monthly Rent	Percentage Rent Rate	CAM	Supervision (%)
Supermarket	52,000	$60,666.67	.015–.75	.4643	10
Drugstore	17,000	17,708.33	.03	.1518	10
Dress store	4,000	8,000.00	.05	.0357	15
Men's store	2,500	4,750.00	.05	.0223	15
Dollar store	6,000	9,000.00	.04	.0536	15
Restaurant	12,500	22,500.00	.06	.1116	10
Cleaners	2,000	3,400.00	.07	.0179	15
Pet store	2,500	4,150.00	.06	.0223	15
Deli	1,800	3,345.65	.05	.0161	15
Bank	5,400	10,560.00	0	.0482	15
Pizzeria	3,000	6,000.00	.06	.0268	15
Jewelry	1,700	3,450.25	.07	.0152	15
Shoes	1,600	2,855.64	.04	.0142	15

Total Gross Leasable Area—112,000 sq. ft.

11.5 acre site, with a community requirement of four square feet of land for every one square foot of building area, can be solved as follows:

Total area in square feet 11.5 acres = 500,940 sq. ft.

To determine building area, divide by five.

500,940 ÷ 5 = 100,188 sq. ft.

To determine remaining land area, subtract building area from total area.

500,940 – 100,188 = 400,752 sq. ft.

Parking Ratios

Some communities require a minimum number of parking spaces per thousand square feet of building area. If the required parking ratio in the shopping center example is five spaces per thousand square feet of building area, the calculation would be as follows:

112,000 ÷ 1,000 = 112

112 × 5 = 560

In this case, the shopping center would require 560 parking spaces. The project architect would then have to determine the feasibility of providing the necessary parking, entrances, exits, and other features within the subject site. The final decision on parking may take into account the types of tenants and the use of compact parking spaces to increase the stalls without having to have all stalls large enough to accommodate full-size cars.

The most definitive resource for proper parking ratios is a publication titled, *Parking Requirements for Shopping Centers, Summary Recommendations and Research Study Report,* published by the Urban Land Institute (ULI) and the International Council for Shopping Centers (ICSC). This publication was the first to indicate that smaller shopping centers do not need the parking allowances that had been the industry standard for years. With fewer parking spaces, a shopping center can add more *gross leasable area (GLA),* which should add to the center's value. This publication is a great tool for a shopping center owner or a real estate manager to use when trying to persuade local planning commissions to reduce parking requirements for a specific shopping center. One should be cautioned, however, that just because one can add square footage does not mean that it is good for a shopping center.

Some shopping centers have been known to add too many outlot or pad tenants that could potentially block the line of sight for in-line merchants and create other problems for existing tenants. Great care should be made that no agreements are violated and that existing tenants are not harmed by the additional space. For instance, a shopping center added an outlot location with a fast-food restaurant which included a drive-through window. The restaurant was quite successful, but at peak times, the line for the drive-through window blocked a nearby driveway and caused traffic problems for the entire shopping center.

Rent per Square Foot

The shopping center industry quotes almost all figures on a per-square-foot basis, making comparisons easy. One of the most basic calculations is rent per square foot, which is the typical approach to determine rental rates. Some parts of the country quote rents per square foot per month while others quote rents per square foot per year. By using a rate per square foot, it is much easier to compare one's shopping center to the others in the area. If a competitive shopping center is collecting $28,000 per month from a similar restaurant, there is no comparison until the square footage of that restaurant is known, in order to calculate the rate per square foot.

The shopping center example in Exhibit 14.1 can serve to illustrate both methods. The restaurant occupies 12,500 square feet, and its monthly rent is $22,500.00. The calculation for rent per square foot per month is as follows (some figures have been rounded):

$22,500.00 ÷ 12,500 = $1.80 per sq. ft. per month

There are two ways to find the rate per square foot per year:

→ **Method 1**

$1.80 × 12 months = $21.60 per sq. ft. per year

→ **Method 2**

$22,500.00 × 12 months = $270,000 annual rent
$270,000 ÷ 12,500 = $21.60 per sq. ft. per year

Using the square footage and the rate per square foot, the real estate manager can calculate the rent:

12,500 × $21.60 = $270,000 rent per year
$270,000 ÷ 12 = $22,500.00 rent per month

Natural Breakpoint

The next logical step is to calculate the breakpoint for percentage rent. Major anchor tenants usually report and pay percentage rent on an annual basis, while small, local, and national tenants generally report and pay monthly with an annual adjustment.

The *natural breakpoint* is the mathematical point at which the minimum rent is the same as the percentage rent given the specific circumstances. The lease agreement requires the tenant to pay a percentage of all sales above the breakpoint as additional rent, referred to as *percentage rent* or *overage rent*—rent paid above the minimum rent. The lease provisions determine whether the percentage rent is to be calculated on a monthly or an annual basis. The natural breakpoint can be determined by dividing the minimum rent by the monthly or annual percentage rent rate.

Annual Natural Breakpoint

For the shopping center's restaurant, the natural breakpoint would be calculated as follows:

Annual rent divided by percentage rent rate equals *annual natural breakpoint:*

$270,000 ÷ .06 = $4,500,000

Therefore, the tenant will not owe any percentage rent until its annual sales exceed $4,500,000.

Same Tenant: Monthly Natural Breakpoint

There are two approaches to obtaining the *monthly natural breakpoint* of $375,000:

→ Method 1

$270,000 ÷ 12 = $22,500.00 per month rent

$22,500.00 ÷ .06 = $375,000
monthly natural breakpoint

→ Method 2

Annual natural breakpoint divided by 12

$4,500,000 ÷ 12 = $375,000

Percentage Rent

All sales above the breakpoint are subject to percentage rental at the rate of 6%—that is, if this tenant reached an annual volume of $3,230,000, no percentage rent would be due:

$3,230,000 × .06 = $193,800

The tenant has already paid $270,000 in minimum rent, so no additional rent is due. If, however, the tenant reached a sales volume of $4,800,000, the calculation would be as follows:

$4,800,000 × .06 = $288,000

Since the tenant has paid a minimum rent of $270,000, a balance of $18,000 ($288,000 – $270,000) percentage or overage, rent is due.

Another way to calculate this is to multiply the overage in annual sales by the percentage rate. In this case, the calculation would be as follows:

$4,800,000 – $4,500,000 = $300,000 sales overage

$300,000 × .06 = $18,000 overage rent due

If the tenant lease provisions required the tenant to report and pay percentage rent monthly with an annual adjustment, anytime the tenant's sales exceeded $375,000, the tenant would report those sales and pay 6% of the amount above $375,000.

At year end, the tenant would owe the overage rent based on actual annual sales and compare it to monthly estimates paid to determine if any refunds are due. If the lease provision required the tenant to report monthly but to pay annually, the tenant would not owe any additional monies as long as total annual sales were less than $4,500,000.

Breakpoint per Square Foot

It is quite common in the industry to refer to sales per square foot because that is a useful figure when comparing tenant rents, sales, etc. Making this calculation for each tenant is helpful in comparing the tenants' sales to each other and to industry standards. The calculations for the shopping center's restaurant on a per-square-foot basis are as follows:

Item	Amount (Divided) by 12,500 sq. ft.	Per Square Foot per Year
Minimum rent	$ 270,000	$ 21.60
Natural breakpoint	$4,500,000	$360.00
Gross sales	$4,800,000	$380.00

Artificial or Negotiated Breakpoint

The parties may wish to change the formula for the percentage rent calculation. The breakpoint is then an *artificial* or *negotiated breakpoint,* rather than the natural breakpoint. Any negotiated figure will work as long as it is agreeable to both parties.

The shopping center owner typically negotiates the artificial breakpoint downward to increase potential percentage rents. On the other hand, a strong, desirable tenant may refuse to pay the asking rent. The shopping center owner, while accepting that position, may ask for a lower breakpoint to receive additional percentage rental revenue and to receive it sooner, thereby increasing the potential return if the tenant does well. Shopping center owners frequently use this tactic when they are required to put in extra *tenant improvements (TIs).* Lowering the breakpoint allows the shopping center owners to recapture money earlier than would be possible with the natural breakpoint. An example follows:

Space	1,300 sq. ft.
Rent	$26,000 per year
Percentage rent rate	5% (.05)
Natural breakpoint	$520,000

The shopping center owner may argue for an artificial breakpoint of $450,000, which would produce additional percentage rent of $3,500 a year if the tenant's sales actually reached the $520,000 original breakpoint.

	Natural Breakpoint	Artificial Breakpoint
Sales	$520,000	$520,000
Breakpoint	520,000	450,000
Sales subject to Percentage rent	-0-	70,000
5% (.05)	-0-	3,500
Minimum rent	$ 26,000	26,000
Total rent	$ 26,000	$ 29,500

An artificially high breakpoint works in favor of the tenant who feels the minimum rent is too high but wants the space anyway. The tenant may negotiate for an artificially high breakpoint to provide a savings on rent if sales go well. Some strong, desirable retail businesses will negotiate a higher breakpoint just because they are much sought after in the industry. The tenant's artificial breakpoint is often based on an *internal rate of return (IRR);* it represents the point at which the store becomes profitable.

Assume a tenant that is interested in a space that is in poor condition and the owner either cannot or is unwilling to make the improvements, the tenant may ask for an artificially high breakpoint to create an opportunity to recover the cost of the improvements.

In the following example, a tenant asked for, and obtained, a breakpoint of $600,000, while the natural breakpoint was $520,000. In that case, the amounts due would be as follows:

	Natural Breakpoint	Artificial Breakpoint
Sales	$575,000	$575,000
Breakpoint	520,000	600,000
Sales subject to Percentage rent	55,000	-0-
5% (.05)	2,750	-0-
Minimum rent	26,000	26,000
Total rent	$ 28,750	$ 26,000

The tenant saved $2,750 in rent by negotiating an artificial breakpoint.

Declining Percentage Rent Rate

Supermarkets are typically high-volume merchants. They are usually quite willing to pay percentage rent, but they have concluded that high-sales volumes are due as much to their expertise and reputation as to the location of the shopping center. These merchants have low-profit margins and pay a very low percentage rental rate. As a result, depending upon the shopping center's location, they may seek to negotiate a declining percentage rental rate. In the shopping center example, the supermarket's natural breakpoint is as follows:

$728,000 ÷ .015 = $48,533,333.00 yearly

This supermarket may negotiate a percentage rent provision as follows:

.015 of sales up to $48,533,333 per year
.01 of sales between $48,533,333 and $56,000,000
.0075 of sales above $56,000,000

If the tenant's sales were $61,000,000 for the year, the percentage rent due would be as follows:

Breakpoint

Sales up to $48,533,333 × .015) = minimum rent of $728,000

($56 000,000 – $48,533,333 = $7,466,667 × .01) = $74,666.67

($61,000,000 – $56,000,000 = $5,000,000 × .0075) = $37,500.00

Total percentage rent	$112,166.67
Plus minimum rent	$728,000.00
Total rent	$840,166.67

If this tenant had not negotiated a declining percentage rental rate, the rent due would have been as follows:

Percentage rent $61,000,000 – $48,533,333 = $12,466,667 × .015	$187,000
Plus the minimum rent of	$728,000
Total rent	$915,000

By negotiating the percentage rent provision, the tenant saved $74,833.34 in rent for the year. The shopping center owner may appear to have lost $74,833.34, but in reality, the shopping owner has done quite well and might not have been able to lease to this tenant by holding to a firm position of demanding a flat percentage rent rate on all sales. Both the shopping center owner and tenant have gained something of value in this situation.

Rents per Square Foot as a Comparison

To compare tenants, the real estate manager generally compares rents on a per-square-foot basis rather than on gross rents. In the case of the supermarket with the split percentage arrangement, the calculation would be based on 52,000 square feet of space, a minimum rent of $728,000, percentage rent of $112,166.67, and total rent of $840,166.67:

Base rent	$728,000 ÷ 52,000 = $14.00 per square foot per year
Percentage	$112,166.67 ÷ 52,000 = $2.16 per square foot per year
Total rent	$840,166.67 ÷ 52,000 = $16.16 per square foot per year

The real estate manager can then compare these figures with those of other shopping centers they own and/or other shopping centers in the area. Within a super regional or regional mall, management typically determines the sales per square foot of each tenant in the mall and, on a monthly basis, compares each tenant's sales per square foot with the sales per square foot of the mall as a whole and with those of like merchants in various categories. Typical categories are women's wear, menswear, shoes, jewelry, food, entertainment, and gifts.

For example, assume in September, women's wear tenants had average sales of $8.30 per square foot—an increase of 15.4% from the same period the previous year. One tenant had sales in excess of $14.00 per square foot for the month, but an increase of less than the 15.4% average. That merchant is doing quite well. On the other hand, a different women's wear store had sales of only $5.50 per square foot for the month. There may be an offsetting reason for this situation, but the figures indicate the tenant and management should discuss the problem. The store may be very large, making the higher volume per square foot more difficult to reach. Perhaps the store has been open for business only one year and is still growing—or it may have management problems. A frank discussion between the shopping center manager and/or owner of the store should help determine if there is a problem and if so, what they might want to do about it. It is also quite possible that the shopping center manager may feel that the sales level is too low, but that the tenant is quite satisfied and may not want to discuss the situation. If that were the case, the shopping center manager may want to reconsider that tenant when the lease comes up for renewal.

Several calculations can help evaluate the sample shopping center set forth in Exhibit 14.1. The shopping center totals 112,000 square feet. The bank does not pay percentage rent, so it must be removed from the calculations to make them meaningful:

Total shopping center less bank equals net shopping center for sales comparison.

112,000 sq. ft. – 5,400 sq. ft. = 106,600 sq. ft.

Assuming that the shopping center had sales of $34,785,678 and the preceding year of $33,129,217, the sales per square foot were as follows:

This year	$34,795,678 ÷ 106,600 sq. ft. = $326.41 per sq. ft. per year
Preceding year	$33,129,217 ÷ 106,600 sq. ft. = $310.78 per sq. ft. per year

The figures can be compared to other shopping centers and industry averages to see how they measure up. There may be valid reasons why a shopping center's sales per square foot fall below the averages. It is helpful to have the sales-per-square-foot information to make an objective analysis.

Split-Level Percentage Rent Rate

A shopping owner and tenant quite often have a difficult time reaching an agreement on the percentage rent rate. The shopping center owner sometimes offers a split rate, that is, one rate to set the breakpoint and another to use for percentage rental calculation. If the shopping center owner was asking 6%, and the tenant wanted to pay only 5%, the compromise might be 6% to the natural breakpoint and 5% thereafter. The following calculations, based on 1,300 square feet, $26,000 rent, and sales of $600,000, show both a fixed and a split-level rate:

	6% to Natural Breakpoint	5% Thereafter
Sales	$600,000	$600,000
Breakpoint	$433,333	$520,000
Sales subject to percentage rent	$166,667	$ 80,000
5% Straight × 5% (.05)	$8,333.35	$4,000.00

The shopping center owner gets the benefit of the lower breakpoint, and the tenant pays only 5% of sales above the established breakpoint. Obviously, a negotiated break point of 5.5% would also be considered a reasonable outcome.

Offsets or Deductions from Percentage Rents

While it is uncommon in newer leases, some older leases, especially with anchor or major tenants, gave the tenants the right to make certain deductions from percentage rent due. Those deductions generally included taxes, insurance premiums, and in some cases, common area costs. The following example uses taxes as a deduction:

Minimum rental	$ 416,000
Breakpoint	27,733,336
Sales	37,500,000
Percentage rent due	102,150
Taxes of $37,500 paid to property owner this year are deductible from percentage rent	(37,500)
Net percentage rent due	64,650
Total rent due	$ 480,650

Even if the tenant's percentage rent does not equal the total taxes and/or common area maintenance (CAM) charges for the year, some portion may be saved as an offset against the percentage rents due. Owners will resist granting such a provision, but some strong anchor tenants have negotiated such a provision. This provision, which was common in the 1960s to the 1980s, is seldom in use today. It is mentioned because anchor tenants typically have 30-year leases with six five-year options. There are some older leases with anchor tenants that have this tenant concession.

Rent as a Percentage of Sales

Shopping center owners and real estate managers often hear tenants complain that they cannot afford the rent. This statement might easily be seen as just a negotiating ploy, but the tenant often cannot afford the rent. Real estate managers and shopping center owners need to determine when such a claim is a fact, and when it is being used only to better the tenant's negotiating position. One way to make this determination is to measure the tenant's occupancy costs in relation to its sales. Typically, if the tenant's occupancy costs are more than twice the normal percentage rent rate for that type of occupancy, the tenant might be facing future difficulties. For example, shoe stores typically pay a percentage rental rate of 6%. If a tenant that normally pays a percentage rent of 6% has occupancy costs much in excess of 12% on an ongoing basis, the possibility is high that this tenant either is or will be a problem for the center.

Shopping center owners and real estate managers must also recognize that some individual stores may have higher occupancy costs but remain in the shopping center and pay rent. Such stores may be part of a chain of stores that considers representation in the particular market important; thus, the store will remain open even if it is not profitable, or at least as profitable as the chain would like it to be. The owner of the store might be making a decent living, even though the total sales are marginal. The store may not currently provide the desired profit levels, but the owner may feel that a customer base is being established and that it will be profitable within a reasonable time.

The following example sets forth important data regarding the tenants in a hypothetical shopping center:

WASHINGTON SQUARE SHOPPING CENTER
Year 2015 Sales/Rental Analysis

Merchant	Current Year Sales	Total Rent& CAM	Rent/Sales Comparison
Children's	675,234	$54,712	8.1%
Jeans shop	722,546	$38,866	5.4%
Shoe shop	192,700	$23,650	12.3%
Bath shop	147,360	$42,600	28.9%
Women's wear	1,235,450	$65,466	5.3%
Drugstore	2,345,000	$102,460	4.4%

In evaluating these merchants, both base rent and CAM charges are included. Some shopping centers use only base rent, but since the merchant has no choice but to pay the extra charges, a conservative approach is to include base rent and CAM charges when calculating the tenant's rent as a percentage of its sales.

The children's shop, jeans shop, and the women's wear shop are clearly at a very comfortable position when comparing occupancy costs to total sales. The shoe shop is slightly above percentage rent level of two times 6%, but the total volume is strong; if the tenant is paying well and appears to be satisfied, there is likely to be no problem.

The bath shop should be evaluated more closely. If the store just opened for business and is building its base, it is probably fine as long as it has the capital to take it through this difficult time. If, however, this is an established tenant, the shopping center manager would want to see if its sales are going down or have stagnated. Has the store made changes that will improve this ratio in the near future? This tenant clearly bears watching and might even merit a discussion to determine where the store is heading.

The drugstore has a very good volume of sales. In spite of the low-occupancy costs, drugstores have a much lower percentage rent rate than other types of tenants. With a typical percentage rent rate of 2%, this store is on the edge of an operating ratio that may cause management some concern. Nevertheless, the typical drugstore today is a chain operation; unless the tenant has voiced a concern, the shopping center manager will need to do nothing.

An annual analysis can be very productive by giving some indication of the health of each merchant in the shopping center and pointing out areas of potential concern in the coming months and years. Some shopping center owners ask for an annual report showing such ratios and then compare them to previous years to look for trends that may be helpful in planning levels of rent, types of tenants to pursue, and possible changes of tenant mix. This type of information, along with the tenant's rental payment history, can be a good gauge of where the tenant may be heading.

As an additional tool, real estate managers can set up groupings of rents as a percentage of sales—such as 5% or less, 5–10%, 10–15%, and 15% and above—then color code the rates and fill them in on the center-plot plan. When this information is compared with overall sales per square foot, it can be a very helpful tool in evaluating the merchants, such as a specific section of the mall or shopping center.

Consumer Price Index (CPI) Calculations for Shopping Centers

Shopping center owners in many parts of the country use a price index to offset the effects of inflation on minimum rentals or, in other words, to keep up with inflation. The lease language should be very specific as to the base rental, base index, timing of the index, and schedule for increasing the rent. The base index should be clearly identified in the lease agreement; it is usually a government index.

The most common index is the CPI published by the United States Department of Labor Bureau of Labor Statistics. Published monthly for most parts of the country and available online (*www.bls.gov/cpi)* it is tailored to specific areas of the country. In addition, the index has two areas: (1) All Urban Consumers and (2) the Urban Wage Earners and Clerical Workers. CPIs can be obtained for any period in the past by logging on to the CPI website.

The following calculations are based on the earlier example of 1,300 square feet at an annual rental of $26,000; base index 237.63; new index 241.43. There are two ways to calculate this index. The answers will differ slightly because the calculator carries the numbers several places, but the result is accurate in both cases:

→ Method 1

Divide the rent by the old index and multiply that times the new index:

$26,000 ÷ 237.63 x 241.43 =$26,415.77

This figure is lower than the result of the next method due to internal rounding of the calculator. The new rent of $26,415.77 represents a rent increase $415.77 or 1.6%.

→ Method 2

First, calculate the percentage of change in the index and then apply that to the base year rental:

241.43 ÷237.63 = 1.016 (or 1.6% increase)

1.06% (rounded up) $26,000 × 1.016 =
$26,000 + $415.77 = $26,415.77
(or a 1.016% increase)

Multiplying the old rent by 1.016 eliminates a step and gives the new rent in just one step:

$26,000 × 1.016 = $26,416.10

It is recommended that the calculation be made both ways and that the lower figure be used to bill the tenant.

In most cases, unless negotiated otherwise, the breakpoint for percentage rent goes up as the rent increases. In this example, using a 5% rate, the breakpoint increases as follows:

Previous rent	$ 26,000.00
Natural breakpoint	$520,000.00
New rent	$ 26,415.77
New natural breakpoint	$528,315.00

Again, analyzing the figures in terms of a per-square-foot-per-year basis can be quite helpful. The calculation is as follows:

Item	Per Square Foot	Amount Per Year
Original base	$26,000 ÷1,300	$20.00
New rent	$26,415.77 ÷ 1,300	$20.32
Natural breakpoint	$26,000 ÷ .05	$520,000
National breakpoint per square foot	$520,000 ÷ 1,300	$400
Natural breakpoint new rent	$26,415.77 ÷ .05	$528,315.40
Natural breakpoint per square foot	$528315.40 ÷ 1,300	$406.40

Consumer Price Index: Floor and Ceiling

A sophisticated tenant may agree to a CPI rental increase, but ask for an upper limit (ceiling). Generally, the property owner who grants the upper limit also requires that the tenant agree to a minimum increase (floor). In a typical lease provision, the tenant agrees to a CPI increase with a minimum of 4% and a maximum of 6% each year. The effect is as follows:

- If the actual CPI is between 4% and 6%, the rental increase will be the actual percentage of the increase in the index.
- If the actual CPI is less than 4%, the rental increase will be 4% per the lease agreement.
- If the CPI is above 6%, the actual rental increase will be limited to no more than 6% per the lease agreement.

The following examples show the calculations:

Base Rental	Base Index	1-Year Index	Percentage Increase	New Rent
$26,000	237.53	247.70	4.28	$26,000 × 1.0428 = $27,112
$26,000	237.53	243.23	2.40	$26,000 × 1.04 = $27,040
$26,000	237.53	263.35	10.87	$26,000 × 1.06 = $27,560

CPI increases are frequently limited to 4% per year, as in the example, but then increased to the full CPI on each fifth anniversary of the lease. The calculation would be as follows:

$26,000 × 1.04 =$27,040

$27,040 × 1.04 =$28,122

$28,122 × 1.04 = $29,246

$29,246 × 1.04 = $30,416

At the start of year six, the rental would increase to the full CPI index over the previous five years which would assume to be 25.6%.

$26,000 × 25.6% = $6,656 increase

New rental will be $32,656

Merchants' Association and/or Marketing Fund

Merchants' association dues and marketing fund contributions are often subject to CPI increases to prevent erosion of their buying power. The typical lease sets the tenant's contribution during the first year, which will be subject to either a CPI or a negotiated increase annually. The calculation is the same as for rents.

Assuming a 1,000-square-foot tenant space and a dues structure of 10 cents per square foot per month in the first year, the dues for that tenant would be $100 per month (1,000 sq. ft. × .10 = $100). The lease would specify the index to be used and the effective date of the change. The calculation would be as follows:

Current dues	$100.00
Base index	237.63 (given)
One-year index	241.46 (given)
Percentage increase	1.61

241.46 ÷ 237.62 = 1.61%

New dues $100 × 1.0161 = $101.61

Some owners would round up or down to the nearest full dollar. In this case, the number would be rounded up to $102.00.

Fixed Increase on Merchants' Association Dues or Marketing Fund Contributions

Many merchants do not like the idea of a CPI because it is an unknown and has no real relationship to their type of business. Negotiating a fixed increase each year is often much easier. A common figure is 5%. Each year, the dues increase by 5% as follows:

Current dues	$100.00
Negotiated 5% increase	5.00
Next year's dues	$105.00
Following year	$110.25
Following year	$115.76

Merchants' Association or Marketing Fund Budget

The income for the merchants' association or for the marketing fund is subject to the lease negotiations.

Typically, the smaller merchants all have the same contribution per square foot, while major anchor tenants have either negotiated a different amount or do not pay dues at all. Frequently, the shopping center owner also contributes to the merchants' association or marketing fund. This example uses the sample shopping center introduced at the beginning of this chapter. It has a total of 112,000 square feet. The supermarket will contribute $6,000 per year, the drugstore will contribute $3,000 per year, the small merchants will contribute 10 cents per square foot per month (assuming 5% vacancy on small shops), and the owner will contribute 30% of the dues collected. The budget for this year will be as follows:

Supermarket	$ 6,000
Drugstore	3,000
Small shops (43,000 × .10 × 12 × .95)	49,020
Total from tenants	$58,020
Owner contribution ($58,020 × .30)	17,406
Total budgeted income	$75,426

Common Area Maintenance (CAM) Billbacks

CAM billbacks can be complicated and can cause more shopping center owner/tenant problems than any other source. There is no standard way to calculate CAM costs, but the following approaches are some of the proven ways to make effective billings. The property shopping center owner and the real estate manager should take great care to follow the lease agreements and to be sure the billbacks are accurate, timely, and fair.

A neighborhood shopping center had one master water meter for all small merchants. The lease provided that each tenant would pay his or her share based on the square footage of the shops. The shopping center manager decided that this was unfair because the beauty shop and a veterinary clinic were larger users of water, so the manger checked with the city and found what those tenants normally consumed and adjusted their bills upward accordingly. Those tenants objected, sued the owner, and won. The manager cannot make an arbitrary decision against the lease in the name of fairness. Management should provide the tenants with reasonable detail so they know what was spent and how the shares were calculated. This example uses the prior shopping center example and for simplicity, assumes the following expenses.

If all of the leases were the same and every tenant used all the services, prorating the expenses would be easy. However, three merchants in this shopping center pay only a 10% supervision or administrative fee, and the rest pay 15%. The lease stipulates the amount of this fee, which the tenant pays the shopping center owner to cover the administrative expenses associated with the common areas. The fee covers the following services:

- Bidding contracts
- Preparing proper contracts
- Supervising the work
- Analyzing and paying bills for the common areas
- Preparing the billings to the merchants
- Working with merchants to answer questions they may have relative to the billings.

At least two calculations are necessary:

Merchant	Total costs ($)	Store Share (%)	Store Share ($)
Supermarket	107,400.00	46.43	49,865.82
Men's store	107,400.00	2.23	2,395.02

Merchant	Super vision (%)	Super vision ($)	Total Billing ($)
Supermarket	10	4,986.58	54,852.40
Men's store	15	359.25	2,754.27

The calculations can become much more complicated. For example, a supermarket may have its own trash removal and not contribute to the trash-removal cost of the center. In addition, a supermarket may agree to a supervision fee but exclude taxes from that fee. In this case, the calculation would be as follows:

Total costs	$107,400.00
Trash removal costs	(18,500.00)
Net costs	88,900.00
Supermarket share (88,900 × 46.43%)	41,276.27
10% supervision (excluding real estate taxes) (88,900 – 37,500 = 51,400 × 46.43% x 10%)	2,386.50
Total billing	$43,662.77

The real estate manager may occasionally encounter an older supermarket lease in which the tenant agreed to pay a *pro rata* share of the CAM costs, not to exceed a given amount. This example assumes the tenant has agreed to a pro rata share but limits the total billing to 80 cents per square foot per year. This limit is known as a cap, ceiling, or lid. Once costs have exceeded the 80-cent figure, the real estate manager might be inclined to send the tenant a bill for the amount due; however, that is not acceptable to most anchor tenants. They want to see the full calculation, as follows:

Total costs	$107,400.00
Supermarket share 46.43%	49,865.82
10% supervision	4,986.58
Total billing	$54,852.40
Subject to a maximum of 80 cents per foot per year (52,000 sq. ft. × 80 cents)	$41,600.00

CAM Costs as a Percentage of Sales

In newer leases, provisions limiting CAM cost reimbursements to a percentage of the tenant's sales are not common, but some older leases had such provisions. The tenant who pays monthly CAM estimates may have a refund coming at year-end. Using the drugstore as an example, assume the tenant has agreed to a pro rata share of all costs, but that is limited to a maximum of 1.75% of sales each year.

Total costs	$107,400.00
Drugstore share 15.18%	16,303.32
10% supervision	1,630.33
Total	$17,933.65
Subject to a maximum of 1.75% on sales of $974,500	$17,053.75

CAM Based on Leased or Occupied versus Leasable Area

Another seldom-used approach to calculating common area real estate tax, insurance, and maintenance charges for shopping centers is the use of leased space or occupied space as the denominator instead of the GLA. The impact on final billings can be significant to the tenants. From the shopping center owner's point of view, this method is likely to generate a larger net recovery of expenses. In theory, the approach is valid because the tenants in the leased spaces are the only ones using the services provided, and they should pay for 100% of those services, rather than spreading the costs over the vacant spaces. Tenants will object and claim they should not be penalized because the shopping center owner cannot lease the vacancies.

To make the concept a little more understandable, the example considers a 120,000-square-foot shopping center that is 90% occupied and/or leased. The tenant in the example has a 2,400-square-foot space. The CAM, taxes, and insurance expenses are $8.00 per square foot per year.

Pro rata CAM share based on *leasable* area:

Tenant's share 2,400 sq. ft. ÷ 120,000 = 2%
Tenant's share of total expenses
$960,000 x 2% = $19,200

Pro rata share based on *leased* area:

Leased sq. ft. 120,000 sq. ft. x 90% = 108,000 sq. ft.
Tenant's share 2,400 sq. ft. 108,000 = 2.22%
Total expenses $960,000 × 2.22% = $21,200

As previously mentioned, the leased square footage is not used in the industry, however, occasionally a property owner will include the leased square feet in the CAM and bill-back provision in the lease. The leasable square feet is the industry standard method, and owners and tenants believe this is the fair approach to determine a tenant's pro rata share of the CAM and bill-back charges.

Exceptions to Common Area Billings

Common area billings are one of the most difficult areas of management for the commercial real estate manager. Concessions granted to individual merchants during the negotiation of shopping center leases complicate the calculations. Anchor tenants in malls often negotiate to have their shares of common area charges based on a smaller percentage of the mall than they actually occupy. An anchor may well agree to a pro rata share of the common area charges and then negotiate a maximum that is below its actual share.

Some anchor tenants agree to pay their pro rata shares of common area charges but omit certain items such as security, major repairs, and parking lot sealing. Anchor tenants in the mall often agree to pay a flat annual amount which is significantly less than their pro rata share. Unless the lease language specifically allows the owner to pass the costs of concessions on to the other tenants, the costs are made by the owner.

For malls, the owner will state in the other tenants leases that tenants whose square feet exceed for example, 50,000 square feet, are excluded in the denominator for calculating the tenant's pro rata share of the common area expenses. This enables the owner to recover the cost of the common area charges from the non-anchor tenants.

Multiple Denominators

Strong national retail tenants along with anchor tenants may negotiate limitations and/or exclusions in the CAM billings that complicate the calculation of the common area bill. Property owners and real estate managers would all hope for straight pro rata allocations for all of their shopping centers, but that is not likely except in the strongest of shopping centers—and even then, anchor tenants may negotiate to exclude certain expenses or cap some expenses. The administration of the common area billbacks can understandably become extremely complicated when different groups of tenants utilize different services. When all tenants use the services equally, which seldom happens, the entire shopping center uses one denominator, and all of the expenses are billed equitably on a pro rata per-square-foot basis.

For instance, anchor tenants may arrange for their trash pick up while the other tenants are billed for their trash pick up in their common area charges. An anchor tenant may self-insure its building while the property owner insures the rest of the shopping center and charge all the other tenants for their pro rata share of the building's insurance. Unfortunately, many tenants have specific requirements that create the need for exceptions. Most property owners do not want to lose a good tenant just because the tenant's exceptions to the common area billings are inconvenient for administrative personnel.

Even small shopping centers may have up to seven denominators for the allocation of common area costs. In one shopping center, security was allocated to everyone except the anchors; building water and electricity were billed on a building-by-building basis; trash removal was shared by about 80% of the merchants; building insurance was allocated to about 70% of the total square footage; roof maintenance was allocated to about 65% of the tenant spaces; and heating, ventilation, and air-conditioning (HVAC) maintenance was shared by about 50% of the small shop spaces. Each of these variations required the development of a different denominator for the spreading of expenses.

This situation is seldom seen in other type of commercial buildings except where a tenant may negotiate for a cap on their pass-through expenses. A bank or a restaurant in an office building is likely to provide its own janitorial services and the restaurant may have a separate meter for water, gas, and electricity. These tenants' pro rata share of the pass-through expenses would need to be adjusted to reflect the cost they are paying directly or separately.

Operating Income and Value

As a rule, each $1 of NOI creates between $5 and $10 in value. Therefore, each $1 of income lost through poor common area administration results in a loss of value for the shopping center of approximately $5 to $10. The real estate manager can easily understand why a property owner might become upset if he or she finds costs that should have been billed to the tenants have not been billed or have been handled so carelessly that income has been lost. The real estate management company is responsible for accurately billing each tenant its pro rata share of the building's operating expenses and rental charges in accordance with its lease obligations.

Midcity Plaza Example

The following is an example of a typical neighborhood shopping center and the common area billing variances a real estate manager may have to contend. Fortunately, this is not a typical example but one that hundreds of real estate managers have encountered throughout the years and will continue to experience because of the negotiations between property owners and tenants. The examples use a percentage allocation rather than a cents-per-square-foot approach because the latter generally poses more rounding problems. The best allocation basis to use is a percentage of the whole carried out to four places past the decimal.

The hypothetical neighborhood shopping center (shown in Exhibit 14.2) is Midcity Plaza. It has an area of 104,742 square feet, including the anchors and one restaurant pad. The anchors own their own sites but contribute to the overall maintenance of the shopping center. The pad tenant owns its site. All

EXHIBIT 14.2

Midcity Plaza Site Costs

Merchants Who Own Their Parcels	Footage	% Total	% Bldg	Trash Removal	HVAC service	Real Estate Taxes	Admin Fee
Supermarket	47000	0.4487	0.0000	(1)	(2)	(3)	10%-Not on Real Estate Taxes
Drugstore	18000	0.1719	0.0000	(1)	(2)	0.0901	10%-Not on Real Estate Taxes
Totals	70200	0.6702	0.0000		0.0000	0.4018	
Shop Spaces							
Ice Cream	800	0.0076	0.0232	0.0316	0.0365	0.0139	15%-Not on Real Estate Taxes
Cleaners	1800	0.0172	0.0521	0.0710	(2)	0.0312	15%-Not on Real Estate Taxes
Pet Clinic	1580	0.0151	0.0457	0.0623	0.0720	0.0274	15%-Not on Real Estate Taxes
Nail Salon	660	0.0063	0.0191	0.0260	0.0301	0.0114	15%-Not on Real Estate Taxes
Real Estate	1140	0.0109	0.0330	0.0450	0.0520	0.0197	15%-Not on Real Estate Taxes
Yogurt	1400	0.0134	0.0405	(1)	0.0638	0.0242	15%-Not on Real Estate Taxes
Beauty Salon	1120	0.0107	0.0324	0.0442	0.0510	0.0194	15%-Not on Real Estate Taxes
Jewelry	982	0.0094	0.0284	0.0387	0.0448	0.0170	15%-Not on Real Estate Taxes
Print Shop	1260	0.0120	0.0365	0.0497	0.0574	0.0218	15%-Not on Real Estate Taxes
Shoes	1360	0.0130	0.0394	0.0537	0.0620	0.0236	15%-Not on Real Estate Taxes
Karate	1560	0.0149	0.0452	0.0616	0.0711	0.0270	15%-Not on Real Estate Taxes

EXHIBIT 14.2 *(CONTINUED)*

Pool Supply	1460	0.0139	0.0423	0.0576	0.0665	0.0253	15%-Not on Real Estate Taxes
Restaurant	3600	0.0344	0.1042	(1)	(2)	0.0623	12%-Not on Real Estate Taxes
Sewing Ctr	2100	0.0200	0.0608	0.0829	0.0957	0.0364	15%-Not on Real Estate Taxes
Watch Shop	600	0.0057	0.0174	0.0237	0.0273	0.0104	15%-Not on Real Estate Taxes
Pizza	4200	0.0401	0.1216	(1)	(2)	0.0727	15%-Not on Real Estate Taxes
Dental	3000	0.0268	0.0869	0.1184	(2)	0.0520	15%-Not on Real Estate Taxes
Fast Food	1160	0.0111	0.0336	0.0458	0.0529	0.0201	15%-Not on Real Estate Taxes
Travel Agt	1160	0.0111	0.0336	0.0458	0.0529	0.0201	15%-Not on Real Estate Taxes
Video Shop	3600	0.0344	0.1042	0.1421	0.1641	0.0623	15%-Not on Real Estate Taxes
Shop Total	34542	0.3280	1.0000	1.0000	1.0000	1.0000	
Center Total	104742	1.0000					

(1) These merchants provide and pay for their own trash removal Denominator 25,342
(2) These merchants provide and pay for their own HVAC service Denominator 21,942
(3) Supermarket has own tax parcel—all others combined under one parcel

tenants in the shopping center pay their actual pro rata shares of the site costs. Only the spaces occupied by the small shop tenants, which are owned by the developer, pay their pro rata shares of what management calls "building costs."

- **Trash removal:** Three shop tenants have negotiated the right to handle their own trash removal; all three are in the food-service business and need wet-garbage removal. They do not contribute to the shopping center's trash removal.
- **HVAC:** Four tenants prefer to maintain their own HVAC service. They negotiated exclusions from the shopping center providing this service and including the cost in the common area billings.
- **Real estate taxes:** The supermarket owns its site. It receives that bill on a direct basis and pays the tax authorities directly.
- **Supervision fee:** The three tenants who have direct control of their buildings and land—the supermarket, drugstore, and freestanding restaurant—have negotiated a supervision or administrative fee at the rate of 10%, which does not include real estate taxes. The shop tenants, with one exception, have a supervision fee of 15%; it does not apply to real estate taxes because they are spelled out in a separate provision in the lease, and no supervision fees were part of that provision. The one exception to the 15% supervision fee is the restaurant, which is part of the shop spaces—it has a 12% fee. The restaurant is a strong national business with many locations and was desirable enough to the shopping center for the property owner to make this concession.
- **Common area budget:** All of the tenants have paid into the common area budget based on a budget provided by the owners of the shopping center, and in the example, Midcity Plaza is at year's end with the common area adjustments based on the actual expenses for the year.

The Midcity Plaza example includes a model for the CAM and tax expenses showing each tenant's share and any exceptions to the billings. This model can be set up and computed on a spreadsheet, but for these examples, the calculations are done by hand. The expenses are separated into site expenses and building expenses. Real estate taxes are shown as a separate line item because they are allocated using a different denominator.

Supermarket

The supermarket occupies 44.87% of the entire shopping center and because the supermarket did not negotiate adjustments to that figure, it pays that share of the site expenses (Exhibit 14.3). Had the supermarket negotiated the right to pay a lesser percentage of the expenses, for example, 38.5%, all of the expenses would have been calculated using that figure. If there were no language to the contrary in the tenant leases, the property owner would absorb the difference in costs that are represented by the gap between the 44.87% and the negotiated 38.5%.

If anchor tenants negotiate a lower percentage than the actual occupancy, some shopping center owners allocate the balance to the small merchants—meaning that the small merchants are paying the gap amount between the anchor tenant negotiated to pay and its pro rata share based on its square footage. If that is permissible in the leases of the tenants, it is a perfectly legitimate approach. However, if the leases indicate the shop tenants will pay their pro rata shares, they should not pay the anchor tenant's shortfall. In such instances, if the property owner bills the tenants for the shortfall, the owner is deliberately overbilling for CAM expenses.

The supermarket, drugstore, and pad restaurant, maintain their own buildings; provide and pay for their insurance; handle items such as trash removal, HVAC maintenance, and other direct maintenance expenses; and pay their shares of the site costs, which represent the services for the entire shopping center. Building insurance, under-canopy lighting, and alarm charges apply only to the shop tenants because the anchors pay their own.

EXHIBIT 14.3

Midcity Plaza Current Year: Actual Cam Expense

CURRENT YEAR: ACTUAL EXPENSES		
Site Expenses	**Expense**	**Per Sq. Ft.**
Landscaping	$16,860	.1610
Sweeping	18,000	.1719
Repairs	8,420	.0804
Parking lot lighting	9,400	.0897
Landscape water	7,360	.0703
Liability insurance	4,750	.0453
Steam clean walks	1,600	.0153
Total site expenses	$66,390	.6338
Building Expenses		
Water	$3,860	.1117
Electricity	5,670	.1641
Repairs	8,300	.2403
Roof repairs	4,360	.1262
Insurance	9,840	.2849
Fire alarm	2,260	.0654
Trash removal	12,630	.3656
HVAC service	3,200	.0926
Total building expenses	$50,120	1.4510
Real estate taxes expense	$151,876	2.6303

Some anchor tenants will negotiate to have the CAM budget submitted in advance with the right to approve the entire budget or expenses above a specific amount. It's important to ensure that the invoices back up the legitimate charges if any tenant questions specific expenses, CAM costs, or other charges. If an invoice is unclear or appears not to be an allowable charge per the tenant(s) lease, the tenant(s) are not to pay the charge.

Some anchor tenants may agree to a supervision fee of, for example, 10%, but not for insurance or utilities. The following shows the calculation with no exceptions or exclusions. If exclusions were applicable, the calculation would be as follows:

Total site expenses (inclusive of taxes, insurance, and building expenses):	$66,390
Tenant's share (.4487 × $66,390):	$29,789.19
Supervision (10%—but not on insurance or utilities):	$2,013.77
$66,390 – $4,750 – $9,400 – $7,360 =	$44,880
$44,880 × .4487 =	$20,137.66
$20,137.66 ×.10 =	$2,013.77

Instead of paying 10% on its entire pro rata share, the tenant would pay only $2,013.77, which is $965.15 less than the full pro rata share. This is a common situation with anchor tenants, and the person preparing the bill must be sure the lease is followed to the letter. Some property owners have been known to send out a bill showing just the net amount due under the assumption that the tenant knows the monthly estimates and can calculate the difference. It's better to present the entire picture with the final bill and save the tenant a lot of research to verify the numbers.

Drugstore

The drugstore also owns its own parcel and contributes to CAM, but it shares a parcel with the shopping center for tax purposes. This is not a common situation, but it illustrates a point. Like the supermarket, the drugstore pays its pro rata share of the site expenses and a 10% supervision fee on those expenses. However, the tax portion of the billing is shown as a separate line item.

If the supermarket were also part of the shopping center parcel, the taxes could be included in the site costs because the percentage of allocation would be the same. However, when some tenants are excluded from an item, the item must have a different denominator—unless all tenants should be paying the expense but have been excluded by negotiation. If, for example, security was contracted for the shopping center, but the drugstore had excluded security from the costs that it would pay, the allocation would be on the basis of the entire center, but the actual cost would be excluded from the drugstore billing. Unless there were agreements to the contrary, the property owner would absorb the drugstore's portion of security and not pass it along to the other merchants.

It is important to note that the 10% supervision fee the drugstore pays does not apply to the real estate taxes, so when site costs are allocated, the supervision fee is allocated to appropriate costs only, and then the taxes are allocated and included. If the drugstore requested copies of invoices for its charges, the real estate manger would provide them.

Shop Spaces

Midcity Plaza has a variety of shop spaces. Several of them provide additional examples of the variety and complexity of common area billings.

- **Ice Cream Store:** The ice cream store has no exceptions, so it pays its full pro rata share of all expenses. However, because other merchants have exceptions to some items, the denominators of those items will be different since fewer merchants use those services. For example, the ice cream store pays its full pro rata share of site costs and building costs, but the denominator is different for each of these items because the anchors pay part of the site costs but none of the building expenses. Trash removal and HVAC maintenance both have exclusions and therefore are separate line items. These items are subject to the 15% supervision fee, so they are separately calculated and are added to the site and building charges before adding on the supervision fee. The taxes are then calculated separately because they represent a different set of merchants, and they are added after the supervision fee because they are not subject to that fee.

- **Pizza Parlor:** The pizza parlor requires a slightly different billing approach because it does not use the trash removal or the HVAC services, so it does not have a line item for those two services. Many owners would make up a standard invoice that would include these items and then zero them out for the actual billing. In this case, the line item is eliminated to avoid confusing the tenant. All of the expenses that are subject to the supervision fee are totaled up and the fee is added. Last, the real estate taxes are added, and the invoice is completed.
- **Restaurant (Shops):** The restaurant illustrates an additional variation in billing. It is the only shop space that has negotiated a supervision fee of less than the 15% the other shops pay. In addition, the restaurant takes care of its own trash removal and HVAC maintenance. The bill could be prepared with all of these items included and then adjusted out, but eliminating them completely avoids confusion when the bill arrives.

General Comments

The real estate manager should be aware of a few other issues when preparing the common area billings. Regardless of the real estate manager's idea of what may be fair or reasonable, the lease language prevails. For example, roof repairs can cause much billing confusion. The lease language determines how roofing repair expenses are allocated. Using Exhibit 14.2, assume that the first five tenants are in Building A of the shopping center, the next six shops are in Building B, and the last nine shops are in Building C. If the leases indicate that roof repairs will be allocated on a pro rata square-foot basis for all the shop spaces, the denominator would be the same as the other building expenses as shown in Exhibit 14.3.

However, if the shopping center allocates roof maintenance on a building-by-building basis, the denominator would be the square footage of the building the tenant occupies. In the case of Building A, the denominator would be 5,980 square feet for the building, so the ice cream store would pay 13.38% of any roof repairs for that building (800 square feet divided by 5,980 square feet). Building B would have a total space of 7,682 square feet, and Building C would have a total space of 20,880 square feet. If the leases called for a building-by-building allocation and the real estate manager decided allocating roof repairs on the basis of all of the small shops would be fairer, a tenant would likely object. If that tenant were paying more because of the allocation decision, the tenant would demand, and rightly so, that the real estate manager or property owner comply with the lease provisions.

Concluding Considerations

Common area allocations have become extremely complicated, and budgets and billings must be prepared carefully. The tenants should receive a fair and equitable distribution of the expenses so they are not billed for expenses that their leases exempt them from paying. Building owners should receive all of the money due in accordance with the leases. The real estate manager has an obligation to both parties to be sure expenses are allocated accurately according to the lease agreements. Any deviation from the agreements could create a liability for the real estate manager for the overbilling of tenants or the loss of income to the property owner. An inaccurate billing to one tenant caused not creating the correct formula or template to bill all the tenants may result in inaccurately billing several or all of the tenants.

FINANCIAL ANALYSIS FOR OFFICE BUILDINGS

Office building owners, managers, and leasing agents rely heavily on math for their day-to-day operations. Rents are quoted on a per-square-foot basis, either monthly or yearly, depending on the area of the country. Operating costs are compared on a per-square-foot, per-year basis. Operating statements can be converted to a square-foot basis to make them easy to compare with those of other office buildings in the area because value per square foot is a measure of comparative value. This section analyzes calculations that are unique to office buildings or that may be determined differently for shopping centers and office buildings.

Rent per Square Foot

The financial analysis section for shopping centers explained the calculation of rents per square foot per month and per year. Office buildings and industrial buildings use the same calculations. The only variations are in the area of load factors for office buildings.

Many office buildings add a *load factor* to the tenant's usable square footage to cover the costs of common areas of the building (e.g., restrooms, electrical rooms, entryways, hallways). In addition to the space that tenants actually use *(usable area),* they also pay for a share of the common areas and usable area *(rentable area).* For example:

Area	Square Feet
Total building	55,000
Hallways, restrooms, etc.	(5,000)
Spaces meant for occupancy	50,000
Common areas	5,000
Tenant spaces	50,000
Load factor	10%

If a tenant leases 1,000-square-foot space (usable area) and the building has a 18% load factor, the tenant will pay rent on 1,180 rentable square feet.

The standard for measuring office buildings and office space is provided by the Building Owners and Managers Association (BOMA) and is shown, in part, in *Chapter 4: Office Building Management.* The inclusion of a load factor has no effect on the building operating expense billbacks because the relationship of the footages remains constant. The variable is the base rent. If the rental rate is the same for usable and rentable square feet, the monthly base rent for the rentable square feet is higher than the rent for the usable square feet.

A building with a higher load factor will change more rent for a building with a lower load factor assuming the rent per square foot is the same for each building. A building with a large load factor of more than 20% may need to lower its base rent or use an arbitrator lower load factor to be competitive.

Rental Comparisons: Usable versus Rentable

A valid comparative survey of two or more office buildings requires an understanding of any load factors involved in order to reduce all buildings to the same terms. For example, assume the following:

Building A is 55,000 square feet, including a load factor of 10%. The annual rent is $19.50 per square foot per year of rentable space.

Building B is 70,000 square feet and does not have a load factor. The annual rent is $21.00 per square foot per year of usable space.

Using rents as the only factor, which building would be the best deal for a prospective tenant seeking 1,000 square feet of usable space? Leasing 1,000 square feet in Building A means paying for 1,100 feet of space times the lease rate of $19.50. To compare this to the building without a load factor, the prospective tenant would multiply the rent by the footage with the load factor and then divide by the usable footage:

$19.50 per sq. ft. × 1,100 sq. ft. = $21,450

$21,450 ÷ 1,000 sq. ft. = $21.45 per sq. ft.

No load factor is involved in leasing 1,000 square feet in Building B, so the stated rate per foot is the actual rate per foot, which is $21 per foot per year. Based on rents only, Building B offers the tenant a better deal.

Operating Expense Billbacks

Property owners try to protect their income streams by passing along all—or at least most—of their operating expenses to tenants in the form of operating expense billbacks. These billbacks have taken various forms over the years and have acquired a broader scope. The real estate manager must understand not only the specific lease provisions regarding billbacks, but also the theory behind each provision. A given building may use two or more formulas in determining billbacks at any given time because of different tenant lease requirements or because the property owner has changed the methodology. The following hypothetical building has 66,000 square feet, including a load factor of 10%. The expenses are as follows:

Item	1st Year	2nd Year
Management	$ 54,700	$ 55,900
Janitorial service	55,600	57,800
Insurance	20,200	22,100
Real Estate Taxes	62,500	64,700
Electricity	67,400	68,300
Water	9,000	9,600
Landscaping	22,000	23,200
Repairs	51,600	59,600
Total expenses	$343,000	$361,200

Base-Year Calculations

The theory of base-year lease provisions is that the rent is set in the base year, and the operating expenses are included in the rental figure because the property owner should know the building's expense levels at that time. If expenses increase in future years, the tenant should pay a share of those increases, thereby keeping the property owner's investment competitive. Assume that a tenant leases 1,100 square feet, rentable, in the hypothetical building described in the previous section, and that the first year is its base year. The second-year billing for operating expenses would be as follows:

Tenant's share of the building 1.67% (.0167)

1,100 sq. ft. ÷ 66,000 =.0167

2nd-year expenses	$361,200
1st-year expenses (base year)	343,000
Amount subject to billing	18,200
Tenant's share (.0167)	$303.94

If, in the third year, the total building expenses went up to $385,400, the base year would remain the same and the tenant would owe the following:

3rd-year expenses	$385,400
1st-year expenses (base year)	343,000
Amount subject to billing	42,400
Tenants share (.0167)	$708.08

Base Year with a Cap

A specific tenant may agree to a base-year provision but may want to negotiate an upper limit, or cap, on the amount. The tenant may negotiate for its pro rata share not to exceed a 5% increase of the costs above the previous year. Using the preceding example, the calculation would be the following:

2nd-year expenses	$361,200
1st-year expenses (base year)	343,000
Percentage increase	5.31%

Increase limited to 5% of previous year's expenses

($343,000 × 1.05 = $360,150)	360,150
Less base year	343,000
Subject to billing	17,150
Tenant's share .0167	$286.41

The tenant saved $17.53 by putting an upper limit, or cap, in the lease agreement. Obviously, the property owner lost the $17.53, but had to consider the possibility that the tenant might not have leased the space without the concession.

Base Year with Cap on Controllable Costs and No Cap on Noncontrollable Costs

The building's owner and its brokers may counter the tenant's request for a 5% cap on the increased operating expenses by offering to cap the controllable expenses (e.g., janitorial services, management fee, repairs, landscaping) and not cap the uncontrollable expenses (e.g., insurance, taxes, snow removal).

Assume the tenant has negotiated a limit of 5% per year on controllable expenses and no limit on the taxes and insurance. The bill-back expense calculation are more complicated, but that is part of the price of obtaining particular tenants. Using the preceding example, the real estate manager first breaks down the expenses, which would be carefully specified in the lease provisions:

Item	1st Year	2nd Year
Controllable costs		
Management	$ 51,300	$ 52,500
Janitorial service	47,520	49,600
Electricity	63,300	65,700
Water	7,000	7,600
Landscaping	18,000	18,000
Repairs	42,000	51,000
Totals	$229,120	$244,400
Percentage increase: 6.7%		
Maximum percentage allowed: 5.0%		
Adjusted figures	$229,120	$240,576
Uncontrollable expenses		
Taxes	59,400	62,300
Insurance	17,300	19,400
Total allowable expenses	$305,820	$322,276
Subject to billback		$16,456
Tenant's share (.0167)		$274.82

If the expenses decrease when compared to the base year in most leases, the tenant does not get a refund.

Expense-Stop Clause

An alternative to the base-year lease is the *expense-stop clause,* which is an agreed amount of operating costs established in the lease that the property owner would pay; the tenant would agree to pay a pro rata share of any increase above that amount. The expense-stop clause figure should represent a fair estimate of the costs of operating the building at about 95% occupancy, when the tenant takes occupancy, or when the building opens—which ever is applicable.

Assume that a expense-stop clause of $7 per square foot per year was negotiated in a lease. The tenant would owe a share of any increase in operating expenses more than $7 per square foot per year, including the first year of the lease. The following example assumes a first-year expense of $478,000 and a second-year expense of $491,700. The calculation is as follows:

First-year expenses	$478,500
Divided by 66,000 sq. ft.	
$7.25 per sq. ft.	
Stop clause	$7.00 per sq. ft.
Subject to billing	.25 per sq. ft.
Tenant's share (1,100 sq. ft. × .25)	$275.00
2nd-year expenses	$491,700
Divided by 66,000 sq. ft.	
$7.45 per sq. ft.	
Stop clause	$7.00 sq. ft.
Subject to billing	$.45 per sq. ft.
Tenant's share (1,100 sq. ft. × $.45)	$495.00

Gross-Up Calculations

The gross-up provision allows the owner to gross up operating expenses that are affected by the building occupancy, which may include utilities, some service contracts, janitorial costs, management fees, and property taxes. It is common to gross up operating expenses in office and medical office buildings (MOBs), but the concept is often misunderstood by the tenants. Some tenants have the mistaken belief that the owner is padding expenses when the building's pass-through charges are grossed up, although the purpose of grossing up the operating expenses is to have the tenants pay their fair pro rata share. The following list demonstrates why the gross up is a fair approach:

- The example office is 100,000 square feet.
- The tenant occupies 10,000 square feet.
- The tenant pays a 10% pro rata share of the operating expenses.
- Janitorial costs are $1 per square foot.

- The cost of janitorial services at 100% building occupancy would be $10,000 (10,000 square feet × $1 per square foot).
- The building is only 50% occupied.
- The cost of janitorial services for the half-occupied building is $50,000 (50,000 square feet × $1 per square foot).
- If the tenant is charged his pro rata share of 10%, the charge is only $5,000 ($5,000 × 10%) for janitorial services, while the actual cost to clean the tenant's premises is $10,000.
- When operating expenses are grossed up to 100% occupancy, the cost for janitorial services is stated at $100,000 (100,000 square feet × $1 per foot), and the tenant is billed $10,000 which is the actual janitorial cost for the tenant's space regardless of the building occupancy level.

Additionally, a gross-up benefits tenants who have a base-year lease. Since these tenants pay their share of the increases after the base year, they benefit from higher operating expenses during the base year of the lease. If the tenant's lease is not a base-year lease, the tenant may negotiate for the gross up to be at 95% building occupancy since a building is seldom fully occupied at all times—a 5% vacancy factor is the standard vacancy rate used for a building's pro forma. Higher base-year operating expenses benefit tenants with a base-year lease, but they also benefit owners who use other methods of billing operating expenses. The purpose of this provision should not be to bill the tenant for the maximum tenant charges allowed, but to charge tenants for their fair share of the building operation costs.

Over-Standard Utility Billings

Office buildings are frequently master-metered for utilities, such as electricity, but have one or more tenants that use much more than the standard amount of certain utilities for their spaces. Having the other occupants pay for this overuse is unfair, and therefore, the lease must provide a way to bill tenants for utility use above the norm.

There are several ways to determine excess utility usage. If the system will allow, a check meter can be installed and an average usage can be determined. The tenant would pay the difference between the meter amount and the average usage in the building. If a check meter cannot be installed, a utility company representative can generally survey the tenant's premises and determine the likely average usage. Using that determination, the building management can then calculate the monthly billing for the tenant. The average monthly electrical usage in the hypothetical office building is $.09 per square foot. A survey by the utility company establishes that one tenant (1,100 sq. ft. of space) uses an average of $.13 per square foot per month. The calculation would be as follows:

$$\$0.13 - \$0.09 = \$0.04$$

$$\$0.04 \times 1{,}100 \text{ sq. ft.} = \$44.00 \text{ monthly}$$

Absorption Rates

New development in any market generally requires that there be demand for that proposed property. One of the ways that the demand is measured is by the *absorption rates* in that market. The absorption rates effects both the development in the area as well as rental rates. For instance, assume that a market has 3,000,000 square feet of office space available, and in the previous year, 750,000 square feet of office space has been leased or absorbed. Assuming that the current absorption rate will continue, it is said that the market still has 2,250,000 square feet of space to lease, and that would be a three-year supply of office space. That is a lot of space to lease, and it is likely that this factor alone would discourage any new development until that absorption increased substantially.

On the other hand, if the market has 1,500,000 square feet of space and just over 1,000,000 square feet were leased in the last year, there would only be a six-month supply at those rates—this would more than likely spur new development. Most office markets are monitored very regularly, on a quarterly and an annual basis by some of the brokerage firms in the area to see how the absorption rates have changed and what this may mean to development possibilities and to the changing of rental rates.

FINANCIAL ANALYSIS FOR ALL COMMERCIAL PROPERTIES

Many of the calculations property owners and real estate managers use can apply to any type of commercial property.

Estimating Maximum Loan

To determine the loan that may be available on any property, the real estate manager must estimate the value of the property and then apply current lending standards. The steps follow:

Establish the estimated income and expenses to arrive at *net operating income (NOI)*:

Annual gross possible rents	$1,331,500
Vacancy, credit loss, lost rents 5%	(66,575)
Common area income (.33 cents × 95%)	35,112
Total income	1,300,037
Owner non-reimbursable expenses	(91,000)
Tenant pass-through expenses (Taxes, insurance, maintenance)	(36,960)
Net operating income	$1,172,077

NOI does not take into consideration debt service, capital improvements, or the property owner's income taxes. It is the income from the property's operations only.

To compare this property with others that may be of a different size, converting the figures to a dollars-per-square-foot approach is helpful. Using 66,000 square feet for this building, the calculation follows:

Operating Statement Item	Per Square Foot	Amount Per Year
Annual gross possible rents	$1,331,500	$20.17
Vacancy, credit loss, lost rents	(66,575)	(1.01)
Common area income	35,112	.53
Total income	1,300,037	19.70
Owner non-reimbursable expenses	(91,000)	(1.38)
Tenant pass-thru expenses	(36,960)	(.56)
Net operating income	1,172,077	17.76

By applying industry standard *return on investment (ROI)* numbers at the time of the calculation and using three different capitalization rates, it is then possible to estimate the value, based on the NOI of $1,172,077. The *capitalization rate* is defined as the desired rate of return. It must be noted that as the cap rate decreases, the value increases; as the cap rate increases, the value decreases. An investor who is willing to take a lower ROI is willing to pay more for a given NOI:

Net operating income	Cap Rate	Indicated Value
$1,172,077 ÷	.08	= $14,650,962
$1,172,077 ÷	.09	= $13,023,078
$1,172,077 ÷	.095	= $12,377,653

The value depends on many factors, such as what similar properties are selling for at the time of the valuation and what alternative sources of investment are returning. If a lender would lend 80% of the value of the project, the *loan-to-value (LTV) ratio,* the calculation would be as follows:

Value	Loan-to-Value (LTV) Ratio	Loan
$14,650,962	.80	$11,720,769
$13,023,077	.80	$10,418,461
$12,377,652	.80	$9,902,122

To compare the hypothetical building with others in the same area, converting the figures to a dollars-per-square-foot basis may be helpful. The building is 66,000 square feet. The calculation is as follows:

Estimate of Value	Value per Square Foot (Divide by 66,000)
$14,650,962	$221.98
$13,023,077	$197.32
$12,377,652	$187.54

Loan Available	Loan per Square Foot
$11,720,769	$177.59
$10,418,461	$157.86
$ 9,902,122	$150.03

Debt Coverage Ratio

Lenders are likely to have a minimum *debt-coverage ratio*. For example, a lender may want $1.20 in NOI for every $1 of debt service to provide a cushion of 20 cents on each dollar for potential lost revenues or higher-than-anticipated expenses. This is called a 1.2 to 1 debt-coverage ratio; it is calculated by dividing the NOI by the ratio as follows:

Net operating income	$1,172,077
Debt coverage ratio 1.2 to 1	
$1,172,077 ÷ 1.2 =	$976,730

The figure of $976,730 is available to service the debt, based on this lender's requirement. Debt-service ratios vary from lender to lender and depend on the developer, type of project, strength of leasing, lender requirements, etc.

Taking the smallest loan figure the lender is likely to give allows the property owner to see if the property meets the lenders requirements. Assume a 10% interest rate and a 25-year term for the hypothetical building described above. With the help of a financial calculator, the property owner or the real estate manager can easily determine that the debt service on the desired loan of $11,720,769, using the described parameters, would be $1,278,080, and it is not supported by the requirements. If the lowest loan cannot be supported, the larger ones will not meet the requirements either.

To see what size loan the 1.2 ratio will support, take the available funds of $976,730 and, using that as the payment, calculate the loan that can be supported, using a financial calculator or software program. In this situation, the loan would be $8,956,083.

To make the deal work, the building's owner must do one of the following:

1. Put in more equity dollars to reduce the loan amount
2. Lower the interest rate by either negotiation or buy-down
3. Increase the term of the loan
4. Restructure the loan completely

Net Leases

Commercial leases have evolved throughout the years toward tenants paying full pro rata shares of all costs of operating properties. Originally, property owners negotiated gross leases, receiving rent from tenants, and paying all operating costs.

Throughout the years, tenant participation in the operating costs of the building has steadily increased to offset erosion of the owner's income stream.

Single-Net Lease (Taxes)

Years ago, as taxes started to increase at an alarming rate, causing excessive loss of rental income, property owners began to pass a share of the taxes onto their tenants. The typical calculation would be the following:

Year	Taxes	Tenant's Share (%)	Tenant's Share ($)
1	$59,400	.0167	991.98
2	$62,300	.0167	1,040.41

The property owner would continue to pay all other operating expenses in a *single-net lease.*

Double-Net Lease (Taxes and Insurance)

Year	Taxes	Insurance Premiums	Total	Tenant's Share (%)	Tenant's Share ($)
1	$59,400	17,300	76,700	.0167	1,280.89
2	$62,300	19,400	81,700	.0167	1,364.39

Triple-Net leases (Taxes, Insurance, and Maintenance)

Year	All Expenses	Tenant's Share (%)	Tenant's Share ($)
1	$305,820.00	.0167	$5,107.19
2	$326,100.00	.0167	$5,445.87

Management fees are a typical pass-through operating expense. Some shopping center owners charge both the administrative fee and the management fee—though most of them charge just the management fee and pass-through charges. Using total first-year expenses, including the management fee, the same tenant's share would be as follows:

Year	Total First Year Expenses	Tenant's Share (%)	Tenant's Share ($)
1	$305,820.00	.0167	$5,107.19

If, however, the lease did not allow the owner to pass along the management fee, but did allow for a 15% supervision fee, the calculation would be:

Total expenses (less the management fee)	$254,520.00
15% supervision fee	38,178.00
Total for billing	$292,698.00
Tenant's share (.0167)	$ 4,888.06

Triple-Net Lease

Owners prefer the triple-net lease also know as the fully-net lease. For some property types, the triple-net lease has become the standard—not to say that all buildings are able to negotiate a triple-net lease. This lease allows the property owner to bill-back all operating expenses. Many property owners are including the cost to replace capital improvements in the common areas, such as carpeting and wall treatment in the halls of office buildings. For triple-net leases, the property owner is responsible for leasing commissions, capital improvements that represent additions to the building or TIs, legal fees for the owner, contributions to merchant's associations or marketing funds, and the common area costs attributed to vacant spaces.

The property owner's attorney should review the language to be sure the lease language for the pass-through charges represents the owner's intent and is current with market pass-through charges. Net leases can be defined differently in different parts of the country. When discussing the net-ness of a lease, the property owner and the real estate manager should always be sure the other party is using the same definition of the type of net lease.

Calculating Reserves for Future Maintenance or Capital Improvements

Some property owners are including in their lease the right to create a reserve account for future major maintenance. They believe this is fair for two reasons: (1) The tenants and their customers are using and wearing out certain components of the property while use of equipment and building features wear out over time, and (2) the property owner prefers to bill the tenant over time for a major charge than billing the entire charge at one time. This can be burdensome for many tenants. The formula to determine the amount of reserves that should be set aside is straightforward:

- Determine the systems that are likely to need major repair or replacement.
- Estimate the amount of money that will be needed at the time of replacement.
- Reduce that figure by the interest that will be earned on the moneys that have been set aside.
- Divide the total figure by the years available to set aside the moneys.
- Divide the annual amount by the number of square feet to arrive at a square-footage figure.
- Divide by 12 if a monthly reserve figure allowed in the lease and is preferred

The 112,000-square-foot shopping center example used at the beginning of this chapter can serve as an example. Assume a hold period of five years, replacement of the roof, and major repairs to the parking lot. In this example, the roof will have to be replaced at the five-year point, and it will cost $112,000 at that time.

Cost of job	$112,000
Interest to be earned	(12,000)
Net cost of job	$100,000
To be set aside on an annual basis	$ 20,000
Reserve per square foot per year ($20,000 ÷ 112,000)	$.1786
Reserve per square foot per month (.1786 divided by 12)	$.0149

Next, assume the parking lot will require major repairs at the end of three years and they will cost $65,000.

Cost of job	$65,000

Interest to be earned	(4,500)
Net cost of job	$60,500
To be set aside on an annual basis	$20,167
Reserve per square foot per year ($20,500 ÷ 112,000)	$.1830
Reserve per square foot per month (.1830 ÷ 12)	$.0153

These figures would be rounded and would represent the money that must be set aside for the work. If these reserve amounts are to be collected from tenants, the lease must have a provision allowing for the creation and billing for reserves. Most major tenants will not contribute to reserves, but they will pay their pro rata shares in a lump sum—assuming that their leases require them to pay their share of the expense. Major tenants may have the right to pre-approve any major expenditure, such as those in the previous examples.

A more sophisticated analysis can be made by discounting the future cash needs by the interest earned, rather than just estimating that amount. Assume the money can be invested at a bank at 5% interest. The property owner needs $112,000 in five years. The property owner would place $1,646.91 in the bank each month to have the required $112,000 in five years. Multiplying the monthly payment by 60 months (five years) shows that the amount actually set aside was $98,814.69 and that the rounded interest made up the difference. On this basis, the monthly reserve would be $.0147 per square foot per month. Another approach is not to include interest earned in the calculations and the interest that is earned may be used as a contingency if there is a cost overrun.

Energy Conservation Payback

Many commercial properties can benefit from retrofitting of lighting fixtures, air-conditioning systems, and controlling devices. While in most cases the saving on utilities is a good enough reason to proceed, property owners and some tenants will want to know the payback period.

Some owners or tenants may want to see additional financial analyses on energy conservation improvements. These include IRR and the NPV of the expected cash flow contributions resulting from the energy project.

The solutions providers working on the energy conservation improvements should be able to conduct this financial analysis prior to project approval. In some cases, the owner's asset manager or sustainability team will have determined which energy conservation improvement make financial sense for the property. In these cases, the real estate manager plays a critical role in project management and ensuring that solutions providers work together with building operations staff to get the best results from the energy conservation improvement.

Payback with Even Returns

As an example, assume a 100,000-square-foot office building has 120 100-watt incandescent light figures on the exterior. All of the fixtures can be replaced with 32-watt fluorescent fixtures at a cost of $8,400. Further investigation shows that the monthly savings on energy will be approximately $210. This will result in a savings of $2,520 per year, with no consideration for increased rates into the future. The payback period is 3.33 years:

$8,400 ÷ $2,520 = 3.33

In most areas, this would be a good payback period and the property owner would probably go ahead with the job. However, if other alternatives will provide a faster return of the cost, the property owner may proceed with an alternative program. The right payback period is not an absolute; rather, the energy conservation program is a system that looks at alternatives. In addition to the monetary savings, the building will also be known for having a concern for the environment, the program may contribute to the building earning a specific energy conservation award, and it will be another component in the marketing of the building.

Payback with Uneven Returns

Using the previous example, the energy savings

program will cost $8,400. Assume the initial savings will be $1,200 per year and will increase each year thereafter. Using these assumptions, the real estate manager can calculate the payback. However, in this example, dividing by the return does not work because it changes each year. To evaluate uneven returns, the real estate manager must deduct each year's return from the total cost until the entire debt is retired. The calculation is as follows:

Original cost of improvements	$8,400
First-year income – 1,200	7,200
Second-year income –1,300	5,900
Third-year income – 1,400	4,500
Fourth-year income – 1,500	3,000
Fifth-year income – 1,600	1,400
Sixth-year income – 1,700	
Partial sixth-year income	
1,400 ÷ 1,700 = .82 of the year	

The payback period will be five years and 10 months (.82 years is 9.88 months, rounded to 10). The equivalent rate of return is 17.2%, without considering compounding. It should be noted that this is the return *on* investment, not the return *of* investment.

Management Fee Calculations

Many methods of calculating management fees are possible, but the most important consideration is accuracy. The client should not have to keep reminding the real estate manager that the fees have been calculated incorrectly. In most markets the management fees are based on a percentage of the monies collected. In a hypothetical situation, assume a small unanchored strip shopping center has the following monthly income:

Base rents	$112,000
Percentage rents	12,000
Common area reimbursements	33,000
Miscellaneous income	3,000
Total monthly income	$160,000

Using a management fee of 5%, the following alternatives are available:

1.) 5% of gross income, minimum fee of $2,500

Gross income	$160,000
Management fee—5% (.05)	8,000

(This fee exceeds the minimum, so no adjustment is necessary.)

2.) 5% gross rents only, minimum fee of $2,500

Base rents	$112,000
Percentage rents	12,000
Total subject to management fee	$124,000
Management fee—5% (.05)	$ 6,200

(This fee exceeds the minimum, so no adjustment is necessary.)

Next, assume the shopping center just opened, the management fee is 5% of gross income with a minimum of $2,500.00, and the first month's income was as follows:

Base rents	$7,000
Percentage rents	-0-
Common area reimbursement	2,000
Total income	$9,000
Management fee—5% (.05)	450
Minimum fee	$2,500

The minimum fee would prevail until the income increased enough to generate a fee larger than that amount. In such a situation, the minimum fee protects the real estate management company if the vacancy of the property increases.

Calculating Leasing Commissions

Leasing is a critical component of the success of all commercial properties. Leasing agents' compensation can take many forms. The following examples are provided for illustrative purposes only; they do not suggest appropriate compensation. There are no standard leasing commissions because they are fully negotiable. The amount of the commission is negotiable, along with the formula to determine the lease commission and the timing of the payment of the lease omission. There may be other components of the commission that needs to be negotiated.

Assume a space of 2,500 square feet at a rental rate of $21 per square foot per year and a five-year lease term. Leasing commissions are typically not based on building operating expense income, common area costs, or options. Some leasing commission agreements may be structured as follows:

- 6% of the 1st-year rental
- 5% of the 2nd-year rental
- 4% of the 3rd-year rental
- 3.5% of the 4th- and 5th-year rentals
- 2% of the 6th- through 10th-year rentals

The commission on the annual rent of $52,500 for a five-year lease for the space described above would be calculated as follows:

Year	Commission
1	$52,500 × .06 = $3,150.00
2	52,500 × .05 = 2,625.00
3	52,500 × .04 = 2,100.00
4	52,500 × .035 = 1,837.50
5	52,500 × .035 = 1,837.50
Total commission	$11,550.00

If the same lease were negotiated for 10 years, with the last five years at 2%, the commission would be as follows:

First five years as in preceding example	$11,550
Years 6–10: $52,500 × 5 = $262,500 × .02	5,250
Total commission	$16,800

The commission may be negotiated at 5% on the first five years, with nothing earned after that time. The commission on that basis follows:

$52,500 × 5 years = $262,500 × .05 = $13,125.00

For the previous example, a commission is not paid on the value of free rent. Using the preceding sliding scale and assuming six months' free rent, the commission would normally be the following:

Year	Commission
1 (6 months only)	$26,250 × .06 = $1,575.00
2	52,500 × .05 = 2,625.00
3	52,500 × .04 = 2,100.00
4	52,500 × .035 = 1,837.50
5	52,500 × .035 = 1,837.50
Total commission	$9,975.00

One broker negotiated a variation on the theory that the free rent period should be ignored and the commission should be computed from the first day of the rental payment. That calculation follows:

Year	Commission
1 (6 months only)	$52,500 × .06 = $3,150.00
2	52,500 × .05 = 2,625.00
3	52,500 × .04 = 2,100.00
4	52,500 × .035 = 1,837.50
5	26,250 × .035 = 918.75
Total commission	$10,631.25

This gave the broker a slightly higher commission than would have resulted with the previous calculation.

Some property owners do not want the length of the lease to determine the amount of the commission. They may prefer a shorter lease and are concerned the leasing agents prefer a longer lease because a longer lease will earn the leasing agents a larger commission. Most leasing agents will act in the best interest of their clients. As a result, some owners pay commissions based on "so many dollars per square foot." In these cases, the broker receives a stipulated amount—a range of $4.00 to $4.50 per square foot, for example, based on a minimum term which is typically three years, regardless of the rental income. Using a 2,500-square-foot space, the commission would be calculated as follows:

2,500 sq. ft. × $4.00 = $10,000
2,500 sq. ft. × $4.50 = $11,250

Referring back to the example with the sliding scale, the commission was $11,500. A comparison of the commissions on a square footage basis shows that they are much the same:

$11,500 ÷ 2,500 sq. ft. = $4.60 per sq. ft.

Rent Concessions: The Real Cost

Property owners often provide rental concessions either to make a new lease or to renew a tenant. Even if the property owner has no choice in the matter, he or she should understand just what the concession costs. Knowing the real cost may suggest a better alternative and dissuade the property owner from the deal. Granting a concession will impact the cash flow and value of the property—the property owner should evaluate both:

1. Cash flow is lost in the actual amount of the concession for that period.
2. The value of the property is reduced, based on the cap rate.

For instance, the lost of value typically will be 10 times the loss of the cash flow due to capitalization of income, assuming a cap rate of 10%. The loss of value can be higher if the market cap rate is lower.

In the previous example, assume the property owner is negotiating a 2,500 square-foot-office space and is asking $21 per square foot per year, which is the market rate. A tenant prospect offers $19 per square foot. If the deal is accepted at $19 per square foot per year, what is the cost to the building?

Market rent $21 × 2,500 sq. ft.	$52,500
Proposed rent $19 × 2,500 sq. ft.	47,500
Lost cash flow	5,000

(Income lost each year of the lease in which the lower rent remains in effect.)

The loss of value is much more dramatic. Using a capitalization rate of 10% to estimate value, the owner finds:

$5,000 lost revenue ÷ 10% (.10) = $50,000
(reduced, value of the property)

As long as the reduced rental remains in effect, the value of the building has been reduced by $50,000, using the capitalization of income approach to value. If the property owner grants this concession, it will create a loss of $5,000 in cash flow and $50,000 in value each year that the concession is in place. Because of market conditions, the property owner may elect to make the deal or may look for an alternate proposal that gives the tenant a break, but lessens the reduction of cash flow or value.

Caps on CAM Costs

National or anchor tenants may negotiate limits on CAM costs. Although the limits may appear to be small, they will effect the cash flow and have a greater effect on the value of the property. The tenant that leases the 2,500-square-foot space in the preceding examples should pay $.53 per square foot per month for the operating costs of the property, but has negotiated a maximum of $.45 per square foot per month. What does this limit, or cap, cost the building?

Lost income

Income loss is $.08 per square foot per month

$.53 – .45 = .08 × 2,500 sq. ft. = $200 monthly

$200 × 12 = $2,400 yearly loss

(This is the lost income each year the limitation is in effect.)

Lost value

If the owner uses a capitalization rate of 10% (.10), the value of the building is reduced as follows:

$2,400 lost revenue ÷ 10% (.10) = $24,000

(This is the lost value each year the limitation is in effect.)

Tenant Improvements (TIs)

TIs play a major role in office building leasing as well as in the leasing of industrial buildings, and, to a lesser extent, in shopping centers. In all cases, however, it is important to understand what is being spent and what impact the spending will have on the project.

Calculating the effect of TIs on a dollars per square foot sometimes offers a clearer picture. Consider the preceding project. TIs of $5,000 do not seem exorbitant because the cash flow is almost $400,000. However, a very small tenant of 400 square feet requires $5,000 in TIs and wants only a two-year lease. The annual rental is $8,400. The square footage comparison follows:

Per Square Foot	
Rent	$21.00
Improvements	
($5,000 ÷ 400 sq. ft. ÷ 2 years)	(6.25)
Net effective rent	14.75
Mortgage from above	16.70
Property owner out of pocket	($1.95)

The property owner may still make this deal for many reasons, but at least he or she will be fully aware of the cost of the deal.

Time Value of Money (TVM)

With the exception of calculating the net set aside for a future expenditure, this chapter has not considered the *time value of money (TVM).* If a transaction is being concluded today, a dollar is a dollar. However, if funds are to be received in the future, those funds are worth less today than a dollar paid or received today because of the impact of interest on that dollar. Several years ago, pre-calculated tables were used to determine the current worth of a dollar to be paid in five years and also to determine what today's dollar would be worth in 10 years at a given rate of interest. Today, real estate professionals use a financial calculator or software program.

First, look at the value of $10,000 dollars in five years invested today at a rate of 10%. If money had no TVM, simply multiply the $10,000 times 10% times the five years, and add up the figures. However, take into consideration the compounding of the interest. As the result, the $10,000 will grow to $16,105.10 if left in the account for five years at 10% interest.

Next, look at how much has to be put in the bank today in order to have $10,000 at the end of five years at an interest rate of 10%. By placing $6,209.21 in the bank today at 10% interest, the desired $10,000 will be obtained at the end of five years.

Net Present Value (NPV)

The concept behind *net present value (NPV)* is to use the TVM to analyze the current value of an investment. Assume purchasing a building for $1 million, cash, and leasing it for the following amounts:

$100,000 the first year
$110,000 the second year
$120,000 the third year
$130,000 the fourth year
$140,000 the fifth year
$150,000 the sixth year

The building will be sold at the end of the sixth year for $1,100,000 cash. The investor wants a 13% return. Will this investment meet his requirements? Using a financial calculator: NPV = $13,923

The result is a positive $13,923, indicating that the goal of a 13% return will be reached, if all assumptions hold true. These calculations are only as meaningful as the accuracy of the original assumptions on which they are based.

Return on Investment (ROI)

Because there are alternative ways in which to invest money, calculate ROI to compare the alternatives. Simply put, ROI is the comparison of income earned to the amount of money invested. On all cash investments, the return amount will be the NOI. An example follows:

Office Building purchased	$1,000,000
Net Operating Income	82,000

Return on investment 82,000 ÷ 1,000,000 = 8.2%

This is a *cash-on-cash return*. A total of $1,000,000 cash was paid, $82,000 cash was received after expenses, and the result is an 8.2% return.

In another situation, the same building was elected to be financed. The *equity* (down payment) must then be compared to the *cash flow* (the NOI less debt service)—assume a 30-year, 7% loan of 70% of the value, or $700,000. The annual payment is $55,885.41. The calculation is:

ROI: $26,100 = 8.7% of $300,000

Because the property owner was able to borrow the funds at a lower rate than the ROI, the rate of return also increased. This is positive leverage.

Take the same situation with mortgage rates of 9% rather than the 7%—the result would be a reduction in the ROI as follows:

Cost of building	$1,000,000
Mortgage	700,000
Equity	300,000
Net operating income	82,000
Debt service	67,588
Cash flow	14,412
ROI:	$14,412 = 4.8% of $300,000

Because a higher interest rate was paid to borrow the funds than was received as the ROI, the net result was a reduction in the rate of return, known as negative leverage.

Incremental ROI

If the building is owned, but improvements are to be made, the cost is generally evaluated for the new improvements and the additional income to be generated, rather than looking at the totals in both cases. Using the previous building as an example, assume that a decision have been made to install an air-conditioning controller that will monitor demand and outside ambient air temperature. The cost will be $70,000 and the estimated savings will be $480 monthly, after all expenses. Our incremental return will be:

$480 × 12 = $5,760 = 8.23% of $70,000

Budget Projections

In the preparation of a budget, real estate managers are often called upon to estimate future expenses. As discussed in *Chapter 15: Budgeting, zero-based budgeting* can be used—i.e., forget everything that has been spent in the past and look at the individual line items with no historical consideration. On the other hand, take historical information and extrapolate it forward by evaluating current contracts and examining industry data to arrive at figures. Averaging the data for the past several years also helps to arrive at a useful figure. For example, if the landscaping contract for the past five years has cost $1,400, $1,400, $1,500, $1,500, and $1,200, the average annual cost would be $1,400. However, the last year was well below that figure. The last year's figure could be used and a factor for inflation could be added to arrive at a figure for the budget, but that figure might not be satisfactory either.

Another approach is to use the weighted average, which allows the real estate manager to look at each figure under consideration and decide how it fits into the situation. In this case, assume that the $1,200 figure is more likely the annual landscaping cost, possibly because the landscaper indicated no change in the agreements. It's important to be sure that whatever final weights that are used, the total is 100. It should be mentioned also that the weighted average approach is very subjective. However, a figure may carry more confidence if it is the result of a weighted average rather than a best guess. One approach to the calculation might be the following:

Year	Contract	Weight	Result
Five	$1,400	.20	$ 280
Four	1,400	.20	280
Three	1,500	.10	150
Two	1,500	.10	150
One	1,200	.40	480
Totals		1.00	$1,340

We would then review the current situation and adjust that figure by known considerations, such as needed services in the project and/or possible contract changes. Another approach is to weigh the changes and add them to the last year. Assume that the lighting maintenance for the building has cost the following amounts over the past five years:

Year	Amount	Change
Five	$12,600	
Four	14,400	+1,800
Three	17,200	+2,800
Two	19,100	+1,900
One	18,200	-900

In reviewing all the contracts and lighting systems, it's decided that the last year's costs should carry the heaviest weight, so it's assigned a weight of .50. The fourth year is very unrealistic, given the direction of the expenses and the age of the equipment, so it's given the least weight of .10. The second and third years are close enough to assign equal weights, so they are both assigned .20. The total of the weights to be assigned to the increase equals 1.00. The calculation is as follows:

Contract	Weight	Result
$1,800	.10	$180
2,800	.20	560
2,800	.20	560
1,900	.20	380
-900	.50	-450
Totals	1.00	+670

Taking the last year's expenses of $18,200, plus the weighted average increase of $670, the coming year's cost would be budgeted at $18,870. Like everything else, weighted averages must be calculated, evaluated, and quite often adjusted.

Break-even Analysis

When leasing up a building or a rehab in which the occupancy has gone down during rehabilitation, it is often very helpful to know at what point the building will *break even*—that is, when the income and the expenses will be equal to each other. By using two formulas, the break-even occupancy rate can first be determined by dividing the total operating expenses (not including the items passed back to tenants as operating expenses), plus the annual debt service by the gross potential income. The formula is as follows:

Break-even occupancy rate (%) = Total annual operating expenses
+ Annual debt service
÷ Gross potential income

By way of example, if the total annual operating expenses, exclusive of operating expense reimbursements, are $120,000, our debt service is $135,000, and our effective gross income is $310,400, the calculation would be as follows:

120,000 + 135,000 = $255,000 ÷ 310,400 = 82.15% break-even occupancy rate

To find out how many square feet that would be, multiply the break-even occupancy rate by the square footage of the building, as follows:

Total Building Square Footage	21,000
Occupancy Rate	.8215
Square Footage Needed	17,252

This is a very helpful figure in the lease-up process and may help in specific decisions regarding tenant leases. In an office building, the variable expenses may change as the occupancy levels of the building change, which must be considered in the final calculations. If, for instance, all variable expenses are calculated as though the building were 95% or 100% occupied, the break-even point arrived at with this approach will be higher than should be expected in reality. In contrast, if the expenses are understated, the break-even point will be lower than should be expected, and that can cause problems in terms of cash flow and funding.

Financial Analysis: Tenant Operating Statements

Property owners and real estate managers frequently ask prospective tenants for their balance sheets and operating statements to determine if they are good financial risks. A tenant may be asked to provide the same information if the tenant appears to have trouble paying the rent and/or asks for rent relief—especially in retail properties. Exhibit 14.4 is a statement of income and expenses for a hypothetical tenant. The tenant operates her own business and hires relief help only when needed.

This tenant is doing well and her sales are increasing. Her expenses appear to be in control. Profit margins are excellent for an owner-operated business. In addition to the satisfactory margin of profit (24% in 2015) the property owner is taking a salary in the area of $50,000, which makes the business very profitable overall. The 2016 gross income is growing nicely. Better yet, the operating expenses are up a modest 1.9% overall. The return on sales increased dramatically between the years, providing a better cushion as time goes on.

In evaluating statements of income and expenses, the real estate manager should be on the lookout for declining sales and examine the reasons for the decline. The problem could be short term or long term. For instance, it could be that new competition is not going away or a temporary distraction that is now over and will let things get back on track. The problem could be seasonal. Runaway expenses are also a warning sign. Newer tenants often invest in new equipment, new ideas, and/or promotional items to build the business but let the ratios get out of hand. Look for a financial cushion. Does the tenant have the staying power to overcome a short-term problem? If this were a retail tenant, look at the cost of goods sold and compare it to industry averages to see how the tenant is doing in terms of markup. Smaller businesses must closely monitor

EXHIBIT 14.4

Johnson's Postal Express

STATEMENT OF INCOME AND EXPENSES	2015	2016	% Change
Income			
Gross sales	$ 85,000	$91,000	+7.1%
Outside accounts	31,000	36,000	+16%
Miscellaneous supplies	4,300	4,600	+7%
Total income	$120,300	$31,600	+9.4%
Expenses			
Rent	$ 16,000	$17,000	+4.9%
Telephone	1,400	1,600	+14.3%
Insurance	1,300	1,400	+7.7%
Wages and benefits	61,000	61,000	-0-
Advertising	3,600	3,800	+5.5
Repairs and maintenance	900	1,050	+16.6%
Supplies	1,400	1,700	+21.4%
Outside accounting	2,400	2,400	-0-
Utilities	3,800	4,100	+7.9%
Total expenses	$91800.00	$94050.00	+1.9%
Net income	$28,500	$37550	+32%
Return on sales	24%	26%	+8%

their end markup, for they often cannot compete with the discounters who are their competition.

Balance Sheet Analysis

For all types of commercial tenants, financial statements are requested from prospective new tenants and from any tenant that is having financial difficulties and/or is asking for rent relief. Exhibit 14.5 shows a balance sheet to illustrate poor relationships in order to explain the various tools used in the analysis.

First, look at working capital, i.e., the relationship between current assets and current liabilities. This tenant's working capital is negative:

Current assets – current liabilities = working capital
$93,700 – $110,600 = -$16,900

This tenant may have too much money tied up in inventory, most of which appears to be financed. Even if the inventory were turned, this tenant would not be in a good cash position. Ideally, a healthy tenant has a good positive margin between current assets and current liabilities.

Although there is no magic working capital number, the tenant should be able to operate and pay the bills for 60 to 90 days without needing strong sales to support expenses or having payments on current liabilities wipe out all of the needed cash flow.

The *current ratio* is the relationship, on a percentage basis, between current assets and current liabilities:

Current Assets	Current Liabilities	Current Ratio
$93,700	$110,600	85%

The current ratio should be 100 for a tenant to have a strong position in a difficult market. The tenant in the example has excessive debt. This tenant could not come close to covering current liabilities with current assets. Given that many of its current assets are not that liquid, the tenant is in an even worse position.

EXHIBIT 14.5

Immediate Photo World

STATEMENT OF NET WORTH

Assets		Liabilities	
Cash on hand	$28,500	Accounts payable	$44,600
Doubtful accounts	(1,800)	Loans payable	56,000
Inventory	67,000	Tax liability	10,000
Current assets	$93,700	Current liabilities	$110,600
Photographic equipment	80,000	Second mortgage	45,000
Furniture and fixtures	30,000		
Company truck	18,000		
Total fixed assets	128,000		
Total assets	$221,700	Total liabilities	$155,600
Net worth	$66,100		

The net worth of a tenant is always of interest to the property owner. In the illustrative case, the tenant has total assets of $221,700 and total liabilities of $155,600, leaving a net worth of $66,100. This tenant has a weak net worth. It does not have a sufficient asset base to carry it through tough times. If the tenant encounters any months of poor sales, it will be asking for rent relief or (more likely) will pick up and leave. Additionally, the assets the tenant does have would probably be worth a lot less than the value stated if they had to be sold off to meet obligations. This tenant will have a minimal net worth under any circumstances.

The current-debt-to-equity ratio measures the percentage of the net worth one would have to use up to pay off the current liabilities.

Current Debt (liabilities)	Equity	Ratio
$110,600	$66,100	1.67

This tenant actually owes almost twice its net worth. In looking for a solvent tenant, a property owner or a real estate manager hopes for equity that is at least twice current liabilities, which would indicate the ability to meet current obligations without going broke. Although this tenant may not be faced with having to meet current obligations without additional income, the tenant is considered very weak.

The total-debt-to-equity ratio gives a long-range view of the tenant's position. In the previous case, the two ratios do not result in much of a distinction. The tenant is in poor financial condition and looking at the total debt-to-equity ratio reinforces that view:

Total Debt (liabilities)	Equity	Ratio
$155,600	$66,100	.42

This tenant could not meet all of its obligations without liquidating the company, and even liquidation would probably fall short. Unless all items sold for book value, this tenant might be in a negative net worth position.

The final statistic is the total-debt-to-total-assets ratio. Again, the focus is looking for the ability to meet financial obligations. In this case, the picture is a little more positive, but most assets are not worth what the book amounts in a liquidation situation.

Total Assets	Total Liabilities	Ratio
$221,700	$155,600	.7018

This ratio means it would take 71% of the tenant's assets to pay off the debt if everything were liquidated at the book value. A property owner would like to see more flexibility in the financial condition of tenants and/or prospective tenants.No fixed ratio measures are either acceptable or unacceptable under all circumstances. At the very minimum, looking at the financial or operating statements and taking into account these relationships will help put the analysis of a tenant or prospective tenant in the proper perspective.

CONCLUSION

In commercial property management, mathematics is a critical element of both decision making and financial analysis. While much of the mathematical analysis is more of an art than a science, the quantification of information is helpful in making comparisons. Much of the decision-making process is analyzing which is the best option among several, and going with that approach. As institutions and REITs assert more influence on the real estate management process, mathematical analyses will become increasingly important.

CHAPTER

15

Budgeting

The effective budget is a financial road map for the property. While the final budget, especially for a larger property, is a very complex document, it is not that difficult to prepare if one does the proper research and analysis prior to putting the budget together. This chapter outlines the steps in preparing the budget.

The purpose of a budget is to provide financial guidance to the real estate manager and the property owner. A well-planned budget allows the manager to anticipate and properly respond to financial changes. For example, if the property does not have sufficient funds to pay the first real estate tax installment, this will be obvious when the budget is developed. The property owner then has sufficient time to plan for the cash shortfall. Conversely, if the property will generate a positive cash flow by midyear, the property owner can plan how the funds will be used. The decision as to what is to be done with funds generated above the budget is that of the owners and not the real estate manager. Without a budget, these two situations would go unnoticed until the property ran out of funds or the owner realized more cash was available than anticipated. Even then, the owner wouldn't know if he or she would be able to use the funds for additional projects or would need them to operate the property later in the year. The real estate manager is responsible for minimizing or eliminating surprises for the property owner.

The budgeting process has become increasingly sophisticated. The *real estate investment trusts (REITs)* and institutions, which emphasize the financial aspects of the properties, have brought a well-considered approach to budgeting. Generally, their budgets are prepared on a spreadsheet program, such as Microsoft Excel, or an accounting program with a fully integrated set of schedules, such as a lease-up schedule, bill-back allocations, or a remodel schedule.

TYPES OF BUDGETS

Two general categories of budgets are operating budgets and capital budgets. An *operating budget* lists all income and all expenses anticipated from the operation of a property over a given period—usually the coming year. A *capital budget* is a long-term plan for major improvements or replacements to a property, generally, five year, but in some cases it will be a longer period of time. This text discusses both types of budgets.

Budget formats can change dramatically depending on the client and the purpose of the budget. Lenders and most major property owners have specific requirements for the budgets that they must consider. Partnerships often have breakdowns within the budget structure unique to that legal structure. Publicly traded companies often have additional requirements based on governmental reporting requirements. Most often, one document can incorporate all of these needs, but occasionally two budgets are necessary: one for the daily operations and one for the special needs of the client.

Sub-budgets comprise the entire budget. In a complex situation, a property can have several sub-budgets, which fall into two categories: (1) expense and (2) income.

Expense Sub-Budgets

Complex commercial properties may use all of the following expense sub-budgets; simpler properties may use only a few.

1. **Capital expenditure budget:** The capital portion of the budget includes those items that are

not generally expensed in one year and that are amortized over more than one year. These include major repairs, leasing commissions and new additions to the property. While *tenant improvements (TIs)* and leasing commissions are generally included in this budget, they may have sub-budgets of their own. Capital budgets are discussed in greater detail later in this chapter.

2. Owner's expenses: Expenditures paid by the owner that are not reimbursed by tenants. Owner's expenses for some shopping centers generally include merchants' association or marketing fund contributions, legal expenses, business licenses, office expenses, costs to maintain vacancies, and possibly property management fees.
3. Common area parking lot for shopping centers: In an enclosed mall, all tenants commonly share the parking lot expenses. Parking lot expenses are exterior items of maintenance, including but not limited to parking lot sweeping, landscaping, security and utilities for the parking lot, and the property management fee, if the lease allows.
4. Common area mall for shopping centers: Tenants whose stores open onto the mall generally share the expenses. Major tenants are not always required to share mall *common area* expenses, which include but are not limited to janitorial services, air-conditioning, maintenance, utilities, security, and interior landscaping.
5. Operating expenses for office buildings and industrial properties: Office tenants share the expenses of operating the building. These escalation charges include janitorial service, building repair, insurance, property taxes, pest control, utilities, and usually, property management fees.
6. Merchants' association and marketing fund for shopping centers: The property owner's contribution to the merchants' association or the marketing fund is generally budgeted in this category. If the property owner collects the merchants' dues and pays the bills, the marketing fund is generally not a part of the overall property budget but is handled separately.
7. Property taxes and insurance: Most owners of shopping centers and industrial properties want a careful evaluation of the taxes and insurance paid and the percentage of such expenses that are recaptured from the tenants. In the typical commercial lease, tenants reimburse the property owner for their pro rata shares of these expenses. Taxes and insurance are included in office building operating expenses.
8. Utility reimbursement: The owner may pay for the utilities in bulk (known as a *master meter*) or have a central plant and recover the costs from the tenants on a pro rata basis.
9. Reimbursement for repairs: Large properties often have an on-site maintenance staff that provides repairs for tenants for a fee. Shopping centers tenants are usually billed separately for the cost to maintain their *heating, ventilation, and air-conditioning (HVAC)* units or other repairs specific to their spaces.
10. Debt service: The amount of principal and interest necessary to meet the mortgage requirements for an existing loan.
11. Lease-up budget: The marketing and advertising cost to lease a building.
12. TI budget for capital expenditure budget: The cost to build out or fit out premises for renewing and new tenants.
13. Food court budget for shopping centers: The cost to clean and maintain the seating, common eating utensils, and trash removal aspects of the shopping center's food court. Usually only the food court tenants are charged for the food court maintenance costs. Some property owners charge the food court cost to the shopping center or mall *common area maintenance (CAM)* budget because they believe it is a draw and an amenity for the shopping center or mall.

Income Sub-Budgets

Income sub-budgets vary according to the type of commercial property involved.

1. Base rent for shopping centers: It is the required monthly rental described in the lease agreement—exclusive of all other sources of income.
2. Percentage rent: Applies mostly to shopping centers and retailers and restaurants in office buildings and industrial parks. The income derived from the provisions for the property owner to receive tenant revenues Percentage rent income is additional rent based on tenant sales.

3. **Reimbursement of tenant charges:** The income from tenants for such items as common area charges, tax, and insurance billbacks.
4. **Merchants' association and/or marketing fund income:** The income generated by lease requirements from the tenant leases per tenants' leases for marketing and advertising for the shopping center.
5. **Parking income:** The income derived from on-site parking charges. Generally, this is a net item. The gross parking income is reduced by the expenses involved, and the net is the parking income.
6. **Miscellaneous income:** This item includes late charges, interest on late rents, vending machine income, high-speed internet, and Wi-Fi services sold to tenants, etc.

BUDGET DEVELOPMENT AND EVALUATION

One important factor in evaluating a real estate manager's performance is his or her ability to develop accurate income and expense projections. The property's financial records provide the real estate manger with the income and expenses to date, and the real estate manager estimates the income and expenses for the balance of the current budget period. Although the budgeting process is not difficult, it can be time consuming, and it requires a thorough knowledge of budget development and evaluation.

The budget must be consistent with the property owner's goals and objectives. This means the real estate manager must meet with the owner to discuss both short- and long-term goals. Was the property purchased for long-term appreciation? If so, the property owner will want to invest in *preventive maintenance* and *capital improvements.* On the other hand, does the property owner have cash flow problems or live off the property's income and need all the cash for personal use? In either of these situations, the owner would be reluctant to spend any more money than was necessary to maintain the current status of the property. It is up to the real estate manager to advise the owner of what is best for the operation of the property, but in the final analysis, the real estate manager must work to meet the owner's goals.

The real estate manager should bring to the property owner's attention all of the major maintenance needs and capital improvements and justify the need for the work—even if the real estate manager is sure the property owner does not have funds to correct the problems or may be unwilling to do so. The real estate manager should distinguish between those maintenance items that are cosmetic or done for marketing purposes as opposed to safety-oriented needs. The real estate manager reviews the necessity of the work and recommends which items should be completed in the budget period and which can be deferred. Developing a budget and then discovering that it is not consistent with the property owner's goals and objectives for the property is an exercise in futility.

Budget Team

Developing an accurate budget requires the input of several members of the real estate management company and may include outside consultants. The real estate manager is primarily responsible for developing the budget. The real estate manager should use the knowledge and experience of maintenance personnel, contractors, accounting department, leasing agent, the property's insurance agent, consultants, and the manager's supervisor. Getting the input of the various departments before the budget is completed makes more sense than waiting until it is done only to learn it does not meet the property's major needs.

The maintenance supervisor is often most familiar with the maintenance and mechanical operations of the property, yet this person's input is sometimes overlooked when the budget is developed. The main tenance supervisor should meet with maintenance personnel to review the property's condition and then submit a brief status report to the manager.

Smaller commercial properties seldom have on-site maintenance personnel. They generally contract all maintenance, whereas most large properties contract only specific maintenance. Prior to preparing the budget, the real estate manager should meet with all contractors to review their areas of maintenance and solicit their opinions on future maintenance needs. For example, the HVAC service contractor may make recommendations for repairs beyond the preventive maintenance contract or recommend upgrading the filters or adding energy conservation features or equipment.

Consultants may be added to the budget team for specific expertise, such as parking lot, roof maintenance, energy conservation, and recycling programs. Consultants are hired to analyze, make recommendations, develop specifications, and estimate costs for specific work.

The leasing agent should provide the leasing projections. The real estate manager must know the occupancy level in order to estimate janitorial and utilities costs in an office building. To project commission expense, the manager also needs to know which spaces are likely to be leased, what the required TIs are, and how much space will be leased and renewed.

The real estate manager and the insurance agent should meet with the owner to discuss the existing insurance program and the cost of alternative insurance coverage.

The accounting department is an integral part of the budget team. The bookkeeper provides historical expenses and actual expenses for the current period. They are combined with the real estate manager's estimate of the expenses for the balance of the current budget period. The result is the estimated expenses for the current year or budget period.

Besides calculating the tenants' charges and reimbursements, the bookkeeper may be asked to determine specific expenses, such as real estate taxes. An estimate of the expenses for the current budget period is an excellent reference when preparing for the next budget period.

Budget Schedule

A budget is developed over a two- to four-month period. Each commercial property has multiple income components and several operating budgets. Every source of income in each income component and every line item expense in each operating budget must be analyzed to prepare an accurate *net operating income (NOI)* projection.

The budgeting process must be planned, communicated to everyone involved in the budgets, and monitored. As a first step in developing the plan, the controller, in larger companies and the manager in smaller properties reviews the management agreements to determine when each budget is due to the owner. The controller and/or real estate manager then prepares a proposed timeline for each budget. The timeline is developed in reverse chronological order, starting with the date, the budget is due to the property owner. It includes the following steps:

- E-mail budget to the property owner
- Complete final review and corrections
- Submit for review by the real estate manager's supervisor
- Write and edit narrative
- Obtain income and expense data from the real estate manager
- Obtain historical and current data from the accounting department

The timeline should be distributed to all staff members involved in the budgeting process and progress should be monitored. The schedule in Exhibit 15.1 illustrates a proposed calendar for a budget timeline for which the budget and management plan are due December 15.

One staff person, such as an administrative assistant, can act as coordinator to keep the process flowing smoothly. Delays should be identified and corrected immediately. Staff members should also be recognized for meeting each deadline.

Owners rarely approve a budget on the first attempt. Generally, one or two meetings or phone

EXHIBIT 15.1

REAL ESTATE MANAGER'S BUDGETING CALENDAR

Date	Action
August	
15	Complete market survey and report results to owners
September	
1	Talk to property owners and get parameters for budget
10	Develop income and operating expenses; send to accounting for calculating tenants' reimbursement of common area maintenance (CAM) charges
11	Start writing management plan
14	Have accounting send complete budget to real estate manager
15	Review first draft budget with executive real estate manager
30	Complete first proposed budget; send to owners
October	
10	Send management/business plan narrative to executive ~~property~~ real estate manager for review
15	Receive owner comments
16	Revise management plan narrative if owners make changes to budget
30	Revise budget; send back to owners
November	
15	Change budget if owners made corrections; send to owners for final budget approval
20	Send management plan and budget to owners
30	Receive final approvals from owners; input budget into the system
December	
15	Implement budget

conversations take place regarding the budget figures, adjustments are made, and after one or two revisions, the parties agree upon a final budget.

Budget Format

All property owners require accurate budget forecasting. Most institutional owners have their own format requirements and software specifications. A detailed month-by-month budget provides a monthly NOI forecast. When the property's debt service and capital expenses are included in the budgeting process, a monthly cash-flow projection can be developed. Exhibit 15.2 shows the net operating income formula.

Each income component—base rent, percentage rent, and recovery of operating expenses from the tenants—is budgeted separately. Operating expense budgets, owner's non-reimbursable expenses, common area maintenance (CAM), building escalation expenses, and other expenses are also budgeted separately. Most real estate

EXHIBIT 15.2

Net Operating Income (NOI) Formula

Start with gross possible income from rents:

minus	–	Vacancy and rent loss
plus	+	Miscellaneous income
equals	=	Effective income
minus	–	Stabilized operating expenses
equals	=	Net operating income

Taking the NOI formula one step further, we calculate cash flow as follows:

minus	–	Debt service
equals	=	Cash flow

management software programs include budget formats. When each income component and each operating expense is budgeted and totaled and the expenses are subtracted from the income, an NOI forecast is produced.

The budgeting process is straightforward—but time consuming. Creating the proper procedures, budget formats, and forms assists in developing an accurate and timely income and expense analysis.

Chart of Accounts

A *chart of accounts* classifies or arranges account items by type of income or expense. Real estate management firms developed and used their own charts of accounts for segregating and identifying income components and operating expenses. Exhibit 15.3 shows a commercial real estate management firm's chart of accounts listed numerically. Exhibit 15.4 presents the same chart of accounts listed alphabetically. (These forms would have to be modified for use with residential properties.)

When institutions became the major owners of medium- to large-sized commercial properties, real estate management firms found, to their dismay, that many of their clients would no longer accept their standard charts of accounts and financial reports. Institutional owners contract with numerous real estate management firms. They cannot operate efficiently and develop their internal reports if every real estate management firm reporting to them uses a different chart of accounts and reporting format. Real estate management firms must be able to accommodate the financial reporting requirements of each client and potential client. However, some clients—primarily private investors, developers, and some institutional owners—will accept the real estate management firm's standard chart of accounts and financial reports.

Almost all commercial properties have two or more operating budgets, so the real estate management firm must develop a simple method of identifying which expenses are the property owner's non-reimbursable expenses, escalation expenses, or CAM. This can be accomplished by adding to the expense account number a prefix that identifies the particular budget.

For instance, "1" is the property owner's nonreimbursable budget prefix; "2" is the shopping center CAM/parking lot budget; "3" is the shopping center CAM/enclosed mall budget; "4" is the office building and industrial property operating budget; "5" is the merchants' association/marketing fund budget, and so on. In the chart of accounts in Exhibits 15.3 and 10.4, the account number for "Window maintenance"

EXHIBIT 15.3

Chart of Accounts—Numerical List

Administrative—71000

71100	Advertising
71101	Merchants assoc. contributions
71105	Entertainment & promotion
71110	Contributions
74105	Automobile lease expense
74108	Parking/ferry tolls
74110	Automobile repairs & maintenance
74810	Management fees
74875	Management fees—cash
75510	Insurance expense
76100	Air freight
76105	Bank charges
76110	Dues and subscriptions
76115	Office equipment rental
76120	Office supplies
76125	Postage
76130	Repairs and maintenance
76135	Telephone expenses
76140	Miscellaneous expense
77100	Accounting fees
77105	Consulting fees
77110	Legal fees
77115	Architect fees
77120	Leasing commissions
78100	Business tax
78105	Licenses
78110	Permits
78115	Personal property tax
78120	Real estate tax
78125	Sales tax on capital additions
79100	Air fare
79105	Car rental
79110	Lodging
79115	Meals
80100	Salaries
80105	Payroll taxes
80110	Profit sharing expenses
80115	Insurance—life
80120	Insurance—medical/dental
80130	Gasoline
80135	Management training

Utilities—81000

81100	Electricity
81200	Gas
81300	Oil
81400	Water
81500	Sewer
81900	Other utilities

Building supplies—83000

83100	Licenses & permits
83150	Alarm
83200	Music
83300	Signs
83350	Supplies
83400	Tools/equipment/uniform
83450	Rentals
83500	Trash removal

Repairs, maintenance & contract service—84000

84110	Salaries
84120	Payroll taxes
84130	Employee benefits
85100	Building repairs/ maintenance
85200	Flooring
85300	Ceilings
85400	Landscaping
85410	Window maintenance
85500	Roof
85600	Elevator/escalator
85700	Plumbing/sprinklers
85800	Parking lot
85900	Security
86000	Janitorial
86100	Painting
86200	Sweeping/snow removal
86300	Electrical
86400	HVAC
86500	Insurance damage
86600	Reserve account

Tenant costs—89000

89100	Tenant repairs
89200	Tenant improvements
89220	Landlord improvements
90000	Rent expenses
96000	Federal income tax expense

EXHIBIT 15.4

Chart of Accounts—Alphabetical List

Administrative—71000	
Accounting fees	77100
Advertising	71100
Air fare	79100
Air freight	76100
Architect fees	77115
Automobile lease expense	74105
Automobile repairs & maintenance	74110
Bank charges	76105
Business tax	67100
Car rental	79105
Consulting fees	77105
Contributions	71110
Dues & subscriptions	76110
Entertainment & promotion	71105
Gasoline	80130
Insurance—life	80115
Insurance—medical/dental	80120
Insurance expense	75510
Leasing commissions	77120
Legal fees	77110
Licenses	78105
Lodging	79110
Management fees	74810
Management fees—cash	74875
Management training	80135
Meals	79115
Merchants assoc. contributions	71101
Miscellaneous expense	76140
Office equipment rental	76115
Office supplies	76120
Parking/ferry tolls	74108
Payroll taxes	80105
Permits	78110
Personal property tax	78115
Postage	76125
Profit sharing expenses	80110
Real estate tax	78120
Repairs & maintenance	76130
Salaries	80100
Sales tax on capital additions	78125
Telephone expenses	76135
Building supplies—83000	
Alarm	83150
Licenses & permits	83100
Music	83200
Building supplies (cont.)	
Rentals	83450
Signs	83300
Supplies	83350
Tools/equipment/uniforms	83400
Trash removal	83500
Repairs, maintenance & contract services—84000	
Building repairs/ maintenance	85100
Ceilings	85300
Electrical	86300
Elevator/escalator	85600
Employee benefits	84130
Flooring	85200
HVAC	86400
Insurance damage	86500
Janitorial	86000
Landscaping	85400
Painting	86100
Parking lot	85800
Payroll taxes	84120
Plumbing/sprinklers	85700
Reserve account	86600
Roof	85500
Salaries	84110
Security	85900
Sweeping/snow removal	86200
Window maintenance	85410
Tenant costs—89000	
Federal income tax expense	96000
Landlord improvements	89220
Rent expenses	90000
Tenant improvements	89200
Tenant repairs	89100
Utilities—81000	
Electricity	81100
Gas	81200
Oil	81300
Other utilities	81900
Sewer	81500
Water	81400

is "85410." The cost to wash the windows in a vacant shopping center space would be a property owner's nonreimbursable expense "1-85410," while the cost to wash the windows on the mall entrance would be a CAM/mall expense "3-85410."

OPERATING BUDGETS

As mentioned, commercial properties usually have several operating budgets. All real estate managers must prepare operating budgets—this chapter considers them in detail.

Property Owner's Operating Budget

All properties have a property owner's *operating budget* for expenses that are not reimbursed by tenants. These expenses include legal fees, partnership audits, utilities cost for vacancies, leasing commissions, mortgage payments, the cost to clean vacancies, and the shopping center's owner's share of the merchants' association or marketing fund dues.

Operating Budgets for Charges Billed to Tenants

Office buildings have a second operating budget for the building's operating expenses or charges billed to the tenants. Multitenant industrial properties may have a common area operating budget that is charged to the tenants.

Shopping centers can have multiple operating budgets. A non-enclosed shopping center, (also referred to as an *open shopping center* or a *strip shopping center*) will have a CAM budget. If the shopping center is an enclosed mall, a second CAM budget is developed for the enclosed mall. The reason for two CAM budgets is that tenants who are not in the mall—such as a bank or a fast food restaurant located on a pad, an outlot, or splitter building—will not be charged for the cost to maintain the enclosed mall common areas. If the mall has a food court, a third common area budget for operating and cleaning the food court may be charged to the food court tenants. Major department stores, often negotiate to pay only CAM for the parking lot and not for the mall areas. The major tenant contends that it does not need the draw of the mall and that its customers have access to the store from the parking lot, however, many property owners disagree with this position. During lease negotiations, department stores are usually in a stronger negotiating position, and they often negotiate to pay no enclosed mall CAM charges or just a nominal amount.

Merchants' Association or Marketing Fund Operating Budgets

Most regional and *super regional malls, life style centers, outlet centers* and specialty centers will have either a merchant's association or marketing fund. Merchant's associations were created when shopping centers became popular in the 1950s with the purpose to promote and advertise the shopping center. Almost all merchant's associations were replaced with marketing funds in the 1980s. There are some merchant's associations in operations in older shopping centers.

Each of these organizations need an annual budget. Their source of income comes from the dues or additional rent paid by the tenants and a financial contribution by the shopping center or mall owner. The dues the merchants and the property owner pay cover these costs. The shopping center's marketing director develops this budget. If the shopping center does not have a marketing director, the real estate manager develops the budget. Quite often, the marketing budget is separate from the shopping center's or mall's operating budget. In such cases, the merchants' dues may be included in the marketing budget, and only the owner's contribution shows up in the property's operating budget.

DEVELOPING THE OPERATING EXPENSE BUDGET

Each item in the operating expense budget should be analyzed on a month-by-month basis to arrive at the total expenses for each month. By listing each expense for each maintenance item monthly, the manager develops a month-by-month operating expense. Combining all the operating budgets and the property owner's nonreimbursable expense budget with the expenses for taxes, insurance, and any other expenses provides a month-by-month operating expense budget. When the monthly operating expenses are subtracted from the monthly income components, the result is a month-by-month NOI projection.

With this budget format, the real estate manager can identify in advance any month with a potential negative NOI or negative cash flow after debt service and capital expenses and shift the timing of some expenses, especially major nonrecurring expenses, to a period with positive cash flow. Identifying months with negative cash flow allows the property owner to plan for cash shortages. Conversely, positive cash-flow projections can be monitored for cash-management planning. The real estate manager must consider 10 elements before arriving at expense numbers, which are explained in the following sections.

1. Inspections

Developing an accurate and meaningful budget is practically impossible without inspecting the property. The real estate manager reviews prior inspection forms and notes items for future maintenance items and capital improvement. The manager then inspects the property. If major maintenance or capital improvement, such as roof repair or replacement is needed, a consultant may be hired to analyze the problem.

2. Budget Input Form

Much software is available to assist in budget preparation and analysis. Most of the popular programs for property management accommodate inputting an annual operating budget and producing budget reports. Many real estate managers find a spreadsheet program to be very effective for annual budgeting. Using spreadsheet formulas in the budgeting process is highly recommended and expected. It eliminates errors and provides a tool to see the "logic" behind the formula created. Different areas of an operating budget demand the use of more complex formulas, but most are simple to understand and use. Multi-year budgets may warrant more sophisticated software to forecast over longer periods using more complex economic variables.

3. Historical Data

One method of developing an operating budget is to add an inflation factor to the current year's budget. However, this method does not take into consideration nonrecurring expenses, capital improvements, the market's impact on the property, and major cost adjustments for specific expenses such as substantial increases in electrical rates or real estate taxes. This budget approach is not usually accurate or acceptable.

Former President Carter popularized the *zero-based budget* that required analyzing each expense without consideration for past or current expenditures. The budget method that will be outlined in this chapter is similar to a zero-based budget. However, historical expenses and current expenditures will provide a frame of reference when developing the operating budget, which is outlined as follows:

- Comparison of the proposed budget to prior budgets on a per-item basis ensures that an expense category is not missing from the proposed budget and highlights expenses that are significantly over or under the prior year's expenses.
- Expenditures over several years can be used for reference to validate bids. If the janitorial costs have been around $1.20 per square foot per year, and the janitor's new bid is in the high $1.40 range, the present janitorial contractor may be overly confident about winning the contract award. In this case, additional bids are necessary. Many property owners will require three bids for all maintenance jobs. This is a very prudent approach to operating properties.
- Historical data can indicate that the maintenance specifications are wrong or that a contractor misinterpreted the bids. For instance, if a full-service landscaping service costs $1,500 a month and some bids are coming in at $1,000 to $1,200 a month, check the bid specifications against the contractor's specifications for missing items such as pruning or weed control.

4. Publications

Publications distributed by real estate associations are other sources for comparing operating expenses. The Institute of Real Estate Management (IREM) publishes *Office Buildings Income and Expense Analysis* as well as *Income and Expense Analysis for Shopping Centers.* These publications analyze office building and shopping center operating expenses for every major metropolitan area and several secondary cities in the United States. Analyses are classified by the size and age of the buildings.

A major variance in an expense category from one of the publications indicates that the real estate manager should further analyze the expense. For instance, if real estate taxes in any of these publications average $1 per square foot per year for the city in which the property is located, and the current projected tax expense is $1.50, this variance should be analyzed further.

The real estate manager may need to hire a tax consultant to compare the assessed valuation with the comparable building valuation. This approach, along with a comparison of like properties in the area, should give management a good idea if the property is properly valued. If no justification for the variance is apparent, the taxes should be appealed.

5. Comparing Expenses with Other Buildings in the Area

Real estate managers commonly seek information from each other, and information is shared freely in the real estate management profession. Active membership in IREM, the International Council of Shopping Centers (ICSC), and the Building Owners and Managers Association (BOMA) provides opportunities to meet other real estate managers and share experiences.

Being a part of a professional network is invaluable when developing a budget for a building—especially when historical expenses are not available due to a building being under construction or if there is a proposal for construction at the building.

6. Current Year's Expenses

A budget is usually developed and finalized a month or two before the current budget period ends. Some of the most helpful information for developing a budget can be obtained from the current budget period's actual and estimated expenses. The actual expenditures and estimates of the expenses for the remaining budget period are the best guidelines for preparing a budget.

Take the current year's expenses to date and estimate the expenses for the remaining budget period. Actual and projected expenses are combined to obtain accurate estimates for the current year's budget.

7. Budget Explanations

As the budget is prepared, make assumptions as to the income and expenses for the coming year. Those assumptions should be listed at the end of each line item in the budget. If the rent on spaces leased is to be increased by the *consumer price index (CPI),* that should be noted along with the percentage assumed. If electricity is expected to be five percent higher than last year, that should be noted as well. As the year unfolds, the real estate manager is able to see where assumptions were accurate or above or below the reality of the situation.

8. Major Job Schedule

A real estate manager can easily overlook budgeted items that occur several months after the budget is developed. Major jobs—those that require planning, bidding, and scheduling in advance—should be included in a major job schedule. The real estate manager is able to plan, bid, and administer the budgeted nonrecurring expense items by periodically referring to the schedule throughout the year.

9. Competition's Impact on the Budget

Outside influences may impact a building's operating and capital budgets. This in turn affects the marketing and leasing of the building. New developments and upgrades of existing competitors' properties always require careful analysis of a building's marketing features. The real estate manager should drive through the area in which the competition is located to look for new and upgraded buildings. These buildings should be toured, compared, and assessed for their affect on the subject building. A site that is vacant when the budget is developed can become a competing building ready for occupancy during the budget period. Low-rise office buildings, industrial properties, and shopping centers can be constructed in less than a year.

In formulating a building's leasing and occupancy projections, the real estate manager should consider additional competition from new developments and upgraded buildings. The city or county building department will usually provide information on plans for new developments. Analyze the potential impact of these plans on the building and decide whether additional improvements to the subject building must be included in the operating budget or the capital budget.

10. Market Conditions

Market conditions affect the operating and capital budgets and the income projections. In a soft leasing market, capital improvements and/or upgrading maintenance are often necessary to maintain or improve the building's market position. A market survey, which is part of the management or business plan, should be conducted in the early stages of the budget process. The market survey provides the data necessary to project leasing activity and occupancy, which in turn are needed to project all of the income components and some of the operating expenses, such as janitorial and utility expenses for an office building. This information is helpful when determining whether to upgrade the common areas and the exterior of the building.

ANALYZING OPERATING EXPENSES

Each expense item is analyzed separately. When analyzing each expense, do not determine the annual cost and divide the number by 12 to arrive at a monthly expense. Since an expense is seldom a constant amount every month, each expense has to be analyzed on a month-by-month basis. Even when a maintenance contract has a fixed monthly price for full service, such as landscape maintenance, periodic maintenance, and emergency repairs, which are usually are not included in the base contract. For example, landscape water expense is highest in the summer and parking lot lighting expenses are highest in the winter.

Budgets are developed a few months before they go into effect. Each property has at least two operating budgets: (1) the CAM or building operating budget and (2) the property owner's nonreimbursable budget. Each budget has multiple expense categories. Multiply the amount of data for each budget by the number of properties managed by a real estate manager, and it becomes obvious that it is almost impossible to remember all the budgeted items, why they were included, how each expense was determined, and when each expense is to be incurred.

An expense explanation notation for each line item is most commonly made after that line item, or it may be on a separate schedule. For example, under the landscaping category for a mall, a monthly $3,900 maintenance expense is budgeted, but lilies are added at Easter at a cost of $1,600, poinsettias are added in December at a cost of $2,800, and new plants are added in January for $2,250. The budget explanation provides a quick and accurate rationale for each expense item and is a reminder of why an amount was budgeted.

Once the real estate manager understands the process and rationale behind each item, any expense item can be analyzed and budgeted. The following sections provide an analysis of expense components.

Audit Fees

The property owner's expenses may include a partnership audit fee. Consult with the property owner for the cost of this service. Retail tenants' sales should be audited periodically to ensure they are submitting accurate sales figures and paying the correct amount of percentage rent. After determining the number of tenants to audit, the real estate manager can obtain cost estimates from firms specializing in tenant audits.

Commissions

Commissions are estimated by first determining the amount of new space that will likely be leased and the amount of space that will likely be renewed. Then, the rent for the new tenant is estimated and the length of the new tenant's or renewing tenant's leases is projected. Next, the real estate manager reviews the leasing agreement to determine the commission schedule for new space, renewals, and pad or out-parcel tenants. The variables are used to estimate the commission expense.

Elevators

Most real estate managers are not knowledgeable about elevator maintenance or HVAC maintenance, so they usually rely on a maintenance contractor. Bid specifications must be carefully prepared; if they originate with the bidders, they must be carefully compared. Will the contract be a full maintenance contract? If a local small contractor with a lower bid than a national contractor is hired, the real estate manager must determine if the contractor has an adequate supply of parts and sufficient service people available for emergency and after-hours service. Should the real estate manager enter into a long-term maintenance agreement, of usually five years, to receive a discount?

All of these issues must be considered when developing elevator maintenance costs. A light-load credit should be negotiated in the contract. This provides a discount if occupancy in the property falls below a certain level. It is usually a series of discounts based on different occupancy levels.

HVAC Maintenance

When bidding the preventive maintenance, the contractor usually provides the maintenance specifications, which can vary significantly. Each bid must be compared for frequency of maintenance, the items to be inspected, frequency of inspections, and the type of filters the contractor provides.

The real estate manager may hire a consultant to develop the preventive maintenance specifications. The manufacturer of the equipment may also provide such specifications. Some buildings have on-site building engineers to perform all HVAC maintenance. The HVAC contractor can accurately estimate the cost of nonpreventive maintenance work and work not covered in the maintenance contract.

Insurance

Insurance expense is based on the type of coverage and its cost, which depends on the type of building, the method of construction, the building's features, and its location. The property owner determines the type and limits of coverage for the building, and the insurance agent provides the estimated cost of the coverage.

Janitorial Costs

Janitorial costs for office space may be determined by dividing the cost into two parts: (1) common areas and (2) occupied spaces. The cost to clean the common areas is usually not affected by occupancy unless a floor is vacant. Obtain a cost, either a dollar amount or a cost per square foot, for the common area. Then, obtain a cost per square foot for occupied space. The common area cost for occupied floors is added to the cost to clean the tenants' spaces, which is determined by multiplying the cost per square foot of space cleaned per month by each month's projected occupancy. Another approach is to obtain a price to clean the entire building based on 100-percent occupancy and allow a credit for each square foot of vacant space.

Shopping centers have only common areas and vacant spaces to clean. The real estate manager determines the number of janitors needed each day and their schedule. The number of janitors required varies for weekdays, nights, weekends, special promotional activities, and peak-selling seasons. The janitorial company bids on the hours and the specifications for cleaning. If the janitorial service is in-house, the real estate manager can calculate janitorial expense by determining the payroll cost of each janitor, the number of hours worked each week, and the cost of the supervisor.

Landscaping

The landscape expense has three components: the monthly maintenance contract fee or monthly in-house maintenance cost, periodic maintenance expenses, and the cost of replacing and upgrading planting materials, including the addition of color at appropriate times of the year. When developing the monthly maintenance cost, the real estate manager must carefully review the contractor's specifications. Some specifications may provide for full maintenance, including pruning, weed control, and spraying, while others may provide for the minimum monthly maintenance. After calculating the monthly charge, the real estate manager must determine the cost of the periodic maintenance, pruning, and weed control if it is not included in the monthly maintenance service.

To determine the third variable—plant replacement and upgrading—the real estate manager should inspect the property with a landscaper, checking for plants and trees that have been damaged or stolen. Review the landscaping needs and decide if upgrading is necessary to maintain the property's image or to be more competitive in the market. Since many projects add color on a regular basis to enhance the ambience of the property, these costs must be included as well. An estimate from a landscaper is submitted with the list of new planting materials.

Legal Fees

Legal fees usually result from eviction proceedings, owner-tenant disputes, or lease negotiations. The real estate manager should review current cases with an attorney to estimate the cost of resolving the disputes. Delinquencies in rent payments should be reviewed to determine which will require legal action and to determine an estimate based on current costs. Legal expenses can be a common area expense or a bill-back item. The need for a legal opinion on common area parking signs would be a bill-back item. The need for a legal opinion to determine whether it were necessary to close off part of the common parking would be a common area expense.

Maintenance Payroll

Maintenance employees' costs include salaries, payroll costs, and employee benefits. They are estimated by determining the following:

- Specifications or job requirements
- Number of maintenance personnel needed
- Salaries for each person
- Number of hours each staff person will work
- Cost of overtime
- Hours for replacement help for vacations and sick leave

The cost is usually constant each month except for additional personnel added for specific maintenance jobs, seasonal needs such as the holiday period for shopping centers, possible bonuses or incentive pay, and periodic salary reviews. Third-party managers are often paid a payroll supervision fee, which is a percentage of the payroll; that fee should be included in the budgeted expenses. Legal costs for tenant disputes or a lease negotiations are non-reimbursable expenses and charged to the property owner's non-reimbursable budget.

Management Fee

The management fee is relatively easy to estimate for properties with high occupancy. Management fees are generally a percentage of income collected, a flat fee, or the greater of a percentage of the income or a base minimum fee.

The real estate manager should review the *management agreement,* which defines how the management fee is calculated. If the fee is a percentage of income, it is a percentage of the base rents and percentage rents collected or a percentage of all income collected. All income includes the base and percentage rent in addition to the income from tenant charges, such as operating expenses, reimbursements for CAM charges, and reimbursement for taxes and increased expenses.

After the real estate manager estimates the income components, which should be multiplied by the management fee percentage. This formula is applied to each monthly income projection to arrive at a monthly management fee. If the building is in a lease-up stage, the process is the same, but the accuracy of the estimated management fee is based on the accuracy of the lease-up projections. When the management fee is a minimum fee rather than a percentage, the minimum fee is budgeted each month. It is quite common to have a minimum management fee until occupancy reaches a given level and it then reverts to a percentage of the gross.

Merchant's Association/Marketing Fund

If the shopping center has a merchant's association or marketing fund, the property owner is usually a major contributor. The tenant's lease generally stipulates both the owner's and the tenant's obligation. Owners usually pay between 25 and 33 percent of the amount the merchants contribute.

The real estate manager must first total the contributions from all the merchants and then multiply this amount by the percentage of the property owner's contribution. If the shopping center opens with a low occupancy, the owner may be willing to pay dues based on 100-percent occupancy or make a contribution to the marketing efforts, in order to provide the association or fund with operating capital.

If the shopping center is new, the merchants and property owner may have a grand opening assessment. In this case, the method for calculating the owner's obligation is the same. If the shopping center is opening with a low occupancy, some owners contribute the merchant's grand opening assessment for the vacant spaces and collect the amount from merchants that open within one year of the center's grand opening. However, it is difficult to collect grand opening dues from merchants who will open a year later—although they, too, will benefit by a strong grand opening.

Painting

Painting expense consists of contract painting and supplies. Before developing the numbers for the budget, the real estate manager inspects the property, identifies areas that need painting, and then bids the jobs. On-site maintenance personnel need painting supplies for small jobs and touch-ups. Painting the common areas is a CAM or bill-back expense, while painting a vacancy is a non-reimbursable expense.

Parking Lot Maintenance

The parking lot must be thoroughly inspected for signs of cracking, raveling, or alligatoring. If major repairs are needed, a parking lot consultant may be engaged to develop specifications for repairs and estimate the cost. If only minor repairs are needed, a reliable asphalt or concrete contractor can provide a cost estimate for the budget. A month or two before the work begins, the job should be bid by three or more contractors, including the contractor who provided the estimate for the budget.

The Asphalt Institute in College Park, Missouri, has produced an audio and visual tape series on asphalt maintenance (*www.asphaltinstitute.org*). This series is excellent for an in-house seminar. Such instructional materials help the real estate manager identify problems and take corrective action. Accurate projections of parking lot maintenance costs are essential in developing this line-item expense.

Parking Lot Sweeping

Parking lot sweeping is usually contracted. The real estate manager determines the frequency of sweeping, develops sweeping specifications, and accepts bids. In many areas, sweeping is dependent upon the weather. Sweeping is not needed when snow is on the ground, but a major spring cleanup is necessary to remove dirt and gravel that build up during the snow season. In other areas, sweeping is needed more frequently during the winter months than in the summer months.

Repairs and Maintenance

This category is often divided into several accounts, such as plumbing, electrical, and painting. If no major problem exists or is anticipated in these areas, historical expense data are usually good references in estimating the expenses for the next budget period. If inspection or service requests indicate major problems in any of these areas, a consultant or contractor should inspect the building to determine the problem, possible solutions, and the estimated cost for each solution.

Roofs

The process for budgeting roof maintenance is the same as budgeting for parking lot maintenance. Building managers often have the roof inspected and evaluated by means of infrared cameras. In most cases, that cost would be billable to the building occupants.

Security

The security needs of the building must be assessed regularly. Security can be provided by a drive-by patrol, part-time to full-time on-site guards, and monitoring devices. Once the real estate manager has analyzed the building's security needs, the security program is bid. If on-site guards are part of the security program, the real estate manager must determine the hours per day the guards will be on site, and provide the schedule to security companies bidding the assignment. Most security contracts are bid on an hourly basis. The rate for drive-by security patrols is usually based on the number of times the property is visited each night. (See *Chapter 17: Safety, Security, and Emergency Procedures*.)

Snow Removal

Snow removal is one of the most difficult expenses to estimate because it is primarily dependent upon the weather. However, even with this uncontrollable factor, it's still possible to develop an economical strategy.

Calculate the costs required for pushing the snow to a different area of the parking lot, to haul the snow off site, and to clear the sidewalks. Then, determine how often per month each of the snow-removal services will be required during a normal year's snowfall. It can also be helpful to consult with weather projections to determine if there are any changes in the normal snow patterns for the coming year. It may be wise to add a contingent amount for an unexpected heavy snowfall.

Supplies

Paper supplies are provided by the janitorial company and included in the janitorial costs or purchased by the real estate manager. The amount of paper products the tenants use depends upon the occupancy of the building. The company that supplies the paper products can usually provide a fairly accurate estimate of the amount of paper products that will be used if the real estate manager tells the supplier how many people work in the building. Another approach to estimating paper cost is to compare the estimated occupancy for the budget period with occupancy for the current year, and then to adjust the cost of paper products accordingly.

The amount of paper products used in a mall's common area does not change significantly from one year to the next, unless the mall expands or the occupancy level drops. If the amount of products consumed is approximately the same, the other variable to consider is a change in the cost of the product caused by a price increase or by changing suppliers.

Other types of supplies, such as hardware, tools, or uniforms, are usually insignificant expenses that do not vary significantly from year to year, but they must be estimated and included in the budget.

Taxes

Estimating real estate taxes is similar to estimating utility costs because not all of the information is available when the budget is prepared. The two factors required for estimating this expense are: (1) the assessed valuation and (2) the millage rate.

Assessed Valuation

The value of a building may be determined using several methods, the income approach, replacement value, and the market approach. The safe method of estimating the assessed value for a new building is to combine the cost of construction and the land value and multiply this amount by the projected millage rate. It is highly unlikely that the first year's assessed value will exceed this estimate.

When a building is assessed while it is under construction, the assessed value represents the value of the land and the cost of the construction as of the date the building is assessed. In this situation, the real estate manager confirms with the assessor's office the date the building will be assessed and estimates the cost or value of the construction as of that date. Some municipalities assess all buildings on the same date—December 31, for example. Existing buildings have the benefit of the current year's valuation for reference. Budgeting property taxes for a building that is fully assessed may be based on a percentage increase from the current year's tax payment. Some states have a maximum limit property taxes may be annually increased, such as two percent.

Millage Rate

The other factor is the *millage rate*—a property tax rate for which the assessment basis is $1.00 per $1,000 of assessed property value. This rate is set by the city or county government. If the new millage rate has not been established, the real estate manager can review the changes in the millage rate over the past five years to establish trends. Reviewing proposed increases as reported in the local newspaper is also helpful. Multiply the millage rate by the assessed valuation to determine the tax amount.

If the property was recently sold, the assessor may use the sale price as the market value and hence the assessed value. The real estate manager must constantly monitor the property's assessment to ensure that it is fair and consistent with the assessment of comparable properties. Budgeting the real estate tax estimate provides an additional opportunity to review the current year's assessment. The real estate manager can review the fairness of the assessed value when the assessment is received.

In preparing the budget, the real estate manager must be aware of net-leased buildings within the overall building site that may pay their own real estate taxes directly to the taxing agency. The owners may want to reflect the total tax liability and then offset for the tenant paying directly. Free-standing restaurants, banks, and other anchor businesses often fall under this category.

Telephone and Answering Service

A few telephone charges can be classified either as escalation/CAM expense or as property owner's expenses. All elevators should have a telephone connected directly to a 24-hour answering service or a 24-hour guard station. The telephone and answering service expense is a building operating expense. If the building has an on-site management office, the answering service, which is needed for after-hours emergencies, is generally a building expense.

Trash Removal

Seldom does the real estate manager select the trash removal company. Either the municipality removes trash or a private contractor has an exclusive contract with the municipality to serve an area. Rates are determined by frequency of service and/or volume of trash removal. The municipality establishes or approves dumping fees.

The volume of trash removed from the building is determined by the building's occupancy level and use. The real estate manager must determine the frequency of trash pickup and/or the size and number of trash receptacles. After this is determined, the trash removal company can quote a monthly fee. Community and regional shopping centers may need to budget for additional trash removal during the holiday season and other peak selling periods.

Utilities

The two factors to consider when estimating utility expense are the billing rate and consumption. Keep in mind that billing rates can change during a budget period and that consumption during lease-up of an office building is difficult to predict.

Billing Rate Estimate

When estimating the rate, the real estate manager

should contact the utility company's representative for the area. The representative can provide the current billing rate and information concerning any proposed rate increase during the budget period. Since this information usually cannot be obtained by simply calling the utility company, it's important to develop a working relationship with the utility company's local representative. One way to build rapport is to request an energy audit of the building. Another opportunity is to work with the utility company when developing the building's emergency procedures.

If the utility company does not provide projected rate increases, the real estate manager can project a rate increase by analyzing the increases during the past three to five years. Special note should also be given to recent rate adjustments and news stories about the local and national cost of energy as well as to the financial condition of the utility company.

Consumption Estimate

The other factor in estimating utility cost is estimating the building's monthly consumption, which are based on the number and types of fixtures, mechanical equipment, occupancy rate, and type of occupant.

Estimating utility consumption for a shopping center differs from estimating an office building's consumption. A shopping center's utility costs include common areas, vacancies, and utilities that are master metered to all the tenants.

The parking lot common area utilities include electricity for lighting and water for irrigation. To estimate parking lot lighting, calculate the hourly kilowatt usage and the number of hours the lights will be on each month. The type and number of fixtures will provide the amount of kilowatts consumed each hour. Then, estimate the hours the lights will be on each day. In the southern part of the United States, these hours will be fairly constant year round; in the northern states, parking lot lighting hours vary as much as four-to-five hours per night from summer to winter. Another and simpler method is to obtain the utility costs for similar buildings in the area.

The formula for determining water consumption is not as simple as that for electricity consumption. The total expense for water can usually be obtained from the landscaper or the water company's representative. If the property is more than a year old, both the electricity and the water usage amounts are available for the prior 12-month period. In this case, apply the projected billing rate to the prior year's usage. Obtaining the water cost from comparable properties is another method to arrive at the cost of the property.

The utilities for an enclosed mall are the lighting, water for irrigation, and the gas/electricity for the HVAC units. The manufacturer or installer of the HVAC equipment can estimate the kilowatts of electricity or BTUs of gas that will be consumed in an hour, and the number of hours the equipment will operate each month. This information, along with the billing rate, provides the utility cost for the HVAC equipment. Again, if the shopping center has been in operation for more than a year, the historical utility consumption is available.

If a utility—water, for example—is master metered, the real estate manager can provide the utility company with a list of the types of businesses in the center, and the utility company will estimate the average consumption for each business. Shopping center tenant spaces are separately metered for electricity, but the shopping center may have master meters for gas and water.

In an office building, utility consumption includes interior common area lighting, parking lot or garage lighting, lighting for occupied spaces, gas or electricity to operate the mechanical systems, and water consumption. The common area lighting and mechanical systems usage is estimated just as the shopping center common area utilities and HVAC units are estimated. The occupied space consumption is based on the average usage per 1,000 or 10,000 square feet, with adjustments for tenants with over-standard usage.

Another way to estimate usage for new buildings

is to request utility consumption records from real estate managers who manage similar buildings in the area. Estimating utility consumption on existing buildings with a history of usage is fairly simple; estimating consumption for a new building or a building in lease-up is difficult. The cost of utilities varies each month based on consumption, and the monthly variance can be significant.

If the building has reached stabilized occupancy starting with the current year's utility cost and adjusting them for any of the previously mentioned factors, it will provide for a reliable estimate of the next year's utility expense.

Vacancy Expense

Vacant spaces incur expenses. Vacancies in shopping centers and industrial properties have more direct expenses than vacancies in office buildings. Because of the separate utility metering and the street frontage of shopping center and industrial space, these spaces have a utility cost. Both water and electricity should be maintained in vacant retail stores and industrial spaces so they can be shown to prospective merchants at any time. Most municipalities assess a minimum meter charge whether the utility is used or not. In cold-weather regions, the space must be heated during the winter to prevent water from freezing in the pipes. Since retail spaces are street-front spaces, the exterior of the windows should be washed monthly or quarterly, and the inside windows should be washed semiannually.

It is important to the leasing effort that all vacancies be placed in condition to show as soon as possible because a dirty and unattractive space is difficult to lease. Accumulations of business cards, junk mail, cobwebs, and expired insects must be removed regularly, or they will create a very negative image for the prospective tenant. The interior of all vacant spaces must be cleaned periodically. Some spaces may need to have walls or ceilings repaired and painted and windows and floor coverings cleaned. Vacant spaces in office buildings need to cleared periodically and walls may be painted to better show the space to prospects.

Window Washing

In an office building, the real estate manager must determine how often interior and exterior windows should be washed and whether the ground floor windows should be cleaned more frequently. Check the leases for larger businesses to see if they have a minimum number of times the windows must be washed annually. After developing the specifications, the real estate manager requests bids from contractors.

Industrial and shopping center tenants are responsible for cleaning their windows. For a mall, the real estate manager budgets the window washing in the common areas. Some smaller strip shopping centers contract for regular window washing for all small merchants and bill it back through the CAM charges to give the center an overall "clean" look.

CAPITAL BUDGET

A *capital expenditure* is an expense that is expected to yield benefits in future accounting periods. Capital expenditures are recorded as assets, and they are amortized over the periods believed to be benefited. What is or is not deemed a capital item can vary for different clients, therefore, it's important to understand each client's accounting philosophy.

Most capital improvements to a property are major expenses, but they are usually nonrecurring expenses. Examples include carpeting over a concrete mall floor, replacing a roof, remodeling a lobby, installing extensive energy conservation or life-safety equipment, and making TIs.

The same principles used in developing an operating budget are applied to developing a capital budget. All budgets start with a property inspection. Many capital improvements, such as the ones listed above, require an expert's opinion and recommendation since few real estate managers have an in-depth knowledge of construction and engineering. When a consultant is needed, the expense should be budgeted for the consultant's time.

Capital improvements to marketing features of the

building, such as lobbies, restrooms, elevators, and lighting in a building's exterior and center court areas, have a direct impact on leasing. Maintaining a building's competitive position is essential to maintaining its occupancy level and rental rates. The real estate manager, whether serving as the leasing agent or not, must continually analyze market conditions and be aware of the building's position in the market. One way to keep apprised of the building's position in the market is to compare its features with the competition's features.

After inspecting the building and determining its position in the market, the real estate manager compiles a list of suggested capital improvements and develops estimates to present to the owner. The real estate manager must thoroughly prepare for this meeting to be able to explain why the expenditures are necessary. The property owner often takes the real estate manager's recommendation under advisement and considers the expenditure in relation to the goals of the property and the property owner's ability and willingness to fund the cost of the improvements. When the owner approves any of the recommended capital improvements, the real estate manager has specifications for the work prepared and bids the job.

Property owners and their accountants do not always agree on whether an expense is a capital expense or an operating expense. One property owner may take an aggressive position on how an expense should be treated, while another may take the opposite view. It's important to understand how each owner treats these expenses.

DEVELOPING INCOME PROJECTIONS

In addition to analyzing the operating expenses and the capital expenses, the real estate manager must analyze each income component and then project the property's income on a monthly basis—in order to develop a month-by-month NOI and cash flow.

The first step in developing the income projection is to review the tenants' lease summaries, which state the obligation to pay rent, percentage rent, and tenant charges. The information from the lease summaries is used to estimate income from rents and tenant chargebacks. The real estate manager must also estimate income for leasing the vacancies.

Occupancy

It is best to analyze for occupancy before rents and chargebacks are considered. The occupancy analysis is almost identical to the base-rent analysis (discussed next), but the entries are the tenants' square footages and not their base rents. The analysis includes lease expirations and new leases and most often has a calculation for average occupancy at the footing of the analysis.

Base Rent

The base rent is the easiest income component to verify. Software programs can project the rents for each tenant for any period from the imputed lease summaries.

Monthly Rent Computation

The real estate manager reviews the leases or lease summaries to determine the monthly rent during the budget period. Careful attention is given to any fixed step-ups in the rent. If a lease expires during the budget period, the real estate manager ascertains whether the tenant will renew and estimates the renewal rate. If the tenant is not renewing, or if the property owner refuses to renew the tenant, estimate how long and during which months the space will remain vacant. Since it is wise to initiate renewals at least six months before the lease expires, only tenants whose leases expire later in the budget period need to be contacted.

Payment History

The tenants' rent payment histories are another factor in projecting base rents. Financially weak tenants may move out before their lease expires, they may make only partial payments, or they may stop paying rent altogether. If any tenants fall into this category, decide what course of action to take. If a property has one or more weak tenants, the owners may want to increase the reserve in the bad debts account or project loss of income from a specific space or project a higher vacancy.

Every effort must be made to collect the moneys due, and if that proves to be difficult or impossible, decide on a further course of action. For instance, a retail tenant may be offered rent relief if the market conditions and the area's economy warrant such an action. In any case, consider the financial impact of such adverse situations on the base-rent income projections.

Base Rent Income Projection

When all factors have been considered, each tenant's monthly rent for the budget period is recorded on the budget form, and the proper entry is made in the budget notes at the end of that line item. After calculating the income that will be received each month from each space, total each monthly income column, and print a monthly projection.

If a merchant's rent was increased in April, the increase should show in that month; the old and new rent for the year should not be averaged. Vacancies are shown by unit by month with income starting in the month that a new tenant commences paying rent. If the tenant receives a period of free rent, the base rent is usually shown as rental income for the months involved, and a rent credit is shown elsewhere in the budget as a rental concession or no income os projected for the months the tenant receives free. Adding the rent for all tenants for the month provides the monthly base rent income projection.

A similar analysis is prepared for percentage rent, operating expense reimbursement or CAM income, reimbursement of taxes and insurance, and any other income components. Adding all the income component budgets together provides a month-by-month income projection.

Percentage Rent

The rent paid in excess of the base or minimum rent is known as *percentage rent* or *overage rent* (rent in excess or over the minimum rent). Percentage rent is a significant income component in many shopping centers. Office buildings and multitenant industrial buildings can have percentage rental income from retail or service tenants, such as restaurants and health clubs.

Percentage Rent Estimate

Percentage rent is a difficult income component to project because the real estate manager has limited, if any, influence over the tenant's sales volume. A quick way to project percentage rent is to increase every tenant's sales by a given percentage over the prior year and compare that estimate with the tenant's breakpoint. In a retail lease, the *breakpoint*, also known as the *natural breakpoint,* is the point at which the tenant's sales are multiplied by an agreed percentage rate to equal the base rate set forth in the lease. Beyond that point, the tenant will begin to pay percentage rent. The breakpoint is determined by dividing the tenant's annual rent by the agreed percentage rate. The amount of sales in excess of the breakpoint is multiplied by the percentage rate to arrive at the percentage rent owed. The breakpoint can also be a negotiated figure, which would be included in the lease summary or the lease document.

A more accurate way of estimating percentage rent is to analyze each tenant separately to estimate its sales for the budget period. The first step in this process is to compare each tenant's breakpoint with its sales for the most recent 12-month period. Tenants whose sales exceed or are within 20 percent of their breakpoints are then analyzed further. The other tenants have little if any chance of their sales exceeding their breakpoints and paying percentage rent.

The following lists several criteria used in estimating the sales of those tenants who are likely to pay percentage rent:

- **Sales projections:** This is the best source on which to base percentage rents, but some store managers and store owners will not share this information.

- **Sales trends:** If the tenant's sales have increased between six percent and eight percent during each of the past five years, a similar increase is probable.
- **New competition:** A local hamburger restaurant may be experiencing 10 percent increases every year, but if a new McDonald's comes into the area, the local restaurant's sales will undoubtedly drop in the short run.
- **Tenant mix:** If a shopping center is adding another major tenant, the shopping center will have additional traffic, and the other tenants' sales can be expected to increase. Conversely, if a major tenant vacates the shopping center, the other tenants' sales will probably decline.
- **Product demand:** Be aware of fads in the marketplace. Hula hoops and drive-in carhops on roller skates were popular in the 1950s, and in the early 1980s, tanning salons and take-and-bake pizza operations were popular. In the 1990s, bagel shops, juice bars, and cupcake shops were popular. However, novelties wane over the years, and many businesses that were once the rage lose their popularity and close.
- **Managerial change:** An exceptionally good store manager may be promoted to regional manager and be replaced with an inexperienced and less capable person. Or, the reverse can happen—a store with poor sales growth may replace its management with an aggressive person, and sales may increase dramatically.
- **Merchandise or design changes within the store:** Figure out of the store recently remodeled or added new lines of merchandise. If so, has merchandise of lesser quality replaced higher quality items? These moves will affect sales.

Use these sources of information to estimate the tenant's sales for the budget period. If projected sales exceed the breakpoint, the amount in excess of the breakpoint is multiplied by the tenant's percentage rate.

Tenant Concessions

Before the estimated amount of percentage rent can be included in the income projection, check the tenant's lease to ascertain whether the tenant has rights to recapture certain charges from percentage rent. In the 1950s and 1960s, many national tenants—especially major tenants—negotiated the right to recapture some or all of their tenant charges, such as CAM, taxes, insurance, from their percentage rent.

For example, if a retail tenant owes $10,000 in percentage and its pro rata share of the real estate taxes is $8,000, the tenant pays only $2,000 in percentage rent and the remaining $8,000 is off set from its real estate tax payment. This right has seldom been granted to a tenant since the 1970s; however, older anchor tenant leases may still contain this concession and sophisticated retailers and restaurateurs who are in great demand by shopping center owner's may attempt to negotiate this concession.

Months with Percentage Rent Payments

After estimating the percentage rent, project for which months the tenant will pay percentage rent. Remember, percentage rent is paid when sales are reported—usually a month after they take place. Most shop tenants pay their percentage rent monthly. Major tenants usually pay annually. Most tenants who owe percentage rent pay in December and January for the November and December sales. Some tenants, such as candy stores, which experience sales peaks in February, April, June, November, and December, may pay percentage rent several months of the year. On the other hand, a restaurant's sales and percentage rent can be constant each month. The tenants' monthly sales indicate the months they are likely to pay percentage rent.

Percentage Rent Refunds

The last factor to consider in this income component is percentage rent refunds. Even though most tenants report sales figures monthly and pay percentage rent monthly, their sales are annualized. If a tenant's sales exceed the breakpoint one month, and the tenant pays the appropriate percentage rent the following month, that percentage rent paid must be refunded if sales are below the breakpoint on an annualized basis. A tenant's breakpoint is determined by dividing the agreed percentage rate into the annual rental rate for the annual natural breakpoint and dividing the result by 12 to determine the monthly breakpoint. Some owners will collect percentage rent only after the tenant's sales have exceeded their annual breakpoint.

Consumer Price Index (CPI)

The *consumer price index (CPI)* is a monthly measure of changes in the prices of goods and services consumed by urban families and individuals. Compiled by the Bureau of Labor Statistics, the index is based on about 125,000 monthly quotations of prices, rents, and property tax rates collected from about 65,000 sources. The items range from food to automobiles and from rents to haircuts. The relative importance given to individual items in the index is based on periodic surveys of consumer expenditures. In the late 1990s, prices were expressed as a percentage of average prices from 1982 to 1984, but the 1967 base-year figures were still being published. The monthly index is prepared for the nation as a whole, for each of 17 large metropolitan areas, for individual items, and for commodity and service groupings. All data are published in the United States Department of Labor's *Monthly Labor Review (www.bls.gov/mlr)*.

Many leases have rent adjustments based on the increases in the CPI. The tenant's rent can be adjusted over any period—such as annually or every three years. The increase may be based on the percentage increase in the CPI or on a fraction of that increase. Any leases with a CPI adjustment will have a ceiling (the maximum amount the rent cam be adjusted) and a floor (the minimum amount the rent may be increased). For example, the rent will increase by the adjustment in the CPI index but not to exceed five percent and be no less than two percent.

Most commercial leases use the CPI for metropolitan areas. All items are indexed to the nearest geographical area that is published for the population area of the property. The CPI adjustment is determined by comparing the current month's index for the selected city with the same index in the preceding year. An example of an adjustment in the CPI follows:

To calculate the percentage adjustment in the CPI, divide 2.60 (the index adjustment) by 161.9 (the preceding year's index) for an increase of 1.61 percent. If a tenant's rent was $1,000 per month, with an annual increase based on the January CPI increase, the increase in base rent would be $16.10 ($1,000 x 1.61%). The tenant's adjusted monthly rent would become $1,016.10. If the increase were based on two thirds of the increase in the CPI, the increase would be 1.08 percent (1.61% x 0.67%). The increase in monthly rent would be $10.80.

Common Area Maintenance (CAM) Income

The real estate manager reviews the lease provisions to determine what percentage of the CAM budget will be collected. Each tenant's lease summary states the tenant's share of the CAM budget. The percentages for all tenants are totaled for each month. The CAM budget is divided by 12, and each month the percentage of the total space that will pay reimbursements is multiplied by one month's CAM budget. Several software programs, including many spreadsheets, can perform these calculations. If a tenant is not required to pay a pro rata share of a particular expense, such as security, the property owner will not be reimbursed for that portion of the expense. The real estate management fee is generally an CAM or bill back expense.

A common area calculations form should be created as a model for future calculations; it should be designed for easy calculation of each tenant's pro rata share of all tenant charges. The form should indicate how each calculation was derived. Note that the denominator for the CAM expense can be larger or smaller than the denominator for taxes and insurance. It is common for a shopping center to have five or more denominators for various CAM expense items. For example, some tenants may provide their own trash removal, so that tenant would not participate in the center trash removal costs. An anchor tenant in a shopping center may own its building and the parking in front of the building and pay its real estate tax directly to the taxing authority and pay for its insurance but share in the overall CAM costs. After the percentages are established, tenant charges can be calculated in dollar amounts for common area allocation and common area estimates.

Building Operating Expense Reimbursement

Building operating expense income is billed to office building tenants in one of three methods: (1) base year, (2) stop clause, or (3) triple-net charge. Determining each tenant's share of the operating expenses is a three-step process:

1. First, develop the building's operating expenses.
2. Second, review each tenant's lease summary to determine the method of billing and the expense items that are treated as reimbursable operating expenses. When reviewing the lease summary, checks for caps on the operating expense charges. For instance, a tenant may pay its full pro rata share of the operating expense charge, not to exceed $11.00 per square foot, during each of the first three years of the lease.
3. Third, calculate each tenant's pro rata share of the operating expenses.

The next sections present the three methods of billing for building operating expenses. In addition to leased spaces, remember to factor in potential income from lease-ups and vacancies.

Base Year

If the tenant pays a *base-year escalation,* establish the expenses for the base year and subtract them from the projected operating expenses for the budget period. Then, multiply the increase in operating expenses above the base year by the percentage of space occupied by the tenant to determine the tenant's share of the operating expense budget. For example, the tenant's base year is the year it moved into the building. The operating expenses for the base year are $12 per square foot. The next year expenses increased to $12.65 per square foot. The tenant will pay the increases above the base year which is 65 cents per square foot per year. In theory, the owner will factor in the based-year expenses, $12 per square foot. However, the market conditions determines rental rates.

Expense Stop

An *expense stop* in an office lease requires the owner to pay operating expenses up to a certain amount per square foot per year; tenants must then pay their agreed pro rata shares of the expenses that exceed the stop amount. When the operating expense stop is used, the dollar per square foot of the stop is subtracted from the dollar per square foot of operating expenses for the budget period. The tenant's square footage is multiplied by the increase in operating expenses per square foot above the expense stop. The resulting number is the amount of operating expenses the tenant will pay. For example, if the expense stop is $10 per square foot per year and the next year's expenses are $10.35 per square foot per year, the tenant pays 35 cents per square foot in additional rent for that year.

Triple Net

In a *triple-net lease*, the tenant agrees to pay a prorated share of all operating expenses (including CAM). Triple-net leases are common in industrial properties, shopping centers, and some office buildings. The tenant's percentage of occupancy of the building is multiplied by the building's operating expenses. This is the method property owners prefer and the market conditions will determine what approach they will use.

Lease-Up

A source of operating expense reimbursement income that is easy to overlook is space that will be leased during the budget period. The lease-up projection should be reviewed, and tenants that will occupy space (that was recently vacant and that will commence paying escalation charges in the budget period) should be included in the operating expense reimbursable income projections.

Operating expense income, like all other income components, is estimated on a month-by-month basis. It's important to be aware of tenants that may have free rent but may still be obligated to pay their share of the operating expenses.

Taxes and Insurance

Real estate taxes and building insurance are not included in the shopping center CAM budget. They are both billed as separate line items, and are usually billed separately in industrial properties. Although most office buildings include these expenses in their operating expense budgets, some office buildings separate either or both of these expenses from the operating expense budget. In each of the above situations, except where such expenses are included in the operating expense budget, management must bill the tenants separately for real estate taxes and insurance expenses.

Most commercial leases require tenants to pay their full pro rata shares of these costs. In years past, tenants often paid these expenses above a base year. Both of these methods of charging tenants are explained in the operating expense reimbursement section.

Most leases allow for a special tax assessment, known as a *Local Improvement District (LID)* or bonded indebtedness. This is a charge for street improvements, such as traffic lights and sidewalks, that are included in the real estate tax billings.

Lease-Up and Vacancy Projections

Vacancy and lease-up projections are the most complex income projections. They are more likely to be accurate if time is taken to study the market, know the building and its competition, evaluate the leasing effort, analyze the marketability of each vacancy, and understand the owner's ability to make a deal.

Estimate when the space will be leased, at what rate, and when the rent will commence. The leasing agent should be consulted for this projection. Conducts a market survey to determine the property's market rental rate range and the rate for each space in order to project the amount of space and which spaces will be leased in the building and when. Each vacant space must be analyzed for its desirability, the rental rate it can command, and its probable lease date. For example, a shopping center has four vacancies: two 1,400 square foot spaces, a 1,800-square-foot space, and a 5,500-square-foot space. The Real Estate Manager projects that one 1,400-square-foot space will be leased in March with the tenant opening May 15 with one and one-half months' free rent. Rent payments begin July 1. The 1,800-square-foot space is projected to be leased in July with tenant occupancy in November and rent to commence November 1. There is little demand for the odd-shaped space of 5,500 square feet, which is projected to be leased in November with three months' free rent, which extends beyond the budget period. No base rent is projected for this space during this budget period. The second 1,400-square-foot space is expected to remain vacant during the entire budget period.

The lease-up of a new office building is projected in a similar way, except the manager looks at square footage instead of spaces leased. For instance, a 95,000-square-foot office building opens with 30,000 square feet occupied. With 7,500 square feet per month projected to be leased during the first six months and 5,000 square feet per month projected to be leased over the next three months, the building's occupancy is expected to stabilize at 90,000 square feet. Just as in the shopping center example, after projecting the amount of space that will be leased each month, anticipate how long building out the tenant's space, including plan check and approval by the building department, will take, when the tenants will move in, how much free rent will be offered, if any, and when the tenants will commence paying base rent.

OFFICE BUILDING EXAMPLE OF A BASE-YEAR MODEL

The theory behind using the base-year approach to determine a tenant's pro rata share of expenses is that the minimum or base rent incorporates the operating expenses for the first year of the lease. The tenant pays any increases in operating expenses.

Although very few base-year leases are currently negotiated in shopping centers, many older shopping center, office building, and industrial property leases have these provisions. To be accurate, trace the base-year expense back to the original calculation. This figure should be included in the formula. Then, the current expense, taking into account the proper base-year information, should be calculated.

The tenant's lease states the base year. It is usually the year the tenant moves into the building. If a tenant is in a strong negotiating position, the base year may be the year after the tenant takes occupancy of the leased premises. The base-year method for determining a tenant's share of an expense can be used for real estate taxes, insurance, office building operating expenses, or a shopping center's CAM charges.

The base-year model for allocating operating expenses is used as an ongoing record of the cost of operating the building and of each tenant's specific agreement relative to those costs. The source document for the base year is the lease. Once the base year has been established, the actual costs for that year are recorded. When the current year's costs are known, the base-year costs are subtracted and the individual tenant's percentage of space occupied in the building is applied to that figure. Exceptions to the costs are generally noted after the percentage allocation so everyone is aware of them. Typical costs that are allocated to office building tenants are detailed in the next sections.

Insurance

Carefully review the lease provisions pertaining to the tenant's insurance to determine if the tenant pays a pro rata share of all of the property owner's insurance coverage. Some leases—especially with major retail tenants—exclude certain coverage or place a limit on the amount of liability insurance they will reimburse the owner.

Tenant Extra Services

Office building leases allow for a charge if a tenant requests extra services. These services can consist of over-standard janitorial services, maintenance that is the responsibility of the tenant, and other miscellaneous jobs. This income component is projected by reviewing the tenant's extra service charges in the current year and determining if any new tenants are likely to have similar needs.

Utility Income

In the past, several types of developments—particularly enclosed malls—billed electricity to tenants for a profit. The developer contracted with the utility company to purchase electricity that was metered on one master meter. The developer then paid the cost to run lines to submeters for each tenant. Tenants were billed the same rate they would be charged if the tenant purchased the power directly from the utility company. The developer earned a profit by purchasing the electricity at a bulk rate (similar to a wholesale rate) and charging the tenants a retail price. Developers justified their profit by stating that it was a return on their investment of installing the utility lines and submeters at their cost.

When managing a property with this situation, monitor the billing rate to ensure the tenants are billed based on the correct rate. Have on staff or on contract an expert on electrical and/or gas meters to read the meters, prepare the billings, and monitor the meters for accuracy. In some states, property owners are not allowed to bill tenants for electricity based on the meter readings and most of the properties use a negotiated dollars-per-square-foot basis for charges. Few property owners are purchasing from utility companies and charging commercial tenants for the utilities they purchase.

Over-Standard Utilities

Some office building tenants consume more utilities than normal for their space size, and most leases allow the property owner to bill the tenants for their over-standard usage. This extra usage is usually the result of special equipment, an excess of equipment consuming an inordinate amount of electricity, or after-hours use of lighting and HVAC service. It's important to monitor the tenant's use of utilities.

When a tenant has additional utility requirements, a consultant may be called in to determine the amount in excess of standard usage. The income received is credited to the building's escalation expenses because the expense will be charged to the building's operating expenses.

In some shopping centers, the anchor tenant's operate on a 24-hour basis and require the parking lot lights to be on all night. That tenant will generally pay a fee for the over-standard cost of providing the service.

Over-Standard HVAC

Tenants who must keep their offices open beyond the building's hours of operation and tenants who need supplementary cooling require over-standard HVAC. Determines an hourly cost for HVAC that includes the cost of electricity, the wear on the equipment, and the cost of the building engineer's time (if he or she is required to be on site while the equipment is operating). The income generated is credited to the building's operating expenses because that is where the expense is charged.

Tenant Improvement (TI) Profit

When the building owner or real estate management company performs TI work, a profit is generally added to the cost of the work. The profit is the typical profit a general contractor would earn. It is credited to the building owner or the real estate management company, or it is shared between the two entities.

Estimates the amount of TI work based on the amount of space that is projected to be leased and renewed, the type of tenant build-outs that new tenants are likely to need, and the improvements, if any, that will be required to renew leases. TI fees are usually a percentage of construction costs. Office tenants and most industrial tenants in multitenant buildings require that the property owner perform TIs. Shopping center tenants usually perform their own TI work. Retailer have a formatted design and usually one or two contractors in an areas that build out their stores.

Interest Income

Interest income is a component that can easily be overlooked. Income received from each property, in excess of normal operating costs, should be deposited in an interest-bearing account. Determines the average balance each month and multiply this number by the interest rate paid on that account.

RESERVES FOR REPLACEMENT

In any large income-producing property, major components must be replaced or major repairs will be needed at some point. Estimating these needs, quantifying them, and setting aside sufficient cash to cover them is prudent. As a practical matter, a recent survey of commercial property owners determined that only a small percentage of owners actually set aside reserve funds.

Many owners choose not to set aside cash reserves. They prefer to use available moneys as they are earned and to worry about major repairs or replacements when they are needed. This is not an irresponsible approach. The owner is generally counting on increased cash flow, the likelihood of refinancing, or the probability of secondary financing or a line of credit.

Even if the final decision is not to reserve cash for replacements, estimate the reserves that may be needed and share the information with the property owner. Real estate managers often evaluate the cash flow and arbitrarily set aside a percentage for reserves. Such a figure is more likely to be what the real estate manager believes the property can afford, rather than what the property may really need. Taking a slightly different approach, set a reserve based on cents per square foot per year.

Needs Estimate

The most effective method of determining the necessary reserves is to consider each major building component. First, reviews which major components must be analyzed.

For example, in a strip shopping center, these components include the roof, parking lot, and exterior painting. Tenants are generally responsible for the HVAC unit.

The holding period of the property must be taken into consideration. No owner is going to worry about what work will have to be done after the property is sold—unless it will have an impact on the sales price. For easy calculations, our example will be a 100,000-square-foot strip shopping center. The owners will hold the center for 10 years. The following explains the evaluation of each component:

Roof

An evaluation of the roof indicates that it is generally in good condition, but one large 25,000-square-foot section will have to be replaced within five years. The estimated cost for this repair in five years is $50,000. To reserve for this cost, the $50,000 is divided by the five years available to accumulate the moneys; that requires an annual reserve of $10,000. Dividing the cost by the square footage of the center (100,000 square feet) provides a reserve of 10 cents per foot per year.

Exterior Painting

A physical inspection indicates that the entire shopping center will need painting at the end of the eighth year. The estimated cost will be $80,000. Again, $80,000 divided by the years to accumulate the reserve indicates $10,000 per year will be needed. On a square footage basis, the reserve is 10 cents per square foot per year.

Major Parking Lot Repairs

The parking lot is sound, but it will need patching, resealing, and restriping after three years. The cost is estimated to be $45,000. The annual reserve is $15,000, and the per-square-foot reserve per year is 15 cents.

Collection of Reserves

To establish a reserve fund, the shopping center manager would set aside 25 cents per square foot for the next three years, 20 cents per square foot for the following two years, and 10 cents per square foot for the next three years. These funds would probably be held in an interest-bearing account. The real estate manager would calculate the interest to be earned and reduce the amount to be set aside by the interest earned; the interest and the actual reserves would provide the needed cash. Another approach would be to allow the interest to accumulate as a cushion in case the original cost estimates were too low.

If the reserves for common area items are to be paid by the tenants, the method of calculation is the same. However, the leases must permit charging the tenants for a reserve for replacement. Most major or anchor tenants will not pay into a reserve. They will pay their pro rata shares when they are due, rather than have the property owner hold their funds.

If leases allow for the collection of reserves, those moneys should be placed in a trust or escrow account earning interest and held on the tenants' behalf until major work is done. If the shopping center is sold, the trust account should be transferred to the new owners to be held on behalf of the tenants. If a tenant has paid into the reserves but vacates before the moneys are spent, the tenant does not receive a refund of the reserves paid.

REVIEWING AND REVISING THE BUDGET

About 60 days before the budget period begins, complete the budget based on the best information available at the time. The property owner reviews and approves the budget, which will ideally be accurate throughout the entire year and no revisions will be necessary.

However, changes may occur that will require revisions. A major tenant may move out. An unusually heavy snowfall may result in being significantly over budget. A long-term, difficult vacancy may be filled unexpectedly. A major replacement of a building component may substantially reduce operating expenses. In such cases, the budget should be revised because the change is likely to be significant. When such a change occurs, incorporate the new assumptions into the budget, date the budget, and give the property owner a new NOI and cash flow projection.

Monthly Comparisons

Because of the very real possibility of large swings in the cash flow of commercial properties, it is critical that the actual figures be compared with the budget on a monthly basis and that those comparisons be analyzed for significant differences. Most owners accept a variance between five and 10 percent in any one line item without too much concern. Quite often, the real estate manager is not even asked to comment on variances of less than 10 percent. However, the current monthly variance may be indicative of a larger problem to come. Be sensitive to this possibility and inform the owner—even if the current variance is within the agreed range.

When the monthly operating statements are forwarded to the property owners, the statements should contain a narrative report that evaluates the numbers for them. Numbers by themselves do not always give a complete picture.

Midyear Evaluations

Even if no major changes have occurred, the budget should periodically be evaluated. Some property owners of income property zero out all budgets at midyear. The actual income and expenses become the budget for that period, and all accounts are in balance, or zeroed out. This is intended to prevent the property owner's staff or the real estate manager from borrowing from one account to support another. Any excess funds are automatically withdrawn.

More commonly, however, the real estate manager prepares an analysis of income and expenses at midyear, evaluates what the current position means for the balance of the year, and reports that position along with recommended changes to the owner. Such a midyear adjustment allows the real estate manager and property owner to plan the balance of the year so the desired goals will be reached. Programs that were not approved for lack of funds can be reconsidered, given the existing circumstances.

Should income be running ahead of budget, and should it appear that such will be the case at year-end, the decision may be made to proceed with some capital expenditures that were shelved due to lack of funds. Conversely, if funds appear to be running behind schedule, some discretionary expenditures may be eliminated from the budget for the balance of the year. An owner with "deep pockets" may not be too concerned that the budget is under expectations for the year, whereas a "cash flow" owner may be keenly aware of every dollar. It's important to understand the owner's position and be sure the owner is informed of anything that might have an impact on that position.

ADDITIONAL BUDGET SCHEDULES

In addition to the basic budget, many back-up schedules detail the basis for the final budget figures. Common additional schedules follow:

Percentage Rent Analysis

A *percentage rent analysis* reviews the sales from each tenant who has a percentage rental lease provision. The current year's sales are extrapolated to a full year, an estimate is made for the sales for the coming year, and an estimate is made of any percentage rental that may be due by comparing the projected sales to the tenant's breakpoint. The percentage rental estimate is entered into the budget in the month that payment is expected.

Shopping Center Common Area Allocation

Once the common area operating budget has been established, a schedule is prepared showing the actual allocation of the expenses to categories of tenants, such as major retail tenants and shop tenants. In an enclosed mall, the division may be between those who contribute only to the mall expenses and those who contribute to the entire site expenses. This is not a breakdown by individual tenant.

Shopping Center Common Area Estimates

After the common area expenses are allocated to the categories of tenants, a schedule is prepared to allocate the costs to each specific tenant based on that tenant's lease provisions. This schedule takes into account any lease limitations or exclusions.

Property Tax Summary

A property tax summary identifies all tax parcels that are part of the property. Generally, this schedule includes the tax parcel numbers, identification of the taxing authority, dates of the current tax bills, appraised value of the parcels,taxes assessed, and payment due dates. If any delinquent taxes are due, that is generally noted along with the reasons for the delinquency. The schedule includes any parcels for which the tenant is directly responsible for the taxes even though the shopping center owns the parcels. This schedule is also used to note tax appeals.

Capital Improvement Schedule

Capital improvements require special attention. This schedule shows the improvements anticipated for the coming year, the months in which they are anticipated, and the amounts of money allocated to them. Starting and completion dates are also included.

Monthly Leasing Schedule

The leasing schedule is used to estimate all vacant-space prospects as well as renewal negotiations. This schedule estimates the date of lease and rental commencement, the rental rate, any leasing commissions due, and any TI work anticipated.

Personnel

In any property that has on-site personnel, a separate schedule is generally prepared showing all site personnel and their current and proposed wages or salaries. Other costs, such as medical/dental and/or retirement plan costs, are also detailed in this section of the budget. If additional personnel will be needed in the coming year, the information is provided here. This portion of the budget is often kept in a separate file that is not available to all personnel.

Budget Summary

Some property owners will ask for a summary of the budget that includes only major categories of income and expenses and serves as a tool for a quick analysis of the year's figures.

Budget Comparison

Many clients and property owners want to see a comparison of the proposed budget to the actual figures for the past year as well as the original budgeted figures for the past year. Such an analysis can be helpful in spotting trends or unusual patterns in the income and expenses of the project.

List of Contracts

Providing a list of all contracts for services that are active at the property is useful. This listing generally includes the name of the contractor, service provided, amount of the monthly contract, and expiration date of the contract.

Lease Expirations

One of the most helpful schedules is a listing of all tenants' lease expirations shown in chronological order by years. This schedule helps spot opportunities to combine spaces as well as potential problems such as a large number of leases expiring in a short time.

CONCLUSION

Budgeting is not a difficult process, but it can be time-consuming. Once the real estate manager understands how to determine each income and expense component, he or she can develop the accurate NOI or cash flow projection that is needed to maintain financial control over the property.

CHAPTER

16

Efficient and Cost-Effective Maintenance Management Programs

Maintenance management is a critical element to the success of all income-producing properties. A new building often commands the best rent in the market place because it is new, looks great, and is expected to look great for a long time. As a building ages, it can still be very competitive, but it must continue the image and reputation that was created when it first opened. An important component of each of those two elements is a good maintenance management program. Maintenance management encompasses repairs, replacements, energy efficiency conservation, and operational efficiency.

The tenants' leases will determine how the operating expenses are allocated to the owner and the tenants. In a *triple-net lease* all the operating expenses are paid by the tenants. The exception is the owner will be responsible for the vacancies *pro rata* share of the operating expenses. In a *gross lease,* the tenants are not billed for any of the operating expenses. There are other forms of net leases where the tenants pay only their pro rata share of the real estate taxes, or the real estate taxes and insurance.

Some tenants negotiate to carve out specific operating expenses from their obligation to pay these expenses while other tenants will negotiate to limit the annual increases in operating expenses. A maintenance management program should be developed based on the operational needs of the property and the property owner's goals and objectives. The decision on the level of maintenance should not be determined by whether the owner receives full or partial reimbursement from the tenants. There are times when an owner cannot afford a planned expense and will defer it to another period in the year or another year.

Competition is fierce among commercial properties, and an effective maintenance management program is essential for a building to maintain its competitive position in the market and the efficient and cost-effective operations of the property. As institutions and *Real Estate Investment Funds (REITs)* have become major owners of commercial properties, this need has become even more acute. Institutions and REITs are conscious of their images, and the need to earn a good return on their investors' funds.

Institutions typically have adequate funds to maintain and improve their properties. The investors in smaller properties are more likely to occasionally encounter tight financial situations that places a strain on their cash flow or ability to fund some repairs. Generally, this situation can be best handled with continual inspections, long-range budgets, and annual budgets, setting aside reserves for future needs and evaluating and reprioritizing planned and scheduled maintenance when funds are lifted. Without a doubt, the highest priorities are for those items that involve the safety and security of the building. Failure to adequately maintain the property will ultimately result in the *deferred maintenance* and deterioration of the building and its position in the market, thus affecting the leasing and rental rates.

The physical condition of a property has a major impact on its net operating income (NOI) and value as well as on the surrounding community. As new buildings are developed, older buildings often look less desirable. If older buildings are not maintained, and/or updated, the contrast is even more striking. If an "A" building is not properly maintained and is allowed to age, it can quickly become a "B" building, along with lower rents and higher vacancy factors. This chapter explains the process of developing and implementing a maintenance management program that will allow the property real estate manager to maintain control over the appearance and operations of a property and impact the property's safety and security. A well-conceived program includes *preventive maintenance* services, routine maintenance, *corrective maintenance,* and a plan for emergencies—as well as energy-saving and conservation programs.

IMPORTANCE OF A MAINTENANCE MANAGEMENT PROGRAM

A good maintenance management program enhances the leasing effort and improves tenant relations. A prospective tenant will not be impressed with the building if told, for example, that the peeling fascia boards will be painted shortly or the worn carpet in the common area is not budgeted to be replaced this year. Tenants occupy their spaces up to 50 to 70 hours a week. Every defect, every item of deferred maintenance, and every day spent waiting for service convinces the tenant that the real estate manager or property owner either does not care or is unable to cope with the property's needs.

Most likely, tenants are contributing to the cost of the building's daily maintenance. And since the tenant has little or no say about common area standards in commercial properties, it is up to management to set reasonable standards and see that they are met. An effective maintenance management program will go a long way in maintaining a good relationship with tenants, the public, prospective tenants, and even the civic authorities.

A sound maintenance management program also preserves the building's physical life and, therefore, should command higher rents to maximize the value of the asset. The longer the physical life of the property is maintained, there is a stronger potential for a longer economic life. A well-conceived maintenance management program reduces the cost and frequency of major repairs, helps maintain a pleasant building exterior to the public, and stabilizes the daily operating expenses.

Safety is another reason for upholding a strong maintenance program. Certainly, no property owner or real estate manager wants someone injured on the property especially an incident caused by lack of reasonable maintenance.

Last, pride of ownership is one of the greatest values any real estate manager can deliver. Commercial properties are often very visible, and they are an asset to the community. An effective maintenance program helps ensure community support. City officials, civic leaders, and the public often take great satisfaction in the condition of the commercial properties in their areas.

MAINTENANCE INSPECTIONS, SCHEDULING, AND WORK ORDERS

Inspections are essential to maintenance management, and they should be a routine part of the program. Maintenance work is scheduled based on maintenance needs the inspections identify. Additionally, each maintenance request from a tenant should generate a work order and a quick, efficient response.

Inspecting the Property

Inspecting the property is the fastest way to become familiar with a new management account. The astute real estate manager will do as much of an inspection as possible before presenting a proposal to a prospective client to be sure that he or she fully understands the needs and complexity of the property before committing to a management program. Inspections are the heart of a maintenance management program and are undertaken for three reasons:

1. Inspections are the fastest way to become familiar with a new management account, and assess the property's condition to provide a comparison with competing properties.

2. Inspections identify current and future maintenance needs. For instance, an inspection may identify a need to re-stripe a parking lot in six months.
3. Inspections are one of the preliminary steps in developing an operating budget and establishing capital improvement expenditures.

Upon taking over the management of a commercial property, meet with each tenant. This visit is an opportunity to question the tenant about the effectiveness of current maintenance and to ask for suggestions to improve the service. When the management account is up and running, maintaining an open line of communication with the tenants is recommended. It is not uncommon to visit tenants on a regular basis just to discuss how things are going, and if the tenant has suggestions for improvement.

The real estate manager generally does not conduct a structural or mechanical inspection unless he or she is qualified to do so by education and/or training. However, real estate managers are trained to conduct a visual inspection of the property and hire consultants to conduct inspections for major structural, mechanical, and maintenance problems. Some maintenance agreements, such as the elevator and *heating, ventilation, and air-conditioning (HVAC)* agreements, include regular inspections by the contractor's staff.

Frequency of Property Inspections

Inspections should be a routine element in the property's maintenance management program. The following lists several factors that determine the frequency of inspections:

1. A property in poor condition must be inspected more frequently than a property in good condition, and older buildings have a greater need for repairs.
2. If the property is located in an area with a high incidence of vandalism, it must be inspected more frequently. For example, a regional mall has considerably more traffic and more wear and tear, especially in common areas, in comparison to a garden office building.
3. An on-site manager can inspect the property more frequently than a real estate manager who is located hundreds of miles away. Every time the on-site manager walks around the property he or she should be inspecting all aspects of the property's conditions.
4. The real estate manager with a large portfolio of properties has less time for inspections than the real estate manager with fewer properties has. However, this should not serve as an excuse to reduce or eliminate reasonable inspections.

An ideal inspection frequency is monthly, although not all properties need inspections that often. However, whenever the real estate manager is on the property for any reason, he or she should be conducting an informal inspection of conditions with the goal of stopping small problems from becoming larger and more expensive. This is also a good time to ensure that prior problems have been corrected. It is also quite helpful to have one or two tenants in each property who will act as your eyes and ears and to report to you anything they see on the property that may need attention. Tenants often take more pride in the property due to his or her participation.

Personnel Involvement with Inspections

When an on-site real estate manager is the only person who conducts the inspections, items may be overlooked because the real estate manager may be too familiar with the property. It's important to alternate inspections with the maintenance personnel and administrative staff. If the leasing is in-house, the leasing agent—observing the property with a marketing perspective—should be encouraged to observe and report any maintenance needs.

Each person has a different perspective and may see things the others might miss. The administrative staff may be more attentive to cleanliness, the leasing agent looks at marketing and merchandising features, and maintenance staff look for wear and tear to the property. No matter who does the inspection, having a copy of the most recent inspection form is helpful in providing a point of reference.

Inspection Forms

Inspection forms provide a column for the inspector's comments on each item evaluated. This helps to ensure a thorough inspection. Each vacancy should be inspected along with the rest of the property and should be maintained in a broom-clean condition. Using a vacant space as a work room or a store room will lessen the chances of the space being leased. Most prospective tenants will have a difficult time seeing beyond the work areas and stored materials to completely understand the size of the space and any amenities it may have.

The completed inspection forms are provided to the real estate manager who expedites the maintenance work. After the work is completed, the forms are kept on file for reference when developing the next budget. In slip-and-fall law suits, the inspection forms provide evidence the property has a maintenance management program; however, if maintenance items are identified and corrective action is not taken, the form may be evidence of neglect.

Decision Between Repair vs. Replace

As properties age, a decision is made on the difference between the maintenance costs verses the cost to replace the item. If a piece of equipment has been the cause of larger bills, then it might be a candidate for replacement rather than continuing to pour money into old equipment.

Is the money saved on operating expenses and fewer repairs a good use of the funds required to replace or repair the equipment? Keep in mind that utility costs are going to continue to rise and this should be factored into the equation. If the maintenance records are complete and accurate, it should be fairly easy to make an informed decision as to repair or replacement.

Scheduling Maintenance Requests

Once maintenance needs have been identified, the work should be scheduled. Maintenance is divided into two categories: (1) preventive and (2) routine. Preventive maintenance allows potential problems to be prevented—or at least detected. They can be solved before major repairs are required. Routine maintenance is ongoing maintenance. It includes a variety of maintenance tasks, from mowing the lawn to sweeping the parking lot, to emptying waste receptacles. It's important to periodically review the routine maintenance schedule with the maintenance staff to determine if the frequency and job specifications are adequate. Meet regularly with the contractors performing routine maintenance to see if they have any ideas for improvements and to share any problems areas.

Develop maintenance specifications from the information from equipment manufacturers, service contractors, consultants, published articles, and trade associations. Maintenance specification manuals are provided with most equipment. Hire consultants to develop preventive maintenance programs for individual components of the building, such as the roof and the parking lot.

The contractor's bid package should include maintenance schedules. When reviewing the bids, it's important to compare apples with apples. For instance, in reviewing bids for HVAC maintenance, compare the type and frequency of filter changes, the list of items covered by each preventive maintenance inspection, and the frequency of inspections. Preventive and routine maintenance schedules are normally developed for a one-year period that coincides with the budget period. Major preventive maintenance, such as roof or parking lot maintenance, may be scheduled for one year or throughout a five-year period.

Whether the real estate manager has a portfolio of several properties, or serves as the on-site manager for a commercial building, several preventive and routine maintenance tasks must be performed monthly or periodically. It is easy to budget for several maintenance tasks—most of which will be performed well after the budget is developed—and then to forget to perform some of them.

Additionally, larger jobs must be scheduled and all maintenance personnel should be aware of those jobs. To keep track of all maintenance orders, each recurring routine maintenance item should be included in the maintenance schedule—schedules may differ depending on the software program used. For example, if one is to reseal the parking lot, it is not a job that can just be set up for a specific date and carried out without advance preparation.

First, the funds must be available. Then, one must write up a bid package and submit it to qualified contractors for bids. If major tenants have approval rights for larger jobs, they must be contacted and give their approval for the job. In coordination with major tenants, as well as the tenants as a whole, the schedule should be determined so there will be minimum disruption to the tenants and visitors.

Once the final bid is approved and the schedule is set, tenants should be notified of the specifics of the job. If security is to be present, that will have to be set up by either the real estate manager and/or the contractor, and that information should be shared with the tenants. Finally, on the day of the job, it is a good idea to be on site to help with any problems that may come up. The major job schedule keeps these jobs in the minds of everyone involved and allows them to do the pre-planning necessary to make sure the job is completed on time.

COMPUTER-AIDED MAINTENANCE MANAGEMENT PROGRAMS

There are many software programs that will assist in the inspection program, oversight, scheduling, and completion of maintenance tasks and are designed especially for the commercial property field. Most programs are designed to track the maintenance process from inspection; request for services; forward copies of the request to the appropriate employee or contractor; receive messages indicating the problem has been solved; or that specific parts need to be ordered; and to complete the file on the call.

A list of the calls is compiled at the end of each day for review by supervisory personnel and for any further action necessary. Additionally, these maintenance management programs are set up to maintain an inventory list of parts on hand and to alert management when stocks may be running low.

More sophisticated programs are designed to be completely integrated with other administrative functions of a real estate management company. All entries can be compared to budget estimates to check against contracts; keep track of specific employees and specific jobs; tie into the profit and loss statements and be integrated into tenant billings for common area costs; and even for specific maintenance to be billed back to tenants, such as a repair inside a retail tenants shop.

Regardless of the property size, the owner and real estate manager should find a system that fits his or her needs.

One of the major benefits of the computer-aided maintenance management programs is the feature showing when a job has been completed. This feature is especially important when interfacing with a tenant who is waiting for a repair and has no idea if it will be done immediately or if it will take more time.

Work Orders

The need for maintenance services falls into two general categories: (1) routine maintenance on equipment such as air conditioners, sump pumps, door openers, elevators, security equipment, and escalators, as well as requests for janitorial service; and (2) servicing repairs or breakdowns. Requests should be handled promptly. When a tenant registers a complaint about a broken system, rather than ignoring the problem, it is to the building owner's advantage to fix it immediately. Most tenants spend 60 to 70 hours on the premises most weeks. When a job is not completed or reasonably delayed, the tenant can easily come to the conclusion the owner and real estate manager do not care about the tenants. Many repairs start out as small problems but can develop into major repairs if ignored.

Once a maintenance request is received and recorded, a work order, whether paper or electronic, can be used to route the request to the maintenance personnel or contractor and to follow up on the work. A work order accomplishes five objectives:

1. Serves as a notice that the periodic operation is to be performed
2. Provides authorization for the expenditure of labor and materials in performance of the work
3. Furnishes a document for recording that the operation was performed
4. Provides a document for the written feedback of other information, such as materials used and other work that was or may be required
5. Indicates problems that need further attention from management if not returned within a specified time

When a maintenance request is received, it is written on a two-part work order form, or on a computer-generated work order. The building maintenance person receives the original. If the maintenance request is e-mailed or phoned to the maintenance staff, he or she completes the work order and calls back the status of the request. This information is then added to the work request. When a contractor is to complete the work, the same procedure is followed. If the management office is on site, the maintenance person may pick up the work order. In such cases, the tenant should sign the work order when the work is completed.

The second part of the work order is placed in a "tickler file." If the request arrived on Monday, for example, and the work should be completed by Tuesday, the second copy is placed in the "reminder file" or in the computer follow-up file for that day. If notification of work completion or the status of the work does not return by Tuesday afternoon, the maintenance person is again contacted.

Sometimes work cannot be completed until a part has been ordered. In this case, the tenant should be informed of the reason for the delay and assured that the request is being processed. If the maintenance person orders the part, but does not tell the tenant or the real estate manager about the delay in completing the work, the tenant will believe the request is being ignored, and the real estate manager will believe the work was completed. The follow-up system will eliminate such an occurrence. Most maintenance software programs have a built-in reminder when it appears that a work order has been open too long.

When the work is completed, the original work order is placed in the tenant's paper or electronic file, and the second part is kept with other work orders and periodically reviewed to identify maintenance problems or trends.

Recording Maintenance Requests

Maintenance requests from tenants must be handled quickly and efficiently. Each maintenance call is recorded, addressed, and noted when completed. Usually, the administrative assistant or the real estate manager receives the request and records the date, location, and the problem on the maintenance request form. Some calls should always be referred to the real estate manager, while others can be handled by the assistant. Other than emergency situations, maintenance personnel should not be authorized to perform maintenance tasks or respond to tenant complaints without approval from a supervisor.

If the tenants are used to directly being able to get the maintenance personnel to immediately react to their complaints, they are likely to make requests beyond their lease parameters. Logging the requests provides documentation and starts the follow-up process. Retaining the log helps develop a history and pattern of maintenance needs. This list can be analyzed to identify recurring maintenance problems that might lead to future problems.

HVAC service requests are known as "hot-and-cold calls," which is a special list for complaints about the HVAC systems. The hot-and-cold log should periodically be reviewed with the HVAC service contractor. General and HVAC service forms should periodically be reviewed with the maintenance staff. This information is helpful when developing the property's operating budget.

When preventive or corrective maintenance is performed on mechanical equipment, the work is recorded in the equipment's service report card or computer file. The noted information includes the problem, the maintenance performed, the date, and the person who performed the work. The service report card should be located near the equipment.

When the equipment breaks down, the service person can quickly review the history of the equipment's problems and better identify the cause of the breakdown. This lowers repair costs and gets the equipment up and running more quickly. This is also used as the basis for repair or replace decisions. If a property has eight air-conditioning compressors, and one of them is requiring an inordinate amount of repairs as indicated by the work orders, it may be prudent to replace that unit rather than continue to make costly repairs and eventually replace the unit.

COORDINATING AND COMMUNICATING WITH TENANTS

In the rush to implement segments of the maintenance management program, it is easy to overlook the tenants who must continue to operate their businesses while the maintenance work is performed. Of most concern to the tenants are HVAC service and access to the property, common areas, and parking lot. A shopping center tenant's visibility is important to the store's sales volume. Blocking the store's visibility with equipment when replacing or repairing a roof, for example, can be detrimental to the tenant's business.

Tenants should receive sufficient written notice of any maintenance that may disrupt or interrupt their businesses. Sealing a parking lot, core drilling, and major roof or HVAC repairs disrupt a building's normal operations and may disrupt its tenants' operations. In the communications, inform the tenants of the nature and timing of the work, the reason it is required, how it might affect their day-to-day business operations, and what will be done to mitigate or prevent disruption to the tenant's business.

Steam-cleaning sidewalks in front of the tenant's business can be very disruptive and if not done properly is likely to stain their windows. This work should be done before store hours and the windows should be protected. In many major repairs, such as parking-lot sealing and/or re-striping, it may be necessary to have a traffic control guard stationed in the parking lot or entrance to the property to help customers and employees find appropriate routes and parking.

Some maintenance work requires special consideration to avoid disruption. To seal a shopping center parking lot in one day, the entire lot must be closed. This can be avoided by dividing the lot into three sections and sealing each in one day, allowing customer parking on two thirds of the lot and continual operation of the stores. Major HVAC repairs that require shutting down the system should be scheduled in the evenings, on weekends, or when the building is closed. The tenants should be notified of the work and informed that it should be completed before the next business day. If the work is not completed on time, the tenants should be notified of the delay, the reason for the delay, and given a new completion time if it is known. Keeping the tenant informed is likely to reduce any friction between management and the tenant involved.

Tenants seldom object to the timing of maintenance work, and when they do, their objections are usually valid. Of course, emergency maintenance must be handled on the spot. An effective maintenance management program minimizes emergencies.

Emergency Phone Numbers

Nothing is more frustrating than receiving a call at home after business hours for emergency maintenance and not being able to contact a service contractor. Delays in responding often result in additional damage and expense. Every real estate manager should develop a list of all the contractors serving the building and of others, such as glass contractors, that are not used regularly but that would be needed in an emergency.

Companies that do not have a 24-hour answering service must provide the mobile number or home phone numbers of several of their service personnel. If the contractor will not provide an after-hours contact number, the real estate manager should select another contractor. Remember, emergencies happen at all hours of the day and night, and maintenance is often needed immediately.

In addition to the contractors' phone numbers, the list should include phone numbers of at least two employees of each tenant, the original construction contractor and subcontractors (if available), the utility companies, police and fire department, and all real estate management company employees. An emergency phone list for each property may be stored in a tablet or Smartphone with plans for the property and organized by property name. Each real estate manager, assistant, and everyone on the real estate management company's answering service call list should have electronic access to this information.

Real Estate Manager's Availability

When the property owner transfers management of the property to the real estate manager, he or she expects the real estate manager or the staff to be available 24/7 to respond to the property's needs. Therefore, the real estate management company must have a 24-hour answering service. An answering machine can be used as long as the greeting includes the name and number of a staff member who is able to handle emergency situations. Many larger companies have one real estate manager assigned daily to emergency situations for all properties. This approach gives the other real estate managers a break from possible late-night calls.

The answering service should have a list of people and contact numbers—including cell phone numbers—to call for each property. The list should be prioritized, with the real estate manager heading the list and the names of other real estate managers and staff assistants following. All staff members on the list should be familiar with the property and should have the emergency phone list. The real estate manager should be available so when an emergency arises after hours, he or she can be reached immediately.

MAJOR MAINTENANCE TASKS

Several types of maintenance require special training, skills, and/or equipment. The real estate manager must develop an effective maintenance plan for each major maintenance area; such plans frequently involve hiring outside contractors to perform the maintenance.

Snow Removal

Some real estate managers never have to deal with snow and ice management; however, those who *do,* will need an effective plan to provide a safe environment, and to facilitate the tenants' business activities. A real estate manager in areas with snow fall who do not have a snow-removal program have little or no control over that aspect of the budget when snow removal becomes necessary. In addition, tenants and visitors will be susceptible to accidents ranging from minor slips and falls to automobile accidents, and the property owner may have increased liability. If customers avoid a shopping center or other retail property because the parking lot and sidewalks are blocked with snow or ice, the merchants' sales will slump.

Developing an effective snow-removal plan requires several steps. Some larger properties have the capability of handling snow and ice management in house; however, medium and smaller properties will very likely have to rely on contract services. The first step is to contract with a reliable snow-removal contractor. Sweeping companies and construction contractors with earth-moving equipment may provide snow-removal services to keep their equipment and workforce busy during the off season.

Contractors should be checked for reliability to ensure they have sufficient equipment. Most snow-removal contractors monitor the weather and likely snow fall, and are often on the property as early as 4:00 or 5:00 a.m. in order to clear the snow before the employees arrive to work—for shopping centers, before the stores open for business. Some real estate managers will have their own contacts with firms that monitor the weather, and when needed, the real estate manager will call the contractor and arrange for snow removal for those days when snow is expected. When accepting bids, carefully check the contractor's references and inquire whether the contractor owns or rents its equipment. If the equipment is rented, the equipment might not be available when needed. Since damage may occurs during snow removal, the contractor must have adequate insurance.

The contract fee can be negotiated based on an hourly rate, the amount of snowfall, or on a flat rate per snow removal. After selecting the contractor, inspect the parking lot together. The purpose of the inspection is twofold:

1. It identifies existing damage that can be repaired or noted, thus, protecting the contractor from blame after the snow season.
2. It identifies curbs, signs, speed bumps, and other features that would be hidden under the snow and could inadvertently be damaged during snow removal. Many of these features must be identified with markers. In addition, drains must be located and marked so they can be cleared when the snow melts. Parking lanes may need to be marked as reference points.

Removing snow from the entire parking lot is not always necessary. Many lots have areas that are seldom used. An office building with many vacancies uses only a portion of the parking lot. A community or super regional mall needs the entire parking lot during the holiday season, but only a portion of it in January and February. Analyze the property's parking needs, divide the lot into sections, and determine which sections must be kept clear of snow during which months.

Snow can be piled onto the sections of the lot that are not needed for parking. However, piling snow too high around the perimeter of a shopping center can block its visibility. Such piles can also become dirty and unsightly. As the snow melts, debris that surfaces must be removed. If the snow cannot be piled anywhere in the parking lot, obtain permission to use nearby vacant lots. Hauling snow to an off-site location, depending on the distance, can become quite expensive.

The maintenance staff should ensure that the chemicals and salt used on the sidewalk and parking lot do not damage those areas or the building lobby if they are tracked inside. Sand and hot gravel can be used on the parking lot to reduce its slickness and provide traction for cars. After the thaw, the lot will need a spring cleanup to remove sand, gravel, and debris.

The real estate manager bases the snow removal budget on an average or slightly above-average annual snowfall. An entire season's budget can be spent in one month, but a good snow-removal plan can minimize the chances of this occurring. Even when the entire budget is spent in a month or two, the real estate manager must continue to maintain a safe parking lot that has adequate parking for tenants, visitors, and customers.

Maintaining Roofs

Few systems in a building cause more problems than roofs. If possible, have a set of the plans and specifications for the roof. Is it tar and gravel, or is it built up with a cap sheet, rubber membrane, or shake? Each type of roof requires a different approach for major repairs.

Traffic on the roof should be minimized. A roof holds up quite well if no one steps on a bubble or crushes something through the membrane. Special paths built into or onto the roof can be helpful, but workers often prefer the shortest path between two points, negating that precaution. If antennas, exhaust-fan ducts, and satellite dishes are installed, the building owner's roofing contractor should properly seal the penetration—generally this is the tenant's expense. The lease should prohibit the tenant from installing equipment on the roof without the property owner's approval.

The real estate manager should ensure that the roof is carefully inspected twice a year and checked from time to time in between. Inspections should be performed before winter and again in the spring. Select and retain a qualified, reliable roof maintenance company. Infrared inspection and analysis are becoming important tools for the overall maintenance plan for all commercial properties. Inspections should identify splits, bubbles, low spots, new penetrations, and blocked drains.

Asphalt Parking Lots

Parking lots pose another potential maintenance problem in real estate management. Many deteriorate because of poor care and heavy traffic. Water and non-use are two big enemies of asphalt parking lots. Good drainage is essential. Small cracks should be cleaned and sealed before water flows into the substructure and destroys the surface from below. Employee parking should be concentrated in seldom-used areas to keep them from deteriorating.

Annual inspections of parking lots are essential and should be supplemented with more frequent checks for potential problems. Overlays and seal coatings can solve some minor problems and extend the life of the parking lot, but when the subsurface has broken down, the only answer is to remove and replace it.

Landscape Maintenance

Landscaping is one of the most advanced systems in commercial properties. An attractive, well-planned system is expensive to install, and its maintenance should not be trusted to beginners.

The landscaping on a commercial property requires definite, detailed specifications. A general landscape maintenance contract for a stated fee may result in some landscaping responsibilities being overlooked or charged as extra items at a premium price. The real estate manager should analyze the landscaping to be sure that native plants are used where possible. He or she should be knowledgeable about disease, infestation, fertilizing, and pruning.

A well-operating irrigation system is also critical to the health of the landscaping system. Generally, a landscape contractor assumes responsibility for the repair and maintenance of the irrigation system as part of the overall landscaping contract. The use of native plants and a drip system can reduce the cost of the landscape maintenance. Additionally, lawns are very expensive to maintain and can often be replaced with plants that have low-water requirements, rock, or mulch.

HVAC Maintenance

Most shopping centers, small office buildings, and many multi-tenant industrial properties are serviced by rooftop HVAC units. The owner of the multi-tenant industrial property assumes the maintenance responsibilities for the HVAC units and either directly bills the cost of maintenance to the tenants or assumes the costs.

Many shopping center leases state that the property owner will provide service for the HVAC units and the tenants will be billed directly by the maintenance service company, or by the real estate management company for the service. Many buildings have central systems that can be controlled in individual spaces or units that are connected to the main building system.

An important component of an effective HVAC maintenance program is the maintenance specification portion of the service contract. Thorough maintenance specifications ensure that the maintenance contractor or in-house staff is accountable. A common, but expensive maintenance problem, is repairing or replacing a compressor. Frequently, when a compressor stops functioning, it must be replaced.

One method of ensuring that the tenants fulfill their lease obligation to maintain their HVAC units is for the real estate manager to contract with the maintenance service company and bill the tenant for the cost. This is common in shopping centers. To eliminate tenants complaining that they are paying for a service they are not receiving, every time their HVAC unit is serviced, the maintenance person should leave a service card with the tenant.

When service is required, the HVAC contractor should give the real estate manager a complete report on the repairs to the equipment. When the HVAC equipment is installed, the installer should be required to perform a start-up inspection and provide the real estate manager with evidence of the work.

Since few tenants have any knowledge of what is needed to service their HVAC units, they are often confused regarding maintenance requirements. When the tenants are billed for the HVAC service, they may be unaware that the unit was serviced and may be reluctant to pay the bill. To avoid this situation, explain the HVAC maintenance service procedures to the tenants. Many commercial properties provide their tenants with a tenant handbook or manual upon move in, which includes information on the tenant's responsibilities. It will also include contact information for the real estate manager for both daytime and after-hour emergencies.

The first opportunity to explain HVAC maintenance service procedures is during lease negotiations. The next opportunity is when the tenant receives the property's tenant handbook. When the tenant moves into its premises, send a letter explaining who services its HVAC unit, how to call for service, and how the tenant will be invoiced. To prevent tenants' complaints that their HVAC units are not being maintained, the tenant should receive a notice each time the unit is serviced.

Janitorial Maintenance

A strong janitorial program starts with good janitorial specifications, a reliable company, and adequate supervision. The janitors must be supervised by the janitorial company, which in turn must be supervised by the real estate manager. In larger malls and medium- to high-rise office buildings, the real estate manager should walk the building each week with the janitorial supervisor. For low-rise buildings, a monthly walk-through is usually sufficient.

Janitorial contractors should be screened thoroughly before they are invited to submit a proposal. In screening a contractor, visit at least two of the contractor's present accounts that pay a similar cost per square foot in order to determine if the quality of the contractor's work is at a level that meets the building's requirements. A visit to the contractor's business offices can also give a sense of the company's professional capability to provide training to its hourly and supervisory employees.

A janitorial contractor's proposal should include previously agreed-upon specifications as well as the contractor's intended staffing and workload plans. Each contractor should include a specific plan for cleaning services, the name and background of the project manager—if the size of the job warrants such a position—and the amount of management time that would be devoted each month to smaller projects. In addition to reviewing the terms, conditions, and the operations plan, compare the proposed service costs with a city industry average. Twenty percent below or above that average could indicate a misunderstanding, misrepresentation, or misbid.

After evaluating all of the contractors and bids, make an intelligent decision. Once a contractor is selected, allow two weeks to ensure that all details about the property have been shared with its management, crew assignments and workload plans have been established, keys and other security clearances have been arranged, and equipment and supplies have been purchased for delivery the day before the new contractor's term begins.

The contractor should require janitors to wear identification badges and uniforms, and it should supply its crews with their own equipment. Ask the contractor to submit a price for restroom supplies. If the price is competitive, the contractor should order all restroom paper supplies and bill the building for actual supplies used each month.

In many buildings, different standards are required for different areas or tenants. The Building Service

Contractors Association International (BSCAI) published "How to Select a Building Contractor," which defines the following three levels of cleaning standards:

1. **Prestige cleaning**—A cleaning standard that will provide unsolicited compliments from tenants, occupants, employees, or visitors, and one that will make the cleaning complaint a rarity.
2. **Adequate cleaning**—A standard that will provide neither compliments nor serious criticism. Some tenants will complain from time to time, but not to the point of threatening to seek other office space or not pay their rent.
3. **Minimal cleaning**—A standard that results in criticism from tenants, occupants, employees, and visitors. Complaints from tenants would be common, to the degree that some may threaten to move to another building.

When negotiating a janitorial contract, the janitorial firm provides a list of specifications that are usually very general and limited in the scope of janitorial service. Develop specifications tailored to the needs of the building and its tenants and use them as part of the bid package. Prepare specifications that keep the building clean at a reasonable cost. The more extensive the specifications and the more frequently work is performed, the higher the janitorial cost .

Elevator and Escalator Maintenance

Elevator and escalator maintenance is an area most real estate managers know little knowledge. Again, specifications must be developed and bid by at least two reliable companies. It's important to be sure the service company has an adequate supply of parts on hand and has the staff to respond to emergencies and after-hour breakdowns. Generally, the installer of the elevators and escalators perform the maintenance services during the warranty period, but once that period is over, it is wise to rebid the work to be sure that the contractor is providing competitive pricing.

Graffiti Removal

Graffiti is usually a major problem, and removal is expensive for property owners and communities. Graffiti was originally associated with subway trains and economically depressed areas, but today, graffiti is a universal problem. Graffiti may be the result of an impulse while waiting for a bus, the enthusiasm of a graduating class, or the ruthless and intentional act of a gang marking out its territory by using distinctive symbols known as "tags." Whether the graffiti consists of initials carved in a paneled elevator wall, a date painted on a wall, obscene or racist remarks, the results are the same: destruction and vandalism. Buildings covered with graffiti are uninviting places to work, shop, and visit. There is also sufficient evidence that existing graffiti invites more graffiti.

Graffiti may be removed with ordinary cleansing, chemicals and abrasive additives (some of which are hazardous), high-pressure washing, sandblasting, and sanding. The method to use depends upon the type of graffiti marker used and the type of surface material vandalized. Some graffiti removal chemicals are flammable and are irritants. They are hazardous substances that can injure maintenance personnel and damage surfaces. The health and safety of the maintenance personnel and others in the area is the first consideration when attempting to remove graffiti. Only experienced, qualified contractors and maintenance personnel should be allowed to work with hazardous chemical agents. Governmental regulations may address the use of some removal agents. An effective method that is the safest, most gentle process is the best choice for each graffiti attack.

When graffiti appears, a picture should be taken for the police, and then the graffiti should be removed immediately. Many communities have a graffiti taskforce that has become familiar with graffiti signatures and can track down the persons responsible for the damage to your building.

After years of subway trains and buses being covered with graffiti, many major cities initiated graffiti removal and prevention policies on their public transportation vehicles. Stiff penalties to individuals and gangs caught marking the vehicles and stations along with an immediate graffiti removal response have all but eliminated the graffiti problem. Good lighting acts as a deterrent to random acts of graffiti vandalism. Adjusting the schedule of maintenance and security personnel to place them in specific areas during certain times of the day or night (for example, in front of a building when school lets out) serves as a deterrent.

Though some people see graffiti as art, most people, including those whose properties are vandalized by graffiti, see it as a criminal act undertaken to deface and destroy public or private property. Some properties may have areas, such as the back or side of a building, where local artists are hired to paint a mural on the building.

CONTRACT SERVICES VERSUS EMPLOYEES

When establishing or evaluating a maintenance program, the real estate manager must decide whether to contract the maintenance work, to provide an in-house maintenance staff, or to use a combination. Seldom can all maintenance be handled in-house, so most real estate managers contract maintenance or use a combination of in-house and contract services. Local circumstances, such as the size of the property and its proximity to other properties in the portfolio, quite often influence who performs the maintenance work. Smaller properties have the problem of not having enough work to do to employ a full-time person, and if they do, that person may not have all of the skills necessary to complete all of the repairs required.

Contract Services

Contract services have the advantage of built-in supervision and a fixed price. If one of the contracted company's employees becomes ill, the contractor must find a replacement. Likewise, if the equipment breaks down and needs repair, the contractor must deal with it, not the real estate manager.

Technical knowledge is one of the main reasons to use contract services. An in-house maintenance person is unlikely to be able to fill all of the property's maintenance needs, which range from air-conditioning to roof repair to landscaping to elevator and escalator maintenance and repairs. By using contract services, the real estate manager can hire a specialist in the area needed, receive expert attention, and pay accordingly.

The smaller the project, the more practical contract services are. A 400,000-square-foot office can support staff specialists, but a 40,000-square-foot commercial property cannot. In addition, smaller projects generally do not have a secure place to store equipment. Owning equipment also means ongoing repairs, replacements, and insurance costs.

Finally, contract services eliminate all the responsibilities of hiring, firing, training, and payroll administration. Some in-house maintenance jobs in commercial properties have entry-level salaries and have a very high turnover. This can cause gaps in efficiency and productivity.

In-House Maintenance Staff

An in-house maintenance staff also has several advantages. It is generally less expensive than hiring a contractor, and additional personnel are available for emergencies. For example, the landscape staff can be deployed to clean up a spill or barricade a dangerous area if the need arises.

One main advantage of an in-house staff is direct control. Maintenance personnel are a critical part of the building image, and an outside contractor that has no understanding of tenant relations at a specific property can make negative or inappropriate comments that could harm the tenant/management relationship. For example, an air-conditioning contractor might tell tenants the units are not the best available and no amount of work will make them function properly. The real estate manager can instruct the in-house staff on the importance of good tenant relations. With a minimum of training, the in-house staff can learn to handle tenant requests that are beyond the property owner's obligations.

If the real estate manager manages only smaller properties, the real estate management company might have an in-house maintenance staff that can cover a number of locations on a roving basis. Maintenance personnel with trucks can handle several properties and respond to most general emergencies. When the real estate manager employs the maintenance personnel directly, providing uniforms and identification is wise. The uniform gives a more professional appearance at a reasonable cost.

If the third-party real estate management company is going to use a maintenance company owned by the real estate management company to do repairs and bill the client, this fact must be revealed to the client ahead of time. Often, a third-party maintenance company can be more cost effective, but if the relationship between the maintenance company and the real estate management company is not disclosed in advance, the client relationship is likely to be damaged and there could be an ethical issue for the real estate management company.

The real estate manager must monitor the work and behavior of maintenance staff. In most commercial properties, the majority of the operating expenses are billed back to the tenants. If tenants observe workers malingering, they may be reluctant to pay common area or building operating charges when billed. As always, the real estate manager should use good judgment in hiring relatives for contract services or as employees because that can give the impression the real estate manager is taking care of a relative rather than obtaining the best service for the property.

Contractor's Insurance

The property owner and the real estate management company will require contractors to have insurance coverage for their protection of all parties. Most contracts require the contractor to obtain the following coverage:

1. Workers' compensation
2. Liability insurance
3. Automobile liability
4. Fidelity bond
5. False arrest and invasion of privacy

The contractor should provide the property owner with insurance certificates as evidence of the required coverage. The property owner and the real estate management company should be named as additional insureds, and the certificate should provide for 10 to 30 days' advance notice before cancellation.

Named insured endorsements are usually issued at no additional charge in most markets and can be obtained in a matter of hours. Some small contractors will argue that this endorsement will increase their cost of insurance, but the real estate manager should not forego the insurance requirement as it places both the real estate management company and the client at risk. The additional costs can be included in the contractor's bid. This usually is not an issue for the contractor since almost all property owners and real estate managers have the similar requirements for contractors.

THE MAINTENANCE AGREEMENT

The final step in securing a maintenance contractor is negotiating a maintenance agreement. The real estate manager may use contractors' maintenance agreements or have a maintenance contract developed. It is best for the real estate management companies to use their maintenance agreement, which is developed to protect the property owners and the real estate management company.

Usually, the maintenance contractor proposes an agreement designed to provide maximum protection to the contractor. If this agreement is used, the real estate manager should realize that almost everything in the contractor's maintenance agreement is negotiable. The terms that receive the most attention are the length of the agreement, the fee, the contractor's insurance requirement, *indemnification* or *hold-harmless provisions*, cancellation rights, automatic renewals, and maintenance specifications.

Maintenance agreements are usually for one year; however, some major service contractors, such as elevator and HVAC contractors, may offer a discount for a longer term, such as five years. The cancellation right is essential. The real estate manager must have the right to terminate an agreement if the contractor does not perform or the property is sold. In addition, the indemnification and hold-harmless provision must be carefully reviewed to ensure that the property owner does not assume needless or unwise liability.

The real estate manager may provide the maintenance agreement, which protects the property owner and the real estate management company, is designed primarily for nontechnical maintenance, such as janitorial, parking lot sweeping, and snow removal, etc. As with the contractor's agreement, it is negotiable. A carelessly negotiated maintenance agreement jeopardizes the quality of maintenance and exposes the property to potential maintenance problems and costly liabilities. The maintenance agreements can be summarized on a form for quick reference. The summary form provides a place to list the most frequently negotiated terms and conditions of the agreement, such as the fee, expiration date, and frequency of service.

Contracts provide direction to everyone involved in managing and leasing commercial properties and are the foundation of commercial real estate management. From the basic lease to the management contract, and from the employment contract to the maintenance and services contract, these documents memorialize the agreements between the parties. If the documents are flawed, the relationship has the potential to be flawed. Just the exercise of negotiating a contract sets out the parameters of the relationship, but the well-crafted and negotiated contract will go a long way to minimize future disputes and ill will.

Contract negotiation is one of the commercial property manager's basic responsibilities, yet few real estate managers receive any training on negotiating contracts. Although some real estate managers learn negotiating techniques from a more experienced co-employee or supervisor, most real estate managers learn by doing. The art of negotiating contracts is not to obtain an advantage in the contract terms, but to ensure that the contractor will provide the services the building needs at a fair price. The real estate manager must understand the maintenance agreement and which provisions can or must be negotiated.

The real estate manager must have a full understanding of how the property operates and how the various services interrelate so he or she can make convenient scheduling part of the maintenance contract. For example, to have the windows in a shopping center cleaned one day and to have the sidewalks steam cleaned the next is not a good idea. The real estate manager must understand the specific services being contracted.

Sample Maintenance Agreement

A maintenance agreement provided by a contractor is of course designed to protect the contractor. Such contracts, which are typically a couple pages, favor the contractor and cover only the basic issues. The real estate manager can accept the contractor's agreement and negotiate additional provisions to protect the building's owner. A preferred alternative is for the real estate manager to develop a general maintenance agreement that can be used, with modifications, for most maintenance jobs. As with the contractor's agreement, it is negotiable. Exhibit 16.1 shows a sample maintenance agreement. Several provisions in the agreement are worth noting.

Provision 2 states that the contractor is an independent contractor and not an employee or agent of the property's ownership or real estate management firm. Independent contractors usually have a business license, carry proper insurance, and control the manner in which they get the job completed. A real estate manager may hire an individual and call the person an independent contractor to avoid payroll costs, workers' compensation insurance, and other administrative responsibilities of an employer. However, just calling a person an independent contractor does not make the person an independent contractor. If a person is injured on the job and files a worker's compensation claim against the real estate management firm and the firm has

EXHIBIT 16.1

Maintenance Agreement

THIS MAINTENANCE AGREEMENT is made this day of _____ 20 ______, and between ______________ (hereinafter referred to as the "Owner") and __________ (hereinafter referred to as the "Contractor").

WHEREAS, the Owner is the owner or ground lessee of that certain real property situated in _____________ County, _____________ as set forth in the legal description thereof attached hereto as "Exhibit A" (the "Property") which Property is improved for commercial purposes (the "_____________"; and

WHEREAS, the Owner has employed _____________ a Washington corporation (the "Agent"), to provide the overall management and operation of the property and all improvements constructed thereon; and

WHEREAS, the Owner desires to employ the Contractor and the Contractor desires to accept such employment, for the purposes of providing the services set forth herein; and

WHEREAS, the Agent shall direct the performance and activities of the Contractor hereunder and is authorized to act for and on behalf of the Owner in all respects;

NOW, THEREFORE, in consideration of the mutual terms and conditions herein set forth and for other good and valuable consideration and receipt of sufficiency of which is hereby acknowledged, the parties hereto hereby agree as follows:

1. Incorporation of Recitals. The foregoing recitals are incorporated herein as if set forth at length at this point.

2. Employment and Work. The Owner hereby appoints and hires the Contractor, as an independent contractor and not as an employee or an agent, and the Contractor hereby accepts such employment as an independent contractor and agrees to furnish and properly perform the necessary services, labor and other activities (collectively the "Work") at the times and in the manner with respect to the Property as is more completely set forth in the Specifications of Work attached hereto and made a part hereof as "Exhibit B." The Contractor agrees to furnish, at Contractor's sole cost and expense, all necessary labor, supplies, equipment, and other materials required to properly perform the Work. Contractor warrants that it has a sufficient number of qualified personnel, materials, and equipment to perform the Work in a first class manner.

3. Term. This Agreement shall commence on ______________ 20_____, and shall terminate at midnight on _____________ 20_____, (which period is referred to herein as the "Term"); provided that this Agreement may be terminated at any time during the Term hereof by Owner upon not less than ten (10) days' written notice to Contractor, or by Contractor as of the last day of any calendar month during the Term hereof upon giving not less than thirty (30) days' prior written notice to Owner. In the event of such termination, all payments due hereunder shall be prorated to the date of termination.

4. Performance. Contractor shall perform the Work on the days and at the lines as set forth in the Specifications of Work; provided, that the hours of completion at the Work are subject to such changes as Owner may direct from time to time. Contractor shall at all times perform the Work in a first-class, professional manner and to the satisfaction of Owner.

5. Fee. The Owner shall pay Contractor for the performance of the Work the sum of $_______(the "Fee"). The Fee shall be paid either (i) in one lump sum upon completion of the Work pursuant to the Specifications of Work; or (ii) per month, in arrears, on the last day of each month. No Fee, or part thereof, shall be paid until the amount due is substantiated by the job verifications described in the Specifications of Work.

(continued)

EXHIBIT 16.1 *(CONTINUED)*

6. Storage. The Contractor shall neither store any supplies, equipment, or materials nor permit any equipment to be left on the Property without the prior written consent of Owner.

7. Notices. All notices required or desired to be given under this Agreement shall be given in person or served upon the parties hereto by certified mail, postage prepaid, return receipt requested, and addressed to Owner as follows, c/o______, and if to the Contractor:

____

____

____

or such other place or places as may be provided in writing from time to time.

8. Attorney's Fees. In the event litigation is filed to enforce any of the provisions of this Agreement or by reason of a breach hereof by a party, the prevailing party shall be entitled to recover all attorney's fees as well as costs and expenses as may be granted in such litigation.

9. Compliance with Law. The Contractor, at its sole cost and expense, shall comply with all federal, state, and local statutes, laws, ordinances, executive orders, rules, and regulations applicable to it, the Work, its employees, and to the use of its equipment and; further, the contractor at its sole cost and expense shall procure and maintain in full force and effect any and all necessary permits and licenses and shall pay all fees or charges in connection therewith, together will all workman's compensation and union benefits, if any, applicable to its employees. The Contractor shall pay in a timely manner all taxes, assessments, and charges of every nature whatsoever levied upon Contractor's equipment, its use or operation.

10. Assignment.

(a) No Assignment By Contractor. It is specifically understood and agreed that this Agreement is personal to the Contractor and shall not be assigned by Contractor without the prior written consent of Owner, which consent, if given, shall be subject to such conditions as may be deemed appropriate by the Owner.

(b) Assignment By Owner. The Owner may assign this Agreement without the consent of approval of the Contractor.

11. Use of Name. The Contractor shall not use the name of the Owner, Agent or any of their affiliates or the Property in any sign, advertisement or written communication without the prior written consent of Owner or Agent.

12. No Waiver. The failure of the Owner to seek redress for violation of, or to insist upon the strict performance of, any term, covenant, condition, provision, or agreement contained in this Agreement shall neither (i) prevent any subsequent act or failure on the part of the Contractor which would have originally constituted a violation from having all the force and effect of an original violation, nor (ii) be deemed a waiver of any of said terms, covenants, conditions, provisions, or agreements unless such waiver shall be in writing signed by Owner.

13. Entire Agreement. This Agreement contains the entire agreement and understanding and recites the entire consideration given and accepted by the parties.

14. Amendment. Any modification, change, or amendment hereafter made relating hereto shall be ineffective unless in writing and signed, by the party against whom enforcement of the change, modification, amendment, waiver, or discharge is sought. All provisions of this Agreement shall remain in full force and effect throughout the Term hereof.

15. Insurance and Indemnity.

(a) Insurance Coverage. The Contractor shall at its sole cost and expense maintain the following insurance covering every aspect of the Work and operations described in this Agreement during the entire Term:

(1) Workman's Compensation Insurance in accordance with law and Employer's Liability Insurance with limits of not less than $ 1,000,000;

(2) Comprehensive General Liability Insurance including Broad Form Contractual Liability and Completed Operations Insurance with the following limits of liability:

(i) Coverage for personal injury to or death of one or more persons, with a single limit of not less than $ 1,000,000 per occurrence (which insurance shall additionally include, but shall not be limited to, coverage in the event of false arrest, libel, slander, assault, battery, and invasion of the right of privacy);

(ii) Coverage for injury to or destruction or loss of property of others with a single limit of not less than $ 1,000,000 per occurrence (including but not limited to theft or vandalism or malicious mischief perpetrated by any person including, without limitation, any servant, agent, representative, or employee of the Contractor);

(3) Complete Automobile Liability Insurance containing personal injury, death, and property damage coverage with a single limit of not less than $ 1,000,000 per occurrence;

(4) Broad form Fidelity Bond Insurance in limits of not less than $ 100,000 per occurrence covering all servants, employees, agents, and representatives of the Contractor.

(b) Original Policies. All insurance shall be written only as original policies and shall be placed only with companies of recognized requite. Each policy shall name Owner and Agent as additional named insureds.

(c) Delivery of Certificate of Insurance. Certificates of insurance with respect to the Contractor's insurance shall be delivered by the Contractor to the Owner at least thirty (30) days before the commencement of the term of this Agreement, or at such other times as the Owner may direct. Renewal policies of said insurance shall be delivered by the Contractor to the Owner at least thirty (30) days prior to the expiration date of each of such policies. Should the Contractor fail to deliver such Certificate of Insurance within the time aforesaid, the Owner may, at its option, procure such insurance and pay the premiums therefor, in which case the Contractor shall promptly reimburse Owner for the cost thereof or the Owner may deduct the cost of insurance from the Contractor's Fee. Each Certificate of Insurance shall name the Owner and Agent as additional named insureds.

(d) Termination. The Contractor agrees to notify the Owner at least thirty (30) days prior to the expiration date if any policy of insurance is not to be renewed upon precisely the same basis as the preceding policy. The Contractor assumes complete responsibility for its materials and equipment and relieves each of such indemnified persons of any liability whatsoever in connection with such materials and equipment, whether arising from theft, loss, damage, or otherwise.

(e) Indemnity. The Contractor shall completely indemnify and defend (or cause its insurance companies to completely defend) the Owner and Agent (and their respective employees, agents, officers, directors, and partners) promptly and diligently, at its or their sole cost and expense, against any claim, action, loss, damage, injury, or expense (including attorney's fees) or proceeding brought, incurred, or claimed by any person against Owner and/or Agent with respect to any and all of the matters referred to in this Agreement (including but not limited to liability imposed by law or by breach of any statutory duty of administrative rule or regulation, false arrest, libel, slander, death, or injury to persons or destruction of or damage to property, the refusal or failure of Contractor to perform its obligations hereunder or otherwise) and the Contractor shall pay, upon the demand of any insured party, any and all attorney's fees, costs, and other charges incurred by any of the insured parties to be afforded insurance or indemnity protections pursuant to this Agreement in the event the Contractor fails to give such a complete defense.

(continued)

16. Subrogation. Contractor agrees that in no event will any right of subrogation be asserted against any of the insured parties to be afforded insurance or indemnity protection for any damage, loss of injury, whether arising from negligence or otherwise.

17. Hazardous Substances.

(a) Presence and Use of Hazardous Substances. Contractor shall not, without Owner's prior written consent, keep on or around the Premises and Common Areas, for use, disposal, treatment, generation, storage, or sale any substances, wastes, or materials designated as, or containing components designated as hazardous, dangerous, toxic, or harmful and/or which are subject to regulation by any federal, state, or local law, regulation, statute, or ordinance. With respect to any such Hazardous Substance, Contractor shall:

(1) Comply promptly, timely, and completely with all governmental requirements for reporting, keeping and submitting manifests, and obtaining and keeping current identification numbers, and submit to Agent true and correct copies of all reports, manifests, and identification numbers at the same time as they are required to be and/or are submitted to the appropriate governmental authorities;

(2) Within five (5) days of Agent's request, submit written reports to Agent regarding Contractor's use, storage, treatment, transportation, generation, disposal, or sale of Hazardous Substances and provide evidence satisfactory to Agent of Contractor's compliance with the applicable government regulations;

(3) Allow Agent or Agent's representative to come on the area in which Contractor is working or which is covered by this contract at all times to check Contractor's compliance with all applicable governmental regulations regarding Hazardous Substances;

(4) Comply with minimum levels, standards, or other performance standards or requirements which may be set forth or established for certain Hazardous Substances (if minimum standards or levels are applicable to Hazardous Substances present on the property or any part thereof, such levels or standards shall be established by an on-site inspection by the appropriate governmental authorities and shall be set forth in an addendum to this Contract); and

(5) Comply with all applicable governmental rules, regulations, and requirements regarding the proper and lawful use, sale, transportation, generation, treatment, and disposal of Hazardous Substances. Any and all costs incurred by Agent or Owner and associated with Agent or Owner's inspection of the property and Agent's monitoring of Contractor's compliance with this Section, including Agent's and/or Owner's attorneys' fees and costs, shall be due and payable by Contractor upon demand by Agent and/or Owner.

(b) Cleanup Costs, Default, and Indemnification.

(1) Contractor shall be fully and completely liable to Agent and Owner for any and all cleanup costs, and any and all other charges, fees, penalties (civil and criminal) imposed by any governmental authority with respect to Contractor's use, disposal, transportation, generation, and/or sale of Hazardous Substances, in or about the Property.

(2) Contractor shall indemnify, defend and save Agent and Owner, and their respective officers, directors, shareholders, and employees, harmless from any and all of the costs, fees, penalties, and charges assessed against or imposed upon Agent and/or Owner (as well as Agent's and/or Owner's attorneys' fees and costs) as a result of Contractor's use, disposal, transportation, generation, and/or sale of Hazardous Substances.

(3) Upon Contractor's default under this Section, in addition to the rights and remedies set forth elsewhere in this Contract, Agent shall be entitled to the following rights and remedies:

(i) At Agent's option, to terminate this Contract immediately; and/or

(ii) To recover any and all damages associated with the default, including, but not limited to, cleanup costs and charges, civil and criminal penalties and

(continued)

EXHIBIT 16.1 *(CONCLUDED)*

fees, loss of business by Agent and/or Owner and by tenants in the property, any and all damages and claims asserted by third parties, and Agent's and/or Owner's attorneys' fees and costs.

18. Binding Nature. This Agreement shall be binding upon the parties hereto, their successors, and assigns.

19. Law. This Agreement shall be interpreted pursuant to the laws of the State in which the Property is located.

20. Agent. It is specifically understood and agreed that the Owner has employed the Agent to provide overall management and operation services with respect to the Property. The Agent has the right and authority to speak for and bind the Owner on all matters covered by this Agreement.

21. Precedence. This agreement will take precedence over any document attached.

IN WITNESS WHEREOF, the parties hereto have caused this instrument to be executed by their duly authorized representatives the day and year first above written.

OWNER:

By its Agent:

____

____

By: ______________________________________

Title: ____________________________________

CONTRACTOR:

____

____

By: ______________________________________

Title: ____________________________________

Exhibit 16.1 is a sample maintenance agreement and is designed to be used as a reference only. It is important to have an attorney review any agreement before using it.

not provided worker's compensation insurance coverage for the injured person, a lawsuit may ensue against the real estate management firm. The governmental agency that hears the case will apply standard criteria to determine whether the person was an independent contractor or an employee of the real estate management company. The real estate manager, who hires an independent contractor, who does not meet the requirements, may have a liability problem if the individual is injured on the job. It is not sufficient for the worker to agree that he or she is an "independent contractor." The person must meet the legal standard.

Typically, a maintenance agreement is for one year. Provision 3 accords the property owner the right to terminate the agreement for cause with 10 days' notice. If the owner has an early termination right, it is only fair that the contractor have a similar right. The contractor may cancel the agreement for any reason with 30 days' notice.

Some contractors may need to cross out Provision 6. This provision states that the contractor shall not store any supplies, equipment, and so forth on the property. A janitorial contractor may need to house an adequate supply of cleaning materials and most of its equipment on-site. A parking lot sweeping company will not need to store supplies and equipment at the property. Outside contractors often try to store materials in the mechanical and electrical rooms, but in most jurisdictions, that is against the fire codes and is not a good practice.

Provision 9 requires the contractor to comply with all laws. This provision applies even to laws enacted after the agreement commences—such as mandatory recycling.

Provision 10 prohibits the contractor from assigning the agreement without the prior written consent of the owner. Contractors are selected based on their reputation and experience as well as price. Many contractors are small, independent firms that are selected for the personal service and expertise they offer. When contractors sell their businesses, the buyers want the maintenance contracts assigned to them. This is a fair request and one to which the real estate manager will probably agree; however, the real estate manager wants the right to check new company owners with the same due diligence used in checking the original contractor.

To avoid a misrepresentation of the relationship between the owner and the contractor, Provision 11 prohibits the contractor from using the name of the property owner or the real estate management firm as advertising without prior written consent. If the contractor provides poor work, the real estate management firm and the property owner do not want to be listed as satisfied customers or without their permission to be seen as endorsing a contractor.

Provision 15 provides the contractor to have specific insurance coverage and to name the property owner and the real estate management firm as additional named insureds. The nature of the work determines if higher liability limits are necessary.

Provision 17 addresses hazardous substances. Every maintenance agreement and lease form has grown two to three pages longer with the addition of this important provision.

The Bid Package

A bid package, prepared for each firm invited to submit a proposal for services, clarifies possible misunderstandings between the real estate manager and the contractors. Each contractor will be bidding on the same specifications. A standard letter inviting a firm to submit a bid and stating the date the bids are due should accompany the bid package.

Some bid specifications, such as those for parking lot sweeping and sidewalk cleaning, are usually simple and can be developed by the real estate manager. Other specifications, such as those for major roof or parking lot repairs, may need to be developed by a consultant. All specifications must be tailored to the property's requirements.

The real estate manager should generally have potential contractors bid the specifications as written and then bid any proposed changes separately. This strategy allows the real estate manager to evaluate all proposals on the same basis before considering alternatives.

CONTRACT NEGOTIATING TIPS

Few shortcuts are possible in the maintenance of commercial properties. The fact that property owners pass many of the expenses along to the tenants emphasizes the importance of receiving value for the money spent. Preventive maintenance, when properly performed, extends the life of the system and reduces breakdowns. Below are more negotiating suggestions to help the real estate manager maintain an efficient, cost-effective maintenance program.

Elevator and Escalator Contracts

Usually the elevator and escalator maintenance firms provides the real estate manager with a maintenance agreement. If the agreement will be used to service the equipment, the real estate manager must read it carefully and negotiate provisions as needed. The elevator maintenance firm's account executive may inform the real estate manager that the contract is the firm's "standard" agreement and the firm will not accept changes to it. However, all contracts are negotiable.

The agreement may be for a long term, for example, five years. The advantage to a term longer than one year is that the service company will probably offer a discount of five to 10 percent for a longer agreement. A long-term agreement may be advantageous if it includes a 30-day cancellation privilege for the property owner. The contractor may argue that a cancellation provision negates the benefits of a long-term agreement. The real estate manager can counter with an offer to pay a penalty—possibly the difference between the discount and the non-discount price for the period the contract was in effect—if the property owner cancels the agreement.

The agreement may have an automatic renewal provision. If the real estate manager does not intend to renew the agreement, but inadvertently misses the period to terminate the agreement, the contract will automatically renew. This provision is usually near the end of the agreement; it should be stricken.

The agreement may also include a provision whereby the property owner holds the contractor harmless for any actions. Imagine the contractor's service personnel getting angry and punching a visitor while in the building. According to some "standard" hold-harmless provisions, the building's ownership might be responsible for this act of the contractor's employee. The hold-harmless agreement should be reviewed and possibly negotiated.

The real estate manager must carefully review the insurance provision to ascertain that the contractor has adequate insurance coverage and that the property owner and the real estate management firm are additional named insureds on the contractor's insurance policies. Regardless of the length of the agreement, the contract may call for an automatic rate increase based on increases in the *Consumer Price Index (CPI)* or union wages. This provision should be reviewed and properly negotiated. If union maintenance personnel receive a salary increase, the contract fee should not increase by the percentage of the union contract increase. It is unlikely that the administrative and management personnel of the contracting firm received the same percentage increase. In addition, the percentage of the union wage increase is often higher than the percentage increase of the firm's general and administrative overhead.

Is the contract a full-service contract, including labor and parts but excluding emergency and after-hours calls, or are parts charged separately and a limited number of service calls included in the base fee? If emergency and after-hours service calls are an extra charge, the agreement should include the rate for that service. The agreement may require the contractor to keep an adequate supply of all the parts needed to service the equipment.

If the building has a low occupancy, a light load credit might be negotiated. For instance, if the building is 70-percent occupied, a 10-percent credit or reduction in the contract price might be obtained. The credit or reduction is a sliding discount that increases as occupancy decreases. A low occupancy reduces the use of the elevators and the wear and tear on the equipment.

Janitorial Contract

Good janitorial specifications are the first step toward good janitorial service. A real estate manager who has never written a maintenance specification should ask a contractor for its specifications and modify them to meet the property's needs. Real estate managers of similar commercial buildings in the area may be another source for janitorial specifications. Real estate managers are usually willing to share specifications, forms, procedures, and experiences. The one exception to this willingness to share is a complete set of policy and procedures generated by a company. Most real estate managers will share small parts of the policies and procedures, but will not let anyone copy their entire book.

The next requirement for good janitorial service is frequent communication between the janitorial supervisor and the real estate manager, followed by periodic building walkthroughs. Janitorial firms often provide a two-page specification sheet that is inadequate and limited in its scope of work. Review the level of service and special janitorial services needed and develop specifications tailored to the building and its tenants.

The janitorial contract should require that janitors wear an approved uniform and have a photo identification badge. If the building has a lobby guard, the janitors should sign in when they arrive and sign out when they leave. Requiring janitorial staff to sign in and out—even when the building does not have a guard—is an important means of checking the number of janitorial staff working in the building.

Some contracts require a specific number of janitorial staff working a minimum number of hours each night. When a staff member is ill or on vacation, the janitorial firm may be tempted not to replace the person and to have the other janitorial staff assume the duties of the absent worker. When this happens, the level of service often drops. The sign-in and sign-out requirements help eliminate this problem.

If the janitorial company is unable to replace the missing personnel, a credit against the monthly fee may be appropriate. It is a good idea for the real estate manager to visit the property at odd hours to check on the services. This includes looking into janitor activities, the parking lot sweeper hours and results, and even the landscaping company activities.

Recycling is an important issue to discuss with the janitorial firm. Many buildings have implemented recycling programs, and some municipalities mandate recycling in commercial buildings. If the building has, or will have, a recycling program, will the property owner or the contractor pay for the recycling equipment? Will an extra janitor be needed for the any additional work created by a recycling program? An efficient pickup or separation of materials may not require extra personnel.

Several formulas are used to determine the janitorial costs in a partially occupied building. The contractor and the real estate manager must agree upon a formula to credit the monthly contract fee for vacant space. The contract may provide for a fee based on 100-percent occupancy and a credit each month based on a cent per square foot for each vacant square foot.

Security Agreement

One of the most important issues to resolve in a security agreement is whether the guards will be armed or unarmed. Most real estate managers insist the guards be unarmed. In the rare case when a guard is armed, the guard is often an off-duty police officer. The contract may be directly with the police department or the police officers' union for a special security need. If the guards are armed, the contract should require that the guards receive periodic firearms training.

Another issue to negotiate is the type of uniform. If an authoritative presence is needed, a military-style uniform is preferable. If the security presence is being down played and a public relations stance is needed, a uniform consisting of a blazer and slacks would be appropriate. The security agreement should also specify the type of equipment the guards must have (e.g., pager, cell phones, vehicle) and who will pay for the equipment.

The insurance provision in the security contract should include false arrest and invasion of privacy in addition to the standard contractor's insurance requirement. What will be the hourly rate for additional guards, holidays, and overtime shifts? Will the contract specify the number of times the guard's supervisor must visit each guard's shift? Will the guard have a sign-in procedure and/or a procedure to monitor the areas the guard patrols? Must a daily log be submitted to the management office?

The real estate manager should retain the right to have a guard replaced for poor performance. To ensure that quality personnel serve as guards, the contract may require that the guards be paid no less than a specific hourly wage and that the guards assigned to the account be maintained on a consistent basis rather than moving them to another of the guard company's accounts. The guards should be required to submit a written report for each shift to the real estate manager. The security firm should provide a guard manual for the duties of each post which is reviewed and approved by the real estate manager. Periodic meetings and training sessions with the guards may be necessary, and the guards should be paid to attend the meetings—either at the guards' hourly rate or through an extra charge. Again, it is helpful for the real estate manager to visit the property at odd hours to see how well the security service is performing at meeting the terms of the contract.

Slurry Seal Contract

The parking lot is one of the most important, and expensive, components in any commercial property. Because of the heavy traffic on these properties, the parking lot is subject to constant repair to extend its life as well as for safety and aesthetic reasons. While some property owners do not endorse the periodic sealing of the parking lot, many believe that sealing will protect the parking lot and extend its life.

Sealing a parking lot is a rather expensive proposition and is extremely disruptive, even when handled with great care. Because this cost is usually passed along to the occupants of the building, it is important to get the best value for the money and to minimize the disturbance to normal business operations. The negotiation of the sealing contract requires attention to detail on both counts.

Tenants' Approval Rights

One of the first considerations is the major or anchor tenant's possible approval rights. Many anchor tenants in shopping centers or major tenants in other commercial buildings have approval rights on maintenance repairs that will cost more than a predetermined figure, which may be as low as $10,000 in some leases. These tenants negotiate this right because they pay a major portion of the maintenance costs of the property. They want to be sure that the property owner is not excessively maintaining the property at their expense. Their rights may require that the property owner to obtain three bids and grant them approval rights on which the contractor is awarded the work.

The real estate manager must review the major tenants' leases to ascertain whether they have any of the previously mentioned rights. Leases should be checked in advance, and tenants with such rights should be part of the process from the start. Tenants that negotiate these rights quite often have highly developed construction and maintenance departments that can be helpful in planning and implementing such projects. These companies also have experience with many firms for this service and may be able to suggest effective contractors. When seeking approval for such a large undertaking, be aware of dealing with the home office and not just the local store or office manager. Final approvals should be in writing to protect both parties in the event of a disagreement.

Bid Specifications

Bidding all larger jobs is a good practice. Three bids are usually adequate for most jobs; in some areas, however, obtaining three bids is difficult due to a lack of qualified contractors. The real estate manager should screen the contractors carefully to be sure they can do the job right the first time and get it done on time. A contractor may be quite willing to come back to make repairs and/or corrections, but this results in further disruptions. To receive three qualified bids, seek bids from five or six companies.

The specifications about the work required should be very clear. If the asphalt needs to be repaired before application of the slurry coat, the repairs should be detailed on a plot plan. Is it an overlay of two inches, a removal and replacement of an area 10 feet by six feet, and six inches deep, or a sealing of cracks only? The product to be used for the sealing should be specified, and the real estate manager must be sure the material is environmentally acceptable. Unless the real estate manager is experienced in the sealing of parking lots, on larger jobs, the use of the services of a parking lot consultant to determine the scope of work may be advisable.

The real estate manager should analyze the parking lot to be sealed to determine a feasible schedule for accomplishing the work while minimizing the inconvenience to the tenants. Drive lanes may need an additional coat. Although Sunday may be the least disruptive time for tenants in an office building or industrial property, overtime costs must be considered. In a shopping center, the best time is usually early in the morning on Monday, Tuesday, and Wednesday to avoid disrupting Friday, Saturday, and Sunday, which are generally busy shopping days.

Two coats will take additional days because it is usually best to wait at least 24 hours before applying the second coat. The schedule must include time for the contractor to arrive at the property very early in the morning to rope off the work area so the job can begin promptly. The schedule should be part of the bid package so the contractor understands how the job is to be broken up and can reasonably estimate the impact on the final bid.

If the real estate manager wants a materials test during the sealing, the contract should explicitly state who will perform the test and what alternatives will be followed if the materials do not meet specifications. If the contractor is to re-stripe the parking lot after the seal coat, the real estate manager may specify the type of paint to be used, the scheduling of the striping, and what markings are to be included (e.g., new red curbs, directional arrows, handicapped parking stalls, stop-sign bars). It is expensive to have a striper come back to paint items missed in the original contract.

In some situations, having security guards help direct traffic and keep cars out of the areas scheduled for repair is helpful. The real estate manager can arrange for these guards separately or have the slurry contractor provide them as part of the contract. In either case, they will have to work closely with the contractor so they know what areas are to be kept clear and how to direct the traffic for minimum disruption. Temporary signs along with streamers between cones may be needed to keep vehicle and pedestrian traffic out of specific areas.

In addition to bidding the specific requirements, contractors should be encouraged to offer alternatives and the costs for them. This approach allows the real estate manager to compare the basic bids in terms of price and timing, and it allows for creativity from the contractors. If a contractor comes up with an innovative approach, the real estate manager can always go back to the other contractors and have them amend their bids to consider the new approach.

Once the bidding has been finalized and a contractor has been tentatively selected, check current references to verify that the candidate can do the job and that there are no recurring problems with existing work. Obviously, depending on these factors, the low bidder may not necessarily be the best choice. It is not unusual for small contractors to try to bid larger jobs in order for their company to expand; however, many of these contractors are not equipped to handle larger jobs. These smaller contractors may submit a very low bid in trying to get the job, but if they cannot get the job done, the savings will turn into problems for the real estate manager, the client, and the tenants. This can be a win-win situation for the property owner receiving a favorable bid and the contractors having the opportunity to increase the size of its jobs.

Contract Preparation

The more details the contract includes, the fewer misunderstandings are likely to occur as the job progresses. When a contract is complete in all details, the real estate manager and the contractor generally have already discussed all items and each party understands every aspects of the job. The discussion is as valuable as the final contract. The sample form in Exhibit 16.1 may have to be modified for specific requirements of the property owner, the property or requirements specific to the state, and the property location.

Parties and Scope of Work. The final contract must contain the legal names of both parties of the contract (i.e., property owner and contractor). The scope of the work should be spelled out in detail. The first item is the cleaning of the parking lot prior to laying down the sealer. This is usually the contractor's responsibility and can be started quite early on the first morning of the job. If the contractor is using a machine sweeper, make sure there are no local restrictions on how early a sweeper may operate and relay this information to the contractor. The intent of such a restriction is to prevent loud noises in the neighborhood during specific hours of the night and early morning.

Material Specifications. Continuing with the parking lot example above the specific materials to be used must be spelled out, as well as the method of installation, the thickness of materials desired, and—if a second coat is to be applied—the timing between coats. It is also a good idea to specify minimum and maximum temperatures on the dates of installation because that can have a bearing on the successful application of many seals. In many cases, the contractor's bid has this level of detail and portions of the bid may be used as an exhibit for that purpose.

Commencement and Completion Dates. Commencement and completion dates are critical. The contract must emphasize that tenants are to receive advance notice of the dates which are provided by the real estate manager and that the real estate manager must approve any changes to the schedule. If the contractor's work is extended and proves to be disruptive, a penalty may be imposed. Obviously, situations beyond the control of the contractor are excluded.

Contacts. The contract typically calls for a specific contact person for the real estate management company and the contractor. Problem resolution can become difficult if the real estate manager is trying to deal with the person who submitted the bid, a project coordinator, and/or a job superintendent. One person must be the point of contact on both sides, and having everyone's phone numbers on both sides to facilitate communication is quite helpful. The contract should detail the contract price, along with sub-items and their costs, which makes resolution of future problems easier by providing a value to the various elements of the contract.

Payment. The method of payment should be clearly defined. Jobs that take more than 30 days usually have a progress payment based on work completed. A provision for a retainer is a good idea. A retainer of 10 percent of the contract allows for pickup items and for the expiration of lien rights. The contractor generally wants a provision for interest if payments are delayed beyond the agreed dates. Many real estate managers and property owners require that all contractors, subcontractors, and suppliers sign lien waivers before the property owner makes any payments.

Insurance. The contract should call for the contractor to provide certificates of insurance. Minimum coverage was required $1 million of liability for years and property owners and real estate management companies have increased the limits to $2 million or greater as well as automobile liability. The property ownership and the real estate management company should be named as additional insureds on the policy, and a certificate of insurance should be delivered to the real estate manager's office prior to the commencement of work. This insurance requirement also applies to any subcontractors performing any portion of the work. Certificates should indicate a 30 days' advance notice of cancellation of the insurance for any reason.

Plot Plan. The real estate manager should attach a plot plan of the property showing the areas of work. If work is to be done in sections, the plan should clearly define the boundaries and dates for each section. This plot plan can be used to notify tenants of the work schedule, and it is important that the contractor adhere to it.

Logistics

A slurry coat for a shopping center's parking lot may need to be installed over a two- or three-day period to prevent the closing of the majority of the parking lot while the stores are open for business. Customers need access to the parking lot seven days a week.

The real estate manager must balance the added cost of extending the job over two or three days with the needs of the shoppers and the tenants. The tenants should be notified at least a month in advance of the commencement of the work to avoid conflicts with a tenant's special sale or event, such as a major anniversary sale. When sufficient advance notice is provided, tenants have an opportunity to explain how the timing of the repairs may affect a planned event such as an annual sales and provide the real estate manager and contractor sufficient time to reschedule the work.

For example, a real estate manager in southern California planned two months in advance to have a grocery-anchored shopping center's parking lot sealed and gave the tenants plenty of advance notice. The manager of the supermarket immediately called the real estate manager and informed him the week selected was the week leading up to Easter and that is the second busiest week of the year for the supermarket. The real estate manager overlooked this and because the work was planned well in advanced was easily able to reschedule the work to the following week. There would have been a major conflict if the real estate manager did not notify the tenants well in advance.

Some contractors ask for advance payments, but these should be avoided if possible. If the contractor fails to adhere to the terms of the contract or performs a poor job, withholding payment is the real estate manager's most practical recourse. On the other hand, a real estate manager or property owner should pay bills on time and be reasonable in working with contractors, or getting work performed on the property may become very difficult. If a portion of a job is contested, the relationship with the contractor will be better if the uncontested portion of the contract is paid and only payment for the portion of contract that is in dispute is held back.

The contractor should sign the contract first and the property owner or real estate manager should sign last. The real estate manager does not want to have a signed contract in the hands of a contractor who may become evasive.

Finally, real estate managers should have the work inspected prior to payment to be sure the contractor performed the job in accordance with the agreement. If accounting automatically pays the bills it receives, payment to a contractor can easily occur without satisfactory completion of the work. It is also a good idea to have all contracts in the name of the building owners and not the real estate management company.

Should the property owners default on any payments, the real estate management company could be held liable if the contracts are in the name of the real estate manager or real estate management company. Late payment or no payment could have a negative impact on the real estate management company's credit rating. Often, the real estate manager signs contracts on behalf of the property owners and in the name of the property owners.

Roof Replacement

Replacing the roof is one of the largest jobs on many commercial property especially industrial properties and shopping center. Fortunately, with the exception of some noise and the possible blocking of parking spaces and entrances, it is not very disruptive to the building's occupants if handled properly. Before making the decision to replace an existing roof, the real estate manager should have the roof inspected by a company that has no interest in installing new roofs. While a replacement is the proper solution in many cases, real estate managers should be aware that it may be suggested when there are less costly repairs that will solve the problem.

Roofing Consultants

Many good independent roofing consultants will perform a thorough roof inspection, make specific recommendations to help extend the life of the roof, and provide estimates as to what the work should cost. Their reports are very complete and are accompanied by photographs of the problems to help the real estate manager and the property owner understand the recommendations. Architects are likely to know good consultants in the area, as are other real estate managers.

If the roof must be replaced, the roofing consultant will generally recommend the most suitable roofing for the area and type of building. The consultant must also check city requirements regarding removal of the existing roof before installation of a new one and will generally provide a list of qualified roofing contractors in the area as well as a cost estimate. Some consultants will oversee the job to be sure the roof is installed in accordance with the specifications. The real estate manager should consider having the roof consultant provide suggested routine and preventive maintenance.

Bid Specifications

It is important to have at least three bids. The real estate manager or the consultant should prepare the job specification so each contractor can bid the same work. Each contractor should be invited to provide alternatives and indicate the cost of those alternatives as a separate item. The real estate manager can then evaluate the alternatives, and if they have merit, each contractor should submit amended bids to reflect the resultant changes.

The real estate manager and the consultant should walk the roof with the contractors to discuss problems, methods of moving materials, storing of materials, staging areas, discarding of wastes, cleanup procedures, and the possible need to interrupt any services to the tenants' or the building's operations during the work.

For example, one roofing contractor was scheduled to begin a roof replacement wanted an electrician and plumber handy to disconnect and reconnect the units, along with a crane for removing the air conditioner unit. Fortunately, the terms of the contract clearly stated that he was responsible for all work necessary to install the new roof. This requirement should have been discussed during the negotiating process and in addition to being properly spelled out in the contract.

Contract Preparation

Once the real estate manager and the contractor agree on the scope and the scheduling of the work, the real estate manager should prepare the contract. The following sections outline what should be prepared when drafting the contract.

Parties and Scope of Work. Each party must be clearly identified. The description of the work should be quite clear. The real estate manager must be careful there are no conflicts between the contract prepared by the consultant and the contractor's final bid. There can be a statement outlining if there is a conflict between the contractor's final bid and the contract prepared by the consultant, the later will prevail. If the air conditioners, roof hatches, or other items must be moved or adjusted, the contract should clearly identify the specific items along with the detailed plan. The document should describe the result desired to ensure that no critical step is overlooked.

Commencement and Completion Dates. Starting and expected ending dates are very important. The real estate manager must have time to notify tenants, arrange for any other work that may be necessary in conjunction with this job, and provide support such as scheduling extra trash removal and blocking off parking areas. The completion date should be realistic, and the contract should provide a penalty if the job is not finished on time. If the original contractor fails to perform the work as agreed, the real estate manager should have the right, after proper notice, to bring in another contractor to finish the job and to deduct that cost from the contract price. While this may be the ultimate solution when the contractor is not performing, it should only be a last resort. Bringing in a new contractor always costs more than the original bid and adds considerable time to the job. If such problems are likely, the real estate manager must be sure that progress payments do not get ahead of the work at any time.

Payment. The total price of the job should be indicated on the contract along with any sub-prices. If separate buildings are involved, indicating the price for roofing each building may be helpful. In case of disputes or delays, being able to isolate the problem areas will be an advantage. A performance bond and the expected cost of the bond may be added to the cost of the larger or more complex jobs.

If progress payments are based on a percentage of the job completed, the contract should stipulate some standard for that decision. If payment is for materials delivered, how will that be determined? The project architect or the roofing consultant often makes the determination and approves payments based on his or her estimate of work completed. Some large roofing jobs are subject to testing, and payment is withheld until completion of the tests.

The contractor is typically entitled to interest on delayed payments. The real estate manager, per the contract, may withhold an amount at the end of the job to be sure that materials are paid for and that no liens are likely to be filed. These items are all subject to negotiation. It is recommended that pre payments in full be avoided at all reasonable costs. One loses the leverage of withholding funds to assure the job is performed correctly and on time. However, there are some very specialized jobs that only one or two contractors can perform and some of them demand advance payment with little or no alternatives.

Insurance. The roofing contractor, like all other contractors, must provide evidence of satisfactory liability insurance—usually coverage of at least $2 million—with the property owner and real estate management company named as additional insureds. Thirty days' advance notice of cancellation of the insurance policy is also required for the subcontractors. Many contracts call for arbitration in place of litigation to resolve disputes.

Other Provisions. Other provisions of the agreement should cover trash removal. If the contractor is to provide a dumpster for removal of the old roof, the placement dumpster isn't an important issue.

Work hours may be critical, especially if important meetings take place in an office building. The contract should also address workers' vehicle parking because workers typically park where it is most convenient and may take valuable customer, visitor, or tenant parking.

Materials storage must be discussed and determined. Maintenance or construction staging areas should be established in advance and all other areas of the property should specifically be excluded from use by the contractors. Rear entrances are generally designated for the contractors' use to keep them away from the main entrances where they might inconvenience customers and tenants of the building.

A materials warranty from the manufacturer as well as the written contractor warranty may be attached to the contract. If the real estate manager has any doubt as to the contractor's ability to perform the work, the real estate manager may insist on a performance bond. However, a bond is likely to increase the cost of the job. Choosing a strong, reputable contractor that does not require a bond is preferred. Of course, the best solution is a reputable contractor who obtains a bond.

For jobs that will require a large work force, it is not unusual for the real estate manager to insist that the contractors provide and maintain a portable toilet for the workers. If this is not required, the workers are likely to bother the tenants to use their rest room facilities and that can be disruptive for the tenants.

Heating, Ventilation, and Air-Conditioning (HVAC) Contracts

Everyone tends to take HVAC for granted until it stops operating. It is one of the most expensive and highly developed systems in commercial properties. In office buildings, the real estate manager typically has full control of the HVAC system, and the maintenance contract is relatively straightforward. Industrial buildings and shopping centers require the tenants to maintain or pay the property owner to maintain the HVAC units serving their premises.

Office Building HVAC Contracts

Real estate managers generally bill back the cost of maintaining the HVAC system to the tenants in an office building as a line item expense in the building's operating budget. They also have control of the maintenance contract and servicing of the units. One of the most common types of HVAC in modern office buildings is the central unit, generally located on the roof with individual air handlers in each unit controlled by a thermostat in that unit or zone.

Service Company Requirements. This central plant generally requires a very sophisticated system, and hiring a trained and knowledgeable service company or building engineer to keep it performing to specifications is essential. Prior to selecting the service company, ask established companies in the area to submit a résumé, including buildings serviced, types of units under service, availability of parts, response time, method of communication with their service staff, hourly rates, emergency rates, and after-hours availability.

Once the company has been pre-qualified, ask the company to survey the building; identify the equipment that is to be serviced, provide an evaluation of the condition of the equipment, and estimate the cost of monthly service for a one-year period. The service contract should cover a one-year period with a seven-day cancellation provision. The cancellation provision is rarely used unless there is poor performance by the contractor.

If the survey reveals deferred maintenance, ask for a proposal on a "one-time" basis to bring the equipment up to standard and then to proceed with a service contract. Some new companies are willing to perform the deferred maintenance repairs within the service contract. HVAC systems need regular filter service. If the building is new and still has considerable construction activity or if it is located in an area with a lot of construction, the filters should be checked more often. Clogged filters severely hamper the efficiency of the equipment. Request that the service company provide a written report on the HVAC system after each service.

The real estate manager should know what work was performed and should be aware of any potential problems. If a unit has been causing trouble for several months, the real estate manager should hear about it before it is no longer functioning.

Contract Preparation. The real estate manager may prepare the contract using an in-house form. If the real estate manager does not have an agreement for HVAC service, the service company may prepare the contract. The real estate manager must then carefully review the agreement and, if necessary, negotiate specific provisions. Asking for an "all-inclusive" rate on service and emergency calls is a good practice. A basic hourly rate may not include additional charges such as a truck charge, commuting fee, overhead, and profit. The contract should specify the billing rate. If the contract includes the right to increase the rate during the contract term, the real estate manager should retain the right to cancel at that point by giving 30 days' notice.

An agreement that includes a two-hour response time to any emergency calls can be very difficult to obtain because HVAC calls tend to come on very hot days and the demand for service peaks at that time. However, having such a provision in the contract may give the building a slight advantage in getting the service it needs.

Regular service generally includes the following:

- Cleaning the coils and fan blades
- Tightening all screws and bolts
- Lubricating fan bearings and adjusting damper linkage
- Checking fan motor current and voltage
- Calibrating controls as required
- Checking, adjusting, and cleaning pilot and main burners
- Replacing filters

Additional work may be necessary for specific equipment and should be specified in the contract. Routine repairs are done at the time of service and do not have to be cleared with management.

However, the real estate manager should preapprove and request a bid for the work required for replacement of a compressor, an entire unit, for performance of a major repair or repairs above a specific dollar amount.

When replacing a compressor or discussing a major repair, consider energy efficient units as the replacements. At the time of invoicing, the warranty for the new unit must accompany the billing. These warranties are noted on the master equipment list, and prior to approving any new compressors and/or units, check the list to be sure the unit is not under warranty.

Shopping Center HVAC Contracts

The typical shopping center lease requires that the tenant be responsible for the repair or possibly replacement of the air-conditioning unit serving that tenant's premises. Strip shopping centers typically have rooftop HVAC units. An enclosed mall may have central air-conditioning units, which would be maintained in the same manner as office building units and, thus, would be part of the *common area maintenance (CAM)* charges billed back to the tenants. Many enclosed malls have rooftop units serving each store.

Individual tenant units require further consideration. The real estate manager can handle the maintenance of units in tenant spaces in three ways:

1. Tenant responsible for HVAC
2. Management contracts for the service and bills the cost to then tenants
3. Management contract the service with the contractor's direct billing to the tenants

An advantage to the last two approaches is that only one service person walks the roof while servicing the HVAC units. If each tenant had its own HVAC service contract, several service personnel would walk the roof to service the units. Fewer people on the roof equates to less damage to the roof. One contractor servicing all of the units usually offers a quantity discount.

Like other contractors, the HVAC contractor must have liability insurance, automobile liability, and employee bonds; the property owner and real estate management company must be named as additional insureds on the insurance policies.

Fire Sprinkler System

Municipalities will require the fire systems be inspected and tested periodically, and the frequency may be different among municipalities. This test features a flow test to ascertain that water is in the system and that the alarm will trip when there is evidence of water movement. The inspector verifies that the main valve is locked in the open position and that the water pressure is up to the minimum standard. The inspector visually checks all the heads in the system for leaks and for obstructions such as stored materials or unauthorized construction. The real estate manager should inventory the extra valves at this time to ensure an adequate supply is on hand, and to ensure the wrench used to change the heads is in place.

Remember to notify the fire department and the alarm company when a test is to take place so everyone involved understands that it is not a real alarm. If the system includes an outside bell, any tenants who might hear the bell should be notified.

Alarm System

The alarm company usually monitors the alarm system to verify that everything functions properly. The inspection and service of this equipment generally covers the digital controls, water flow switches, outside stem and yoke tamper switches, and post indicator valve switches. Contracts for alarm equipment are available in two forms.

1. Five-year lease: A common form is a five-year lease that covers both equipment and service. At the end of the five-year period, the lease is generally renewed with a change in pricing structure, depending on the need for new equipment.
2. Service only: The alternative is to pay for the equipment up front and have a separate contract for service only.

The lease-service combination is another approach because it eliminates any capital expense at the outset and allows for more flexibility at the end of the contract—especially if new equipment is needed to update the system.

When negotiating a lease-service contract, the contractor's form is usually used. This has to do with the lease of the equipment, rather than with the service portion of the agreement. This contract needs to be carefully reviewed and, if needed, negotiated.

Parking Lot Sweeping Contract

Nearly every commercial property requires parking lot sweeping. The parking lot is the largest area in a shopping center. Some downtown buildings that are built on the entire lot will not have surface parking. Check with the local municipality for ordinances that prohibit sweeping during specific hours for noise control.

The first service issue to consider is the type of equipment the contractors propose. Will the equipment be a vacuum or brush sweeper? Each type of equipment has its advantages and disadvantages. Another issue is whether a water truck will be needed periodically.

The real estate manager determines the frequency the various areas of the parking lot will be swept. Some shopping centers are swept daily others every few days while some industrial properties may need to be swept only monthly. Additional services to discuss with the contractor are whether the firm will empty the trash receptacles and replace their liners, and clean windowsills, phone booths, and newspaper racks. The landscaper or a contractor who cleans the sidewalks may perform these services. Sometimes it is best to have two contractors provide these services if neither of them is on site daily. If the service is performed late at night or early in the morning, the sweeper may be asked to report vehicles parked overnight. The parking lot sweeper often provides snow removal service and spreads sand and de-icing chemicals on the parking lot during the winter.

In smaller properties, combining services for savings and efficiency is often beneficial. Combining landscaping, sweeping, and general maintenance services often results in a more efficient operation and eliminates problems that often arise among these service providers.

Negotiating Tips Summary

The following lists a summary of important tips to consider in negotiating contracts follows:

- Always provide bidding contractors with a very specific description or specifications of what is to be done. If they want to suggest other methods, have those items quoted separately.
- Include as much in the initial contract as possible because changes are usually much more expensive than comparable items included in the basic proposal.
- Consider buying parts such as ballasts, filters, or bulbs and having them installed. The cost of independently purchasing such items is often considerably less than the contractor's price. On the other hand, a national janitorial contractor might sell such items at wholesale prices.
- Combine contracts when possible. In small projects, having the landscapers sweep the lot, replace damaged signs, and remove graffiti is usually economical.
- Require a 24-hour-a-day, seven-day-a-week emergency number from all contractors. Problems that require immediate response can happen at all hours.
- Where possible, select contractors whose businesses are located close to the properties. This eliminates travel time and allows for quick response in an emergency.
- When negotiating an elevator contract, obtain a light-load credit for low occupancy. For instance, if the building is less than 60-percent occupied, a 15-percent credit may be obtained. The credit is a sliding discount based on occupancy.
- Be on the alert for automatic renewal provisions in contractors' maintenance contracts and negotiate them out.
- Carefully read the hold-harmless provision in a contractor's agreement
- Develop a maintenance contract that protects the

property owner and the real estate management company.

- If the contractor's agreement must be used, remember it is negotiable.

UNIT PRICING

Under a unit-pricing system, a fixed price is obtained from contractors for specific maintenance work for a predetermined period—usually one year. The contractors agree to maintain their prices for the predetermined period, and the real estate manager commits to using the contractors—provided the quality of their service is maintained. Unit prices can be obtained on a variety of work, including cleaning carpets, sweeping parking lots, security, and extra janitorial service. Unit prices are frequently used for *tenant improvement (TI)* work on items such as carpeting, installing light fixtures doors and hardware, electrical and phone outlets, and interior reconstruction, such as removing and installing walls, relights, etc.

When developing an operating budget, or when estimating costs for remodeling or building out office space, base most estimates on the unit prices. Using unit prices saves the time required to bid work for each job when negotiating a lease. Unit pricing is efficient in estimating the cost of small TI jobs and non-complicated larger jobs. Unit pricing is an estimate and it is always best to obtain three bids for the job.

EQUIPMENT CONTROL

Equipment, whether kept on-site or with the roving maintenance personnel, must be accounted for and controlled. The equipment should be inventoried and marked with the company or building name. Equipment assigned to a maintenance person should be signed out. Few situations are more frustrating than having a piece of equipment missing when it is needed—especially in an emergency.

Equipment Maintenance

There are three reasons for developing an equipment maintenance program: (1) safety of the users, (2) assurance of proper equipment operation, and (3) extension of the equipment's life. Manufacturers provide recommended maintenance and cleaning procedures for most equipment.

Fire Extinguisher Inspection

Be aware of local fire requirements and, if possible, walk the property with a fire department representative. A schedule should be prepared showing the type of equipment necessary, required locations for the fire extinguishers, and service frequency. Units should be inspected periodically because extinguishers are sometimes stolen or used and replaced in a discharged mode. Extinguishers can also lose their charge. On larger projects, bid the service and obtain competitive rates. Be sure the units are not serviced too early because that usually sets the next service date early as well.

Fire Sprinkler Inspection

Fire sprinkler systems are one of the most important safety systems in a building, and it is imperative that they be fully functional at all times. Most jurisdictions now require regular periodic inspections, and many require a complete analysis of the entire system periodically .

The system must also be checked between inspections. Vandalism to the system may occur because the risers are often behind buildings in an open area. In addition, valves fail and wires become loose.

Lighting Maintenance Procedure

Lighting maintenance is a critical portion of the overall project maintenance program. Good lighting is a deterrent to crime. Burned-out bulbs give the property a substandard, neglected look.

A complete inventory of all lighting fixtures in the project provides the basis of an effective lighting maintenance program. Besides numbering all fixtures, the inventory should include the type of fixture, mounting, light bulb, and date of ballast replacement. However, frequent changes of bulbs or ballasts in one fixture may indicate an underlying problem that is not readily apparent. A lighting inspection form may be used on a periodic basis to determine lighting conditions. Such a form should allow for quick, accurate notation as to which fixture has problems and what type of bulbs or ballasts the maintenance personnel should take with them. Obtaining the as-built drawings for the lighting system would be ideal. Some real estate managers will use an outside service to inspect the lighting on a monthly basis and replace any bulbs or ballasts as needed. An option is for either the real estate manager or a cooperative tenant to look over the lighting on a regular basis and to make a decision when a light bulb or ballast needs replacement.

Plans Inventory

Organizing all building and property plans before they are needed is an excellent time saver. If possible, a full set of as-built drawings should be maintained in the real estate manager's office on site. Drawings should be numbered and cataloged for easy retrieval. If contractors or maintenance personnel need to remove drawings, it is best to provide a copy rather than to take a chance on the plans being returned incomplete—or not at all.

Because problems are often reported to the real estate management office by phone, it is helpful to keep a plot plan in the office showing roof ladders, sprinkler risers, electrical cabinets, main water meters, and so on. If the items are difficult to find, or if a key is needed to obtain entry, this information should be included.

REPORTING INSURANCE CLAIMS

Accidents and insured losses may occur, and it is important that critical information be sent to the responsible parties in the proper format as quickly as possible. The property owner, in conjunction with the respective insurance carrier, should prepare a claims policy and procedure outlining what is expected in case of injury or property loss and provide it to the real estate manager for guidance. Forms for reporting incidents are generally provided with the policy or the insurance agent may provide them.

If a report comes in from a major tenant on its own insurance form, the procedure usually calls for the form to be attached to the property owner's required form and then processed. This ensures that the property owner and its insurance company will have all the information needed to handle the claim properly.

HAZARDOUS MATERIALS

One important issue that can have a serious impact on all commercial properties is the treatment of hazardous materials. No property is immune.

Asbestos

One well-publicized contaminant is asbestos, which is a concern in all buildings built before 1979. Even those built after 1979 can have problems with hazardous materials caused by specific tenant uses. Industrial buildings and shopping centers are more likely to have problems arising from tenant uses involving hazardous materials, but office buildings can also be affected. Horror stories are told in the industry of asbestos removal costs in the hundreds of thousands of dollars.

Asbestos Basics

Asbestos is a fibrous material that can impart fireproofing characteristics to building materials. Airborne asbestos particles are human health hazards. Asbestos can be found in the following:

- Adhesives
- Asphalt tile cements
- Finishing cement
- Insulation cement
- Joint compound
- Caulking putties
- Plaster and stucco
- Mastic
- Spackle
- Roofing asphalt
- Fire and water sealants
- Sheet goods
- Resilient flooring
- Vinyl/asbestos tile,
- Vinyl wallpaper
- Paints and coatings

Because of the potential risk and attendant costs of asbestos and its removal, most investors conduct an extensive inspection of buildings prior to purchase. Usually, the building is placed under contract subject to a satisfactory inspection. Once the inspection is completed, if the existence of asbestos is confirmed, the buyer must decide how serious the matter is. In some cases, the level of asbestos may be so small and easy to contain that the matter is easily handled. In other cases, however, the levels of asbestos are so high and potentially unsafe and very costly to remove or encapsulate that a sale is lost. Sometimes, the parties reach a compromise in which the buyer may assume responsibility, but the seller makes a financial contribution to the solution. Experts originally thought that removal of asbestos was the best solution, but now they favor encapsulating the materials and leaving them in place when conditions permit this approach. This approach is based on the idea that the less the material is disturbed, the less likely it is to cause a problem for anyone.

Asbestos Discovery. It should be noted that remodeling is the most likely activity that would uncover the existence of asbestos. Spaces in office buildings are continually being remodeled or reconfigured, so asbestos is unlikely to go undetected for long. On the other hand, shopping center spaces may see no construction activity for years, so the discovery of asbestos is less likely .

Other Hazardous Materials

While asbestos has received considerable publicity to date, many other hazardous substances are of concern to building owners. For example, the presence of mold in buildings has led to serious health issues. Any complaints about mold from tenants and/or their employees must be taken seriously and be investigated. If mold is present, it must be removed.

Several former service station sites have been contaminated by leaking underground gasoline containers. In many cases, the property owner is required to dig out all contaminated soil and remove it to a designated dumping site where it is often burned. Uncontaminated soil is then put back in and recomputed. The whole process is time consuming and expensive. There may be other solutions to eliminate the contaminations. The property owner may have a claim against the former tenant who caused the contamination if that tenant is still in business and has resources to cover the claim. Another example is medical waste. Medical waste pickup should be contracted with a firm that is qualified and licensed. More information on bloodborne pathogens and medical waste is explained in *Chapter 5: Managing Medical Office Buildings*.

Hazardous Substance Report

In view of all the potentially hazardous materials and the attending liabilities, buyers of buildings inspect for hazardous materials prior to purchase. Lenders may require this inspection. This allows them to evaluate the building on an overall basis and determine whether individual tenants are contributing to the problems. A hazardous substance report can be used as a point of reference for any future problems regarding hazardous materials.

Sample Environmental Audit

An environmental audit can be a revelation for the property owners of a commercial property. Most major cities have firms that conduct such audits at a moderate cost. In a neighborhood shopping center, for example, potential danger can originate from the following:

- Cleaners
- Photo labs
- Print shops
- Beauty supply shops
- Beauty shops
- Engraving shops
- Hardware stores
- Auto parts stores
- Oil-changing stations
- Paint stores
- Chemical companies
- Computer companies
- Plating companies
- Farm supply stores

Hazardous Materials Lease Provisions

As can be seen, hazardous materials may pose potential problems for the property owners and real estate managers of commercial properties. It is prudent to consider hazardous materials when writing new leases or renewing existing leases. For instance, a provision written in a lease for a strip shopping center protects the property owner against possible lease conflicts when the lease with the tenant would not ordinarily allow a billback. If the issue comes up because of environmental considerations and is mandated by a governmental authority, the shopping center's owner will have the right to pass the cost along to the tenant. The provision also allows items such as new equipment that ordinarily might be classified as a capital improvement to be billed back to the tenant. In addition, such provisions take a proactive approach to compliance by requiring the tenant to sign a specific statement indicating that the tenant has not engaged in any environmentally sensitive activities.

CONSERVATION AND RECYCLING

The impetus for recycling is twofold: (1) the lack of land for landfills and (2) the recognition that the world's natural resources are limited. Municipalities around the country are mandating residential recycling and are taking the initiative by establishing their own goals for recycling. More and more municipalities are requiring commercial buildings to reduce their waste and implement recycling programs.

Additionally, some recycled materials may have value and the sale of these materials may offset all or some of the cost of trash removal. Finally, a building that is involved in conservation and recycling is considered to be a good "citizen" of the community. Some municipalities incorporate a recycling requirement into the building design. The ideal time to develop a recycling program is when the building is designed. This allows for equipment such as compactors as well as storage space to contain recyclable materials, to be designed into the project's space.

Real Estate Management and Recycling

Waste reduction occurs through recycling and more efficient utilization of existing materials and products. Recycling saves valuable landfill space, reduces energy needs to make new products, and saves the world's valuable resources. Many municipalities offer free recycling consultant services and videos. The magnitude of the need to recycle is apparent when we review the amount of waste Americans create. Each American generates about four and one-half pounds of garbage a day, or 1.5 tons of garbage per year.

Real estate managers should be proactive in developing and implementing recycling and other waste reduction programs in each building they manage. In fact, recycling some materials may generate revenue, while having less trash pickup often generates cost savings. A recycling program shows the community and the building's tenants that the building is a responsible member of the community and enhances the building's image. A recycling program should become part of the marketing and leasing program as well as part of the tenant-retention program.

A recycling and waste reduction program starts with a commitment from the real estate manager, who should explain the benefits of the program to the property owner. Then someone is assigned the responsibility of developing and implementing the program. That person solicits the support of the tenants. In a mid- or high-rise office building or in a mall or a large industrial property, this responsibility is often assigned to the building's assistant manager or operations manager. The real manager usually assumes this responsibility on a smaller commercial property.

\Recycling companies are selected to participate in the plan. Waste reduction and recycling potential are assessed. The program is promoted and tenants are educated on their roles and responsibilities. The program must be monitored and the communication process must be maintained with tenants.

The Recycling Process

Recycling is a three-step process. First, materials are collected. Second, the materials must be reprocessed and converted into new products. The third step is to purchase and use of the recycled products. The following discussion outlines the basic steps necessary to develop and implement a successful recycling program for all commercial properties.

Starting a Recycling Program

Starting a recycling program for a commercial property is relatively easy. Many tenants' employees already recycle at home. Most communities have governmental agencies, waste management companies, and nonprofit organizations that provide guidelines on establishing a recycling program, and some organizations will conduct an audit of the building's waste stream. Several contractors participate in recycling programs and are not only eager to participate, but can also assist in setting up the program. Trash removal companies and companies that recycle materials will also assist in establishing a recycling program.

Information Gathering

The first step in starting a recycling program is to gather as much information as possible on recycling. Sources for recycling information are:

1. Contractors, such as janitorial and landscape service companies
2. Vendors, such as trash removal companies and recycling companies
3. Real estate managers of buildings with successful recycling programs
4. Governmental agencies

Many municipalities have waste reduction/recycling programs staffed by consultants or contract with a consulting firm to provide free information to businesses. The public library has a wealth of books and periodicals on recycling. A person in the real estate management company or a member of the on-site management or operation staff of a large commercial building may be assigned the responsibility of developing and implementing the recycling program.

Waste Audit

An audit of the waste generated by the building tenants, visitors, and/or shoppers should be conducted. Many public and private recycling organizations will assist in conducting the audit. The audit will assess the type of waste in the waste stream, establish waste-reduction measures, determine which materials can be recycled, provide a financial analysis of the cost and/or savings associated with recycling, and design a system to collect, store, and pick up or deliver the recyclable materials. The contractors and vendors involved in picking up waste, such as janitors, landscapers, and waste-hauling companies should be invited to participate in developing the program.

Financial Analysis

The financial analysis consists of several factors. Will special equipment be needed? If so, will the building or the janitorial company pay for new janitorial double-barrel carts and recyclable trash receptacles for office tenants? Will the waste disposal company provide new dumpsters at no charge, or is there a monthly rental? Will the building purchase a compactor or recycle-collection receptacle for the common areas?

The price recycling companies will pay for recyclable material is determined by the supply of the material on the market and the capacity of plants to store and recycle the materials. The financial analysis for a recycling program includes the income received for the recyclable material or the cost to have it picked up. Another component of the analysis is the savings from less frequent trash pickup. The savings are often greater than the cost to have the material picked up and the amortized cost of equipment purchased for the recycling program.

Tenant Involvement

Once the program has been designed, tenants must buy into and participate in the program for it to be successful. Tenant promotions, training, and follow-up are key components. Meet with each tenant or have a group meeting of all the tenants. Representatives from the recycling organizations that assisted in selling the program, along with building contractors that will participate in the program, should explain their roles and answer questions.

Each tenant should be asked to appoint a recycling coordinator who will attend a training session. Establish recycling and waste reduction goals and ask each tenant to establish similar goals. A questionnaire should be sent to each tenant assessing its level of interest and its waste stream. The questionnaire should ask the type and amount of paper, glass, metals, and plastic the tenant uses, whether the tenant has a recycling program, and if so, what type of equipment or containers it uses. The questionnaire should ask tenants to provide the name and phone number of the person they select to be their recycling coordinators.

The real estate management company can periodically send e-mails to the tenants reminding them of the recycling program, providing a progress report on their efforts, discussing the cost savings (which will reduce the maintenance pass-through expenses to the tenants), and providing additional recycling tips. Give recognition to tenants that have met their goals by congratulating them in the e-mailed to all the tenants and by placing a sign in the building lobby or entrance.

With the enthusiasm of the real estate manager and the cooperation of the building's tenants, contractors, and vendors, every commercial building can have a successful recycling program.

Recycling in Office Buildings

Office buildings are prime places to implement recycling programs. The waste stream from most office buildings consists primarily of materials that are relatively easy to sort, collect, store, and haul away. Office buildings have a captive audience of participants. The low turnover of tenants and employees provides a stable base for a training program. Many tenants have already instituted recycling programs. Several national firms and governmental agencies have taken the lead in business recycling.

Paper

Recognizing that office buildings generate more paper than any other item in the waste stream, the real estate manager must develop an effective means to sort and collect paper. In 2010, more than 60% of paper was used in the U.S., which was an improvement of almost 90% since 1989 and still discarded well over $2 billion of paper. Just a few years ago, office workers generated about a half pound of recyclable paper every day. A successful paper-recycling program starts at the employee's desk. Each employee should receive two small desktop or desk-side cardboard containers: one for high-grade paper and the other for low-grade paper. The cardboard containers are approximately six by 12 inches and may have a design or custom printing. Larger intermediate containers are placed in convenient locations throughout the office. Employees empty their desktop or desk-side containers into the intermediate containers. The janitorial personnel empty the intermediate containers weekly or on an as-needed basis. A container for non-recyclable trash is also located at each employee's desk.

Since the recycling program will reduce the trash pickup cost and, thus, reduce the maintenance charges to the tenants, the cost of the equipment may be included in the building's maintenance bill-back charges to the tenants.

Other Materials

Other items collected in the recycling program include aluminum cans, phone books, glass, cardboard, newspapers, and toner cartridges. Separate containers for aluminum and glass can be placed in the kitchen or lunchroom. Cardboard can be flattened and stacked for nightly janitorial pickup. Many large office buildings have a compactor dedicated to cardboard in the loading dock area. In many cities, specialized companies collect the copier's toner cartridges for reuse or come to offices to refill the toner cartridges.

Efficient Use of Materials

The second component to reducing the amount of trash in the waste stream is to use materials more efficiently. The real estate manager should provide tenants with the following tips on conserving paper:

1. Print with double-sided copies.
2. Reuse single-sided paper for note pads or drafts.
3. Use white paper because it can be recycled more easily.
4. Reuse file folders.

5. Keep mailing lists up to date.
6. Use e-mail rather than sending multiple copies of memos and letters to co-workers and don't print out e-mails if it can be avoided.

Recycling in Shopping Centers

Unlike office buildings, real estate management is not responsible for collecting the tenant's trash for shopping centers. In addition, the type of recyclable materials generated by retail tenants is different compared to office building tenants.

Waste Stream Audit

As with all property types, the first step in establishing a recycling program for a shopping center is to audit the waste stream the tenants generate. Most tenants typically generate a large volume of cardboard. Mixed paper is often the second-highest volume of waste. Restaurants generate glass, tin, aluminum cans, plastic containers, and food waste in addition to cardboard and mixed paper. The shopping center's common areas generate yard waste and mixed trash shoppers throw in the common area's waste receptacles.

Cardboard

Cardboard recycling is the first issue to resolve. For example, supermarkets or department stores have programs to recycle cardboard. These tenants have a compactor dedicated to cardboard in a storage room, on the loading dock, or behind the store.

The real estate manager has several options for working with shopping center tenants in establishing a cardboard recycling program. If the shopping center can justify the cost of a compactor, the tenants can be encouraged to place their cardboard in the compactor dedicated to cardboard, which would be located in a central place behind the shopping center.

In many areas of the country, a recycling company or the trash-hauling company picks up the cardboard and drops off an empty compactor when picking up a full one. If the shopping center does not have a compactor, the tenants flatten the cardboard boxes and stack them in a large bin. A recycling company or the trash-hauling company removes the bin.

If the tenants are unwilling to have their employees take their cardboard boxes to a central location, establish a program in which the shopping center maintenance staff picks up the cardboard from behind the stores each day and takes it to the central compactor or bin. The expense of having a maintenance person pick up the cardboard is often offset by the savings in less frequent trash pickup.

For example, a successful super regional mall on the West Coast generates more than 225 tons of cardboard annually. The mall has eight central locations where the merchants flatten and stack the cardboard. Limited space in the storage areas does not allow for a compactor in each of the eight collection areas, so maintenance personnel collect the cardboard and take it to a central location where it is compacted. The income received for the cardboard, plus the savings in less frequent trash pickup, exceeds the cost of the maintenance personnel needed to handle the cardboard.

Another savings tip is to rent larger dumpsters because they require less frequent pickup than smaller ones. For instance, an eight-yard dumpster will need to be picked up half as often as a four-yard dumpster. Savings from the less frequent pickup are considerably greater than the increased rental cost of the larger dumpster. In addition, dumpsters and compactors should be monitored and pickup should be requested only when they are filled, rather than on a regular schedule. Some waste pickup services are unable to offer on-call pickup service because all their vehicles are on scheduled routes.

Mixed Paper

Mixed paper can be recycled by placing covered mixed-paper containers in trash receptacle areas and encouraging tenants to separate mixed paper from their garbage. Styrofoam peanuts used for packaging can be collected in large plastic bags and returned to the manufacturers if they are located in the area.

Food Waste

Restaurants generate a considerable volume of glass, tin and aluminum cans, and food waste. Restaurants are able to establish recycling programs for their food waste if the area has a company—often referred to as a rendering company that recycles food waste. Vegetables and fruits can be recycled into compost. Grease, bones, and fat are used for high-protein animal feed. Some food waste recycling companies will only pick up grease. Companies that pick up grease may pay for the grease or pick it up at no charge. If the distance to the restaurant is too great, the restaurant staff may have to take the grease to the rendering company. Several small restaurants and tenants in a food court can use one grease container. When grease containers are used, the areas must be kept clean to keep away insects and rodents and prevent foul odors.

A supermarket's food waste includes off-grade fruits and vegetables as well as excessive foliage and trimmings from the vegetables. A typical supermarket may produce 150 to 200 gallons of produce waste per day. This waste can be placed in a container and recycled into compost or used as farm animal feed. Retail tenants will require additional containers and more frequent pickup of recyclable materials during the holidays and other sales seasons.

Community Recycling Center

Community recycling centers can easily be established in a shopping center. Separate collection bins for glass, newspaper, and aluminum can be placed in a corner of the shopping center. The glass container may have separate compartments for clear, green, and brown glass.

One of the real estate manager's primary concerns is keeping this area clean. The first step is to provide attractive, easily usable containers. Next, the containers must be emptied on a regular schedule with an option for special pickups. The shopping center maintenance personnel, whether on-site personnel or service contractors, must monitor the cleanliness of the area.

Another concern is that people may dump trash such as old mattresses, furniture, and so on beside the collection bin. Most shopping center managers whose shopping centers have community recycling centers do not find this to be a problem.

Shopping centers have an opportunity to generate goodwill in the community by informing the community through press releases of their recycling program. Shopping centers can also conduct recycling fairs in which several public and private recycling organizations disseminate recycling information and pamphlets and answer shoppers' questions.

Landscape and Yard Waste

Some commercial properties also develop landscape or yard waste recycling programs. The primary yard wastes are grass, tree, and bush trimmings. When grass is mowed, it can be mulched and left on the lawn to be recycled back into the lawn in the form of soil additives. This eliminates bagging the clippings and paying hauling charges.

Prior to agreeing to mulch grass clippings, the real estate manager must review the purpose and use of the lawn areas. If the tenants' employees use part of the lawn area as a lunch area or if an area is an important component of the curbside appeal of the building, the entire lawn area may be zoned into sections where grass clippings are mulched and sections where they are bagged and removed from the site. Nursery and landscaping industries are the primary markets for compost. Compost may also be used in land reclamation. Stumps, brush, and tree trimmings can be ground up and used for temporary road base, horse arenas, trail mix, and ground cover.

An alternative is to eliminate lawns completely and replace them drout-resistant plants or with decorative rock. This reduces the amount of labor required to maintain that area, but also cuts down on the water usage for the property. There are several firms that will provide water-reduction equipment for commercial buildings.

Pest Control

Pest control is an important issue in most commercial properties. In a shopping center, the real estate manager takes care of any external extermination and may have a regular pest control service that services the property monthly or quarterly depending on the problems experienced. Tenants have lease provisions that require them to handle any pest control problems within their premises and/or caused by their use.

Office buildings present a different situation. Employees within the units frequently bring in food and/or plants that may attract insects. Tenants are required to monitor and correct any problems created by their use of the premises, but many buildings have an overall pest control service to keep the building insect free. If the building management finds that an individual tenant caused an infestation, that tenant should be billed for the cost of the service.

Recycling and the Lease

Many companies—large and small—are responding to the recycling challenge by establishing recycling goals. The ease with which they can achieve their goals is enhanced if the building has a recycling program. Companies like to be associated with success and a positive image. When a building has a successful recycling program, the tenants share in the success and the positive public relations. A recycling program may reduce the building's operating expenses, thus, reducing the tenants' occupancy costs. A building's recycling program should become part of the marketing and leasing plan.

Existing Lease Provisions

To ensure that all tenants cooperate in a building's recycling program, the tenant's lease should allow the property owner the right to implement a recycling program. Most leases have a compliance with law provision, which requires the tenant to promptly comply with all governmental statutes, ordinances, and rules. The lease's use provision also typically states that the tenant will comply with all governmental statutes, rules, and regulations. The rules and regulations provision may give the property owner the right to enforce a recycling program, and many rules and regulations provisions give the owner the authority to establish rules and regulations.

Even if the lease does not provide for the tenant to participate in recycling programs, most tenants are likely to cooperate if approached in a reasonable fashion and advised as to the benefits to them and to the community.

Energy Savings Programs

Without a doubt, energy is one of the highest operating expenses. Even when the costs are passed along to tenants, they have a negative impact on building operations. If tenant occupancy costs are higher than the competition's, tenants perceive that tenancy in the building is more expensive.

Energy savings programs, especially retrofits, are common in shopping centers. While the owner of the shopping center is often obligated to pay for capital additions, the tenants benefit from the resulting savings. For example, if a shopping center owner decided to retrofit the parking lot lights from standard bulbs to low-pressure sodium bulbs, the cost would be considered a capital expenditure—meaning the property owner would bear the cost of the improvements. However, the savings in electrical usage would be to the benefit of the tenants. Even if this were the case, a building owner might decide to go ahead with such a program to reduce the occupancy costs and improve the efficiency of the property.

Even without a retrofit, an owner can lead the effort to conserve energy by controlling the lighting in the common area, such as hallways and parking lots. There are many energy saving light bulbs and ballasts that can be installed every time a light is replaced. All lighting should be on timers with electronic eyes, so they are not coming off before dusk and/or staying on after sunrise. Public restrooms lights can be fitted with electronic sensors to automatically turn on when the facility is occupied and turn off when the facility is empty.

There are many rebate programs for commercial buildings, and it is worth looking into for the building owners. Many retrofit programs do not appear to be financially attractive considering the cost and the benefits derived; however, once the incentives are applied, the programs make financial sense. There are private companies that will analyze your property and recommend specific rebate programs, but the real estate manager can request the utility companies to conduct an audit of the building and make very specific recommendations.

Major malls and office buildings can benefit from the use of control devices on the air-conditioning that monitor the outside temperature and the demand placed on the units and phase the units in and out depending on those conditions. Small shopping centers without central air-conditioning benefit most from controlling the usage on parking lot lights. Most commonly, this is done by switching to a lower-energy bulb and ballast package, and controlling the timing with both a time clock and an electronic sensor.

Even if tenants have the responsibility for their own electrical and gas meters, advising them to save costs by controlling energy usage is still prudent. Such devices and practices as time clocks on hot water heaters, control devices on air-conditioning and heating, wrapping of hot water heaters, and insulating doors and windows are good measures to help control costs and save energy.

Water is the other major item where conservation should be the guiding principal in its use. The most obvious savings of water in commercial buildings is that of landscape watering. Switching as many plants as possible to native plants will cut down on the need for excessive watering. Replacing sprinkler heads that cover a large area can be replaced with a drip system. Removing lawns and substituting hardscape, can also reduce the use and therefore the cost of watering. There are computer control programs to measure the amount of water in the lawns and plants and when the water levels are adequate, the system turns off the water. When the water content goes below the standards set, the system automatically turns the water back on. Low-flow sink fixtures and fixtures that are operated by hands being placed beneath them and going off when the hands are removed can also save water. Most buildings today have low-flow toilets to preserve water.

CONCLUSION

When the real estate management profession was in its early stages, the real estate manager's responsibilities were limited to rent collection and maintenance. Through the changing needs of ownership, the competitive nature of real estate, and changes in the consumer laws and concerns, the real estate manager's responsibilities have expanded to include many specialties. However, maintenance management will always be one of the most important responsibilities of the real estate manager—especially because maintenance costs are part of the expense side of the NOI equation. An effective and efficient maintenance management program reduces expenses and minimizes increases, thus enhancing the value of the property.

CHAPTER

17

Safety, Security, and Emergency Procedures

Safety and security play important roles in many aspects of operating a property and running a real estate management company. The *executive real estate manager* is responsible for developing a safety program for the real estate management company. The real estate manager is responsible for assessing the security needs of the properties in the management company's portfolio and developing a plan to meet the needs of each property. This chapter discusses safety and security issues that may be overlooked, such as conducting security audits, developing an accident prevention plan, implementing a training program to deal with bloodborne pathogens, and instituting an emergency procedures plan.

CONDUCTING THE SAFETY AND SECURITY AUDIT

In today's complex management environment, real estate managers should conduct safety and security audits on their properties, evaluate the results of those audits, and act upon them as necessary. The safety and security audit covers the common areas of the property and, depending on the type of property and its tenant mix, may deal with the interior of tenant spaces—even though the tenants are responsible for security within their premises.

The following sections provide a broad outline for developing a safety and security inspection checklist tailored to a specific property. A checklist is a valuable instrument to ensure that all areas of the property are covered. It's also helpful to ask employees, tenants, and contractors to contribute information.

Information Sources

Many sources are available to help maintain the safety and security of commercial properties. The real estate manager must become familiar with community resources and develop relationships with individuals who can provide information and assistance.

Community Standards

The community in which the property is located provides many of the initial standards of safety and security in the basic construction of the building. Built-in safety devices such as fire sprinkler systems, fire extinguishers, electrical breakers, dead bolts, and special lighting may be part of the community building requirements for safety and security.

Community Disaster Offices

Most counties and/or cities have disaster offices that provide information on safety and security hazards, such preparing for natural disasters, how to deal with them, how to secure the premises, and continuing normal business after a disaster.

Insurance Companies

Insurance companies have a direct interest in promoting the safety and security of buildings to reduce their exposure and to make the building safer and more secure. Some insurance carriers conduct annual inspections of commercial property as part of their due diligence program. The real estate manager should find out when this inspection is to be conducted and arrange to be present. The real estate manager's presence will be helpful to the inspector, and the real estate manager will gain a better understanding of the insurance carrier's concerns. Tenants are more likely to take recommendations seriously when an outside source such as an insurance company conducts the inspection.

Once the final report arrives at the real estate management office, it should be reviewed with the property owner. The property owner and real estate manager may want to discuss the recommendations with the owner's insurance agent before deciding how to address any recommendations.

Police Department

The local police department can be an important source of help in analyzing a property and suggesting ways to improve the safety and security of the buildings. Typical police department suggestions involve proper lighting, good visibility throughout the property, and proper signage for traffic. Most police departments have brochures on preventing crimes such as break-ins, passing bad checks, theft of goods, and physical harm. In addition, most departments have personnel who will come to tenant meetings to discuss local problems and prevention programs.

The police department can assist in dealing with tenants who may be causing problems that endanger other tenants or customers in the building. A review of the past year's crime reports in the area will provide an indication of the likelihood of such crimes being repeated in the near future.

Fire Department

The fire department may inspect the property and make suggestions for fire safety. Typical fire-related issues include adequacy of exits, storage of flammable materials, proper use of electrical cords, maintenance of sprinkler heads, and provision of required safety devices, such as Ansul Systems for restaurant cooking hoods.

Real Estate Managers

Other real estate managers in the immediate area can be excellent sources of information on safety and security issues. They are usually generous in sharing information. They know the types of crimes, if any, that have occurred and the unique characteristics of the area that require special attention.

A nearby school may require additional attention during the lunch hour or after school hours. A bus stop at the entrance to a property may be a positive factor, but it may also be the source of problems at peak hours. Local gang activity may be apparent in graffiti on the premises. Area real estate managers who live with these situations can provide invaluable information.

Building Occupants

Existing tenants are good sources of information about events that have occurred in and around the property. A real estate manager who communicates with tenants regularly can learn their concerns and the types of incidents that have taken place. While discussing these issues with tenants, enlist their help in reporting future incidents, undesirable people in the building or on the property, or other concerns about the safety and security of the property.

External Common Areas

When inspecting a commercial property, safety and security concerns must be firmly in mind. Areas that only employees and/or contractors visit are equally as important as areas the occupants and invitees of the building see and visit. Rooftops, elevators, and electrical rooms are as important as the main lobby of an office building or the grand entrance of a regional mall.

Driveways

Safety and security begins at the entrance to the commercial property. Tenants, their employees, customers, and purveyors of goods must be able to enter and leave with ease.

Traffic Flow

Are the lanes clearly marked? Are there appropriate stop signs? If two-way traffic is present, do the arrows at appropriate intervals show the direction to the property? Are cross lanes within the property clearly marked so two cars coming at right angles will not collide? Yield signs or stop signs should be considered in these locations. Does vegetation block the driver's line of sight?

Truck Access

Are trucks required to drive through or back up through pedestrian areas on the property? Are the truck-loading ramps well marked? Do the tenants who use truck-loading ramps, as well as maintenance personnel and security personnel, check them from time to time to be sure that they are not being used for skateboarding ramps? Is night lighting sufficient to allow use of the area for legitimate purposes?

Parking Lots

Entrances and exits can be sources of problems and should be carefully inspected. Are entrances and exits clearly marked? Some properties have only one area for the entrance and others for the exit. If they are not properly marked, motorists to the building might face oncoming traffic when entering or leaving the property. Stop signs should be clearly marked and lane dividers clear and easy to see—even in poor weather conditions.

Could grade changes between the commercial property and public streets cause a problem with traffic or pedestrians in the area? Are curbs in good condition and are they well marked? Some areas have curbs at the entrances but have no sidewalks. Does this condition pose potential problems for pedestrians? Low shrubs can often serve as a deterrent to pedestrian traffic and reduce certain problems.

Parking Garages

If the property has a parking garage, is the lighting sufficient? Are the ramps clearly marked? Are pedestrian areas well defined for both the motorist and the pedestrian? Is the access to the elevators and/or exit stairs clearly marked? Do company personnel or the local police occasionally patrol this part of the property?

On particularly dark days, are the lights in the garage turned on? Standing water and/or discarded materials may become trip/fall hazards in an area that has little traffic. Are the garage stairwells checked regularly to ensure they are dry and clean?

Employee Parking Areas

Are employee parking areas well lit? Do maintenance personnel or security patrols check them from time to time? The real estate manager should ask the local police to patrol the area from time to time. Just having a police car drive through the property periodically can help keep out undesirables and make employees, visitors, and customers feel safer when leaving their cars in remote areas of the property.

Driveway and Parking Surfaces

The real estate manager must regularly inspect to ensure the surfaces of the driveways and parking areas are properly maintained.

Bumper Blocks. Some parking lots have bumper blocks. Are bumper blocks in place every lane or two to prevent cars from cutting across lanes of parking and causing an accident? Are they easy to see and in good condition? Some bumper blocks are secured with steel rods; when the concrete of the block breaks, the steel rod sticks out of the ground and can cause a trip/fall accident and/or tire damage to customers' cars. Ensure that the bumper blocks are routinely inspected and repaired to avoid such incidents.

Speed Bumps. Are speed bumps installed on long, open driveways to slow down the speeding motorist? If speed bumps are present, are they easily visible to pedestrians, so that the chance of a trip/fall accident will be reduced?

Potholes/Alligatoring. Are potholes and severe alligatoring repaired immediately to avoid trip/fall accidents? Cracks in the asphalt are difficult to see. Are traffic cones or simple barricades available to mark problem areas until they can be repaired? If these items are not kept on site, all personnel should know where to obtain them on short notice in case of unexpected problems.

Cleanliness. Are the parking lots and driveways cleaned to remove debris that could cause a slip/fall accident? All personnel, including outside contractors, should look for potential trip hazards and remove them or call someone in authority.

Grease Buildup. An area of the parking lot sometimes overlooked is the area in front of most parking spaces. Over time, cars will leak oil, and the buildup can become a slip hazard to someone cutting across the lot. Staff should check these areas from time to time, and if the buildup is excessive, these areas can be steam cleaned when the sidewalks are cleaned.

Different Materials. Any area where concrete and asphalt meet can be a source of trip/fall accidents. A potentially dangerous area is where concrete ramps meet the parking lot surface. Because concrete and asphalt expand and contract at different rates, a large gap between the two (or a substantial differential in grade) is common. These areas should be corrected as soon as they are identified because they can be hazards. Similar areas include concrete bus ramps in asphalt lots, concrete pads for trash trucks, and wheelchair ramps.

Utility Boxes

Utility boxes can become hazards—especially when they have been in the ground for a long time and are no longer at grade. They can be trip hazards when they stick up from the ground or when they slip below grade. Covers should be inspected regularly to ensure they are still safe and do not present potential problems for pedestrians.

Snow Removal

Snow removal and proper maintenance of the property during snowstorms and when snow is on the ground are potential problems for a real estate manager. Properties in areas that experience snowfall need a snow removal policy consistent with the potential for snow buildup for the area.

In many cases, a de-icer is all that is needed. The real estate manager should have outside contractors available to clear snow or assign the task to specific building employees.

Signage

All signs should be in keeping with the design of the property and use the wording designated by the local authorities. Signs should be installed high enough that they are not easy to vandalize but are quite easy to see.

Warning Signs. Most would agree that people should not ride bicycles or skateboard in shopping centers, industrial properties, or office building parking lots, streets, ramps, and so forth. However, many properties are attractive areas for this type of activity. While good signage will not stop everyone and may not be needed on all properties, signs may discourage some undesirable activities. They also give those in authority something to point to when the activity does occur. Tenants are more comfortable with signs in place even though they know the signs will not stop everyone.

Customers-Only Signs. Signs may be needed at each entrance indicating that the property is for the use of customers only, and providing the authority to remove those who loiter on the property. In some areas of the country, having someone removed for vagrancy or loitering can be very difficult. Signs are helpful if the police are asked to come on the property to remove an undesirable person.

Signage Condition. All property signage should be inspected regularly to be sure it is still in place and in good, readable condition. Stop signs are popular items for vandalism and theft. Extra stop signs, skateboarding signs, and customers-only signs may be stocked or obtained from suppliers that can provide them on short notice.

Exterior Lighting

Lighting is an important part of any safety and security plan. Proper lighting can help avoid trip/fall accidents and burglaries.

Lighting Levels. Does the light level in the property meet safety standards? The property architect or electrical contractor can measure the lighting levels to be sure they have not become substandard over years of use. Are sufficient fixtures and wattage available to light areas to make it difficult for burglars to hide? Has the conversion to energy-saving bulbs compromised the lighting levels in the property? Are all of the bulbs in working order? In difficult-to-reach areas, installing long-life bulbs is often prudent to reduce the frequency with which they burn out. Are bulbs in low places protected with covers to prevent damage and/or theft?

Lighting Times. Are the lights on long enough? The generally accepted rule is to turn lights on half an hour before dusk and turn them off half an hour after sunrise. In winter months, when darkness falls early and even some days are dark, the lights should be monitored. A good set of timing devices includes a time clock and an electric eye, with the eye overriding the time clock when lights are needed. In larger properties, do security circuits provide some lighting all night as an alternative to leaving all the lights on?

Preventive Lighting. Additional lighting is especially important near ground obstructions such as changes in grade, planters, and underground utility boxes that may be trip hazards.

Landscaped Areas

Landscaped areas certainly add beauty, appeal, and value to any commercial building. Unfortunately, they can also be sources of safety and security issues.

Clear Path. Do the customer and/or tenant have a clear path from the car to the building entrance? Parking spaces next to planters frequently encourages the customers to step into the dirt in the planter to get to the building entrance. If this is the case, the planter could be modified with a concrete walkway, or stepping stones could be installed in a safe manner to provide the walkway. If the walkway is not desired, the parking space or the planter could be modified so the planter is no longer the clear pathway.

Potential Tree/Bush issues. Are low tree limbs hazards to pedestrians or children on bicycles? Are tree roots sticking up in a walkway or causing sidewalks to rise, thereby causing a trip hazard? Do trees and/or bushes stand in the way of pedestrians or motorists seeing potential obstructions, such as other pedestrians, bicycles, or cars? While lush vegetation can be attractive, shrubbery may also pose potential hazards.

Landscaping as a Security Problem. Is the landscaping so high as to create a security hazard that would allow burglars to hide before carrying out their plans? Large shrubs next to outside windows are excellent cover for a burglar. Large shrubs next to ATM machines or building entrances can also provide cover for a burglar. Most police personnel suggest that shrubs be trimmed back so one can easily see between the buildings and the shrubs. At night that makes it easier for the police to shine a light between the shrubs and the building to detect someone hiding.

Landscaping and Lighting. Is the landscaping so high and dense that the vegetation reduces the lighting? When very high light poles provide the light, a large tree canopy can reduce the lighting levels on the ground. Is ivy growing on the walls and covering the wall-mounted light fixtures, thereby reducing their effectiveness? Wall-mounted fixtures light many walkways, but they can be almost useless if the vegetation is allowed to cover them. Are ground-mounted lights no longer effective due to heavy vegetation growth?

Water Problems

Is water spilling over onto concrete or asphalt and causing a puddle that can be slippery and result in a slip/fall accident? Is water sitting on concrete or asphalt where algae can form and become a slip/fall hazard? Do hose bibs leak a long time causing a buildup of algae on the sidewalk and a potential problem in the future? Are hoses used regularly? Are they laid over active walkways where they can cause trip/fall accidents?

Exterior Fountains. A danger with outside fountains is overspill of the water. Many fountains have a very light water fall that a light wind can easily cause to overspill on the sidewalk and cause a slip/fall hazard. The water pressure and path should be carefully studied to eliminate any overspill. Placing plantings so no over-spray onto the perimeter can occur often eliminates this potential hazard. Even an inside fountain can have an overspill problem if not designed properly or if the water flow is not properly regulated.

Other Trip/Fall Hazards. Sprinkler heads and water spigots can be especially dangerous if not properly placed. If the public cuts through planters on a regular basis, sprinkler heads should be evaluated and possibly moved. Sprinkler heads jutting out from wall surfaces can be hazardous to someone walking close to the building. Flush-mounted spigots may be best for the property.

Sidewalks

People generally expect to have a safe area to walk on and do not pay much attention to sidewalks. That very complacency can lead to accidents. To avoid potential incidents, the real estate manager must pay special attention to the condition of the sidewalks.

Slickness. Old sidewalks may become slick from the traffic passing over them. Walks should be checked for slickness. They may not seem to be problems in dry weather, but when it rains or the walks are washed, they could become very slick. Sandblasting them to remove the slick surface is easy.

Cracking. Many areas of the country have very expansive soils that cause sidewalks to crack. Hairline fractures are generally not a problem; however, in many areas, these cracks open enough for high heels to be caught in them. Changes in grade also may occur. These areas must be treated by filling the cracks, grinding the higher portion of the walk, or replacing the section that is causing the problem.

Wheelchair Ramps. Wheelchair ramps can cause trip-and-fall accidents. These areas must meet local codes. They are generally marked with a surface pattern in the concrete, colored paint, or a combination of the two.

Steps. Irregular steps can cause problems. Having steps marked with some sort of nose material showing the leading edge is a good idea. A brass nose-piece can help identify concrete steps or areas painted to highlight where steps begin and end.

Handrails. Ramps for wheelchair access may need handrails on the outside edge to ensure that no one walks off the edge. Handrails should be mounted on both sides of all staircases. Wide staircases may have one down the middle as well. All handrails should be solid and clearly painted.

Recreational Facilities

The presence of recreational facilities such as children's play areas and bicycle racks can make a commercial building more attractive to tenants and their customers. Without careful planning and maintenance, those same amenities can become sources of liability for the property owner.

Children's Play Areas. Seldom, if ever, do industrial buildings or office buildings have children's play areas, but they are popular in shopping centers—especially in large enclosed malls and lifestyle shopping centers. Play areas should be in an open area of the mall and not in an isolated corner.

The equipment in play areas should be carefully selected and the safety of small children should be kept in mind. Hard surfaces should be softened with carpet or similar materials. Equipment designed for climbing should be carefully evaluated for safety. Building personnel should monitor play areas and immediately evaluate any incidents of injury to see if changes in the equipment or setup should be made. The insurance company is a good source of information on both the original equipment and construction and changes to make the area safer.

Bicycle Racks. Bicycle racks are becoming more popular as more people ride bikes to work and to shop. Most bicycle racks are quite safe and easy to see; however, some very small racks that bolt directly to the concrete can be hazards if installed near or in pedestrian areas. Shopping centers often install racks next to walkway posts where they are not easily seen. While some of the racks are quite safe when empty, once a bicycle is locked into them, it may protrude so far into the pedestrian walkway as to be a hazard. The proper location of these racks is an important factor in their safety. Once properly located, they must be firmly secured. Finally, the placement of the racks should be such that pedestrians are not in frequent contact with people riding bikes and looking for places to park them.

Trash Compactor and Dumpster Areas

Dumpster areas represent a potential hazard in commercial properties. Dumpsters are heavy and most are on wheels. People may go through them for cardboard, cans, bottles, and so forth. Trash compactors pose a different set of problems.

Cleanliness. The areas should be kept clean so there is a minimal chance of a slip/fall accident. Keeping the areas clean also discourages odors, insects, and animals.

Gates. If the area has gates, they should be in good repair.

Fire Sprinklers. If the dumpster area is attached to the building and the building has fire sprinklers, the area above the dumpster may have a sprinkler head. It should be installed high enough so that it will be difficult to vandalize or set off as a prank.

Door. If dumpsters are kept inside, the outside doors should be kept locked to prevent these areas from becoming a hangout for criminals. Keeping the doors closed and locked also prevents animals from entering.

Compactors. The power of a trash compactor is substantial. Most have safety devices and are key operated. The safety plan must include a procedure for ensuring these powerful devices are operated properly and safely.

Outdoor Machines, Equipment, and Decorations

Commercial properties may have a variety of outdoor equipment—from ATM machines to seasonal decorations—that can pose safety and security issues. The real estate manager should include such equipment in the security audit.

ATM Machines. ATM machines may become potential problem areas because criminals know that the users will walk away with cash. The owner of an ATM machine should be held to very strict security measures in its placement and installation. The area should be readily visible from pedestrian and/or traffic areas. The area should be well lit and the light bulbs should be protected. Vegetation that may be nearby should be trimmed back so it will not provide cover for a criminal.

News Racks and Vending Machines. News racks should be firmly bolted to the building or the sidewalk. Large vending machines may need to be bolted to the building so they cannot fall or be pulled over. Do racks and/or machines protrude into pedestrian areas where they may cause problems for the building's tenants or customers? Since children may play on or around these machines, they should be made as childproof as possible.

Roof Ladders. While roof ladders are not major problems in office buildings, they can be in shopping centers and industrial parks. Generally, roof ladders are mounted on the outside of the building. Exterior roof ladders may need to have shields that are high enough that children cannot stand on a shopping cart and get over the shield. The shield should be locked at all times. Keys to the ladders can be provided to the tenants, police, fire departments, and contractors so they have full access.

For office buildings, the roof is often accessed through the top floor. This access should be kept locked at all times to prevent children from entering. Additionally, there generally is equipment on the roof that would be subject to vandalism. To avoid many of these issues, in the design of newer properties, roof ladders can be installed in electrical rooms.

Seasonal Decorations. Seasonal displays such as Christmas and holiday decorations must be carefully considered. The installation requires special care. The location of the decorations should be out of normal paths for customers and employees. They should not obstruct drivers' vision, and they should not provide areas where a burglar can hide. Decorations should be secured well beyond what is expected for normal weather conditions. Safety connections may be necessary. A large holiday decoration bolted to a light pole may need at least two connectors. If that is not possible, one strong connector and a heavy wire loop to hold the decoration to the pole may be needed. The connectors must be checked to ensure they have not become loose.

When seasonal decorations require electrical power, the connections should be carefully installed and checked during the season. Electrical cords must be installed out of the normal pedestrian paths and be well secured. The capacity of the breakers should be checked. Some decorations have circuit breakers built into the systems that give double protection. In areas where children may be able to get close to decorations, every effort must be taken to ensure that there is no danger of shock.

Internal Common Areas

Security and safety concerns do not stop at the front door. Common areas inside commercial buildings also pose significant safety and security issues.

Public Restrooms

Public restrooms are another area of potential concern in a commercial property. In the past, public restrooms were not provided unless essential. Today, some municipalities require them in most buildings open to the public, such as shopping centers and office buildings. Most industrial parks have not been required to provide public restrooms.

Neighborhood and community shopping centers typically do not provide public restrooms, but larger shopping centers and malls do. Most office buildings have restrooms for tenants and their employees. Some office buildings lock the restrooms and provide keys to the tenants and security guards. Others have combination locks on the doors and give the combination to the tenants to minimize the activities of vandals and troublemakers.

Most large buildings, shopping centers, and office buildings have janitorial personnel check all restrooms on a regular schedule to clean, restock, and show a presence to minimize potential problems. The fact that someone appears to be checking restrooms on a regular basis may act as a deterrent to vandals.

Reducing or eliminating the items that can be vandalized also reduces the likelihood of such activity. Restrooms can be made vandal resistant by installing polished stainless steel in place of glass mirrors, eliminating towel racks, and putting in hand dryers built into the wall, and putting trash cans in the walls rather than on the floor. A hard-tile surface makes it very difficult to vandalize the walls and is an attractive finish. Lighting can be set behind unbreakable plastic covers.

All employees of the tenants, employees of the building, and outside contractors should be asked to watch for problems and report them immediately to management. Problems frequently occur at a specific time every day; the person responsible may be caught and stopped if the problem is reported in a timely manner.

Elevators and Escalators

Escalators can be the source of some problems, but not to the same extent as elevators. Typically, problems with escalators arise from improper usage. Baby strollers and shopping carts should not be taken on escalators. No one should be allowed to run on escalators—in any direction.

Elevators can occasionally be a source of problems. Most states require that elevators have an alarm available in case of emergencies; however, most states do not require that the alarm be monitored. If it is not, the result could be that someone stuck in the elevator hits the alarm button but it is ignored. The best system is one that is monitored.

In many cases, the telephone has an automatic dialer that is preset to phone the building office, an answering service, the security guard station, or the elevator service company. The elevator phone can also be a hands-free unit where the button is touched and the communication is two-way without picking up the handset.

Electrical/Telephone Rooms

Most commercial properties have phone or electrical rooms that need reasonable access for service. These rooms should be clean at all times; nothing should be stored in them. Lighting should be checked regularly, and the bulbs should be protected from breakage or theft. Long-life bulbs are a worthwhile investment for these areas.

Electrical cabinets should be kept locked at all times. When work is done on the panels, all doors and interior protective panels should be replaced and the outside doors secured. The doors to the electrical or telephone rooms may need to have protected locks and be kept locked at all times. The best lock for this use is one that cannot be set in the open position. The lock should be self-locking anytime the door is closed.

Automatic Doors and Door Swings

Automatic doors on tenant spaces in shopping centers, office buildings, and medical office buildings (MOBs) can be sources of problems. They should be checked regularly to be sure they have a safety device that requires them to open immediately if they encounter a person or an object as they close. Any door that swings out into pedestrian traffic should have a protective railing to both warn and protect a pedestrian in the event the door opens when pedestrian is next to it. Automatic garage-type loading doors should also have protective devices to stop them if they encounter anything in their path on the way down. Such automatic doors are common in industrial properties and to a lesser extent in shopping centers.

Fire Sprinkler Systems

Many communities require commercial buildings to have a fire sprinkler system that is inspected on a regular basis. Additionally, many communities require the system to be monitored electronically at all times. Even when local codes do not require the monitoring, 24-hour monitoring and regular inspections of the system by qualified experts are good ideas. While most real estate managers would be able to tell if major components of the system were not working, very technical portions of the system require an expert evaluation.

Fire sprinkler systems need to be inspected. Undercanopy heads and dumpster heads can easily become so dirty they might jam if activated by a fire. Birds nesting in the bells or loose wires can disable alarm bells. Some communities require that all sprinkler systems be backed up with extra sprinkler heads and a wrench. It is not unusual for these to be stolen or lost; they should be checked regularly to be sure they are available when they are needed.

Tenants should not block the sprinkler heads with stock or place additional dividers in the space that will prevent the sprinkler head from reaching all areas of the space. In areas where the tenants may be manufacturing an item or performing a service, sprinkler heads often become dirty. They must be cleaned on a regular basis to make sure they will operate properly. Inspections by the fire insurance carrier and/or the fire department are likely to turn up such problems.

Specialized Equipment

Security devices add to the feeling of comfort and safety in most commercial properties today. It is critical that all devices be properly installed and checked on a regular basis to be sure they work. Additionally, if the devices require monitoring, as do some ~~TV~~ cameras, the persons doing the monitoring must be trained and diligent.

Cell Phones. When a building has security or security is required to patrol a large area, a cell phone can be provided to the guard along with a list of all tenants and their suite phone numbers. Cell phones with text-messaging capabilities have been shown to relay text messages at times when the system would not support telephone calls. A system of communications is developed for tenants to contact the security guard and/or security company.

Direct to Police Two-Way Radio. Two-way radios are excellent security tools, but not all police departments allow their use. Real estate managers should ask the police department about the availability of such devices.

Two-Way Radios within the Property Only. Many two-way radios now come with microphones that can be clipped to the clothing, allowing for easy calling and receiving without using both hands. They are particularly useful for maintenance and security personnel who may need their hands free for work.

Monitoring Cameras. The cameras are often mounted in out-of-the-way areas such as garages, corridors, and storage rooms. They can be monitored, and a response system can be established in case a problem is detected. The cameras may also be used to record ongoing activity, as they are in banks and some stores. Some cameras are not monitored and provide a video recording and record of activities in a particular area.

Card-Key Entry Systems. In smaller office buildings, a card-key entry system for after hours is an effective security device. Such systems are relatively inexpensive, and they record all entries with the card number and time of entry. They usually allow tenants to "buzz in" visitors after hours.

Phone Override Systems. In some buildings, management staff have the ability to phone all tenants at one time to notify them of a problem. In a shopping center, the problem may be a shoplifting group or someone trying to pass a bad check. In an office building, the problem could be a suspicious person or a fire in a portion of the building.

Security Logs. Completed by on-site or roving security personnel, security logs are a very important part of the safety and security programs of commercial properties. Security reports should be filed daily. They should include anything that could have an adverse effect on the property: suspicious persons, lights out, unlocked doors, unusual noises, or evidence of late-night activity not consistent with normal building activities. All such information should be reported and then evaluated for patterns and/or solutions, if needed.

Tenant Spaces

Most tenants are responsible for their premises; however, the typical lease allows for reasonable inspections by the management staff.

Insurance Inspections

Some insurance companies conduct annual or periodic inspections that cover a variety of safety issues. Inspectors check to see if fire aisles are kept open and if exit signs are properly installed and have the required lighting. Does each tenant have a fire extinguisher that is current and ready for use? In restaurants, most communities require the use of a fire-retarding system, such as an Ansul System, and evidence of inspections on the required schedule. Extension cords are often overloaded, and may represent trip hazards as well as fire hazards.

Inspectors verify whether the tenant has exterior displays (often in violation of the lease) or signage that may create a hazard in pedestrian areas. In some retail properties, tenants may set cardboard boxes and trash out early in the day, which can become a trip hazard for other tenants or invitees of the building. Inspectors determine if doors are kept open or unlocked during business hours as required.

Building Requirements

As a safety measure, building management may require that coffee pots and/or hot plates be connected to a timing device that automatically turns them off after hours. Coffee pots left on all night have caused fires. Some coffee makers provide for making a cup of coffee one at a time without the need for a pot of hot water on a hot plate.

If a store is a likely target for a break-in because of its particular merchandise, such as computers, electronic equipment, expensive eye glass frames, wigs, or jewelry, management may suggest that the store have a security system that has a loud alarm on-site and is directly connected to a monitoring service. The alarm may be monitored by a security company. The ceilings of these stores require special attention because of possible entry from the roof.

Businesses known to have large amounts of cash, jewelry, or other items that make them targets for theft or burglary may need to take extra precautions. Building management may have them install unbreakable windows and interior alarms, locate guards on the premises, provide a safe and take any other precautions the local police department suggests.

Keys

In retail properties, real estate managers seldom maintain keys to the tenants' premises. Retailers have merchandise valued in the tens to hundreds of thousands of dollars in their premises and if merchandise is missing, management does not want to be one of the parties who has a key to the premises. If an emergency occurs and management needed access to the premises, the door or a window can be broken to gain access to the premises.

In some cases, the police and fire departments require installation of a Knox-Box®—a rapid-entry system that provides non-destructive emergency access to commercial and residential property. In such cases, purchase and install the Knox-Box® but request that the police and fire department make direct contact with each merchant, secure a key, and put it in the Knox-Box®. This procedure ensures that management has not touched the keys and will not be suspect in case of a tenant loss.

Office building managers must retain master keys to all suites for maintenance purposes and for access in case of emergencies. In such cases, only the minimum number of personnel should be issued a "grand master" key that opens all doors in the building. Grand-master keys should be numbered, marked "do not duplicate," and signed for by those who need them. All other keys in the building can be set up for access as needed by the janitorial service, leasing agent, and specific contractors.

Elevator service personnel, for instance, may need access to the front door and the elevator room. A key that would not allow access to the tenant suites can be cut for that purpose. Regardless, all keys should be numbered and signed for, and master keys should be closely guarded. The re-keying of a building can be an expensive undertaking.

Vacant Spaces

When spaces are vacated, they should immediately be cleaned and put into condition to re-lease. This serves two purposes: (1) re-leasing will be easier if the space shows well and (2) maintaining security will be easier if the space is clean.

Old furniture should be removed. If the existing carpet is soiled or worn, it should also be removed. A clean concrete floor is more desirable than worn carpet. Some property owners will have the walls painted. Building supplies should not be stored in the area because that makes showing difficult and makes it easy for someone to hide—especially in a larger space. If such materials must be stored in the space, they can be stacked neatly in a corner.

If heating and/or air conditioning is left on, the space should be checked for leaking condensation or potential hazards from the heating system. If the suite has restroom facilities, staff should check for leaking water because that can easily damage the floors below and can potentially cause electrical shorts. Sometimes workers use the bathroom and they should be check periodically. Windows should always be cleaned.

Management should have vacant spaces checked regularly for unauthorized persons. Homeless persons might use the space for living quarters, or potential burglars might use it to gain access to other portions of the building. If the spaces are kept clean, detecting unusual activity is fairly easy.

For example, a real estate management company assumed the facility management of a very large vacant furniture store which had several "rooms" to display furniture. These are areas for people to hide or set up temporary living quarters. The executive of the real estate management company insisted that when this building was inspected, it was done by two staff members for safety reasons.

Many residential sales firms have developed safety procedures for their sales agent when they show homes. The procedures include that the prospective buyers arrive at the agent's office and the agent copies their drivers' license, informing the office manager where they are taking the prospective buyers (in front of the prospective buyers) and recording a description of the prospects. Real estate management firm should review their safety procedures for their real estate managers.

Contract Services

When hiring contract-security services or building and maintenance contractors, real estate managers must follow the commercial property's rules and procedures.

Contract Security Services

Guards should receive complete, detailed instructions regarding their duties include and perhaps more important—what they do not include. Security guards who are not police officers should not make arrests. If an arrest is necessary, the guard should call the police.

Security services must report to the real estate management company any activity that is a potential danger to people or property. The limits of the responsibilities of security personnel should be carefully explained, and their activities should be monitored regularly to be sure they do not exceed the limits of their contracts. As with all contractors, security firms should carry liability insurance and other appropriate insurance for a security company and should name the building ownership and the real estate management company as additional insureds.

Building and Maintenance Contractors

Outside contractors that work on the property require special attention. A contractor may perform dangerous work. The real estate manager must be aware of the risks and be sure that prudent precautions are taken. Landscapers use mowers and trimmers that can throw rocks; sweepers use large equipment that can cause damage or injury; welders use torches that can start fires; construction workers use high voltage equipment and nail drivers; roofers often use hot tar pots; painters may hang off the sides of buildings on scaffolds, and sign contractors and often use rolling scaffolding. Most outside contractors and their employees drive trucks that pose potential dangers. Each time a construction contract is signed, evaluate what is being done and how it is being done to ensure that potential safety problems are being addressed.

The real estate manager must demand that outside contractors observe building rules, discuss their plans in advance, and take safety precautions. For example, building management may specifically prohibit the following:

- Storing materials in pedestrian lanes or the unauthorized areas in the parking lot
- Draping electrical cords or running them for long distances
- Running hoses long distances and/or over pedestrian areas
- Discarding materials from the roof or from upper floors without property protection

Contractors' trucks should be parked only in authorized locations and every consideration should be given to the tenants, shoppers, and invitees of the property. If workers are using high ladders or scaffolds, the area should be cordoned off to prevent falling objects from injuring anyone.

If major parking lot work takes place while the buildings are open for business, develop the overall plan with the contractors to ensure the tenants, shoppers, and their invitees are affected as little as possible. If the job is complicated, placing a guard on-site to guide the public through the process is well worth the extra cost.

Safety and security are always ongoing concerns. Everyone involved in the property, including employees, contractors, insurance personnel, police, fire personnel, tenants and their employees, and customers should be encouraged to report problems to management. Because many properties are open to the public 24 hours a day, potential safety and security problems can occur at any time.

From a humanitarian viewpoint, real estate managers are concerned with the safety and security of their tenants, employees, and invitees. They are not just concerned with potential financial liability should someone get hurt on the property. Real estate managers must monitor their properties on a continuous basis to provide the levels of safety and security appropriate in today's complex environment.

SECURITY PROGRAM

After assessing the property's security needs, develop a program to meet those needs and implements the program in a cost-effective manner. If the property owner questions the cost of the security program, explain that a good security program is a necessary component to maximize the building's cash flow and value. A building's leasing program will not be effective if the building has actual or perceived security problems. Buildings with security threats will have low rental rates with high vacancy rates.

When a shopping center has security problems, neighborhood residents will shop there only when they have no other choices. Retailers' sales will decline and their ability to pay rent may be in jeopardy. Providing a safe environment is the first priority of a security and safety program.

Security Uniforms

Many real estate managers have preferred the soft look for their building's security guards. The soft look—typically a blazer with contrasting slacks and a tie—conveys a combination of a public relations and a security presence. When a security presence is necessary, the hard look, meaning a police-type uniform, is preferred.

Armed Security Guards

For the most part, buildings generally do not need security guards, but the are necessary for high-rise office buildings and regional and super regional malls, which have security personnel on site. Unarmed security guards are preferred and usually adequate for properties that need on-site security, and most security guards contracted by real estate managers are unarmed. However, the increase in violent crimes has caused real estate managers in high-crime areas to rethink the need to arm some or all of the security guards. If security guards must be armed, check with the property's insurance carrier to be sure the property's policy includes the proper liability coverage.

If armed security guards are necessary, their ability and training must be higher than that of the typical unarmed security guard. Psychological screening and regular re-qualification may be necessary.

The most qualified guards are police officers. A few cities contract police service to the public. The city assigns an off-duty, uniformed police officer with a revolver to the property or event.

In an area that does not have such a program, an off-duty police officer is the next best choice. Some police associations contract for security services and serve as the police officer's employer. If the police association does not serve as the employer, find an employment agency or a contractor to serve as the police officer's employer and to provide workers' compensation insurance in case of an on-the-job injury. Otherwise, the real estate manager may have to place the officer on its payroll. The cost of a police officer is usually double to four times the cost of a proprietary security company's guard.

Security Vehicles

Real estate managers of malls that have large parking lots often use a sports utility vehicle with large tires to place the driver above the other vehicles in the parking lot. The vehicle may have security markings and a light bar.

Security Orders

The real estate manager working with a security company provides security orders detailing regular tasks and instructions for specific incidents to each security guard and for each post. Security orders must be tailored to the building's features, tenant mix, and security needs. The security orders are written. They are distributed to each guard, and a copy stays with the security post.

ACCIDENT PREVENTION PLAN

The purpose of an accident prevention plan is to minimize or eliminate on-the-job accidents. Such accidents can upset employees' lives and lower company morale. Replacing injured employees is costly to the real estate management firm and disrupts the many tasks necessary to effectively operate a real estate management firm or a property.

A serious workplace injury can also result in governmental fines and possible criminal action against the employer. Employees deserve to work in a safe environment. To develop an accident prevention plan, each plan must be tailored to the needs of the place of employment. An accident prevention plan includes a five-step program as follows:

1. Develop a plan
2. Establish a safety committee
3. Prepare an accident prevention plan booklet
4. Conduct ongoing safety meetings
5. Maintain occupational injury and illness records

Developing a Plan

Before an accident prevention plan can be developed, the executives of the company must fully endorse the program and assign responsibilities to individuals to develop the program and serve on the safety committee. The program should be viewed as an opportunity for administrative and management personnel to work together to create a better and safer working environment for everyone.

A committee is generally given responsibility for developing an accident prevention plan for the real estate management firm's corporate office. If a property has only on-site maintenance personnel, the real estate manager for that property develops the plan. When the plan is completed, it is sent to branch offices and properties with on-site offices as a guide for each office to use in developing a plan tailored to its workplace. One person is assigned the responsibility of monitoring the program and ensuring that new employees' orientations, periodic company safety meetings, and safety committee meetings are held.

Forming a Safety Committee

A safety committee with representatives from on-site personnel and the real estate management firm's office(s) is established for all property sites. Its purpose is to aid management in identifying unsafe conditions, suggest corrective measures, and enlist the cooperation of all company personnel. The safety committee should consist of representatives from all departments. For instance, a safety committee for a real estate management firm's corporate office may consist of accounting, administrative, and real estate management personnel.

Some states require that every business have a safety committee and that an equal number of administrative staff and managerial personnel be on the safety committee. Either the executive real estate manager assigns a committee chairperson or the committee selects its leader. The committee should meet periodically to review the results of inspections, review and evaluate employees' suggestions, discuss suggested safety procedures and training programs, monitor the safety program's effectiveness, and promote safety in the workplace. Minutes of each committee's meeting should be taken and maintained in the safety book. Minutes should include the following:

1. Date of the meeting
2. Location of the meeting
3. Meeting attendees
4. Review of the minutes of the prior meeting
5. Discussion of and status of action taken on issues discussed at prior meetings
6. Review of new issues, including employees' suggestions, accident and inspection reports, and proposed training programs
7. Determination of the date, time, and place of the next meeting

Preparing an Employee Accident Prevention Booklet

An employee accident prevention booklet is developed, reviewed by the safety committee, and given to all employees at the first employee safety meeting. New employees should be given a safety orientation when they receive their employee benefits booklets and are introduced to the company.

The accident prevention plan may serve as a frame of reference for developing a plan for a building's on-site office or a real estate management firm's regional office and/or headquarters. Each workplace may have different procedures for evacuation, a wide range of job requirements, and different equipment and hazardous chemicals. Each plan must be tailored to meet the needs of the particular workplace.

The accident prevention plan may include the following:

1. Statement regarding the firm's belief in creating and maintaining a safe environment for all its employees
2. Discussion of the firm's safety orientation program for all new employees
3. Purpose and activities of the Safety and Health Committee
4. Emergency phone numbers
5. Location and content of first-aid kits
6. Procedures for assisting injured people
7. Bloodborne pathogens safety procedures
8. Reporting of accidents to the company
9. Statement of each employee's responsibilities
10. Forms

Conducting Ongoing Safety Meetings

The safety committee can develop a series of employee safety training sessions. The issues discussed at these meetings and the frequency of the training sessions depend upon the needs of the job site. Programs can include safety videos, such as the bloodborne pathogens safety video; speakers on fire protection, first aid, and other safety issues; and a review of good safety practices and procedures. For instance, the employees can be trained on the proper use of the fire extinguishers, informed of the location of the first-aid kits and emergency equipment, taught procedures for responding to a bomb threat, informed of safe ways to pick up heavy objects, or educated as to products in the workplace that contain hazardous chemicals.

Maintaining Occupational Injury and Illness Records

The executive real estate manager should determine which records and reports governmental agencies require on workplace injuries.

PROTECTION AGAINST BLOODBORNE PATHOGENS

Occupational exposure to bloodborne pathogens is becoming a major employee safety issue. *Bloodborne pathogens* are pathogenic microorganisms that are present in human blood and can cause disease in humans. These pathogens include Hepatitis B Virus (HBV) and Human Immunodeficiency Virus (HIV). In the real estate management industry, working in medical office buildings (MOBs) pose the greatest exposure and risk to bloodborne pathogens.

The Occupational Safety and Health Administration (OSHA) published standards to protect all workers who are exposed to potentially infectious body fluids such as blood and saliva. The real estate manager should develop a training program for management, administrative, maintenance, and security personnel to minimize their exposure to bloodborne pathogens.

OSHA has defined occupational exposure as a reasonably anticipated skin, eye, mucous membrane, or parenteral (needlestick) contact with blood or other potentially infectious material that may result from the performance of an employee's duties. An exposure incident is defined as a specific eye, mouth, other mucus membrane, non-intact skin, or parenteral contact with blood or other potentially infectious material that results from the performance of an employee's duties. The term universal precautions refers to a method of infection control that assumes that all human blood and specific bodily fluids may be infected with HBV, HIV, or other bloodborne pathogens and should be treated as potentially infectious.

Occupational Exposure to Bloodborne Pathogens, published by OSHA, provides an overview of OSHA's bloodborne pathogens standard and informs employees and employers how to reduce the risks of occupational exposure to bloodborne pathogens. OSHA's fact sheet, "Bloodborne Pathogen Final Standard, A Summary of Key Provisions" (OSHA 92-46), states that all employees who could be "reasonably anticipated" to be exposed to blood and other potentially infectious materials while performing their jobs are covered by the OSHA regulation.

Real estate managers can develop a bloodborne pathogen training program and procedures. Maintenance personnel—especially janitors and landscape maintenance personnel—may encounter situations where blood has been spilled or needles or other objects that may cause puncture wounds have been discarded in trash receptacles or in landscaped areas. The building's janitorial and landscape contractors, as well as other building contractors, should provide bloodborne pathogen training for their employees. This training is especially important for the management and maintenance staff of medical office buildings (MOBs). These employees may be offered the hepatitis B vaccine.

An exposure control plan assumes that all human and animal blood and bodily fluids are infectious. Management should hold an educational session for all employees that includes an explanation of bloodborne pathogens, how they can be transmitted, and precautions in the workplace. Protective equipment should be made available to employees of the real estate management company.

States often have regulations that are more stringent than federal regulations or that are not addressed by OSHA. Real estate managers should be aware of such laws.

Safety Kits

Several companies have developed kits of equipment to be used when blood or other bodily fluids are spilled. The kits are usually in a red nylon bag and contain the following:

- Box with pop-up lid to form a carrying case
- Absorbent pillows for absorption of large spills
- Absorbent sheets for absorption of small spills
- Boxes of tissues/wipes for cleanup in conjunction with spray disinfectant
- Safety glasses for eye protection from splashes
- Hygienic masks for nose and mouth protection
- Disposable plastic aprons to prevent contamination of clothing
- Latex gloves to protect hands
- Bottle of disinfectant with sprayer and instructions on the bottle for refill using common household bleach
- Twelve feet of yellow caution tape for isolating the spill area
- Sealable plastic bags with "Caution Blood/Body Infectious Waste" or "Biohazard" label for collecting the contaminated pillows, pads, and tissue wipes
- Red disposal bags with an attached twist-tie for closure, identified by the "Biohazard" symbol, for final disposal of all contaminated materials, including the apron, gloves, and hygienic mask
- Antiseptic/germicidal wipes for cleaning hands if hand-washing facilities are not available

The kits include directions for use. Employees should be made aware of where these kits are stored. A pocket-size kit, referred to as a single incident kit, contains supplies for a one-time use and attaches to a person's belt.

Staff Training Program

Bloodborne pathogens training programs vary depending upon the type of property, tenant mix, visitors to the property, and other variables. A training program includes, but is not limited to, the following segments:

1. Introduction: The introduction provides an

overview of the goals and objectives of the training program. The trainer must explain how people can contract HBV and HIV and discuss the importance of universal precautions. The American Medical Association's (AMA) video provides a technical explanation of bloodborne pathogens and ways medical professionals should protect themselves from infection. The video clearly makes people aware of the seriousness of this issue. Companies that provide safety equipment may also provide videos for non-healthcare professionals.

2. **Discussion of the concept of universal precautions:** The training program cannot emphasize enough that the bodily fluids of all persons and animals should be considered to contain potentially infectious agents (germs) and that universal precautions must be practiced. Universal precautions or universal blood and bodily fluid precautions refer to the handling of all types of bodily fluids.
3. **Training session records:** A record of all training sessions must be maintained. The record should include the date of the training, who conducted the training session, the session's agenda, and a list of each person in attendance.
4. **Hepatitis B vaccine:** Employees who have occupational exposure to bloodborne pathogens should be offered the Hepatitis B vaccine.

Universal Precautions

Universal precautions require the use of protective barriers that reduce the risk of exposure of the worker's skin or mucous membranes to potentially infectious materials. Examples of protective barriers include gloves, gowns, masks, and protective eyewear. Gloves may reduce the incidence of contamination of hands, but they cannot prevent penetrating injuries due to needles or other sharp instruments. Masks and protective eyewear or face shields may reduce the incidence of contamination of mucous membranes of the mouth, nose, and eyes.

Universal precautions were originally written for staff in healthcare settings and for public safety workers. The following guidelines focus on maintenance, janitorial, and management staff who may be exposed to contaminated blood and bodily fluids.

General Guidelines

In most commercial settings, few staff members are likely to come into contact with bloodborne pathogens; however, knowledge and practice of universal precautions can be useful to everyone—even in daily living. All employees should receive training in basic universal precautions.

Hand Washing

The single most important way to avoid infection is to wash hands frequently and thoroughly. Employees must wash their hands immediately after contact with blood or other infectious materials (even if gloves were worn), before and after using restroom facilities, after removal of gloves, and/or other protective clothing, and upon leaving the work area when blood or other infectious materials are present.

Use of Gloves

The use of gloves is mandatory when cleaning areas or handling objects contaminated with bodily fluids or other potentially infectious materials. Gloves must be worn when an employee has the potential for direct skin contact with any of the following: blood; infectious materials; mucous membranes; nonintact skin; items or surfaces soiled with blood, bodily fluids, or other infectious materials. If an employee has an open cut or abrasion on the hand, the area should be protected with a bandage underneath the glove.

Disposable gloves such as surgical or examination gloves, either vinyl or latex, must be replaced as soon as practical when contaminated or as soon as feasible if they are torn, punctured, or their ability to serve as a barrier is compromised. Hands must be washed after the gloves are removed. Gloves should be placed in a plastic bag and then in a lined trash can, secured, and disposed of daily.

Utility gloves may be cleaned and disinfected for reuse if they show no signs of deterioration. However, they must be discarded if they are cracked, peeling, torn, or punctured. It may be best just to discard them.

Eating, Drinking, and Hygiene

Staff members must not eat or drink in work areas if any risk of exposure is present. This rule extends to smoking, applying cosmetics, and handling contact lenses.

Clothing

Staff members who are likely to be exposed to bloodborne pathogens should keep a second set of work clothes at the workplace. If an individual's clothing is or may have been contaminated, the person should change clothes and properly dispose of or disinfect the contaminated clothing.

Housekeeping and Maintenance Guidelines

Housekeeping and maintenance workers are most at risk of exposure to bloodborne pathogens. Staff members in those departments need extra training to handle potentially hazardous materials and situations safely.

Refuse Containers

Never reach into a trash receptacle or similar container with unprotected hands. Always wear gloves when removing trash liners or other containers from trash receptacles. If gloves are not available, immediately contact a supervisor.

Broken Glass

Never pick up any broken glassware or metal shavings with your fingers. Sharp edges could easily break the skin, allowing pathogens to enter. Recommended mechanical means of cleanup include the use of a brush and dustpan, shovel, or tongs. If the glass container held any infectious material, then the brush, dustpan, broom, or rag used to clean up the glass must be handled as though it were also contaminated, and it must be thoroughly cleaned and decontaminated before reuse. If it cannot be decontaminated, it must be discarded.

Sharps

If needles and other sharp objects are found, they should never be handled by hand. Never break, bend, or recap used blades or needles. The previously mentioned procedure to remove broken glass should be used to remove sharps.

Spill Cleanup

All equipment and working surfaces must be properly cleaned and disinfected after contact with blood or other potentially infectious materials. Isolate the area where the spill occurred by placing tape around it. Broken glassware that may be contaminated must be removed by mechanical means such as tongs. Chemical germicides and disinfectants must be applied at recommended dilutions to decontaminate all spills of blood and potentially infectious materials. Spills must be cleaned immediately, using the following precautions:

1. Wear gloves when wiping up a spill.
2. Use appropriate disinfectant.
3. Avoid spraying or splashing of blood or bodily fluids.
4. Scatter an absorbent on blood and other bodily fluids that are on the floor or other surface.
5. Collect and place the debris in a plastic bag, and dispose of it properly.

Disinfection of Rugs

Apply a sanitary absorbent agent to the rug, let dry, and vacuum. If necessary, mechanically remove bodily fluid with a dustpan and broom, and then apply rug shampoo (a germicidal detergent) with a brush and revacuum. Rinse the dustpan and broom in disinfectant. If necessary, wash the brush with soap and water. Dispose of nonreusable cleaning equipment as previously noted. The vacuum bag or sweepings should be disposed of in a plastic bag that is labeled for hazardous waste or color coded. The broom and dustpan should be rinsed in a disinfectant or discarded.

Care of Cleaning Equipment

Mops should be soaked in disinfectant after use and rinsed thoroughly or washed in a hot water cycle before rinsing. Disposable cleaning equipment and water should be placed in a toilet or plastic bag as appropriate. Nondisposable cleaning equipment (buckets) should be thoroughly rinsed in the disinfectant, and the disinfectant solution should be promptly discarded. All bins, pails, cans, and similar receptacles that have a reasonable likelihood of becoming contaminated with blood or other potentially infectious materials, and are intended for reuse, must be inspected and decontaminated on a regularly scheduled basis. They are to be cleaned and decontaminated immediately and, if necessary, properly discarded.

Biohazard Symbol

If any container, box, or bag has the biohazard symbol imprinted or attached to it, prevent anyone from handling or coming in contact with the object, and immediately contact the appropriate supervisor. The biohazard symbol is required to be fluorescent orange or orange-red.

Exposure and Contamination Incidents

When an exposure incident occurs, the following steps are recommended for immediate action:

1. Cleanse the areas of exposure to minimize the chance of infection.
2. Prevent people from entering the area by isolating it.
3. Notify appropriate staff about the spill cleanup.
4. Follow spill cleanup protocol and observe universal precautions.
5. Assign someone to monitor the site until cleanup is completed.
6. Notify a supervisor to begin documenting the incident.
7. Seek medical treatment and evaluation for anyone exposed.

Training Resources

The more society becomes aware of the risk of occupational exposure to bloodborne pathogens, the more information becomes available. However, the majority of people—including business leaders—are still unaware of this critical issue.

Many publications and articles regarding bloodborne pathogens have been written for the healthcare profession. Some of these publications and training materials can be adapted for use by commercial real estate managers. See the Appendix for resources for establishing training programs and procedures for dealing with exposure to bodily fluids.

EMERGENCY PROCEDURES

Disasters and emergencies are regular occurrences in our society. The real estate manager should approach the issue of emergencies and disasters not as a matter of whether an incident will occur, but rather when it will happen and what type it will be. Emergency procedures are the process of preparing for, responding to, mitigating, and recovering from an emergency or disaster. This chapter provides information for real estate managers on the development of an emergency procedures plan for a commercial building. These suggestions must be tailored to the specific needs and unique characteristics of each building.

A particularly important step toward assuring the safety and security of the property is to prepare and distribute an emergency procedure and tenant kit to tenants. The tenant kit or manual contains most of the information a new or existing tenant needs regarding the property and includes a section on emergency procedures that advises the tenant about responding to an emergency.

The kit provides emergency phone numbers with direction about whom to call for specific emergencies. Depending on the part of the country in which the property is located, the emergency procedures and tenant kit may provide information on earthquakes, hurricanes, tornadoes, floods, and other disasters. Initial preparation of a tenant kit takes considerable time; however, once it is completed, it is easy to update or modify for another property as necessary.

Developing an Emergency Procedures Plan

An emergency procedures plan provides information for responding to the anticipated emergencies and disasters that might occur at a building. The plan is tailored to the characteristics of the building and the profile of its occupants. The emergency procedures plan provides the names and phone numbers of the staff and tenants as well as those of contractors, specialty contractors, and maintenance firms that may be needed during an emergency or during the restoration after an emergency.

The emergency plan includes a site plan of the property indicating the locations of electrical, gas, and water shutoffs. Depending on the type of property, a site plan or floor plans indicating the name and location of each tenant may be included. A list and location of the on-site equipment is included.

The majority of the emergency plan details specific actions to take for anticipated emergencies and evacuation procedures. The plan also provides advice on how to respond to questions from the media and steps for restoration after the emergency. It includes the names and reporting requirements of the insurance carriers.

Tenants' employees and visitors to the building are the primary concern of the building's management during an emergency. Special consideration must be given to disabled persons who work in the building. The on-site building management office should maintain a list of disabled employees, the nature of their disabilities, and their location in the building. A copy of the list is kept in the front of the emergency plan. This list may need to be given to those responding to an emergency.

Determining Likely Emergencies

Before preparing an emergency procedures plan for a building, the real estate manager determines likely disasters and emergencies for the area. For example, a real estate manager in California will prepare for earthquakes, not tornadoes. However, if a tornado did hit the area, information in the building's emergency procedure plan would provide a frame of reference for responding to it. To determine likely disasters and emergencies, the area and the building must be analyzed.

Area Analysis

First, probable natural disasters are listed. Most people already know if their area is prone to earthquakes, floods, forest fires, hurricanes, tornadoes, or other disasters. The weather bureau can provide further information on the history of any natural disasters in the area.

Next, the sociopolitical climate must be assessed. Is the building in a city with civil unrest, radical groups, or activists prone to picketing and unruly demonstrations? Are bombings a distinct possibility? If so, responding to these disturbances will become a major component in the emergency procedures plan. Even if these events are not anticipated, the plan should have sections on how to respond to them.

The criminal activity in the neighborhood of the building is reviewed. The local police precinct can provide information on specific criminal activities in the area. Local real estate managers usually share their building's experiences.

Building Analysis

The building must be evaluated for potential emergencies. First, is the building a high-profile landmark in the community or neighborhood? Next, the tenant mix is evaluated and the profile of the occupancy of the building is reviewed. Embassies, governmental offices, and international corporations are all possible targets of bomb threats, picketing, or civil disturbance. Children, the elderly, and disabled persons require special consideration in the building's emergency procedures.

The type of building, its tenant profile, and visitors will be major factors in determining how the management team will respond to different emergencies. An office building has a group of people who work in the building daily and can be trained to respond to emergencies. A medical office building is likely to have medical and operating procedures performed daily; it has hundreds of visitors daily who are unfamiliar with the building and may have temporary or permanent disabilities. An enclosed mall has hundreds to thousands of shoppers and temporary store workers with a high turnover should be trained by their employer to respond to emergencies. The tenant kit provided by the real estate management staff will provide the tenants with valuable information for training staff.

A building's height is important in developing evacuation plans. Industrial buildings are typically one-story buildings; shopping centers are usually one story buildings, suburban malls are one to two story buildings, urban malls are typically four to six stories, while office and medical office buildings can be one story to high-rise buildings. A building with one point of access, such as an office building, can have a procedure to check everyone who enters; an enclosed mall has multiple entrances, people carrying packages, and no practical way to restrict access to the property.

The building and its structural features must be considered. Is it a wood frame, concrete tilt-up, or steel building? Does it have a fire sprinkler system? What are its life safety features? Is it a vertical or horizontal building? What size is the building? How many people work and visit there? In the event of a bomb threat, a 50-story office building with 5,000 employees will require a far different response plan than a two-story walk-up office building or a strip shopping center with each space having a front and back door.

The building's location is another factor to consider when developing an emergency procedures plan. Is the building in an area that has adequate police and fire protection? Does the fire department have the equipment and training to respond promptly to any type of emergency? During a major area-wide disaster, such as a major killer earthquake, the police and fire departments may not be able to respond to commercial buildings for several hours or even days. Their first priorities are to respond to hospitals and schools as well as facilities and plants that provide necessary community services. Is the building in a congested downtown area with access to only one side of the building? What are the adjacent buildings? Could they be used as staging areas if the building had to be evacuated? Could the police or fire department use an adjacent building as a command station? What is the building's proximity to police, fire, and medical assistance?

Classifying Emergencies

Disasters or emergencies can be classified as natural or man-made and anticipated or unanticipated. A natural disaster includes hurricanes, tornadoes, floods, earthquakes, tsunamis, or any other disaster caused by nature. The National Weather Bureau is often able to give advance warning for some natural disasters such as hurricanes, tornadoes, and floods, but other catastrophes, such as earthquakes, are not as easily predicted. For example, in 2005, Hurricane Katrina was the eleventh named storm and fifth hurricane of the Atlantic hurricane season. It was the costliest natural disaster, as well as one of the five deadliest hurricanes, in the history of the United States. Today, countries are developing or enhancing their systems to predict such a catastrophe and to warn people of the imminent damage of massive waves and flooding.

Man-made emergencies also come without warning. Arson, vandalism, theft, random shootings, hostage taking, assaults, bomb threats, and medical emergencies all occur without warning. Bombings may be an exception, but information prior to a bombing is often sketchy and unpredictable. Since September 11, 2001 (9/11) terrorist attack on the United States, real estate managers have added terrorism to the man-made emergencies for which they must prepare.

Anticipated disasters or emergencies are those known to occur in an area. The building's emergency procedures plan includes a response to man-made emergencies and natural disasters that are likely to occur. Unanticipated disasters or emergencies are events that no one would imagine would happen. They usually are man-made emergencies, but they can be caused by nature.

The most difficult disaster or emergency to respond to is the unanticipated man-made emergency such as 9/11; yet, the real estate manager and the building staff must be prepared to respond to it. Emergency procedures are developed to address the known disaster; the procedures then provide a basic frame of reference for responding to the unexpected emergency or disaster.

RESPONDING TO SPECIFIC EMERGENCIES

The emergency plan details the steps the building staff must take to respond to particular emergencies. Planning and practice can make a positive difference in many emergencies.

Bomb Threats

The bomb threat is one of the more terrifying emergencies that can confront a building's staff and tenants. A caller reporting a bomb in a building is attempting to (1) warn the occupants of an explosive placed in the building, (2) create an atmosphere of fear and panic, (3) disrupt normal activities.

Seldom is a bomb threat real, yet every threat must be taken as a potential explosion. The real estate manager must assess the situation and determine whether the building should be evacuated. A hasty response may result in greater hazard through panic than the potential danger from a blast. Evacuation for every bomb threat may encourage a deranged person to call in a bomb threat daily. Such a situation will be disruptive to the tenants' businesses, and constant evacuation will not be taken seriously by the employees. Yet, the possible danger to people may require the evacuation when a bomb threat is received.

Preparing for a Bomb Threat

The real estate manager and staff must plan for the potential of a bomb threat, including bombs sent through the mail. Part of the planning should include police presentations on bomb threats. The building's staff and a representative of each tenant should attend these sessions. When a bomb threat is received, the police are immediately called. In most municipalities, the police decide whether to evacuate when a bomb or an object that appears to be a bomb is found. Until the police take charge, the real estate manager is responsible and, using the information available, must make the most prudent decision on whether to evacuate.

Receiving a Bomb Threat

Bomb threats are usually received over the phone; the call is usually placed to the building's management office or to a tenant. The staff member or the tenant should be prepared to gather as much information as possible from (and about) the caller. The call should not be transferred. A pre-arranged signal should be used to notify someone in the office that a bomb threat is being received. The caller must be kept on the line as long as possible.

The person speaking to the caller should stress the importance of saving lives and ask him or her to help. Then, the building representative attempts to gather as much information about the caller and his or her intentions as possible. The person should note the caller's exact words, any background sounds, the caller's voice, any indication of the caller's gender, race, or age, and the time of day the call was received. The caller is asked where the bomb is placed, when it will go off, and why it was placed in the building. It is important to remain calm. The recipient of the call should have a checklist to record the above data for the building manager and the police.

Conducting a Search

After a bomb threat is received, a search is conducted. The real estate manager should consult with the police department on who should conduct the bomb search. If the decision is to have the building staff participate in the search, they should be responsible to search in the common areas. These areas include the grounds around the exterior of the building, the lobby, stairwells, restrooms, halls, and any other areas accessible to visitors or tenants.

If a tenant received the call, the real estate manager joins the tenant's representative in searching the tenant's premises. In a high-rise office building or a regional mall, search areas are assigned to different members of the management and maintenance staff. The search starts at either the top or the bottom of the building and works its way up or down systematically from floor to floor. All personnel should be instructed that if a suspicious device or box is found, it must not be touched or disturbed.

While the building's common areas are inspected, the real estate manager inspects the targeted tenant's premises with a tenant representative who will be able to spot any item that does not belong there. During the search, a staff person or security guard is assigned to prevent anyone from entering the building.

Spotting Mail Bombs

The mail system can be an easy means to deliver a bomb to a building. The real estate management staff and the tenants must be informed on how to spot a potential mail bomb. Possible indications of a suspicious package or letter include excessive postage, handwritten or poorly typed address, misspelled words, strange or no return address, powdery substances on the letter or package, oily stains, excessive weight, lopsided or uneven letter or package, strange orders, and wrong titles or names. The package or letter should not be moved.

Weighing Evacuation

Whether to evacuate a building when a bomb threat is received is one of the most difficult decisions the real estate manager will face. A one- or two-story office building, an industrial park, or a non-enclosed shopping center can be evacuated with less risk of injury than can a multi-story building or an enclosed mall. In some high-rise buildings with thousands of employees, it may be more prudent not to evacuate the entire building every time a bomb threat is received.

If a bomb is found, the police take charge of the building. Evacuation can involve the entire building or one or two floors above and below the bomb, or just the floor where the bomb is planted. A first-aid team may be summoned to the building. Utility services such as gas may need to be shut off in the area where the bomb is located or in the entire building. The maintenance staff as well as the elevator and HVAC contractors should be notified.

Knowing people could be injured in an evacuation, the real estate manager must weigh the decision to evacuate against the possibility that the threat is a nuisance call that could become a daily occurrence. Other factors to consider include the information provided by the caller, the building owner's policy, and the location of the building. Since 9/11, real estate managers are more likely to evacuate when a bomb threat is received.

Earthquakes

Most casualties from an earthquake result from falling objects and debris because the shocks can shake, damage, or demolish buildings. Earthquakes may also trigger landslides, cause fires, and generate high ocean waves called tsunamis. The tsunamis created by the earthquake in December 2004 in Asia caused more damage and deaths than the earthquake.

Earthquakes can occur anywhere in the western hemisphere. Injuries or deaths may be caused by falling objects such as roof parapets, brick from the exterior of buildings, flying glass, overturned furniture, and fallen power lines. Aftershocks are usually smaller than the initial quake, but they may be of sufficient magnitude to cause additional damage.

The building should be inspected for objects that may fall or break off during an earthquake. Cracks in the building should be repaired and decorative features and any object that is suspended by a chain or rope should be secured. Tenants should be informed of potential dangers that could be caused by falling items in their premises. Top-heavy shelves or filing cabinets, light fixtures, and hanging plants should be secured.

During an earthquake, people should remain in the building, move away from the windows, and seek cover under a desk or in a doorway. The elevator should not be used because power may be lost. If outdoors, people should move away from buildings and utility lines.

After an earthquake, the real estate manager should check for injuries, signs of possible structural damage, broken utility lines, and damage to the building. If no injuries or damage occurred, the real estate manager should still visit all tenants to reassure them that everything is under control. Checklists of actions to take to prepare for and respond during an earthquake are available from local and federal governmental agencies.

Fires

A fire safety plan is part of every building's emergency procedures. A fire plan has six parts:

1. Develop a plan.
2. Appoint a fire marshal.
3. Form a fire brigade.
4. Provide fire safety education and training.
5. Stage periodic fire drills and emergency evacuations.
6. Work with local or state fire officials.

The fire plan starts with a walk-through of the building with a representative from the fire department. Next, the staff and tenants must be instructed on fire safety in a commercial building. A fire department spokesperson will usually conduct educational sessions for tenants and staff upon request. Topics include evacuation of a building during a fire, location of the fire pull stations, fire equipment required in each suite, and use of the equipment. Floor wardens receive additional training. Fire departments have educational materials that can be used as references when developing this section of the emergency procedures and as handouts for the tenants.

Elevators

Most people feel helpless when they are trapped in an elevator. Whether a person is claustrophobic or not, being trapped in an elevator is a frightening experience. Emergency procedures should address this situation.

The elevator cab should contain a direct-dial telephone connected to an answering service, the elevator service company, or a 24-hour monitored security station. A button that rings an outside alarm may not be heard in the evenings or on weekends. A telephone allows the representative of the building management to keep in constant communication with people in the elevator to assure them that they are safe and that help is on the way.

It is critical that the building's staff not exceed its knowledge and abilities in attempting to assist someone in a jammed elevator. A sudden movement of the elevator during such an attempt can cause serious injury or death. Unless lives are in immediate danger, passengers should not be removed from the elevator by anyone other than a representative of the elevator service company or the fire department. Elevator service companies will provide elevator safety tips.

Civil Disturbances

Civil disturbances are usually riots that result from a celebration, protest march, or strike. Celebrations after major sporting or social events have turned into riots. The real estate manager must be aware of planned protest marches and strikes and anticipate that some sporting events can turn into riots. The real estate manager can check with the police to obtain the route of planned protesters and strikers.

If the building is on or near the route, precautions should be taken in case the peaceful event turns ugly and a riot breaks out. The history of the group that is marching will be an indicator whether an incident is likely. What is their cause, and how many protesters are anticipated? The police may be able to inform you if outside agitators will try to infiltrate the group protesting and cause property damage and possible assaults.

If an incident is likely, the real estate manager evaluates what procedures can mitigate injury to occupants and damage to the building. Plywood may be needed to cover ground-floor windows and doors. All the exterior doors may need to be locked. The elevators may need to be taken out of service. Security guards or additional security guards may need to be placed inside the building.

During the march, the real estate manager monitors the planned event from the roof of the building, by watching reports on television and/or by communicating with the police. If the building is situated where it provides a view of the march, the real estate manager may offer the roof of the building to the police as an observation post.

Crime in a Building

Robberies, assaults, hostage taking, and other crimes can occur in a commercial building. Any crime must immediately be reported to the police. The action the management staff takes depends upon variables that can and cannot be anticipated. Staff members must use their best judgment to determine the extent of their involvement in the incident, and they must always consider their personal safety.

When a crime is in progress, building management staff may be able to make the perpetrator aware that people are nearby and are attempting to assist the victim. If the assailant is observed, a full description will help the police. During the incident, management staff should keep people away from the scene and prevent others from entering the building. A management staff member waits for the police in the building lobby or entrance to direct and/or take the police to the area of the incident. Depending on the type of incident, occupants may be evacuated from the building, or occupants above the floor of the incident may be evacuated to a higher floor.

After the incident, the victim should be offered first aid. Building management staff should preserve the crime scene for a criminal investigation. To prevent a copycat crime, details of the crime should only be released to the police, building management staff, and building ownership. Management should refer questions from the media to the police; anything management staff might say could impede a criminal investigation.

Terrorism

The FBI defines terrorism as "the unlawful use of force or violence against persons or property to intimidate or coerce a government, the civilian population, or any segment thereof, in furtherance of political or social objectives." The U.S. Department of State defines it as follows: "The term terrorism means the premeditated, politically motivated, violence perpetrated against non-combatant targets by sub-national or clandestine agents usually intended to influence an audience."

Two types of terrorism occur: domestic terrorism and international terrorism. Domestic terrorist groups are on both sides of the political spectrum. Radical animal rights groups, extreme environmental groups, hate groups, and right and left-wing extremist groups have destroyed governmental and private properties to advance their causes and gain publicity. Prior to the events of 9/11, many people did not perceive the actions of these groups as acts of terror. Today, U.S. citizens are aware that the battleground for fighting domestic terrorism is our homeland. The battleground for fighting international terrorism can be anywhere in the world—including our homeland. Radical religious groups have attacked and killed scores of innocent people at social gatherings around the world including Paris, Brussels, and even in the U.S, in San Bernardino, California.

International terrorist groups are foreign based; their activities are carried out throughout the world. The structure of such groups consists of leaders who define policy, establish objectives, and develop the plan of attack; terrorists who carry out the attacks; and supporters who provide funds, safe houses, and other logistics necessary for the terrorists to infiltrate countries and carry out their attacks. Terrorists' tactics include suicide bombing, bombing, hostage taking, kidnapping, murder, assassination, cyber terrorism, as well as biological, chemical, nuclear, and radiological attacks. Freedom in democratic countries gives terrorists the freedom to operate.

After the events of 9/11, the United States Department of Homeland Security established a color-coded threat alert system to advise municipalities, citizens, and businesses of the potential for terrorist incidents. Security procedures are heightened at governmental buildings, airports, and other transportation hubs during higher risk periods.

Unanticipated Emergencies

A real estate manager may have to deal with an unanticipated emergency. Since it is impossible to train people to respond to a specific unknown emergency, this section describes and evaluates actions that can be taken during an unanticipated emergency. Preparation for such an emergency is, however, a part of preparation for an anticipated one; the major difference between the two is that one has a detailed step-by-step response procedure, while the other does not.

During an unanticipated emergency, the real estate manager must rely on the building's emergency procedure plan, an understanding of the building and its environment, and good common sense to respond. The real estate manager must immediately evaluate the situation and, based on knowledge and experience, make instant decisions while events are occurring and the emergency is playing out. Factors to consider include the type and size of the building.

For example, strip shopping centers and high-rise office buildings require different responses. The tenant mix, customers, and visitors are also crucial factors. A mall is likely to have children and elderly, while an industrial park will probably have mostly young and middle-aged adults. The profile of the people at the property during the emergency can affect an evacuation. Other factors that affect the response to an emergency are weather conditions; the availability of public services, such as a sheriff or a volunteer fire department in a rural area; and the presence of on-site management and/or maintenance staff. A scenario for unanticipated emergencies cannot be developed; each requires a unique response. The emergency procedures developed for anticipated emergencies serve as a frame of reference for responding to an unanticipated emergency.

DEVELOPING AND TRAINING THE EMERGENCY TEAM

The on-site management team or, in the case of a commercial building without on-site personnel, the real estate manager and his or her administrative staff in the real estate management company office will respond to an emergency. Additional people outside the real estate management staff may be called, depending on the nature and extent of the emergency. The real estate manager develops and trains the first of the two response teams, which consists of the real estate manager, his or her staff, and the building's staff. The second team consists of any person, company, or governmental agency that has specialized skills needed in an emergency.

Primary Response Team

The number of persons on the primary team—those who respond to every emergency—depends on the size of the building. In a high-rise office building, regional mall, or a large mixed-use development, the team will consist of the management and administrative staff, maintenance personnel, and security personnel. For a small strip shopping center managed from the real estate management company's central office, the team will be the real estate manager and the administrative assistant operating from the firm's central or regional office. No matter the size of the property, all personnel involved in the day-to-day management must be trained to respond to disasters and emergencies.

Although property owners are seldom directly involved in actions taken during most emergencies, they must be considered an integral part of the team. They should be informed as soon as possible of the emergency and the activities of the real estate manager and the emergency teams. If the emergency is prolonged, such as a hostage situation, or requires extensive action or restoration afterwards, the property owner may take an active role in evaluating the situation and making decisions.

Training the Emergency Response Team

All members of the primary emergency team, whether on site or at the real estate management firm's central office, must be trained to respond to an emergency. When a commercial property has no on-site personnel, the real estate manager, support staff, and personnel responsible for the building's maintenance should walk the property to become familiar with the building and the parking lot.

A map indicating the location of shutoff valves, electrical panels, and fire equipment should be prepared. A copy of the map should be posted on site, possibly in a maintenance or storage room, and included in the project data book, which is likely to be in an electronic file. A data book is a listing with the contact information of all the tenant, maintenance contractors, and other firms needed in an emergency, governmental agencies, utilities companies, the property owners, and the real estate management company's staff. It may include site plans and floor plans of the building along with any other information that may be needed in the daily management of the property.

Regardless of the size of the property and its staff, everyone must be trained to carry out his or her assigned responsibility. Training begins by walking the property, reviewing the emergency procedures handbook, and becoming familiar with the use of the building's life safety equipment. In addition, the real estate manager may invite the police and fire departments to meet periodically with the building's staff to review specific emergency roles and to conduct practice drills in the building. The drills can be held in the evening or on weekends and should include the building's entire staff.

Staff members in the real estate management firm's central office need special training for bomb threats, building evacuations, and any other emergencies that may occur when they are not on-site to direct the response. When real estate management staff members are not on-site, they are more dependent on members of the secondary emergency team for assistance. On-site staff at a commercial property can respond to every emergency that occurs during the hours the building is staffed.

Assigning Responsibilities

Each person should be assigned a specific responsibility, depending on the emergency. For example, when the staff of a large, suburban mixed-use development in southern California received a bomb threat, staff members were ready to carry out their assigned responsibilities. When the receptionist for the building's management office received the bomb threat, she asked the caller questions designed to provide information on the whereabouts of the bomb, the motivation for the call, and information about the caller. During the call, the receptionist got the attention of another staff member who notified the real estate manager of the incident and called the police. Each person had an assigned duty. There was no panic, and business resumed when the threat proved false. If the real estate manager had elected to evacuate all or part of the building, additional procedures would have been implemented.

If a bomb threat were called in to a tenant, the tenant would call the police and notify the building's management office. The real estate manager would then go to the premises of the tenant who received the threat and conduct a search of the premises with the tenant, looking for suspicious or unfamiliar objects, such as unfamiliar briefcases or equipment. The day porters and maintenance personnel would search their assigned common areas, the stairwells, restrooms, closets, and exterior of the building. The security guards would prevent anyone from entering the building. Additional security personnel from other buildings in the mixed-use development would be called in to assist in keeping people away from the building. The building engineer would reserve an elevator for possible use by the police and fire departments. The assistant real estate manager would wait for the police and escort officers to the suite where the bomb threat was received. Day porters would serve as runners between personnel, since using a cell phone or walkie-talkie might trigger an explosive. The real estate manager's administrative assistant would document action taken during the incident.

Secondary Response Team

The second emergency response team includes anyone who provides expert support services for the real estate management staff. Heading the list are the police and fire departments, which respond to many emergencies. Utility company representatives, contractors, and even tenants and their employees may be part of the second response team.

Utilities, Services, and Contractors

Representatives of water, electric, and gas companies may be need to shut off or turn on service. The building and real estate management company's insurance agents and attorneys may be called in an emergency.

The building's contractors should be ready to respond to an emergency. The janitorial firm is often called upon to provide cleanup immediately after an emergency. The security company may be asked to provide additional security during and after the emergency. The HVAC and elevator contractors may be needed to shut down, repair, or start up their equipment. Specific maintenance contractors, such as electricians, plumbers, and painters, may be needed to restore the property after the emergency. Other contractors, such as a glass company, a company that removes smoke or other odors, and an equipment rental firm, may be called when an emergency occurs.

The building's contractors must be trained in emergency procedures. These people, especially the janitors and the security guard(s), spend most of their time in the building when the real estate management staff is gone and the building is closed. They need to know how to contact the real estate manager and the building's staff, what to do when an alarm goes off, and how to respond to any emergency. Since there may be a high turnover of janitorial and security personnel, their supervisor must be prepared to train new employees.

The real estate manager develops a list of all companies and utilities that could play supporting roles in an emergency. The list of firms must contain complete phone information—including after-hours numbers, and contact persons. For easy access, this information is kept in the property's project or property data book and in the real estate manager's emergency procedures handbook. Electronic copies of these documents can be accessed from anywhere with a smart phone and electronic tablet.

Tenants and Their Employees

The tenants' employees must be instructed on emergency procedures. Their training starts before the tenant takes occupancy, when the real estate manager meets with each office manager, and reviews the tenants' handbook and emergency procedures. The real estate manager or another staff member should walk the building with the tenants' employees to show them the stairs, the exits, and other basic features. Regular training sessions performed by the tenant must be conducted periodically for new employees. Police and fire department representatives lend credibility to the training sessions and provide valuable information. The size and type of the building and the tenant mix, determine the frequency of the real estate managers lead training.

Depending on the building, the tenants may be included on the emergency team. Mid- and high-rise buildings frequently use tenants' employees as floor captains and in other responsible positions during emergencies. Some municipalities require that every floor of the building above a certain height have a floor captain, an assistant floor captain, a person instructed in first aid, and a person responsible for the disabled on that floor. These team members need additional training; they must be replaced if they move out of the building. In some buildings, finding volunteers for these positions is difficult, and the real estate manager must impress upon the tenants the necessity of having people fill these important emergency roles.

Managers of Adjacent Buildings

Real estate managers in adjacent buildings may coordinate and assist during an emergency. For example, during a building evacuation, the tenants may be moved to an adjacent building's garage, or the adjoining building may be used as a command post or staging area for the police, the fire department, or contractors.

DEVELOPING THE EMERGENCY PROCEDURES MANUAL

The real estate manager must tailor an emergency procedures handbook for the tenants to the building's specific requirements. An emergency procedures handbook for a high-rise building will be more complex than one for a neighborhood shopping center or multi-tenant industrial park. Evacuation is a major concern in a multi-story building, while it is usually a relatively smooth process in a one-story building.

The manual informs tenants of the building management's role in an emergency, how tenants should respond to such situations as fire, bomb threats, earthquakes, etc., and provides emergency phone numbers. The emergency procedures manual can be part of the building's tenant information kit or booklet, or it can be a separate publication. Tenants should be encouraged to keep this booklet in a convenient place known to all employees and to require employees to review the booklet regularly. The manual may be provided electronically to the tenant or in hard and electronic formats.

The following lists some of the topics covered in an emergency procedures manual:

1. Emergency phone numbers
2. What to do if you discover a fire
3. Fire safety
4. What to do if you hear an alarm
5. How to respond to a bomb threat
6. How to respond to specific natural disasters, earthquakes, tornadoes, etc.
7. What to do during a power outage
8. How to respond to medical emergencies
9. How to respond to biochemical attacks
10. What to do during a civil disturbance
11. Evacuation procedures

RESTORATION AFTER AN EMERGENCY

After an emergency, the emergency team's activities shift from responding to the emergency to recovering from it. A restoration plan is an integral part of the emergency procedures. After an emergency, the building needs to be back in operation and the tenants need to be back in business as soon as safety will allow. A responsive restoration program minimizes any damage to the building's reputation in the community.

The real estate manager, a consultant, or the fire department must determine when it will be safe to reenter the building and start the restoration. Restoration can be cleanup, cosmetic improvements, structural repairs, or rebuilding. Temporary repairs are often required to prevent future damage to the building; when the emergency is stabilized, permanent repairs are completed. A restoration program reduces the possibility of further damage to the building and reduces the time tenants' businesses are closed.

Areas that need special attention in the restoration program include utility service, checking for safety hazards, and inspecting the roof and roof drains. Several contractors specializing in restoration should be interviewed and listed in the project data book.

Each should be questioned regarding its area of expertise, size of restoration it can handle, size of contractor's staff, equipment owned or accessible, licenses held, and insurance coverage. Access to the building during restoration should be limited to prevent injury and further damage to the building.

If the tenants' premises are vulnerable to theft after an emergency, a security guard or guards should be hired immediately. No one should be allowed into the building without proper identification, and restricted areas should be clearly defined. When the building is safe to reenter, the tenants should be notified when and how they will have access to their premises.

Reports and Documentation

After an emergency, preparation of several reports may be necessary. These reports must be filed with the appropriate agencies and kept in the real estate management company's office.

If damage occurred to the building, an accurate account of the expenditures is necessary to receive the proper reimbursement on the insurance claim. The real estate manager and controller must develop a separate account to which all expenditures can be charged. The real estate management, operations, and accounting staff must be aware of the special account and code all invoices for the emergency.

All employees should track the time—especially overtime—they spend on the emergency. The property's insurance agent should be requested to instruct the real estate manager on which expenses the insurance carrier will reimburse. When in doubt, an expense should be charged to the emergency, and the insurance carrier will decide if it is a reimbursable expense.

The insurance carrier may require a narrative report on the incident. The company's attorney may advise on the type and extent of these reports. Photos and videos can record the damage and the restoration. Depending on the extent of the damage, the real estate manager, the building's maintenance superintendent or chief engineer, or an outside consultant must assess the damage. Formats for all reports should be determined when the emergency procedures are developed.

Public Relations

The press reports most emergencies. The real estate manager must develop an emergency public relations program to provide accurate and timely information to the press, tenants, and community.

Emergency public relations is that portion of overall crisis and disaster planning that ensures that verbal and nonverbal communications carried out during the life of an incident will aid rather than hinder relief, recovery, and rehabilitation. Emergency public relations concerns the second reality in any emergency: what people think has happened and what people perceive.

Appointing a Spokesperson

The first step in developing the public relations program is to appoint a spokesperson or public relations agency to speak with the media. No one other than the assigned spokesperson should be authorized to provide information on the emergency or the building. All of the employees of the real estate management firm and all of the building's contractors, especially on-site security guards, maintenance, and janitorial personnel, should be informed that they are forbidden to discuss the incident with anyone. The information they provide could be incomplete, inaccurate, or sensitive and could hinder a police or fire department investigation, initiate a lawsuit, or present the building in an unfair unfavorable light. Since it is rare for most people to be approached by the media for their opinions, the temptation to answer a reporter's question can be overwhelming. The company's policy must be continually reinforced with all employees and contractors.

If the real estate manager or another representative of the firm is the designated spokesperson, that person should receive training in working with and speaking to the media. If no one in the firm is qualified to be the designated spokesperson, a public relations firm experienced in crisis public relations can be assigned this responsibility. A public relations firm can also be hired to assist in developing contingent public relations plans for various emergencies.

Releasing Information

The real estate manager and the owner should discuss the real estate manager's role in releasing information. For example, if the emergency, cleanup, or restoration extends several days, will the property owner approve all media releases? A plan for releasing the information must be developed. The police or fire department may establish a command post or insist that only their representatives talk to the media. Such a situation is likely if a hostage is held in a building or if an arson or assault investigation is underway. If the real estate manager or public relations firm is disseminating the information, it is best to provide accurate information as soon as possible.

If not all information is available, the message should be, "We don't have all the information to comment on that question, but we are investigating and will release the information as soon as possible." The spokesperson should cooperate with the media and with all police or fire department investigations. A story will be written or broadcast about the emergency whether the spokesperson is cooperative or not.

Information unnecessarily concealed will prompt future media investigation and lead to distrust by the media and the community. Some media questions may need to be referred to a spokesperson for the police or fire department. When information is released, the positive action should also be included in the release. Phrases such as "quick response by the fire department" or "professionally handled by the police" develop trust in the action taken.

Informing Tenants

Tenants need to be informed after a crisis. One or several spokespersons should contact the tenants as soon as possible to explain what happened and what action the building manager is taking. If an earthquake occurs that causes no damage, the building's manager should visit each tenant and explain that. If the emergency damaged the building or required the closing of the building, the tenants should be informed of the action taken by building management and, if known, when the building will be ready for occupancy. If tenants must retrieve materials from their suites or stores, the real estate manager should have them escorted into the building when it is safe.

SECTION

V

Commercial Property Development

CHAPTER 18

The Commercial Real Estate Development Process

Simply put, developers are visionaries and also risk takers. Where others see a vacant lot or dilapidated eyesore of a building, developers envision a new or rehabbed building generating revenue and serving as an asset to the community. Developers are the engine of commercial real estate and one of the leading forces in stimulating local economies. They are a special breed of professionals who are willing to assume enormous risks for the potential to earn tremendous profits by developing a speculative building. Developing a building is a complicated, time-consuming, but also risky adventure.

The profession is a high-risk and high-reward business. The rewards, aside from being purely financial, are unequaled by any other profession in the real estate industry. There are other benefits to developing a project which include the feeling of personal accomplishment, recognition in the community and the real estate industry, and the satisfaction of creating a building in the community that enhances commerce and provides housing for hundreds of families and individuals.

Because the developer often personally guarantees the construction loan to build the project, it comes with many risks. If the development is initially successful or is successful over time, the developer is handsomely rewarded. If the development is significantly over budget, has long construction delays, or the lease up is well below projections, the project will not come close to achieving its *pro forma* and the developer will most likely need to make cash contributions to keep the project's loan current. If the cash drain continues for a long time or is beyond the developer's financial capabilities, the developer is likely to lose the property to foreclosure or deed in lieu of foreclosure. If the developer personally guaranteed the loan, the lender may go after the developer's other assets. Few people are willing to take such risks for the rewards of developing a property. Yet, successful developers are continually taking these risks.

Real estate development activity affects all real estate disciplines. A land broker represents the developer in the acquisition of a site for development; an architect designs the building; a mortgage broker provides financing for the project; a general contractor, along with dozens of subcontractors, constructs the building; a leasing agent markets and leases the building; an investment broker sells the building; an asset manager represents the investor who purchases the building; and a real estate manager manages the building through several real estate cycles and different ownerships. When developers are active, all segments of the commercial real estate industry are active and the industry prospers. When development activities come to a halt, usually due to over-building, a recession, or high interest rates, the commercial real estate industry experiences a mild or severe recession.

INCENTIVES AND RISKS

Though development can be very financially rewarding and provide industry and community recognition, few people have the constitution to take the big risks necessary to develop a building.

Incentives

The primary incentive for any business is to generate income and earn a profit. A successful development can generate enormous profits, and it can generate several income components for the developer. The largest income opportunity is the profit from the sale of the property. The next largest initial income source is the development fee. Developers can also earn leasing, management, construction project management, and financing fees for the ownership group fees. When the developer holds the property for an investment, a successful property will generate monthly cash flow for the developer.

Sale of Property

The largest portion of the profits comes from the sale of the property. Many developers are merchant builders who develop a property with the intent to pre-sell the building or to sell the building soon after it is completed. Other developers intend to retain ownership of the building to realize increased building value from rental increases. They also anticipate regular cash flow from the building. Many developers would like to retain ownership of every property they develop. However, the high front-end cost associated with the long lead-time necessary to start a development—and the carry cost of developments that do not achieve their projections—often forces developers to sell some of their buildings to replenish cash reserves, to fund company operations, or provide capital for more projects.

Development Fee

The developer's development fee is either a percentage of the hard costs (brick and mortar costs) or a percentage of the total development costs (soft and hard costs) of the project. If the hard or soft costs are in excess of a predetermined amount, the development fee may be based on a lower percentage of the cost. The development fee is an expense of the project's pro forma.

The developer usually draws a monthly development fee from the construction loan. If the project requires the developer to front considerable moneys before construction commences and funding begins, the developer may request a fourth to a half of the development fee—plus reimbursement of the funds advanced to create the development opportunity to be paid from the first construction loan draw. The developer's rationale is that the development company's staff spent a year, or much longer, creating the development opportunity and this expense is a major portion of the entire cost to create and develop the building.

Ideally, the development fee will cover the developer's entire overhead and allow for a profit. When a developer has several projects under construction, the company usually has excellent cash flow. When there is no construction, the development company's overhead is paid from other income sources, such as a line of credit from a bank; infusion of capital from the owners; cash flow from completed and retained developments; property management or leasing fees and consulting; cash reserves, infusion of cash from the partners; or the company simply goes out of business.

A four percent development fee on an office building based on hard costs of $30 million is $1.2 million. It is easy to see how such substantial fees can enable a developer with multiple projects in various stages of construction to generate large profits. Of course, the number of projects that must be under construction to cover the company's overhead is related to the cost and size of the projects, and the size and operating expenses of the company.

Fee Development Activities

Developers can also earn income by offering their services as fee developers. An owner of a parcel of land may want to develop a building on a site but lacks the experience and expertise. A developer may offer the expertise of its company, for a fee, to be responsible for the entire development process. The developer has no ownership interest in the project, takes no development risk, and receives a fee equal to a percentage of the project's hard costs as compensation. Fee development activities provide a source of income for developers when speculative development activity is slow or supplements their income during strong markets.

Another opportunity to serve as a fee developer exists when a large user owns a site and wants to develop a building for their business. The owner may hire a developer to complete one, several, or all of the phases of the project, such as obtaining the proper zoning, completing all the entitlement processes, supervising the construction of the building, or coordinating the entire development process. The retailer, such as a supermarket, may have excessive land on the site that it will sell to the developer to construct shop and pad buildings.

A lender who foreclosed on a property that is not complete or needs renovation may hire a developer to complete the project to add value to the building before the lender sells it. The lender often contracts with a developer with whom it has a banking or working relationship. The developer is responsible for the entire development process and reports to the lender.

Although the previously mentioned fee development activities do not provide the large profit opportunities that the speculative development does, they have limited risks and can provide an income stream during both a critical time for the development company and during good markets.

Leasing Fees

Developers who have an in-house leasing team or negotiate all, or the major tenant leases, earn substantial leasing fees. A 50,000-square-foot office building with annual rents at $50 per square foot for five years with a 5% commission schedule would generate commission income of $625,000. If this building were 500,000 square feet, the commission income over five years would be $6,250,000. The developer would have the cost of its leasing team covered and some leases would also be co-brokered. The commission for co-brokered leases is shared with other brokerage firms involved in the transaction. After deducting these costs, the developer would earn a nice profit from in-house leasing.

Another approach to leasing is for the developer to negotiate only the anchor tenants' leases. Since anchor tenants drive most development, the developer usually negotiates the leases for the anchor retail tenants before completing the shopping center design. Developers can generate a rapport with anchor retail tenants because they usually have several of them in their shopping centers. It is more difficult for developers of office buildings and industrial to develop a rapport with the tenants who take large amounts of spaces in these buildings because they typically have just one office in the area.

When a developer leases to anchor tenants, they can earn a substantial commission paid from the loan to develop the project. For instance, if a shopping center has 125,000 square feet of *gross leasable area (GLA)* with a 50,000-square-foot supermarket, a 17,500-square-foot super drug store, and the commission for anchor tenants is $5.00 per square foot, the total commissions for negotiating the two anchor leases would be $337,500. A brokerage firm may be hired to lease the 57,500 remaining square feet of small shop space and pad or out-parcel buildings.

Real Estate Management Fees

Real Estate management fees earned by developers that manage their properties are another source of income. Where management activities are a separate profit center, the developer's real estate management company or division pays a portion of the developer's office rent, the receptionist's salary, and other joint expenses. Though the profits from the real estate management department seldom, if ever, cover the developer's operating expenses, they can cover part of its overhead and are a good source of income during periods when development activities are slow or nonexistent.

Asset Management Fees

A developer may provide asset management services for one of its development that has partners. The developer must report to the partners and possibly provide additional financial reports and other requirements.

Fees are required to cover the developer's overhead and generate a profit for the development company

Equity

Usually the primary reason a developer builds a project is to retain ownership and earn cash flow and the value enhancement of the property over time. The developer may retain ownership of the project for decades or years after the project is completed, sell the project, and harvest the increase in equity that has been created in the project. Seldom can a developer finance 100 percent of the cost to develop a project.

The developer needs to raise equity equal to the difference between the cost of the project and the amount a lender or alternative capital sources are willing to finance the development. The developer may also use its own funds as the equity portion of the development and finance the remaining development costs. A developer may seek equity partners to either contribute towards the needed cash equity and receive a percent ownership of the development or *sweat equity*—when the developer earns a percentage ownership for finding the opportunity, entitling the project with the municipality, and receives a percent ownership for creating the development opportunity.

The development fee covers the development cost or sweat equity in recognition of the value that is created. Investors will contribute all or a majority of the equity needed. The developer receives an ownership interest in the development without contributing to the needed equity. If the developer contributes equity, its share of the ownership will be larger than it's pro rata share of contributed capital. For instance, the developer may contribute 10 percent equity and receive 20 percent ownership of the project. The developer may contribute no equity and receive a negotiated share of the equity and the investors contribute 100 percent of the equity. The sweat equity may be a percentage of the cash flow after the partners who contributed the equity receive a specific return on their equity such as eight percent or 10 percent.

Cash Flow

Many developers will retain ownership of some or all of the properties they develop. Over time, the cash flow from the operations of these properties can be substantial. In addition, the developer may earn real estate management, refinancing, and leasing fees.

DEVELOPMENT RISK

The developer faces many kinds of risks before, during, and after the project is developed. The greatest risk is the *recourse loan*—a loan the developer personally guarantees. If the income from the property is insufficient to pay the mortgage, the developer must make up the difference or the lender can foreclose on the property. If the foreclosure sale price is below the loan balance, the lender can seek a deficiency judgment against the person or persons who guaranteed the loan. Often, a developer will personally guarantee the construction loan and not the permanent loan on the building.

The developer also faces the possibility that excessive construction cost will exceed the amount of the loan or change the *loan-to-value (LTV) ratio*. In such a case, additional capital must be raised from the developer and/or its partners or from outside sources—and that may reduce the developer's ownership interest in the property. Another risk is that income from the property will be insufficient to pay all of project's costs and later the building's expenses, requiring the developer to personally fund the deficit. A developer may incur more than $100,000 in staff time and out-of-pocket expenses pursuing a development opportunity. If the opportunity does not come to, the developer loses the out-of-pocket costs and paid staff to work on a project that never got developed.

One of the big risks is the possibility that the real estate market will turn from good to depressed by the time the building is completed and ready for occupancy. This occurred for many developers just before and during the *Great Recession* through 2013. A medium-size office building or multi-anchored shopping center typically takes three to five years from conception to initial occupancy. Some regional malls take 10 or more years from conception to grand opening. Delays can adversely affect the leasing of the building. The entitlement process, possible community opposition to the development, time the developer needs to raise the project equity, financing market, possible pre-leasing requirements of the lender, availability of contractors, and weather could affect the time required to develop a project. Delays in starting construction—possibly due to contaminated soil or wetlands issues—increase the carrying cost of the land and delay the fees from the development that are necessary to pay the development company's overhead. During delays, the real estate market can change from strong to weak.

A change in the interest rate is likely to impact the building's permanent financing. For example, in the mid 1980s, a developer assembled land for a mall in an oil-patch state when the market was strong, but a few months after construction commenced, the price of oil plummeted, and the leasing activity came to a halt. The mall opened a year later with few tenants. The developer does not have control over the entire development process and all the forces that can affect the development. External forces can have a beneficial impact or bring dire consequences to a project.

TYPES OF DEVELOPMENT PROJECTS

By monitoring and responding to economic and real estate trends, the developer can identify likely opportunities. With the trends in urban living, developers began building more high-rise apartments and condominiums with ground-floor retail space. Mixed-use developments became more popular with residential and office uses over ground floor retail. Almost every suburban city wanted a town center and all cities wanted to enhance their street retailing. Shopping center developers created hybrid retail properties that are a combination of two or three types of shopping centers. Redeveloping buildings on great neighborhood streets through the country and adaptive use redevelopment opportunities were created in urban areas. Developers respond to the needs and preferences of businesses and consumers by developing projects that meet their wants and needs.

There are right and wrong reasons to develop. Classic wrong reasons to develop include covering overhead, paying yesterday's bills, or covering the cash-flow deficit of a previously developed project. A developer sometimes starts a project just to pay expenses—even though the market is soft. The developer may hope that market conditions will improve by the time the building is completed or believe the project is special and will lease up successfully—despite a poor market. "Build it and they will come" can be a common illusion of some developers.

Governmental Request for Proposal

Municipal agencies often have surplus land they will sell or lease. A city may form a redevelopment agency to purchase property, demolish the existing building, and sell the land to a developer for a predetermined project. A school district may have surplus property it will sell or lease. The governmental agency will issue a *request for proposal (RFP)* and developers will either submit a bid to purchase the property or submit a development plan. The agency selects the development plan that best suits the intended use for the property and/or the developer who offers the highest price for the site.

Transit Agencies

Transit agencies develop transit stations in communities and may have excessive land for development. Often, the station is underground and the agency will ground lease the land above the station to a developer. Developments on or near a transit station are known as *transit-oriented developments (TOD).* They are often a mixed-use development with multi-family housing above ground floor retail. Because of the ease of commuting to and from work, these developments are often in high demand. A transit agency will issue an RFP for their development site.

Major Tenant-Driven Developments

An ideal opportunity occurs when a major tenant brings a proposed site to a developer or informs the developer of an area or areas in which it is seeking sites. Since most shopping centers must have a commitment from an anchor tenant and office and multi-tenant buildings benefit by substantial pre-leasing, a tenant's need for space can become a development opportunity. The situation occurs more frequently in shopping center development when an anchor tenant, such as a supermarket, informs the developer of the number of new stores it plans to open, when it plans to open them, and the areas it is targeting. The developer either searches for sites or contacts land brokers to locate sites.

Other Developers' Projects

Occasionally, a developer cannot execute a project. The developer may not be able to obtain financing, equity partners, or pre-leasing activities may not be successful. The developer's option on the site may not have expired, and another developer can assume the option on the land and pursue the development opportunity with the sale of a different proposed project. The first developer may own the site and development opportunity and may be able sell it to another developer. In that case, the due diligence costs of the first developer are usually included in the sale price. Caution is necessary when assuming another developer's proposed project; it may be for sale because it is ill conceived.

FEASIBILITY ANALYSIS

Soon after becoming interested in a potential development opportunity, the developer undertakes a *feasibility analysis.* This study will either support the developer's initial belief that the proposed project is viable (go or no go), or it will indicate which components of the pro forma (the financial projection for the proposed project) do not support the project. The equity investors, who contribute capital for the purchase of the land or the equity required by the lender, review the feasibility analysis to determine if the return on their investment justifies the inherent risk of investing in the development. Lenders require a feasibility study and may commission their own to support the viability of the project and to determine LTV and debt-coverage ratios.

The feasibility analysis has six primary considerations: (1) the demand for the project and its rental rates, (2) rough schematic and layout of the building or buildings on the site, (3) review of the permitting and entitlement process, (4) pro forma, (5) estimate of construction costs, and (6) determination of the project's ability to obtain capital and financing.

Determining the Demand

Determining the demand for the project or the length of time it will take the project to lease up is the most difficult part of the feasibility analysis. Vital factors in projecting future demand are the area's economy, current vacancy rates, historical absorption trends, other proposed projects, and trends in the industry that will affect the project.

Current vacancy rates are relatively easy to obtain. Regional and local brokerage firms, as well as national brokerage firms, publish quarterly vacancy reports for office space and industrial properties. They also provide historical absorption trends and analysis. These reports usually analyze the many micro-markets in the area. A market study by the developer's staff or contracted to a consultant will provide current market data for the neighborhood (apartments), trade area (shopping centers and retail properties), or micro market (office and industrial properties) where the property is located.

Many office markets consist of the *central business district (CBD),* which is where the majority of the new Class A buildings were developed; a historical district near the CBD with renovated Class B buildings; one or two additional areas in the city with a variety of building classes; and several suburban areas with a concentration of Class A and B buildings.

Typically, up to 80 percent of the tenants who lease space in a proposed office building come from a three- to five-mile radius of the site. Thus, the micro-market analysis is more important than the macro-market analysis for office buildings. The trade area for a grocery-anchored shopping center is usually a few miles, and the demand for retail space and specific retailers in the trade area is the determining factor whether to build a grocery-anchored shopping center on a specific site.

The large brokerage firms only conduct shopping center vacancy studies in a few cities because locating and surveying strip shopping centers is more difficult than locating and surveying office buildings or industrial properties. Office buildings and industrial space tend to be concentrated in a half dozen areas, while shopping centers are relatively evenly scattered throughout an entire region with concentrations of retail hubs usually centered around regional malls. The demand analysis for an anchored strip shopping center can be limited to the proposed shopping center's primary trade area because the majority of the shoppers (70 percent or more) will live or work within that area.

Determining Rental Rates

A market survey is necessary to determine the building's rental rates, tenant allowances, and possible concessions. Since the proposed building will not be ready for occupancy for two to five years, the developer projects rental rates for the pre-leasing period and the first year the building is occupied. Typically, rental rates for new buildings establish a new high water mark for rental rates in the area. The new construction costs, which are higher than the costs to build new buildings in the past, and the increased land cost, create the need to charge higher rental rates.

Completing the Analysis

The remaining components of the feasibility analysis (rough schematic and layout, review of the permitting and entitlement process, pro forma, estimate of construction costs, and determination of the project's ability to obtain capital and financing) are discussed throughout the rest of this chapter.

The final components of the feasibility analysis are a projection of the financing cost and a consideration of the project's ability to obtain financing. First, the construction financing, and then the permanent or take-out financing is projected. The pro forma will include projections for an annual *net operating income (NOI),* cash flow after debt service, equity requirements, and rate of return on the investment.

THE DEVELOPMENT PROCESS

From locating a site to develop and drafting a rough schematic of a proposed building through orchestrating a grand opening, the development process requires the experience and expertise of many real estate professionals. The architect and the real estate manager are important members of the development team.

Locating Development Sites

Locating sites for development is essential to the developer's business development plan. Most developers need a continual stream of development opportunities to stay in business, especially in the early years of the company. Potential sites are typically found one of four ways: (1) the developer finds the site, (2) a broker with a listing markets the site to developers, (3) a broker has an assignment from a tenant to find a site and a developer to build the building, or (4) the landowner brings the site to the developer for sale or as a joint venture.

Developer Finds Site

Every development company needs a least one rain maker, someone to generate development opportunities. The developer is the primary rainmaker, but others in the company may also generate development opportunities. Developers usually have excellent contacts in the region and property type. They may be well known in the industry. A retail developer may hire a real estate person from a national major retailer, such as a supermarket, to find development sites for them. This person is not only familiar with the area in which his or her former employer is seeking sites to open new stores, but is also familiar with the areas other anchor retail tenants are seeking new locations.

An anchor tenant for a building may inform the developer of its expansion or relocation plans and ask the developer to locate a site and submit a proposal to develop the building. This happens when a strip shopping center anchor tenant—such as a supermarket—tells a developer it is planning to open a dozen stores over the next few years and indicates the cities, counties, or neighborhoods it has targeted for market penetration.

Broker Finds or Markets Site

The brokerage community is another source of potential development sites. Most land is sold through a broker, and each area has brokers who specialize in land sales. In addition, many commercial brokers who concentrate on leasing or selling properties occasionally handle land sales. By networking and cultivating a rapport with these brokers, developers can ensure they are among the first to learn about land for sale. Most commercial developers specialize in one or two property types—office buildings and/or industrial properties, for example—and when a site zoned for a particular property type becomes available, the interested developer should be among the first to see it.

One of the broker's primary concerns is whether the developer has the ability to execute the project. This may include concerns about the staff's expertise; the ability to obtain capital and financing to proceed through the preplanning process; and the ability to attract prospective tenants—especially anchor or lead tenants. Most developers will option the site to complete their due diligence before purchasing the property.

During the three- to six-month period of due diligence, the property owner takes the property off the market. If the sale cannot be completed, the broker must market the land again. Since that delays the sale of the property and thus payment of the commission the broker earns when a property sells, the broker may not encourage a landowner to tie up a property with a long option if the developer does not have the ability to execute the project. Networking in the commercial brokerage community is an important component of the developer's business development plan.

Landowner Proposes Site

On occasion, landowners will contact developers with a proposal to sell or lease land or to enter into a joint venture to develop the property.

Due Diligence

Regardless of how the developer learns about the property, a thorough *due diligence* (careful examination or evaluation) usually precedes the purchase. The developer will attempt to option the property at little or no cost for as long as possible to conduct the due diligence. Typical concerns include obtaining the proper zoning; acquiring a building permit; conducting wetlands and environmental contamination studies; and, if the site is proposed for a shopping center, obtaining interest and then a lease commitment from one or more anchor tenants.

Ideally, the developer prefers at least a one-year option, while the landowner wants to minimize the length of the option. Several factors necessitate a longer option period. Prior to wetlands and hazardous contamination becoming major issues and hindrances to developing a site, the developer's primary concerns were zoning and tenant interest. A three- to six-month option usually was sufficient to resolve those issues. However, anti-growth opposition in some communities, in addition to wetlands and environmental contamination concerns, have made the three- to six-month period generally insufficient to determine if a site can be developed.

The developer prefers not to pay for the option or the carrying cost of the property, including real estate taxes and insurance, during the option period. The developer's rationale is that the landowner would have to spend the same time to complete the same investigation if he or she were to develop the site. In addition, the developer is spending tens of thousands of dollars in staff time, and company overhead expense to conduct the due diligence plus out-of-pocket expenses.

Consultants may be hired at the developer's expense to investigate potential wetlands and contaminated soil, while architects may be needed to determine the amount of buildable space on the site and a consultant may conduct a market survey. The purchase-option agreement can be negotiated to deduct these costs from the property's sale price. If the property is not purchased, the property owner may reimburse the developer for half to all of these costs for the right to obtain ownership of the consultants' reports if the developer is willing to provide the pre-development investigation information to the property owner.

Since the option period may extend beyond one year, the landowner may provide the developer with a free "look-see" period of three to six months. A developer who needs more time to complete the due diligence may pay a monthly fee to extend the option. There are numerous ways to structure an option to purchase property. The developer wants sufficient time to ascertain that a building can be developed, whereas the landowner wants assurance the developer is diligently pursuing the investigation and the property has not been unduly taken off the market. The landowner may negotiate for the developer to pay for the cost of the real estate taxes on the property during the option period and possibly a fixed or monthly fee.

Rough Schematic

A rough schematic or layout of the proposed building and parcel is necessary to determine its size, leasable area, and placement on the site. The size of the building in terms of leasable area is one of the components that determines its potential income. The more square feet of leasable area, the greater the potential income and square footage to spread the project cost over. The other component used to determine potential income is the building's market rental rate.

Since a greater building area equals a greater income potential, developers often instruct the architect to design the maximum leasable space into a project. A leasing agent or real estate manager should review the preliminary layout and the final drawings to determine if the proposed building has space that will be difficult to lease and price these spaces accordantly.

Difficult spaces may take several months and even years to lease, usually at rates far below the original pro forma.

The building layout and size suggest potential users for the project. The size and configuration of a land parcel proposed for a shopping center determine whether the site can accommodate anchor tenants and, if so, how many anchor tenants the project can accommodate. Since anchor tenants (e.g., 50,000+-square-foot supermarkets and 100,000+-square-foot discount stores or home improvement centers) often require spaces in excess of 200 feet deep with abundant front parking, the configuration of some sites will prohibit or limit the number of anchor tenants.

The Development Team

The vision of the developer goes beyond seeing a building where one does not exist to perceive the market demand for the project and understanding the cost of developing the project and the income it will generate. A developer typically needs multiple teams to bring their vision to reality. These teams include: (1) the developer and developer's associates; (2) the design team; (3) the finance team; (4) the construction team; (5) the marketing and leasing team; and (6) the real estate management team.

Architects and engineers are hired to transform the developer's vision into a building design. A general contractor is hired to assemble the construction team and to build the building. A mortgage broker is selected to find the best financing available based on the developer's financing goals and objectives. One or more leasing agents are chosen to provide market information, project rental rates, develop a marketing plan, and find tenants. A real estate manager is hired or contracted to develop the building's operating budget, review proposed finished materials for maintenance, establish the operations and management, and develop the business plan for the building based on the developer's goals and objectives. Other consultants may be hired to address specific issues and to validate the economics of the developer's vision.

Major tenants may influence the design. The anchor tenants and their architects review and have approval rights over the placement of their buildings within the shopping center. They are concerned with the visibility of their location and sufficient parking spaces in their parking field. Landscaping, mechanical, structural, traffic, and other consultants review aesthetic, structural, environmental, and operational aspects of the project. A general contractor transforms the developer's vision and the architect's design into a building. An attorney is needed for legal advice, negotiating contracts and leases, and dealing with issues that can hinder the development of the project. Each team member has a different perspective, role, and expertise that is needed to successfully develop the project. The developer must maintain a clear focus and lead the team in the right direction.

Architect Selection

The architect has one of the most important roles in the success of a new or rehabbed development and therefore should be one of the first members to join the development team. The architect's expertise is needed to determine if the site for the proposed building is of sufficient size and of appropriate configuration to accommodate the project. A critical component of every development is the amount of *gross leasable area (GLA)* that can be built on the site. The size of the building is one of the components that determines the amount of income the project can generate, and that determines whether the project is financially feasible. If the project is a rehab or an adaptive use of an existing building, the architect determines if the changes to the building, along with the amount of GLA that can be created, will meet the needs of the intended users.

Background and Experience

It is critical that the architect be experienced with the property type to be developed. Each property type—whether office, medical, industrial, or retail—has unique features and design criteria that are important to meeting the needs of the building's tenants. The architect must know not only the latest trends in building designs and features but also the specific requirements of different types of tenants. The needs of office building tenants are different from the needs and requirements of retail tenants. For example, a developer hired a friend who was a shopping center architect to design an office building. The architect was not aware of operational issues in office building, so the architect ultimately designed an office building that had operational inefficiencies that would have increased the cost of the common area maintenance charges. Fortunately, the real estate manager was an early member of the development team who caught the operational deficiencies that were corrected before construction commenced.

Another example is when an apartment architect is hired to design a mid- to high-rise apartment with ground-floor retail space. If the architectural firm does not have a retail property design experience, it is likely the firm will not know the space demands of retailers and to visually separate the retail ground-floor space from the rest of the building. Error in designing the ground-floor space is likely to negatively impact the marketing and leasing of this space and result in a longer lease-up time at lower than pro forma rates. It may be necessary to hire a consulting architect to design the ground-floor space with the apartment architect being the lead architect.

An experienced architect can find hidden value in a building that is to be rehabbed. The architect will make more effective use of existing space: storage areas can be converted to GLA, dead space can be converted to rental storage areas, rooftops can generate income from antennas and dishes, and cubby holes (such as areas under stairs, places for retail carts, or cash machines) can generate additional income. Choosing an architectural firm that has extensive experience with the specific property type that is to be developed or rehabbed is essential.

Interview Process

The interview process allows the developer to meet the architect, see work samples, learn about the architect's experience with the proposed type of property, and evaluate his or her understanding of the latest trends in that property type. The first interview should be at the architect's office. This allows the developer and the real estate manager to see renderings of similar projects the architect has designed, discuss the design process, ask about the challenges of other design projects, and learn how the architect addressed and solved them. While reviewing these projects, the developer and real estate manager can discuss state-of-the-art building features, the latest amenities tenants want and need, and the tenants' occupancy trends (e.g., space planning, technology requirements, etc.). Important real estate management issues to discuss include operational efficiencies and inefficiencies that can be designed into the project and recommended materials that will have an impact on the maintenance and operating costs of the building.

The goals and objectives of the project must be thoroughly discussed. This includes a description of the project, its targeted market, anticipated project time line, financial constraints, market rental rate, and whether the project will be pre-sold, be sold shortly after completion, or be a long-term hold. If the building is being remodeled or undergoing a major rehabilitation, existing tenants' concerns and other issues should be discussed. The scope of the project should be presented, and the architect should review the firm's personnel and the backgrounds of those who will work on the project. The availability of staff and the architectural firm's ability to meet the proposed timeline are critical to the project's success.

The second meeting with the architect should be a visit to the site or the existing building so design concepts can be explored. Other important issues are the proposed budgets and pro forma, the project's proposed timeline, and the availability of the architect's personnel to meet the timeline.

It is important for the owner of the proposed project to convey his or her vision of it. The owner should be comfortable with the skill, creativity, and relevant experience of the architect selected to design the project. Following the interviews, business, and professional references should be requested and checked.

The developer should review the design process with the architect, which includes zoning analysis, conceptual and design presentation drawings, construction drawings, shop drawings, and as-built or recorded drawings.

The real estate manager and the architect may not agree on the choice of building materials. The architect often selects materials based on aesthetic appeal while the real estate manager focuses on maintenance, operations, and cost control. There should be a discussion and hopefully a consensus on the selection of materials.

The architect's proposed fees are one of the last issues to discuss. Several methods are used to determine fees for architectural services. They can be based on an hourly rate, a percentage of the construction contract, the floor area or GLA, or a stipulated sum. The cost of supplementary services including those services of engineers, surveyors, and other professionals must be negotiated. When fees are based on an hourly rate, the developer should inquire as to the hourly billing rate of each person who will work on the project, the percentage of the job each will perform, and an estimate of the total cost of the assignment and other reimburseables—such as cost of copies, mileage, etc. A clear understanding of the fees and out-of-pocket expenses will prevent disputes and hard feelings from developing.

Real Estate Manager's Role

Real estate managers bring valuable expertise and experience to the development team that other team members do not have. Sometimes a developer may forget to include the real estate manager on the development team, even though the real estate manager's understanding of the operations, operating costs, and efficiencies of buildings and knowledge, and of the leasing market may be invaluable to the development team as well as to the success of the project.

The real estate manager should meet with the developer and leasing agent to review their perspectives of the market. These development team members should then meet with the architect and general contractor to review the design, layout, and materials for the project.

At times, real estate managers may find themselves at odds with other members of the development team. Their perceptions of the market may differ from those of leasing agents or developers. The real estate manager may disagree with the architect regarding choices of building materials. The real estate manager focuses on maintenance, operations, and operating cost control, whereas the architect views the building for its aesthetic appeal. Issues when negotiating the lease and criteria for accepting and rejecting tenants (e.g., weak financial statement, incorrect use) may prove to be points of disagreement among the real estate manager, leasing agent, and developer. Fully utilizing each member's expertise and experience helps the development achieve or exceed its short- and long-term financial projections.

To be active participants and add their experience, expertise, and opinions to the development team, real estate managers must understand the development process as well as the motivations, concerns, and perceptions of the other team members—especially the developer/owner. Real estate managers who achieve this understanding will be able to make a valuable contribution by integrating their knowledge and experience with that of the other team members. The final decision of all the recommendations rests with the developer. A prudent developer encourages differences of opinion. This enables the developer to make the best decisions for the project.

Reviewing Market Conditions

The real estate manager's initial involvement with a proposed development should be reviewing the market conditions. Are the projected rental rates and *pass-through charges* (and concession package, if necessary) realistic? When conducting this analysis, the real estate manager must balance the developer's sometimes overly optimistic view of the market and his or her perception. Historical absorption rates, vacancy factors, current and projected supply-and-demand trends, market rental rates, proposed competition, and the possibility of attracting an anchor tenant are factors the real estate manager must consider in projecting the building's market rental rates, pricing each space within the building, and lease-up. The real estate manager's perspective of the market is a good counterpoint to the developer's perspective.

Reviewing Proposed Plans

Reviewing the plans for the proposed building is the second important area in which the real estate manager can contribute as a member of the development team. The real estate manager will focus on three potential problem areas: (1) built-in leasing problems, (2) maintenance issues, and (3) operating expenses. In the effort to maximize the gross leasable area on a site or to make a building's size or configuration conform to the shape and size of a land parcel, space that is difficult to lease can inadvertently be designed into a building. Such spaces take longer to lease and at a rate lower than projected. Space that does not meet the needs of the building's potential tenants is difficult to lease.

The real estate manager also reviews the building's plans for efficiency of operations. Office buildings that lack electrical outlets in the corridors and janitorial closets without sinks require more time to clean. The increased housekeeping time adds to the building's operating expenses. A three-story skylight over a lobby or mall center court is architecturally striking and affords natural light, but the design must include a method to clean the exterior and interior of the glass.

Building materials, especially those in the common areas, must be examined to determine if their appearance can be maintained and at what cost. A review of the plans will enable the real estate manager to develop an estimated operating expense for the project. If the building's tenant pass-through expenses are not competitive in the market, will the building's location or other amenities outweigh, in a tenant's mind, the added expenses?

Continuing Management Responsibilities

When a development project is completed, each member of the development team moves on to another project, yet, most of the real estate manager's responsibilities are just beginning. He or she must successfully guide the property through market cycles, new forms of competition, the latest technology, and ever-increasing government regulations.

Once the project design has passed the development team's review, the real estate manager prepares the building for its opening and ongoing management and operations. These activities include developing a maintenance management program, establishing emergency procedures, administering the leases, preparing a grand opening event, establishing a tenant retention program, developing a risk management program, preparing the building's operating budget and NOI projections, and determining a monthly and annual report format acceptable to the building owner.

Governmental Approvals

For hundreds of years, cities and municipalities have imposed restrictions and guidelines on the development of commercial and residential properties. Land use and construction codes are intended to protect the environment, ensure safety, guard the health of citizens, maintain the natural and man-made beauty of the community, and provide necessary services and recreational activities. As a result, the developer may encounter a myriad of obstacles that may prevent the proposed project from ever being built or being built at a cost that is financially possible.

Consultants, such as permit expediters, can assist in obtaining the countless permits and approvals that are necessary before construction can commence or tenants can occupy the project to conduct business. Each municipality has its own rules, ordinances, zoning laws, and permitting processes. The requirements to develop in one city are often different from the requirements in an adjacent city. The time a developer needs to complete the permitting process (the procedures involved in obtaining all the necessary permits for starting construction) can vary considerably from municipality to municipality. This process, also known as the entitlement process, is one of the most critical periods in many developments. If the project does not receive the necessary permits, it will never become a reality.

The permitting process can be very costly. The developer measures the cost in fees, time and opportunities lost, and carrying costs. Although the fees are not a significant cost in relations to the entire cost of the project, each expense must be managed to achieve an economically successful project. The second expense of the permitting process, time, can be quite costly. There are many ways to measure the cost of time.

During the permitting process, market conditions can change, and a building may lose its competitive position if it opens a year or two later than planned. For instance, the passage of time may allow a competing shopping center to open six months earlier, offer prospective tenants an earlier move-in date, and establish its market position with the shoppers in the trade area. Construction costs can increase, and the financing market can change over a relatively short period. A one or two percent increase in the interest rate for the project's loan can change and dramatically reduce the investors' return. If the rental market becomes soft and rental rates decline, the projected NOI may fall below the lender's *debt coverage ratio (DCR)* and the developer may not be able to finance the project at current interest rates.

Developers earn fees drawn from the construction loan. If a developer is without a continual income stream for an extended period, the development company may be forced to downsize and eventually cease doing business. Another lost opportunity resulting from a lengthy permitting process is the allocation of the profits from the completed project. Ongoing cash flow from the property or the proceeds from the sale of the project may be earmarked for acquiring additional land for other projects, paying prior debts or company overhead, funding existing buildings with negative cash flow, making investments, or conducting personal business. The developer may not be in a financial position to wait out the permitting process before receiving funds to address the aforementioned issues. Finally, the developer must bear the cost of carrying the property during the permitting process. The developer may have a mortgage payment on the land or option payment, and potentially expenses of the consultants and staff necessary to pursue the permitting process.

The following section, while reviewing several elements in the permitting process, is not a comprehensive guide because of the varying requirements of each municipality. However, the information should provide the reader an overview of the major issues a developer encounters when seeking approval from the many jurisdictions that have review and approval rights and obligations.

Zoning

Zoning enables municipalities to control the use of land and the improvements. A zone is an area within a municipality that is intended for a limited or specific use. The municipality determines what can be built, how large a building can be built, and where it can be built on a parcel of land. Most municipalities separate their land uses by categories such as the following:

- Single-family residential
- Multifamily residential
- Retail
- Commercial/industrial
- Mixed-use
- Institutional

Within these general classifications are subcategories. For instance, one single-family area may be zoned for one house per five acres, while another may be zoned for a higher density of five houses per acre. Zoning can restrict the size and height of buildings. In an outlying area of a city, the height limit for an office building may be 50 feet, while the city's CBD area may have a limit of 1,000 feet. Industrial areas may be zoned from light industrial use to heavy manufacturing uses.

Land use codes usually allow flexibility to accommodate the unique characteristics of a project or the parcel of land. The code usually includes provisions for conditional use, special design exceptions, and variances. A *variance* is a change or modification to the in-place zoning standard. For instance, a developer may petition for a variance to change the parking ratio for a shopping center, to reduce the open space requirements for an urban mixed-use development, or to extend the height of an office building.

A developer may petition to change or amend the zoning classification of a particular parcel of property, for example, from industrial to office use. The concerns of the municipality occurs through a hearing for the request for rezoning include compatibility with existing land uses, impact on the area, and whether the change is a response to a public need.

Public notice is required for a change to a land use so citizens have an opportunity to participate in land use decisions. The public may be notified of a hearing on the land use issue by signage on the property, notification in the newspaper, or a direct mailing notice sent to all property owners within a specific distance of the property. The public's opinion is encouraged during the hearing.

Historically, cities and municipalities regulated land use based upon the communities overall economic and residential development plan. During the 1960s and 1970s, many cities developed master plans for land use. Cities realized their master plans would affect each other and other areas of the state. Therefore, many states have enacted growth-management acts that call for urban counties and cities to develop comprehensive plans to control and guide their growth in future decades.

When cities and counties coordinate their land use, they can more effectively address public concerns such as social and economic needs, traffic congestion, adequacy of open spaces and recreational areas, or water and air quality.

Permits

The intent of a construction permit is to ensure that buildings are constructed to recognized standards of structural soundness and fire safety. Several construction-related activities that may require permits include demolition, grading, mechanical issues, building construction, and *tenant improvement (TI)* construction.

During the construction of a building, several mechanical construction activities require separate inspections and permits. The inspections can include plumbing, electrical work, sewer work, sprinkler system, and a fire-alarm system.

A building that is to be demolished may contain asbestos in the ceiling, floor tile, fireproofing, siding, roofing, insulation, or other building materials. The federal *Environmental Protection Agency (EPA)* has determined that asbestos is a hazardous substance. A developer must contract with a professional testing firm to determine whether asbestos is present. If it is, a licensed asbestos abatement contractor must remove the hazardous substance before the building can be demolished.

A grading permit may be required based on the extent of the land clearing, filling, and grading activities proposed for the property. A permit will be required for interior TI for the construction or remodeling of a space within an existing building. Depending on the extent of the TIs, city or county inspections will occur at various stages of the construction process and after the work is completed. When the work has been inspected, if no code violations are found, the governing agency issues a *certificate of occupancy (C of O).* After the certificate of occupancy has been issued, tenants may occupy the premises.

Environmental Review

Every municipality faces the challenge of protecting the environment while allowing and encouraging economic growth. Many municipalities have an environmental review process. An environmental review is often required if a proposed building exceeds a specific size (for example, more than 10,000 square feet of space in a commercial, retail, or industrial zoned area) or if it is planned for an environmentally sensitive area. Environmental issues that development can affect include traffic, parking, drainage, air and water quality, wetlands, erosion, and the cumulative impact of these and other factors.

The environmental review process may involve several stages such as data collection, a public hearing, evaluation, recommendations, and a ruling. Information gathering may be as simple as completing an environmental checklist, or it may involve a lengthy *environmental impact statement (EIS).* The purpose of an EIS is to inform the public and the municipality of the project's effect on the environment and, if necessary, to propose measures to mitigate any adverse effects.

The public is invited to the hearing to express their opinions, concerns, and support of the proposed development. The public may be notified of the hearing by placards placed within a specified distance of the site, a large site sign, a notice mailed to all property owners within a specific distance of the site, a notice on the municipality's website and published notices in newspapers. Depending on the hearing procedures, interested parties may or may not appeal decisions.

The environmental issue of the 1990s was wetlands. The federal government is dedicated to protecting wetlands and species that inhabit them. When a stream, pond area, or an indication of a species indigenous to wetlands areas is present on a site, a wetlands survey may be required. Numerous governmental agencies regulate wetlands.

Though environmental studies may be costly and may delay the start or completion of a project and even increase the cost of the project, developers have a responsibility to protect the environment.

Traffic Management Plan

In heavily congested areas, municipalities may require the developer of a project (usually an office building) to submit and implement a transportation management plan (TMP) for the building. A traffic management plan reduces the number of workers arriving at the building in a single-occupant vehicle (SOV) and increases the number of workers carpooling and arriving in high-occupant vehicles (HOV) or using public transportation. A traffic management plan includes a survey of the tenants' employees to determine their modes of transportation to and from work. The building's real estate manager may coordinate a ride-sharing plan.

The developer of an office building with paid parking may need to provide discounted parking rates for HOV stalls, subsidize some employees' public transportation passes, or provide vanpool vehicles. The municipality may require a quarterly or annual report on the status of the building's traffic management plan. Though most municipalities do not have TMP requirements, mitigating traffic congestion will continue to be an important issue for many municipalities for many years. This issue is a component of the effort to address global warming.

Landscape Requirement

Large commercial properties devoid of landscaping, can appear as a massive, imposing building or as a massive building surrounded by a black sea of asphalt. Many municipalities have ordinances that require a minimum of landscaping, which can accomplish the following objectives:

- Providing a buffer between buildings and incompatible uses
- Mitigating the adverse impact of a building's height, size, and scale
- Reducing drainage problems
- Screening undesirable views
- Interrupting the barren appearance of parking lots
- Enhancing the beauty of the area

Landscaping ordinances may require the developer to provide landscaping on the street frontage and other public property. Environmental benefits of landscaping include reduction of pollution and dust, creation of home and food for wildlife, provision of shade in summertime, and improvement of air quality.

Adverse effects of growth in some areas are an increase in the possibility of drought and/or a negative impact on the area's water supply. Some municipalities require that a certain percentage of the plants proposed for a project be drought-tolerant or require low-water usage.

Sign Ordinance

Municipalities preserve or enhance the appearance of the community by enacting sign ordinances for commercial buildings and businesses. A sign ordinance defines allowable signs and may prohibit other types of signs. Several kinds of signs may be approved, restricted, or denied.

A pole sign is a permanent, multi-faced sign attached to a building or supported by one or more poles in the ground. These signs are usually 20 feet or higher and may have one merchant's name on it, such as a supermarket or fast food restaurant or they serve several merchants. Some municipalities have enacted ordinances requiring that these signs be removed, lowered, or replaced by ground-level monument signs.

A wall sign is placed against the wall of a building or suspended under a canopy. Shopping center tenants locate wall signs above their entrances. A projecting sign extends outward from a building such as a blade sign above a store Roof signs are mounted on a roof.

Municipalities may regulate some or all of the aforementioned signs. Ordinances specify the length, area, and height of the signs, as well as their placement. A commercial building's sign criteria must comply with the municipality's sign ordinances.

Mitigation Fees

The developer may be required to pay mitigation fees to cover the cost of the infrastructure surrounding the development. For example, the increased growth may require new schools and other municipal services be constructed to support the growth both immediate and in the future.

Emergency Procedures

Fire departments in some municipalities require developers to submit and receive approval for an emergency procedures plan for buildings beyond a specific height. The fire department wants assurance that, in the case of an emergency, the building management and occupants are prepared to evacuate the building or to take other appropriate measures. Fire departments commonly require an annual or semiannual practice evacuation of the building. Many municipalities withhold issuing a certificate of occupancy until the fire department has reviewed and approved a building's emergency procedures plan.

FINANCING

Few developers have enough capital on hand to fully pay for the cost of their development projects, so financing is an essential element in the development process. The developer starts with the pro forma analysis and begins seeking financing early in process.

Pro Forma

The pro forma is the financial analysis of a property for a specific period, such as one year or five years, and includes projections of income, vacancy factors, operating expenses, capital expenses, and debt service (loan payment).

Income Projection

The income projection is based on a stabilized occupancy of 95 percent. The price of each space in the building must be based on its value to the user/tenant. For instance, in an office building in the CBD, ground-floor space often leases at a premium—especially if the building is located in the retail core of the CBD. The second-floor space will lease for a low rate, and then the rental rate for each subsequent floor may increase. One side of the building may have water views and command a higher rental rate than the other side. The top floor or penthouse, may have a higher ceiling and the best views, in addition to the prestige of being the highest floor in the building; these features command a premium rate. The price of each shopping center space reflects its size, front footage, bay depth, configuration, visibility, and location in the shopping center. With the exception of small buildings, all the spaces seldom have the same rental rate.

Vacancy Factor

The vacancy factor typically used for the entire building is five percent. Anchored shopping centers often use a five percent vacancy on the shop space and no vacancy on the anchored tenants. The rationale for not applying a vacancy factor to anchor tenant space is that they are credit-worthy tenants on long-term leases with multiple options.

Operating Expenses

The income analysis also includes the recovery of operating expenses, such as common area maintenance and other billback expenses, as well as other income sources (e.g., rooftop and parking income for an office building) and non-reimburseable expenses

Projections. Operating expenses are projected on a stable occupancy rate of 95 percent. The Building Owners and Managers Association (BOMA) publishes its annual *Office Building Experience Report,* and the Institute of Real Estate Management (IREM) annually publishes its *Office Building Income and Expense Analysis* and *Shopping Center Income and Expense Analysis.* Each publication provides operating expenses for buildings in every major city and many small towns across the United States. Income and operating expenses are the components that determine a building's NOI. The NOI formula consists of the building's income minus vacancy and credit loss plus miscellaneous income minus all operating expenses.

In addition to a projection of the building's stabilized NOI, a separate income and expense projection is necessary during the initial lease-up period. This projection calculates the amount of space leased, occupied, and producing rent on a month-to-month basis until the building is collecting rent on 90 to 95 percent of its leasable space. The shopping center industry refers to leasable space as *gross leasable area (GLA);* the office building industry refers to it as rentable square footage. Monthly operating expenses are significantly less during the lease-up of an office building, but they are not necessarily less during the lease-up of a strip shopping center, mall, or a multi-tenant industrial park.

Expenses. Two major expenses of an office building, utilities, and janitorial services, are directly related to occupancy. Depending on the building's size, the on-site maintenance staff may or may not be at full capacity until a significant level of occupancy is attained. A new building frequently is not fully assessed for real estate taxes during its first year or two.

A shopping center's occupancy usually does not have an impact on the *common area maintenance (CAM)* expenses. Landscaping, maintenance, parking lot sweeping, snow removal, exterior lighting, and other expenses are necessary whether the shopping center is half empty or fully occupied. Tenants are responsible for the maintenance and utility costs of their premises. The property owner incurs a nominal cost to maintain vacancies and keep the power on in vacant spaces.

Multi-tenant industrial properties are operated as a hybrid strip shopping center and garden office building. CAM is the responsibility of the property owner, and this cost may be billed to the tenants. Depending on the lease, the maintenance of the tenant's premises is usually the tenant's expense.

If the management fee is a calculated as a percent of the collected income, the fee will be less during a lease up or when the building has a low occupancy. Management agreements may state the management fee is the greater of a minimum fee or a percentage of the collected income. In this situation, the management fee will never drop below a specific amount.

An important component of the lease-up pro forma is the recovery of the CAM or pass-through expenses. The owner will not recover 100 percent of these expenses until the building is 100 percent occupied, with all tenants paying their pro rata shares. Just as the building's rental income increases with occupancy (and after the free rent period expires), the CAM and pass-through expense recovery increase with occupancy. When projecting CAM and pass-through expense recovery, the developer must review the terms of each proposed lease to determine whether it stipulates a cap or limit on these expenses or requires the tenant to pay its full pro rata share. Some tenants may carve out expenses or specific expenses they are not required to reimburse the owner. The real estate manager should be responsible for projecting the building's operating expenses during the initial lease-up period and at stabilized occupancy.

Debt Service

The last important element of the lease-up pro forma is debt service (loan payment). Debt service is discussed in the "Financing Commercial Developments" section in this chapter.

Project Equity

The project equity is the difference between the cost of developing the project and the amount of the loan. Ideally, the developer would prefer to obtain 100 percent financing. That was often possible in the 1970s and early 1980s. In that situation, the developer would have no cash invested and no equity partner but would own 100 percent of the project.

If a developer could demonstrate that the value of a shopping center (or any project) was 133 percent of the cost to develop it, and the lender was willing to provide a loan at 75 percent of value, the loan would be for 100 percent of the development cost (133% x 75% = 100%).

The loan as a percentage of the cost to develop a project will vary depending on several factors including the market conditions, the economy, and policies of the lender. The loan may range from 60 percent to 90 percent of the cost to develop the project.

Equity Partners

Most developers do not have sufficient cash on hand to use as equity for many or all of their development projects. For example, if development of a small project cost between $10 and $12 million, and a lender is willing to finance 70 percent of the project cost, the developer will need $3 million to more than $3.5 million dollars of equity (cash) to obtain financing and complete the project. Imagine the equity needed for a 500,000-square-foot high-rise office building or a million-square-foot super regional mall. Thus, developers have traditionally sought equity partners. Equity partners often contribute 100 percent of the equity required by the lender. The developer's contribution—often referred to as "sweat equity"—includes generating the development opportunity and contributing expertise and time to complete the project. The developer is the general partner and assumes the risks and liabilities of that role.

The developer's rationale for receiving such a share of the project through sweat equity without any cash investment is threefold:

1. Few successful development opportunities exist, and if the project meets or exceeds the pro forma projections, it will be enormously successful.
2. The developer is investing the time of its staff and the cost to operate the development company (although the developer will receive a development fee which is typically a percent of the hard cost).
3. As a general partner, the developer is responsible for cost overruns and the project's operating deficits; in addition, the developer usually must personally guarantee the construction loan and perhaps the permanent loan. Personally guaranteed loans are known as recourse loans.

During the early 1980s, insurance companies were among the primary equity partners for developers building large- and medium-sized commercial properties. Pension funds, syndicators, and partnerships were sources of equity capital. By the mid-1980s, foreign investors became important providers of equity capital. From the late 1980s to the mid-1990s, few investors were interested in real estate development projects. By the late 1990s and early 2000s, investors once again were willing to work with a developer to build projects. Other equity investors are wealthy families and individuals, institutional advisors on behalf of their clients, pension funds, and foreign governments and investors.

Required Returns

Equity partners may require either a guaranteed or a preferential ROI. A guaranteed return provides the equity partner with an agreed guaranteed rate of return on the funds contributed. The guarantee is usually for a limited period, such as two or five years, or perhaps for the entire term of the joint ownership. If the cash flow from the property is insufficient to provide the guaranteed return, the developer must make up the difference from company or personal funds.

Developers prefer not to provide equity partners with a guarantee return and seldom must offer this return on the equity investors funds. A preferential return provides the equity partner the first distribution from the cash flow of the property until it receives a prescribed percentage return (e.g., 10 percent) on the amount contributed. The developer then receives the next distribution from the cash flow, which equals the amount paid (or percentage return) to the equity partner or based on the developer's percentage of the project. Any additional funds are divided based on each party's ownership share of the project.

Land Contributions

In another form of equity contribution, the landowner contributes the land, free and clear, to the development partnership. If the land is worth 30 percent of the cost of the project and the lender loans 70 percent of the development cost, no additional equity contribution is needed. Even with the land being contributed to the development, additional equity capital may be needed. Many projects never begin because the developer is unable to obtain the necessary equity or capital.

Financing Commercial Developments

During a soft market, obtaining financing is one of the most difficult components of the development process. The alternative to obtaining financing is to provide 100 percent of the equity for a project. The period during the 1980s and 1990s is a typical example of a changing financing market. The combination of the savings and loan debacle, low returns on commercial real estate in the late 1980s, and an excessive supply of vacant space in many areas of the country resulted in a credit crunch from the late 1980s to the early 1990s. Few of the traditional commercial real estate lenders were active in the early 1990s. Many lenders significantly reduced the amount of funds they had available for commercial real estate loans. The situation reversed in the late 1990s, and commercial real estate loans were once again readily available and at record low rates. During the Great Recession of 2008 through 2013, construction loans were difficult to obtain, for many developers.

Leverage

Developers have traditionally been able to obtain long-term, fully amortized loans at a fixed interest rate. Such loans are usually for 20 to 30 years. Some loans are for a fixed term, say 20 years, with a balloon payment at the termination of the loan. This would not be a fully amortized loan. Developers may attempt to obtain loans equal to the largest possible percentage of the cost of the project. The goal for many developers is to obtain 100 percent financing, but it is rarely, if ever achieved. Occasionally, developers obtain more when they can demonstrate that the value of the project far exceeds its cost. This occurs when the project's value exceeds 100 percent of the cost of development, and additional financing in the form of a second mortgage is placed on the property. Such a project is said to be "highly leveraged."

Leverage, the use of borrowed funds, allows the investor to realize a profit on the use of borrowed money. If the development is successful, positive leverage will increase the profitability or the return on the developer's equity investment. However, the higher the leverage, the greater the risk. A highly leveraged project has a larger mortgage or debt service payment and must maintain a high occupancy at pro forma rental rates to pay the building's operating expenses and debt service.

Three criteria lenders consider when evaluating a borrower's request for a loan are: (1) the property's or proposed development's debt coverage ratio, (2) LTV ratio, and (3) loan to cost. Each of these criteria measures the risk of the loan.

Debt Coverage Ratio

The *debt-coverage ratio (DCR)* expresses a relationship between the property's NOI and the annual debt service. The NOI is achieved by subtracting the property's operating expenses from the rents collected. (Reminder: the NOI formula is income minus vacancy and credit loss plus miscellaneous income minus operating expenses.) The lender requires more than one dollar of NOI for every one dollar of debt service. For instance, the lender may require 1.25 dollars of NOI for every one dollar of debt service. This would be expressed as a 1.25 to 1 DCR.

This ratio ensures the lender that if the property's vacancy rate increases or the rents achieved are below the pro forma and/or expenses are above, funds will be available to pay the debt service on the loan. Obviously, if rents are dramatically below the pro forma or the property experiences, a high vacancy rate for an extended time, the NOI is likely to be insufficient to cover the debt service. The formula for determining the debt coverage ratio follows:

$$\text{DCR} \div \text{NOI Debt Service}$$

The lender will make a loan whose annual payment is less than or equal to the number arrived by dividing the DCR number of 1.25 into the NOI. The NOI for a property is \$300,000 and the lender DCR is 1.25. The lender will make a loan with an annual payment of no greater than \$240,000.

$$1.25 \div \$300{,}000 + \$240{,}000$$

Loan-to-Value (LTV) Ratio

Another measurement of a loan's risk is the LTV ratio. The amount of the loan is a percentage of the value of the property. For instance, a lender may loan 80 percent of the value. If the property has a $20 million value, the lender would loan $16 million. The LTV formula follows:

Value of the property × percentage of the value

$20,000,000 × 80% = $16,000,000

Cash-on-Cash Return

An investor measures the desirability of an investment and its risk by analyzing the cash-on-cash return of the funds invested. Cash-on-cash return measures the rate of return on the amount of funds invested. A return of $10,000 on a $100,000 investment is a 10 percent cash-on-cash return. The cash-on-cash formula follows:

Return on the Investment ÷ Amount Invested

$10,000 ÷ $100,000 = 10%

Break-Even Analysis

Another analysis the developer uses is the *break-even analysis,* which is the specific occupancy level needed to pay the building's operating expenses and debt service. It can be expressed as the amount of square feet occupied or as the percentage of occupancy. The break-even analysis can change as the market rental rates change. The components of the break-even analysis are rental income, operating expenses, and debt service.

For example, if an office building's break-even occupancy is 83 percent and the average occupancy for similar buildings is 94 percent, the building owner can feel confident that the investment in the building is relatively secure. However, if the break-even occupancy is 96 percent and the average occupancy in the area has not reached 90 percent for several years, the owner's investment may be at risk. There are several factors that will determine a building's occupancy and some are specifics to building, such as amenities and location that will enable a building to outperform the market.

Sources of Financing

Sources of financing include life insurance companies, savings and loan associations, commercial banks, pension funds, *real estate investment trusts (REITs),* real estate syndicates, and private individuals. Commercial banks are the primary source of construction and development loans as banks prefer shorter duration term loans. After a project is completed, the construction loan is replaced with a permanent loan. Any of the preceding sources can provide permanent loans.

The construction loan is usually a recourse loan. The borrower guarantees repayment of the loan. If the lender forecloses on the property, the borrower is usually liable for the difference between the loan and the sale price of the property. The permanent loan is either a recourse or non-recourse loan. The non-recourse loan provides no loan guarantee by the borrower.

The term credit crunch implies that few loans are available and those that are available are based on a low LTV ratio, higher rates, shorter amortization terms (20 verses 25 years) or short terms before the mortgage must be paid off. If development is the engine of the commercial real estate industry, financing and equity are the engine's fuel. While the early 1990s experienced a credit crunch, 20 years later loans were readily available at historically low interest rates. This is another example of the cyclical nature of the real estate business—especially the development industry.

Other Risk Takers

The developer is not the only party who is taking a risk in developing a project. The equity investors who provide the capital for the down payment—the difference between the cost of the project and the amount the lender is willing to loan—are placing their investment at risk. These investors are usually limited partners with less risk than the developer (the general partner). They are not usually required to personally guarantee the loan and may or may not be liable for their pro rata shares of cash calls.

The lender takes the risk that the developer may not complete the project or that the project will have cost overruns that force the developer to increase the amount of the loan to complete the project. The lender who provides the developer with the permanent loan to pay off the construction loan is also at risk. If the developer cannot make the loan or mortgage payments, the lender must foreclose on the property. When the lender acquires ownership of the property, it is often worth less than the remaining principal balance on the loan. That happened to many lending institutions across the country in the early 1990s and during the recession of 2008–2013 and was a major contributor to the financial market crisis at that time.

Another third party at risk is the anchor tenant. If the property is pre-leased and the developer is unable to execute the project, that delays the anchor tenant's expansion plans. This is a major concern to a retail anchor tenant such as a supermarket in a proposed shopping center that may be expanding its market penetration or trying to establish a presence before competition enters the area.

Developer's Reputation

The decision of each party—the equity investor, the lender, and the anchor tenant—to participate in the proposed development is based on the developer's reputation and previous project track record. During a normal real estate market, a developer who has a good reputation for executing successful projects seldom has problems attracting equity partners and lenders' interest. During a recession or an exceptionally poor real estate market, few developers are able to obtain equity partners and/or financing. In many areas of the country during difficult economic times, tenants that normally serve as anchor tenants do not expand. However, when the economy takes an upswing and development activities once again become feasible, developers who have survived and kept their reputations intact are able to resume development activities.

When the commercial real estate market improves after an overbuilt market or a recession, many lenders and investors approached new development opportunities cautiously. Lenders initially placed more stringent requirements on financing speculative projects, requiring larger down payments or capital contributions, which lower the LTV ratio for financing a project. Investors who provided the capital or equity for the project required a larger equity share of the project.

Project Costs

The estimate of the project costs may first include the cost of the land. Additional costs are divided into hard and soft costs. The hard costs, the brick and mortar costs, include the cost for the buildings, parking areas, and so on. Soft costs include architecture and engineering costs, fees and permits, sales tax, commissions, financing, and other nonmaterial costs. The hard costs are usually expressed in absolute dollars as a cost per square foot of the building or leasable area. Soft costs are expressed as a fixed dollar amount, as a percentage of the hard costs, or in dollars per square foot. Each expense line item is then expressed in absolute dollars.

REVIEWING THE DEVELOPER'S PLANS

Since developers *develop* and real estate managers *manage*, the two do not meet until the project is completed and just before it is ready for occupancy. Developers are very creative and often focus on marketing, financing, public relations, and construction, but they spend little time on how the property will be managed. This section discusses operational issues that should be considered prior to construction for shopping centers and office buildings—with emphasis on preventing problems before they are built into the property.

Reviewing Shopping Center Plans

There is an advantage to giving the developer and architect the freedom to create an attractive, marketable shopping center or office building with no concern for operations and then allowing the real estate manager to review the plans and suggest changes that will enhance the day-to-day operations and possibly lower operating expenses. This approach is likely to yield the most creative project, and having the real estate manager make suggestions prior to finalizing the plans is more efficient and cost effective. The following factors would most likely be reviewed by the real estate manager:

- Size of spaces to be built
- Configuration of the spaces
- Fit-out package
- Storefront materials for the shopping center
- Overall lighting specifications and configuration
- Trash removal considerations
- Common utility rooms
- Potential landscaping problems
- Water availability in the common areas
- Impediments to effective parking lot and garage sweeping
- Use of materials that may increase operating expenses
- Need for storage and/or maintenance workshops
- Need for special electrical circuits for maintenance and/or holiday decorations in the shopping center's parking lot
- Employee parking access and lighting
- Internal circulation
- Signage considerations
- Utility master metering or submetering
- Areas to collect recyclable materials
- Recycling issues
- Sustainability issues and energy conservation

Size and Configuration of Spaces

For a strip shopping center, developers will typically build spaces that are 1,200 to 2,400 square feet. Deep spaces are a problem in strip shopping centers. The most effective space arrangements have a frontage-to-depth ratio of 1 to 3; the maximum ratio is 1 to 4. This means that a 60-foot-deep store would have a frontage of 15 to 20 feet. Most smaller retail spaces are built at a depth of not more than 80 feet.

Developing second-floor space in strip shopping centers is tempting, but that quite often does not work unless the building is located in a high, dense urban area. In most small shopping centers, the second floor is used for office purposes; however, such uses may create a conflict over parking and do not generate the image desired by a typical office tenant. Second-floor space in small shopping centers is generally not good space for retailer.

The space requirements for retailers in enclosed or open-air malls are different from those in strip shopping centers. Mall retailers lease larger spaces than strip shopping center retailers and these lease spaces are deeper than spaces in strip shopping centers.

Lighting Requirements

The parking lot and canopy lighting in shopping centers can become quite complicated. Some tenants want all-night lighting for their operations, and some shopping centers require security lighting during the night.

The real estate manager should review the lighting requirements and suggest separate circuits for security lighting and special metering if some lights are left on all night, as in the case of a 24-hour restaurant or supermarket. Some electrical rooms and hallways may need to have lights on 24-hours a day because they get no outside lighting. Timing devices are crucial in such cases. Many projects use a time clock backed up by an electronic eye. Two or three different time clocks may be necessary to serve the needs of various tenants.

Trash Removal

Trash removal is a major cost for any property and can be a problem. Many properties provide trash removal service as part of the CAM program and bill the tenants for this service through the CAM charges. Trash areas must be convenient for all tenants and reasonable to maintain. They must not be an eyesore to the public. Trash enclosures should be out of sight as much as possible. The real estate manager must evaluate any trash removal system for its handling of such items.

Common Utility Rooms

In many shopping centers, electrical meters, telephone switching boards, and alarm stations are installed in common utility rooms. In this case, access by the tenant's must be considered.

Landscaping Considerations

Landscaping is one of the most important features and systems in shopping centers; it can be expensive to install and maintain. One common mistake in landscaping a shopping center is planting bushy trees that will grow and block a tenants' sign and visibility. Large bushes planted along a driveway can create visibility problems for cars moving around the parking lot. The landscape designer should ensure that the landscaping will not cause problems.

In many shopping centers, plants are placed where they obstruct a logical walking pattern from car to store. Unfortunately, the public tends to take the most direct path and will destroy the plants in short order. One shopping center installed more than 20 concrete walkways where the public had determined they wanted to walk. Another shopping center had a 35-foot shopping center sign at the front entrance, but it had two beautiful 50-foot pine trees obstructing the sign. Understandably, the tenants believed the sign to be ineffective. As these examples illustrate, developers and landscapers must always consider the impact the full-grown landscaping will have on the shopping center.

Water for Maintenance

Exterior faucets are essential in a shopping center. One shopping center with over 500 feet of front sidewalk had only one faucet; obviously, a very long hose was needed to do the proper maintenance on the property. Trash areas at the rear of a shopping center should be cleaned on a regular basis, but in most cases, no faucet is nearby to do the job. Many shopping centers that regularly steam clean their sidewalks do not have a convenient supply of water for that service. Always anticipate water needs and recommend the facilities necessary for proper watering of landscape areas and maintenance.

Efficient Sweeping

Shopping centers and malls are typically swept from once a week to daily. The cost to keep the parking lot clean increases dramatically if handwork is necessary to clean part of it. Try to eliminate areas that require the driver of the sweeper to dismount and hand clean. If eliminating all such work is impossible, careful modifications in design can reduce the cost of maintenance. All sidewalks should have ramps providing easy access for the cleaning equipment.

Materials or Systems that Increase Operating Expenses

Evaluate materials to see if alternatives are available that will provide the same aesthetics while keeping operating expenses at a reasonable level. For example, a shopping center in southern California, adobe tile is installed in a pedestrian area. The cost of stripping and cleaning the tile over the years was considerable. In another enclosed mall, a slanted glass canopy high above the entrance was almost impossible to maintain. It regularly became water stained and had to be cleaned using a rig off the roof of the building. Each cleaning was inordinately expensive. Brass railings are very attractive and, when they are all polished, they add a feeling of elegance to the property. However, if they have to be polished on a daily basis, they add to the cost of maintaining the property. An upscale mall may consider the image of the brass railings worth the expense to keep them clean and polished.

Large-scale areas of flowering plants can be expensive. Flowering plants certainly add to the ambience of the property, but such areas should be carefully evaluated with regard to the cost of maintaining them and the image they present for the shopping center. Perhaps the same landscaping effect can be obtained using smaller planting areas and perennial ground cover. Areas handling heavy traffic such as buses, trash removal trucks, or large delivery trucks should be concrete or have a heavier base of asphalt. These surfaces cost a little more to install at the outset, but they will reduce maintenance costs substantially over the years.

Storage and Maintenance Areas

Although strip shopping centers seldom need storage or maintenance areas, malls require them. In one regional mall, the original plans called for a large maintenance area, but the leasing personnel were so efficient, they had a lease out on that space. Fortunately, the real estate manager was able to convince the property owners that a 900,000-square-foot mall would need a maintenance and storage area, so it was put back in the plans prior to construction. Almost every shopping center needs to store small items such as extra signs, safety cones, light bulbs, ladders, and deicing chemicals (in the northern tier of the country).

Special Electrical Circuits for Maintenance and Decorations

Many large strip shopping centers and malls install holiday decorations as well as banners for other events. Arrangements should be made for sufficient electrical outlets for such items during the initial construction. Outlets along the rooflines and on each light pole are comparatively inexpensive to install during construction but are very expensive after the fact. Some exterior outlets should be available for maintenance equipment. These can be on a separate circuit, and the power can be turned off when they are not in use.

Employee Parking

Safe employee parking is important to the success of all shopping centers. The design of employee parking areas should take into consideration lighting, visibility, and employee safety. Employee parking areas should not infringe on prime customer parking areas.

Internal Circulation and Signage Considerations

The parking lot is critical to the operation of a shopping center. If customers are confused on how to get around the parking lot or experience many tight areas and close calls with cross traffic, they will shop elsewhere. While most real estate managers are not traffic experts, they can evaluate difficult situations and then hire experts to devise solutions. One shopping center had a major four-lane entrance with an internal cross street approximately 150 feet inside the property line that carried major traffic within the shopping center. This intersection had no stop signs, and it quickly created major traffic tie-ups within the shopping center. The simple addition of stop signs on the cross street eliminated the problem.

Plans for loading areas, limited-time parking areas, and parking for disabled shoppers must also be reviewed. Try to envision the shopping center in full operation to anticipate potential problems. No one will ever be able to anticipate all the problems, but having the real estate manager in on the initial design review and planning sessions could eliminate many costly mistakes.

Utility Master Metering

A developer may master meter water and/or gas in a shopping center to save construction costs. Since some tenants are heavy users of these utilities (e.g., hair salons, and restaurants), individually metering these tenants is best. If the developer does not individually meter these tenants, the alternative is to submeter them.

Areas for Recycling Materials

Some municipalities require businesses to recycle paper, glass, and metals. Even if recycling is not mandatory, such a program can reduce the cost of trash disposal. The real estate manager should check for locations to build enclosed areas for recycling containers. Some shopping centers provide large enclosed recycling containers for the public.

Reviewing Office Building Plans

The operation of an office building is different from that of a shopping center or mall and warrants special consideration. Office tenants typically receive an allowance for the build out their spaces. The market conditions determine the amount of the building allowance, which is usually expressed in terms of dollars per square foot of leased space.

Most office building maintenance is the responsibility

of the property owners—even though the cost of most or all of the maintenance is passed on to the tenants. Additionally, there is public traffic in the building and the convenience and perceptions of the invitees are very important.

The major operational considerations for an office building follow:

- Floor plate size and configuration
- Air-conditioning and heating systems
- Finish materials in common areas
- Lobby decor
- Security desk for the lobby
- Directories and signage
- Freight elevator and lobby dock
- Landscaping—interior and exterior
- Parking design and perhaps an attendance booth
- Storage areas for janitorial, maintenance, and security supplies and perhaps lockers for the personnel security desk for the lobby

Floor Plate Size and Configuration

The dimensions for the floor plate and bay depths determine whether the building will be tenanted by small-, medium- or large-space users. These dimensions also determine whether the building can accommodate the space plans of small, medium, or large tenants. The developer should make every effort to determine the target market for the building, evaluate their space needs, and have the building engineered to those needs.

Air-Conditioning and Heating Systems

The air-conditioning and heating systems should be zoned to the smallest likely users in the building. The system should have the capability to monitor and bill for tenants' after-hour utility and HVAC usage.

Finish Materials in Common Areas

Because maintenance becomes a big problem as buildings age, putting in first-class materials with low maintenance requirements at the outset can avoid large future expenditures. Installing linoleum in the restrooms is less expensive, but tile will have a better appearance and require less maintenance over time. Tile walls in the restrooms are preferable by many to painted walls for the same reasons. Common corridors hold up better and remain attractive longer if they are wallpapered in a strong, durable paper rather than painted. Elevator interiors should consider how the frequency of cleaning the interior cabs and replacing the wall covering. Every item considered for the building should be reviewed from the point of view of future maintenance needs and requirements along with the image the material creates for the building.

Lobby Decor

The office building's lobby sets the tone of the building for the tenants and their visitors. The lobby should have the same feel as the exterior of the building, and it should be reasonably spacious, well lighted, and professionally maintained. Therefore, each item in the lobby should be considered from a maintenance point of view and the image it creates for the building. Carpeting is attractive but does not hold up as well and requires more maintenance than terrazzo or a glazed tile. Hardwood flooring looks good, but in major traffic areas, it may require additional maintenance to keep it to building standards. Furniture and fixtures in the lobby should be considered for ease of maintenance, wear and tear, and replacement of parts. Often, the image of the lobby is more important than using materials that are easy and less costly to maintain.

Directories and Signage

An attractive signage program with easy-to-use directories enhances the building's image. The architect should develop the design criteria for all building signs. The directory should be large enough to meet tenant needs for additional and above-standard listings and should come from a supplier that can respond to future needs in a timely fashion or be electronic signs. For a tenant to wait two months for a door sign or directory listing is difficult. Many lobby directional are electronic digital signs that can be modified immediately by the management staff.

Landscaping—Interior and Exterior

Interior landscaping is becoming an important aspect of office building. Arrangements must be made to water and service interior plants without harming the flooring area around them. The people servicing the plants must have access to water, and the plants may need to have direct light.

Exterior landscaping should not create hazards to cars in the parking lot. The appearance of the original landscaping should receive careful thought to prevent the problems that arise from over-planting. Drought resistant plants should be considered.

Janitorial Services

Tenants generally have more problems with janitorial services than anything else in an office building—with the possible exception of heating and air-conditioning. Janitorial service needs include equipment storage as well as access to sinks and servicing areas. For example, the original design of one high-rise office building had only one janitor sink—and that was on the ground floor. Fortunately, the real estate manager reviewed the plans prior to construction and was able to correct the situation and have a janitorial sink in a closet area on every floor. Easy-to-clean surfaces should be considered to reduce janitorial costs and keep up the building's appearance.

The janitorial contractor handles the removal of office building trash. Issues to consider include location of the trash receptacles and access to the receptacles by the janitorial and trash removal companies. If the building will have a recycling program, there will need to be a place for storing materials to be recycled until they are picked up.

Parking

Parking can be a difficult issue for any building, but more so for an office building. Parking lots are not attractive, but landscaping can enhance them. The plants must not interfere with traffic circulation or with a driver's ability to see an oncoming vehicle. Paint and good lighting can improve the appearance of a parking garage. Parking garages and parking lots for office buildings need a lighting review similar to that for shopping centers. Painting the ceiling of a garage may increase lighting levels. If the parking area is large, area signs are beneficial, especially for the visitor who may forget where their car were parked. Directional signs should always be clear.

CONSTRUCTION

A reliable general contractor is a critical member of the development or construction team. The construction manager and the general contractor turn the developer's vision into reality. A developer may hire a general contractor to build out TIs for an office or industrial property. A shopping center may have a vacant pad or out-parcel where the property owner plans to develop a shop building. A general contractor may be needed to remodel a building.

The developer usually has a construction manager who manages the construction process. The developer may hire a general contractor or it may own a separate general contracting firm. In either case, the developer and the general contractor enter into a general contract agreement.

Selecting a General Contractor

Developers frequently know and select general contractors for their projects. However, in certain situations, a property owner may ask the real estate manager to recommend or to select a general contractor. For example, a property owner who does not live near the property may not know local general contractors or anyone other than the real estate manager who can refer one. Ideally, the real estate manager will know three or four good general contractors that may bid on a project.

Prequalification

The first step in selecting a general contractor is to prequalify candidates. The prequalification criteria include the following: history of the company; backgrounds of key executives; résumé of completed projects, contracts, and licenses; professional and trade association memberships; references; bonding capabilities; disputes or lawsuits with current or past clients; insurance policies; projects constructed; references; and the company's financial strength.

Interview

The next step is to interview one of the firm's key executives as well as the person who will be the project's construction manager. One of the most important issues is a discussion of the property owner's goals and the objectives of the new development, remodeling, or construction project.

During the interview, ask the construction manager about his or her experience with the type of construction to be performed and/or the type of property to be built. The real estate manager should also discuss the "development" or "construction" team and each team member's role and responsibility.

Another important point to cover is whether the performance of the work in an existing building will disturb the other tenants. Issues that can affect the business of other tenants include the location of the construction staging area, trash, and debris removal, delivery of construction materials, excessive noise during normal business hours, safety practices, and the behavior of construction workers.

The contractor's insurance coverage and bonding capacity should be reviewed. This discussion may include reporting requirements, submittal and approval process of invoices, and, if appropriate, regular construction or project meetings.

References

Business and professional references must be requested and checked. When checking references, two important inquiries are whether past projects stayed within budget and whether they were completed on time.

Other questions of concern are the quality of the work performed, the contractor's responsiveness to completing the "punch-list items," and any disruption of tenants' businesses in existing buildings during the construction. This can be a critical issue when remodeling a building or building out a tenant's space.

Preferred Contractor

Sometimes, a preferred general contractor is selected before the project is designed. Though this eliminates the bid process and may a cost-plus contract, it allows the general contractor to have input into the design of the project. The general contractor may have significant input in valve engineering, selection of materials, and development of a realistic construction schedule.

Construction Contracts

A contractor can use several different methods to charge for his or her services. The following sections list four common construction-contracting methods.

Lump-Sum or Fixed-Price Contract

The awarding of lump-sum or fixed-price contracts is based on competitive bids. The general contractor submits a fixed-price bid based on the design and plans and is allowed to charge additional fees for alterations (known as change orders) to the plans and design.

If the project costs less than the fixed price, the contractor keeps the savings. Likewise, if the bid was less than the actual price, the general contractor is responsible for the additional cost. This form of contract holds considerable risk for the contractor as well as the possibility of handsome rewards.

Cost-Plus-Percentage Contract

A cost-plus-percentage contract is common when the cost cannot yet be determined, such as during the early stages of a renovation project. Until an older building can be thoroughly investigated for hidden problems (e.g., what may be behind the walls), determining a fixed fee or guaranteed price is impossible.

The general contractor charges the developer the actual costs of construction plus a percentage of those figures. When the building's costs can be estimated with some accuracy, the contract may be converted to a fixed-price or other form of guaranteed-price contract.

Cost-Plus-a-Fixed-Fee Contract

A cost-plus-a-fixed-fee contract is the same as the cost-plus-percentage contract except the general contractor's fee is a fixed sum. This contract may be used in lieu of the aforementioned contract to ensure that the general contractor has no incentive to spend more money than necessary to complete the project.

Guaranteed Maximum Price Contract

With a guaranteed maximum price contract, the general contractor guarantees the construction cost will not exceed a maximum price—and shares in the savings. The developer pays the actual cost of the project, not to exceed the guaranteed price, and thus can budget the guaranteed price and share in cost savings.

After estimating the construction costs, the general contractor and the developer work up a critical path schedule including a timeline for each construction phase. The general contractor contracts with subcontractors to build each phase. At least once a month, the contractor submits a construction progress report to the developer. Unless the construction contract stipulates a fixed price, this report provides a running account of the project's costs, including an analysis of cost to date, anticipated costs to complete, and the anticipated total cost as compared with the budget. Each component of the construction budget is analyzed separately.

Insurance

The general, contractor and subcontractors are required to maintain insurance and to include the developer as an additional named insured on their policies. The types of insurance required include general and automobile liability, workers' compensation, builders' risk, bonds, and coverage for equipment.

Walk-Through

After the contractor has completed the project, the construction manager, accompanied by the real estate manager, will conduct a walk-through and compile a punch list of items that require finishing or repair. On completion of the work, the construction drawings and warranties are turned over to the real estate manager, who should develop a list of all subcontractors and material suppliers for future needs.

MARKETING AND LEASING

The developer estimates the cost of five components of the project's pro forma: land cost, construction cost, financing cost, operating expenses, and leasing. The first four can be estimated with a fair degree of accuracy. Often, the fifth component can not be predicted with a fair degree of accuracy.

The first component of the estimate is the land cost. The developer either purchases the land or obtains an option for a stipulated price. The only unknowns are the geotechnical condition of the site and whether hazardous substances are present. A geotechnical survey determines if the site is suitable for building. An environmental survey determines, with a fair degree of accuracy, whether the site is contaminated by hazardous substances. Environmental issues may arise during construction that were not discovered during an environmental study or analysis of the site.

The experienced developer seldom has significant construction cost overruns. A well-designed and executed project will be within a few percentage points of the construction estimate. If the development has several changes to the design or materials used during construction, it is likely the general contractor will not be able to build the project on budget. This seldom occurs so the cost of the development can be estimated with a fair degree of accuracy.

Since construction financing is precommitted, it is a known cost. The permanent financing may be precommitted with an agreed interest rate or tied to a financial index with or without a cap and a floor on the interest rate.

Operating expenses can also be projected, based on the costs to operate similar buildings, with a reasonable anticipated increase in costs between the time of the original estimate and the building's opening.

Leasing, is the most difficult component to project, and has two major components: (1) the rental rates, including concessions, that will be achieved and (2) the time it will take to lease. Leasing projections are based on a thorough analysis of the market or on the developer's "gut feeling" for the market. Two to 10 years may elapse between the time the developer conceives the idea to the day the building opens for occupancy. A small strip center or garden office building typically takes two to four years to develop from conception to occupancy; a high-rise office building requires four to seven years; and a regional mall may take five to 10 years. This period includes the entire development process described in this chapter.

During the time the project is in progress, the market can turn from good to poor. An economic downturn may occur in the area or nationally, causing unanticipated space in existing buildings to come on the market increasing vacancy rates. If the pro forma for a development was created in 2006 and the building commenced construction in 2007 and the building was ready for occupancy in 2010, the rental rates project and lease-up time projected before the Great Recession of 2008 through 2013 was probably different than the actual rental rates and lease up that was achieved in the middle of the great recession.

The merger of two major banks, for example, may result in tens of thousands, even hundreds of thousands of square feet of subleased spaces leased below market rate available and competing with all space on the market. Such an unanticipated event will probably depress rental rates, increase concessions, and slow the lease-up of a new building.

Selecting the Leasing Agent

Three choices are available for selecting the project's leasing team or agent: (1) contracting with a brokerage firm, (2) employing an in-house staff leasing agent, or (3) assigning the responsibility to the real estate manager.

Each approach has advantages and disadvantages. The developer should select the approach that can lease the property the fastest at the best rates. A successful lease-up validates the decision to develop the project.

Exclusive Broker

Leasing agents actively works the area, are aware of tenants in the market for space, and are familiar with the terms of recently completed leases. They typically devote all their time to leasing one property type in a limited geographical area. Since leasing agents receive compensation only when a lease is signed, they must be very aggressive in their marketing and leasing efforts.

The disadvantage of this approach is that after the initial leasing and marketing efforts, if deals are not in play, the agents may spend more time on other properties that generate commission income, since the leasing agents receive no salary. If leasing slows, leasing activities may consist primarily of a sign on the property, an internet listing and little else. When this happens, it is time to find a new leasing agent who will start with new enthusiasm and optimism. The last 10 to 20 percent of a project is often the most difficult to lease, yet this space represents the developer's profit. The agents' efforts to fill this space may not match the intensity of leasing the first half of the project.

When hiring a commercial leasing firm, the developer is best served by giving the company an exclusive to lease the property. Some developers and property owners mistakenly believe that if leasing agents have an open listing on the property, everyone will try to find tenants for the project. The reality is few, if any, commissioned leasing persons will spend time trying to find a tenant when they may find that the space was just leased or someone else was representing the tenant. The leasing community will show a tenant a property with an open listing when the leasing agent represents the tenant. It is a rare exception when a leasing agent will canvass or cold-call for a building without an exclusive listing. An exclusive listing assures the leasing agent that when a lease is executed, he or she will receive a commission.

In-House Leasing Agent

Many developers hire in-house leasing agents who work only on the developer's project. The agents become more familiar with the project, does not reduce its leasing effort when leasing is slow, and are loyal to the developer. Because the leasing agent leases only the developer's properties and there will be periods when no leases are executed, a salary plus an incentive compensation based on leasing activity is common.

The disadvantage to this approach is that the in-house leasing agent may not be as aggressive as the outside agent because of the comfort of a regular salary. Some believe the in-house leasing agent must be as aggressive searching for tenants as the leasing agent for a brokerage company because if the leasing agent is not productive, the agent may be replaced. The agent who is limited to leasing only his or her employer's properties may not be as active in the general leasing market.

Real Estate Manager as Leasing Agent

The real estate manager seldom, if ever, has the time to lease a new project. However, the real estate manager may be the best person to lease the last 10 to 20 percent of the project and to handle the re-leasing of space and renewals.

Leasing Meetings and Reports

Regularly scheduled leasing meetings and reports are critical to the marketing and leasing effort. Leasing meetings, typically held weekly or monthly, keep the entire leasing team focused on the project's objectives. It is a time to review the progress of each deal; discuss and debate negotiating strategies; review the recent leasing and marketing efforts; evaluate the advertising plan; discuss the market conditions; and plan future activities.

This is also the best opportunity for the developer to determine the effectiveness of the leasing agents and whether they are spending sufficient time on the project. The leasing agent presents a leasing report during each meeting.

General Lease Negotiations

Two areas must be negotiated on every lease: (1) the business terms and (2) the lease provisions. The leasing agent negotiates the business terms, which include lease rate, concessions, length of lease, and options subject to the developer's approval.

The leasing agent, the real estate manager, or an attorney negotiates the other lease provisions. Some leasing agents do not have a good understanding of the impact of lease provisions on the operations of the property and do not know how to negotiate these provisions and still provide the property owner with adequate protection.

Some developers prefer to have their leasing agents searching for tenants rather than sitting in a room negotiating these provisions. In either case, if the leasing agent does not negotiate the lease provisions, a real estate manager who understands the lease or an attorney can negotiate the provisions. If the leasing agent or real estate manager negotiated the lease, the developer's attorney should provide a final review and draft any changes.

Major Tenant Lease Negotiations

A primary difference between developing office buildings and shopping centers is that office buildings traditionally have been developed as speculative buildings, with limited or no pre-leasing activities, while shopping centers (except small unanchored strip shopping centers and some specialty or theme centers) need a commitment from one or several anchor tenants (also known as major tenants) before a project can be financed and started. Major tenants, whether office or retail, recognize their importance to the proposed project and use this advantage while negotiating their lease terms.

Seldom do two or more major tenants compete for the same location in an office building or a shopping center. The developer is aware of a proposed major tenant's negotiating strengths and must execute a long-term lease that provides the tenant with sufficient concessions, meets the lender's requirements, and is consistent with the projections in the project's pro forma. Despite any concessions, the major tenant's lease terms, combined with the projected rental terms of the other tenants, must make economic sense for the developer to proceed with the project.

Negotiating Shopping Center Anchor Leases

The anchor tenants for neighborhood and community strip shopping centers are usually one or a combination of the following: a supermarket, super drugstore, discount clothing stores, or home improvement center. Larger community centers may include a junior department store or discount store such as Kohl's or Wal-Mart. Specialty department stores such as Nordstrom or Nieman Marcus or full-line department stores such as Macy's or Dillards anchor regional and super regional malls.

Design and Layout Requirements. When considering a potential location, anchor tenants focus on two design and layout issues: the shopping center's access and the visibility of their proposed store. Access concerns include ease of entry from the street to the parking lot near the tenant's site, whether sufficient parking is available in front of or around the site and their store, and the location of the store's entrances.

Concerns regarding layout are usually about having sufficient land available to design the prototype store. Anchor tenants require a minimum and maximum square footage for their different store layouts. If a developer cannot accommodate the alternative sizes and layouts, the potential tenants will usually reject the proposed site.

Real Estate Transaction Types. If the anchor tenant decides to enter into a real estate transaction with the developer, the anchor has three types among which to choose: lease, ground lease, or purchase.

If the retailer prefers a lease, the developer provides a build-to-suit arrangement. The anchor tenant gives the developer its plans, and the developer builds and leases the store to the tenant. The second approach is a ground lease. The developer creates separate parcels of land from the site to accommodate the anchor tenant's building and required parking. The tenant leases the site and constructs its own building.

The third approach is for the anchor tenant to purchase its site and build its store. The tenant may then package several of its buildings together, sell them to an investor, and enter into a long-term leaseback or retain ownership of the real estate.

Rental Terms and Concessions. The rental terms the anchor tenant can achieve reflect its strong negotiating position. Full-line and specialty department stores receive the best rental terms and concessions when a developer is negotiating to have them anchor a regional or super regional mall. Seldom, if ever, do developers have more department stores interested in their proposed mall than can be accommodated.

The arrangement with a department store can be a "give-away deal." If the store puts up its own building, the mall developer may even sell the site and sufficient land for parking for substantially less than the market value. The developer who builds and leases the building to the department store anchor may provide a substantial contribution, in excess of $1 million, toward the tenant's improvements.

The rental rate charged to the department store is usually equal to or slightly less than the developer's cost to service the debt or mortgage on the premises. The reason the developer offers such a "give-away deal" is that department stores are essential to developing the mall. Even with the "give-away," if the shop spaces lease at or near the pro forma rate and on schedule and the development costs are per the pro forma, the mall will be very profitable.

The anchor in a strip shopping center does not receive as favorable lease terms as the department store in a regional or super regional mall. However, the developer recognizes that the number of potential anchor tenants for the strip shopping center is limited. The developer's objective is to negotiate the lease at par, meaning that the tenant will not receive any concessions and its monthly rent will be equal to the developer's debt service on the building. Even though these are long-term leases with rent increases every five years, there is a possibility in the future the anchor tenant will pay percentage rent in addition to its minimum rent.

Anchor tenants may attempt to negotiate a cap or ceiling on their pro rata shares of the pass-through expenses such as CAM, taxes, or insurance. Anchor tenants may negotiated a cap on those expenses or agree to a fixed CAM charge with a nominal annual increase

Anchor tenants for regional and super regional malls negotiate for and are usually granted an exclusion from paying CAM expenses for the common areas on the mall area. They pay their pro rata shares of the parking lot common area maintenance cost. The mall's shop leases require those tenants to pay all the enclosed mall CAM expenses. The shop tenant's lease states that the denominator for the formula to calculate the tenant's share of the enclosed mall common area expenses consists of the total square footage of all shops facing the mall, excluding the square footage of the anchor tenants.

Favorable lease provisions for the anchor tenant include a long-term lease to amortize the millions of dollars invested in tenant improvements and fixtures. Each store is important to its market penetration strategy. The length of the typical anchor retail tenant's lease is 20 to 30 years, with six to eight five-year options.

Use Provisions and Restrictions. The anchor tenant will want a very broad use provision that will allow it to change its product line and sublet all or a portion of its premises to almost any use. The developer must stand firm and not allow a change from the intended use of the premises. If a supermarket closes and subleases its space to an auto-supply store, fabric store, or any other low-traffic generator, it will do immeasurable harm to the traffic and possibly to the shopping center's reputation. Most shop tenants pay the higher rents of an anchored shopping center because of the customer traffic generated by the anchor tenant or tenants. With the loss of these customers, most shop tenants' sales will decline, and the rental value of these spaces will decrease. Standing firm on limiting use provisions is also justified by the rental and lease provision concessions the developer gives the anchor for generating traffic in the shopping center. These same concessions are not intended or justified for a subtenant that will generate a small fraction of the traffic.

Because of the anchor tenant's concern with visibility and convenient customer parking, it will insist on limiting the number and placement of pad buildings, also known as pad parcels or out-lot parcels, in the parking lot. These small buildings, leased to restaurants and banks, are very profitable for the developer. Tenants pay a premium rent for the visibility, access, drive-through lane, and identity these locations offer.

The developer will negotiate with the anchor tenant to keep some pad sites in the plans for the shopping center. To preserve visibility, a department store may negotiate that a kiosk or cart cannot be within a certain distance of the store's mall entrance. Changes to the layout or design of the shopping center may affect the anchor tenant's visibility and access. The anchor tenant will negotiate the right to approve plans to remodel or expand the shopping center or mall and to change the parking lot's ingress, egress, and layout.

Anchor tenants in strip shopping centers, especially supermarkets, are concerned with long-term parking in the areas in front of or near their stores. They will attempt to negotiate restrictions to tenant uses adjacent to their premises. For example, they may request that office tenants, theaters, bowling alleys, or schools not be located within 100 to 300 feet of their premises. Developers often agree to such restrictions.

Though department and discount stores do not negotiate for an exclusive, supermarkets and super drugstores often receive such an exclusive. The supermarket may negotiate an exclusive for groceries or seek a restriction preventing another store over a specified size (typically 5,000 square feet) from selling groceries, bakery goods, fish, fruits, and vegetables. The latter restriction enables the developer to lease to a typical-sized bakery, or a meat or fish market; however, few of these types of tenants are available today. The super drugstore will negotiate for, and usually achieve, an exclusive to sell prescription medicine.

The anchor tenant will insist on restricting uses that may be detrimental to its image or that of the shopping center (e.g., adult bookstores). Similarly, the developer must not concede to the anchor tenant the right to assign or sublease its space to another use. As previously mentioned, a change of use to a tenant that draws significantly less traffic will have an adverse impact on the shopping center's tenant mix and eventually the rents it can achieve as well as its net operating income and value. The developer should insist that the use of the premises not be changed.

If the anchor tenant wants to close its store (known as "going dark"), a fallback position is for the property owner to have the right to cancel the lease, release the anchor tenant from all future lease obligations, and regain possession of the premises. Such a lease provision will be hotly debated because the anchor tenant knows it often can sublease or assign its lease at a substantial increase in rent. For instance, if a supermarket paying $8.00 per square foot on 30,000 square feet subleases the space for $11.00, it realizes an annual profit of $ 90,000. Moreover, if the supermarket is vacating the premises to open a state-of-the-art, 50,000-square-foot store a few blocks away, it may not want the property owner to re-lease the space to another supermarket, i.e., a discount or specialty market.

Operating Agreement. The developer and anchor tenant or tenants negotiate a shopping center's operating agreement, which places restrictions on the owner's and tenants' use of the shopping center and assigns rights and obligations to the owner and anchor tenants. These restrictions, rights, and obligations are found in the shopping center's common area agreement and/or the *reciprocal easement agreement (REA).* These agreements define the standards of maintenance for the common areas; appoint one party, usually the property owner, as the manager of the common areas; determine each party's portion of common area expenses; define the common areas; and restrict the use of these areas. The agreements also give anchor tenants the right to install pole signs, provide for minimum parking requirements, and allow each party to approve changes to the parking lot and expansion or remodeling of the shopping center.

Negotiating Office Building Leases

Office buildings, unlike medium-size and large shopping centers, are often planned and developed without major pre-leasing. A major office tenant's negotiating position, although strong, seldom has as much leverage as that of a shopping center's anchor tenant. The operation and design of a shopping center definitely impact a retail anchor tenant's business. Those factors seldom affect the office user's business, so a major office tenant's lease has fewer lease provisions to negotiate.

Rental Terms. The major tenant's lease is usually 10 to 20 years, with one or two multi-year options. The developer will prefer to have the rent adjusted to the market rate for each option period. The tenant may negotiate for the rent to be increased by a percentage of the market rate. The tenant's rationale is that the initial lease rate is below the market rate and the rate during the option periods should be a percentage of the market rate. The lease must define how to determine market rate. The lease provision must state which building or types of buildings and what area are used to determine the market rental rate.

Concessions. The office building market conditions in the area determine whether any concessions, such as favorable rental terms, over-standard improvements, and moving allowances, must be negotiated with the major tenant of an office building. Regardless of the market conditions, a developer will offer a major user of office space favorable rental terms—often including free rent or a reduced rate.

The tenant will negotiate for a cap on pass-through expenses, and the developer will try to avoid this concession. If a compromise is necessary, the developer may offer to place an annual percentage cap on the increase of the controllable expenses but not the uncontrollable expenses. The theory is that the developer has control over some expenses, such as maintenance contracts, but no control or limited control over other expenses, such as utility, taxes, insurance, and snow removal. Experienced office building tenants will negotiate specific expenses that should be excluded from the building's pass-through charges, such as artwork in the lobby, cleaning of vacant spaces, and salaries of the property's ownership's personnel that are not on site.

Another common concession is over-standard TIs. The building provides a standard TI package or a dollar-per-square-foot allowance; for example, $65.00 per square foot above the building shell. A major tenant usually requires additional improvements beyond the building's standard package. The developer prefers not to offer over-standard TIs because this concession is expensive and the property owner incurs the cost before the tenant takes occupancy and commences paying rent. Nevertheless, this concession is typically offered to major tenants. A consolation in providing over-standard TIs that the tenant may be more likely to renew its lease because competing property owners may be unwilling to provide similar TIs. If the tenant does vacate, the improvements usually have salvage value.

Only the imagination of the tenant or the tenant's broker limits the concessions that may be requested and negotiated. The major tenant may negotiate for the right of first refusal on contiguous space or contiguous floors, space pocketing (space that is reserved for the tenant's later use), and exterior signage and name rights on the building. Other concessions may include a moving allowance and a grand opening party.

CONCLUSION

Property development is a big risk and big reward business. When a project is built on time and within budget and leases up per the pro forma, it is a tremendous success. The rewards for a successful development are unsurpassed by almost any other business endeavor. However, several things may go wrong and easily and quickly turn a project filled with anticipated success and rewards into a dismal failure.

Delays in the permitting process, unforeseen construction costs and delays, changes in the financing market, a downturn in the economy, or a major tenant's financial woes can cause a project to fail—just to name a few possibilities. Developers can earn millions on one project and lose it all on the next. Some people envy the lifestyle of the successful developer, yet entrepreneurs who risk everything they have on one or more developments are entitled to reap the rewards of a successful venture.

The engine of commercial real estate is the developer. Without speculative development activities, there would be few buildings to design and construct, a reduction in the need for financing, fewer leasing and sales transactions, and limited growth opportunity for the real estate management industry.

When development are active building projects the commercial real estate industry benefits and cities have new places for commerce and an increase tax base.

CHAPTER

19

Renovating, Rehabbing, and Repositioning Commercial Properties

There are excellent value-added opportunities to renovate, rehab, and reposition properties in good and poor real estate markets. Value-added buyers are always looking for opportunities to reposition properties and to greatly enhance their value. Many property owners will analyze their property for value-added opportunities, while others will be unaware of the opportunities or be buried in the challenges of a troubled property. This chapter will review the process to add value to properties by renovating, rehabbing, and repositioning them.

Although a building's physical life may last hundreds of years, its economic life may end well in advance of its physical life. Buildings may become functionally obsolete for their original use, such as older class B office buildings in downtowns, especially in the *central business district (CBD)* that are no longer able to meet the space-planning needs of modern office tenants or have the amenities required of corporations. Even though these older buildings are functionally obsolete, some are still structurally sound and are usually in good locations. However, these buildings, which usually have a large vacancy or are empty, can develop "Empty Building Syndrome."

Retrofitting these buildings to new building codes may be too costly or even structurally impossible. Problem areas may include antiquated wiring and plumbing, inadequate *heating, ventilation, and air-conditioning (HVAC),* poor mullion and column spacing, small floor plates, and noncompliance with the Americans with Disabilities Act (ADA). Some of these buildings may need to be torn down, while others can be redeveloped for the same use or for a new use—also known as, *adaptive use.*

REASONS FOR REHABBING

An office building developed during the early 1900s in the CBD that has 4,000 to 5,000-square-foot floor plates does not meet the needs of most downtown office tenants. Such a building's structural soundness, architectural value, and location can provide opportunities to change its use to apartments or condominiums. Property owners and developers consider rehabbing buildings for a variety of reasons.

Adjusting to Tenants' Changing Needs

Tenants' changing needs may be the reason a building loses its economic life. The best example is shopping centers—the retail industry experiences more change than any other industry. The shopping center properties respond by developing new styles or converting an existing shopping center to a different type. Changes in the *demographics* and *psychographics* of a neighborhood may also require a change in the tenant mix and general design of a shopping center. New shopping centers continue to be developed as a response to changing retail concepts—which are a response to the changing needs and wants of consumers.

Older industrial properties in urban locations that have made a transition to residential areas have been converted to loft apartments and condominiums. If a building's intended use has not changed, but technology has changed the way the tenants conduct their businesses, to be competitive the building may need to be rehabbed to accommodate the new technology.

Modernizing a property is one of the most common reasons to rehab a building. This would include new architectural styles, features, and materials. The building's intended use may still be viable, but the building is outdated and has lost its competitiveness. In an office or medical office building, the lobby, elevator cabs, and hallways are updated. In a shopping center, the building façade, landscaping, and common areas are updated over time. In shopping malls the flooring is replaced and updated, existing landscaping is replaced with new varieties of plants, and furniture is replaced with a design fitting for the new appearance and style.

Additional Leasable Area

Rehabbing to expand a building can present an opportunity to create additional leasable space by adding additional floors, building over a parking structure or area, or acquiring adjacent property. Creating a pad or out lot in the parking lot of a shopping center is a classic example.

In urban areas such as Union Square in San Francisco and North Michigan Avenue in Chicago, the second and third floors of office buildings have been converted from office space to retail space for tenants that can occupy multiple levels. Some ground-floor space in such buildings have been redesigned and remodeled to accommodate retail customers. Retailers will pay a premium for the ground-floor space and a much lower rate for usable basement area and second and third-floor space.

Other additional leasable areas may be found within the building. Can storage areas be converted to leasable space? Can the basement be converted to tenant's space or storage? If the building is in a strong retailing area, could a basement area be converted to retail use and combined with the ground-floor space or leased for an entertainment, or restaurant use with an entrance from the street?

Regardless of the type of building, the rehab process always tries to create new *gross leasable areas (GLAs)*. An espresso stand or small shop may be added to the lobby of an office building, and carts, kiosks, and wall shops, added to a shopping center or mall.

BENEFITS OF REHABBING

The benefits of rehabbing a commercial property are recognized worldwide. In Europe, a rehab is referred to as "refurbishment," and in Asia, it is known as "retrofit." Regardless of what the procedure is called, every modern country is aware of the potential benefits of rehabbing or repositioning commercial properties. These benefits are achieved by extending and/or maximizing a property's economic life, which is threatened when the building's competitiveness erodes. During a Retrofit Seminar in Singapore, Frederick S. Jennett, CBE, stated, "Rehabilitation speaks to America's cultural shift—away from disposable goods and toward creative recycling, renovation, and reuse of the best from the past."[1] This statement was expressed more than 25 years ago and is still valued today.

Although conservation can be a major influence, refurbishment [rehabilitation] is usually economically motivated recognition that the basic value of a well-constructed building outlasts its original or current use. Skillful adaptation and upgrading for new often increases the economic value of the original building. Rehab is good management of the building stock to ensure that the original investment is not prematurely lost.

A well-conceived and professionally implemented rehab of a commercial property extends the building's economic and physical life. In addition to the economic benefits, rehabilitation restores a building to its original splendor and saves its architectural heritage. This occurs in the rehab of older office buildings and manufacturing plants. Few rehabbed shopping centers are old enough to have historical significance. Older warehouses and manufacturing buildings, such as Ghirardelli Square in San Francisco and Faneuil Hall in Boston, have been converted to retail use. In Portland, an old brewery was converted to a multiuse development.

Of the variety of social and economic factors that have contributed to the benefits of rehabilitation,

1. Robert Sheridan, " Turning Old Factories into New-Style Industrial Buildings," *Urban Land* (February 2, 1989), 2–5.

one of the most important have probably been the federal income tax incentives for the rehab of historic buildings.

TYPES OF REHABBING

Rehabilitation can take many forms: remodeling, restoration, renovation, adaptive use, or modernization. Rehabilitate is defined as "returning a structure to good use through proper maintenance and remodeling. Physically improving a property to take on the characteristics of a more up-to-date building." Remodeling is described as "changing the plan, form or shape of something to correct functional or economic deficiencies," while modernization is explained as "the act of remodeling; bringing up-to-date, to modernize, to repair and renovate a building so it has more of the character of contemporary design."

The purpose of *restoration* is to refurbish a building's original architectural details as closely as possible. The *renovation* of a building refers to the physical upgrading of materials and support systems while retaining the original use. *Adaptive use*, on the other hand, is the process by which structurally sound older buildings are developed for economically viable new uses. Such buildings may be historically important, architecturally distinctive, or simply under utilized structures that exhibit signs of life under a façade of age and neglect. One or more of these forms of improving a building's value and its economic life are often components in successfully repositioning a building.

Well-known examples of adaptive use include Ghirardelli Square in San Francisco, which was converted from a chocolate factory to a mixed-use development of retail, restaurant, and entertainment uses. Faneuil Hall in Boston was converted from a group of warehouse buildings to a festive market, and Trolley Square in Salt Lake City was converted from a trolley barn to a specialty shopping center.

Eventually, every building will be upgraded or demolished because of age, wear and tear, changes in tenant needs, evolution of neighborhoods or technological advancement. The rehab design must take into consideration the fact that the building will probably be rehabbed again—possibly even several times—during its physical life. The design must be flexible, anticipate future trends, and be able to adapt to ever-changing technology.

THE REHAB PROCESS

The rehab process usually starts with an older building and, within cost restraints, converts it into an attractive and economically viable property. The rehab process requires more planning and additional management from all the members of the rehab team than if they were to develop a new building. A building that is occupied during the rehab process requires additional planning.

Rehab Analysis

The first question to consider is *"why?"* Is the rehab an effort to:

- Save a failed project?
- Maintain the property's market position?
- Improve a building's market position?
- Capture a new market?
- Increase the property's income and value?
- Fulfill an obligation to the community?
- Display pride of property ownership?

Whatever the reason, a market survey must be conducted to determine if the proposed rehab will meet its objective and be an economic success. Two key elements of the market survey are (1) demand for the product and (2) market rental rates. If the property is not economically successful, the project will ultimately fail.

A major component of the rehab analysis is the *pro forma*. First, the property owner or developer considering a rehab must determine the maximum amount of income the rehab project can generate after allowing for vacancy and credit loss. Next, estimates are calculated for the amount that can be borrowed, based on the proposed project's available income to support the loan. By knowing the maximum amount of the loan and the capital investment, the scope of the project and the maximum amount of funding available for construction can be ascertained. With rehab projects, the capital stack may have many pieces, including tax credits, tax incremental financing, and/or historical tax credits. It can be difficult to structure some rehab project with just equity and debt. Construction costs must be estimated and contained. If costs exceed the loan and the capital investment, alternative solutions, such as substitution of materials or elimination of features, may be necessary. The property owner or developer then determines if the construction loan and equity is sufficient to complete the rehab to the design specification necessary to achieve the projected income.

Rehab Team

A successful rehab project requires the input of a team of experts, each with a different discipline. The rehab team is led by the property owner and includes an architect, general contractor, leasing agent, and real estate manager. The property owner may assign its role to a project manager, the property owner's representative, or the property's real estate manager. The team members must bring their expertise to the project with their vision of what will make the building successful. Depending on the plans for the property, consultants such as historical; structural and mechanical engineers; environmental consultants; technology and telecommunication experts; energy and security experts; and others may join the rehab team.

Team Member Selection

Rehab team members have different agendas, and although their perspectives vary, each is necessary for a successful project:

- Architects view the project for its function and aesthetic value.
- General contractors focus on cost containment, quality construction, and schedule requirements.
- Leasing agents see a fast lease-up at market rates
- Real estate managers are concerned with existing tenants and the long-term efficient and cost-effective operations of the property
- The property owner's representative protects the interest of the property owner and aligns all of the team members efforts.
- The property owner weighs the risk versus the reward elements of the project.

Several years ago during a roundtable discussion on rehab, builder Seymour Cohen emphasized:

> ... This business of renovation and restoration is really a highly specialized business, and I think it requires highly specialized knowledge from the architect, the engineers, the construction manager, and the contractors themselves ... I think we all ought to gear ourselves for this work because it is the wave of the future. As has been said, 'there is no room in this kind of work for adversary positions.' The architect, engineers, construction manager, and builders don't just have to be experts, they all have to be in on the job early in the game. Contractors with good experience have a lot of help to offer the architect and property owner during the design phase[2]...

Since the need and the opportunity to rehab properties will always exist, Seymour Cohen's comments will always be valid. His message is essential for a successful renovation and/or repositioning of a property.

Team members must be flexible and work together to meet the property owner's objectives while keeping the project within budget. Everyone on the team must understand the roles of the other team members and assist them in accomplishing those goals. Without a solid team approach, the probability of a successful rehab diminishes. Every opportunity to develop a successful rehab project has a corresponding opportunity to fail.

Team members should be selected according to their expertise in the rehab's current or planned property type. Each property has unique characteristics, and only a professional with expertise in the specific property type fully understands how these characteristics can be incorporated into a building

2. *Architectural Record Digest,* December 1982.

to make it marketable. For instance, office tenant requirements differ from those of retail tenants. The differences include size and depth of space, amenities, utility requirements, location, visibility, access, and the targeted market.

A shopping center architect would not have the same understanding of office tenants' requirements as of retail tenants' requirements, though some professionals have extensive experience with multiple property types. This concept generally holds true for general contractors, leasing agents, and even real estate managers.

Real Estate Manager's Role

The real estate manager is the only team member whose involvement begins before the rehab starts and continues long after the rehab is finished. Every other rehab team member moves on to another project after completing his or her assignment. During the property's entire economic life, the real estate manager has the responsibility of seeing that it meets the property owner's objectives.

The real estate manager's knowledge of managing, marketing, and leasing provides a unique contribution to the development of a successful rehab. If the real estate manager has been managing the property under consideration, he or she is intimately familiar with all its aspects, including the building's position in the market, its strengths, and its weaknesses—necessary information when analyzing the proposed rehab's potential.

The following unique insights position the real estate manager as a valuable member of the rehab team:

- Familiarity with the tenants and their likes and dislikes about the building
- Understanding of the building's strengths and weaknesses, its position in the market, its present market niche, and the market rates it can command
- Knowledge of the building's maintenance problems and the materials or features that are difficult and/or expensive to maintain
- Ability to envision the future of the building, its acceptance in the community, its competitiveness (especially compared with new competition), the cost to operate the building, its income, its *net operating income (NOI)*, and ultimately its present and future value

Because of the potential for unknowns in a rehab project, team members must be experienced and adaptable to unforeseen situations. They must also be able to avoid design and construction mistakes that would affect the marketing and leasing program and, thus, the success of the project.

Design Considerations

Several design issues must be considered before the architect starts drawing plans for the proposed rehab. If the building has historical significance, historical research should precede the design. When attempting to restore the building to its original grandeur, the developer might use old photos revealing decorative features that have been covered or removed. The history of the site should be researched. During a roundtable discussion of leading architects, Irving Fischer said:

> The time spent probing the building with the architect and the engineers and the subcontractors is the most productive part of the design process for everyone involved. Without detailed study of the building before any other work gets started, you simply don't know what you are facing. Without detailed study, the architect just designs away and it will never get built the way he or she designed it; and the property owner ends up with costs that bear no resemblance to the budget.
>
> On any job where we are construction managers, we insist on spending the money for a thorough survey before anything else starts—including the structure, the locations of all openings, the location, and condition of services. You can't take old drawings and assume it was built that way, or that no changes have been made that can drastically affect the new work. Dimensions have to be checked; the condition of materials (and particularly the structure) has to be field confirmed to the drawings.[3]

3. *Architectural Record Digest*, December 1982.

This was great advise when it was given and it is still valuable advice today.

Other design considerations include a phase I or II environmental study. This includes researching prior uses for the site. The current land use and zoning requirements must be considered. If a land-use variance is needed, will there be community opposition? Will there be significant delays when seeking a variance? A building survey will determine if the building meets current building codes. If major rehab is undertaken, will the construction trigger a requirement to bring the building into compliance with current or proposed building codes?

Discussions and negotiations with building officials may be necessary to request exceptions to the building code. An old building may not structurally be able to comply with modern building codes, yet the building may have historical value to the community. An audit of the building for design inefficiencies may uncover areas that can be converted to leasable areas, tenant storage areas, maintenance storage, or even a management office.

The design should consider future renovation. For instance, conduits could be oversized to allow for future technological equipment if they are needed with ever changing technology.. The rehab design process is a rare opportunity to correct prior mistakes and prepare the building for the future.

If construction costs exceed the budget, a change in the project's scope may be necessary. Reducing the scope of the project to remain within budget requires an analysis of the impact on the marketing and leasing program, the projected rental rates, and the gross income the building will generate. The outcome is a balanced equation between the rental rates that produce the building's income stream, the rehab cost translated into the debt service and the capital investment, and ROI.

Controlling the Site and Building

The real estate manager's role in the design process starts with reviewing existing leases and other documents that may place restrictions on remodeling, expanding, or rehabbing the property.

In shopping centers and malls, the major tenants commonly have approval rights on issues they believe can affect their business. Major retail tenants want to protect their visibility, sight lines from the street, their parking field, and their customers' convenient parking—all of which translate into sales. These tenants believe their investment of several million dollars in their stores and their long-term leases justify receiving these rights.

The major tenants' approval rights often include changes to the layout of the parking lot, the addition of buildings to the site (including pad or out-parcel buildings), redesign of the buildings, and changes to the common areas. The major tenants' leases may also prohibit certain uses within the shopping center or mall or within a defined distance from their premises. These uses, such as theaters and offices, usually generate long-term parking—if they are not prohibited, they may be restricted to a specific location on the property.

The real estate manager must review all the tenants' leases for approval rights, restrictions, and exclusives. Although small shop tenants rarely have these rights, their leases must be reviewed as well. The developer may want to add a box store anchor, such as an office supply store or a pet supply store, but one of the tenants may have an exclusive for that product line.

Retail projects often have common area agreements or *reciprocal easement agreements (REAs)* giving the signatories to these agreements—usually the property owner, major tenants, and sometimes the lender—rights of approval for any changes or remodeling to the common areas. If such agreements or restrictions exist, the rehab team must receive approval in writing from the agreements' signatories before commencing the rehab. Tenants may have the right to expand, relocate, or even cancel their leases if the building is rehabbed or expanded.

Monitoring Construction Activities

The rehab process often produces unforeseen construction situations. Even when the building's original plans are available, surprises can occur when walls are opened, false ceilings are removed, and buildings are demolished. Sheer walls, bracing, and even hazardous materials may be discovered during construction. Storage tanks or contaminated soils may be revealed with an environmental study (Phase I or II).

Dealing with the unknown is the critical issue for the general contractor who initially may be reluctant to provide a fixed or guaranteed construction bid until all details are determined. The first bid may be a cost-plus proposal. As the job progresses and all factors are determined, the contractor may be willing to provide a fixed price or guaranteed maximum price (GMP) with shared savings for the balance of the work.

The construction requires preplanning. The general contractor and subcontractors must be aware of the impact their work has on existing tenants. When unanticipated issues arise, the property owner, architect, and general contractor must be able to make quick, informed decisions. The job must be scheduled, and the construction work must be phased in. Some rehab work may require more skilled workers than new construction. The general contractor may assign a senior superintendent to work with tenants and the property owner, who may be dealing with unknown costs.

Hazardous Substances

Throughout the rehab, safety is of paramount importance. If hazardous materials are present, the rehab team must use state and federal laws as the guide to decide whether to remove the materials, encase them, or allow them to remain in the building in its present state. The rehab team must thoroughly review and obey the laws regarding hazardous materials. Other considerations in deciding whether to remove hazardous materials are the cost to remove material now versus in the future, the concerns of potential lenders and buyers, and the impact on the marketing and leasing program. The degree to which lenders are willing to finance the project or the price a buyer is willing to pay for the project may be influenced by the presence of hazardous materials. If the decision is made to remove the hazardous substances, the proper permits, documentation, and reporting must be completed, and a licensed contractor who specializes in the removal of hazardous materials must be chosen to remove them.

Tenant Issues

The rehab of retail properties often occurs with merchants still open for business. This happens when a regional mall is converted from an open-air center to an enclosed mall, a second level is added to a single-level enclosed mall, or a strip shopping center receives a major facelift. Even some office buildings are renovated while tenants are in place. In each case, as a requirement of the tenant's lease in the "Quite Enjoyment" provision and possible other provisions, it is imperative not to disturb the tenant's business during construction.

If tenants occupy space in the building during the rehab process, construction activities may affect their ability to use their premises and conduct business. In such cases, depending on the property type, the rehab team must address the following questions:

- How will the contractors have access to the building?
- Where will construction workers park?
- Does the building have a loading dock?
- How will materials and equipment be taken into the building?
- Will a passenger elevator be assigned to the contractors if the building does not have a freight elevator? What hours may they use passenger elevators?
- Will flooring and other existing building materials be covered for protection?
- Will core drilling and jack hammering need to be scheduled before the tenants open for business

or after the building is closed?

- Where will the construction staging area be set up?
- Where will construction trash dumpsters be located, and how will they be emptied or picked up and removed?

The real estate manager must be involved in placing construction barricades and protective walks to maintain the retail tenants' visibility and access. Additional directional signage may be needed throughout the project.

Adjacent Building Issues

Another concern is the possible impact on tenants in adjacent buildings during the construction phase. First-floor retail and service tenants' businesses in nearby buildings may be disrupted. Construction barriers can change pedestrian traffic patterns. Noise and dust can create problems for the tenants and their customers. The rehab team must analyze these issues and take appropriate action to mitigate disruption to neighboring tenants' businesses. The real estate manager should study the adjacent tenants and their hours of operation and meet with the project manager and/or general contractor to discuss these issues.

Design Constraints

Rehabbing a building places constraints on the design. These constraints force design decisions because of limited alternatives. Design constraints may compel decisions to maintain structural components of the building because of their integrated role, or because of budgetary concerns about the cost of removing and replacing them. Another design constraint may be the cost or inability to match existing materials. In many situations, old materials are discolored and cannot be matched. Manufacturers may have discontinued features such as tile or railings.

Local and Federal Codes and Restrictions

The application of building codes often complicates the rehabilitation of older structures. These codes have traditionally been written for new buildings, and their requirements may be unduly onerous when applied to historic buildings undergoing restoration. Moreover, prescriptive provisions of building codes designed to protect health and safety may necessitate measures that jeopardize character-defining features of historic structures. Therefore, a property owner contemplating rehabilitation should first determine whether the local building code will become applicable as a result of the anticipated work, and, if so, to what extent. If code requirements will apply and are likely to be difficult to meet, property owners should explore whether exceptions or variances are obtainable. Finally, special provisions of local codes, or entirely separate state or local provisions, may apply to historic structures, partially or totally in lieu of general building standards.

If the building is located in a National Register Historic district, federal restrictions may govern the type of rehabilitation work that can be undertaken. A complex rehabilitation project may require one or more levels of environmental and historic review and involve legal issues such as code compliance, zoning regulations, and local, state, and federal preservation and environmental regulations.

Renovating an older building that is not a historical structure may also have difficulties conforming to new codes. The redevelopment team should meet to arrive at alternative solutions. After they arrive at practical solutions they meet with the building department and present alternative solutions. If one of the alternative solutions meets the safety requirements of the build code the building official may agree to the proposed solution.

Logistics

The real estate manager reviews the building for space for the general contractor's office. The real estate management office may need to be relocated, possibly several times, as the construction progresses through the building. If office space is not available in the building, temporary trailers can be set up in the building's parking lot or adjacent to the building. An alternative to using trailers is leasing ground-floor space in an adjacent building. In addition, a fenced construction staging area can be situated in the building's surface parking lot.

After the construction has been completed, the real estate manager should obtain "as-built" plans and warranties. If a portion of the building envelope, such as the roof, has been penetrated, the real estate manager must know the warranties for the work. The real estate manager and leasing agent coordinates with the construction contractor regarding promotional and marketing activities during the construction phase, the activities of tenants operating in the building during the rehab process, tenant move-ins, and the grand opening.

Marketing

A critical element in the analysis of rehabbing an office building is determining its market. If the building is going through a complete renovation, its rental rates will be significantly increased. The existing tenants may not be willing or able to pay the pro forma rates needed to justify the renovation. The rehab team must remember that commercial space is never leased at the developer's pro forma rate; rather, space is leased at market rates. A pro forma rate that exceeds the market rate jeopardizes the economic viability of the rehab project.

The feasibility study must identify the targeted market, the anticipated rental rates and possible concessions, and the anticipated building lease up velocity to a stabilized occupancy rate. In other words, it must identify the building's market niche and price the building to the niche. Relevant considerations include the following questions:

- Who will the tenants be?
- Will the building be targeted to service, professions, small businesses, or governmental agencies?
- What are the space requirements, open or closed office plans, types of businesses, or unusual requirements?
- The employees profile of the targeted industries may indicate specific building amenities they prefer.

As stated, one of the first steps in the rehab process is determining the amount of income a building must be able to generate to pay the building's operating expenses, service the building's loan, and return a profit commensurate with the developer's investment and risk. The market analysis must take into consideration space in the building that is less desirable and possibly difficult to lease. Each floor in the building should be analyzed for its bay depth, mullion spacing, distance from elevators, length of corridors, window size, view, and configuration. Each floor and the areas and spaces on each floor should be individually priced to establish market rates. This will provide a realistic income projection for calculating an accurate absorption or lease-up rate.

The marketing plan should consider whether tenant concessions are necessary to lease the building. Will the tenant concessions be in the form of free rent, over-standard tenant improvements, moving allowances, or contributions to the tenant's operating costs, such as paying for an open house, a new phone system, or the tenant's stationery and other printed materials?

Another component of the marketing plan is whether the office building will be leased on a usable or rentable basis. Usable square footage is determined by measuring the tenant's space within its demising walls and from either the center or interior of the outer and corridor walls. Rentable square footage takes the same measure and adds a load factor (a percentage of the common areas) to arrive at the tenant's square footage.

The rehab is an opportunity to re-measure the building and possibly change the method of calculating future and renewing tenants' square footage. The load factor of the building may change. The industry standard is to use rentable measurements. Both usable and rentable can work by dividing the total amount of operating expenses over 100 percent of the usable space or 100 percent or the rentable space—where a loss is collecting rent on the pro-rata share of the common area with the use of rentable method. An important consideration is determining the standard in the market.

Rehabbing with Tenants in Place

Rehabbing a building with tenants in place allows for an important and often necessary source of revenue. However, tenants occupying a building during rehab can cause design and construction constraints that may lead to additional project costs. When remodeling a commercial building, in particular one with retail tenants, the rehab team must remember that the existing tenants must continue to conduct their businesses during the construction phase. The tenants must understand what is going to happen, why it must happen, when it will happen, how long it will take, how it may impact their businesses, and what will be done to mitigate the impact on their businesses and their customers.

Communicating with Tenants

The real estate manager can ensure that tenants remain informed by conducting general meetings to explain the construction sequence and scheduling to them. The first meeting should be an announcement and review of the proposed rehab. This could be planned as a dinner or cocktail party with the architect and either the developer or the real estate manager as featured speakers. The speakers can introduce the rehab concept, the goals of the project, and the rehab team. The architect can provide renderings of the project and explain what the new design will accomplish, the construction sequence, and the timing of the project.

The real estate manager can address the tenants' primary concerns, such as disruption to their businesses. It is important that existing tenants, especially retail tenants, be supportive of the rehab because prospective tenants often visit and discuss the project with existing tenants. At informational meetings with existing tenants, it may be best that a tenant's particular needs not be discussed during the presentation; rather, tenants should meet with the real estate manager individually to resolve individual concerns.

Tenants can also receive information through a biweekly or monthly e-mail and frequent visits by the real estate management staff. As the construction sequence and schedules change, the tenants need to know what is happening next in their area, as well as in the entire building. Tenants should be encouraged to call the real estate manager with their concerns.

If tenants move into the building during the remodeling, the real estate manager should meet with them to explain what has happened so far as well as the timing and sequence of the remaining work. In addition to obtaining a tenant's certificates of insurance and estoppels, and approving a tenant's exterior signage, the real estate manager may be responsible for approving the tenant's layout or construction plans. If the tenant is a retailer, the real estate manager should monitor the tenant's construction to ensure that it meets the agreed store opening date. The building's new emergency procedures plan should be reviewed with the tenants before they move in.

Ensuring a Smooth Transition

In addition to respecting possible restrictions that tenants' leases may place on the rehab process, the real estate manager must develop a plan that allows existing tenants to operate their businesses with as little interruption as possible, and this plan should be incorporated into the tenant retention program. Issues that require special attention include noise, dust and dirt, protecting the building's materials delivery, storage of construction materials, access to and throughout the building, parking, and signage.

Whenever construction occurs in an enclosed building, it can create excessive noise that can prevent tenants from conducting their businesses. Core drilling, jack hammering, and other construction activities that generate excessive noise should be scheduled before or after the building's normal business hours. On most construction projects, the workers clean the site at the end of each working day.

Because construction workers will be walking throughout the building and dust and dirt will be tracked in, a day porter or construction laborer may be assigned to keep the common areas clean. The flooring, walls, and the ceilings may need protective coverings. The general contractor must inform subcontractors of their responsibility to keep the area as clean as possible during their activities.

Tenants and their visitors need easy, convenient access to the building and their premises. The construction area should include convenient storage areas for equipment and materials. Elevators the construction crews use should be padded, and the floor covering and ceiling materials should be removed or protected.

A nearly ideal situation took place in Orange County, California, during nine months of construction to enclose an open-air regional mall. Only one merchant was closed on a Saturday morning for two hours, and even that could have been avoided with better communication with one subcontractor. During the mall enclosure, barricades were designed to provide customers with a view of the construction activities to generate interest and curiosity. The lower half of the eight-foot-high barricades was constructed of plywood; the upper half consisted of a framed heavy-gauge wire mesh. Modular graphics on the barricades allowed the barricaded areas to be enlarged or reduced without disrupting the graphic presentation. The barricades also displayed directional signs for the stores, ensured tenants' and customers' safety, allowed the stores to remain open, and expedited the construction work.

Tenant Buy-Outs

The tenants' occupancy rights within the building and on the site of the proposed rehab are major concerns with rehabs—especially office building rehabs. Violation of any of the tenants' rights can be costly. Will any tenants located in the building or on the site obstruct the rehab development? Do these tenants have leases that will expire after the commencement of construction? In all buildings especially an office building, the developer must review the tenants' leases for options, space pocketing, first rights of refusal, and rights of relocation. If any of these situations exists, the tenants may need to be bought out of their leases or relocated—or their leases mutually amended or cancelled. Otherwise, two possibilities exist: delaying the project until the leases expire, which may prevent the building from opening on or near the projected dates, or conceiving a plan to rehab the project with the tenants in place.

A buy-out analysis (the decision whether to buy out a tenant's lease) is complex. If the buy-out occurs too soon and the project does not actually begin until after the lease's expiration date, an unnecessary cost is added to the project. On the East coast, a retailer on the ground floor of an old downtown low-rise building located in the center of a block of buildings to be rehabbed was offered a lease buy-out in excess of a million dollars. The tenant refused the buy-out and attempted to negotiate a larger settlement. The permitting process and the obtaining of construction financing extended the construction commencement date two years, and the tenant's lease expired just prior to the commencement of construction. Fortunately for the developer, the buy-out negotiations were never completed, and the tenant vacated at the lease expiration date with no buy-out.

If the developer does not reveal news of a proposed rehab in order to negotiate a more favorable buy-out with tenants, and the tenants find out about the rehab, they may and probably will negotiate better terms for their buy-outs. Some tenants can make more money from a buy-out than from operating their businesses. The developer or real estate manager must find out what motivates each tenant before negotiating a buy-out. Is the tenant interested in bettering its location, upgrading the interior of the premises, seeking a "fair" settlement, or looking to make a quick fortune?

A possible alternative to buying out a tenant's lease is to find a suitable or even better location for the tenant. Most experienced retail tenants are reasonable in their negotiations with the developer in this regard because they consider improving their business the most important element in any negotiation.

Relocating to a better location would be a prime concern. Depending on the remaining term of the lease, the property owner may have to contribute to the relocation costs of the tenant.

Another consideration in the buy-out analysis is the tenant's intent in occupying the premises. In some situations, the tenant may be willing to buy out its lease. This may occur when a retailer's business is poor or an office tenant reduces or eliminates its operations in the building and the tenant is unaware of the property owner's plan to rehab the property. A real estate manager who discovers a tenant in this position should approach the tenant with an offer to cancel the lease upon payment of a penalty fee. For example, prior to the announcement of the rehab and enclosure of an open-air mall in California, the property owner was willing to offer $100,000 to a national tenant to vacate a strategic center court location. The tenant's sales were poor, and the real estate manager asked if the tenant would like to have the lease canceled. The tenant offered the owner $75,000 for that privilege.

Before any discussion with a tenant regarding a buy-out, the developer should prepare a timeline for the commencement of construction and construction activities. If the rehab team cannot gain control of all the spaces before construction commences, the team must develop a plan to accomplish the rehab work in phases. Such a plan would be based on the location of the tenant or tenants in the building or on the site and their lease expiration dates.

ADMINISTRATION AND MANAGEMENT RESPONSIBILITIES

The new product created by the rehab will require the real estate manager to analyze and reevaluate the management and operations of the building. The first area to analyze is management staffing. If the rehab is a change of use, is the present staff qualified and experienced enough to assume the management and marketing responsibilities of another type of property? Converting a group of warehouse buildings into a retail project, such as Faneuil Hall in Boston, or into a mixed-use development requires an understanding of a different tenant mix, marketing techniques, promotions program, and tenant requirements. If the rehab has a retail component, the property's trade area must be thoroughly analyzed. When a change of use occurs, individuals with specific areas of expertise may have to be added to or hired in place of the existing staff. The management and marketing of a specialty shopping center requires different skills and expertise than the management and marketing of a warehouse or an office building, and vice versa. The real estate manager must also analyze the maintenance staff. Are additional maintenance personnel with specific skills needed? Which services will be contracted?

A rehab inevitably calls for a new lease form. The new lease may have different tenant requirements for insurance, signage, late charges, rent due dates, estoppel, certificates of occupancy, maintenance responsibilities, building escalation or common area charges, percentage rent, reporting sales, and sales audits. Each lease must be carefully reviewed and summarized to administer each tenant's and the property owner's requirements. Common area maintenance, real estate taxes, insurance, and building operating expense pass-through and other tenant charges must be developed and accurately assessed to each tenant.

Energy Audit

Most buildings being rehabbed, especially office buildings, present an excellent opportunity to improve the building's energy efficiency. An energy audit may be necessary to determine and evaluate opportunities to reduce the building's energy consumption. The goals of an energy conservation program should include substantial and permanent reduction in energy usage and general improvements in the comfort and environmental conditions for the building's occupants.

Two areas that have significant potential for energy savings are lighting and the HVAC system. Consultants specializing in each of these areas may be added to the rehab team. More energy conservation opportunities are available in office buildings than in shopping centers. To lower energy and operating costs for office buildings, specific activities can be divided into three general categories: (1) operational and maintenance procedures that provide immediate no-cost or low-cost energy and cost-saving opportunities; (2) modification of existing equipment and systems that generally require engineering design; and (3) design and operation of energy management control (EMC) systems that can be interfaced with existing equipment and procedures. Solar panels and water reclamation features may be included in the new design of the building.

In addition to the savings in operating expenses, an energy reduction program usually increases the building's value. The amount of value enhancement depends on whether the tenants are on gross leases that call for the property owner to pay all the building's expenses, on triple-net or modified-net leases that require the tenants to pay all or a portion of the building's operating expenses, or whether the tenants pay for their utility consumption.

For example, if a 10 percent cap rate is used for valuing a building, every dollar of reduced operating expenses the property owner pays will result in a $10 increase in building value. If the tenant pays all the operating expenses and the building's tenant charges can be reduced, the tenant's occupancy costs are lowered, thus making the building more competitive—or allow the building owner to collect more base rent as tenants look at the total rent they pay in the market place. If the tenants are paying lower operating expenses, their rents may be increased proportionally to these savings when their leases renew. The tenant's occupancy costs may still be competitive to the occupancy costs for competing buildings. This is in addition to the increase rent due to changes in the market conditions. Computerized energy management programs can be designed to monitor tenants' energy usage, allow the property owner to bill tenants for over-standard energy usage, and to control the heating and cooling of the building from an on-site or off-site location.

Operating Expenses

The rehab of a commercial property will inevitably affect the building's operating expenses. Maintenance costs increase in older buildings as they become less and less efficient. Reducing energy usage can achieve significant savings. Another potential area of savings is through more efficient maintenance. The rehab process provides an opportunity to analyze and correct areas of unusually high maintenance cost. Inefficient mechanical systems and hard-to-clean flooring are just two examples of the many opportunities to reduce a building's operating expenses.

On the other hand, the rehab of a commercial building is likely to increase the building's overall operating cost. The increased value created by the rehab will increase the building's insurance cost and real estate taxes. Upgraded areas, such as landscaping and common areas, may result in increased maintenance. A rehabbed building may require an overall higher level of maintenance standards.

When a rehabbed office building goes from a class C to a class B building or from a class B to a class A building, the maintenance standards will also increase. A mall converted from an open-air center to an enclosed mall will experience a significant increase in common area maintenance expenses when enclosed mall common areas are added. In addition to the HVAC maintenance expense, expenses will be added for cleaning skylights, entry doors, and glass; for upgrading flooring and landscaping; and for improving janitorial standards due to increased mall traffic.

Maintenance and Operations

The proposed rehab presents a unique opportunity to review areas of the building that are costly and/or difficult to maintain. This analysis should start with a discussion with the maintenance staff and maintenance contractors. Next, each of the building's operating expense items should be reviewed and compared with average expenses for buildings in the area as found in such publications as the *Experience*

Exchange Report from the Building Owners and Managers Association (BOMA), or the *Income Expense Analysis for Shopping Centers and Office Buildings* from the Institute of Real Estate Management (IREM).

The building design should be reviewed for efficient and cost-effective maintenance and operations. Does it have excessive common areas that will add to the cost of operation? Does it contain materials that are expensive to maintain? Will the building's pass-through operating expenses or common area maintenance costs be competitive? The rehab design should consider the cost to maintain the building. Over a 10-year period, the cost to maintain a building can exceed its rehab cost. Each operating expense item should be analyzed in relationship to the proposed rehab.

Tenant Billing Formula

Since commercial tenants typically pay all or a portion of the building's operating expenses, the formula for tenant billings must be reanalyzed. This analysis starts with reviewing the building's standard lease and then summarizing each tenant's operation expense bill back provisions. The rehab may have created additional GLA, thus, changing the denominator in the formula for calculating each tenant's pro rata share of the operating expenses.

If the project is an office building, a new tenant's lease may have converted the building from a usable to a rentable formula for calculating the tenant's square footage. The office building's efficiency or load factor, the ratio of common area to usable area, may have changed, thus resulting in a change in the rentable formula.

Operating Expense Formula

If the rehab is for a mixed-use development, a formula for each building's share in the operating expense of the overall project must be determined. If the project is a single building with similar uses, the formula will probably be simple. However, if the project has several buildings with different uses, or one building with several uses, a formula fair to all tenants must be determined for allocating common area cost and/or operating expenses. When the project includes several buildings with different uses, each building must be charged its equitable share of common expenses.

Expenses that may be allocated to each building are security; building engineers and day porters; landscaping; parking lot repairs and maintenance; exterior areas' utility expenses; and real estate management costs. Once a formula has been developed and tenants are charged their pro rata share of expenses based on the formula, the formula should not be changed unless GLA is added or deleted from the project or an error is discovered.

Evaluating Emergency Procedures

The building's emergency procedures plan must be reevaluated. First, what new life-safety features will be added to the building? Next, will the building's employee profile change? Will visitors or customers increase?

If the rehab has a residential component, a separate emergency plan must be developed to handle a building that operates 24 hours a day and has children and elderly residents. The on-site manager for the residential component of the project must be aware of community resources for referrals for emergency housing, spouse and child abuse, substance abuse, and other civil and domestic problems.

If the project remains entirely commercial, the proposed tenant mix and employee count may alter the emergency procedures plan. Governmental agencies and international corporations are likely targets of picketing and bomb threats. Evacuation procedures may need modification. The real estate manager should meet with building officials to become familiar with possible changes in the building's codes for life safety and preparedness. Police and fire department officials may become involved in formulating the emergency procedures plan. The building's security needs must be reassessed. In addition, new tenants' power or utility requirements must receive consideration. IREM has published *Before and After Disaster Strikes,* which is designed to assist real estate managers in developing emergency procedures for commercial and residential properties. *Chapter 17: Safety, Security, and Emergency Procedures* has more information about developing an emergency procedure plan for commercial buildings.

Insurance

The insurance program for the property will change. The rehab will create additional value, use changes may create new risks, and the magnitude of the project may require augmenting coverage and increasing limits. During the rehab process, the real estate manager must review insurance policy requirements. Determine whether the insurance policy contains any notification provisions. For example, if the sprinkler system is shut down temporarily during construction, must the insurance carrier be notified ahead of time?

If the insurance policy contains a notice provision and the carrier is not informed, the building may have no coverage when the sprinkler system is shut off. For example, the agreement with one of the department stores at a mall being rehabbed required the property owner to notify the store manager 72 hours in advance if the main water line to the store were to be shut off and to post a fire watch during the shut-off period. If the property owner had failed to notify a tenant who experienced a fire loss because of the sprinkler system being deactivated during rehab work, the property owner might have been liable for the loss.

Other considerations include whether any safety hazards are present and whether safety signs are installed where needed. Determine if all rehab team members, contractors, vendors, and consultants have proper insurance coverage. The general contractor, all sub-contractors and vendors should include the property owner and the real estate management company as additional named insureds on its policy. No contractor, construction, or maintenance people should be allowed on the property without proof of proper coverage. Vendors and contractors are usually required to have at least $2,000,000 or more in property and liability insurance coverage. This amount may be increased if their work is hazardous. For example, the work of a subcontractor is hazardous when installing a roof over the common area for a mall enclosure while the mall is open for business. Finally, the property's loss of rental income insurance must be reviewed.

Leasing Plan

No other aspect of the rehab process is as unpredictable as leasing. Design, construction costs and timing, and the building's operating costs can be estimated with a comfortable degree of accuracy. However, leasing is subject to such factors as changes in the economy, overly optimistic views of the market, over-built markets, the impact of interest rates on potential tenants, new competition, and the acceptance of the rehab by the project's targeted market. The building's image is another factor that can affect the leasing program. Changing a property's poor image may take longer than the rehab process.

Clearly, no other factor has a greater impact on the property's NOI and value than its marketing and leasing program. A property with an effective program will be able to maintain its rent at market rates and enjoy maximum occupancy. A successful leasing program validates the rehabilitation of a commercial property.

Leasing Plan Development

The initial step in developing the leasing plan is to determine the property's market niche. Frequently, this niche is different from the market the property originally targeted—for example, a small enclosed mall converted to a power center, an obsolete Class B office building converted to a hotel or apartment building with ground-floor retail space, or a tired community shopping center converted to a lifestyle shopping center.

Once the market niche has been determined, all facets of the property must be compared with the competition, including location, features, design, and, for a retail project, major tenants. This analysis helps determine the building's market rental rates, which building features to emphasize, and which existing features are weak. After the building is positioned in the market, the developer can initiate a marketing and leasing program.

If the rehab is a retail project, an analysis of the demographics and psychographics of the shopping center's expanded trade area is necessary. From this analysis, the real estate manager can develop the ideal tenant mix and identify merchants to contact to fill the tenant mix. The existing tenant mix and merchants should be evaluated to identify the project's present strengths and weaknesses. The real estate manager must determine which existing merchants can operate successfully and contribute to the synergism of the tenant mix of the rehabbed project.

Merchants in older shopping centers often pay low rent and may not be able to generate sufficient sales in the rehabbed shopping center to pay higher rents when their leases expire. If a retailer's sales are significantly below the shopping center's sales average for that merchandise category or national averages for that business category the tenant probably cannot generate sufficient increased sales to support the rental rates the property owner will require to renew the lease. These tenants will move out at lease expiration, seek a mutual cancellation of their lease, or try to negotiate a lease buy-out.

Difficult Spaces

The redesign of the building(s) must be reviewed from a marketing and leasing perspective. Will there be difficult space to lease? Will some retail space have poor visibility? What is the depth of the retail spaces or the distance from the corridor wall to the curtain wall of an office building? What is the size of the floor plate? Each of these issues will assist in targeting the right tenant(s) for these spaces.

The rehab may include a change of use if the property was originally designed for the needs of one type of tenant. For example, a loft building may be converted to another use, such as an office building or a specialty shopping center. As a result, the bay depth may be too deep, the building core may be in a less convenient location, and other design problems may cause leasing challenges. Difficult spaces must be identified, and their correct market rental rates must be established.

The project's income projections must reflect the rental rates charged for space that is difficult to lease. Areas that are difficult to lease do not meet the needs of the majority of the target market, and these spaces will not lease at the rental rate charged for the rest of the building. The rehab team must recognize the need to discount the rental rates for such spaces. Moreover, the rehab process presents an opportunity to reanalyze the marketability of each space and each area for lease. To eliminate or minimize difficult space to lease, the leasing agent, real estate manager, and architect must thoroughly analyze each space in the proposed project.

In retail properties, difficult spaces to lease include those that are too deep or too large and those with limited frontage or visibility. In office buildings, difficult spaces to lease include those with overly deep bay depths, incorrect mullion spacing, odd sizes, limited window area, and too much distance to the elevators.

Co-Tenant Effects

In retail properties, another important issue is the effect that each tenants' operations have on one another. If some retail tenants remain in place and in operation during the rehab, will the relocation, removal, or temporary closing of other tenants—especially major or anchor tenants—negatively impact their businesses? When a major tenant or several small shop tenants relocate within a shopping center or leave the center, the pedestrian traffic changes dramatically. The developer must weigh the impact of such changes on the existing tenants. Possible options to overcome concerns include adjusting tenants' rents to percentage rent only, providing a lower base rental rate, or even waiving rent during part or all of the rehab process or until a specific tenant moves in, or the building achieves a certain percentage of occupancy. These are difficult choices for a property owner, but in some situations, they may be necessary for the survival of the tenants and the continuation of the tenant's rental stream. If tenant loss occurs, additional advertising and promotion will probably be necessary to generate additional traffic to the shopping center.

Leasing Updates and Meetings

One of the first questions the leasing agent or a prospective tenant asks is, "When will the building be completed?" The leasing agents and prospective tenants want to know when the space can be turned over to the tenants for their improvements or when the tenants can move in their equipment, fixtures, and inventory, and when they will be able to open for business. If at any time these dates are likely to change, inform all interested parties. In the leasing agent's enthusiasm for the project and desire to lease the space, he or she must be careful not to make promises that cannot be kept. One of the advantages to rehabbing a building is that it usually can be brought into the market sooner than a newly constructed building.

The architect, leasing agent, and real estate manager should meet frequently throughout the rehab process to review tenant needs. The leasing agent must know which walls can be removed and which walls are sheer, or are integral to the design. Pre-leasing activities may place constraints on the design of the project. Once a tenant signs a lease for a space, the design of the rehab must take into consideration the new tenant's occupancy rights.

SHOPPING CENTERS

When people think of rehabbing a property, they usually think of an older building. Even though many shopping centers are just 30 to 50 years old, some are prime candidates for rehabilitation because many of them are obsolete. Their *obsolescence*, whether *curable* or *incurable*, is the result of changing retailers' requirements and space needs and/or outmoded design, signage, and features. From strip shopping centers to enclosed malls, most shopping centers usually exhibit some obsolescence in design and space configuration by the time they are 20 years old. Many no longer perform at their maximum potential, and they can present excellent opportunities for rehab and possibly expansion.

Advantages of Rehabbing Shopping Centers and Malls

In many communities, limited parcels of land are available in the size necessary to develop anchored strip shopping centers and malls. A new grocery-anchored neighborhood shopping center needs a site of five acres or more, while a super regional mall may need 40 to 100 acres, depending on whether it is a horizontal or vertical mall and whether it has surface or deck parking. Other obstacles may prevent the development of new shopping centers, such as wetlands and environmental concerns, poor demographics, existing competition, or community resistance. Some communities object to the development of a new shopping center—especially a regional mall. The residents are concerned that the mall will generate increased traffic through the area, thereby creating increased congestion and noise in their neighborhood.

The rehab of a shopping center or mall usually does not encounter the previously mentioned obstacles and frequently meets with community support. As the demographics and/or psychographics in a shopping center's trade area change, the shopping center or mall must be repositioned to adapt to its customers' changing needs. The community welcomes the rehabilitation of an older shopping center or mall. In addition to modernizing and rehabbing the shopping center or mall, the project usually results in new merchants, an improved tenant mix, and additional tax revenues for local and state municipalities through increased property and sales taxes and greater employment opportunities.

Property and sales taxes from shopping centers are major sources of income for many municipalities. For instance, if a neighborhood shopping center of 125,000 square feet generates $500 per square foot in taxable sales with a sales tax of eight percent, the shopping center will produce $5,000,000 in sales taxes. If a regional mall of 1,000,000 square feet in the same community produces taxable sales of $825 per square foot, the mall will generate $66,000,000 in sales taxes. The real estate tax assessment for these properties will be another major source of revenue for the municipality. The proceeds are usually shared among the city, county, and state governmental bodies and other taxing authorities.

The rehab of a shopping center has a greater effect on the community than the rehab of an office building or industrial property. Residents in the community visit shopping center properties more frequently than most other commercial properties, and it can affect individuals' daily lives.

The shopping center—especially a mall—with its promotions, community activities, and merchandising events becomes a focal point of the community. In contrast, residents of the community seldom visit an office building. Unless a rehab includes the exterior of an office building, the public may never know that the interior was renovated.

A rehabbed shopping center or mall generates additional jobs. New, more successful merchants may need additional employees. Further, the shopping center may need to be remerchandised. The existing tenant mix may need adjustment to meet the needs of changing demographics and psychographics in the shopping center's or mall's trade area. Customer research, such as on-site intercepts, questionnaires, focus groups, and telephone surveys may be necessary to analyze a changing trade area and to reposition the shopping center or mall.

Issues in Rehabbing a Shopping Center

Two areas that have significant impact on remodeling a neighborhood or community shopping center are the building's front elevation and the size of the tenants' premises. A change to the facade or elevation has a major influence on the appearance of the shopping center. Other areas to consider are the shopping center or mall's visual, physical, topographical, and functional conditions as well as management and operational concerns.

Exterior Changes

Visual conditions to consider are the shopping center's appearance and style, the buildings' color, signage, landscaping, directories, mall amenities, lighting, flooring, and artwork. Physical conditions include the quality and/or obsolescence of the materials and mechanical systems. Topographical considerations are the layout of the parking lot, driveway and drive lanes, drainage, and landscaping. Functional considerations include the parking lot and interior mall lighting, ingress and egress, and pedestrian circulation.

Management and Operational Issues

Management and operational issues include the location of the on-site management office and maintenance workshop for larger shopping centers and malls, storage, lighting, energy conservation, deliveries, maintenance of special features such as skylights, and standard maintenance such as flooring and roofs.

Tenant Space Changes

Another area that affects the shopping center's success is adjusting to and meeting the retailers' ever-changing requirements. Space demands have changed significantly in the past 10 to 30 years.

Supermarkets—the primary anchor tenants for neighborhood and community shopping centers—have evolved from the 20,000- to 25,000-square-foot grocery stores of the early 1970s to the 35,000- to 45,000-square-foot superstores of the early 1980s to stores of 60,000 or more square feet in the 1990s, and back to 50,000 square feet. "Hypermarkets," which first developed in Europe and entered the United States market in the Midwest, are stores in excess of 100,000 square feet and include a supermarket as well as other retail merchandise. The larger Target and Walmart stores are examples of such superstores.

Many small shop tenants have downsized their stores to reduce occupancy costs. With more efficient merchandise delivery systems, retailers discovered they did not need the mezzanine and large stockrooms they designed into their stores up to the 1980s. It became common that by merchandising the entire cubicle—i.e., floor, walls, and ceilings—they could produce the same or more sales in less square footage.

An enclosed mall anchored by a supermarket and a junior department store with shop space may be de-malled and converted to a strip shopping center. The back of stores that fronted the mall and backed to the parking lot are reversed and the store fronts face the parking lot. The row of mall stores across these stores are either leased to a use that does not need frontage, such as a governmental agency, or college off-campus site. These spaces may be combined with the row of stores across the mall common area and leased to much larger retailers.

Sometimes, all the shop space is gutted and converted to box retail space. The rehab of a mall may include vertical expansion, in which case the major tenants should also expand their spaces vertically. Each level of the mall would benefit by having major tenants' entrances. Space in an enclosed mall that is too big or that was vacated by a major tenant can be converted to a food court, leased to box retailers, divided into large specialty or fashion forward retailers, or developed as an entertainment center. Deep spaces can be converted to non traditional uses.

Effect on Tenants' Businesses

The major concern of existing shopping center merchants during the rehab is how the construction activity will impact their businesses. Many merchants anticipate that their sales will decrease; however, the result is often just the opposite. Many merchants, especially those in a regional and super regional malls, will experience sales increases for several reasons.

First, the community is curious about the rehab. Additional customers will respond to merchants' aggressive advertising and promotional campaigns. In addition, the developer will budget funds in the pro forma for advertising and marketing to maintain or increase customer traffic. Some merchants will remodel and upgrade their stores to have a new, fresh look to coincide with the new look of the mall or shopping center. Finally, during the construction phase, new retailers are moving into the shopping center or mall, thus improving its tenant mix and synergism.

A successful re-opening depends on the percentage of tenants open when the project is completed. The real estate manager must ensure that the maximum number of tenants are open and operating. This is especially important if the rehab is a retail building. The rehabbed shopping center or mall must have sufficient merchants open to create the synergism necessary for success. The general contractor, tenants' construction coordinators, and the architect must hold weekly meetings to facilitate the tenants' construction.

The rehab process generates both curiosity and excitement in the community. Construction activities provide several opportunities for publicity: the initial announcement of the rehab; selection of the general contractor, architect, leasing agent, real estate manager, and lenders; ground breaking; major tenants signing their leases; demolition of a building; adding an art object to the project; topping off; construction progress reports; a pre-grand opening charity event; and the grand opening.

The real estate manager can raise community awareness by providing a scale model and/or a PowerPoint presentation that shows the shopping center or mall before the rehab and its projected appearance afterward. The real estate management staff can go into the community to speak to community groups such as home owner' associations, social and business organizations, chambers of commerce, and high school and college classes about the rehab of a tired, obsolete shopping center or mall in the community.

Pre-Leasing and Tenants' Rental Rates

The shopping center's leasing activities start prior to the commencement of the rehab. It's important to determine how to structure a tenant's rental rate when the tenant moves in before a rehab is completed. This situation occurs when the leasing program has been successful and a proposed rehab is delayed due to financing, changes in the interest rates, difficulties in raising capital, or inclement weather. The delays could be as long as two or three years.

In such a case, the tenant does not want to pay the market rate for a rehabbed center before it is rehabbed, but the property owner wants rental rates to support the shopping center. An equitable solution is to charge the tenant the market rate for the shopping center in its current condition during the time the work is in process, with a predetermined automatic rental increase the day the rehab is completed. For instance, a tenant may have an initial rental rate of $35 per square foot with a three-percent annual increase until the rehab is completed. At that point, the rate automatically increases to $50 per square foot with a three-percent annual increase.

Tenant Analysis of Potential for Success

The tenant must consider several factors to determine whether its product will be successful in the rehabbed shopping center. To assist, *Store Magazine* published the following 10 questions a retailer must consider when analyzing whether to lease space in a rehabbed shopping center:

1. Is the cost of setting up a retail business in such a project "in the ball park"?
2. Will the property owner provide any financial help in setting up shop?
3. Can the retailer handle the cost of doing business once the doors are open?
4. Is the retailer prepared to handle the swings and sways of traffic flow?
5. Is the retailer's line of goods suitable for the location?
6. Will the retailer work well in a historical setting?
7. Can the retailer deal with physical limitations?
8. Does the retailer have the financial staying power to last through the early years of a project?
9. Can the retailer compete with other attractions?
10. What's the bottom line?

Tenant failure and tenant turnover occur in every shopping center, even the most successful ones. Selecting the wrong tenants for a shopping center compounds this factor.

Timing of Construction Activities

A major consideration for rehabbing a shopping center or mall is the timing of the construction activities. Most retailers generate 25 to 30 percent of their annual sales during the Christmas holiday season, which traditionally starts the day after Thanksgiving and extends through Christmas Eve, and for some, even until New Year's Eve. However, many retailers start their holiday promotions and sales in early November. A major disruption to the tenants' businesses during this period can be the difference between a profitable or not profitable year for most retailers. Some independent merchants cannot survive poor holiday sales.

Ideally, the rehab of a shopping center should commence as soon as weather permits after the first of the year and reach completion prior to Thanksgiving. If the rehab must extend into the holiday season, the rehab team should give special consideration to minimizing its impact on shoppers and tenants. In addition, some retailers will open new stores only during specific dates or windows during the year. These retailers have blackout periods when they will not open a store. If the shopping center's re-opening occurs during their black-out period, the retailer may delay its opening.

Parking Ratio

During the rehab, an opportunity is available to increase the size of the shopping center by reducing the shopping center's parking ratio. Many older shopping centers were built with a six-to-one parking index. This ratio means that six parking stalls are provided for every 1,000 square feet of GLA.

A center of 150,000 square feet that has a six-to-one ratio would require 900 parking stalls. If the parking requirements were reduced to four to one, only 600 parking stalls would be necessary. The additional area created by the reduced parking index could support additional square feet of GLA, depending on the layout of drive lanes and landscaping requirements. This added space could be in the form of a pad or out-parcel building or an addition to an existing building.

The Urban Land Institute (ULI) report, *Parking Requirements for Shopping Centers: Summary Recommendations and Research Study Report,* provides recommendations for how many parking stalls and the different types and sizes that shopping centers and malls need. It also analyzes how multiplex cinemas, food courts, and entertainment features affect the number of parking stalls required. ULI's publication *The Dimensions of Parking,* provides information on parking development and operations.

Municipalities establish parking ratios, and, when necessary, the real estate manager must work with the city to change its parking code or obtain a variance. Most major tenants' leases and some small shop tenants' leases may require a minimum parking ratio or index. The shopping center's common area agreement or reciprocal easement agreement must also be reviewed for parking index requirements. The signatories to any agreement with parking ratio requirements must approve changes and amend either their leases or the common area agreements. Violations of these agreements can be—and usually are—very costly.

OFFICE BUILDINGS

A survey conducted by *Buildings Magazine* found that more office buildings were modernized or rehabbed than any other property type. Office building tenants are less concerned with a specific location than retailers or even industrial tenants because the success of office building tenants seldom depends on the building's amenities or location.

Advantages of Rehabbing Office Buildings

The office building tenant has very little loyalty to a building, while the retail tenant may jeopardize its success by relocating its business too far away from its customer base. A retailer establishes an identity in a particular location selected for the neighborhood's demographics and psychographics, and it seldom moves to a nearby shopping center. The office tenant, on the other hand, is periodically solicited by the brokerage community to relocate to an adjacent building, a building down the street, or a building in another area of town or even in another city. The office building property owner is in a more competitive environment than a shopping center property owner. A significant component of the office building's tenant retention program is providing a satisfying environment for the tenants and their employees and modernizing and/or rehabbing the building can contribute to that goal.

Another reason for the continually increasing activity in rehabbing office buildings is that it affords property owners and developers the opportunity to take an older structure and create an efficient and marketable office building. Taking a proposed new office building concept through the development process to the first tenant's move-in may require two to five years, and in some cases, longer. Rehabbing older buildings allows local developers with smaller staff members to participate in redeveloping well-located, high-quality buildings. These developers might not have the opportunity, the staying power, or the financial backing to acquire major downtown parcels of land and go through the myriad hurdles involved in developing major buildings on prime locations.

Issues in Rehabbing an Office Building

The office building renovation or rehab can present more risks and be more complex than rehabbing a shopping center or an industrial property. The office building is a vertical structure, often of multiple stories, interwoven with mechanical and electrical systems.

Due to the nature of a vertical building, the following are integral components: energy conservation, accommodating the requirements of new technology, and life-safety systems. Architect, Tom Fridstein, during a roundtable discussion several years ago among architects, engineers, construction managers, and building owner, stated:

> In the renovation/rehabilitation of existing office space there are really three aspects you must begin with. The first is to improve the functioning of the space. The second is to improve the aesthetics or the atmosphere of the space so that it looks up-to-date, improves productivity, and is attractive to customers. The third, extremely important today, is to cut down on energy usage.[4]

Since that conference was held an additional issue of importance is sustainability.

Office Building Components and Systems

When developing the design of an office building, six areas must be considered.

1. Exterior: Landscaping, signage, art objects, entry, parking areas, elevators in the building and in the parking garage, and lighting
2. Interior: Building products, hardware, accessories, carpeting, floor and wall coverings, ceiling, furniture, directory, signage, and restrooms. Within the interior, the common areas represent 10 to 20 percent or more of the building. "The renovation of these areas symbolizes the developer's approach to his project, setting a tone and establishing an ambiance that will permeate throughout the building." The lobby is the first place that a statement—possibly a dramatic statement—can be made.
3. Building envelope: Windows, doors, curtain walls, roofing, insulation, and re-facing
4. Controls: Environmental control and, energy management systems, life-safety systems, intelligent building systems, and communication systems
5. Electrical: Emergency power and lighting, security and alarm systems, electrical distribution systems, and lighting
6. Mechanical: HVAC, sprinkler system, and sanitary system. New mechanical systems may create additional space and raise the ceiling heights. Using very wide, shallow ductwork allows for additional height in tenants' spaces.

4. "The Special Design and Specification Problems in Rehabilitation and Re-Use," *Architectural Record* (December 1982), 28–35.

One commentator stated:

> Mechanical systems are not isolated or separate entities from the other areas of the office building. What is done to building envelopes, environmental upgrades, hazard and fire protection, lighting, roofing, and energy management control systems will have a direct impact on the operating characteristics of the HVAC piping and air distribution systems that turn structures of glass, iron, and stone into living edifices.[5]

Building Codes

Consideration must also be given for all types of properties to possible changes to the municipality's building code that have been made since the original construction of the building that is proposed for rehab. The structure must be thoroughly analyzed to see if it can meet current building codes regarding seismic life safety, updates to the Americans with Disabilities Act, energy conservation, and environmental concerns.

INDUSTRIAL PROPERTIES

Industrial properties are seldom considered when discussing rehabbing. Yet, unique opportunities exist to rehab older, large single-use industrial buildings and multi-tenant industrial buildings developed since the 1960s.

Advantages of Rehabbing Industrial Properties

In nearly every city in the nation, facilities can be found that are monuments to the past glory of industry. Changes in manufacturing patterns, transportation systems, location and skills of the labor force, and market patterns and demands have caused many industries to relocate their operations to new sites. Empty and lifeless, abandoned industrial buildings have a negative visual and social impact on an area and represent lost tax revenues. When recycled into new industrial space, they can again contribute to the vitality of a city.

5. P.G. Barrett, "Renovating Mechanical Systems," *Commercial Renovation* (April 1990).

Large inner-city industrial buildings of 200,000 square feet or more, formerly occupied by one tenant, are candidates to be subdivided into multi-tenant buildings. In desirable areas where a mix of commercial and residential buildings has evolved, some of these old industrial buildings have been converted into loft residential buildings.

ISSUES IN REHABBING AN INDUSTRIAL PROPERTY

Industrial tenants, just like retailers, have been searching for ways to operate more efficiently. To meet production schedules, industrial tenants and manufacturers become more efficient through computerized inventory control and precise timing of parts and supplies delivery known as just-in-time (JIT) delivery. As a result, some industrial space requirements have decreased while the requirements of the space have changed. As an example, ceiling heights have increased which allows for more efficient operations and storage and, thus, a better use of space for many users.

Feasibility Study

The developer must analyze the market to determine whether a demand for rehabbed industrial facilities exists and whether the proposed site is appropriate. Several factors must be considered. The environmental condition of the site and the building are among the first issues to study. Industrial sites have a greater probability of harboring pollution from former users than office buildings or shopping centers. Underground storage tanks, storage of chemicals for manufacturing purposes, or the by-products of the manufacturing process are just a few of the potential contaminants. The building must be inspected for asbestos and polychlorinated biphenyls (PCBs) as well as other hazards associated with industrial use. The expense of cleaning up a site may make the rehab cost prohibitive.

Other site-related factors to consider in a feasibility analysis are accessibility to freeways and rail transportation. If the site is in an inner-city area, security may be a concern. Of course, the zoning classification of the site will restrict potential users. The building must be studied to determine the types of users that could operate efficiently in it.

Industrial and Office Parks

Many multi-tenant suburban and office parks have already lost their competitive edge. Industrial users, especially those with smaller space requirements, are looking for efficient, modern environments for their businesses. With creative rehabbing, an older, tired-looking project can be brought into the mainstream of modern business properties and compete successfully with the newer planned industrial communities.

Many improvements to an industrial park are considered cosmetic rather than actual remodeling. Such improvements include painting the buildings in contemporary colors, creating a coordinated landscape, adding an organized signage program, and providing the project with new identity signs and directories. Improvements to landscaping provides an instant new look to an otherwise uninteresting project. Interior space improvements include increasing the ratio of office space to warehouse space, installing new ceilings and wall treatments, painting and carpeting in up-to-date colors, and adding limited kitchen facilities. Including an on-site management and/or leasing office encourages a substantial increase in existing and potential tenant contact, as well as more broker contact.

RENOVATION AND REHAB OPPORTUNITIES

Property owners and developers rehab commercial buildings for a variety of reasons from accommodating tenants' changing needs to creating additional leasable space to create additional cash flow and property value. The property owner leads the rehab team. The real estate manager is an essential part of the team and the only member whose duties continue after the completion of the project. Other team members include an architect, general contractor, and a leasing agent. The rehab process can involve years of work from design through construction to marketing the rehabbed building. The most frequently rehabbed commercial buildings are office buildings and shopping centers; however, industrial properties can also benefit from the rehab process.

REPOSITIONING COMMERCIAL PROPERTIES

The true definition of repositioning is rebranding a product. A commercial property may be rebranded and marketed to the same target market or to a different target market. A property is repositioned to maximize its value or for defensive reasons. The property may no longer compete in its market and needs to be rehabbed or remodeled to stop the value erosion and regain its market share with increased rents. Repositioning a property enables it to once again be in competition and regain its market position and market share.

A property that is competitive in the market may be positioned for offensive reasons. The property will become superior to its competition and outperform the market in terms of rental rates, occupancy and tenant turnover. A property that is repositioned will either be targeted to a different segment of the property's existing market or it will target to a totally different market. A property repositioned that is targeted to a totally different market is a property has been converted to another use. This is referred to as adaptive use.

The repositioning process includes the following components but not necessarily in this order:

1. Property acquisition
2. Building analysis
3. Market analysis
4. Determining the building's position in the market
5. Develop repositioning alternatives
6. Testing and financial analysis of each alternative
7. Selecting an alternative to reposition the building
8. Preliminary plans or architectural concepts
9. Developing a pro forma
10. Determine and raising required equity
11. Financing the project
12. Hiring consultants and professionals (architects, general contractors, leasing agents, etc.)
13. Developing a marketing and leasing plan
14. Communicate with existing tenants and develop a plan to mitigate disruption to their businesses
15. Final design and construction drawings
16. Construction contract
17. Entitlement process to obtain necessary permits
18. Construction
19. Staffing
20. Establishing the management and operations
21. Grand opening

Analyzing the Property

The property must be thoroughly analyzed to determine why it has lost its market position and potential opportunities. The analysis will include a review and/or inspection of the site plan, building layout and design, and the configuration and size of each space. The analysis includes a structural inspection and a marketing analysis. A thorough inspection is the first step in analyzing the building.

The inspection starts with the exterior of the building and the grounds. What is the property's curbside appeal? What is the condition and appearance of the exterior common areas? These items would include the landscaping, sidewalks, lighting, parking lots, parking garage, and exterior amenities. The building and grounds are inspected for deferred maintenance and obsolescence. Depending on the age and the tenancy over the life of the building an environmental report may be needed.

An older commercial industry building, especially a manufacturing building, may be leased to tenants who used materials and chemicals that were not considered hazardous substances years ago, but are now considered hazardous. An older shopping may have had a dry cleaners or a film processing store and the site could be contaminated. The building must be analyzed from a marketing and leasing perspective. The inspection will provide insight into the cost to renovate or demolish the building. The analysis should identify functional obsolescence.

Functional obsolescence includes conditions that can be modernized or rectified but usually at a great expense. Functional obsolescence almost always negatively effects the marketing and leasing of the building and places downward pressure on rental rates. Examples are often found in older strip shopping centers built prior to the 1980s. These shopping centers have deep shop spaces and are often 100 feet deep, while today's shop tenants prefer spaces between 65 and 75 feet deep. When determining the rent for these spaces, 25 to 35 square feet is discounted and the blended rate for the entire space is reduced.

The analysis of the property and the building may discover an opportunity to add leasable area. There may be unused space in an office building that can be leased as storage space. A shopping center, business, or industrial park on a main street may have room in its parking lot to add a pad or out-parcel building for a fast-food restaurant, bank, or a smaller espresso drive-through stand. The more people with different expertise and skill sets that walk, inspect, and analyze the building, the greater chance of discovering hidden leasable space and creative ways to improve the building. An architect and a space planner, along with the management and leasing teams, should be among those analyzing the building and property.

The following lists other questions to consider when analyzing the financial status of the property:

- Does the property have insufficient cash flow?
- Can the property ownership continue to fund negative cash flow?
- Do the partners have funds for renovation or remodeling?
- Are the partners willing to invest in the property?
- Will the partners assume the risks of a major investment to improve the property and/or add additional leasable space or buildings on the site?
- What are the short- and long-term goals of the property ownership and of each partner?

Review the Tenant Mix

What is the make-up of the existing tenants? Are the tenants willing to raise rents to support the cost of renovating or modernizing the building? If the building is being repositioned with tenants in place, their rents and lease expiration dates must be reviewed. The real estate manager will determine which spaces are likely to be released.

Retail properties and shopping centers will need a more thorough analysis of each tenant in place. There are two issues to review and evaluate with the retail tenants: (1) the tenants' use and (2) current and past sales. When reviewing a retailer's use the quality and price points of their merchandise, ask the following questions:

- Will the retailer complement the new tenants to create a strong synergism at the property?
- Is the retailer or restaurant performing at a sales level that will support the new rents when the lease expires?
- Are the tenant's sales sufficient enough to be a contributor to the synergism of all the tenants?

Anchor tenants have long-term leases with multiple five-year options. Determine what are their sales are and how they compare to sales at other stores and national averages for their category. Poor performing anchor tenants may need to be replaced by either a mutual-lease cancellation or more likely a owner buy out of their lease.

When tenants are in-place, the leasing team and the property owner need to decide which tenants should remain after the property is repositioned and which tenants' leases expire.

Some tenants may be under performing and others may be in strategic locations that can be leased to better retailers or restaurants, and their leases may need to be bought-out.

Competitive Analysis

Just about every troubled property has a T and R problem. The T is time and the R is rate. The building is taking too long to lease or release and the rental rates are depressed. When determining the building's competitive position, first analyze its location in relation to its competition and its intended use. Next, the architecture design is reviewed for historical significance, out-dated design, and obsolescence.

Each space should be evaluated for its marketability. Can spaces be combined or divided into smaller spaces? What is the depth of retail spaces, what are the ceiling heights for manufacturing buildings, and what is the distance between the corridor wall and the curtain wall in an office building? These are just a few issues to consider when evaluating the marketability of the spaces in a building. When the target market is determined, the developer will compare the spaces in the building to the wants and needs of the target market.

Market Analysis

The first analysis is that of the micro market for an office building, industrial property, or the trade area for a shopping center. Demographics are evaluated for all property types and psychographics are evaluated for retail properties and shopping centers. Competing buildings are identified and studied. A market survey is conducted. A visit to the municipality's planning department will reveal proposed new and to-be renovated buildings. These buildings may be new competition to the subject property. Once the market has been studied, the marketing team and the property owner can determine or confirm the subject building's position in the market.

Analysis of Alternatives

After the building and market has been analyzed and the subject building compared to the competition and positioned in the market, the real estate manager and leasing team will address the building's deficiencies, attributes, and opportunities to reposition the building. An important component of the analysis of alternatives is to evaluative the property in its "as-is" condition. This is the base line for comparing the performance of the property to alternatives. If the property is managed and operated in its current condition and correcting deferred maintenance, how will the property perform in the short and long term. The other alternatives include minor to major renovations, rehabbing the building, and changing the building's use. A detailed plan for each alternative must be developed, and if the changes are not significant, the real estate manager can cost out the changes. If the renovation or rehabbing the property requires significant changes, a contractor is needed to estimate the costs.

Testing Alternatives

Each alternative must be tested and compared to the other alternatives to determine which one provides the best return and an acceptable level of financial risk that the property ownership is willing to accept. Two critical components of testing of alternatives are; (1) the financial analysis and (2) the marketing analysis.

An income and expense model is developed for the property in "as-is" condition. This model will include correcting deferred maintenance and the cost of current and future capital improvements. Each alternative being considered also needs a financial model. These models will include capital expense for remodeling or renovation. If additional leasable space can be added, construction costs will be included on a separate budget. A real estate manager working with an architect, the leasing agent, and general contractor will develop the specifications for the additional space or building(s) and the general contractor will develop the construction budget. If one of the alternatives is an adaptive use, the first analysis is to determine if the current zoning will allow the new use. If not, can a variance or conditional-use permit be obtained from the municipality?

An income and operating expense pro forma is developed for the property when it reaches a stabilized occupancy. This will provide the property's NOI and its value can be estimated. A timeline for each alternative is developed and is used when developing the leasing and income projections along with the financing cost of the project.

The final analysis is a comparison of each alternative financial models that will include *cash-on-cash return,* the *internal rate of return (IRR),* value enhancement, and the value of the property at different intervals throughout the next several years.

Equity and Financing

If the chosen alternative is to renovate or remodel the property, the owner will either refinance the property, restructure the existing loan, or the partners will contribute additional equity for the cost to reposition the property. If the property will be expanded or converted to another use, a significant capital investment will be required. The property's ownership will need to refinance the property or restructure the loan and contribute additional equity.

If the property has a loan balance considerably less than the value of the property, additional capital may not be necessary if the property's pro forma and NOI meets the lender's underwriting requirements—measured by a debt-coverage ratio and/or an LTV ratio. If the cost of the renovation or adaptive use is too great, or the risks are beyond their tolerance level, the owner may consider selling the property for a premium as a value-added opportunity.

Recommendations

The testing of alternatives will provide the basis for a recommendation. After the completion of a thorough analysis of the alternatives, the property owner will meet with the real estate manager and other real estate professionals to review each alternative, their financial projections, or pro forma, and evaluate the pros and cons of each alternative. The analysis of each alternative will be based on the property owner's goals and objectives. The following lists some of the issues that are considered when arriving at a recommendation:

- The time frame of how and when changes will be implemented—which eventually becomes the operating plan for the property
- Description of the perceived risks and exposures
- Discussion of how the recommended solution will be financed
- Description of the recommended marketing and leasing plan necessary to achieve the desired results
- Anticipated date for implementing the recommendation, along with the anticipated date the recommended action plan should be achieved
- The results of the testing of alternatives
- Explanation of how the recommended action best addresses the goals and objects of the property's ownership

After one of the alternatives is selected, which may be to maintain the property in "as-is" condition, the real estate manager develops and implements a business plan to achieve the goals and objectives of the desired alternative.

Business Plan

The business plan establishes a course of action to reposition the property in accordance with the property owner's goals and objectives. It will become the short- and long-term plan of action for the property. The plan is updated each year and changes are made that reflect changes in the market, leasing activities, and the economy. *Chapter 2: The Business Plan* reviews the process or writing and the content of a business plan.

Marketing Plan

The marketing plan often starts with a market analysis and includes a market survey. The plan explains the property's current position in the market and the benefits repositioning will have on the leasing, rental rates, and occupancy of the property. More information on the market analysis and many leasing issues can be found in *Section III: Marketing and Leasing.*

There are two main elements that are essential to include when it comes to write the marketing plan: (1) A statement explaining the purpose of the plan with a short narrative about the short- and long-term occupancy, and when the financial goals will be achieved, and (2) A definition of the target market, which identifies the prospects—both demographically and by business type—along with an explanation of the reason this market qualifies as the target and the data upon which this assumption is based.[6]

The property owner will hire a marketing and leasing team to create and implement the marketing plan. The existing leasing team must be evaluated for their past and current performance and recognizing that an unsuccessful performance may be the result of the property's poor position in the market for so many years. Can this team create and successfully implement a new marketing plan targeted at the new targeted market? The property owner needs to hire the best leasing team to lease the repositioned property. If the use of the property will change, a new leasing team that specializes in the new use will need to be hired.

Management and Operations Staffing

When a recommended alternative is selected, the real estate manager establishes the management and operations plan for the property. A staffing plan is created that may or may not include all or some of the existing staff. New skill sets may be required, but ideally, all or most of the existing staff would be retained.

A new maintenance management program and emergency procedures plan needs to be developed. Each maintenance and service contract must be evaluated and, if appropriate, renegotiated or terminated. An operating budget is created taking into consideration new building materials that need to be maintained, possible change in the number of maintenance personnel at the property, increase frequency of contracted maintenance, and a higher standard of maintenance. These changes will increase the operating expense of the property. There may be energy savings due to new and more efficient mechanical equipment, lighting, and irrigation systems. Insurance will increase to reflect the cost to insure the renovated building with will have a higher replacement value. The increase in value will cause the real estate assessment and real estate taxes to increase. If the property has new equity partners, they may require more complex financial reporting. If tenants are in-place during the renovation, a plan must be developed to inform them of the improvements to the building, the timeline for the activities, how the construction or remodeling may affect them, and what will be done to mitigate possible disruption to their business.

If the alternative selected has an impact on the neighborhood, the community will want to know the plans for the property. A renovated retail property or shopping center with new retailers, service tenants, and restaurants will be welcomed by the community. Renovating the interior of an office building will have a limited impact on the community. Regardless of the extent and the impact to the community, the plan to reposition the property should be a story the real estate manager is continually telling the community.

The real estate manager should develop a PR program to inform the community and the brokerage community of the plan and the timeline to complete the repositioning of the property. The program may include press releases to the media, e-mails to the brokerage community, presentations with photos of the property, and renderings of the improvements to community groups and home property owners' associations. This will generate community interest and support and assist in the marketing and leasing of the property.

CASE STUDIES

There are thousands of stories of properties that have been successfully repositioned. Each property that has been repositioned encountered and overcame unique issues to the property and possibly its property ownership. It is wise for the team responsible for the repositioning to meet with the property ownership, management and leasing team of other properties that have been repositioned. A frame of

6. Lawrence W. Baiamonte, John N. Gallagher, Kenneth Goodacre, Kathleen M. Harmon, Richard F. Muhlebach, *Troubled Properties: A Practical Guide for Turning Around Trouble Assets* (Chicago: IREM, 2011).

reference and a list of dos and don'ts can be learned from every building that has been repositioned. The following are a couple of properties that have been successfully repositioned.

Case Study: Specialty Retail Pier

An older specialty retail pier with one level of ground-floor retail and two levels of parking was developed on the water front of a major coastal city. The waterfront tourist district and all the tourist activity moved many years prior a mile down the street from the subject property. With no tourist activity, the retailers located in the subject property suffered. The property experienced a high vacancy with high tenant turnover and rent-collection problems.

The property's lender petitioned the court to appoint a *receiver* and place the property in *receivership*. After a year in receivership, the lender acquired title to the property. The real estate manager was hired to be the receiver because the real estate management firm had extensive experience managing and leasing retail properties, strip shopping centers, and enclosed malls.

The property ownership struggled with the property for many years and did not have the funds to reinvest in the property. The executive of the firm suggested to the bank, after it acquired title to the property, it be converted to an office building. The repositioning was too risky for the lender and the property was sold to a developer.

The developer repositioned the property by remodeling the building and converting it to an office building. This repositioning is known as an adaptive use. The property was repositioned by converting it from one use, specialty retail, to another use, office building.

Case Study: A Small or Mini Enclosed Mall

A small enclosed mall on the East Coast was developed in a small city an hour's drive from a metropolitan area. The mall was' anchored by a national supermarket, a regional drugstore, but a third-anchor space was not leased, nor was 50,000 feet of the enclosed shop space. A typical mall is defined by having two rows of stores facing each other separated by a walk way. In this situation, the supermarket and drugstore faced the main parking lot.

The lender petitioned the court for a receiver and the property was placed in receivership. The received was a shopping center manager and her company specialized in managing large multi-anchored shopping centers and enclosed malls. The lender acquired ownership of the mall. The receiver knew that the interior space of 50,000 square feet was not of sufficient size to attract several fashion retailers to create a synergism that would draw shoppers to the mall. She also knew that a supermarket and a drugstore are not mall-anchored retailers. They do not draw the traffic that supports mall retailers.

She suggested the property be de-malled and converted to a grocery-anchored, strip shopping center. The lender believed this was a relatively low-risk alternative and could create additional value that would exceed the balance of its loan. The bank hired a shopping center developer to de-mall the small enclosed mall. The row of interior shop space backing up to the main parking lot was reversed by adding store fronts and entrances on the parking side of these stores. Customers no longer needed to enter the mall to enter these stores. The stores now had signage above their store fronts facing the parking lot with great visibility from the street.

The challenging issue was what to do with the row of stores on the other side of the mall. The developer's leasing team knew that retailers, service tenants, and restaurants would not lease this space. The leasing team leased the space that is located right off the mall entrance in the interior of the mall to a day-care center and the adjacent long row of interior shop space to the community college for their off-campus classrooms. The bank sold the property and earned a profit in excess of the value of their loan balance. This property was repositioned to a different type of shopping center that offered a different shopping center experience and leased to specialty food and service tenants and the community college.

THE FUTURE OF REPOSITIONING PROPERTIES

There are scores of stories of office buildings being converted to hotels, apartments, or condominiums because the office buildings were old with obsolesce and no longer competitive, yet their downtown locations are exceptional for a residential use. Apartments have been repositioned as condominiums, industrial building into loft apartments, dated and uncompetitive enclosed malls into power centers, older community shopping centers into life style centers, and many other types of repositioning through adaptive use or renovation, remodeling and rehabilitation.

Structurally, most properties can last for many decades and even hundreds of years with proper maintenance. There are buildings in the United States that are as functionally sound today as they were when they were built in the 1700s and 1800s. There are buildings in Europe and Asia that are several hundreds of years old that are in use today and will remain in use for many years to come. Most properties will need renovation and/or remodeling to continue their economic life. There will always be value-added opportunities to reposition properties in good real estate markets and in poor real estate markets. The creative real estate professional will identify these opportunities, reposition these properties, and harvest their increased cash flow and equity.

Glossary

Absorption rate: The amount of space of a particular property type that is leased compared to the amount of that same type of space available for lease within a certain geographic area over a given period of time, accounting for both construction of new space and demolition or removal from the market of existing space. Also used in reference to the rate at which a market can absorb space designed for a specific use (e.g., office space). Absorption rate can be computed as follows:

Units or square feet vacant at the beginning of the period	
plus	units or square feet constructed new during the period
minus	units or square feet demolished during the period
minus	units or square feet vacant at the end of the period
equals	units or square feet absorbed during the period.

Accrual-basis accounting: The method of accounting that involves entering amounts of income when they are earned and amounts of expense when they are incurred, even though the cash may not be received or paid. All certified audits must use accrual accounting.

Adaptive use: A process whereby a structurally sound older building is redeveloped for a new, economically viable use, as refitting an office building or warehouse space for use as rental apartments or condominium units; sometimes called ***change of use.***

Alteration provision: A lease provision that prohibits a tenant from making any alteration or improvement to the leased premises without ownership's express consent, usually required to be in writing.

Annual sales statement: A required sales report submitted to real estate managers by tenants at shopping centers.

Arbitration: A process of dispute resolution in which a neutral third party (arbitrator) renders a decision after a hearing at which both parties have an opportunity to be heard, often employed as a means of avoiding litigation. Arbitration provisions are common in collective bargaining (union) agreements and often required in commercial contracts. When arbitration is voluntary, the parties to the dispute select the arbitrator who has the power to render a decision, called an award, that is binding on the parties.

Arrearage report: A report indicating the part of a debt that is overdue after missing one or more required payments. The amount of the arrears is the amount accrued from the date on which the first missed payment was due.

Artificial breakpoint: A negotiated breakpoint that requires a retail tenant to pay percentage rent before (or after) the natural breakpoint is reached. See also ***breakpoint.***

Asset manager: One who is charged with supervising an owner's real estate assets at the investment level. In addition to real estate management responsibilities that include maximizing net operating income and property value, an asset manager may recommend or be responsible for or participate in property acquisition, development, and divestiture. An asset manager may have only superficial involvement with day-to-day operations at the site (e.g., supervision of personnel, property maintenance, tenant relations).

Assignment: The transfer, in writing, of an interest in a bond, mortgage, lease, or other instrument. The transfer of one person's interest or right in a property (e.g., a lease) to another. Also, the document by which such an interest or right is transferred. Specifically, the document used to convey a leasehold is called an *assignment of lease.* The assignor of a lease remains liable unless released by the landlord. Compare ***sub-lease; sublet***.

Assignor: One giving some right or interest. The person making an ***assignment***.

Base rent: The minimum rent as set forth in a (usually commercial) lease, excluding passthroughs, percentage rents, and other additional charges. See also ***minimum rent***.

Base-year expense: In a commercial (office, retail, industrial) lease, the stated year that is to be used as a standard in determining rent escalations. In subsequent years, operating costs are compared with the base year, and the difference determines the tenant's rent adjustment.

Billback items: Another name for ***pass-through charges.***

Bloodborne pathogens: Pathogenic microorganisms that are present in human blood and can cause disease in humans. These pathogens include Hepatitis B Virus (HBV) and Human Immunodeficiency Virus (HIV). In the real estate management industry, working in medical office buildings (MOBs) pose the greatest exposure and risk to bloodborne pathogens.

Breakeven analysis: A financial technique used to determine when income will cover all operating costs. Calculation of breakeven may include or exclude debt service.

Breakeven point: The point at which income covers all operating expenses plus debt service. In rental real estate, the number of units or the square footage that must be occupied by tenants (or the amount of income that must be generated) to cover a property's operating costs plus debt service. In retailing, the sales volume at which revenues and costs are equal.

Breakpoint: In retail leases, the point at which the tenant's volume of sales multiplied by a predefined percentage rate is equal to the base rent stated in the lease and beyond which the tenant will begin to pay percentage (overage) rent; also called ***natural breakpoint.*** (Natural breakpoint is calculated by dividing the tenant's annual base or minimum rent by the established percentage rate.) Sometimes a tenant and owner will negotiate an ***artificial breakpoint*** that requires the tenant to begin paying percentage rent either before or after the natural breakpoint is reached.

Building standard: A uniform specification that defines the quantity and quality of construction and finish elements a building owner will provide for build-out of space leased to commercial tenants.

Build-to-suit: An arrangement in which a land owner constructs (or pays for constructing) a custom building on the land, and both land and building are leased to the tenant; a frequent arrangement in shopping centers (e.g., for pad or outlot spaces) and industrial properties.

Business interruption insurance: A form of property insurance which provides coverage against the loss of profits (indirect loss) resulting from damage to the building or contents (direct loss), as by fire or other peril.

Buy-out: A form of concession whereby an owner or developer arranges to pay the rent for the rest of a tenant's lease term so that the tenant will relocate to the owner's property or move out of a space that the owner wants to use for another purpose.

Canvassing: Contacting prospective tenants by telephone or in person in order to interest them in leasing commercial (office, retail) space. See also ***cold calling***.

Capital budget: An estimate of costs of major improvements or replacements; generally a long-range plan for improvements to a property. Also used in referring to a long-range financial plan for acquiring and financing capital assets.

Capital call: A call for additional equity investment by shareholders or partners in order to fund cash shortfalls in development or operations, or to compensate for the falling value of noncash assets, and the need to increase cash so that liabilities do not exceed assets.

Capital expenditure: Spending on capital assets, such as major improvements, large equipment, additions to buildings, buildings themselves, and land.

Capital improvement: A structural addition or betterment to real property that increases its useful life or productivity or extends the life of a building or its equipment. The improvement must have a life in excess of one year in order for the cost to be recovered (depreciated) for income tax purposes.

Cap rate: A rate of return used to estimate a property's value based on that property's net operating income (NOI). This rate is based on the rates of return prevalent in the marketplace for similar properties and intended to reflect the investment risk associated with a particular property. It is derived from market data on similar, recent, sales (NOI ÷ property value/sales price = capitalization rate) or from calculations based on expected returns to debt and equity.

Cash-basis accounting: The method of accounting that recognizes income and expenses when money is actually received or paid; also called ***cash accounting.*** Compare ***accrual-basis accounting.***

Cash flow: The amount of spendable income from a real estate investment. The amount of cash available after all payments have been made for operating expenses, debt service (mortgage principal and interest), and capital reserve funds; also called ***pre-tax cash flow*** to indicate that income taxes have not been deducted.

Cash-on-cash return: A measure of the productivity of an investor's initial investment that compares the yearly cash flow of a property with its initial investment base: cash flow ÷ initial investment base. The result is given as a percentage.

Ceiling rent: In public housing, a cap on the amount of rent a family can be charged; sometimes called *maximum rent.* Ceiling rent caps the ***total tenant payment (TTP),*** which is the amount a family must pay to cover both shelter and a reasonable amount for utilities.

Central business district (CBD): The central shopping or business area in an urban environment, usually the place where real estate values are highest; also called ***downtown.***

Certificate of occupancy (C of O): A document issued by an appropriate governmental agency certifying that the premises (new construction, rehabilitation, and alterations) complies with local building codes and/or zoning ordinances. Some jurisdictions require a certificate of occupancy for apartments based on inspection of units between each tenancy.

Change of use: The process of changing the function of a structure without changing its exterior dimensions. See also ***adaptive use.***

Chart of accounts: A classification or arrangement of account items by type of income or expense (e.g., rent, advertising, insurance, maintenance), as well as assets and liabilities, accounts receivable, and accounts payable.

Cold calling: Calling on prospects with whom the representative has had no previous contact in order to interest them in leasing (commercial) space or employing property management services. See also *canvassing.*

Commission: A fee paid to an agent or employee for transacting a piece of business or performing a service. In real estate, the fee paid to the party or parties responsible for generating the business (e.g., the fee paid to an agent or broker for negotiating a sale or rental). The amount and payment of the fee is usually established via a written (commission) agreement. The fee may be a percentage of the transaction amount, an agreed-to fixed amount, or a rate per square foot. Real estate sales commissions are documented in a listing agreement; in real estate management, leasing commissions may be identified as separate compensation in the management agreement. See also ***schedule of commissions***. The term is also used in referring to a group of individuals empowered by a government or other entity to exercise specific authority, as a state real estate commission that oversees real estate activity.

Common area: Areas of a property that are used by all tenants or owners. In commercial properties, the lobbies, public corridors, and service areas of office buildings and enclosed shopping malls.

Common area agreement: A separate agreement, usually between an anchor tenant and a shopping center owner, that sets standards for maintenance of the common area and states how the related expenses will be distributed between the parties. It may also prohibit the shopping center owner from making changes to the common areas (e.g., relocating entrances or adding a pad or outlot building) without the written approval of each signatory to the agreement. (Often, a shopping center common area agreement is incorporated in a ***reciprocal easement agreement.***) Such an agreement may also be established among multiple owners of a mixed-use development (MXD) or other similar property, in which case it may also address removal of the common area manager for nonperformance.

Common area maintenance (CAM): The amount that a tenant will pay to maintain the common areas of the property (e.g., landscaping, parking areas, sidewalks, roadways). In leases for office buildings and industrial properties, CAM costs may be paid along with other property operating expenses as ***pass-through charges.*** More specifically, a provision in a retail lease that stipulates how much the tenant will pay for maintaining the common area of a shopping center or mall (mall corridors and center court, courtyards, sidewalks, skyways, parking areas, landscaping, elevators, escalators, etc.).

Community room: A large room usually found in malls, sometimes a converted vacant space, offered as a free meeting place for community groups and for a small fee to businesses in shopping centers.

Community shopping center: A shopping center commonly anchored by a junior department store, discount store, or variety store and having 100,000–500,000 square feet of ***gross leasable area (GLA),*** often configured as a large open-air strip with three or more anchors.

Comparison grid: A form used to compare the features of a property with those of other properties in the same market that are similar in size and use. The form lists features and amenities of the properties in a column at the left and includes columns to identify the characteristics of the subject property and to evaluate those same characteristics in the comparable properties. The user usually also assigns a value to each item, an estimate of how much additional rent a tenant might willingly pay to have the feature. For rental apartments, a comparison grid should be completed for each different type and size of apartment. In commercial properties, the basis for comparison would be the square footage of an office suite or store space. Usual practice is to identify at least three comparable properties. The form is often used in determining a market rent for the subject property and usually included as part of a management plan.

Compounding: In banking, calculation and payment of interest on the principal and on any previous interest.

Computer-aided design (CAD): A computerized system used by architects, space planners, and building managers to facilitate space planning and building design; sometimes also called ***computer-assisted design.*** A CAD system makes it possible to create space plan drawings and make revisions to them much more quickly than can be done using traditional methods.

Concession: An economic incentive granted by an owner to encourage the leasing of space or the renewal of a lease. Concessions are usually related specifically to the rental rate (e.g., a month's free rent). In office buildings, shopping centers, and industrial properties, they may also relate to the tenant improvement allowance. For retail tenants, a concession may be a lower percentageofsales requirement. Concessions usually affect the total economic value of a lease and, therefore, are subject to negotiation.

Condemnation: A declaration that a structure is unfit for use. The taking of private property for public use by governmental power of eminent domain, including payment of just compensation. Also, the official act to terminate the use of real property for nonconformance with governmental regulations or because of hazards to public health and safety. See also ***eminent domain.***

Construction management: The supervision of construction of tenant improvements to commercial space by a space-planning department or a firm specializing in this activity.

Consumer Price Index (CPI): A way of measuring consumer purchasing power by comparing the current costs of goods and services to those of a selected base period; formerly ***cost-of-living index.*** Sometimes used as a reference point for rent escalations in commercial leases (i.e., as a measure of inflation). The CPI is published monthly by the U.S. Department of Labor, Bureau of Labor Statistics.

Continuous occupancy clause: A lease clause that requires the tenant to occupy the space continuously throughout the lease term.

Continuous operation: A shopping center lease provision that requires the retail tenant to operate the business throughout the term of the lease (sometimes including reference to established operating hours of the shopping center, but ***store hours*** are usually addressed in a separate lease provision); also called ***operating covenant.*** A continuous operation requirement may not be viable in jurisdictions where the courts will not enforce the lease provision but rather take the view that the landlord can recover money damages for a breach of the lease. In a shopping center, maintaining a continuously operating viable mix of retail businesses is key to the success of the center as a whole and that of all the individual tenants; money damages paid to the landlord are not adequate compensation in the event a tenant does not comply. A shop tenant will sometimes try to negotiate to have the continuous operation requirement apply contingent on a specific anchor remaining in operation; if the anchor is allowed to ***go dark,*** the continuous operation provision in the shop tenant's lease would not apply.

Continuous operation clause: A retail lease clause that requires tenants to keep their stores fully stocked at inventory levels equal to (1) when they first opened for business, (2) their stores in other locations, or (3) stores offering similar merchandise in the area. There may also be requirements regarding store hours, staffing, and business name.

Corporation: A legal entity that is chartered by a state and treated by courts as an individual entity with the ability to buy, sell, sue, and be sued separate and distinct from the persons who own its stock. For purposes of taxation, the Internal Revenue Service (IRS) differentiates regular corporations subject to corporate income tax under Subchapter C of the IRS Code from those whose taxable income is taxed to their shareholders per Subchapter S of the Code.

Cost of living adjustment (COLA): The money cost of maintaining a particular standard of living in terms of purchased goods and services.

Covenants, Conditions, and Restrictions (CC&Rs): One of the documents that governs participation in a condominium or homeowners' association, CC&Rs are enforceable rules and regulations that protect the economic value, architectural uniformity, and long-term desirability of the property. In shopping centers, CC&Rs restrict the use of the property.

Curable obsolescence: Reversible deterioration of a building that is a result of deferred maintenance. Also, remediable loss of value due to a property becoming outmoded or noncompetitive.

Current ratio: A measure of a company's ability to pay its current liabilities from its current assets; a measure of ***liquidity.*** Calculated by dividing the value of current assets by the value of current liabilities.

Debt-coverage ratio (DCR): Used by lenders as a measure of financial risk. A measure of the amount of debt service that can be carried on a property pledged as collateral for a loan. The ratio is calculated: annual net operating income ÷ annual debt service payment (principal plus interest), and the result is written as a decimal (e.g., 1.55). The closer the resulting value approaches to one (1.0), the riskier the loan.

Default: Failure to fulfill an obligation (as a mortgage or other contracted payment) when it is due. The non-performance of a duty, such as those required in a lease or other contract.

Deferred conditions summary: A tool for tracking future changes in the terms of the leases. The information is listed on the month and year of the change.

Deferred maintenance: Ordinary maintenance of a building that, because it has not been performed, negatively affects the use, occupancy, and value of the property. Also, an amount needed for repairs, restoration, or rehabilitation of an asset (e.g., real property) but not yet expended.

Delinquency: Failure to make payment on a debt or obligation when due. A state of being overdue. A debt on which payment is in arrears, as of mortgage principal or interest or rent under a lease.

Demographics: The statistical analysis of populations, using information derived primarily from census records, including overall population size, density, and distribution, birth and death rates, and the impact of immigration and outmigration. Also included are age, gender, nationality, religion, education, occupation, and income characteristics of people who live in a geographically defined area. Used to characterize discrete markets. Residential property owners and managers are also interested in such concurrent data as household size, numbers of children and their ages, and levels of homeownership because they relate to requirements for living space in the form of rental apartments. Retail tenants are interested in population and household data within a prescribed ***trade area*** to help establish price points, merchandise mix, and marketing focus. A tool of ***marketing research.***

Denominator: The sum of the square footage of the premises of all the retailers that are billed for a particular expense.

Discounting: Calculating how much a future sum of money would be worth at present.

Drip-line methodology (Method B)*:* Measures to the most exterior drip line at the perimeter of the roof system to calculate areas. Method B is generally intended for wall-less industrial structures.

Due diligence: The duty of a seller to ensure that the offering statement does not misstate or omit pertinent information. The appropriate or sufficient level of care and attention that should be given during the examination or evaluation of a property, either as preparation for financing or refinancing or in an effort to identify environmental problems that must be addressed.

Easement: An interest in or right to land that is owned by another person. A legal right to use land owned by another person or business for a specific purpose. An easement may be granted by a deed or created as a result of actual use that was not prohibited ***(easement by prescription).***

Escalation expense: In a lease, a provision for increases in rent based on increases in operating costs, changes in a standard economic index such as the ***consumer price index (CPI),*** or an agreed upon schedule stated in the lease, commonly used to account for inflation over the lease term or to maintain the rent at market levels. A provision in a mortgage or loan agreement under which the entire amount of the debt becomes due immediately in the event of a specified occurrence such as missing a set number of monthly payments or other default. (A similar provision in a lease that would make the full amount of rent for the remainder of the lease term due under specified circumstances such as default. Most courts will not allow the remaining rent to be escalated in this fashion.)

Effective income: Determined by subtracting the lost income from the anticipated vacancy and credit loss, which is either the actual number of vacancies, a historical factor that appears to be reasonable in the marketplace, or a projection of which spaces will be vacant and for how long during the budget period.

Effective rent: In residential property management, the rent per month reduced by the monthly value of any leasing concessions computed on a per-month basis for that unit. The cumulative rental amount collected over the full term of a lease. Also, the amount of rent a commercial tenant actually pays after base rent is adjusted for concessions, pass-through charges, and tenant improvements. The effective rent differs from the quoted base rent set forth in the lease. See also ***base rent.***

Eminent domain: The right of a government or municipal quasi-public body to acquire private property for public use through a court action called condemnation in which the court determines that the use is a public use and determines the price or compensation to be paid to the owner. (The owner of the property must be fairly compensated, usually based on an appraisal of the fair market value.) See also ***condemnation.***

Encumbrance: Any lien, such as a mortgage, tax lien, or judgment lien; also, an easement, a restriction on the use of land, or an outstanding dower right which may diminish the value of property.

Endorsement: Signature placed on the back of a check transferring the amount of that instrument to someone else. An attachment to an insurance policy that provides or excludes a specific coverage for a specific portion or element of a property or makes additions or changes to the existing terms of a policy.

Entertainment shopping center: Typically range from 200,000 to over 500,000 square feet. They are now being referred to as "shoppertainment." They are anchored by large multi-screen stadium-seating theaters and theme-oriented retailers and restaurants.

Environmental impact statement (EIS): An analysis of the anticipated effects of a development or action on its surroundings. Such an analysis may be required prior to development under federal or state law (e.g., under the National Environmental Policy Act of 1969, an EIS is required for federally supported developments). An EIS can reveal impediments to development (e.g., the presence of underground tanks or toxic waste).

Environmental Protection Agency (EPA): An independent agency of the U.S. government established in 1970 to enforce laws that preserve and protect the environment.

Equity: The value of real property in excess of debt. The interest or value that an owner has in real estate over and above the mortgage and other financial liens against it; outright ownership. In accounting, the excess of a firm's assets over its liabilities.

Errors and omissions (E&O) insurance: A form of liability insurance. In the case of the property manager, E&O insurance protects against liabilities resulting from honest mistakes and oversights (but provides no protection in cases of gross negligence).

Estoppel certificate: A document by which the tenant states the terms of the lease and the full amount of rent to be paid for the entire term of the lease, commonly requested by the landlord in conjunction with a transfer of ownership or in relation to financing or refinancing.

Exclusive: A right granted to the tenant that restricts the owner from leasing space in the same shopping center to other retailers that sell similar merchandise or provide similar services, usually defined in an ***exclusive use clause.*** Care must be taken in granting exclusives because limitation of competition violates anti-trust regulations. When granted, exclusives must be taken into account when prospecting for and leasing to additional retail tenants.

Exclusive use clause: A clause preventing the owner of a shopping center from leasing space to other retailers who sell merchandise or provide a service similar to that specified in the tenant's lease. (Because state laws on this sensitive issue vary, advice of legal counsel should be sought before using this type of clause.) See also ***exclusive.***

Executive real estate manager: Another name for ***real estate supervisor.*** Also sometimes used in referring to the chief executive officer (CEO) of a (usually small) real estate management firm.

Exit strategy: The method by which a property owner intends to get out of an investment that he or she has made in the past. It is a way of "cashing out" an investment.

Expense: Any business-specific cost incurred in operating a business (or investment real estate). For income tax purposes, costs that are currently deductible from income, as those for goods or services.

Expense-stop method: In an office building lease, a clause obligating the property owner to pay operating costs up to a certain amount per square foot per year; tenants pay their pro rata share of any costs in excess of that amount. When used in a retail lease, a clause obligating the tenants to pay a pro rata share of operating expenses up to a certain amount per year; the owner pays any costs in excess of that amount.

Experience exchange: A compilation of operating data on comparable properties generated through annual or other regular surveys of property managers. IREM publishes ***Income/Expense Analysis®: Conventional Apartments, Income/Expense Analysis®: Federally Assisted Apartments, Income/Expense Analysis®: Office Buildings, Income/Expense Analysis®: Shopping Centers,*** and ***Expense Analysis®: Condominiums, Cooperatives, and Planned Unit Developments*** annually. The Building Owners and Managers Association (BOMA) International publishes an annual ***Experience Exchange Report*** on office buildings. The National Association of Industrial and Office Properties (NAIOP) publishes ***Industrial Income and Expense Report*** every other year. ***Dollars and Cents of Shopping Centers*** is published every other year by the Urban Land Institute (ULI). Shopping center operating data are also published periodically by the International Council of Shopping Centers (ICSC).

Exterior wall methodology (Method A): Measures to the outside of exterior walls (measure line) to calculate areas. Certain features of an industrial building are excluded from the calculation of area, including canopies, unenclosed connecting links, unenclosed exterior staircases or fire escapes and unenclosed shipping/receiving platforms. The main condition for an area to be excluded is that it exists beyond the measure line.

Feasibility analysis: Analysis done to discover the practicality, possibility, and reasonableness of a proposed undertaking (e.g., real estate development), especially regarding proposed costs and revenues.

Fee simple: The most complete type of private ownership of real estate which gives the title holder the right to possess, control, use, and dispose of the property without time limitation, including the unlimited right to divide the property among one's heirs.

Festival (or theme) shopping center: A type of specialty shopping center, usually located in an historic section of a city, which creates a unique shopping environment using imaginative architecture and nearby natural resources. Customers are drawn mostly from the tourist trade, and merchandising is concentrated in restaurants and souvenir-type goods. This type of center may be anchorless.

Floor area ratio (FAR): The relationship between the total amount of usable floor area that a building has, or has been permitted for the building, and the total area of the lot on which the building stands. This ratio is determined by dividing the total, or gross, floor area of the building by the gross area of the lot.

Floor plan: Architectural drawings showing the floor layout of a building and including precise room sizes and their interrelationships. The arrangement of the rooms on a single floor of a building, including walls, windows, and doors.

Force majeure: An event or effect that cannot reasonably be anticipated or controlled. A clause commonly included in construction and other contracts to protect the parties in the event that part of the contract cannot be performed due to events or causes beyond the parties' control (e.g., weather, natural disaster, war, strikes, or riot).

Functional obsolescence: A condition of obsolete design or use of a property. Defects in a building or structure that detract from its value or marketability. Such defects may be curable or incurable.

Future value (FV): A concept derived from the time value of money that describes how much an investment will be worth after a specified time span at a given rate of interest.

General contractor: An individual or company that undertakes the construction or renovation of a property and agrees to perform (provide) or procure all of the various construction disciplines necessary to complete the building of the structure and install the necessary mechanical and other equipment and systems. A construction specialist who enters into a formal agreement or contract with the owner of real property to construct a building or complete a remodeling project.

Great Recession: A severe global economic problem that began in the United States in December 2007, affecting the entire world economy, and is often characterized by various systemic imbalances and was sparked by a liquidity shortfall in the United States banking system. The Great Recession has resulted in the collapse of large financial institutions, the bailout of banks by national governments, and downturns in stock markets around the world.

Green lease: Align the financial and energy incentives of building owners and tenants so they can work together to save money, conserve resources, and ensure the efficient operation of buildings.

Gross building area: Area equal to length times width of the building(s) times the number of living floors, expressed in square feet.

Gross lease: A lease under which the tenant (lessee) pays a fixed rent. The landlord (lessor) is responsible for paying all property expenses (e.g., taxes, insurance, utilities, repairs, etc.), and these costs are factored into the rent paid by the tenant. Compare ***net lease.***

Gross leasable area (GLA): The amount of floor space available to be rented in a commercial property. Specifically, gross leasable area is the total floor area designed for tenant occupancy and exclusive use, including any basements, mezzanines, or upper floors.

Gross up: In commercial leasing, adjustment of variable operating expenses that are passed through to tenants in a new building or one that is not fully occupied to more closely reflect those expenses under full occupancy (usually around 90 percent; in shopping centers, between 80 and 90 percent).

Ground lease: A lease for land only, it gives the tenant the right to use and occupy the land under a property. Under a ***subordinated ground lease,*** the owner offers the land as collateral for the mortgage commitment on the property. If the ground lease is ***unsubordinated,*** the land will not become collateral for the mortgage, and the lender will be in a second lien position.

Guaranty: In real estate management, a pledge by a third (outside) party who agrees to assume responsibility for a tenant's obligations under a lease in the event of tenant default, including payment of rent and performance of all other terms, covenants, and conditions of the lease. The arrangement is specific to a particular tenant and the lease for specified premises. The individual or organization making such a pledge is called a *guarantor.*

Health Insurance Portability and Accountability Act (HIPAA): An Act to amend the Internal Revenue Code of 1986 to improve portability and continuity of health insurance coverage in the group and individual markets, to combat waste, fraud, and abuse in health insurance and health care delivery, to promote the use of medical savings accounts, to improve access to long-term care services and coverage, to simplify the administration of health insurance, and for other purposes.

Heating, ventilation, and air-conditioning (HVAC) system: The combination of equipment and ductwork for producing, regulating, and distributing heat, refrigeration, and fresh air throughout a building.

Hold harmless: A declaration that one is not liable for things beyond his/her control. A clause in contracts (e.g., management agreements) through which one party assumes liability inherent in a situation and thereby eliminates the liability of the other party.

Holdover tenancy: A situation in which a tenant retains possession of leased premises after the lease has expired, and the owner, by continuing to accept rent from the tenant, thereby agrees to the tenant's continued occupancy as defined by state law. Some leases stipulate that such holding over may revert to a month-to-month tenancy, often at a higher rent.

Hybrid shopping center: A large development with a big-box element, entertainment district, restaurant row, and neighborhood center within the complex.

Income/expense analysis: Evaluation of the relationship between gross income and operating expenses.

Income/expense projection: An estimation of income and expenses for a future specified time period.

Incurable obsolescence: Irreversible loss of value of a building because of changes in style or market preference. This type of loss may be physically impossible or financially unfeasible to improve.

Indemnification: Legal exemption from responsibility for a loss that may occur in the future or for a loss or damage already suffered. The condition of being indemnified. The action of indemnifying.

Indemnify: To exempt from incurred liabilities or penalties. To secure against harm or damage or loss. Contracts and insurance policies usually include an indemnification clause.

Industrial park: A controlled park-like development designed to accommodate specific types of industry (e.g., manufacturing) and usually located at a distance from the center of a city. Often, such properties are also specially zoned for heavy manufacturing or for light manufacturing and warehouse operations.

Industrial district: An area where workers of a heavy industry (ship-building, coal mining, steel, ceramics, etc.) live within walking-distance of their places of work.

In-kind gifts: Contributions of goods or services, other than cash grants that are offered along with, or in lieu of, cash grants. Examples include computers, software, furniture, and office equipment.

Internal rate of return (IRR): The rate of return at which the discounted value of all benefits received during ownership is equal to the value of the owner's equity in the investment. The true annual earnings of an investment expressed as a percentage. A method used by investors to determine cash returns in relation to cash invested. (The calculation assumes that the annual ***proceeds*** can be invested at the same rate as the IRR.) In financial analysis, the specific discount rate for which the net present value (NPV) is zero, which gives a percentage that indicates the viability of a project or the profitability of an investment.

Insurance provision: A provision in commercial leases that requires the tenant to obtain specified types and amounts of insurance, including a certain amount of liability insurance, and to include the building owner as an additional named insured party on the policy.

Key money: When an existing vacancy has substantial improvements and the retailer may be required to pay for those existing improvements.

Kiosk: A booth or stall set up in a shopping center, sometimes on a temporary basis, to sell goods such as tobacco, newspapers, magazines, seasonal merchandise, candy, keys, and other small impulse-purchase items.

Late fee: A fee charged for late payment of rent.

Lease amendment: A written revision of a lease specifying changes to the basic document that have been agreed to by the parties to the contract.

Lease outline drawing (LOD): The material prepared for the tenant, showing the demised space and its relation to adjacent spaces and the location as a whole. The illustrated floor plan also documents the proposed and/or certified square footage of a commercial space being leased also known as ***rentable square footage.***

Lease restrictions summary: A separate listing of all lease restrictions that may have a future impact on the leasing and management of the property.

Leasing agent: The individual in a real estate brokerage firm (or management organization or development company) who is directly responsible for renting space in assigned properties. In some states, leasing agents must have a real estate broker's license unless they are employed directly by the property owner. Residential leasing agents may be called ***leasing consultants.***

Letter of intent (LOI): A letter or document stating the intention of the parties to take (or not take) a particular action, sometimes contingent on certain other action(s) being taken. In commercial leasing, a preliminary step to finalizing specific lease terms.

Leverage: The use of borrowed funds to increase one's purchasing power. In real estate, use of borrowed funds to purchase investment property with the expectation of realizing a return that exceeds the cost of the borrowed funds. Also used to describe how effectively an investor is using debt. Positive leverage means that debt increases return on equity. Negative leverage decreases such return.

Licensing agreement: Provides the retailer the right to use space, but it does not create an owner-tenant relationship. This means the tenant of the space does not have all the protection of state landlord-tenant laws.

Lien: A claim against property by a creditor under which the property becomes security for the debt owed to the creditor. The legal right of a creditor to have his/her debt paid out of the property of the debtor. Mortgages, mechanic's liens, and tax liens are monetary liens against a property for the satisfaction of debt.

Lien release: A document executed by a provider of contract services (labor and materials) under which the contractor relinquishes the claim imposed against the property where its services are being performed.

Lien theory: In some states, a lending practice in which title to the mortgaged property remains with the borrower and a lien on the property is given to the lender by means of the mortgage.

Lien waiver: A voluntary relinquishing of a subcontractors' right to make a claim against a property for payment of labor or materials already provided. Such waivers are required for release of construction loan funds from the lender. Also, an agreement between management, contractor, and subcontractor that no liens will be placed against the property for failure to meet the contract terms.

Lifestyle shopping center: A type of strip shopping center composed entirely of destination tenants. Such centers may or may not include anchor tenants.

Limited liability company (LLC): Created by state statute, a business ownership form that functions like a corporation (its members are protected from liability) but for income tax purposes is classified as a partnership. Income and expenses flow through to the individual members. The arrangement offers considerable flexibility in its organization and structure.

Load factor: The percentage of space in a (usually commercial) building that is added to its usable area to account for lobbies, corridors, and other common areas; sometimes also called ***add-on factor.*** In utility consumption, the ratio of the average load carried by a power station for a given period to the maximum load carried during the same period (kilowatt-hours ÷ kilowatts of demand consumed). The ratio between the capacity of an elevator (weight of passengers or freight) and its actual utilization, stated as a percentage.

Loan-to-value (LTV) ratio: A measure of the lender's risk of loss in making a loan. The relationship between the amount of the principal of a loan and the market value of the real estate securing it; usually expressed as a percentage using the formula: loan amount ÷ property value. The value may be the price being paid for the property or the appraised value. An LTV above 85 percent would be considered high risk.

Local Improvement District (LID): A method of financing capital improvements constructed by the city that provide a special benefit to the properties within the boundary of the LID. The LID formation process leads to the sale of bonds and the retirement of those bonds via annual payments paid by the property owners within the district. The LID assessments become liens on the benefitted properties.

Loss leader: In retailing, an item sold at a lesser markup than would normally be obtained on that item in order to attract customers in the hope that they will buy more-profitable items as well.

Management agreement: A contractual arrangement between the owner(s) of a property and the designated managing agent, describing the duties and establishing the authority of the agent and detailing the responsibilities, rights, and obligations of both agent and owner(s).

Market rent: Rent that a property is capable of yielding if leased under prevailing market conditions; ***economic rent.*** Also, the amount that comparable space would command in a competitive market. Often used interchangeably with ***street rent*** and ***contract rent.*** (By definition, the latter is the rent stated in a specific lease.) For office buildings, the basis would be dollars per rentable square foot; for retail space, it would be dollars per square foot of gross leasable area (GLA).

Market research: Collecting information about consumer wants, needs, and preferences by surveying consumers directly. A methodology used to explore product design, packaging, size (quantity), and other marketing-related issues, including price. In shopping center management, the gathering of information about a trade area and a particular retail site pertaining to population, economy, local industries, per capita expenditures, competing retail sites, and sales potential. Specific information about shoppers is often gathered via ***focus groups,*** telephone interviews, and ***intercept surveys.*** Compare ***market survey.***

Market survey: A detailed and comprehensive evaluation of a given market that provides market research data. Collection and analysis of up-to-date information on other products distributed in a given area. See also ***market research.*** In real estate management, the process of gathering information about specific comparable properties for comparison to data about the subject property in order to weigh the advantages and disadvantages of each property and establish a market rent for the subject. In the office building market, a survey is made of comparable buildings located in the subject property's neighborhood and includes such information as number of stories, net rentable area, building features and amenities, rental rates, and load factors. For shopping centers, a market survey of competing centers would include location specifics, ***gross leasable area (GLA),*** anchor and ancillary tenants, rental rates, and sales volumes. Amount and availability of parking are important considerations in market surveys for all types of properties.

Master meter: A single meter, owned and operated by the utility company, which measures the total amount of energy from one source that is required to operate an entire building. When a master meter is in place, individual tenants' spaces may be submetered to measure their discrete energy use.

Metes and bounds: Boundaries of a tract of land established by referring to natural features or man-made constructs (e.g., a river, a road) as the point of origin. This is differentiated from boundaries established by measuring from a fixed starting point and stating specific distances in reference to compass directions.

Millage rate: A property tax rate under which the assessment basis is one dollar for every one thousand dollars of assessed property value (1 mill = $1/$1000). Thus, the owner of a property with assessed valuation of $100,000 and property taxes assessed at a millage rate of 20 mills would pay $2,000 in property tax.

Minimum rent: In retail leasing, the rent which will always be due each month in a tenant's lease term, regardless of sales volume and exclusive of any additional charges. Often used in conjunction with a percentage rent arrangement; sometimes called ***fixedminimum rent.*** See also ***base rent***.

Modified-accrual accounting: A method of accounting in which items that repeat at regular intervals are accounted on a cash basis while those requiring accumulation of funds toward a large dollar payout are accounted on an accrual basis.

Month-to-month tenancy: An agreement to rent or lease for consecutive and continuing monthly periods until terminated by proper prior notice by either the landlord or the tenant. Notice of termination must precede the commencement date of the final month of occupancy. State law usually establishes the time period of prior notice.

Natural breakpoint: Another name for ***breakpoint.***

Negative cash flow: A deficit or loss. When operating expenses and debt service exceed revenues collected (effective gross income).

Negotiated breakpoint: Refers to situations where tenants do not accept the ***natural breakpoint*** as the starting point for percentage rent payments.

Neighborhood center: A shopping center typically anchored by a supermarket or drugstore and having 30,000–100,000 square feet of ***gross leasable area (GLA).***

Net lease: A lease under which the tenant pays a prorated share of some or all operating expenses in addition to base or minimum rent. The terms net-net (or ***double-net***) and net-net-net (or ***triple- net***) are also used, depending on the extent of the costs that are passed through to the tenant. Used most often for commercial tenants, the definitions of the terms vary with location and type of property (e.g., office, retail, industrial). In retail leasing, the tenant pays a prorated share of property taxes under a net lease, prorated shares of both property taxes and insurance under a net-net (or double-net) lease, and prorated shares of all operating expenses (including common area maintenance) under a net-net-net (or triple-net) lease. Compare ***gross lease.***

Net operating income (NOI): Total collections (gross receipts) *less* operating expenses; may be calculated on an annual or a monthly basis. More broadly, cash available after all operating expenses have been deducted from collected rental income and before debt service and capital expenses have been deducted.

Net present value (NPV): The difference between the cost of a real estate or other investment and the discounted present value of all anticipated future fiscal benefits of that investment. In financial analysis, a method that discounts expected future cash flows to their present value using a predetermined desired rate of return. NPV is calculated by subtracting the present value of the capital outlay from the present value of the expected returns.

Non-controllable expenses: Operating expense items over which property management has no control (e.g., real estate taxes, insurance premiums, labor-union wages).

Obsolescence: Generally speaking, a loss of value brought about by a change in design, technology, taste, or demand. Also used in referring to the process by which property loses its economic usefulness to the owner/taxpayer due to causes other than physical deterioration (e.g., technological advancements, changes in public taste); an element of depreciation. See also ***curable obsolescence; incurable obsolescence.***

Occupancy cost: The tenant's total cost for the leased space. For commercial tenants, this includes base rent plus a pro-rata share of property operating expenses (e.g., insurance, real estate taxes, utilities, common area maintenance, and management fees) and may include reimbursement of a tenant improvement allowance. In addition, retail tenants may pay percentage rent (usually as overage) and contribute to a marketing fund or merchants' association.

Off-price shopping center: A type of specialty shopping center comprised of tenants offering name-brand merchandise at large discounts (20–60 percent) off normal retail prices because special bulk purchases allow cost savings to be passed on to the customer. Compare ***outlet center***.

Operating budget: A listing of all anticipated income from and expenses of operating a property, usually projected on an annual basis. While funds for accumulation of capital reserves would be deducted from net operating income (NOI) in an operating budget (and the accumulated funds would be recorded as a capital or asset item), actual expenditures of such reserve funds would be anticipated in a ***capital budget.***

Operating expenses: The normal costs of running a business. In real estate, the expenditures for real estate taxes, salaries, insurance, maintenance, utilities, and similar items paid in connection with the operation of a rental property that are properly charged against income. More broadly, all expenditures made in connection with operating a property with the exception of debt service, capital reserves (and/or capital expenditures), and income taxes. At commercial properties, increases in operating expenses are often used as a basis for rent increases. Items included for this purpose can vary by property type and geographic location.

Option: The right to purchase or lease something at a future date for a specified price and terms. The right may or may not be exercised at the option holder's (optionee's) discretion. Options may be received, negotiated, or purchased. In a lease, the right to obtain a specific condition within a specified time (e.g., to renew at the same or a pre-agreed rate when the lease term expires; to expand into adjacent space at a pre-agreed time when that space is expected to be available; to cancel the lease).

Outlet center: A type of specialty shopping center comprised of at least 50 percent factory outlet stores offering namebrand goods at discounted or wholesale prices. Usually the manufacturer will operate the store, eliminating the retail markup. Merchandise is usually manufacturers' surplus (e.g., seconds, irregulars, factory overruns). Compare ***off-price center***.

Outlot: In a shopping center, a site that is not attached to the main center; also called ***out parcel*** or ***pad space.*** The term is often applied to freestanding space in the parking lot. Outlot tenants usually include restaurants, gas stations, and driveup banking services.

Overage rent: In retail leases, rent payments in excess of a guaranteed minimum, usually a percentage of the tenant's sales; also called ***percentage rent.***

Owner's expenses: Expenditures paid by the property owner and not billed back to the building occupants.

Parking area ratio: The relationship between the size of the parking area and the size of the building it is intended to serve.

Pass-through charges: In commercial leasing, operating expenses of a property that are paid by the tenants, usually on a pro rata basis in addition to base rent, including real estate taxes, insurance on the property, and common area maintenance (CAM) costs.

Parapolice program: Offered by cities to allow the police guild to assign uniformed off-duty officers to patrol at the shopping center's expense.

Payback period: The amount of time required to recover the cost of a capital investment.

Percentage rent: In retail leasing, rent that is based on a percentage of a tenant's gross sales (or sometimes net income or profits), often compared to the guaranteed minimum or base rent under the lease and paid as ***overage*** (i.e., the amount of percentage rent in excess of the minimum or base rent due). A percentage rent provision may also be written such that the tenant in a shopping center is required to pay a percentage of gross sales in lieu of minimum rent under certain circumstances (e.g., loss of an anchor tenant).

Performance bond: A guarantee or assurance by a third party (surety) that a contractor will perform and complete the contract as per agreement; a type of ***contract bond.***

Planned employment center: Includes a variety of offices and service uses to serve the industrial businesses in the master-planned area and in the community at large. The planned employment center is a multiuse district to provide for employment needs of urban areas.

Planned unit development (PUD): A type of development that usually includes a mixture of open space, single-family homes, townhouses, condominiums or cooperatives, rental units, and recreational and commercial facilities within a defined area under a specific zoning arrangement. Generally, PUDs are large in scale and built in several phases over a number of years. Typically, all infrastructure for the site is constructed before the improvements are built. Also, a ***zoning*** classification that allows flexibility in the design of a subdivision, usually setting an overall density limit which allows clustering of units to provide for common open space.

Present value (PV): The current dollar value of a sum of money to be received in the future which has been discounted by a given percentage rate. The amount one would have to invest today at a given rate for the period to yield the future sum.

Preventive maintenance: A program of regularly scheduled inspection and care that allows potential problems to be prevented or at least detected and solved before major repairs are needed.

Promissory note: A written promise to pay a specified sum of money to a specific person or firm under specified terms (a stated interest rate, a schedule of payments, and a due date).

Property manager: A knowledgeable professional who has the experience and skills to operate real estate and understands the fundamentals of business management. The person who supervises the day-to-day operation of a property, making sure it is properly leased, well maintained, competitive with other sites, and otherwise managed according to the owner's objectives. The chief operating officer or administrator of a particular property or group of properties.

Property tax: A tax levied on various kinds of real and personal property by state and local governments based on the nature of improvements to the land, fair market value, and assessed valuation.

Pro rata: For commercial leasing, based on the size of individually owned or leased spaces in relation to the whole. Commercial tenants commonly pay proportionate shares of operating expenses and other costs. See also ***pass-through charges.***

Pro rata share: A retail tenant's share of operating expenses—e.g., HVAC charges, common area maintenance (CAM) fees, taxes, insurance, etc.—computed as a percentage by dividing the gross leasable area (GLA) of the tenant's space by the GLA of the shopping center.

Psychographics: A qualitative methodology for compiling information about people's individual personalities and lifestyles, it goes beyond demographics to uncover personal preferences and attitudes that numbers alone do not reveal; a tool of market research. In leasing, used to determine what factors about a property are likely to appeal to particular prospective tenants (more specifically applicable to individual consumers in regard to apartment leasing). See also ***market research.***

Power shopping center: A large strip shopping center anchored by several large promotional, warehouse, or specialty stores that dominate their merchandising categories and having very few small shops.

Power town: Power shopping centers with an expanded tenant mix that may include a theater, higher parking ratios, and more customer amenities. The power town is usually larger than a power center, which often maxes out at 800,000 square feet.

Punch list: A list of office space improvements, both building standard and tenant paid, that should be finished or accounted for before move-in. Used for reference by management to guide final inspection of built-out premises before delivery. A marked punch list documents that the items punched were completed by the contractor in a good, workmanlike manner in respect to the contract documents and makes clear the items yet to be completed.

Quiet enjoyment: The use of real property by a tenant without illegal or unreasonable interference or annoyance by the landlord or others. A right granted under landlord-tenant law—the right to privacy, peace and quiet, and use of the leased space, common areas, and facilities. A clause included in most leases stating that the tenant has a right of possession of the leased premises without undue disturbance by others (the owner, other tenants).

Radius clause: A provision in a retail lease that prevents a retailer from opening and operating a similar—and therefore competitive—business within a certain radius (distance in all directions) from the shopping center, normally expressed in miles.

Real estate investment trust (REIT): An entity that sells shares of beneficial interest to investors and uses the funds to invest in real estate or real estate mortgages. Real estate investment trusts must meet certain requirements such as a minimum number of investors and widely dispersed ownership. No corporate taxes need to be paid as long as a series of complex Internal Revenue Service qualifications are met.

Recapture: An income tax term describing money taken back or forfeited; a kind of tax penalty. For example, if a tax deduction was taken but does not meet all conditions, the deduction will be disallowed and the taxpayer will be required to pay tax on the income that had been offset by the deduction. This money is said to be recaptured by the taxing body.

Receiver: An individual appointed by a court to manage a property that is the subject of a pending bankruptcy or foreclosure. A receiver's role is to preserve property that has been abandoned or for which there have been allegations of fraud or mismanagement by the owner. In some states, property is assigned to a receiver during the statutory redemption period after a foreclosure sale.

Receivership: Court-ordered turnover of a property to an impartial third party ***(receiver)*** so that it may be preserved for the benefit of the affected parties. A special trust set up to hold and administer property under litigation.

Reciprocal easement agreement (REA): In shopping centers, an agreement between anchor tenant(s) and landlord regarding rights of use of each other's property, specifically the use of each other's parking area for customer parking.

Recourse loan: A loan provision that allows the lender to require the borrower to pay the debt out of his/her own personal assets. In the event of default, the lender can claim other assets of the borrower in addition to the property pledged as collateral for the loan.

Regional mall: A large shopping center anchored by two or three major retailers, at least one of which is a full-line department store, and usually developed as an enclosed mall having 250,000–900,000 square feet of *gross leasable area (GLA)*. See also *super regional center.*

Regional shopping center: Range from 400,000 to 1 million square feet of *gross leasable area (GLA).* Anchored by at least one full-line department store and tenanted predominately by fashion, gift, and general merchandise stores and restaurants.

Rentable area: In a residential property, the combined rentable area of all dwelling units. The rentable area of a unit is calculated by multiplying length times width of the apartment, with no discounts for interior partitions, plumbing chases, and other small niches. Balconies, patios, and unheated porches are not included in these measurements. Sometimes called ***net rentable area.*** In an office building, the area on which rent is based and which generally includes the space available for tenants' exclusive use plus identified common areas less any major vertical penetrations (air shafts, stairways, elevators) in the building. The term is applied to the building as a whole, to individual floors, and to portions of floors. Compare ***usable area.***

Rent relief: Designed to help a retailer overcome financial difficulty. Commonly used rent relief programs include deferred rent, percentage rent only, waived rent, and use of the security deposit.

Request for proposal (RFP): Written specifications for services to be provided by a bidder, often including the scope of work and details of design and use and asking for specifics regarding materials, labor, pricing, delivery, and payment.

Reserve fund: Money set aside to provide funds for anticipated future (usually capital) expenditures.

Reserve replacement fund: An escrow account used to help defray the costs of replacing a property's capital items. In regard to government-assisted and/or subsidized housing, HUD and Rural Development provide guidelines on initial amounts required to establish the fund, maintenance and monitoring of the fund, and withdrawal of amounts from the fund for capital expenditures.

Reserves: Funds set aside for foreseeable expenses or charges. For a condominium, funds set aside to enable the association to meet nonrecurring and/or major expenses (a requirement in most states).

Retail merchandising unit (RMU): A portable sales/display structure, similar to a ***kiosk,*** used in selling goods in the interior common area of a mall.

Return on investment (ROI): The ratio of net operating income to the total investment amount, for a given time period, which provides a measure of the financial performance of the investment. A measure of profitability expressed as a percentage and calculated by comparing periodic income to the owner's equity in the property (income ÷ equity = % ROI). A measure of cash flow against investment, it can be calculated either before or after deduction of income tax. ROI measures overall effectiveness of management in generating profits from available assets; however, it does not consider the ***time value of money.***

Right-of first offer: Related to a ***right-of-first refusal,*** but is considered to favor the rights holder.

Right-of-first refusal: A right sometimes sought by a commercial tenant (and granted by the landlord at initial leasing or lease renewal) that allows the tenant to lease previously defined additional space within a specific time period after the space becomes available for lease to another tenant or after the landlord has received a bona fide offer to lease that same space from another potential tenant (a third party). Usually the lease terms require the landlord to notify the tenant of the availability of the space or of the terms of the third-party offer, and the tenant must lease the space at market terms or under the terms of the third-party offer (if appropriate) or refuse the space so that it can be rented to the third party. This type of lease provision may also be written granting the tenant the right of first refusal to lease a particular space within a defined time period at a negotiated rent (often market rate) when that space becomes available. This may be sought by the tenant as an alternative when the landlord will not negotiate an option to expand the tenant's space.

Rules and regulations: Guidelines for tenants who lease space in a building, usually outlining requirements specific to rent payment, tenant maintenance responsibilities, and the like; also called ***house rules and regulations.*** Specifics are usually incorporated in the lease, either as a specific provision or as a rider, and they vary by property type. As an example, rules for rental apartments may include other specific requirements, such as policies regarding the keeping of pets (use of leashes, cleaning up etc.). Those for an office building are likely to address operational issues (security requirements or after-hours access). Shopping center rules address issues of conformity (uniform shopping hours).

Security deposit: A preset amount of money advanced by the tenant before occupancy and held by an owner or manager for a specific period to ensure the faithful performance of the lease terms by the tenant; also called ***lease deposit.*** (Local or state law may require the landlord to pay the tenant interest on the security deposit during the lease term and/or hold the money in an ***escrow account.***) Part or all of the deposit may be retained to pay for rent owed, miscellaneous charges owed, unpaid utility bills, and damage to the leased space that exceeds normal wear and tear. Limitations on withholding may be imposed by local and state ordinances.

Schedule of commissions: A document that outlines the terms of a commission agreement stating how and when the fee is to be paid. See also ***commission.***

Sign restriction provision: A provision in a shopping center lease that limits the use of outdoor and indoor advertisements and other graphic displays. More specifically, it requires the tenant to comply with specific sign criteria regarding sign placement, size, and graphics and to submit the plans for exterior signs for the landlord's approval; such signs are installed and maintained by the tenant. Sign criteria may be governed in part by local laws that regulate size, materials, and positioning.

Single-net lease: A commercial real estate lease agreement in which the tenant is required to pay property taxes in addition to rent. A single-net lease is a form of pass-through lease in which taxes associated with the property become the responsibility of the tenant instead of the property owner. The owner is responsible for the other operating expenses incurred of the property.

Site plan: A plan, prepared to scale, showing locations of buildings, roadways, parking areas, and other improvements. A drawing of a retail site as it will look when it is completed, including individual tenant spaces, common areas, elevators, escalators, food courts, service areas, parking, and access routes.

Smart building: A building which provides a productive and cost-effective environment through optimization of four basic elements: structure, systems, services and management, and the interrelationship between them.

Space planning: The process of designing an office configuration for maximum functional efficiency based on a prospective tenant's space utilization needs, aesthetic requirements, and financial limitations.

Specialty shopping center: A type of shopping center often dominated by food and gift tenants and having 50,000–300,000 square feet of ***gross leasable area (GLA).*** There may be no conventional anchor tenant. Many such centers have been created by conversion of an existing old building ***(adaptive use)*** in a tourist-oriented area, usually perpetuating an architectural theme suggested by the site; also known as ***theme*** or ***festival shopping centers.***

Stark law: A limitation on certain physician referrals. It prohibits physician referrals of designated health services ("DHS") for Medicare and Medicaid patients if the physician (or an immediate family member) has a financial relationship with that entity

Strip shopping center: A type of shopping center designed in a single, unenclosed strip of stores set in a row facing the street.

Subordinated ground lease: See ***ground lease.***

Subordinate loan: Secondary financing. In the event of default, it is junior to any previously recorded mortgage lien against the property.

Subordination: The process of lowering the rank of a legal claim; for example, giving a lease a lower priority than a mortgage lien, which then subordinates the lease to the mortgage lien. The condition whereby a tenant's lease is transferred to the mortgagee in the event of a foreclosure on the owner's mortgage.

Subordination clause: A lease covenant in which the tenant agrees to take any action required to subordinate his/her claims against the property to the rights of the lender under a first mortgage or deed of trust, so long as it does not affect his/her right to possession.

Super regional shopping center: In excess of one million square feet of ***gross leasable area (GLA),*** super regional shopping centers are anchored by four or more full-line department stores, major discount retailers, and/or a multi-screen theater, and have more than 100 small shops like those in a ***regional mall.***

Temporary tenant: A retail tenant that rents for a short period of time, often on a seasonal or month-to-month basis, usually occupying a kiosk or cart in the common area of a shopping center, or a vacant space in an enclosed mall, office space, or industrial space.

Tenant improvement (TI) allowance: In commercial leasing, an amount a landlord agrees to spend (office) or grants to the tenant (retail) to improve the leased space before tenant move-in or as a condition of lease renewal. The exact amount, if any, is negotiable. A ***standard tenant improvement allowance*** is a fixed dollar amount allowed by the owner for items that may be installed in the leased premises at no charge to the tenant. Payment for tenant improvements is part of the lease negotiations.

Tenant improvements (TI): Fixed improvements made to tenants' office space, usually based on specific building standards determined in advance by ownership; specifics are often negotiable, especially in a slow market. In apartment rentals, additions or alterations to the leased premises for the use of the tenant, made at the cost and expense of the tenant and becoming a part of the realty unless otherwise agreed to in writing.

Tenant mix: The combination (or types) of businesses and services that lease space in a shopping center or office building or (sometimes) industrial park.

Time value of money (TVM): The concept that a dollar in hand today is worth more than a dollar that has been promised at a future date. The basis of compounding to determine future value or discounting to determine present value. Growth of an investment over the years, especially as measured using such concepts as ***compounding, discounting, present value,*** and ***future value.***

Total tenant payment (TTP): The total amount the HUD rent formula requires the tenant to pay toward the gross rent. In public housing, TTP is defined as the monthly amount a household must pay toward shelter and a reasonable amount toward utilities. This does not include charges for excess utility consumption or other miscellaneous additional charges agreed to between the owner and the tenant (e.g., charges for the use of a garage).

Transit-oriented development (**TOD**): A mixed-use residential and commercial area designed to maximize access to public transport, and often incorporates features to encourage transit ridership.

Transmittal letters: A formal document that provides information about a usually lengthier accompanying document. The sender uses the letter to transmit the attached document to the recipient.

Transportation Management Plan (TMP): A TMP lays out a set of strategies for managing the work zone impacts of a project. Because work zone objectives, needs, and issues vary from project to project, the scope, content, and degree of detail in a TMP will also vary. It is ultimately up to individual agencies to establish and implement TMPs that best serve the mobility and safety needs of the motoring public, construction workers, businesses, and community.

Triple-net lease: Also called net-net-net lease. See ***net lease.***

Turnkey operation: A concession whereby the owner agrees to provide a completely finished space for a commercial tenant.

Usable area: The area in an office building that is available for the exclusive use of a tenant; compare ***rentable area.*** On a multitenant floor, the area remaining after the area devoted to core facilities (public corridors, elevators, washrooms, stairwells, electrical closets) is subtracted from the gross area of the floor. On a single-tenant floor, usable area excludes ducts, stairwells, elevators, and the building elevator lobby on the floor if such exists, but includes washrooms and electrical closets.

Use clause: A lease provision that restricts the use of the rental space. In an apartment lease, the stated use would be a private dwelling. In an office lease, the type of business operation would be cited. In a retail lease, the use clause restricts the tenant's use of the rented space by indicating what types of goods can and cannot be sold.

Use factor: The number of hours a building operates in relation to the total number of hours in a given time period. The term is generally applied in office building operation and management.

Use restrictions: In a condominium or other common interest development, rules and regulations, often prohibitive in nature, that regulate the behavior of unit owners and others in common areas and govern relations between neighbors.

V**ariance:** A deviation from the set of rules a municipality applies to land use and land development, typically a zoning ordinance, building code, or municipal code. The manner in which variances are employed can differ greatly depending on the municipality.

Window mullion: A vertical element that forms a division between units of a window, door, or screen, or is used decoratively. When dividing adjacent window units, its primary purpose is to provide structural support to an arch or lintel above the window opening. Its secondary purpose may be as a rigid support to the glazing of the window. In the commercial door industry, the term "floating mullion" is also applied to an interlock profile which is fitted in between a pair of double swing doors.

Work letter: An addendum to the tenant improvement clause of an office or retail lease that lists in detail all the work to be done for the tenant by the owner.

Zero-base budgeting: A method of budgeting for private businesses and government agencies that requires justification of all expenditures, not just those that exceed their allocation for the prior year. In this practice, all budget line items begin at a zero base and are funded for the upcoming period according to their individual merits.

Zoning: A public regulation to control the character and intensity of land use by areas or zones. A legal mechanism whereby local (municipal) governments regulate the use of privately owned real property to prevent conflicting land uses, promote orderly development, and regulate such conditions as noise, safety, and density. Zoning regulations are specified in ***zoning ordinances.*** Establishment of independently controlled sections within an HVAC system such that the temperature and other conditions in each zone (space or group of spaces) are regulated by a separate control.

Zoning ordinance: A type of law passed by a municipality to regulate and control the character and use of property.

Zoning variance: An exception made to a prevailing zoning ordinance that does not constitute a change in the legally applicable zoning.

Index

A

B

C

D

E

J

K

L

M

O

P

S

T

U

V

W

Y

Z